American Foreign Policy Making and the Democratic Dilemmas

American Foreign Policy Making and the Democratic Dilemmas

FIFTH EDITION

JOHN SPANIER
University of Florida

ERIC M. USLANER
University of Maryland

Brooks/Cole Publishing Company
Pacific Grove, California

Brooks/Cole Publishing Company
A Division of Wadsworth, Inc.

Printed in the United States of America

10 9 8 7 6 5 4 3 2 1

LIBRARY OF CONGRESS
Library of Congress Cataloging-in-Publication Data

Spanier, John
    American foreign policy making and the democratic dilemmas / John
Spanier, Eric M. Uslaner.—5th ed.
        p.   cm.
    Bibliography: p.
    Includes index.
    ISBN 0-534-11087-8 (pbk.)
    1. United States—Foreign relations administration.   I. Uslaner,
Eric M.   II. Title.
JX1706.A4 1989
353.0089—dc19   88–25059
                                                                        CIP

In memory of
William and Liesel Spanier
and
Abe and Irene Uslaner

Preface

This fifth edition of *How American Foreign Policy is Made*, appearing as the Bush administration begins, focuses on the dilemmas that the United States faces as a democracy conducting its foreign policy. Although this issue was introduced in the first edition, our discussion of it in this edition is more elaborate and is analyzed more explicitly, hence the change of the title.

Our original purpose in writing this book was to explain the ways in which foreign policy (further subdivided into crisis and noncrisis security policies) is made differently than is domestic policy. At that time, most texts on the policy process focused on *domestic* policy making. *American Foreign Policy Making and the Democratic Dilemmas* was written to fill the need for an introduction to the actors and elements in the foreign policy decision process and to the analytic approaches most useful in understanding and criticizing it. In the second edition, we added intermestic policy as a further category to our two types of foreign policies because of the increasing erosion of the distinction between foreign and domestic policy in this area. This threefold distinction is examined in greater detail by additional case studies.

Contemporary conflict over foreign policy demands, too, that we not only deal with the processes of foreign policy making, but also confront the question of whether the outcome of these processes can be both effective and democratic. We felt this issue critical enough that we have explained it at greater length in what we call the *three dilemmas* of democratic policy making. For this purpose, we examine the variations in the constitutional and political power of the president and Congress in both domestic and foreign policy formation. We also examine the actual access to foreign policy decision roles and various possible participants; the parts that may be played by members of Congress, political parties, and interest groups; and the impact of the media and expressions of public opinion.

The rational-actor and bureaucratic models of decision making are suggested as aids to a clearer understanding of the interaction of all these forces. The utility of the rational-actor model is demonstrated in case studies of the Cuban missile and Iranian hostage crises. The bureaucratic model elucidates policy making on SALT II and such "intermestic" issues as energy, trade, and agriculture.

The new edition includes not only new case studies (trade and agriculture), but also greatly expands on our previous treatments of older issues. Legislative–executive relations are treated at considerable length; the subject has its own chapter (Chapter 3). We discuss the historical context of the interactions between the two branches and offer a detailed case study of the Iran–Contra affair. Our analysis of public opinion (Chapter 5) is greatly expanded, including a detailed analysis of how the public reacted to the Iran–Contra affair. We also consider interest groups in foreign policy in greater detail in Chapter 6. The actors we consider range from economic to ethnic interest groups. We also deal with lobbying by foreign governments and the role of political action committee contributions by groups primarily concerned with foreign policy. We consider whether such groups are dangerous to democratic decision making. In recent years local activists—ranging from independent citizen groups to mayors and governors—have played increasing roles in foreign policy making from trade issues to protests over American policies in South Africa and Latin America. This is a topic that has not received much attention. We focus on it in Chapter 6.

The new edition also greatly expands the role of the democratic dilemmas in our coverage of many issues. More so than in the past, we relate each chapter to these three dilemmas. Additionally, in Chapter 9 we consider whether these dilemmas can be resolved within our present constitutional system or whether fundamental reforms, as urged by leading analysts of American government, are required. We also focus on the lessons from the Iran–Contra affair for democratic accountability and contrast these morals with those of the Lend-Lease Act during World War II.

The recent past suggests that presidential dominance has become a given in American foreign policy making, so our concluding chapter returns to the question: Can policy formulation be both effective and democratic? Drawing on American foreign policy experience we ask: How might events have been altered by enlarged congressional participation? Would the outcomes in fact have conformed to the democratic expectations of today's reformers?

These are complex issues, and we do not claim to have resolved them. Rather, our goal is more modest: to outline for the introductory student of American government or of American foreign policy the foreign policy-making process and to highlight the problems we believe are the most important. In any such endeavor, particularly a joint one, some arguments are bound to remain incomplete in the eyes of the specialist. Our problem was somewhat compounded by differing views on what would constitute a "good" foreign policy—and, indeed, on how much of a say Congress should have. Such disagreements have led us to produce balanced arguments on different sides of critical issues—and also to examine the feasibility of proposed reforms regardless of our personal biases.

We are grateful to Frank Kessler, Kevin Mulcahy, Martin Sampson, and Paul Watanabe for their helpful comments in reviewing the manuscript, and to all those involved in bringing the manuscript to fruition.

John Spanier

Eric M. Uslaner

Contents

Chapter One

Foreign Policy in a Democracy

THE THREE DILEMMAS OF DEMOCRATIC FOREIGN POLICY

The United States officially has one president, but he occupies two presidencies.[1] One deals with the domestic political system, the other with the international one. Inherent in that division lies one of the three major dilemmas the United States, as a democracy and as a superpower, faces as it conducts its foreign policy. This fundamental dilemma might be summed up as *governmental checks and balances versus concentration of presidential power*. In domestic matters, it has always been considered vital to limit presidential power to preserve the constitutional design of American democracy. The nation's historical tradition has been one of fear and suspicion of concentrated power, whether it existed in the governmental or economic area. The possession of power has been equated with its potential abuse, and power was therefore domestically distributed vertically between the federal government and the states; within the federal government it was separated horizontally among the executive, legislative, and judicial branches.

By contrast, the conduct of foreign policy—whose principal aim is safeguarding the nation's security so that life may be preserved and enjoyed—requires a concentration of executive power. In the international, or state, system, in which each state is its own protector and must rely primarily on its own resources and strength, the chief executive is usually considered the defender of the "national interests." This was as true in America in the days before democracy, under the rule of the British Crown, and it is true in contemporary democracies, and in authoritarian and totalitarian states. Survival in an essentially anarchical international system whose principal rule is self-help requires a single source of authority so that a state can, if necessary, act speedily, secretly, with continuity of purpose or, when demanded, with flexibility. From the beginning of the modern state system it was taken for granted that legislatures, especially as the democratic representatives of the people, were incapable of conducting foreign affairs; public opinion was felt to be too ignorant, too impassioned, and too unstable. Par-

1

liaments as legislative institutions were by their very nature thought to be incapable of rapid decisions; to pass wise legislation, they were expected to debate at some length and reconcile conflicting interests and viewpoints. In short, the primacy of the executive in foreign policy was essentially a response to the nature of the state system.

Because of the domestic system's requirements to restrain executive power and the state system's need for ample executive power, tension between these two aspects of the presidency in the United States is inevitable.[2] On the one hand, if the president is limited sufficiently to protect American democracy, the danger is that he might also become so enfeebled that he will not be able to defend effectively the nation's interests. On the other hand, if the president accumulates enough power to act with the necessary authority, dispatch, and secrecy to protect the nation, he might become so powerful that he will erode the restraints on his power that were intended to preserve the constitutional nature of the American political system. Thus, what is a virtue domestically might become a vice internationally, as the nation falls victim to its democratic organization; and what is a virtue externally might become a vice internally, as the nation loses its democratic soul in seeking to protect its democratic order from foreign threats.

Interestingly, this fundamental dilemma—how to preserve a democratic order at home while investing the government and especially the presidency with enough authority to effectively guard the nation's security and welfare—was first noted by the English political philosopher John Locke, who is usually regarded as the theorist whose political philosophy underlies the Declaration of Independence and the Constitution. Locke asserted that man possessed certain natural or inalienable rights that in society would be protected by the election of representatives who, through the legislature, would restrain the executive from abusing these rights and undermining the democratic nature of society. Externally, however, nations continued to live in a "state of nature" with one another. Therefore, the executive—which in the conduct of foreign affairs Locke called the federative power—could not be similarly contained.

> These two powers, executive and federative, though they be really distinct in themselves, yet one comprehending the executive of the municipal laws of the society within itself . . . ; the other the management of the security and interests of the public without . . . . And though this federative power in the well or ill management of it be of great moment to the commonwealth, yet it is much less capable to be directed by antecedent, standing, positive laws than the executive; and so must necessarily be left to the prudence and wisdom of those whose hands it is in, to be managed for the public good.[3]

It was Locke, then, who first distinguished between the two presidencies—the executive and the federative—both embodied in one person, the president, situated at the crossroads where the domestic and international systems meet and overlap.

The second, and closely related, dilemma might be summed up as *process versus output*. The American government is supposed to represent the "will of the people." This will is expressed in many different ways. A nationwide election is held every four years for president, the only nationally elected figure in the United States; elections are held every two years for one third of the Senate and the entire House. And those who hold grievances are able to organize themselves, express their legitimate interests, and, as interest groups, can strive to achieve their goals by supporting candidates for office during elections and, in between elections, by bringing their influence to bear at the legislative, executive, and judicial levels of government (both state and federal). Clearly, in domestic policy, the emphasis is on widespread participation of many different groups and interests in society and government and the reconciliation of their diverse and conflicting interests as they are reflected in the bureaucracy, Congress, and competing interest groups. The preferences of the majority emerge through this political process.

In foreign policy, as in domestic policy, the executive and legislative branches share responsibility and power. This does not, however, necessarily produce the "right" policies. The concern for producing "correct" foreign policies—or at least not the wrong ones—is certainly understandable, especially in this highly volatile era. President John F. Kennedy once said that foreign policy can kill us, while domestic policies can set us back. This description may be overdrawn. Not all foreign policies are likely to result in nuclear war nor are all domestic policies necessarily salvageable and correctible if mistakes are made. But Kennedy did state a simple truth underscoring the difference between foreign and domestic policies: the first, unlike the last, may be irreversible and result in the destruction of American society, indeed, much of the world. Kennedy's own estimate in the early 1960s was that 100 million Americans, 100 million Europeans, and 100 million Russians would become casualties in the opening hours of an all-out American–Soviet nuclear war. A Carter administration study placed U.S. casualties at 140 million and Soviet casualties at about 110 million.

From the beginning of the Cold War in the late 1940s there was agreement that foreign policy should therefore be decided differently than domestic policy. Indeed, there was some precedence. During World War II (1941–1945), the balance between the president and Congress was virtually suspended, and the president was given emergency powers for the duration of the conflict. After hostilities had ceased, the Congress reasserted itself. Not surprisingly, the concentration of power in the presidency was therefore considered the most effective way to deal with the Soviet Union. Partisan rivalry and executive-legislative conflict—the norms in domestic policy—would play havoc with foreign policy. Presidential primacy and congressional and bipartisan support would provide a more effective pattern.

The Cold War, being neither war nor peace (as usually understood), meant that the president had to wield a kind of emergency power on a continuing basis. This was a novel situation. The United States had overnight become the leader of the "free world," with extensive and long-term commitments. Many of the situations it confronted, and could expect to confront, needed speedy decision and action, for delay could be costly, and the issues that had to be dealt with were varied and complex. American foreign policy required that the president be given the authority he needed. Only he had the capacity to act quickly and, thanks to the large bureaucracy whose responsibility it was to deal with the world beyond America, he also possessed the expertise. He did, however, need legislative support, for "correct" policies were not always popular. Conflicts between the president and Congress on the one hand, and between the Democrats and Republicans on the other, would undermine such support and were, therefore, intolerable. "A nation which excuses its own failures by the sacred untouchableness of its own habits can excuse itself into complete disaster."[4] The domestic ways of making policy were unfit for making foreign policy.

Successive presidents—with the general support of Congress—expanded the powers of the office to avoid such disaster. After the United States became deeply involved in the Vietnam War in the 1960s , however, it was precisely this growth of presidential power that was called into question. The "imperial presidency" was said to be responsible for a policy that had overcommitted the United States and led to "global policemanship" beyond the capacity of America's "limited power." Vietnam was considered the logical conclusion of the unchecked growth of presidential power. In turn, the imperial presidency was said to be the offspring of the disregard for prescribed procedure. Senator J. William Fulbright (D-Ark.), chairman of the Senate Foreign Relations Committee during the 1960s, said:

> Out of a well-intended but misconceived notion of what patriotism and responsibility require in a time of world crisis, Congress has permitted the president to take over the two vital foreign policy powers which the Constitution vested in Congress: the power to initiate war and the Senate's power to consent or withhold consent from significant commitments. . . . So completely have these two powers been taken over by the president that it is no exaggeration to say that . . . the United States has . . . become . . . a presidential dictatorship.[5]

Recent presidents, Fulbright said, had claimed the unlimited right to use the armed forces as they saw fit under an inflated interpretation of their powers as commander in chief and had ignored Congress' authority to declare war.[6] Similarly, the Senate's treaty power had been weakened by the president's contracting obligations with other nations by executive agreements or declarations; the interpretation of existing treaties in "extravagant and unwarranted ways"; and the revision of treaties by executive agreements after Senate approval of the treaties.[7] Fulbright's charges were widely accepted at the time.

By the late 1970s, however, as disillusionment with U.S.–Soviet détente grew, demands arose for the weakening or removal of at least some of the restraints placed on presidential power in the wake of Vietnam. These restraints seemed to be obstacles to the conduct of a more vigorous assertive foreign policy seemingly required by the continued expansion of Soviet influence, the demands of developing nations for a new international economic order, and the growing importance of and tensions in the Persian Gulf–Indian Ocean area for American and Western security and economic viability. The fear now was that the imperial presidency had become the "imperiled presidency," and that if the shift of power from the presidency to the Congress that occurred after Vietnam was not partially reversed, the United States' ability to define and defend its vital security and economic interests might be jeopardized. In short, greater congressional participation in foreign policy was compatible with a more limited American role in the world, but this larger legislative involvement, or what the critics called congressional "interference" and "restraint," was not deemed compatible with the enlarged global role that seemed to be the lot of the United States in the 1980s.

The third dilemma follows from the other two: *broad democratic participation versus foreign policy making by a small elite.* The ethos of the American political system points to the widespread involvement of the many actors involved on a particular issue. Certainly domestic policies follow this practice. The emphasis is on representativeness. In foreign policy, however, it is on expertise. Too many cooks spoil the broth seems to be the adage. Most cooks are assumed to be amateurs. The small number who are professionally skilled in foreign affairs should be in charge and be the president's advisers. By contrast, the foreign policies of a president who feels he must reflect public opinion, as represented by the polls and Congress, will be short term and erratic, for the public's mood tends to change rapidly. We are then condemned to "diplomacy by dilettantism," as one expert has called it.[8]

The degree of participation is critical in the two principal models of decision making presented in this book (Chapter 5); bureaucratic/governmental politics and rational. The first part of the former is so named because the most important domestic policies and virtually all foreign policies are initiated in the executive branch; whether the ideas for the policies are the president's own brainchildren or not, it is the bureaucracy that spells out the details of proposed policies (and later administers them). Governmental refers to the wider participation in the policy process of other actors such as Congress, interest groups, and affected segments of public opinion. And the word *politics* is included because with so many actors with different views and interests at stake, the only way of arriving at a decision is by negotiations and compromise—that is, politics. If the necessary accommodations are attained, most of the participants will gain something, although most likely not all they wanted. Such an accommodation, then, is considered a satisfactory solution even though the policy output may not be the best one in terms of solving a particular problem. There clearly is no such thing as a "correct" policy. The issue is how to reconcile conflicting interpretations of what the correct policy ought to be. The result of the compromises made is bound to be a watered-down version of what rationally would be the best (although not necessarily the correct) policy solution. In short, bureaucratic politics involves multiple actors. The decision-making environment is decentralized and the focus is on both the conflictual nature of and the necessity for accommodation if decisions are to be made.

The rational model refers to the *best* solution to a particular problem. The focus, instead of being on the internal dynamics of the decision-making process, which democratically allows all major actors to participate in formulating policy, is on the specific issue at hand and the most appropriate way of enhancing the chief value or goal that the policy makers select and seek. Which way, for example, can they best attain a goal such as the nation's security or welfare? Of the several possible alternatives usually available, which option is the most likely to achieve this end? The search is for a successful policy, not necessarily a popular one; the emphasis is on the solution to the problem, not the attempt to satisfy the many actors involved, which all too often results in a policy that no participant fully favors. The assumption is that the government is a unitary actor and rationality refers only to choosing the best among several ways of attaining a specific aim. In fact, decision making is highly centralized, made by those policy makers occupying the "command post positions." In real life, of course, the assumption underlying rational decision making—that these policy makers have the time and information to consider all aspects of a problem before deciding on the best possible solution—falls short.

In our scheme, the bureaucratic/governmental politics model best explains the domestic policy process, while the rational actor model is most useful in explaining foreign policy crisis situations. Our other two policies, noncrisis security policies and intermestic policies, the last a mixture of *inter*(national) and (do)*mestic* policies,[9] are also best understood in terms of the bureaucratic/governmental politics model. While rational policy stands largely by itself, the other policies are part of a continuum.

Crisis policy is made by the few deciding rationally (see Table 1–1); other policies by the many arriving at a decision politically. The more a policy resembles domestic policy, the larger the number of actors and the more intense the bargaining is likely to be. At the cost of some repetition, let us be clear about the distinction. Crisis policy focuses on the external situation confronting the nation and on finding a correct response in that after a full examination of the alternative ways in which the national security or welfare can be protected in the situation at hand, the most effective means of achieving that goal at the least possible cost is chosen. Noncrisis security and other policies, by contrast, focus on the preferences of the

TABLE 1–1

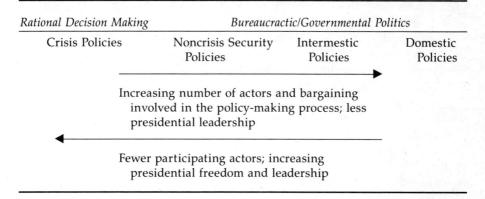

Rational Decision Making		*Bureaucractic/Governmental Politics*	
Crisis Policies	Noncrisis Security Policies	Intermestic Policies	Domestic Policies

Increasing number of actors and bargaining
involved in the policy-making process; less
presidential leadership

Fewer participating actors; increasing
presidential freedom and leadership

many participating actors in the bureaucracy and legislature, their varying and differing policy preferences, purposes and power, the negotiations among them, and the policy "outcomes" that occur as a result of the compromises struck. In short, the last emphasizes the dynamics of the decision-making process and its central feature, the constant bargaining and trade-offs arranged among the players. It ought to be added that crisis policy, decided quickly by a few at the pinnacle of the executive branch, resembles policies made by authoritarian regimes, while noncrisis policy, characterized by the widespread participation of the bureaucracy and Congress over a fairly lengthy time period, tends to be highly democratic.

Our third dilemma for most security policies has been summed up as follows.

> A democratic government must accomplish two tasks: On the one hand, it must pursue policies which maximize the chances for success; on the other hand, it must secure the approval of its people for these foreign policies. . . . The necessity to perform these tasks simultaneously faces a democratic government with a dilemma; for the conditions under which popular support can be obtained for a foreign policy are not necessarily identical with the conditions under which such a policy can be successfully pursued. A popular foreign policy is not necessarily a good one.[10]

THE GROWTH OF PRESIDENTIAL PRIMACY

In an effort to strike a balance between the demands of the state system—or what Paul Seabury has called the "intrinsic authoritarian necessities of foreign affairs"[11]—and the democratic needs of the internal order, the framers of the U.S. Constitution vested exclusive responsibility for the conduct of foreign policy in the federal government and then divided its authority in this field, as in the domestic, between the president and

Congress. The president could receive and send ambassadors—that is, deal with representatives of foreign powers—but the Senate had to give its consent to treaties by a two-thirds vote as well as confirm top diplomatic, military, and political appointments. The president was appointed commander in chief of the armed forces, but only Congress was empowered to declare war, appropriate funds for the maintenance of military forces, and regulate commerce with other nations. It could also investigate the operations of the various executive departments, including those that participated in the formulation and implementation of the foreign policy of the United States.

Thus, while this sharing of the foreign policy power by separate branches was intended to ensure a check on presidential power, the president clearly was constitutionally the nation's chief diplomat and commander in chief. But a number of changes in the social and economic environment increasingly have upset the balance between the executive and legislative branches and shifted power toward the president. Most of these new conditions have affected the conduct of both foreign and domestic affairs in all nations, but particularly in those of the West. First, and perhaps most fundamental, is the general growth of "big government"—which has usually meant *executive* government. Running a highly urbanized, complex, industrial society has required big government and large bureaucracies to serve its manifold needs. The mass vote and the mobilization of new groups and classes into the political process have multiplied demands on government for services ranging from unending economic growth, high employment, subsidies of all types, stabilization of the economy, and the redistribution of power, status, and money to create a more equitable society. The list is endless.

Indeed, it was the growth of the role of the government in the domestic economy, as much as any international event, that, in the United States, marked the sharp shift in the balance between the president and the Congress. The Great Depression of the 1930s focused people's attention on Washington. The traditional forces of the marketplace had failed to readjust themselves to an era of great economic crisis, and the administration of Franklin D. Roosevelt, which began in 1933, committed the national government to direct intervention in the economy. Even during the pre-World War I administration of Woodrow Wilson, known for his liberal economic policies (which he called the "New Freedom"), total federal expenditures constituted less than 2 percent of the gross national product—(GNP), the value of all goods and services produced in the country. Half of those expenditures went for defense. By the 1930s, the figure for total spending rose to 7.7 percent, most of which (4.9 percent) was domestically oriented. The federal share of the GNP has continued to rise so that it was approaching 25 percent by the early '80s. This great increase in federal spending gave broad new responsibilities to the national government—and to the president who proposes and (at least indirectly) administers the programs. And, until

Ronald Reagan, presidents have not shied away from claiming credit for these programs, thus enhancing their power even further.

Presidents and prime ministers in the relatively open societies of the West, as leaders of political parties from whom the electorate expects the satisfaction of certain demands, have become the central figures; as heads of their party and government, they draw up the social and economic programs, as well as foreign policies, and it becomes their responsibility to submit and shepherd bills through their respective legislatures. For the most part, legislatures do not act on their own. They wait for the executive to submit a program. And it is on this record of achievement that the parties and their leaders run in the next election and seek to renew their mandate to govern. The fact is that presidents have become the authors of and spokesmen for national legislative programs and, by the 1980s, trillion dollar budgets.

Even nations that are neither democratic nor economically developed share this global trend toward executive government. States that do not possess a constitutional tradition (for example, the Soviet Union) may have a legislature, but such a body has no independent status and power. The executive has complete authority and governs unchallenged. In the new, former colonial, economically developing countries power also tends to be centralized in the executive. One-party governments and military regimes exist throughout the Third World; parliamentary bodies, with few exceptions, are in decay, if they still survive. Executive dominance, whether justified by efficiency, ideology, or impatience, has everywhere emerged as the way to ensure results or for an individual to retain power.

In the case of the United States, another obvious fact needs to be noted in this regard. The president is nationally elected, and he, more than any other figure, represents the national mood and is the spokesman for the nation's interests, domestic and foreign. Congress, on the other hand, represents local interests; its representatives in the House and "ambassadors from the states" in the Senate respond mainly to their constituents' interests. By contrast, in Great Britain, elections are organized around the parties and their national platforms. One votes for a member of Parliament because he or she represents one of the parties whose leader, if the party wins, becomes prime minister. But, unlike in Britain, the U.S. chief executive is also chief of state. He is more than a partisan leader and chief of government. In short, when he occupies the office of the presidency, he becomes the symbol of national unity and can thus draw on most citizens' patriotism and loyalty. In a nation increasingly diverse and fragmented, that symbolic role is very important. In Britain, the monarch is chief of state and stands above politics and differences over public policy, while the prime minister is chief of government. Therefore, a United States citizen may often feel politically schizophrenic, hating and loving the president at one and the same time (as a partisan and American). In Britain, the citizen can hate the prime minister and still love, respect, and feel patriotic about the king or queen.

Only the president can instantly communicate with the people. Television, especially, has done much to expand the president's powers, but even in the days before the widespread use of radio, Theodore Roosevelt referred to the White House as a "bully pulpit." This is all the more true today when the people look toward the president for everything from national defense to social justice. Harry Truman once said that the president is the lobbyist for all the people. As chief of state, whether receiving a distinguished foreign dignitary or visiting other nations, he is covered by the press and television cameras and therefore can remain first in his nation's eyes, if not always in its heart. In either capacity, whether he attends a summit conference with other Western leaders or Soviet leaders, or wishes to make a statement to the public via a press conference, television is present and is his to command; he has no problem getting on the nightly news.

Presidents play many roles: chief of state, chief executive, chief legislator, chief of party, chief diplomat, and commander in chief. But President Reagan added a new role: chief pastor. On several occasions when servicemen or civilians were killed (as in the Challenger space shuttle explosion in 1986), the president attended the services, eloquently eulogized those who had died serving their country and afterward, spent a few minutes, together with Mrs. Reagan, embracing and consoling each of the bereaved families. These moving ceremonies were clearly "a byproduct of television and the constant airing of foreign policy, which effectively makes the president personally responsible for its outcome, including casualties."[12]

Since World War II and the advent of the nuclear era, the president's foreign policy role has reinforced his central role in government to the point where he is no longer merely the "first among equals"; during the Cold War he became, as one writer has said of the English prime minister, the "sun around which planets revolve."[13] The Constitution gave the presidency specific grants of authority with a great potential for expansion. These grants, such as that of commander in chief, were written in such a way that they were open to future interpretations as circumstances changed. In a real sense, what was not said in the Constitution "proved ultimately more important than what was."[14] Often called the Constitution's "great silences," they gave presidents—especially strong presidents such as Lincoln, the two Roosevelts, Truman, Kennedy, Johnson, and Nixon—freedom to do what they thought needed to be done in unprecedented circumstances on behalf of the nation's interests as they defined these and to test the powers and limits of the office.

They were, to put it simply, "missing powers" in the Constitution. For example, the Constitution did not say where the powers to recognize other states or to proclaim neutrality were located. If the president and Senate must cooperate in the negotiation and ratification of a treaty, did they both have to agree also on when to terminate a treaty or can the president do so on his own? If Congress must declare war, does it also make peace? Who proclaims neutrality, the president because he is commander in chief or Congress because of its authority to declare war and regulate commerce? Does a president have to authority to send U.S. troops into Korea, Lebanon, or Grenada, or launch air attacks on Libya, or conclude military base agreements with foreign nations? Could a president, some ultimate day, believing Moscow was about to attack the United States, launch a preemptive strike on his own authority? One frequent manner of determining who exercises these powers has been to assume that the foreign affairs powers explicitly granted imply other powers: The president's power to appoint and receive ambassadors, for example, implies the power to recognize or withhold recognition from other states. The "implied powers" doctrine, however, leaves much room for struggles between the executive and legislative branches for control of the conduct of foreign affairs—as the former enhanced its powers, especially during this century. As Louis Henkin has noted, the powers specifically allocated to the president are so few that "a stranger reading the Constitution would get little inkling of such large presidential authority, for the powers explicitly vested in him are few and seem modest, far fewer and more modest, than those bestowed upon Congress."[15] "It seems incredible that these few meager grants support the most powerful office in the world and the multivaried, wide-flung webwork of foreign activity of the most powerful nation in the world."[16] One obvious reason for this is that the Founding Fathers did not foresee the United States soon playing an active and major role in international politics. In his farewell address, President Washington counseled his countrymen to take advantage of America's "detached and distant situation" from Europe and stay isolated from the "toils of European ambition, Rivalship, Interest, Humor or Caprice."[17] Today, the president is not only leader of the United States but in a sense, of the West. And whether he provides firm or fumbling leadership, his actions will have global consequences. Television coverage of foreign policy crises, dramas, and glamor magnifies the public's awareness of the president's leading role and its need for his leadership.

Thus we return to our question. Can a democratic American domestic order be reconciled with an executive powerful enough to safeguard the nation's security so that it can continue to enjoy its way of life? Former Senator Fulbright admitted he was a pessimist. "I for one am fairly well convinced that neither constitutional government nor democratic freedoms can survive indefinitely in a country chronically at war (presumably the Cold War), as America has been for the last three decades. Sooner or later, war will lead to dictatorship."[18] Has post-World War II American foreign policy—the means to protect the security of American democracy—subverted the very aims it was intended to serve? Let us take a closer look at the basic types of policies and the principal characteristics of each corresponding foreign policy process. It is our contention that there are three different types of foreign policies and that each is made in a different way.

THE DIFFERENT TYPES OF POLICIES

Security and Crisis Policies

All states need a foreign policy because they all exist in an essentially anarchical world in which each state lives in fear and must seek its own security.[19] There is no world government to protect individual states. Each must guard itself in a system in which states tend to view each other as potential adversaries rather than friends. The analogy is the proverbial town of the "old West" where there was no "law and order" and where men lived in fear of one another and wore guns to protect themselves against those who might want to rob them, take away their land, or who were just plain ornery and mean. State A might look at its neighbor B and see it is arming itself. Is B strengthening itself to deter a possible attack (a defensive action), or is it preparing to attack (an offensive action)? State B might declare that its intentions are peaceful and that it is increasing its military power only to ensure that A or other states will not attack it. But why should A believe that statement? Once B's capabilities have grown, it may attack; the declaration of peaceful intent may have been deceitful. Or, even if B had been sincere about its defensive intentions earlier, it can, after all, change its mind once it realizes its improved power position.

The point of this simple analogy is that, in general, states distrust one another. Even when one state extends the hand of friendship, the other wonders why. Is one state trying to deceive the other to strike later? Where their security is concerned, if not their survival, states are cautious and careful. No one guarantees them either; each is its own guardian. States, therefore, rarely take chances; the stakes are too high. The basic rule is "protect yourself." This is fundamental since security is regarded as the prerequisite for a nation to preserve its way of life. Forgetting this basic rule is to risk endangering one's territorial integrity and political independence.

The principal mechanism to ensure state security is in fact the balance of power. If one state matches another in strength, neither is likely to attack the other; but an imbalance may entice the stronger one to attack. Consequently, in the state system, in which each state sees an increase in power and security of another state as a loss of power and security for itself—a loss it regards as unacceptable—preserving the balance of power constitutes the heart of foreign policy. American foreign policy since World War II has been largely concerned with the central balance with its principal adversary, the Soviet Union, and a series of regional balances in Europe, Asia, the Middle East, and, since the 1970s, sub-Sahara Africa. Thus the United States is involved in virtually every area of the world, with many different nations as adversaries, allies, and developing countries. Military power—the threat and the actual use of force—has played a major deterrent and coercive role in this foreign policy, although other instruments, such as economic aid to strenghten an ally, have also been used widely.

American foreign policy is primarily concerned with assuring the nation's security, but there are more *specific* policies that also seek to preserve the nation's security. These include (but are not limited to) such policy areas as the defense budget (procurement and deployment of arms and personnel), arms control, limited war, alliances, arms transfers to allies and other countries, economic and technical aid, and intelligence operations against other states. Most of these policies are continuing ones because they involve long-term interests. The United States, as one of the world's two nuclear superpowers, has an additional interest in not only balancing Soviet military strength but in seeking to reduce the intensity of the arms competition and stabilize the balance in an environment of rapid technological innovation in weaponry. Foreign aid programs and arms transfers go on from year to year, although the recipients and the amounts they receive may change. Limited wars obviously—and fortunately—are not an everyday concern, but when they have occurred, as in Korea and Vietnam, the fighting has gone on for periods of three to eight years and they have consequently required major commitments of troops, arms, and money. And the use of force in other contingencies remains a constant possibility.

Crisis policies, by contrast, are distinguished by their relative infrequency and their short duration, but they make up for the lack of numbers by their utter seriousness and atmosphere of great danger. Frequently characterized by surprise, crisis policies are even more prominently featured by the perceived threat to a nation's vital interests and the lack of time the policy makers feel they have to deal with it. If they do not act quickly, the crisis situation, which in all probability took them by surprise and is in any case seen by them as endangering the country's fundamental security, will go against them. In these circumstances, the most critical element of a crisis is that the possibility of the threat or actual use of force—which underlies much of traditional international politics—is very high. In short, the likelihood of war erupting suddenly becomes a real danger. Even if in the case of a Soviet–American crisis (most crises in which the United States has been involved since World War II have been with the U.S.S.R.) the initial clash is at the level of threats or low levels of force, the possibility of escalation to a nuclear confrontation is always present. The art of crisis management is, therefore, defending the interests threatened (usually by invoking the threat of force) while simultaneously avoiding nuclear war.[20]

Intermestic Policies

If these two security policies comprise what is sometimes today called the "old" international politics, the increasingly important "new" foreign policy revolves around economics, specifically the issue of prosperity. Earlier, we noted that the major domestic cause for governmental growth, and especially the power of the presidency and executive branch, has been the increasing demand by citizens for more and more services. Governments all over the world, especially in democratic states where the electorate can hold its representatives accountable, are held responsible for the welfare of their peoples and for satisfying their ever higher expectations. This "welfare state" must, therefore, concern itself with economic growth, creation of jobs, higher incomes, and social programs for the disadvantaged. If political leaders do not want to lose office, their concern with social services must be at least as great as the military services. Security issues, except in moments of crisis, rarely touch the mass of the electorate personally, even if they are aware of important foreign policy events from watching television news or reading newspapers. But employment, salaries, and prices affect their pocketbooks. Bread-and-butter issues arouse them quickly, certainly in time for the next election.

Most nations do not have the natural resources or industrial/agricultural capacity to ensure their own prosperity. They must import raw materials, manufactured goods, and food items. Nations, and especially their economies, are thus increasingly a part of an interdependent world. Even a government like that of the United States, a country possessing many of the resources it needs, an enormous industry, and productive agriculture, no longer completely controls its economic destiny. Ever since 1973 and the dramatic increase in oil prices, it has become clear that the economic prosperity of the United States is both sensitive to events overseas and increasingly vulnerable in a more and more interdependent world.[21] America's welfare can be undermined if, for example, a less developed country possessing a vital resource such as oil withholds that resource or dramatically raises the price. OPEC's 1973 price increase and the 1979 jump after the Shah of Iran was deposed lowered America's living standards at the time, increased inflation, precipitated the worst recession since the 1930s and made it more difficult to resume a rapid rate of economic growth.

Only after oil prices had shot to close to $35 a barrel did this country begin a serious policy of conservation, switching to non-OPEC oil and greater use of coal; in addition, the closing of factories and production cutbacks helped lower oil imports. Lower American, as well as European, demand suddenly produced an oil surplus and a price reduction to $29 a barrel. Later, oil prices plummeted briefly to below the 1973 level of $12 per barrel before they once more rose to $18 per barrel.

The oil issue erased the distinction between international and domestic policies. Caught up in both, it could best be characterized as "intermestic." In an increasingly interdependent-world, no nation any longer fully controlled its own economic destiny; what Washington decided to do about inflation or recession might be less important than what Saudi Arabia or Iran decided. Because jobs and income were involved, these intermestic issues became critical to the electorate, which was profoundly affected by more than the oil policy. The United States, for example, used to be the world's breadbasket; American farmers were the most productive in the world. During the 1970s agricultural exports were a main source of earning dollars, paying for some of the imported oil, and keeping the resulting trade imbalances—the difference between what is spent on imports and earned on exports—from widening further. But by the 1980s, other countries had also become productive food producers and were exporting as well. Some of these countries, such as China, Australia, France, and other members of the European economic community (Common Market), were friends and allies. As they undercut one another's prices, tensions between these nations grew, affecting their political-military relationships. A collective solution to the problem was widely promoted since no national one was possible: to cut the subsidies farmers received to produce their staples. But that was a difficult solution, given the political power of farmers in all countries.

U.S. and other farmers were not the only group that was upset; so too were U.S. workers. American industry, once the world's most powerful and prosperous, had never depended on exports or been threatened by imports. U.S. goods were well made—items labeled "Made in the U.S.A." were sought after throughout the world—and because they were mass produced, they were more affordable than equivalent foreign-made goods. But during the 1970s this changed drastically as foreign—especially Japanese—cars poured in during the oil crisis while American-made cars were in the main poorly assembled, unreliable gas guzzlers. Never having had to be competitive in the world economy, the United States suddenly found itself immersed in that economy and unable to compete effectively. Foreign labor was usually less expensive and often more educated and skillful; foreign products were desirable, well made and finished, and competitively priced. America, confronted not only by an economically revived Europe but, more competitively, by Japan and other export oriented economically developing Asian states such as Taiwan and South Korea, suffered in the international marketplace. The Reagan administration's decision to cut taxes drastically while financing a large increase in military spending resulted in an enormous budget deficit of over $200 billion, and a jump in the value of the dollar. These factors made American products too expensive for foreigners while rendering imports more affordable. The resulting trade deficit had a disastrous impact on workers and farmers, increasing unemployment and contributing to the foreclosure of farms. One long-term consequence, even though the dollar has since gone down, somewhat reduced the huge monthly trade imbalances, and made United States' products less expensive, has been political pressure for protectionism. The basic problem remains the uncompetitiveness of the United States' economy in the world economy.

POLICIES AND STAKES

A key element in any situation in which any of these governmental policies may be invoked is how the various actors involved in decision making perceive the consequences of their actions. The differences between foreign and domestic policy making are due, at least in part, to the different stakes involved and how the actors perceive them. In domestic policy making, participants can often differentiate between the "winners" and the "losers." In foreign policy making, on the other hand, the entire nation is usually seen as either "winning" or "losing." Most foreign policy decisions do not result with one group in the population gaining at the expense of others.* In domestic policy, the most clear-cut example of the winners-losers dichotomy may be antipoverty programs, which are specifically designed to provide aid to an identifiable group in the population (the poor), who are classified as losers by such standards as income or housing. The poor are viewed as a "have-not" group, and the debate surrounding antipoverty programs is marked by arguments about what the government should do to aid disadvantaged groups at the expense (in taxes or prerogatives) of the "haves" in society—those people who have more or less "made it." The goal, then, is to turn some of the losers into winners.

On the traditional issues of foreign policy, however, decisions are not generally viewed in terms of winners against losers. Foreign policy decisions are more frequently viewed based on the entire country (rather than any particular group in the population) winning or losing. This is most noticeable when a country goes to war or is involved in a crisis. The winners and losers are the nations (or alliances) involved, not specific groups like the oil companies, the farmers, or the poor. Tensions within the country on domestic legislation are put aside as the population "rallies around the flag" in support of the president's actions as commander in chief.[22] Simply stated, the stakes are very different in foreign and domestic politics.

In domestic politics, there are a multitude of interest groups concerned with the decisions of government and attempting to influence them. Each group wants to be a winner rather than a loser. Even though the president initiates more domestic legislation than does Congress, the chief executive's hands are tied to a much greater extent in domestic politics than in foreign politics. Groups and individuals looking out for their own interests attempt to influence Congress on how money should be spent, which tax loopholes should be closed or left untouched, and how business and labor should be regulated. The process of raising revenue and spending it for domestic programs is marked by a relatively high degree of conflict among the groups contending for special benefits. The mediating actors in domestic politics are Congress and the executive departments that draw up the federal budget. To some extent, the very large scope of the demands made can also serve to moderate these demands made by interest groups. The president simply cannot spend his time listening to all of these demands. He must in many cases give up a large part of his power to Congress.

---

*Not everybody sees foreign policy in this way. Notably, radical critics (on both the left and the right) do see foreign policy decisions as involving domestic winners and losers. Critics on the left, for example, may view foreign policy decision making as a conflict between capitalists and the workers (just as they do in domestic politics).

All of these conflicts and more are found on intermestic issues. In addition to the aforementioned actors on domestic policy, we find the president trying to balance a whole series of conflicting interests: the vitality of the American economy, the coherence of American policy, and the various pressures from multinational companies who often have divided loyalties. The president will have to balance the American demand for oil against the traditional policy of providing strong support for Israel. Oil companies, as well as other businesses operating abroad, find themselves active participants in the intermestic policy process. To meet their goals of making as large a profit as possible, they might pursue policies (such as advocating a tilt in Middle Eastern policy toward the Arabs) that might be at odds with that of official U.S. policy.

There are, then, so many different actors, foreign and domestic, and the issues involved may be vital to the nation's security and certainly to its economic well-being. International politics and economics, as well as intermestic policies, clearly involve very high stakes. There are "winners," "losers," and sometimes "nonwinners" as well—groups that might not be affected by a particular change in policy through careful strategic planning or simple happenstance. Indeed, we find not only winners and losers but also many "high rollers"—actors willing to take major risks, such as the oil-producing nations, which steadily raised their prices during the 1970s in the belief that their strategic position was superior. What makes intermestic politics so complicated is that it encompasses not only the divisions we find on domestic policies, but also the "we-they" conflicts of foreign policy.

The situation is quite different with crisis and, to a large extent, security policies. Since foreign policy decisions are not perceived either by the public or by the decision makers as involving methods of "dividing up the spoils," the conflict over decisions made will involve a much smaller circle of actors. Interest groups become mobilized only when they see the potential to "win" something for themselves, but on most foreign policy issues either the entire country wins or the country loses. This is not to deny that some citizens or groups may differ vastly on foreign policy questions from other citizens or groups. But, significantly, each group views its own position as the one that is in the "national" (or even "international") interest.

The basic distinction then, between conflicts over domestic and foreign affairs concerns the way participants view the stakes of the policy process. On most domestic policies, including intermestic policies, there are more likely to be winners and nonwinners than winners and losers. These policies, also called "distributive" policies, are "perceived to confer direct benefits upon one or more groups [but are] determined with little or no conflict over the passage of the legislation but only over the size and specific distribution of the shares."[23] On crisis decisions, however, the whole nation either wins or loses, and the nature of the conflict on such policies will be quite different. Conflict on these crisis decisions is most likely to resemble the less frequent but loudly argued cases of domestic policies that propose to redistribute income from the haves in society to the have-nots, where again we see a clash between inevitable winners and losers. Security policies involve many actors who may have diverse goals and different perceptions of the stakes involved. Crisis decisions, on the other hand, involve only a small number of actors, and the stakes involved are generally quite clear. Indeed, the high stakes involved in crisis decisions are a key reason why the president is the dominant actor in this area. The president is the only actor in the American political system capable of the swift and decisive action required in crises.

CHARACTERISTICS OF FOREIGN POLICY DECISION MAKING

The principal characteristics of decision making in the foreign policy sphere may be summed up as follows.

1. The actors and processes of foreign policy decision making differ for each of the three types of foreign policy decisions: crisis decisions, security decisions, and intermestic policy decisions.

Crisis decisions, as noted, usually involve an element of surprise. The leaders have not been anticipating a threat from a foreign power; when the threat does occur, they perceive the need for a quick response lest the situation deteriorate to the detriment of the nation's security and violence ensues. For this reason, crisis decisions are made by the small number of actors at the very top of the executive "policy making machine."

Security decisions, on the other hand, involve long-term policies. Most security policies, although formulated by the president and the various foreign policy bureaucracies, involve money and thus require congressional approval. Because many actors must participate, these policies may require lengthy deliberation. Furthermore, because security policies express continuing goals and commitments, they tend to involve stable sets of actors.

Intermestic decisions may involve both short-term and long-term considerations. Energy, for example, is an issue of enduring importance but it may also be subject to short-term factors such as an oil embargo or temporary loss of supplies. These issues affect both relations among nations and politics within nations. Intermestic issues, therefore, mobilize all the actors that domestic policies usually do: the executive agencies whose jurisdiction is basically domestic, Congress, interest groups, and public opinion. Consequently, the State Department, articulating the "national interest," will hardly be heard above the din of voices of the Departments of Treasury, Agriculture, Labor, and Commerce, their respective congressional committees, and interest groups in each of these and other policy areas. All these actors feel expert in these areas, possess major stakes and can articulate their viewpoints, and usually have a good deal of clout, since they represent specific, well-organized, and well-financed groups who normally represent millions of voters.

2. The foreign policy elite is a relatively small group located in the executive branch, primarily the political leadership and the professional officers of the principal foreign policy bureaucracies. More specifically, this includes the president (who is elected), special assistants on national security affairs, secretaries, under secretaries and assistant secretaries (political appointees), as well as senior professional officers of both the Departments of State and Defense and the Central Intelligence Agency. On a secondary level, there are the upper ranks of the Arms Control and Disarmament Agency, the U.S. Information Agency, and the Agency for International Development, as well as other departments and agencies that have an intermittent interest in specific foreign policy issues, for example, the Department of the Treasury's interest in monetary policy or the Department of Agriculture's desire to export food products.

3. Most noncrisis foreign policy decisions are arrived at through bureaucratic politics. Different bureaucracies have different perspectives and training for their professional staffs, a need to enhance their prestige, budgets, and influence—the more so if they are convinced of the importance of their contribution to the nation's security and well-being. The different departments and agencies, in short have their own biases and tend to see the same problem differently, or even focus on different parts of the same problem and therefore come up with varying and conflicting policy recommendations. The result, on the one hand, is bureaucratic conflict; on the other hand, the need to make a decision produces a "strain toward agreement or consensus."[24] Policy, therefore, results from a process of bargaining and compromising. This is particularly the case on intermestic issues, where even more diverse interests are involved than we find for security policy or most domestic issues. This multiplicity of actors, many of them outside of the executive branch, makes bargaining particularly difficult—and there is no guarantee that a satisfactory compromise will be reached. Stalemate remains a strong possibility.

4. The central and key figure in the foreign policy process is the president. Although noncrisis policy is largely the product of bureaucratic conflict, this does not mean—as models of bureaucratic struggle often imply—that the president is merely one player among many, one chief among many departmental chiefs. He is more than merely a first among equals; he is by far the most important player.[25] He, after all, appoints the chiefs; presumably to a large degree they reflect his values and owe him, as well as their departments, a degree of loyalty. They

can be fired if they no longer serve the president's purposes. He can also "stack the deck" by assigning a policy to a particular chief and department or set of people. If he selects "hawks" to investigate whether to intervene militarily in Vietnam, as Kennedy did, he is likely to receive a report favoring intervention; had he chosen "doves" he would in all probability have gotten back quite a different answer.

Moreover, many problems require the consideration of so many political, economic, social, and psychological elements that nowhere short of the presidential level can these factors really be balanced off against one another and integrated into an overall policy. But perhaps the most important factor—in an era in which presidents have grown increasingly fond of being their own secretaries of state—is that presidents will seize for themselves specific areas of policy (for instance, arms control) or policies (for instance, negotiating an end to the war in Vietnam). "The ability of bureaucracies to independently establish policies is a function of presidential attention. Presidential attention is a function of presidential values. The chief executive involves himself in those areas which he determines to be important."[26] Bureaucratic power is thus to a large degree a function of presidential—and, even further, congressional and public—inattention. In practice this means bureaucracy plays its largest role in routine day-to-day matters, its smallest during crisis periods.

The comparative presidential ability to gain legislative support for his foreign as distinct from his domestic policy has been summed up by one leading scholar of American politics as follows.

> The president's normal problem with domestic policy is to get congressional support for the programs he prefers. In foreign affairs, in contrast, he can almost always get support for policies that he believes will protect the nation—but his problem is to find a viable policy. . . .
>
> In the realm of foreign policy there has not been a single major issue on which presidents, when they were serious and determined, have failed. The list of their victories is impressive: entry into the United Nations, the Marshall Plan, NATO, the Truman Doctrine, the decisions to stay out of Indochina in 1954 and to intervene in Vietnam in the 1960s, aid to Poland and Yugoslavia, the test-ban treaty, and many more. Serious setbacks to the president in controlling foreign policy are extraordinary and unusual.[27]

On intermestic policies, not surprisingly, the president's ability to initiate, lead, and maneuver will, as in domestic policies in general, be more constrained than on security issues. As one writer, referring to the growth of intermestic issues, which he calls nondefense issues, has said:

> There is likely to be an increasing emphasis on *nondefense* foreign policy issues, most of which will have a great impact on *domestic* politics and great attraction for domestic interest groups. Problems with the mone-

tary system, trade deficits and surpluses, energy policy, and the import or export of things such as inflation, unemployment, technology, and pollution will consume more and more of the foreign policy effort. This will occur . . . because these nondefense issues will have a larger absolute impact on American society. . . . As post-Vietnam foreign policy becomes more oriented to nonsecurity affairs, the president's choices will become more constrained, on the one hand, by independent foreign actors he will not be able to outmaneuver, such as economic institutions and foreign governments' economic policies, and on the other hand, by the fact that his decisions will have real domestic impact. . . . Indeed, the seamlessness of the distinction between foreign economic and domestic economic policy may simply extend the president's weakness in domestic policy to foreign policy as well.[28]

Whereas in foreign policy, presidents can usually take the initiative and gain great satisfaction from the role they play on the world stage—an opportunity few can resist—in policies that affect the domestic arena, presidents find themselves more constrained by the Congress, interest groups, and media, and on some issues, public opinion.

5. The role of parties in foreign policy has been defined in terms quite different from those applied to domestic policy by politicians themselves as well as by journalists and scholars. Largely stirred by the memory of the defeat of the Versailles treaty following World War I in the conflict between a Democratic president and a Republican Senate, the post-World War II partisanship mood was one of the usual type of political considerations that, it was held, had no place in the conduct of foreign affairs. The national interest was to be placed ahead of party interest. In protecting the nation against external threats, the president deserved the support of both parties. "Bipartisanship" became the new slogan and the patriotic policy to follow; partisanship was to be confined strictly to domestic affairs. Executive–legislative hostility and party controversy over foreign policy might undermine the stability and continuity of U.S. policy, make it impossible to speak with one national voice in world affairs, and erode the nation's credibility in its dealing with friends and foes.

Since Vietnam, bipartisanship has been on the decline. As the Democrats swung more to the left and Republicans to the right, the gap between the parties grew. One pursued "world order politics," focusing on the interdependence between the industrial Western democracies and the less-developed countries of Asia, the Middle East, Africa, and Latin-America. The other continued to concentrate on the U.S.–Soviet rivalry; the Cold War, far from being over, had entered a new and more competitive phase. While security issues were increasingly subject to partisan conflict, intermestic issues like trade remained partisan. For instance, the Democrats have traditionally supported lower tariffs while Republicans have sought to protect industry; today, the Democrats are more disposed to support protectionism while the Republicans oppose protective tariffs. Still, on these types of issues, regional and economic interests may cut across party lines. But on security issues, party differences have become clear, especially during the four Carter and eight Reagan years.

6. The Congress has been traditionally supportive of the president in foreign policy. Legislators to a large extent felt a lack of familiarity and sense of incompetence on foreign affairs. Viewing them as esoteric matters beyond their personal experience, in contrast to farm or labor problems, confronted with expert civilian and military witnesses at committee hearings, they usually have tended to subordinate their own presumed expertise—political judgment of the feasibility and acceptability of administration policies—to that of the president and his phalanx of bureaucratic help.

But since Vietnam, Congress has become more assertive and less willing to accept presidential dominance on foreign policy. There has been a renewed concern for the establishment of a balance of power between the president and Congress in policy making, although this reassertion of congressional power does not mean that the legislature has become an equal partner with the president. While more members of the Congress are more interested in foreign policy today than at any time in recent history, they are still a substantial minority within the Congress. Most legislators remain primarily concerned with domestic policies—and with their own reelection campaigns. Most foreign policy questions are not salient to voters, so members of Congress tend to downplay their importance and devote their time to issues and services that are more rewarding. Thus, only a minority of the legislators are strongly concerned about foreign policy and even they tend to be supportive of the president in crisis situations.

There are more challenges than before on security decisions, but the greatest congressional involvement is found on intermestic policies. These issues (energy, trade) have great impacts on the day-to-day lives of the people in members' districts and the stakes are perceived as very high. Members see themselves as the only protectors of their districts' interests. The key intermestic policy battles are fought in the legislature, where presidential programs are often held hostage and do not always escape alive. Regional and economic controversies surrounding intermestic politics are clearly reflected in the localism of Congress and its decentralized (many say parochial) system of committees and subcommittees.

7. Interest group representation, articulation, and influence, while pervasive in domestic politics, are not nearly as extensive or intense in the traditional area of foreign policy concerned with security issues. In this area interest groups tend to lack the interest, experience, and above

all, the knowledge they possess on domestic issues. Nonetheless, ethnic groups in a nation of immigrants have often pressed for policies favorable to the former mother country. In contrast, as already suggested, on intermestic issues so many groups have interests in the outcome of policies and see the stakes as so high that these groups may control much of the policy process. Businesses, banks, agricultural and shipping interests, and labor organizations have a natural interest in trade, foreign investment, and tariff issues. Virtually nobody fails to perceive a critical interest in energy policy (Chapter 6).

8. The public has, like the Congress, largely been supportive of the president's conduct of foreign policy, particularly before Vietnam. One reason is that most Americans simply are poorly informed and uninterested in foreign policy issues. Their knowledge and experience, like that of most senators and representatives, relate to affairs nearer home, such as family and professional life; the political opinions they do hold are more likely to be about national politics. At best, policy makers may sense a general mood, which may set broad limits on what they regard as feasible and permissible, but they do not receive specific operational cues. In general, it would be more accurate to say that public opinion on foreign policy is a response to the policy makers' decisions and to public presentation of the issues. On intermestic issues, however, much of the public does not make a clear-cut distinction between domestic and foreign policy considerations. Thus, these issues can easily become a source of great controversy, since citizens may expect that domestic political considerations will determine how to resolve questions involving the state of the economy. The public is less supportive of the president during times of domestic hardship, for they expect him to provide immediate relief for these sorts of pocketbook problems and display little patience when he cannot do so.

We can sum up these characteristics with the following diagram of concentric circles. In these circles (see Figure 1–1), the central decision-making locus on foreign policy is the president and his key advisers. In the second circle are the major foreign policy agencies and the armed services, the second-rank and less-influential foreign policy departments, presidential and other executive departmental advisers, and cabinet members whose primary responsibility is in the domestic sphere but who may be consulted on foreign policy questions. The innermost circle is composed of a select few members of the administration; the outer circles have successively more members and correspondingly less impact on foreign policy decisions. Congress is in the third circle, while political parties, interest groups, "personal diplomacy," public opinion, and the mass media are in the fourth circle. But the issue is not solely one of numbers and how close the various actors are to the inner circle; it is also a matter of time. The longer a policy is debated and the more prolonged the process of making policy, the more likely that

FIGURE 1–1   The Concentric Circles of Power in Foreign Policy Decision
          Making

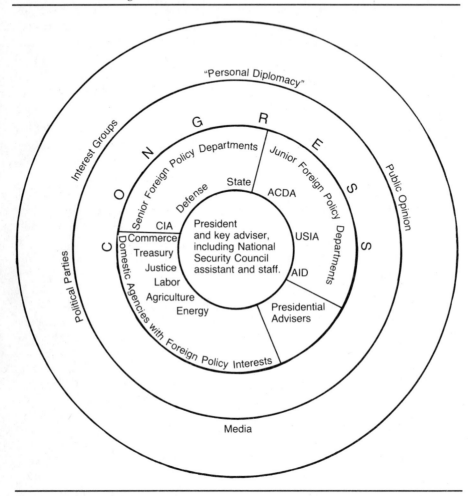

SOURCE: Adapted from Roger Hilsman, *To Move A Nation* (New York: Doubleday Publishing, 1967), pp.
541–44.

it will spill from the inner circles to the outer circles and become part of the
public debate. On intermestic policies, of course, the outer circles tend to be
involved early and may be more influential than the inner circle, circumscribing presidential leadership.

   All three types of policies revolve around the central question of democratic decision making on foreign policy. How much participation, and by
which actors, do we want or can we tolerate? The larger the number of participants involved in making decisions, the more difficult it will be to reach

a concensus on what ought to be done. That is why in a crisis, participation is kept narrowly confined. More broadly, the question is whether American democracy, with its checks and balances and its goal of preserving individual freedom and preventing political tyranny, can also effectively protect and enhance the nation's security and well-being in a dangerous and more interdependent world.

NOTES

1. Aaron Wildavsky, "The Two Presidencies," *Trans-Action* (December 1966), p. 7.
2. Paul Seabury, in *Power, Freedom and Diplomacy* (New York: Vintage, 1967), p. 189, elaborates on this tension.
3. John Locke, *Two Treatises of Government* (Cambridge: Cambridge University Press, 1960), pp. 383–84 (italics and capitalization of nouns omitted).
4. George F. Kennan, *American Diplomacy 1900–1950* (Chicago: University of Chicago Press, 1951), p. 73.
5. J. William Fulbright, *The Crippled Giant* (New York: Vintage, 1972), p. 193.
6. Ibid., p. 198.
7. Ibid., p. 218.
8. Kennan, *American Diplomacy*, pp. 93–94.
9. Bayless Manning, "The Congress, the Executive and Intermestic Affairs: Three Proposals," *Foreign Affairs*, January 1977, pp. 306–24.
10. Hans J. Morgenthau, *A New Foreign Policy for the United States* (New York: Praeger Publishers, 1969), pp. 150–51.
11. Seabury, *Power, Freedom and Diplomacy*, p. 196.
12. Henry G. Graff, "Presidents Are Not Pastors," *New York Times*, May 27, 1987.
13. Ivor W. Jennings, *Cabinet Government* (Cambridge: Cambridge University Press, 1951), p. 183.
14. Seabury, *Power, Freedom and Diplomacy*, p. 196.
15. Louis Henkin, *Foreign Affairs and Constitution* (Mineola, N.Y.: The Foundation Press), p. 37.
16. Ibid., p. 41. See also his "Foreign Affairs and the Constitution," *Foreign Affairs*, Winter 1987/88, p. 284–310.
17. Quoted by Felix Gilbert, *To the Farewell Address* (Princeton, N.J.: Princeton University Press, 1961), p. 145.
18. Fulbright, *The Crippled Giant*, p. 241.
19. John Spanier, *Games Nations Play*, 6th ed. (Washington, D.C.: *Congressional Quarterly*, 1987 chaps. 2 and especially 5.
20. Ibid., ch. 9.
21. Robert O. Keehane and Joseph S. Nye, *Power and Interdependence* (Boston: Little, Brown, 1977), pp. 11–15.
22. See Kenneth N. Waltz, *Foreign Policy and Democratic Politics* (Boston: Little, Brown, 1967), pp. 274–75, and John E. Mueller, *War, Presidents, and Public Opinion* (New York: John Wiley & Sons, 1973), p. 211.
23. Robert H. Salisbury, "The Analysis of Public Policy: A Search for Theories and Roles," in *Political Science and Public Policy*, ed., Austin Ranney (Chicago:

Markham, 1968), p. 158. See also Salisbury and John Heinz, "A Theory of Policy Analysis and Some Preliminary Applications," in *Policy Analysis and Political Science,* ed., Ira Sharkansky (Chicago: Markham, 1970), pp. 39–60.

On the original distinction between distributive and redistributive policies in the literature of political science, see the pioneering article by Theodore J. Lowi, "American Business, Public Policy, Case Studies, and Political Theory," *World Politics,* July 1964, pp. 677–715. On the applicability of distributive and redistributive policies to the study of foreign policy, see James N. Rosenau, "Foreign Policy as an Issue Area," in *Domestic Sources of Foreign Policy,* ed., Rosenau (New York: Free Press, 1967), pp. 11–50; and Lowi, "Making Democracy Safe for the World: National Politics and Foreign Policy," in ibid., pp. 295–331.

24. Roger Hilsman, *To Move a Nation* (New York: Doubleday Publishing, 1967), p. 541.

25. See Stephen D. Krasner, "Are Bureaucracies Important?" *Foreign Policy,* Summer 1972, pp. 159–79, for an incisive critique of the bureaucratic model.

26. Ibid., p. 168.

27. Wildavsky, "Two Presidencies," pp. 7–8.

28. Donald A. Peppers, "The Two Presidencies: Eight Years Later," in *Perspectives on the Presidency,* ed., Aaron Wildavsky (Boston: Little, Brown, 1975), pp. 463–64, 469.

Chapter Two

Presidential Preeminence in the Making of Foreign Policy

PRESIDENTIAL PRIMACY IN FOREIGN AFFAIRS

The preeminence of presidents in the domain of foreign policy is visible in the names attached to specific policies: Washington's Farewell Address, Jefferson's Embargo, the Monroe Doctrine, Theodore Roosevelt's Big Stick, Wilson's Fourteen Points, Franklin Roosevelt's Good Neighbor Policy, the Truman Doctrine, the Eisenhower Doctrine, the Nixon Doctrine and the Reagan Doctrine. During his years in office, President Nixon even issued an annual State of the World message to supplement the yearly State of the Union message. (The last formerly included a president's assessments and general recommendations on foreign and domestic policies; Nixon separated the two.) President Carter, after the Soviet invasion of Afghanistan in 1979, declared the Carter Doctrine, which committed the United States to preserving the independence of the oil-producing states bordering the Persian Gulf. The Reagan Doctrine embodied U.S. support for guerrillas trying to overthrow Marxist regimes in some Third World countries.

Indeed, between the end of World War II and Vietnam, most of our presidents have been primarily interested in and concerned with foreign policy issues. Truman had little choice; circumstances made it necessary for him to give most of his time to foreign policy. President Eisenhower, the general who had led Allied armies to victory in Europe, was elected during the protracted Korean War, which he promised to end. John Kennedy left no doubt that he sought his fame and reputation by his handling of foreign policy; in his inaugural address he confidently asserted that the United States "shall pay any price, bear any burden, meet any hardship, support any friend, oppose any foe to assure the survival and the success of liberty."[1] President Nixon, too, clearly considered foreign policy his particular area of expertise and showed far less interest in domestic affairs. Before his

27

inauguration, he was quoted as saying that the country needed a president for the conduct of foreign policy; the cabinet could take care of domestic policies. His reorientation of American policy toward Communist China and his negotiations with the Soviets on a broad front from arms control to trade preoccupied the president in his attempt to lay the foundation of a "generation of peace."

By contrast, President Lyndon Johnson's fate tragically symbolized the plight of a president whose principal experience was domestic and whose fundamental wish was to enact a social reform program to rival that of his mentor, Franklin Roosevelt. Unfortunately the world would not go away. Thus Johnson, on succeeding President Kennedy after the latter's assassination, pushed more liberal social legislation through Congress than any president in the twentieth century, including Franklin Roosevelt. But foreign policy proved his undoing. Feeling inexperienced in this area, he kept Kennedy's advisers, all of whom had been counseling the escalating intervention in Vietnam and therefore had a vested interest in the success of the Vietnam policy; he thereby almost unthinkingly committed himself to a larger intervention. Johnson refused to do what he should have done—appoint men he knew and whose judgments he trusted. Thus, when it was too late he appointed one such man, Clark Clifford, as secretary of defense. Clifford, after reevaluating the war effort, recommended deescalating the war and beginning peace negotiations. But feeling cowed by what he called Kennedy's "Hahvuhd" types, Johnson kept them around, believing they had the knowledge and experience he lacked; he was mistaken. Johnson paid for his mistaken judgment; he decided not to run for reelection in 1968.

Gerald Ford, Nixon's successor also had little experience in foreign policy. After long service in the House, he became president only by the rarest of circumstances. First, the vice president was forced to resign because of kickbacks he had taken while governor of Maryland and, second, the president left office because of a pending impeachment proceeding in the Congress. Ford, however, had a very experienced and forceful secretary of state in Henry Kissinger. Carter was the first governor in the postwar period to become president. Even though he had served on the Trilateral Commission, the purpose of which was to bring about closer relations between the United States and its democratic and industrial allies in Western Europe and Japan, he had no foreign policy experience and relied heavily on a number of advisers. The point, however, is clear: whatever the president's background and however much or little he is interested in foreign policy, he soon becomes immersed in foreign policy issues. One of the ironies of the Carter presidency in this respect was that the president was widely perceived as having failed as a manager of the economy and that his achievements really were in the foreign policy area: the Panama Canal treaties, Camp David and the Israeli-Egyptian peace treaty, the official recognition of the People's Republic of China, and the SALT II treaty (even though the Senate never ratified it). President Reagan, another former governor, also focused on domestic policy during most of his first administration. More than any of his predecessors, Reagan was uninterested in foreign policy matters; at press conferences he frequently displayed his ignorance by making gross factual errors when asked about international events—errors that later had to be "corrected" or explained by White House statements. A strong anti-Soviet, Reagan would issue broad directives such as a military buildup, while avoiding the specifics of policies (except in the cases of his involvement in the covert war against the Nicaraguan government and his proposal for Strategic Defense Initiative). He believed in delegating authority to the responsible cabinet officers. Yet it was Reagan the "great communicator" who, with his patriotic speeches and generally tough rhetoric stirred the nation. He made Americans feel good about themselves again, and gave them pride that the United States was once more "standing up" to the Soviet Union and terrorists (only to weaken the credibility of his administration by trading arms for hostages with Iran).

THE SELECTION AND CAMPAIGN FOR THE PRESIDENCY

The Recruitment of Presidential Candidates

The central role of the president in foreign affairs has been reflected during the post-World War II period—from the eruption of the Cold War to the end of the war in Vietnam—by the pattern of recruitment of presidential candidates. Until World War II, the governorship had supplied a long list of presidential candidates. Since the end of the Civil War, the list included, among others, Wilson, Theodore Roosevelt, Coolidge, and Franklin D. Roosevelt. While the United States was largely an isolationist country, this training ground for presidents was incomparable. It was at the state level that they gained experience in dealing with the problems of pre-Depression domestic America; four of the presidents since 1945 have served in the Senate. At a time when the United States was one of the two leading powers in the world, when nuclear weapons would mean the deaths of tens of millions of Americans if war erupted, this is not really surprising. The expertise for dealing with these key issues of war and peace was in Washington, not state capitals. And in Washington, the Senate is the senior legislative body and is more involved in foreign policy making than the House. Thus the emergence of the Senate as a launching platform for presidential candidates is natural. Truman was a senator, although he was not selected by Roosevelt as vice president in 1944 because of his knowledge of foreign affairs. But what is striking about post-Truman presidential and most vice presidential candidates until 1976—especially the winners of each nomination in both parties—is (1) the predominance of U.S. senators and (2) membership of those senators on either the Foreign Relations Committee or the Armed Services Committee, with a slight edge for the first. The standout exception was Eisenhower, a military officer and public servant with much experience in foreign policy and diplomacy.

Two senators who were unsuccessful in their first tries for a place on their parties' national tickets and were successful the second time had in the interim become members of the key Senate committees. John Kennedy (D-Mass.) in 1956 was a member of the Senate Government Operations Committee when he sought the Democratic vice presidency; four years later, when he became his party's presidential nominee, he was on the Foreign Relations Committee. Barry Goldwater (R-Ariz.), unsuccessful in 1960, was successful in 1964 and had in the meantime become a Senate Armed Services Committee member. Edmund Muskie (D-Maine), the Democratic vice presidential candidate in 1968, joined Foreign Relations before the next election, when in the early going he was considered the front-runner for the Democratic presidential nomination.

In contrast George McGovern did not become a member of the Senate Foreign Relations Committee until after he had lost his race for the presidency in 1972. McGovern's concern for foreign policy was said by his opponents in Senate races in 1974 and 1980 to lead to a neglect for his constituents' concern with domestic issues (see Chapter 3 for a more general discussion of this theme). In 1980 he lost his Senate seat but remained an active voice in Washington, particularly on foreign policy; indeed, his 1984 quest for the Democratic nomination stressed international issues. Almost all of the Democratic aspirants in 1984 had foreign policy experience, ranging from service on Senate committees to former Florida Governor Reuben Askew's position as Carter's special trade representative. Only the Reverend Jesse Jackson, who had not held public office, lacked an active foreign policy background. To compensate for this, he, as Carter did in 1976 and Reagan did before the 1980 election, toured Western Europe before announcing his candidacy. He later gained the release of first an American navy flier shot down in an engagement with the Syrians in Lebanon and then some Americans (mainly alleged drug runners) and a number of Cuban political prisoners while visiting Castro in Cuba.

Governors were generally unsuccessful presidential aspirants from 1945 to 1976—until after Vietnam and the resulting disillusionment with foreign policy and increasing domestic economic concerns. Two governors were nominated during the Cold War: Thomas Dewey (R-N.Y.) in 1948 and Adlai Stevenson (D-Ill.) in 1952 and 1956; the last had some foreign policy experience. State executives who made bids for the presidential nomination and failed—Nelson Rockefeller, William Scranton, and W. Averell Harriman— had considerable foreign policy experience. But most governors did not; because their experience was primarily domestic, they were not even nominated. A state's chief executive who demonstrated an interest in foreign policy but also an inability to handle international problems was even worse off than a governor who stressed domestic concerns almost to the exclusion of foreign policy. A case in point is former Michigan Governor George Romney. Romney was considered the front-runner for the Republican nomination in 1968 until he stated that the Johnson administration had succeeded in "brainwashing" him on the proper course of action in Vietnam. The charge backfired on Romney, who appeared to many to be too gullible on any policy. The first governor actually elected on a national ticket in the postwar years was Spiro T. Agnew in 1968 and 1972, who had not aspired to the post and was surprised at being selected by candidate Nixon in 1968 to balance the GOP ticket geographically and ideologically. Both Nixon and Agnew, of course, left office involuntarily; Agnew was then replaced by Nelson Rockefeller who, as noted, had considerable foreign policy experience (indeed, he introduced Henry Kissinger to national political life). At the time of his nomination, Rockefeller was serving as the head of a self-financed research organization analyzing both foreign and domestic policy alternatives.

As surveys indicated a declining trust in the federal government by the citizenry, Washington experience became a less critical factor for candidates seeking the presidency. In 1976, former Governor Jimmy Carter of Georgia gained the Democratic nomination for president by running against the "Washington establishment." Four years later, facing Carter the incumbent, former Governor Ronald Reagan of California won the Republican nomination, which had so long eluded him in the days when Washington experience was more highly valued. To be sure, each candidate benefited from the extensive use of the media in presidential campaigns and from the party reforms of the 1970s, which more than doubled the number of presidential primary elections held throughout the nation. The campaign for president now extended over almost an entire term, with formal announcements occurring as early as two years before the election. As wealthy men with no formal commitments, Carter and Reagan were able to pursue the nominations of their parties full-time for two years, while their challengers in both 1976 and 1980, such as Frank Church (D-Idaho), Edward M. Kennedy (D-Mass.), and Howard Baker (R-Tenn.), remained tied to their Senate duties. But the success of outsider candidates goes beyond the long campaign: George Bush, with considerable Washington experience and an extensive foreign policy background (former director of the Central Intelligence Agency and U.S. representative to the People's Republic of China), did not fare well in the campaign against Reagan. Bush throughout the primary campaign had heavily stressed his Washington experience and was perceived, perhaps unfairly, to be out of step ideologically with the Republican party of 1980. Four years later, it was an ex-vice president, who had spent the interim years building his campaign organization and campaigning actively even before the primaries began, who emerged as the Democratic presidential candidate—although not without a struggle against Jesse Jackson, who mobilized most of the black vote in the primary states, and Senator Gary Hart, who quite successfully represented himself as the candidate of the future in the initial primaries in New England.

Foreign policy continued to be of interest to many of the candidates in 1988. However, only two candidates (Senator Albert Gore and former Colorado Senator Gary Hart) had served on either the Foreign Relations/Foreign Affairs or Armed Services Committees in either house in recent years. (Former Delaware Governor Pierre S. Du Pont had served on the International Relations Committee in the House, but he left the Congress in 1977.) Table 2–1 shows some of the foreign policy experience of candidates for the presidency. Robert Dole (R-Kans.), like Lyndon Johnson, served as both majority leader and minority leader in the Senate. Representative Richard Gephardt (D-Mo.) served as chair of both the Democratic Caucus and the Ways and Means Subcommittee on Trade, while Senator Albert Gore, Jr. (D-Tenn.) also was a member of the trade subcommittee on Commerce. Yet, the striking fact about the 1988 candidates is their lack of experience on the national political scene. Only Bush (who served in the House, ran for the Senate unsuccessfully, served as director of the CIA, and was Reagan's vice president), Dole, and Gephardt could be considered "Washington insiders"; and Gephardt downplayed his Washington role in his campaign, preferring to stress his populist stand on trade. Former and sitting governors—Dukakis, Babbitt, and Du Pont—were among the prominent players. Several governors who chose not to run—most notably Mario Cuomo (D-N.Y.) and Bill Clinton (D-Ark.)—could claim substantial blocs of support within their parties. Other than Dole, even the senators who ran—Gore, Simon, and Hart—were either in their first terms or were not judged as powerhouses in the legislature. The ultimate Democratic nominee, Dukakis, selected Senator Lloyd Bentsen (Tex.) as his vice-presidential candidate, at least in part to reassure those who believed that the Massachusetts governor had too little experience in foreign policy. Bentsen served on the Select Committee on Intelligence and the Commerce, Science, and Transportation committee, where he emerged as the leading spokesman on trade legislation in the Senate. Bush selected Senator J. Danforth Quayle (R-Ind.), a junior member of the Armed Services Committee.

From Truman to Reagan, presidents had been so involved with foreign policy problems, including crises when the threat of nuclear war became especially acute, that domestic problems were bound to suffer neglect. The fact that there are only so many hours in a day and that the president can pay attention to only some of the many problems that he should deal with (had he unlimited time) means that he has to make a choice, and when the external danger is perceived as high by the president and his advisers, foreign policy will preoccupy them. Since throughout most of the post-1945 period the threat from the Soviet Union and China (from 1950 to 1972) was seen as global in scope, it is not surprising that before Reagan domestic affairs were delegated to a secondary status. One analyst even asserted that "foreign policy concerns tended to drive out domestic policy."[2] Indeed, in a situation where even potential foreign crises like Vietnam did not receive sufficient attention, and therefore tended to blow up into full-fledged crises, domestic affairs often seemed to gain consideration only when they too became critical. Sometimes, in fact, it appeared that only domestic violence would attract sufficient attention and bring results, as, for example, when rioting during the 1960s dramatically demonstrated the frustration and anger of American blacks at their status and treatment 100 years after the Emancipation Proclamation.

This subordination of domestic to foreign policy has occurred with increasing frequency during this century, as America has more and more become involved in world affairs. Every president who has come into office bent on reform at home has sooner or later found himself confronted by external threats that came to preoccupy his attention and led to the subordination of domestic problems. Wilson's New Freedom program was overtaken by the German menace and World War I; Franklin Roosevelt, or "Dr. New Deal," as he called himself, became "Dr. Win-the-War" early in his third term, as Hitler, Mussolini, and Tojo made it impossible to complete domestic reforms; after 1945 Truman's Fair Deal quickly became subordinated to the policy of containment; Kennedy's New Frontier became a victim of one foreign crisis after another; and Johnson's Great Society was devoured by Vietnam.

This does not mean that, without the appearance and perception of external threats, presidents supported by Congress would have spent the resources used up by recurrent military preparations on domestic problems and reforms of various kinds. Roosevelt's New Deal was stalled in Congress by 1938. Truman's Fair Deal made modest progress in 1949 and 1950, but was overshadowed by congressional criticism of the Korean War in the last two years of his administration. Eisenhower had no social program to speak of, and Kennedy's New Frontier remained largely rhetoric since Congress wanted no part of it. Johnson's Great Society was the exception. It was made possible by the exceptional circumstances of his immense persuasive skills, a landslide presidential victory that also elected a sizable number of Democratic congressmen, and the president's concentration on the enactment of his social legislation. Simultaneously, he conducted the escalating Vietnam War in a business as usual atmosphere that demanded no sacrifices from the American people. This strategy worked until the 1966 midterm election and the recapture by the Republicans of many of their former House seats. Nixon, in his turn, had few domestic interests except to dismantle some of his predecessor's social programs.

But the widespread disenchantment with foreign policy and increasing concern with domestic affairs in the late 1970s meant that senators no longer had the inside track on being nominated for the presidency. The first challenge came from the ranks of governors. Carter, of course, was renominated in 1980 despite a strong challenge from Senator Edward Kennedy. Reagan in

TABLE 2-1 Major Party Presidential and Vice Presidential Candidates 1952–1988

Year	Presidential		Vice Presidential	
1952 DEM	Stevenson*	Sen. A.S.	Sparkman	Sen. F.R.
	Kefauver	Sen. F.R.		
	Barkley	Sen. A.S.		
	Russell	Sen. A.S. (Chairman)		
	Harriman	Sec. of Commerce and Committee on Foreign Aid (in executive to evaluate U.S. capability for Marshall Plan aid)		
1952 REP.	Eisenhower		Nixon	House Un-American, Select Committee Foreign Aid, 80th Congress
	Taft			
1956 DEM.	Stevenson	See 1952	Kefauver	See 1952
	Harriman		Kennedy	Sen. Gov't. Operations
	Kefauver		Humphrey	Sen. F.R.
1956 REP.	Eisenhower		Nixon	See 1952
			Stassen	Disarmament adviser
1960 DEM.	Kennedy	Sen. F.R.	Johnson	Sen. A.S.
	Humphrey	Sen. F.R.		
	Johnson	Sen. A.S.		
	Symington	Sen. A.S.		
1960 REP.	Nixon	See 1952	Lodge	Sen. F.R. 80th U.S. Ambassador to U.N.
	Goldwater			
	Rockefeller			
1964 DEM.	Johnson	See 1960	Humphrey	See 1960

Year / Party	Candidate	Note	VP nominee	VP note
1964 REP.	Goldwater	Sen. A.S.	Miller	
	Scranton			
	Rockefeller			
	Romney			
	Lodge	See 1960		
1968 DEM.	Humphrey	See 1960	Muskie	Sen. Gov't. Operations
	McCarthy	Sen. F.R.		
	R. Kennedy			
	McGovern	Director, Food for Peace		
1968 REP.	Nixon	See 1952	Agnew	
	Romney			
	Rockefeller			
	Reagan			
1972 DEM.	McGovern	See 1968	Shriver	Director, Peace Corps
	Muskie	Sen. F.R.	Eagleton	
	Humphrey	See 1960		
	Jackson	Sen. A.S.		
	Wallace			
	Lindsay			
1972 REP.	Nixon	See 1952	Agnew	
1976 DEM.	Carter		Mondale	Select Sen. Intelligence
	Brown			
	Church	Sen. F.R. Select Sen. Intelligence, chairman		
	Udall			
	Jackson	See 1972		
	Wallace			
1976 REP.	Ford		Dole	
	Reagan		Schweiker	Select Sen. Intelligence

35

TABLE 2–1 (concluded)

Year	Presidential		Vice Presidential
1980 DEM.	*Carter*	See 1976	*Mondale* See 1976
	E. Kennedy	Chairman, Senate Judiciary Committee, Subcommittee on Immigration	
	Brown		
1980 REP.	*Reagan*		*Bush*
	Bush	Director, CIA, U.S. Envoy, China	Director, CIA, U.S. Envoy, China
	Baker	Sen. F.R.	
	Connally	Sec. of Treasury, Sec. of Army	
	Dole		
	Crane		
	Anderson		
1984 DEM.	*Mondale*	See 1976	*Ferraro*
	Glenn	Sen. F.R.	
	Cranston	Sen. F.R.	
	Hollings	Sen. Appropriations, Defense subcommittee	
	Hart	Sen. A.S.	
	McGovern	Sen. F.R., 1973–1981	
	Askew	Special Trade Representative	
	Jackson		

Year/Party	Nominee	Positions	VP Nominee	VP Positions
1984 REP.	*Reagan*	See 1980	*Bush*	See 1980
1988 DEM.	*Dukakis*		*Bentsen*	Select Sen. Intelligence; Senate Commerce
	Gephardt	Chair, Democratic Caucus		
	Jackson			
	Hart	Senate A.S.		
	Simon			
	Babbitt			
	Gore	Senate A.S., Commerce		
1988 REP.	*Bush*	Vice President	*Quayle*	Sen. A.S.
	Dole	Senate Minority Leader		
	Haig	Secretary of State, 1981–82		
	Du Pont	House International Relations		
	Kemp	House Appropriations Subcommittee on Foreign Operations		
	Robertson			

*Party nominees in italics; F.R. = Foreign Relations Committee; A.S. = Armed Services Committee.

the Republican party had the field virtually to himself; he was an old campaigner, the darling of the conservatives, and had almost taken the nomination away from President Ford in 1976. After his nomination in 1980,
presidential candidate Reagan, inexperienced as he was in the area, stressed
foreign policy heavily.

Like Carter, it was predictable that Reagan would have to give much of
his attention to foreign policy. He would, like his predecessor, have to learn
on the job. As already noted, there is an irony to Carter's record as president: if he had any successes they were in foreign policy, not domestic
affairs. He was the father of the Israeli–Egyptian peace treaty of 1979; he
negotiated a strategic arms limitation treaty with the Soviets; he formally
recognized the People's Republic of China; he negotiated a new status for
the Panama Canal; and he was active in seeking a peaceful solution to the
Rhodesian problem. He also energetically promoted human rights and
responded strongly to the Soviet invasion of Afghanistan. By contrast, the
energy problem, unemployment, and inflation grew worse under Carter—
not because Carter did not devise programs to manage these problems, but
because Congress and the president were unable to agree on approaches
to these complex issues. Carter was widely perceived as an incompetent
president and, most ironic of all, it was his handling of the Iranian hostage
issue and Afghanistan that rallied the country around him, helped stifle
Kennedy's campaign on domestic issues, and helped the president survive
the late presidential primaries.

Carter, with a limited background in foreign policy, chose a running
mate in 1976 with a Washington background and foreign policy experience
and capitalized on Ford's blunder in a foreign policy debate. He campaigned
as an outsider against the "Washington establishment" candidate. Four years
later, he found himself the "insider" candidate against Reagan, who also
chose a running mate with Washington experience and an extensive foreign
policy background. Reagan's campaign against Carter very much resembled
Carter's against Ford in 1976. Reagan attempted to make up for his lack of
foreign policy background by attracting knowledgeable assistants and issu-
ing policy statements. Experience itself would be gained on the job. Even as
incumbent in 1984, Reagan continued to campaign as an "outsider," and
stressed Mondale's role as Carter's vice president in attacks that most analysts felt were important to his reelection. President George Bush is a de-
parture from this pattern. In his campaign, he stressed his experience in
foreigh policy as vice president (see Chapter 5). Immediately after the election, he met with German Chancellor Helmut Kohl and British Prime Minister Margaret Thatcher; prior to his inauguration he met with Soviet leader
Mikhail Gorbachev. Bush's first cabinet appointment was Secretary of State
James A. Baker.

Candidates who lack foreign policy background have sought to overcome this handicap by making trips abroad and hiring foreign policy experts as consultants. Gary Hart visited the Soviet Union to hold talks with
Soviet party leader Mikhail Gorbachev in 1986. Jesse Jackson made a trip to

Damascus where he arranged the freedom of American pilot Robert Good-man, who had been shot down in Lebanon, and later paid a surprise visit to the Geneva summit between Reagan and Gorbachev; he engaged in a brief televised dialogue with the Soviet leader. While contemplating running, Mario Cuomo hired many foreign policy experts and used his position as governor of New York to meet with visiting heads of state such as Italian Prime Minister Bettino Craxi and Garrett Fitzgerald of Ireland; he also made a trip to Moscow. Even if candidates have no direct foreign policy experience, it is important that they try to establish some background so that they appear equipped to handle crisis decision making.

The increasingly key problem is that American presidents have to learn on the job. In parliamentary systems, the prime minister almost always is a person who has served many years as a member of parliament and later served in one or more cabinet positions. In such positions he or she acquires the administrative experience of running a department of government and dealing with problems of coordinating and implementing policy. American presidential candidates with Washington experience, to be sure, are not innocent of some experience. Service in the Senate and House exposes them to foreign and defense policy debates, and many gain a good knowledge of some specific area in which their respective committees and subcommittee specialize. They usually have a sense of what policies are politically feasible and publicly acceptable. They often have a feel for the problems involved in coordinating the executive-legislative branches to make policy and are familiar with the bureaucracy. Still, serving in the Senate and the House is different from governing a nation, running a vast bureaucracy, and devising effective policies, mobilizing congressional support for them, and satisfying public opinion. And to the degree that presidential recruitment continues to include former governors, they will in all likelihood have little knowledge or experience in the foreign policy-defense areas, although their experience in such key areas as trade and attracting foreign investments is growing.

PRESIDENTIAL CAMPAIGNS AND FOREIGN POLICY

Conventional wisdom contends that the outcome of a presidential race turns primarily on domestic or "pocketbook" issues. Foreign policy issues are not similarly relevant to most voters. Others argue for the salience of foreign policy and point to the elections of 1952 and 1968, when the Korean and Vietnam wars seemed to exert a major influence on voting behavior; or to 1980 when the electorate reacted to Iran's holding of U.S. hostages and President Carter's inability to gain their release. What seems beyond dispute is the fact that the voters are very much concerned over the relative capacity of rival presidential candidates to deal effectively with foreign policy issues, even though they may have little knowledge of, or concern with, the substance of these issues. Clearly, presidential candidates themselves believe this to be the case. One of the chief ways in which presidential hopefuls demonstrate their qualifications for the high office they seek is by exhibiting knowledge and competence in matters affecting the national security of the United States. When a candidate fails to radiate a reassuring image in foreign affairs, his campaign is gravely damaged.[3]

What is not debatable is that presidential campaigns can have critical impacts on foreign policy.[4] One negative impact, as we have already stressed, is that the election campaign may bring to the fore inexperienced leaders. Another negative is the use of a particular issue to beat the opponent; a "loss of China," a "missile gap," and other specious issues that divert attention from the real issues, yet afterward may have profound—largely negative—effects on the conduct of foreign policy (see Chapter 3). Additionally, the campaign can lead to promises that simply cannot be or are not kept, such as Eisenhower's pledge to liberate the then Soviet satellites in Eastern Europe, or Lyndon Johnson's statement that American boys would not be sent to Vietnam to do the job Asian boys should do. In domestic policy Congress is the principal obstacle, but in foreign policy it is Congress *and* 160 other nations. Promises rashly made may lead to cynicism and disillusionment when they remain unfulfilled. Each presidential candidate is increasingly tempted to criticize his opponent and promise that he can do better—much better; the gap between promises and achievements is almost inevitable, as is later public disillusionment and cynicism.

This temptation to promise easy and painless solutions is exaggerated by two aspects of the campaign: the increasing number of primaries and the use of television appearances and radio/television advertisements. Complex issues are boiled down to simple solutions and catch phrases that can be presented in a minute and a half on the evening news; in a long campaign, there tend to be lots of such phrases and broad promising generalities. These changes in presidential campaigns have led increasingly to an emphasis on personality rather than on policies (see Chapter 5). While personality is not unimportant, it must be stressed that this emphasis denies voters ways of assessing the various candidates' knowledge of foreign affairs and their sense of judgment on foreign policy issues. Personality is often just "image making"; a candidate seeking votes does not state his views but rather takes polls to find out what he should say or not say. As Robert Strauss, Democratic National Committee chairman from 1972–77 has said:

> There can be no laboratory test in foreign policy. . . . U.S. history is full of surprises about the men who have become presidents. Most often these have been pleasant surprises, as was the case with Harry Truman. Yet trusting to luck is not enough. However imperfect a basis it is for judgment, the amount and quality of information available to the American people about prospective presidents and their foreign policy capabilities and intentions must be increased.[5]

One more negative aspect of the campaign needs to be discussed, namely, the temptation to avoid controversial topics that might cost votes. For example, no candidate for the presidency is likely to advocate a peace process between Israel and some of her Arab neighbors that would require the United States to pressure Israel to be more accommodating on territorial issues and perhaps the Palestinian situation in exchange for peace. Despite the enormous difference in power, and Israel's dependence on U.S. military and economic assistance and diplomatic support, U.S. presidents—who have usually taken an evenhanded position between the Israeli and "moderate" Arab points of view—have little leverage, except possibly in the second and third years in office. A president running for reelection is unlikely to be so bold as to take a tougher position with Israel as reelection time nears (or election time for his successor); if he were to do so, the opposing candidate would criticize him for endangering Israel's security. It has become almost a ritual for presidential candidates to visit Israel and express their commitment to her security and welfare. Israel is obviously not the only controversial issue.

In fact, former Secretary of State Cyrus Vance has so despaired of the heavy intrusion of domestic politics into foreign policy issues that he had advocated one six-year presidential term. Since it takes a president from six to nine months to learn his job and feel comfortable in it, Vance said, he can operate with assurance only for the next eighteen months.

> But during the last year or so, he is running for reelection and is forced to divert much of his attention to campaigning. As a result, many issues are ignored and important decisions are deferred. Sometimes bad decisions are made under the pressures of months of primary elections. And at home and overseas, we are frequently seen as inconsistent and unstable.[6]

Presidential campaigns can also have positive effects. Despite the greater salience of domestic issues, the campaigns every four years can bring to the public's attention some of the key issues facing the nation, such as Soviet–American relations, arms control, the military budget and U.S. military strength, trade (and jobs), and American policy toward South Africa or Central America. Some of these issues do raise differences between candidates in the primaries, as well as between the two final contenders in the presidential debates that have become part of the campaign ritual every four years, and may thus educate the electorate about some of the foreign policy alternatives.

Instead of putting off critical issues, campaigns may advance them because some presidents see these issues as helping them get reelected. President Nixon's overture to China and summit conference in Moscow, which concluded the SALT I agreement and antiballistic missile treaty, were all-important foreign policy achievements that created the public perception of a creative statesman deserving reelection. They counteracted much of the criticism for Nixon's continued conduct of the Vietnam War. (Nixon, too, countered that criticism by advancing the diplomatic process enough to enable Henry Kissinger, his national security adviser, to say that "peace is at hand" just before the election.) President Ford might have been reelected in

1976 had he signed SALT II and not been frightened off by right-wing criticism of détente and arms control from Ronald Reagan, who was vying with Ford for the Republican nomination. And President Carter might have benefited from his extraordinary risk taking in personally brokering Israeli–Egyptian differences and moving these countries toward peace had it not been for the adverse consequences for him of Iran's seizure of U.S. hostages in Teheran and the administration's subsequent floundering and inability to gain their release in time for the president to benefit.

A critical advantage of the election is that it compels presidents and candidates to move toward the center of American politics. This has become especially important because since Vietnam, as we shall see below, the two parties have taken more divergent approaches to foreign policy. President Reagan is particularly instructive in this respect. The darling of the conservatives, strongly anti-Communist and antiarms control, the president had, by the time of his reelection campaigns, shifted to accepting the necessity for a strategic relationship with Communist China against the Soviet Union, despite earlier statements suggesting closer U.S. relations with the Nationalist Chinese regime on Taiwan. Then he began to talk of the importance of arms control and of his commitment to a summit conference with the new Soviet leader, Mikhail Gorbachev in 1985. In this way, fears that Reagan's recklessness and cowboy approach to foreign policy might get the U.S. into war were allayed. He did not send the marines into Nicaragua or El Salvador, only into Grenada (which was very popular with the American public); and in Lebanon, Reagan pulled the marines out before battle casualties rose, thereby maintaining a high performance rating in the public opinion polls.

More fundamentally, election campaigns can sometimes educate the American public to the necessity for change. Franklin Roosevelt took the lead in 1940 by slowly shifting public opinion from isolationism to the need for supporting Britain after France's defeat by Germany that year; and that effort continued after the election. The president took risks in adopting his position, but he was an effective leader of a public shocked by the defeat of France. The 1948 and 1952 campaigns contributed to the death of isolationism and the mobilization of public opinion in favor of the United States playing a leading role in the world. Conversely, campaigns allow candidates to gain a better sense of the issues that are on the electorate's mind. Reagan's shift toward arms control was undoubtedly in large part a response to widespread concerns that were conveyed to the president by, among other things, his travels around the nation and the popularity of the nuclear freeze movement. In the 1984 primaries, all of the Democratic contenders but one (Senator John Glenn) favored the nuclear freeze; the president needed to defuse the peace issue and identify himself with it, as he had begun to do by 1983.

An interesting phenomenon is that other countries increasingly seek to exploit the open nature of the U.S. political system, especially the presidential campaigns, for their own purposes. North Vietnam was particularly shrewd in this respect, launching major offensives in 1968 and 1972 to affect the course of the war and American opinion. The Tet offensive in 1968 was especially successful because it undermined public support for the war with the result that the subsequent presidential campaign focused not on winning the war, but on deescalating and getting out. While it was clearly North Vietnam's purpose to strengthen pressure in the United States to withdraw, South Vietnam's was the opposite. In the peace negotiations that had just started, they resisted any concessions in the hope that the Republicans would win and that they would get a better deal from Nixon. In 1972, with mounting criticism of Nixon and unrest in the country at the continuing U.S. involvement in the war, the Democrats nominated Senator George McGovern as the peace candidate. But Nixon's moves toward China and Russia, and the fact that the war appeared close to being over favored Nixon. North Vietnam played the election cleverly. It made some key concessions in the now four-year-long peace negotiations; then, before they were concluded, the North Vietnamese announced diplomatic breakthroughs and the imminent end of hostilities. Once it became apparent that McGovern, who might offer them better terms, would not win the election, they were clearly keen on getting the administration committed to end the war before the election. They feared that Nixon's reelection for a second and final term would allow him first to continue the heavy and damaging use of U.S. airpower against North Vietnam (U.S. ground troops had largely been withdrawn from the fighting by then); and second to offer less favorable terms than before the election. After the United States withdrew from Vietnam in 1973, the big North Vietnamese offensive to finish off South Vietnam was reportedly scheduled for 1976. The election campaign would presumably ensure against reintervention by the United States. In fact, however, South Vietnam had collapsed in 1975 under its own incompetence in dealing with the daily fighting.

In 1980, the Iranians played the same game. Having seized the U.S. embassy and its occupants in Teheran in early November 1979, the Ayatollah Ruhollah Khomeini's Islamic regime held these hostages month in and month out. Nothing seemed to gain their release. Only after Iraq attacked Iran in September 1980 did Iran's attitude begin to change. The U.S. presidential election campaign also played a role in finally gaining freedom for the hostages, for Ronald Reagan had strongly denounced the Iranians, calling them "barbarians," and the general sense was that Reagan, unlike Carter, might take strong military action. Just as the North Vietnamese had wanted to commit Nixon before the election in the expectation of getting better terms, so now the Iranian leaders calculated that a president fighting for his political life would be more accommodating than one assured of four years in office—if Carter were reelected. The Iranians proposed ending the crisis by November 4, but internal quarrels and the war with Iraq delayed them several weeks and Carter was unwilling to accept a number of the conditions submitted on November 2.[7] Had a settlement been reached at a dramatic last moment, would Carter have been reelected? Once Reagan was elected, the Iranians were determined to end the crisis before he took office; in fact, the hostages were released on the day of his inauguration.

The Soviets took the opposite tack in 1986–87. In part to slow down the Strategic Defense Initiative (SDI), President Reagan's plan for a defense of the United States against nuclear missiles, and in part to slow down the arms race so that he could divert funds into the stagnating Soviet economy, Soviet leader Mikhail Gorbachev was eager for arms control agreements, both on intermediate-range missiles based in Europe and on strategic arms (intercontinental missiles and bombers). He appeared particularly anxious because he correctly assumed that if he and Reagan signed an agreement, the president would be able to mobilize the two-thirds vote necessary for a treaty in the Senate. In 1979–80, Carter had been unable to muster the necessary sixty-seven votes, partly because of the unhelpful Soviet invasion of Afghanistan. Gorbachev clearly believed that if the strongly anti-Soviet and previously antiarms control Reagan signed a treaty, most conservative Republican senators would be in no position to oppose the treaty, as they might have been with a more liberal Democratic president. Reagan's anti-Communist credentials would ensure the necessary votes. Gorbachev's calculations proved to be correct: the arms control agreement on intermediate nuclear forces (INF), signed in December 1987, was passed by the Senate by a vote of 93–4, despite the fierce opposition of a few die-hard Republican conservatives.

PRESIDENTIAL STAKES IN FOREIGN POLICY

Foreign policy and presidential authority are organically and intimately tied together. The welfare state is one reason for the enormous growth of presidential power, but foreign policy is the primary one. Presidential power has clearly grown with America's global role; during the Cold War, presidents achieved a clear-cut primacy, while Congress subordinated itself to a secondary, if not peripheral, role. In the post-Vietnam, Watergate period, congressional attempts to restrain the president were linked to attacks on America's Cold War role as "global policeman." A more limited presidential role was tied to a policy more consistent with America's "limited power" as an institutionally greater congressional role. In short, the executive-legislative conflict revolved around America's world role. A strong presidency had a vested interest in not retreating from its overseas commitments; a strong Congress—reasserting itself at the cost of the presidency—had a vested interest in precisely such a retreat to what was called a more responsible, discriminating foreign policy.

It may also be true that while Democratic presidents have been in the forefront of expanding executive authority, it has been Republican presidents before Reagan who have had an even greater vested interest in making foreign policy their strong suit. Democrats were in power when the United States became involved in World Wars I and II, the Korean War, and the Vietnam War and were sometimes accused of being the "war" party." Democrats could, however, also run on their domestic record—the New Deal, the Fair Deal, the New Frontier, and the Great Society. By contrast, the Republicans, the party of Herbert Hoover and the Depression, had no domestic record on which to run; they had to run on foreign policy and demonstrate to the nation that they could more effectively manage the country's foreign affairs. Thus Eisenhower was urged to run in 1952 by the eastern, moderate, internationalist wing of the Republican party. Senator Taft (R-Ohio), the leader of the dominant conservative, nationalist-isolationist, Midwestern wing of the party, was favored in 1952 as the Republican presidential candidate. Eisenhower, elected after three years of the Korean War, was followed eight years later by Nixon, elected after three years of the Vietnam War. Nixon's only interest was foreign policy. Détente with the Soviet Union, with SALT I as its centerpiece, rapprochement with Communist China, a gradual disengagement from Vietnam which left the anti-Communist Thieu regime in power in Saigon, was the foreign policy record that Nixon successfully ran on in 1972. And Reagan sounded the alarm once more about Moscow after years of détente, Vietnam, and the humiliation the United States suffered in Iran in Carter's past year; he summoned the country to "stand tall" once more and successfully appealed to its pride and patriotism.

A president's interest in foreign policy is a matter of personal and political self-interest. A president's foreign policy record allows him to establish a reputation for leadership and effective stewardship of the nation's affairs which, in turn, also helps his party's reputation and fortunes. Until the Vietnam era, foreign policy was the one area in which the president was able to exercise a degree of initiative and autonomy that did not exist in domestic affairs. By and large, the president could count on public support and congressional deference on foreign policy issues. The temptation to be an activist president in foreign policy is thus very great. After Vietnam this temptation remained great, even if congressional support was no longer always a certainty. For one thing, a president's historical reputation remained tied to his foreign policy accomplishments. Not only did President Nixon's reputation as a foreign policy leader restore some of his luster after he was forced to resign the presidency in disgrace, but President Reagan's eagerness for arms control agreements with the Soviets, after years of opposing such agreements, testified to his desire (and reportedly, even more Mrs. Reagan's) to leave a record of important accomplishments in the key area of war and peace.

CONDUCTING FOREIGN POLICY

The Inner Circle: The National Security Council

At the center of the inner circle, helping the president conduct foreign policy, is the National Security Council (NSC). In addition to the president, its members are the vice president and the secretaries of state and defense, plus three advisers: the director of Central Intelligence, the chairman of the

Joint Chiefs of Staff, and the director of the Arms Control and Disarmament Agency. All are statutory members whose appointments were designated by Congress when it organized the National Security Council. Two additional categories of officials have been appointed from time to time. One consists of those officially designated by the president—for example, the National Security Adviser (NSA), the director of the Office of Management and Budget, the secretary of the Treasury, the chairman of the Council of Economic Advisers, the permanent U.S. representative to the United Nations, the director of the United States Information Agency and the secretary of energy. A second category of officials includes those whom the president informally asks to attend occasional meetings, such as the White House chief (or deputy) of staff, the president's press secretary, and the president's counsel. For example, during his second term, Reagan chose to include Attorney General Edwin Meese, Secretary of the Treasury James Baker, Budget Director James Miller, and United Nations representative Vernon Walters.

The National Security Council was founded in 1947 by the same act that established an independent air force, the Defense Department, and the Central Intelligence Agency. The rationale behind its establishment was to centralize decision making on national security issues, to ensure that the political, military, and intelligence strands of foreign policy issues would be more related to one another than previously, and to make certain that the major foreign policy advisers would be included in the decision-making process. Under Franklin D. Roosevelt, the decision regarding which high officials or agencies to include or exclude in a specific decision was entirely in the president's hands. As a result, political and strategic issues had often not been coordinated. The NSC was supposed to be a check against such presidential discretion and lack of coordination. The fact that the NSC was placed in the White House reflected the president's roles as chief diplomat and commander in chief, and the recognition that the president must lead the country and formulate a comprehensive and integrated foreign policy.

Nevertheless, presidents have not used the council as either the formal or actual locus of foreign policy making. Truman, Eisenhower, Johnson, and Ford relied heavily on their secretaries of state. Both the Truman–Dean Acheson and Eisenhower–John Foster Dulles relationships were close, and both secretaries jealously guarded the relationships against interlopers. Johnson relied heavily on Secretary Rusk and Ford was very dependent on Kissinger. Kennedy relied on his Secretary of Defense, Robert McNamara, as well as his brother, Attorney General Robert Kennedy, and close staff aides like Theodore Sorensen, less than on his secretary of state. It was during this period that the NSA first gained a degree of influence and prominence, largely because he was McGeorge Bundy, a well-known academic from Harvard who took an active role. His predecessors, especially during the Eisenhower years, had not only not been prominent public figures but had confined their role to managing the council and ensuring that policy decisions were left for the president. Bundy, however, became a major player in the policy process because Kennedy encouraged him to state his own views on foreign policy. President Johnson retained most of the Kennedy people and also consulted from time to time with a group of "wise men," individuals with extensive foreign-defense policy background who no longer held formal positions in the government (the best known of these was Dean Acheson). President Nixon restricted his circle of advisers largely to Henry Kissinger, the NSA from 1969 to 1975 and secretary of state from 1973 to 1977. During the years he was not secretary, Kissinger was clearly the most important foreign policy official, far more influential than the secretaries of state and defense; as secretary of state, Kissinger continued to dominate, especially during President Ford's administration. Nixon transformed the NSA's role from that of being one of several key policy figures to that of the president's chief adviser on foreign policy. Both Presidents Carter and Reagan, however, vowed that their primary foreign policy adviser and spokesman would be the secretary of state, but their efforts were not always successful. Secretary Cyrus Vance and NSA Zbigniew Brzezinski—like Kissinger a well-known academician, and an articulate man of strongly held views—were often in conflict. Even the initial reduction of the NSA's authority and prominence, including the appointment of a number of undistinguished NSAs and two prominent secretaries of state during the Reagan years, did not fully restore the secretary of state's position as the president's primary policy maker and spokesman.

This brief review of who the president relied on for foreign policy advice suggests two conclusions. One is that the president consults pretty much whomever he wants; his informal circle of advisers is likely to include both key NSC officials and others with whom he has a close relationship. In short, membership on the NSC does not guarantee any official a place in the inner circle. Among President Carter's closest non-NSC advisers were his wife Rosalynn, Chief of Staff Hamilton Jordan, Attorney General Griffin Bell, press secretary Jody Powell, and Robert Strauss (who held a variety of positions from chairman of the Democratic National Committee to chairman of the 1980 reelection campaign). Just as Carter relied heavily on the people he had come to know and trust in Georgia politics, so Reagan relied heavily on longtime friends and officials from his California days, especially during his first administration: White House Chief of Staff Edwin Meese; his deputy Michael Deaver; William Clark, his second NSA and later secretary of the interior; Secretary of Defense Caspar Weinberger; and, although he shied from publicity, William Casey, director of the CIA. The only non-Californian who gained access to this group was James Baker, a Texan who in 1980 had been George Bush's key aide, and who became chief of staff after Meese left that position. President Bush continued this trend, naming Baker as secretary of state; two other Texans also appointed were John Tower as secretary of defense, and Robert A. Mossbacher as secretary of commerce.

A second conclusion is the increasing visibility of the NSA and his emergence as a rival to the secretary of state. This perhaps is not as surprising as it sounds. As presidents in this century have become more and more preoccupied with foreign policy issues, they have also increasingly wanted—or felt compelled—to become their own secretaries of state. Wilson set the precedent; he clearly overshadowed William Jennings Bryan, the former Democratic presidential candidate and great orator, as well as Bryan's successor, Robert Lansing. Franklin Roosevelt paid very little attention to his secretary of state, Cordell Hull. During World War II, in his meetings with Churchill and Stalin, he usually left Hull at home and uninformed. Kennedy deliberately selected a relatively weak secretary of state, Dean Rusk, a former assistant secretary of state during the Truman years, and from 1969 to 1973 Nixon chose a friend, William Rogers, precisely because he had no experience in foreign affairs. Nixon replaced Rogers with Henry Kissinger, a strong figure, at the beginning of his second administration and Kissinger remained as President Ford's secretary after Nixon resigned in 1974.

As presidents have increasingly exercised their authority as the nation's chief diplomat, they have also come to rely more and more on a personal adviser who, starting with Eisenhower, came to be called a special assistant on national security affairs. Wilson had his Colonel House, and Franklin Roosevelt his Harry Hopkins. Kennedy appointed Bundy, Johnson appointed Walt Rostow from MIT after Bundy resigned, and Nixon chose Kissinger, who, like Bundy, came from Harvard. Under Nixon the position became institutionalized, and a sizable foreign policy staff of about fifty was assembled in the White House (Bundy had twelve). This growth marks perhaps better than anything else the pre-Reagan shift of the locus of foreign policy decision making from the State Department to the White House. Even when appointed secretary of state, Kissinger kept his White House position until 1976 when he gave up the national security post because of political pressure on Ford. Yet, the new security adviser was General Brent Scowcroft, Kissinger's deputy. Carter followed the past pattern of employing an academic adviser on foreign policy, Brzezinski of Columbia University, whose staff was about forty. Ironically, the staff grew to its largest, about seventy, when the NSC and NSA were at their most ineffective. By 1986, the NSC's main function almost appeared to be giving everyone a title: one NSA, one deputy assistant, one assistant to the president who doubled as special counselor, three additional deputy assistants, one special assistant, fourteen senior directors, forty directors, and nine deputy directors! There were five committees dealing with U.S.–Soviet affairs, and the staff had become involved with bureaucratic minutiae "at the cost of providing strategic direction and imposing policy coordination."[8] Something similar appears to be happening in the contemporary Soviet Union, where the current leader, Mikhail Gorbachev, has reportedly shifted some authority for the making of policy toward the United States and the Western allies from the Foreign Ministry to the Communist party's Central Committee. Anatoly Dobrynin, initially was placed in charge in the latter, and has served as Soviet ambassador to Washington for twenty-four years. As Gorbachev's foreign affairs strategist, the international department of the Central Committee has developed into an alternative center for the development of foreign policy options. Earlier, the international department had managed only relations with foreign Communist parties, not major foreign policy issues.

Secretary of State versus National Security Adviser

In a real sense, the national security adviser had become a second secretary of state. This was not the original intention; the NSA was merely to arrange meetings of the National Security Council (NSC) and manage the paperwork. Created in 1947 to coordinate the political and military strands of foreign policy, the NSC did not initially play a prominent role. Truman's and Eisenhower's assistants remain unknown figures; these two presidents relied on strong secretaries of state. But Kennedy, wishing to play a more direct foreign policy role than his two predecessors—especially wanting to be his own secretary of state—made the NSA's position more prominent by appointing Bundy. The latter, however, largely remained out of the limelight. The NSA's job was to ensure that the president would receive all the necessary information and the full range of options he needed to make decisions, coordinate the work of all departments involved, and ensure that presidential decisions would be carried out. He was to be a largely anonymous manager. It was Kissinger, serving a president whose principal interest was foreign policy, and Brzezinski (with a somewhat smaller staff of about thirty to thirty-five), who gave the position public prominence. Kissinger was in charge of the Vietnamese peace negotiations, SALT, China and, after the 1973 Yom Kippur War, the first Israeli–Egyptian steps toward peace in the Middle East. Brzezinski was not quite as dominant, although he was active, especially on policies toward the Soviet Union and China. A hard liner concerned about the Soviet's rapidly growing military power and expansion of influence, his advice became more prominent after the Soviet invasion of Afghanistan disillusioned Carter with U.S.S.R. behavior and Secretary of State Cyrus Vance's more accommodating stance. His position was reinforced by Vance's resignation in 1980; had Carter been reelected, Brzezinski would undoubtedly have been his primary foreign policy adviser.

Thus, one result of appointing a prominent national security adviser has—with two exceptions*—been friction with the secretary of state, officially the president's chief foreign policy adviser. Conflicting policy statements from the president's adviser and the secretary of state also raise questions among friends and foes about what U.S. foreign policy is and who is in charge. Another result is tension with Congress, which does not confirm the assistant's appointment; as the president's assistant he cannot be

---

*One was the period when Henry Kissinger occupied both positions during the second Nixon administration; and then when President Ford (who succeeded Nixon after his resignation in 1974), during his last months, replaced Kissinger with retired Air Force General Brent Scowcroft, Kissinger's former deputy at the NSC.

called on to testify before congressional committees, even though he may give television or newspapers interviews. A cabinet officer is confirmed and must testify (at best, the assistant meets informally with the Senate Foreign Relations Committee, for instance, or individual members of Congress). Perhaps the greatest danger is that the NSA, if he is someone with strong policy preferences, will not ensure that all points of view on issues reach the president. It has been said that Rostow, who was considered a hawk, shielded Johnson from critical views on the Vietnam War. The NSA cannot be both policy advocate and neutral policy manager. Institutionally, it is impossible; it is not primarily a matter of personality.

Not surprisingly, it has been suggested that the NSA's position should be either abolished or downgraded to that of a basically neutral manager and that the secretary of state should be restored to the position as the president's chief adviser on foreign policy. Interestingly, after he left office Kissinger himself came out against a strong NSA and recommended a strong secretary of state. An active adviser, he said, is bound to reduce the secretary of state's prestige and influence. If the president does not have confidence in his secretary of state, Kissinger claims, he should replace him. Secretary Vance too, after resigning from office in 1980, urged that there be only two spokesmen for the government on foreign policy issues: the president and the secretary of state. Reagan, who reflected on the frequent Vance (and later Muskie)–Brzezinski tugs of war during his predecessor's tenure, chose as his first secretary of state General Alexander Haig, Kissinger's former assistant and later NATO commander in chief. Haig, a strong personality, was to be Reagan's chief foreign policy maker and spokesman and prevent the rise of a rival like a Kissinger in the White House. The appointment of Richard Allen, not previously well known as a foreign policy activist—he had been an economic consultant, largely in matters of trade, after a brief stint as a political science professor at Georgia Technological University—was to emphasize the secretary of state's primacy in foreign policy. The fact that the NSA would no longer report directly to the president as did his predecessors, and that the president's counselor, Edwin Meese, would serve with cabinet rank and would be in charge of both the national security and domestic policy staffs, underlined the determination to avoid having what amounted to two secretaries of state.

This arrangement did not, however, work out well in practice, as might have been foreseen. A strong secretary of state may not be able to avoid conflict with the national security assistant.[9] First, departments deal with policy only from their own perspectives; this is as true of the State Department as of other departments. Brzezinski, in his memoirs of the Carter administration, has said that the State Department tends to confuse foreign policy with diplomacy, but diplomacy is only a tool, as is the use of force or covert operations. Political considerations must be integrated with military, intelligence, and economic/commercial/financial factors. But this cannot be accomplished from a departmental perspective; each will fiercely resist giving another department the lead in formulating policy. Given the fierceness of bureaucratic politics, the institutional fragmentation of policy in Washington, and the weakness of political parties, the NSA can provide a degree of balance by centralizing policy direction.

Second, the State Department is reputed as cautious, often timid, unimaginative, and slow. This reputation for lack of risk taking and avoidance of controversial issues has been strengthened by the history of those foreign service officers who, in the 1940s, went out on the proverbial limb by predicting Nationalist China's collapse and suggesting that the United States make overtures to the Chinese Communists, who would shortly control mainland China. The careers of most of these officers were destroyed as they were charged with wanting that outcome and abetting it in the anticommunist hysteria of the 1950s. Other officers who favored a specific policy in other areas have found their careers set back when a new administration favoring a different policy has come into power. In short, prudence dictates caution, "going along," and "getting along" rather than "getting out in front."

In addition, the State Department lacks the capability for long-range planning. Its Policy Planning staff has neither the power nor the prestige to do so and gain the cooperation of other responsible departments. This raises a question about the desirability of State acting as the president's chief adviser on foreign policy; indeed, Presidents Kennedy and Nixon questioned whether State had the ability to act in any advisory capacity. One reason for the growth of the NSA's authority is precisely that presidents have felt they could not depend on State for quick or sound advice. Recent presidents have felt the need for someone other than the secretary of state to ask for judgments and independent opinions not influenced by departmental biases and perspectives; the NSA has been that individual.

Third, the State Department is surprisingly weak in the very areas that ought to be its strengths. Perhaps because foreign service officers are supposed to be generalists, they often lack area expertise despite frequent rotation in a particular region, as well as knowledge of foreign languages, especially Russian, Chinese, Japanese, and Arabic dialects. In an era of increasing specialization, the State Department also misses other skills that it needs to hold its own against other departments: science and technology, international economics and, to a lesser extent, political-military expertise. The last illustrates the point: the State Department has had to bring in outside experts because foreign service officers still lack sufficient knowledge of defense and arms control policies.

Fourth, even if the department should be the primary spokesman, it would not be the only one—or the most powerful. Defense, Central Intelligence Agency (CIA), and—now that economic issues have become as prominent as political-strategic ones—Agriculture, Treasury, Commerce, and Labor are all more powerful spokesmen for their viewpoints than is State. These agencies all represent major sectors of the society and economy such as the defense industries, farming, labor, and the banking or business community, all of which have political clout and can mobilize support for their views in Congress and among the public in general. State, even though it may claim to represent the "national interest," has no constituency. Its chances of determining policy through coordinating the varying views of the different departments is, therefore, likely to be contested. By contrast, the NSA, as the president's alter ego, is in a better position to coordinate the many strands of policy and the conflicting views on what policy should be, and to impose on foreign policy the direction the president wishes. As Richard Allen perceptively noted later about Secretary Haig's difficulties:

> Haig, an experienced and exceptionally skilled operator within the bureaucracy, clearly believed that the conduct of United States diplomacy was actually synonymous with the broader, presidential concept of "national security." In the 1980s, "national security" is in itself an all-encompassing term too often narrowly construed as having to do only with foreign policy and defense matters. In reality, it must include virtually every facet of international activity, including (but not limited to) foreign affairs, defense, intelligence, research and development policy, outer space, international economic and trade policy, monetary policy and reaching deeply even into the domains of the Departments of Commerce and Agriculture. In a word, *"national security" must reflect the presidential perspective, of which diplomacy is but a single component* [italics added].[10]

The NSA cannot only represent that perspective, but if it is known that he has the president's personal confidence and can speak authoritatively on his behalf, he can resolve the bureaucratic conflicts and impose some order and direction on U.S. foreign policy consistent with the president's wishes.

Fifth, the very fact that foreign and domestic policy have become intertwined on so many issues means that the president is, by definition, paying constant attention to foreign policy. Not only do traditional security policies have an impact on domestic policy because of the demand for money and personnel, but such issues as energy or farm or environmental policies have both foreign *and* domestic policy implications. The NSA, sitting next to the president, can keep the president far better abreast of what is happening so that he can calculate the domestic feasibility and costs of a particular policy as, for example, on trade matters in which a president has to calculate which domestic constituencies are benefitted or hurt. The secretary of state does not sit at the crossroads between the "two presidencies." Only the occupant of the White House does.

Last, the very qualities that constitute the "essence" of its work do not help the State Department in its struggles for influence on policy among other departments in Washington. Diplomacy requires that foreign service officers be sensitive to the interests of the countries to which they are posted. After all, the State Department represents America's desire to get along with other nations. In Washington, however, the department has acquired the perhaps unfair reputation of representing foreign interests at home rather than U.S. interests abroad. More to the point, however, the department's skills are supposed to lie in compromising differences and accommodating conflicting perspectives and interests. But being influential in Washington requires an aggressive, pushy style. Bureaucratic politics is a rough game.

And hardly least—perhaps it should be first—presidents want action and results in order to demonstrate their leadership capacity. Given State's slow work habits, its tendency to produce fudge, and its reacting to White House proposals with an emphasis on professional caution and experience, advising one step at a time (clearly suggesting that the president's men should leave the conduct of foreign policy in their expert hands), presidents soon look elsewhere and are tempted to go around the department. Foreign policy is also a glamorous field. Its innate importance, especially at critical moments, the crucial contribution of foreign policy to a president's historical reputation, the ability to act on security issues with less opposition from Congress and interest groups than in domestic policy (although that is declining), draws almost immediate presidential attention. And when it comes to political judgments, no president is going to take second place to "a bunch of bureaucrats." So presidents do not hesitate to make bold and innovative suggestions and take the initiative in the conduct of foreign policy.

Thus the NSA is likely to remain in a powerful position, helping the president achieve an overall view and giving the president counsel when he seeks it. It is the president, at whose pleasure the assistant serves, who defines the job and the balance he wants between his assistant and his secretary of state. He may dislike conflict and appoint a figurehead to the State Department, as Nixon did during his first administration; or he may, like Carter, welcome diverse advice and conflict, which leaves him greater freedom to choose. (Franklin Roosevelt regularly encouraged conflict among *all* his advisers.) Or he may not give him direct access, as Reagan did initially with his first NSA. But it is unlikely the president can do without the NSA, for in the words of the Senate Subcommittee on National Security Organization:

> The president at all times should have the help and protection of a small staff whose members work outside the system, who are sensitive to the president's information needs, and who can assist him in asking relevant questions of his departmental chief, in making suggestions for policy initiatives not emerging from the operating departments, and in spotting gaps in policy execution.[11]

These reasons may be reinforced by differences of opinion among the president's cabinet members and White House staff. In the absence of a consensus, the NSA may well be the person asked by the president to present the options and his own preferences. Thus, conflict between the NSC adviser and the secretary of state may be unavoidable, not because of the personalities involved but because of the structure of decision making. Perhaps it would be more appropriate to say that the increasing impingement of the world on the United States makes such conflict almost inevitable; this century has forced American presidents to become ever more involved with the conduct of foreign policy. As chief diplomats, commanders in chief, and chiefs of state, they have had no choice but to become activists in foreign policies. In doing so, they have looked for assistance from within the White House. The rise of the powerful national security adviser reflects the leading role the United States plays in the world and that increasingly, presidents want—or feel compelled—to be their own secretaries of state, qualified or not.

The Reagan Administration Melee

Conflict between secretary of state and national security assistant was evident very early in the Reagan administration. This was so despite President Reagan's determination to make his secretary of state his number-one foreign policy man and to demote the NSC. One reason for the conflict was that Alexander Haig was suspect by the Reaganauts, the ideological conservatives who had come with Reagan from California and who ran the White House. Haig had served Kissinger, who was associated in their minds with détente and arms control, policies the Reaganauts condemned even though they had been in effect during a previous Republican administration. Haig was therefore denied frequent access to the president; he saw him only once a week and then always with a White House staffer present. In these circumstances, Haig was unable to achieve the type of relationship that Dean Acheson had stated was necessary for the effective conduct of foreign policy: a close relationship in which the secretary of state has the president's confidence and meets alone with him regularly so that the two can and do speak frankly to one another about the state of the world. Acheson had that kind of relationship with Truman and so, Haig observed, did Kissinger with Nixon. But Haig claimed to be "mortally handicapped" by his lack of access to Reagan, meaning he had to formulate policy without knowing the president's thoughts and methods, or having the opportunity to discuss policy details with him.[12]

What made the Reagan–Haig relationship even more difficult was that Haig took the president literally when Reagan said that his aim was to restore the secretary of state as his "vicar"—as Haig called his role—of foreign policy. And, as already noted, the secretary was not modest about defining the scope of his jurisdiction. Virtually all matters beyond the nation's borders were included; this encompassed not only traditional policy areas such as defense but also economic policy. Clashes with the secretary of defense, a close personal friend of the president, soon erupted; so did other conflicts, such as with the secretary of commerce when it came to negotiating limits on Japanese automobile imports. But most of all, tension occurred with the White House, where the staff felt that Haig was attempting to overshadow the president, perhaps to establish his own reputation in preparation for a run for the presidency. (He was a weak candidate in 1988).

The result of this infighting was the worst of all systems for conducting foreign policy, one that fell somewhere between the secretarial system of a Truman and Eisenhower and the presidential system of a Kennedy and Nixon (see Table 2–2). Not only did the NSA report to the principal domestic adviser (who had no foreign policy competence) instead of directly to the president, as had become custom, but the White House, while asserting that crisis management was, as in the past, within its jurisdiction, placed Vice President Bush in charge. Since the vice president is not involved in daily foreign policy making, how could he take charge at critical and dangerous moments when he had not participated in decisions that preceded the crisis? Moreover, since the vice president has virtually no staff of his own, would he not have to depend on the president's NSC staff during a crisis? Clearly, the early Reagan system was a confusing and disorganized one in which the secretary of state frequently found himself at odds with—and checked by— the White House.[13]

Of course, the fundamental problem was Ronald Reagan himself. He was completely inexperienced in foreign policy; his prime area of concern— the one in which he had both experience and a sense of competence—was domestic policy. The president, to be sure, had strong feelings. For example, he was militantly anti-Communist and committed to a large military buildup. However, some specific policies ran headlong into his inexperience, unfamiliarity, and lack of interest on most issues. His press conferences revealed a startling lack of knowledge of the details of policies; and what was later politely to be called his *management style* was one of "hands off."[14] In late 1986, when a foreign policy scandal, referred to by such names as Irangate, Iranamok, Contragate, and Contra(de)ception (see Chapter 3 for case study), broke out the president repeatedly defended his ignorance of events by claiming that his aids had not told him! His predecessors would all have demanded to know what was going on. Thus while the secretary of state was not in fact given the authority to be Reagan's spokesman and number one policy maker, the president's lack of interest and competence in foreign policy meant that the conflicts that naturally erupt in any

TABLE 2–2   Organization for Foreign Policy—President and National Security Assistant

Presidential System	Falling in between	Secretarial System
Kennedy (Bundy)	Carter (Vance–Brzezinski)	Truman (Acheson)
Nixon (Kissinger)	Reagan (Allen–Haig–Clark/	Eisenhower (Dulles)
	McFarlane/Poindexter/Carlucci/	Johnson (Rusk)
	Powell–Shultz)	Ford (Kissinger)

administration were usually not resolved. The result was that the secretary of state, secretary of defense, CIA director (the last two being Reaganauts), and others were continuously feuding. Instead of a battle between the secretary of state and NSA, the Reagan administration ended up with a confused melee.

Efforts to resolve this matter were only partially successful. The initial step taken was to replace Richard Allen with William Clark after one year. Clark, a California rancher, close Reagan friend, and executive assistant to the president when governor of California, had later been appointed to the California Supreme Court. He too had no foreign policy knowledge or competence but had gained some familiarity and experience when he was appointed the number-two man in the State Department. But his service there was short and he had none of the intellectual background and expertise Bundy, Kissinger, and Brzezinski had brought to the NSC position. He was expected to be essentially a good manager and mediator and to reduce the amount of conflict among the president's principal foreign policy advisers, especially between the White House and the secretary of state, his former boss. Clark was given access to the president, and the NSC position was upgraded so that Clark's authority was equal to that of the other principal White House officials. Second, Haig was replaced in the second year after the White House made several decisions he had opposed. His replacement, George Shultz, a former professor of economics at the University of Chicago and secretary of Labor and the Treasury under Nixon, had a calm personality and was more sensitive to the presidential need to show who was in charge. This new arrangement with Clark and Shultz appeared initially to provide the president with a system more comfortable to him for the conduct of foreign policy.

As Clark gained a degree of foreign policy knowledge and experience, however, he became more assertive, especially on Central America, Middle Eastern, defense, and arms control issues; and, at the end of eighteen months as the NSA, he had become the Reagan administration's most influential foreign policy figure and the Clark–Shultz relationship had become more strained. At this point, Clark, not totally comfortable in his foreign policy post, opted to become secretary of the interior. He was replaced by ex-marine Robert McFarlane, a loyal staff officer who had gained some experience and knowledge in foreign policy. But McFarlane was not a member of the Reagan inner circle and soon found himself in trouble with the president's chief of staff, Donald Regan, who was determined to run the White House as he had run Merrill Lynch—as a corporation, hierarchically organized, with the president as chief executive officer, the chief of staff as chief operating officer, and all others in a subordinate role. Any staffer who sought to play an independent role or have his own power base was not tolerated. In short, all access to the president went through Regan.[15]

As if this were not bad enough, McFarlane was also confronted with the ongoing rivalry between the secretary of state and secretary of defense, a rivalry that was more than institutional or ideological. The NSA was never given the authority to resolve this bitter personal conflict and to make decisions; the result, in McFarlane's opinion, was paralysis and drift in policy. Moreover, as McFarlane reported, "I had countless times with the president when I felt he wasn't absorbing what I was telling him. He did not have a good deal of interest in foreign affairs." He quit in frustration after two years, convinced that while he knew more about these affairs than anyone else in the cabinet, "I wasn't being listened to because I didn't qualify to be in the inner circle." In McFarlane's words:

> The president is a man who admires men who have accumulated means and become wealthy and demonstrated considerable accomplishments in a chosen endeavor. . . . I haven't done that. I had a career in the bureaucracy. I didn't really quite qualify. It didn't do any good to know a lot about arms control if nobody listened.[16]

The problem was that the president would not resolve the Shultz–Weinberger disputes; it was not Reagan's style to knock heads to resolve differences. The absence of a strong-minded NSA placed a premium on cabinet offices being combative to win the president's personal support. This style of decision making did not change with McFarlane's replacement, Vice Admiral John Poindexter, who, like his predecessor, lacked clout. He also lacked foreign policy experience. While a nuclear physicist by training, he had picked up the military's post-Vietnam distrust of the press and Congress. A man without political experience as well, highly secretive in the conduct of his job, he was soon caught up in the Iran–Contra scandal and resigned. Reagan's fifth NSA in six years, Frank Carlucci, a veteran of government service in the CIA and Defense Department, was the first genuinely competent person to occupy that key position during the Reagan presidency. But by the time of his appointment in late 1986, Reagan was not only entering his last two years in office, but he was gravely weakened by the Iran–Contra affair. When Carlucci succeeded Weinberger as secretary of defense, he was followed by General Colin Powell, the third military man out of six NSAs in seven years. In the Bush administration, Secretary of State Baker had held no previous foreign policy positions, while NSA Brent Scowcroft had served in the same position in the Ford administration. Conflict between two men with different institutional histories was thus a real possibility.

The succession of weak NSAs did not, however, solidify the secretary of state's position as the president's "vicar" on foreign policy. Secretary Shultz's position was always a somewhat tenuous one. He did not have Haig's aggressive personality to prevail in the bureaucratic struggle, and he was not, like Kissinger, a conceptualizer. His principal skill was that of a negotiator; he had been a labor relations expert concerned with collective bargaining. A good secretary of state has to have a broader vision and be an architect; negotiating skills by themselves are not enough. Although a man of undoubted personal integrity, Schultz's accomplishments have been basically negative.[17] After watching his first efforts at diplomacy—arranging for

Israel, Syria, and the Palestinian Liberation Organization to leave Lebanon—end in disaster with the killing of 241 marines in 1983, he did not try any new initiative in the Middle East until very late in the second term. Four visits to the area did not advance the peace negotiations one iota. The Contra war in Nicaragua and the Strategic Defense Initiative (SDI), the proposed shield for protecting America's population in a nuclear war, were managed by the NSC and the Defense Department. While Shultz basically washed his hands of Central America (although his Assistant Secretary of State for Latin-American Affairs Elliott Abrams largely managed the covert war together with the director of the CIA and the NSC staff) he loyally supported the president's policy, despite his own apparent preference for a negotiated solution.

Shultz sought to make arms control his issue and, given his lack of expertise, he took the unprecedented step of hiring a veteran, Paul Nitze, as his own adviser. Nevertheless, Shultz's success was rather mixed. He fought a rear-guard action on SDI, opposing the Defense Department's effort to reinterpret the 1972 antiballistic missile treaty to allow testing of SDI components in space; but he lost that one eventually to Secretary of Defense Caspar Weinberger. Shultz also opposed the Defense Department's efforts to abandon the SALT II limits on strategic weapons, arguing that this would publicize the president's lack of interest in arms control; Weinberger won that one too in November 1986. Moreover, at the 1986 Iceland summit meeting between Soviet leader Gorbachev and President Reagan, Shultz was unable to prevail over Weinberger or persuade the president to use SDI as a bargaining chip and compromise on SDI research and development so that the United States could accept the Soviet proposal of a 50 percent reduction in Soviet and U.S. missiles (see the case study in Chapter 8). Nor was he able to follow up on this potential "grand compromise" because Weinberger's freedom to negotiate on strategic arms was severely restricted.

Later, he did achieve a significant arms agreement, eliminating Soviet and U.S. intermediate-range missiles in Europe. This accomplishment was mainly the result of Gorbachev's unexpected willingness to accept an American proposal and the president's sudden need for a major achievement in the wake of the Iran–Contra scandal and the serious damage it had done to his reputation. Ironically, Shultz's effort to separate himself from this scandal, which damaged his standing in the White House, strengthened Weinberger's influence even though he too had distanced himself on this issue. Shultz' major preoccupation, largely a result of the marine deaths in Lebanon, was terrorism. He repeatedly urged the need to use force and exact a price for terrorism against Americans. Weinberger opposed such a use of force, even reportedly aborting a planned U.S.–French air strike against the terrorist camp following the killing of 241 American marines and 59 French paratroopers. Shultz, the leading advocate of attacking Libya's Colonel Qaddafi, was successful on this issue after Qaddafi provided the provocation. But on the whole, the secretary of state was eclipsed by the secretary of defense, especially on arms control issues, so he largely confined himself to damage limitation. Although he was successful in persuading the president to moderate his strong anti-Soviet language, Shultz's overall record was a negative one.

The Reagan foreign policy record contains no diplomatic achievements like his predecessor's Panama Canal treaties, the SALT II agreement, the Camp David accords, or the official recognition of Communist China. It consists largely of the invasion of a tiny Caribbean island, an attack on Libya, the support of a number of anti-Marxist guerrillas against Marxist governments (mainly in Nicaragua, Angola, and Afghanistan), and, because of Gorbachev, an agreement on intermediate-range missiles in Europe. It is notable too that the secretary of state, despite his professional interests and background, including having been President Nixon's secretary of the treasury, did not exert himself on issues such as the protection of U.S. industries, the huge debt problem of Latin-American and other less-developed countries and other economic issues. Neither did he challenge the Treasury's primacy in international economic policy. Even in his own area, as noted, he distanced himself from the Iran hostage crisis when it became clear that Reagan was determined to try to swap the hostages for arms. He apparently did not see it as his responsibility to continue to object and, if he could not dissuade the president, he did not feel he should resign. Yet, as one observer has noted:

> The case of . . . George Shultz is probably illustrative of the maximum influence future secretaries can expect to have. . . . Shultz's prominence is due to an unusual combination of factors. Reagan has had no desire to act as his own secretary of state, no deep personal interest in international affairs and little knowledge of the subject. Fortuitously, the secretary of state's frequent competitor, the NSA, has been strapped by presidential preference. Reagan's NSAs, except William Clark, have had their policy advisory roles restricted, and some NSAs were weak and ineffectual or unschooled and inexperienced in foreign policy. Despite this, by January 1982, the NSC, not State, had the primary interagency coordinative function.
>
> Moreover, Shultz is a skilled, experienced, bureaucratic operator regarded highly by Congress and by many within the administration. His effectiveness was further enhanced . . . by his self-effacing, team-playing style. . . . Above all, Shultz has developed an unusually cordial personal rapport with the president . . . always a crucial factor.[18]

There are, of course, problems with the NSA's domination of foreign policy as well.[19] Any system run out of the White House risks not availing itself fully of the bureaucracy's expertise; a staff of 30 to 50 people is not a substitute for the large body of experts throughout the executive branch. Moreover, to the degree that the White House runs policy and bypasses interested bureaucracies, the danger is that the president and the NSA may not gain support for their policies in the executive, let alone the Congress and the public. Third, the president and the NSA can only manage a certain number of policies. These are likely to be the ones that they judge as key issues and/or those that need be handled immediately; other important and long-term issues are postponed and neglected. Finally, if the NSC is abused by the use of covert operations, as in Irangate, the operation, narrowly held and not subjected to sufficient criticism from the experts, is likely to turn into a disaster (see Chapter 3).

The NSC's original functions need therefore to be reemphasized: preparing options for the president, acting as a neutral arbitrator in finding compromises between departments, ensuring that presidential decisions are implemented, selecting issues for the president's attention, and providing the president with independent judgment on what policy the administration should adopt.

> The degree to which the NSA should also be a policy adviser to the president also must be resolved. A major concern is that the NSA cannot be both an influential policy adviser and a neutral arbiter. Moreover, an assumption of the former role would invite friction with the secretary of state. On the other hand, to be an effective manager and institution the NSA must have an advisory role. This gives the NSA the stature and political clout to deal with powerful members of the cabinet. . . . Many presidents will naturally solicit advice from NSAs with whom they are in daily contact. Yet the NSA must not usurp the rightful role of the secretary of state.[20]

This clearly will not be an easy task. But since in the next century the United States will be even more deeply involved in world affairs, and both its national security and economic well-being will be intimately related to events and decisions made beyond the nation's borders, pressure for the NSA to play the central role in foreign policy making is likely to grow as well. Presidents will continue to take the leading foreign policy role because of their constitutional responsibility, the benefits such a role brings them politically, and the necessity to do so in the nuclear age. It is also only at the White House that a view transcending the various foreign policy bureaucracies can emerge and be imposed on policy. Thus the NSA can no longer be only or mainly a "manager"; he cannot avoid being a policy advocate also.

Obviously, whether this occurs or not, it would not mean the end of the rivalry between the NSA and the secretary of state, as well as others. That is normal. Such a system, given capable men, can serve the president well. The battles royal and guerrilla warfare Secretary Shultz talked of during the Iran-Contra hearings, are almost commonplace and not necessarily unhealthy, for they expose the president to a range of options and the cost, risk, and opportunities of each option. But if the system is abused, as in the Iran-Contra affair, when the NSA with little foreign policy experience seeks to make policy by cutting out the secretaries of state and defense who had opposing views, and transforms the NSC into an operating agency, it will fail the president and U.S. interests. But in the final analysis, if the system is to work well, it needs a president who does more than give general guidance; he must show continued interest in policy, including the details of some key issues, ask critical questions, demand policy reviews if policies do not work, and not exclude the foreign policy experts in the bureaucracies.

Brzezinski has suggested that the NSA's role should be openly acknowledged so that it can be legitimated and to avoid the current perception that the NSA is usurping the secretary of state's rightful functions. He further urges that the NSA's position be institutionalized by requiring Senate approval for his nomination, as for other leading officials.[21]

The Second Circle: The Bureaucrats

While the secretaries of state and defense—and often their under secretaries and assistant secretaries—and the CIA director are attending meetings of the president's inner circle, one may wonder, Who's minding the store? Each department has a set of second-rank officials including assistant secretaries and other officials. There are also the ambassadors who report back to the State Department, the ambassador to the United Nations, and the military and civilian officials in the army, navy, and air force in the Pentagon. In addition, there are junior foreign policy agencies. These cannot match the political influence of State, Defense, and the CIA. These less influential foreign policy bureaucracies include the Arms Control and Disarmament Agency (ACDA), the United States Information Agency (USIA), the Agency for International Development (AID), and the major foreign policy bureaucracies (the foreign service and the military services), and the scientific and academic advisers to the executive branch. These advisers include the Rand Corporation, a "think tank" for scientists—and social scientists— in California; the Harvard Center for International Affairs and centers at other major universities; and the largely Washington-based professionals (see below).

Another set of actors in this second circle are cabinet members whose departments are only partially concerned with foreign policy issues. The Department of Commerce plays a major role in all aspects of international trade as well as in matters of immigration. The Department of the Treasury is a key actor in such decisions as the valuation of the dollar in the international money market and, of course, has an abiding interest in the cost of U.S. foreign policy. The Agriculture Department is consulted on such issues as wheat sales to the Soviet Union and China and the use of surplus commodities in the foreign aid program. Indeed, food exports have become a major issue. In the 1970s the United States was the "food basket" of the world; in the 1980s, after the European Common Market countries, India, China, and others had stepped up their production of everything from grain to butter, U.S. exports declined sharply. Washington found itself under great pressure to help agricultural exports, resulting in strained relations with allies ranging from France to Australia. Other departments with an interest in foreign policy are Labor and Energy (see Figure 2–1).

FIGURE 2-1 Administration of U.S. Foreign Affairs

	Foreign Affairs Branch			
Political Affairs (general foreign policy and conduct of relations with foreign countries)	Politico-Military Affairs (mutual defense, strategic policy, arms control)	International Commercial and Economic Affairs (trade, investment, monetary affairs, foreign aid)	Information and Educational and Cultural Exchange (contact with foreign audiences through government media; promotion of people-to-people relations)	Intelligence (collection and analysis of information bearing on the conduct of foreign relations)
		Departments and Agencies Involved		
Department of State	Department of Defense, Arms Control and Disarmament Agency	Departments of Agriculture, Commerce, Energy, Labor, Treasury; Export-Import Bank; International Trade Commission; Overseas Private Investment Corporation; U.S. Trade Representative; International Development and Cooperation Agency; Agency for International Development	United States Information Agency	Intelligence Community

Responsibilities in all foreign affairs branches

Interagency Policy Coordination

National Security Council

Flexible system of interagency committees at various levels and of varying composition depending on subject matter

Constitutional Responsibility

President

Head of government/Head of state

SOURCE: United States Department of State, Bureau of Public Affairs, *Atlas of United States Foreign Relations, 2d ed.,* (Washington, D.C.: U.S. Government Printing Office, 1985), p. 5.

Compared to the inner circle, there is greater continuity among the lower-level officials. A new administration does not result in massive changes in the executive departments. In particular, the military service personnel are quite durable. The country desks at State, the scientists at the Pentagon, the small staff at ACDA, and many career diplomats who have obtained their posts by rising through the Foreign Service remain in place as the people at the top change. The second circle thus provides a continuing organizational basis for foreign policy decision making at lower levels. However, the bureaucrats at the various country desks (for instance, the African desk, the Western Europe desk, and so forth) at State and in the three services at Defense also develop vested interests to protect. They served in their departments before their respective secretaries, under secretaries, and assistant secretaries were appointed and have established their own standard operating procedures.

A change in those at the top may mean at least a minor shakeup of bureaucratic procedures. The lower-level officials may attempt to resist such changes, as the services did under Secretary of Defense McNamara. In addition, if a member of the inner circle is occupied with settling problems and conflicts in his own department, he faces the problem of presenting a unified departmental position to the White House. The problem is particularly acute for secretaries of state. The State Department is divided into various "desks," each dealing with a different geographical or functional area: African Affairs, Inter-American Affairs, East Asian and Pacific Affairs, Near Eastern and South Asian Affairs, and International Organization Affairs, as well as Economic and Russian Affairs, Oceans and International Environmental and Scientific Affairs, International Narcotic Matters, Humanitarian Affairs, and Politico-Military Affairs. The various desks not only have their own operating procedures, but also their own policy positions, and these are often in conflict with each other, as well as with the views of the secretaries. The Middle East desk, for instance, has long been charged with displaying a pro-Arab and anti-Israel bias, while most secretaries of state have been disposed the other way.

The function of the second circle is to provide ideas, information on policy alternatives, and to make policy recommendations that the members of the inner circle can then debate. The second circle also carries out the daily operations of the nation's foreign and military policies. It does not play a direct role in crisis decision making or even in most foreign policy decisions, but it serves the members of the inner circle by providing background information and analyses for decision makers.

How well the members of this second circle perform their information functions may affect how influential their spokesmen in the inner circle are. Presidents normally want accurate information and sound analysis from their principal advisers (although on rare occasions a president is determined to do something to which some of these advisers object, as in the case of President Reagan's determination in 1986 to exchange arms with Iran for the release of U.S. hostages seized by pro-Iranian terrorists in Lebanon). These men, in turn, depend on the professional people, such as the Foreign Service or Officer Corps. The State Department has fared less well than Defense in the role of providing key information to its top-level bureaucrats. The large bureaucracy at State leads activist presidents to circumvent the department in making foreign policy innovations. Because the department is compartmentalized, there is the insurmountable problem of coming up with a unified position on foreign policy. There are simply too many vested interests in the department to achieve a consensus on what ought to be done and to arrive at one set of recommendations on how to do it (see Figure 2–2). The policy statements that the secretary of state receives from his subordinates therefore often take a long time to write and tend to be ambiguous. On the other hand, the policy recommendations of Defense tend to be produced relatively quickly and are quite specific, reflecting the military's characteristic "can-do" attitude.

The Pentagon is not without its own vested interests: there are *inter*service rivalries and vigorous *intra*service rivalries (such as that between the Strategic and Tactical Air Commands in the air force or between the carrier navy, the rest of the service navy, and the nuclear submarine navy). But the Defense Department's policy recommendations to the president are usually more specific than those of State, because, despite the rivalry among the services, the military's analysis emphasizes the "threat" and potential danger, and preparations to counter it. The focus, in short, is on capability, specifically the enemy's hardware and on the American forces that would be needed should a confrontation and possibly a war occur.

The State Department, by contrast, begins its analysis with another country's intentions and the general context of a particular problem or dispute. Its professional bias is the opposite of the military's, namely, to have the best relations with other countries, which tends to make it minimize problems and discount threats. To the foreign service officer, the military's stress on capability, action, and quick solutions may seem simplistic, but to the military, the former's concern with the intentions is too general, vague, and unlikely to bring about a resolution. In addition, if one of the services sharply disagrees with the recommendations of the secretary of defense, its chief of staff can state his objections directly to the president, for the Joint Chiefs of Staff are almost always in the inner circle. In contrast, the secretary of state *may* be the only representative of that department in the inner circle. Even if the under secretary and assistant secretaries are on occasion in the inner circle, they do not ordinarily have the same influence as the Joint Chiefs.

Interestingly enough, though, Defense is not necessarily the most influential when it comes to the use of force. The military advisers have usually been divided, as were their civilian counterparts. ". . . military leaders were less anxious than the majority of involved civilians to initiate United States commitments about as often as they were aggressive. Joint Chiefs of Staff

FIGURE 2-2 Responsibilities in the Department of State

			Duties				
Leadership and overall direction	Policy development and coordination	Development of policy toward and conduct of relations with foreign countries and international organizations	Policy development and conduct of relations in special fields	Policy development in and conduct of consular affairs (passports, visas, citizens' services overseas)	Specialized support	Congressional, media, and public liaison	Management of the department
			Responsible Officers				
Secretary of State Deputy Secretary of State	Under Secretaries for Political Affairs, Economic Affairs, and Security Assistance, Science and Technology Counselor of Department	Assistant Secretaries for (heads of bureaus of) African Affairs, Inter-American Affairs, East Asian and Pacific Affairs, European and Canadian Affairs, Near	Assistant Secretaries for (heads of bureaus of) Economic and Business Affairs, Oceans and International Environmental and Scientific Affairs, International	Assistant Secretary for Consular Affairs	Legal Adviser Assistant Secretary for Intelligence and Research Chief of Protocol	Assistant Secretary for Legislative and Intergovernmental Affairs Assistant Secretary for Public Affairs and Spokesman of the Department	Under Secretary for Management Inspector General Assistant Secretary for Administration Assistant Secretary for Diplomatic Security

Director of Policy Planning Staff

Eastern and South Asian Affairs, and International Organization Affairs

Narcotics Matters, Human Rights and Humanitarian Affairs, and Politico-Military Affairs

Directors of Bureau of International Communications and Information Policy and Bureau for Refugee Programs

Director General of the Foreign Service and Director of Personnel

Comptroller of the Department

Director of Management Operations

Director of Foreign Service Institute

67

(JCS) members' views were virtually the same as the dominant civilian attitude more than half the time. . . . In no case did a fully united set of military advisers oppose united civilians." The real difference was that once a commitment was made, the military wanted to employ force massively and quickly to win. Ironically, the "only cases in which military recommendations on use of force were considered irresistible were the instances in which they opposed intervention.[22] In the post-Vietnam years, the military was united in resisting further intervention. During the eight years of the Reagan administration, there was a consistent pattern, whether in Grenada, Lebanon, Nicaragua, or elsewhere: the secretary of state took the lead in advocating the use of force, with the secretary of defense usually resisting.

The difficulties the State Department has in developing clear-cut policy proposals further weaken the stature of its department in the inner circle by leading activist presidents to assume the political functions of the department. After all, diplomacy is something presidents think they know something about. Bargaining and accommodation between conflicting interests are the essense of the political process, and its summit is reached in the White House. This preemption further lowers departmental morale. As Henry Nash has stated: "To the extent that crises in Asia and the Middle East have been 'managed' by the president's White House staff, the skills of state have eroded through disuse."[23] Kissinger himself argued the following before becoming NSA and, later, Secretary of State in the Nixon administration:

> Because management of the bureaucracy takes so much energy and precisely because changing course is so difficult, many of the most important decisions are taken by extrabureaucratic means. Some of the most important decisions are kept to a very small circle while the bureaucracy happily continues working away in ignorance of the fact that decisions are being made, or the fact that a decision is being made in a particular area. One reason for keeping the decisions to small groups is that when bureaucracies are so unwieldy and when their internal morale becomes a serious problem, an unpopular decision may be fought by brutal means, such as leaks to the press or to congressional committees.[24]

We thus have a kind of vicious circle in which the frequently ambiguous policy recommendations of State are often rejected and in which this rejection leads to a further weakening of the influence of State in the inner circle. The public's image of State is a function of the department's performance, of what people believe it stands for, and of how the department is viewed in comparison with Defense. The public, including Congress, sees State as representing foreign interests rather than American labor, business, agriculture. State brings a troubled world in which there are no quick and easy solutions to the door of American citizens. But instead of facing the world as it is, the public and especially Congress make State a scapegoat. The department is frequently called *Foggy Bottom.* Originally this term referred to the haze surrounding the department's building in a valley in the District of Columbia; in more recent years, the term has been used to characterize the type of thinking in the department. If State thought "correctly" and represented American interests abroad more vigorously, it seems to be suggested, there would be no foreign policy problem. State represented foreign headaches because it brought world problems to the United States, and the department was supposed to find the aspirin to make them disappear. The public's view of State is not one of admiration. Francis E. Rourke has noted that

> The nonmilitary sector of the foreign affairs bureaucracy has been on the defensive before the bar of public opinion, confronted with a deficit of public support rather than the surplus which the military ordinarily enjoys. Over virtually the entire period of the cold war the State Department had been in a precarious position with respect to its public image.[25]
> On the other hand, "the military role exerts a symbolic appeal that is as rare among bureaucratic organizations in the United States as it is in other societies. The identification of the military with national pride and achievement—in a word, with patriotism—is a quite extraordinary bureaucratic resource—setting the Defense Department apart from all other executive agencies in the country."[26]

This does not mean that the Defense Department does not have its own severe problems; it does, largely in the operational area. Since Korea, the military has been criticized for its consistently poor performance, whether in Vietnam, the rescue of the merchant ship *Mayaguez* seized by the Cambodians in 1975, the humiliating and botched-up rescue of U.S. hostages in Iran in 1980, the avoidable 1983 tragedy in Beirut, Lebanon, in which 241 marines were killed, the successful but poorly planned Grenada invasion, also in 1983, or the shooting down of an Iranian airliner with 290 people aboard by the USS *Vincennes* in the Persian Gulf in 1988. The problem has been essentially "grossly overelaborate planning . . . supervision by vastly overstaffed headquarters very remote from the scene of combat . . . with no real center of higher decision." The Joint Chiefs of Staff were basically only a committee of service chiefs, resulting in clumsy planning for combat because "the interests of each service must be accommodated, . . . because everything must be done by committee, bureaucratic compromises displace tactical ingenuity, operational art, and sharp choices that strategy always demands."[27] To try to dampen interservice rivalry and plan and execute military operations more effectively, in 1986 Congress passed a defense reorganization bill. Its purpose was to make the chairman of the Joint Chiefs the principal military adviser to the secretary of defense and the president rather than, as in the past, being merely a first among equals; to improve the quality and timeliness of military advice that had too frequently represented a bland consensus; to strengthen the authority of theater commanders, whose forces would include troops from all the services to reduce interservice disagreements; to make these commanders responsible only to the chairman of the Joint Chiefs and secretary of defense, thereby shortening the chain of command and clarifying who was responsible for actions taken; to pay more attention to strategy, roles, and missions of the various services and for the more efficient use of resources, especially money; and to reward rather than punish officers who place the national interest above service interests by promoting officers to generals and admirals only if they have previously served in a position on a joint staff.

While State is usually less influential in the inner circle than Defense, there are even weaker agencies in the second circle. The functions of ACDA, concerned with arms control, overlap with those of State because it is concerned with the overall diplomatic position of the United States, and Defense, which is charged with devising military strategy and evaluating the level and kind of armaments needed to defend the country. Therefore, ACDA, small by comparison with State and a midget compared to the giant-sized Defense Department, must walk a very thin line between these agencies and at the same time serve the president. ACDA's fortunes have gone up and down. In the 1960s, as arms control became a prominent issue, its influence rose; in the SALT I negotiations, its influence reached its highest levels (although much of the negotiating on key issues was done not by ACDA's director but by Kissinger negotiating in the back channels with the Soviet ambassador in Washington). After SALT I, its influence declined as Kissinger completely took over the arms control negotiations. Under Carter, ACDA's director conducted most of the negotiations. But with the growing disillusionment with detente, the renewed emphasis by the president and Congress on rebuilding military strength, and the death of SALT II in the Senate, the stature of ACDA declined sharply. The question was even raised of whether it was needed at all; the agency could be integrated into the State Department or abolished altogether. Influence varies, among other things, with time and circumstances. During the Reagan administration its influence was small, symbolized by the initial appointment of a hardliner who had opposed SALT II; when he was fired he was replaced by Kenneth Adelman, a young inexperienced, and politically uninfluential figure who shared the administration's generally negative attitude toward arms control.

The second circle thus provides decision makers with information on policy questions. It also runs the bureaucracies, which in turn gather the information for the mid-level officials. This circle has its own sphere of decision making as well, but its decisions concern more routine types of foreign policy questions, which the president and his inner circle have neither the time nor the inclination to answer. Will the administration agree to a particular request for foreign aid? Will it send a trade mission to a newly emerging country? These are the questions usually reserved for the bureaucracies.

The distinction between the actors in the first or inner and second circles is not clear-cut over all decisions on foreign policy issues. Because the first and last circles may at times overlap, a sudden crisis in a remote area in the world can elevate a bureaucrat—for example, a Soviet specialist—to the inner circle. Or, if one president pays more attention to the recommendations of his secretary of state and another to his secretary of defense, different policy areas or issues may find the same actors in different circles.

In this connection, it is worth emphasizing a function of the NSC that is normally overlooked. A lower-level official may write a policy paper on either a current policy or a future issue. As it slowly makes its way up the vertical channels to the top of the department or across the horizontal channels between departments sharing responsibilities for a problem, it is likely increasingly to be watered down or, at some point, buried. It is NSC staff members, dealing with specific areas, who usually know other members throughout the executive branch also working in these areas. They can cut across bureaucratic lines (in our concentric circles), establish informal links with those they believe able (given these links, the last will also take the initative and send their papers or talk to the NSC staff), thereby enlisting the "best and brightest" in the process of policy formation. A good NSA encourages this process to make sure that good ideas do not get lost somewhere in the bureaucratic maze. Establishing such links should not be regarded as an act of insubordination; it is intended to ensure that senior officials gain access to the best information and ideas.

PRESIDENTIAL POWERS AND PRIMACY

The Ability to Act: Information as a Political Resource

One reason why the president is looked to for leadership on foreign policy and why Congress has generally played a subordinate role is his advantage over Congress in foreign policy in the vast amounts of information he has at his fingertips. "Power is knowledge," and the foreign policy bureaucracy possesses such knowledge. The president can call on the State and Defense Departments, the Central Intelligence Agency, the Arms Control and Disarmament Agency, the U.S. Information Agency (propaganda), the Agency for International Development (economic aid), and the foreign staffs in such other departments as Commerce, Treasury, and Agriculture. All these agencies are represented in the embassies abroad and participate in the making of foreign policy in Washington; abroad, they are also amply represented outside the embassies, often by delegations of at least equal size to that of the State Department's foreign service. Indeed, the State Department, of the senior agencies, is the smallest one. In the White House alone the president has the help of special bureaus on a whole range of topics— including the National Security Council, Office of the U.S. Trade Representative, Office of Science and Technology, Council of Economic Advisers, Council on Environmental Quality and, not least, the Office of Management and Budget.

It is not surprising that in these circumstances Congress should be dependent on the executive for its information. This is particularly true when compared to domestic affairs. Here, as already noted, a representative or senator can call on the appropriate executive departments dealing with the problem as well as on numerous interest groups, or can rely on his or her own familiarity with the problems being considered by the committee (for instance, congressmen from agricultural areas may serve on the agriculture committee). A member of Congress has, in brief, means not only to check out what the facts really are, but also experience from which to gain a sense of perspective on executive policy recommendations. But on foreign policy issues Congress has relied—and largely still does—primarily on information supplied by the president and the foreign policy bureaucracy. And given the facts of life for most congressmen—that they must devote a lot of time to their constituents' affairs, that they are members of one or more committees in which most of Congress' work is accomplished, and they feel that they usually have less competence and knowledge of external than of internal problems—this reliance is understandable.

This dependency is, in fact, twofold. First, it applies to the "facts" that most congressmen do not even have the time to digest. The year 1987 was the fortieth anniversary of the Marshall Plan for the reconstruction of postwar Europe, a highly imaginative policy that signaled a revolutionary shift of American policy from its prewar isolationism to a postwar commitment to Europe (a course Congress had rejected in 1919). During the hearings on it, this exchange occurred between the staff director of the Republican Policy Committee and Republican Senator Homer Ferguson (Mich.):

Mr. Smith:

> Now, Senators, for your amusement as well as to bear out my point on the impossible work load put upon members of Congress, I have gathered here a group of the books and reports, limited solely to an official character, which you should be reading now on the Marshall Plan.
>
> [Mr. Smith here presented a stack of material 18-inches high.]
>
> You are going to take the momentous step in the history of this country when you pass upon the Marshall Plan. . . . That is what you ought to be studying. It contains the Krug report, the Harriman report, the State Department report, the reports of the Herter committee, the Foreign Relations Committee digest; it includes part of the hearings just completed of the Foreign Relations Committee. It does not include hearings yet to be held by the Appropriations Committees. This is one work load you have now on a single problem out of the many problems you have to decide.

Senator Ferguson:

> How long would it take in your opinion . . . for a person to read it?

Mr. Smith:

> Well, Senator, I have been reading for the last 35 years, nearly all my life, in the field of research; and if I could do an intelligent job on that in two months of solid reading excluding myself from everything else. . . . I would credit myself with great efficiency.

Senator Ferguson:

> A normal person would probably take four to five months.[28]

How in these circumstances can a legislator become familiar with such intricate problems as the strategic arms control negotiations, the nature of nationalism in a Third World region, the intentions of the Soviets toward the major non-Communist states, or the strategic doctrine and force structures of the U.S. military? These and the multiple other issues confronting Congress are issues on which even the experts may not have all the facts and on which, even with sufficient facts, they would disagree about meaning, consequences, and policies.

Of course, all of this assumes that Congress gets the information. After it was disclosed in 1973 that the United States had been secretly bombing Cambodia during 1969–70, a number of senators were critical of Secretary of State Rogers for not discussing this issue with them fully at the time. A State Department spokesman said in reply that Rogers had mentioned the raids on two occasions while testifying before the Foreign Relations Committee, although he admitted the secretary had not volunteered information on the magnitude of the raids. He added that if Rogers had been asked for details of the bombing, the secretary would have provided any requested information. But how were senators to ask questions about a military operation of which they were unaware and about which they had learned only a few details from the *New York Times?* This utter dependence of senators on executive information was also vividly demonstrated when in 1983–84 it became public that the United States was involved in mining Nicaraguan harbors, a warlike act but a matter mentioned so briefly before the Senate's supervisory committee on intelligence activities that the senators felt deceived. If the executive withholds information, Congress is likely to remain ignorant. This was starkly revealed when the administration's efforts to privatize foreign policy after the Congress cut off military assistance for the Nicaraguan resistance fighters, or Contras, in 1984 became public. Clearly, information was withheld to maximize the administration's freedom of action and minimize congressional interference (see Chapter 3).

But Congress is dependent on the executive not only for the facts but for their interpretation as well. For example, in 1947 the Truman administration had to reach a decision about intervening in the eastern Mediterranean, where the Soviet Union was putting great pressure on Turkey for control of the Dardanelles and on Greece, where a civil war involving the Greek Communists was raging. There was little precedent for American involvement in that area of the world. While Congress had become increasingly anti-Soviet during spats with Moscow in 1946, it was also in a fierce budget-cutting mood and averse to vast expensive external commitments in January 1947. Thus when in February the British informed the State Department that they could no longer support both endangered countries, the Truman administration decided that American power had to contain what it perceived to be Soviet expansion. Western Europe was drained by war, and Britain's role as a major world power was ending; in its place, the postwar bipolar balanced emerged.

On the Eurasian continent, the Soviet Union was emerging as the dominant state; only the United States, separated from Eurasia by the Atlantic and Pacific oceans, could supply the countervailing power. President Truman called together a congressional delegation to declare his intentions, but it initially reacted skeptically and interpreted Truman's proposed action as one of pulling British chestnuts out of the fire. Secretary of State George C. Marshall and Under Secretary Dean Acheson contested this interpretation, and Acheson particularly stressed American security considerations. Convinced, the congressmen insisted Truman explain his dramatic reversal of traditional American policy before Congress and the nation. In an address to a joint session of both houses, Truman informed Congress of the situations in Turkey and Greece and then outlined the basis of the new containment policy. He disguised the basic power realities motivating U.S. actions, however, and justified them on ideological grounds.[29] The Truman Doctrine was, for the United States, the beginning of the Cold War.

Another pertinent example is the American involvement in Vietnam. Johnson inherited a situation in which only ad hoc decisions had been made in response to immediate problems. The Kennedy administration, Arthur Schlesinger, Jr., has suggested, was occupied with other more urgent issues, such as the abortive Cuban invasion, the Berlin Wall, crises in Laos and the Congo, the Alliance for Progress, and the limited nuclear test ban.[30] Only piecemeal economic and military commitments had been made; each constituted the minimal step necessary to prevent a Communist victory. At no point were the fundamental questions and long-range implications of an increasing Vietnam involvement analyzed: Was South Vietnam vital to American security? Would its fall represent the consolidation of one country under a nationalist leader or constitute a "falling domino" in the communization of all of Southeast Asia? Did the political situation in South Vietnam warrant or preclude American intervention? Were political conditions both in the United States and in South Vietnam conducive to effective military action? How large a commitment would the United States be required to make, and what costs should be expected? What role should Saigon and its forces play?

If these questions were even asked by President Kennedy and his advisers, the answers did not provide guidelines for the policies that were ultimately followed. The assumption was that South Vietnam was vital, a test of the credibility of America's commitments and power. Policy was built on that assumption. The approach was incremental and, as the overall situation deteriorated badly, Johnson, like Kennedy, continued to react to the symptoms of the problem and applied short-range solutions: first covert operations, then increasingly frequent air strikes against North Vietnam, followed by around-the-clock bombing and, finally, the use of U.S. ground forces in South Vietnam.

What is noticeable, in restrospect, is not only the administration's lack of questions, but also Congress'.[31] Congressmen may not always know the

facts or be sufficiently expert in foreign policy, but their expertise is supposed to be something more fundamental, a political judgment about the
viability of policy, an ability to question the experts' views based on specialized knowledge. But neither the Senate nor any of its committees, including Foreign Relations and Armed Services, raised any of the fundamental
questions that should have been answered before the 1965 intervention. As
before, the Senate and House followed the executive's lead; their criticism
came after the intervention, and then only after the intervention went sour.

It is unlikely that the information and interpretation "gap" between the
executive and legislative branches will disappear. It has, to be sure, been
narrowed as congressional committees have obtained larger and more expert
staffs to develop their own sources of information and policy advice, taken
more investigative trips abroad, and have been critical in cross-examining
administration witnesses. The Vietnam War has led the Congress to concern
itself more with the assumptions underlying specific policies and the likely
consequences of their adoption. Still, the resources of the executive remain
overwhelming by comparison. An administration that insists its policies are
of vital importance to the national interest and can make a convincing case
for its position still usually prevails, as Carter did in extending U.S. commitments to the Persian Gulf and Reagan did despite a great deal of justified
skepticism in Congress about his policies toward El Salvador, Lebanon, and
reflagging Kuwaiti oil tankers in 1987.

The Willingness to Act

The Chief Diplomat and the Constitution.   Besides the advantage of
knowledge, the president possesses the further advantage of being able to
act. It is, of course, this capacity to initiate action—especially the commitment of U.S. forces when the president deems it necessary—that has been
greatly responsible for the expansion of presidential power in foreign policy
since the Nazi and Japanese threats of the late 1930s; and it is this capacity
that is at the heart of the contemporary controversy over the extent of presidential powers. Not that this expansion started in the 1930s. For example,
the Constitution states that the president can receive and send ambassadors.
President Washington, for example, interpreted this as conferring on the
presidency the power of diplomatic recognition when he received Citizen
Genêt of the French Republic. Congress, of course, has on occasion exerted
its influence in this area, as it did after 1949, when it consistently warned
successive presidents not to extend recognition to Communist China. Still,
a determined President Nixon visited China in 1972 and in effect established
all but formal relations with the People's Republic.

President Carter extended full diplomatic recognition in 1979. The decision did not go unchallenged. Opponents of the recognition of China,
which involved withdrawing our embassy from the Nationalists on Taiwan,

took the issue to the courts. Senator Barry Goldwater, who brought the lawsuit, argued that since the Senate had given its consent to the 1955 mutual security treaty with Taiwan (the treaty would be null and void one year after the transfer of recognition), the Senate had to consent to ending the treaty and, by implication, the recognition of the People's Republic of China.[32] A federal judge ruled that the Senate had to approve the president's decision by a two-thirds vote or a majority of both houses of Congress, even though the treaty contained the standard clause allowing either party to withdraw from the treaty at any time after proper notification of the other party (a clause approved by the Senate with the rest of the treaty). But on appeal, the judge was overruled, and the president's right to recognize a nation by accrediting diplomats was upheld. This is a legal right that a president will exercise when political circumstances are favorable or, at least, not hostile to a recognition.* On China, Congress had for thirty years opposed recognition and made it very clear that the president would recognize Peking as the legal government of China at his risk. The resulting Asian policy bordered on the irrational, reflecting emotions, even hysteria, not hard calculations of what American national interests required. But presidents refused to exercise their power for fear of Congress. Only after a costly and divisive war and the election of a conservative president who could never be accused of appeasement was U.S. policy once more set on a path of rational calculation—and then only gradually.

Presidents not only exploited the "great silences" of the Constitution to "make foreign policy" and enhance the powers of their office, but also used their position as the nation's chief diplomat to strengthen their position against Congress. In this connection, presidents have long resorted to setting policy through declarations or by means of a variety of individual initiatives. A Monroe announces his famous doctrine or a Truman declares, as he did in early 1947, that it must be U.S. policy to support free peoples who are resisting attempted subjugation by armed minorities or outside pressure, and more recently, the Carter Doctrine committed the United States in the Persian Gulf–Indian Ocean area. Or a president may visit West Berlin, as Kennedy did, thus reinforcing in the minds of his NATO allies and Soviet adversary the American commitment to that city and Western Europe; he may visit the capital of a nation not previously recognized, as Nixon did on his trip to Peking, signaling a radical shift of policy; or go to the Middle East to indicate U.S. interest in the area and a more "evenhanded" policy between Israel and the Arab states. Or he may, as Carter did after the Soviet invasion of Afghanistan, decide that the United States should boycott the 1980 summer Olympic games in Moscow.

---

*The Supreme Court has never ruled on the question of the president's right to extend recognition. The judges have always hesitated to interfere in foreign policy and left such issues to be settled politically.

President Reagan, early in his administration, announced that the United States would not permit Saudi Arabia to fall into the hands of any internal or external forces threatening to cut off oil supplies to the West. The president, clearly trying to suggest to the world that his administration had more resolve than his predecessor's in defending America's friends, said that "we will not permit [Saudi Arabia] to be an Iran."[33] Reagan's words were immediately seen as a broadening of the Carter Doctrine, which had seemingly committed the United States to Saudi Arabia's defense against external threat. Now the United States also appeared to be committing itself to the defense of the ruling royal family against domestic revolution or insurrection. The president's words were followed by the stationing of four AWACS (Airborne Warning and Command System) planes on Saudi soil to protect that country from potential air strikes from Iran, which was then at war with Iraq and hostile toward Saudi Arabia. Later, against great opposition in Congress, the administration sold the Saudis five of these planes. Both moves were cited by the administration as evidence of a deepening American commitment.

President Reagan, like earlier presidents, also expressed his support for Israel. Thus, although no formal treaty of security existed between Israel and the United States at the time, repeated presidential pronouncements over several decades have constituted a de facto defense treaty despite the absence of Senate approval. Indeed, congressional figures often protest such presidential "commitments." One congressman complained that Reagan's statements had "spelled out a dangerous strategic doctrine. . . . They have asserted, in effect, a right to commit United States prestige, power, and military might to the defense of remote areas of the world without the advice, much less the consent, of the Congress." Many in Congress, if not most, were skeptical of Reagan's commitment in 1987 to protecting Kuwaiti oil tankers in the Persian Gulf, but they were reluctant to oppose him outright after the president had already announced U.S. policy (see "Labor Powers Resolution" section).[34] Presidential words, as well as acts, create obligations.

The point of these examples is threefold. One, the president, by what he says and does—and, on occasion, by not saying or not doing—sets the direction and tone of U.S. foreign policy. Two, by exercising his initiative, the president usually leaves Congress with little option but to follow him, unless it wishes publicly to humiliate him and undermine his position as the nation's spokesman in international affairs. He may also keep the Congress ignorant. This was starkly revealed when the administration's efforts to "privatize" foreign policy after the Congress cut off military assistance for the Nicaraguan resistance fighters, or Contras, in 1984 became public. Clearly, information was withheld to maximize the administration's freedom of action and minimize congressional interference (see Chapter 3). And three, the president has an array of tools—informal, such as discussed above, as well as more formal ones—at his disposal, which enable him to use his advantages.

One of the more formal tools the president can use to draw public attention to certain issues and his suggested solutions is the draft treaty. Although the Senate may be consulted during the drafting and negotiating of a treaty and may give its consent when it is submitted, the end of the negotiating process really commits the United States, unless the Senate wants to erode other nations' confidence in the president's ability to represent and articulate America's international interests. Ever since defeat of the Versailles Treaty concluding World War I, the Senate has been reluctant to deny ratification. For example, when a president negotiates a limitation on strategic arms, the publicity alone by the time the treaty reaches the Senate floor may make the draft difficult to defeat. Arms control measures are probably unique in this respect. If an administration has initialed a draft treaty that has the support—or at least the acquiescence—of the various interested executive agencies involved, such as the Joint Chiefs of Staff, it is likely to be able to "sell" such measures to Congress and the public. (Arms control often takes on the appearance of a combination of motherhood and salvation and can be easily identified with that most cherished of values, peace.) When such a measure is signed in Moscow by the president himself, as Nixon did in 1972 with the Strategic Arms Limitations Treaty (SALT I) and the event is fully covered by television (as were the president's return to the United States and his immediate journey to Capitol Hill to report the success of his negotiations in building a more stable "structure of peace"), who can really do more than raise some objections and then approve such a clearly worthy enterprise, especially when, in effect, the president has already gone over Congress' head to the country?

SALT II, however, reaped considerable opposition even though the Carter administration consulted Congress, especially the Senate, far more than had Nixon or Ford for the earlier arms control negotiations. Despite that opposition, which ranged from liberals who thought the number of strategic weapons allowed each side were too high to conservatives who felt that the treaty ratified Soviet strategic superiority and endangered U.S. deterrence capability, to moderates who found the treaty acceptable if the administration would simultaneously increase defense spending 5 percent per year, Carter was short of the votes needed for ratification when other events overtook him and jeopardized passage of the treaty. Carter used these other events—the Shah's fall in Iran, the Soviet invasion of Afghanistan, among others—to toughen his policy toward the Soviet Union, invoking a number of diplomatic and economic sanctions, and withdrawing SALT II before the Senate—in its anti-Soviet mood—defeated it (see Chapter 6). By contrast, Reagan's public signing of the INF agreement in December 1987, in Washington, D.C., where the summit was covered by the television networks, gained overwhelming public support for the treaty, even among most conservatives.

Although some of the most fundamental U.S. policies since 1945 have been submitted to the Senate to let the American people know what commitments their government has undertaken on their behalf and to signal to the adversary the nature of American interests, treaties are few and far between. Presidents often bypass the Senate, where a two-thirds majority is required for approval of treaties. In a Senate representing fifty states, it takes only 34 votes out of 100 to defeat a treaty. That means a majority of senators may in fact favor a treaty, which was certainly true of SALT II. Indeed, given the fact that a highly urbanized state with a large population has the same representation as a rural state with a smaller population, the thirty-four senators opposing the treaty may in fact represent less than 5 percent of the population. The two-thirds majority required for treaties in fact places a premium on opposition so that the president, to mobilize those sixteen votes he needs over a fifty-one majority, has to literally "buy" these votes by acquiescing or supporting policy decisions such as increasing the defense budget or a pet project that a senator wants for his state. These may add millions, if not billions, to the nation's federal budget.

Given the uncertainty of Senate treaty approval, it is understandable why presidents prefer to use executive agreements that do not need legislative approval. (Executive agreements may, of course, also be negotiated and signed in pursuance of a particular objective authorized Congress—for instance, specific tariff agreements with individual countries after Congress has approved a general tariff bill.) Indeed, executive agreements outnumber treaties by 17 to 1 (see Table 4–3, Chapter 4). The vast majority of these were executive agreements to implement congressional legislation or congressional–executive agreements; and only a small minority were executive agreements based on the executive branch's constitutional authority. But these agreements may be the most significant of all the executive agreements and indeed more important than most of the treaties, for they may commit the United States to the defense of other countries or involve the use of force. Thus, for example, a series of executive agreements with Spain for American military bases since 1953 are tantamount to a military commitment to Spain, even though the Senate in 1970 adopted a nonbinding resolution expressing the view that the 1970 executive agreement signed by Spain and the Nixon administration should not be construed as a U.S. commitment to the defense of Spain. In 1976, an agreement for the continued use of American bases in Spain was finally put in treaty form giving the United States the opportunity to deny the existence of a defense commitment to Spain. The issue of a bilateral U.S. defense is now moot. Spain, finally a democratic state, is now a full-fledged member of NATO.

The trend toward executive agreements on important issues is demonstrated by two other Nixon agreements: The Paris peace agreement of 1973 ending the Vietnam War (at least, officially) and the five-year freeze on offensive arms negotiated as part of the SALT I package; both of them were executive agreements. But no executive agreement is ever likely to be more dramatic than the destroyer deal arranged by President Roosevelt in 1940. One more example, perhaps more of presidential ability to commit the

United States than of executive agreement, was a letter President Nixon sent President Thieu of South Vietnam to soften his opposition to the Vietnam peace agreement. While such letters do not usually constitute executive agreements, Nixon assured Thieu that if North Vietnam did not abide by the terms of the agreement, he would "take swift and severe retaliatory action."[35] Nixon repeated this assurance at a later date. Confronted by these reassurances and faced with U.S. determination to go ahead and sign the cease-fire agreement on its own and disengage from the war, Thieu signed too. Nixon had just been reelected by a very large majority; he had won all states except Massachusetts. With Nixon at the zenith of his power, Thieu obviously believed his promise was credible. Watergate and the congressional war powers resolution were to undermine that promise.

Nixon had also embodied the SALT I five-year freeze on offensive nuclear arms in an executive agreement, while the antiballistic missile agreement was incorporated in a treaty. When President Carter began to note mounting opposition to SALT II as the negotiations proceeded, he stated that he might make the document an executive agreement. But after vociferous objections from the Senate, he backed down and submitted it to the upper chamber as a treaty, only to find he had to withdraw it when it became clear he could not mobilize the two-thirds approval required for treaties (see Chapter 8 for the SALT II case study).

The Commander in Chief Wields the Sword.   The president's authority as commander in chief has become the greatest source of his expanded power in this century. In 1900 President McKinley sent troops to China to join an international army to crush the Boxer Uprising, which had besieged foreign embassies in Peking. Theodore Roosevelt, Wilson, and Coolidge used the marines at will throughout the Caribbean. Woodrow Wilson sent troops into Mexico to pursue Pancho Villa and had Vera Cruz bombarded before the outbreak of World War I. In early 1917, when the Germans declared unrestricted submarine warfare on all shipping, belligerent and neutral, to starve Britain into submission, Woodrow Wilson armed American merchant marines taking supplies to the British. Wilson acted after the Senate refused to sanction his request to authorize armaments for the self-defense of the ships. When, during the Russian Civil War of 1918–1920, the Japanese sought to exploit that conflict and establish themselves in Siberia by landing troops, Wilson sent American troops to counter the Japanese and to protect allied interests in western Russia against the Germans. After the eruption of World War II and the fall of France, President Roosevelt, as we already know, used American warships to escort the English and Canadian merchant ships as far as Iceland, where the British Royal Navy took over, and ordered American ships to "shoot on sight" at German raiders or submarines.

Since World War II, recurrent crises—many with the potential of exploding into nuclear war—as well as two limited wars, have built on these precedents and further expanded the president's authority as commander in chief. When the Soviets blockaded Berlin in 1948, President Truman responded with an airlift to supply the population of the western half of the city. When the North Koreans attacked South Korea in 1950, the president ordered first air support for the South Korean army and then the landing of American ground forces in Korea when the air support seemed unable to stem the invaders. Congressional leaders were informed of these decisions by the president, but he did not ask for their approval. Truman felt that as commander in chief he already possessed the authority to commit U.S. forces when he believed American security was endangered. After Communist China's intervention in Korea, he sent several divisions to Western Europe to enhance Western strength and deter a possible Soviet move in Moscow's "front yard" while America was becoming more deeply involved in Asia; again Congress was not asked for approval.

Both Eisenhower and Kennedy, as we know, made commitments to South Vietnam. The first initiated a large-scale program of economic and military assistance to support the non-Communist government there. "The United States had gradually developed a special commitment in South Vietnam. It was certainly not absolutely binding—but the commitment was there."[36] Kennedy would enlarge this into what the Pentagon Papers refers to as a "broad commitment"[37] and would leave his successor feeling that the commitment was virtually binding. Kennedy also launched the Eisenhower-planned invasion of Cuba in 1961 and blockaded the island a year later to compel the Soviets to withdraw their missiles. After his assassination, his successor intervened in the Dominican Republic in 1965 with troops to forestall "another Cuba" (Eisenhower had earlier, in 1954, covertly used the CIA, rather than the marines, to overthrow the government of Guatemala when it was feared to be moving in Moscow's direction). And in 1983, President Reagan sent the marines and Rangers into Grenada.

It was, however, the increasing unpopularity of America's first modern limited war, the Korean War, that led President Eisenhower, after the Democrats had been defeated in 1952, to ask for congressional resolutions granting him legislative support to use the armed forces when he felt this was necessary in the national interest. The administration's idea was that "the resolution process, by involving Congress in the takeoff, would incriminate it in a crashlanding."[38] In other words, a principal purpose was to ward off the type of later congressional criticism and retribution that had hurt the Truman administration. These resolutions did not, however, indicate that Eisenhower, any more than his predecessors or successors, felt that in the absence of congressional support he lacked the legal authority to use the armed forces as he saw fit—as, for example, in Lebanon or the Formosa

Straits. In any event, Congress gave him virtually a blank check; in fact, it was more an expression of approval than a grant of authority.

In 1964, Johnson received a similar broad grant known as the Tonkin Gulf Resolution, after the gulf where North Vietnamese torpedo boats allegedly attacked two American destroyers. It reads, in part:

> [Be it] Resolved by the Senate and House of Representatives of the United States of America in Congress assembled, that the Congress approves and supports the determination of the President, as Commander in Chief, to take all necessary measures to repel any armed attack against the forces of the United States and to prevent further aggression.
>
> The United States regards as vital to its national interest and to world peace the maintenance of international peace and security in Southeast Asia. Consonant with the Constitution and the Charter of the United Nations and in accordance with its obligations under the Southeast Asia Collective Defense Treaty, the United States is, therefore, prepared, as the President determines, to take all necessary steps, including the use of armed force, to assist any member or protocol state of the Southeast Asia Collective Defense Treaty requesting assistance in defense of its freedom.[39]

Johnson, unfortunately for the nation as well as himself, was neither lucky nor shrewd and wound up using force.[40] Both he and Eisenhower requested congressional resolutions for the areas in which action was contemplated when tensions there appeared to be quite high. In each case Congress, once the president had publicly requested its support, had acceded. Eisenhower, however, was either lucky or shrewd. In neither crisis was he required to use force overtly. In the Middle East, troops landed in Lebanon but were not involved in any fighting, and in the Formosa Straits the Seventh Fleet "showed the flag" but did not need to shoot. Johnson, however, was drawn deeper and deeper into war.

Johnson had hoped that the Tonkin Gulf Resolution, passed by the Senate with only two dissenting votes and by the House unanimously, would be read by Hanoi as an indication of American determination to prevent a Communist takeover of South Vietnam. But nothing, including escalating military force, led Hanoi to "leave its neighbor alone," as Secretary of State Dean Rusk phrased the American objective. More punitive moves, it was felt, were needed to attain this aim. Sustained air attacks that avoided bombing cities were launched in the spring of 1965; when those also did not frighten off Hanoi, Johnson felt he had no choice but to send American troops into South Vietnam as the military situation there deteriorated rapidly and the Vietcong appeared to be within reach of victory. But as the increasingly Americanized war dragged on and victory seemed more and more distant, congressional and public support for the war declined, as it had earlier for the war in Korea. As the criticism mounted, the Tonkin Gulf Resolution offered no protection to Johnson. The conclusion would, therefore, seem to be that congressional support in the form of a resolution for presidential use of force is politically largely immaterial, especially if the conflict turns against the United States. If a president is successful, he will receive little or no criticism—indeed much praise—even without a congressional resolution; if he is unsuccessful, he will reap large amounts of criticism and abuse, even if he has hundreds of congressional resolutions.

In any event, once the country is involved in a war, whether it is legally declared by the Congress or not, presidents make the basic political decisions and choose the appropriate military strategy to achieve the chosen political objectives. Thus, Roosevelt during World War II decided that Germany should be defeated before Japan since Germany was the stronger power and the United States, as a belligerent, had allies whose existence was threatened primarily by Germany, not Japan. Later, Roosevelt chose to invade continental Europe through France rather than, as Churchill wanted, to drive into the Balkans from northern Italy and Yugoslavia, thereby trying to limit the Soviet army's advance and the establishment of Soviet influence to Eastern Europe. A cross-channel invasion, which would come to grips with the German army on the plains of Europe, where it could be defeated, seemed to Roosevelt a more feasible way to end the war quickly; it undoubtedly was, but it did mean that the Soviet army had reached the heart of Europe by the time of Germany's collapse.

During the Korean War, President Truman, who had already made the key decisions to drop two atomic bombs to force Japan's surrender and to intervene in Korea, made two further significant decisions: one, to cross the 38th parallel dividing North and South Korea after the North Korean army had been pushed back; and two, not to extend the war even farther by bombing and blockading China after the Chinese had responded to the U.S. invasion of North Korea by intervening, just as the North Korean invasion of the South had precipitated American intervention. This brought Truman into a fierce confrontation with the commanding general, Douglas MacArthur, a great war hero who was supported by the conservative and dominant wing of the Republican party in Congress. When MacArthur refused to stop publicly criticizing the administration's policy and strategy in Korea with the assertion that there was "no substitute for victory," Truman fired him amid a public furor.[41]

For Johnson, of course, all the decisions in Vietnam proved fateful: the decision in 1965 to escalate the American intervention with air power and troops until U.S. forces in Vietnam stood at over 500,000; further decisions to escalate to appease congressional hawks and deescalate to satisfy the doves; and the decision to fight a "painless war" until 1967 by deferring many students from the draft and postponing a war tax to counter the rising inflation, among other measures. But as the intervention turned sour, it precipitated an executive-legislative struggle, badly divided the nation, deeply divided the Democratic party, and helped the Republicans win the presidency that year.

After President Nixon came into office, the Senate repealed the Tonkin Gulf Resolution not once but twice! Nixon even supported this move, claiming that he did not need it, and thereby added insult to the injury the Senate already felt at what it claimed was Johnson's deception at the time he requested the resolution. Although it had given him a broad grant of authority, senatorial critics now asserted, it had done so on the assumption that Johnson would use it only for retaliatory strikes, *not* to justify the widening of the war with large-scale American intervention.[42] But Nixon, whose policy was to withdraw U.S. ground forces gradually while letting the South Vietnamese army increasingly take over the fighting, claimed that as commander in chief he had the authority to use the armed forces in any way he wished to protect the remaining American forces in Vietnam.

As more and more U.S. troops were pulled out and Hanoi's temptation to attack in South Vietnam increased, Nixon undertook a number of actions—vigorously criticized in the Senate—under the authority he claimed as commander in chief. He ordered American forces into Cambodia to search for and destroy North Vietnamese supplies and Vietcong headquarters. (Before this action in 1970, as noted earlier, U.S. bombers had carried on bombing attacks in Cambodia, which were hidden from congressional and public scrutiny.) Nixon also sent American planes from time to time for "protective reaction" raids on the North; authorized the mining of North Vietnamese ports and the heavy bombing of Hanoi and Haiphong after Hanoi launched a large conventional attack on South Vietnam; and, when the Paris peace negotiations stalled, launched B-52s during the Christmas season to compel a settlement (in January 1973, a settlement was signed). After the Paris peace agreement, when the understanding that a cease-fire and withdrawal of U.S. forces from South Vietnam would be followed shortly by cease-fires in Laos and Cambodia failed to materialize in Cambodia, B-52s were used to stem the successful Communist forces. Since the president could no longer invoke his need to protect American troops after they had departed, he claimed that the failure of the Communists to abide by the Paris agreement meant that he could wage the war in Cambodia until a cease-fire had been agreed on. He had possessed the authority to wage the war in Vietnam; this authority continued until the war in Cambodia ended as it had in South Vietnam. The Congress disagreed and cut off funds for further bombing in 1973.

In an attempt to terminate the bombing even before the cutoff date, a suit was brought in federal court on the basis that Congress had not declared a war in Cambodia and that consequently the president's action was unconstitutional. A similar suit was brought to the courts by over 100 congressmen trying to compel President Reagan to invoke the War Powers for his commitment of the U.S. Navy in the Persian Gulf. Both suits were unsuccessful, but at some point it is likely that the Supreme Court will have to rule on the whole issue of the president's war power. In the past, the Court has generally been reluctant to challenge the president's exercise of his power, even when he has exercised it in unprecedented ways. Whether it can or will continue this general abstention on the crucial central issue of the use of force remains to be seen.

THE WAR POWERS RESOLUTION

In the wake of the Vietnam War, the Congress took a number of actions to hold the executive more accountable. Collectively, they constituted a congressional assertion to play a larger and more active foreign policy role than before and, simultaneously, to restrain the president from presumably getting the country into "another Vietnam." "No more Vietnams" was the slogan and the mood of the country throughout the 1970s. Closer congressional supervision of presidents was viewed as the best means of keeping the country out of new and costly overseas adventures. America was no longer to be the world's policeman; it was to play a more limited role only. To ensure this was Congress' responsibility.

Congress' determination to play a more energetic part in the process was reflected in the following actions.

1. The War Powers Resolution, which was passed by the Senate and the House over President Nixon's veto in 1973, was to restore Congress' role in decisions involving the use of force.

2. Executive agreements had to be reported to Congress, and the Congress has tended to insist that important agreements be submitted as treaties.

3. An increasing number of restrictions have been imposed on security or military assistance, including a congressional veto of specific arms transfers over a few million dollars.

4. Intelligence operations—that is, CIA covert interventions or subversions—must now be reported to a number of Senate and House committees.

We shall focus on the War Powers Act because it is as commander in chief that presidents have enormously expanded the powers of their office, and because it was the Vietnam War that led the Congress to assert its responsibilities on the use of force. The resolution states that in the absence of a declaration of war the president shall consult the Congress before introducing U.S. armed forces "into hostilities or into situations where imminent involvement in hostilities is clearly indicated by the circumstances." The resolution also provides for three emergency situations in which the president can commit American forces without prior congressional declaration of war: to repel or forestall an attack on the United States; to repel or forestall an attack on American forces located outside the country; and to rescue endangered American citizens in carefully defined circumstances. Beyond these emergency categories, the president would need "specific statutory authorization."[43] This requirement aims to replace the blank-check resolution with precisely worded authority, jointly devised by Congress and the president. Even when the president uses his emergency powers, the War Powers Act requires that he immediately make a full report to Congress and obtain congressional authority to continue the action after sixty days, with an extension of thirty additional days if troops are in danger. If he fails to receive legislative concurrence, he must terminate the action at that time. Even before this sixty-day deadline Congress can terminate the action through a concurrent resolution, which would not be subject to a presidential veto. As one of the bill's sponsors said, "The real danger is that presidents can—and do—shoot from the hip. If the collective judgment of the president and Congress is required to go to war, it will call for responsible action by the Congress for which each member must answer individually and for restraint by both the Congress and the presidents."[44] The War Powers Act, in short, grants the Congress the potential to play a greater role in decisions involving the use of force through the use of the legislative veto. Indeed, to be more precise, the resolution no longer permits Congress to avoid its political responsibility.

The Ford–Carter Years

The act, in one sense, recognized "reality," for it changed the Constitution from reading that war cannot be waged without the consent of Congress to the president can wage war until Congress stops him. When the U.S. merchant ship *Mayaguez* was seized in what the American government claimed to be the high seas by the Cambodians shortly after the final collapse of South Vietnam in 1975, President Ford used American military forces to recover the ship and its crew on the island where they were and, to prevent any retaliation, ordered some bombing of certain airfields and port targets on the mainland. The president did inform the Congress, as the War Powers Act required, of what had occurred and what he intended to do. But he no more consulted Congress than had his predecessors. The ship and crew were recovered, although at the time the rescue operation began, unknown to the United States, the crew was being released. Despite loss of life and equipment, the action was generally applauded as successful and as saving a tattered American prestige that had been badly deflated by the fall of South Vietnam to the communists.

The lesson from this incident appeared clear and was probably of no comfort to the proponents of the War Powers Act. If a president is unsuccessful when he uses force, he will be damned even if he has legislative support; if successful, he will be acclaimed even if he does not possess congressional support. Subsequently, there were a number of more ambiguous tests of the War Powers Act. One incident that, ironically, failed to become a test was the abortive 1980 rescue mission of the American hostages held by the Iranians in Teheran (Chapter 7). While there were some mutterings in Congress about President Carter using military forces, which Carter termed a "humane mission" rather than a military one, no one was really willing to bring the issue to a head. The mission's failure, the loss of life among the rescuers, and the humiliation of the whole affair were apparently considered tragic enough. Yet this rescue mission had anticipated the possibility of escalation. The marine-piloted navy helicopters, with their armed men aboard, were backed up by a powerful carrier-based group of naval ships; careful preparation had been made so that the mission would be undiscovered not only by the Iranians but the Soviets. There was some concern about Soviet intervention.

Reagan and Lebanon

During Reagan's eight years in office, force was used on several occasions but the president, like his predecessors, refused to invoke the War Powers resolution. One incident was the U.S. involvement in Lebanon from 1982 to 1984. Since 1975, Lebanon had been a nation in turmoil deeply divided within by ethnic and religious quarrels among Christian and Moslem factions, then occupied by Syria, and finally, in 1982, invaded by Israel to destroy the Palestine Liberation Organization (PLO). In the hope of ending the fighting by protecting the withdrawal of the PLO fighters, the United States together with France, Italy, and Britain sent an "international peace-keeping force," as it was called, to the capital city, Beirut, in 1982. Later, in 1983, the United States tried to assist the new Lebanese government to establish and extend its authority to the city and, hopefully, beyond. The marines then ended up in the middle of the civil war. When in 1983 several marines died in the shelling of their position, the president refused to invoke the War Powers Resolution. Lebanon was a peace-keeping operation, he said, not a war. The Congress, however, insisted that he had to do so since the marines were involved in a combat situation and naval gun fire was used to support Lebanese government forces. The issue was resolved by compromise.

The president, on the one hand, did not recognize the authority of the War Powers Resolution. *Congress*, however, determined it was in effect. This meant that the president did not have to send Congress formal notification, and Reagan thereby avoided directly acknowledging the validity of the act as it applied to Lebanon. Indeed, in signing the legislation authorizing the marines to stay in Lebanon, he specifically said that he could not cede any of the authority he already held as commander in chief, in fact suggesting he really did not need congressional approval to keep the marines there. On the other hand, the Congress was willing to authorize the continued deployment of the marines in Lebanon for eighteen months rather than sixty or ninety days, after which the president would have to go back to the Congress for authority to keep them there another two or three months. This longer term would, it was expected, give the president the time to both secure his objectives in Lebanon and avoid injecting Lebanon as an issue into the 1984 presidential election campaign. But in early 1984, after a terrorist drove his truck filled with explosives into the marine barrack in late 1983, killing more than 241 men, the president pulled the marines out; so did the other "peacekeepers," leaving most of Lebanon under Syrian influence and a southern strip on Israel's borders under Syrian control. Despite the eighteen months' mandate, congressional and public pressure to withdraw from Lebanon was too intense to resist in an election year.

Reagan and Central America

Concurrent with the crisis in Lebanon, President Reagan undertook another action as commander in chief: he sent the Marines into the tiny Caribbean island-nation of Grenada (110,000 inhabitants). Here a pro-Cuban regime was deposed and the prime minister murdered by an even more radical faction. The United States acted, the president said, to protect the 1,000 Americans on the island—most of them medical students—and to forestall a possible Iranian-style hostage seizure. He also responded to the concerns of several eastern Caribbean states about instability in the region resulting from a Cuban military buildup in Grenada. A third, and real reason, was U.S. concern about Cuban control of Grenada, which lies in the southern part of the Windward Islands in the Caribbean, just north of oil-rich Venezuela. Additionally, the use of U.S. troops was intended to send a message to the Sandinista regime in Nicaragua that the United States might some day use force against it as well.

The president sent Congress a letter informing its leaders of the invasion, as he is required to do by the War Powers Resolution, but he did not invoke the resolution. Again, Reagan insisted that the law could not tie his hands as commander in chief. Democrats, particularly in the Senate, were especially critical of the president's action. Both houses of Congress insisted on invoking the War Powers Act, forcing the president to remove the troops within sixty days unless Congress approved an extension. But a showdown was avoided when Congress—especially the Democratically controlled House whose leader, Speaker Thomas O'Neill, denounced the invasion as "gunboat diplomacy"—seeing how popular the invasion was with the public and viewing the returning students fall on their knees to kiss American soil, decided not to push the issue. In any event, U.S. troops had been withdrawn before the sixty-day limit. When United States planes attacked Libya in 1986 to retaliate for its reported involvement in terrorist attacks in which Americans were injured and killed, the Congress did not even bother to insist on the War Powers. The president's action was greeted with great enthusiasm.

The Central American situations in which the United States supported the government of El Salvador against left-wing guerrillas and the Contra guerrillas in their war to overthrow the Sandinista government in Nicaragua, also ironically failed to become tests of the War Powers Act. Neither involvement ever gained much public support and Congress throughout remained anxious lest the United States become involved in another Vietnam. Congressional concerns certainly made it impossible to use United States forces, especially in Nicaragua. Thus the War Powers Act may have had an indirect effect but, probably even in its absence, the Reagan administration would not have intervened directly. There would have been considerable domestic opposition and, if United States forces had not quickly succeeded in toppling the Sandinistas, the resulting turmoil might have been reminiscent of the Vietnam days. Hence in Nicaragua, the administration became involved in a covert war that ended in a major scandal. (See Chapter 3 for a more detailed discussion.)

In brief, the Central American situation arose from the administration's perception that events there were part of the broader Soviet–American rivalry. Therefore, it sent fifty-five military advisers to El Salvador to assist government forces. Because of congressional concerns about increasing the size of this group—a buildup of advisers had preceded the United States military intervention in Vietnam—the administration sent the additional advisers to neighboring Honduras. But legislative concerns remained high about the possibility of the conflict escalating and about intervening in a country whose civil war seemed the result mainly of decades of governmental political repression and social injustice. While it reluctantly went along with the president's requests for military and economic aid, the administration stilled some of the criticisms by finding and supporting centrist and democratically inclined political leader Napoléon Duarte. It also made clear its opposition to the powerful political right wing, which had long dominated El Salvador with its death squads that were indiscriminately killing "communists," including centrist political and religious figures. Congress played an important role in this respect: by making its aid conditional on a greater respect for human rights, it compelled the administration to pay more attention to these matters and made the Salvadoran army restrain its own forces' often unnecessary killings of civilians and, perhaps even more important, restrain the death squads with which the army was often involved. With training by the United States, the Salvadoran army became more of a professional fighting force and achieved greater success in its war, although the civil war continued.

The situation in Nicaragua, however, increasingly became the focus of the Reagan administration's efforts. Nicaragua was controlled by the Sandinista government which, after the ouster of the American-supported Somoza regime in 1979, increasingly suppressed criticism, ousted its moderate partners, and turned toward Cuba and the Soviet Union. The Reagan administration accused the Sandinistas of permitting arms from the Soviet bloc to flow through their country to the Salvadoran rebels. The administration, through the CIA, organized the opponents of the Sandinista regime, and provided them with arms and other assistance in their camps in Honduras and Costa Rica in an effort to pressure the Nicaraguans to cut off arms shipments. The CIA was thus involved in an undeclared war against the Sandinistas that, despite administration denials, seemed aimed mainly at overthrowing the Nicaraguan government. This kind of covert operation, in brief, fell between the cracks of resolving an issue either by diplomatic negotiation or the direct use of American military forces.

Therefore, the congressional restriction on actions aimed at overthrowing the Nicaraguan government became hard to enforce. Where exactly was the line to be drawn between actions that blocked the supply of arms from

Nicaragua to the Salvadoran guerrillas and those that destabilized the Nicaraguan regime? The first presumably was legal, but the last was not. Moreover, while the president officially maintained that the United States only wanted to stop the flow of arms, he called the anti-Sandinista rebels "freedom fighters" opposing a government that had betrayed its original democratic commitments, including the promise to hold genuinely free elections. Reagan also said it would be difficult to bring stability to Central America if the Sandinistas remained in power. One result of these and similar statements was a stalemate: the Democratically controlled House voting repeatedly to cut off funds for the CIA's covert activities in Nicaragua, and the Republican-controlled Senate going along with the administration. But even the Senate rebelled when it was revealed that the CIA had been active in organizing and directing the mining of Nicaraguan harbors. Opposition to the covert war thus mounted in both Houses.

The congressional cutoff of funds for the Contras in 1984 and 1985 (except for $27 million for "humanitarian" assistance, which by definition was not to include the buying of arms) did not, however, discourage the administration. Convinced of the correctness of its actions, it did an end run around Congress, shifting the direction of the conduct of the Contra war from the Central Intelligence Agency to the National Security Council to avoid congressional oversight while replacing congressional funding of arms with private and foreign government funding. In essence, it privatized the conduct of the war. To say the least, this was a novel idea but since, according to the Constitution, U.S. foreign policy was supposed to be made by the president and Congress, the discovery in November 1986 of what was going on, after years of suspicion and rumors, led to a major crisis for the Reagan administration (see Chapter 3).

Reagan and the Persian Gulf

The administration also refused to invoke the War Powers Resolution in the Persian Gulf where Iraq and Iran were waging their war. In this war, which had started in 1979 with an Iraqi attack to exploit Iran's instability in the early days of the Islamic revolution after the fall of the Shah, the odds were with Iran as the war dragged on year in and year out after the Iraqis failed to win a quick victory. Iran's population was three times larger than Iraq's and while Iraq had better and more arms, Iran could and did sacrifice more of its men in battle than Iraq. Iraq even used poison gas, but that too did not bring an end to the war. (Had Israel not taken out its atomic reactor in 1981, would Iraq have used nuclear bombs?) In desparation, the Iraqis in 1984 began attacking ships going to and from Iran where they loaded oil; the aim was to strangle Iran financially so that it would have to call off the war rather than continue the fighting until it had achieved its declared aim of deposing the Iraqi regime. Iran retaliated, starting in late 1986, by attacking ships to and from Kuwait, not just Kuwaiti-owned shipping, thus setting off a tanker war. It also intermittently threatened to close the Persian Gulf to all shipping, which would have shut down oil exports from the various Arab countries on the Gulf, who were pro-Iraqi in sentiment and supported it with financial aid. The Iranian acquisition of Chinese-made short-range missiles and their emplacement at the mouth of the Gulf was therefore considered an ominous sign.

The United States repeatedly reaffirmed its commitment to keeping the Gulf open: the navy, which had been in the Gulf since 1949, would ensure this goal. But freedom of the seas was never threatened, for Iran depended on the Gulf for its oil exports; it was in fact Iraq, which used pipelines, that threatened this freedom with its attacks on ships carrying Iranian oil. A more obvious reason was U.S. support of the pro-Western oil sheikdoms, all of whom feared an Iranian victory and the spread of Islamic fundamentalism. In the war itself, while declaring neutrality, the United States in fact favored Iraq because an Iranian victory was not in America's interest. However, since Iraq could not win, the U.S. preference was for a stalemate.

It is in this context that the president's thoughtless, if not reckless, sale of arms to gain the release of a few U.S. hostages in Lebanon became pertinent. Among other consequences, it shocked the Arab Gulf kingdoms and other Arab states who feared that the United States was tilting toward Iran. One result was that Kuwait, lying to the south of Iraq and an ally of Iraq, turned to the Soviet Union for help. Moscow agreed and chartered three of its tankers to Kuwait. Kuwait was basically a city-state with oilwells and a port through which Iraq's trade and arms flowed. Kuwait was in all but name an ally of Iraq. The United States, which had also been asked for its protective services in December 1986 but had not given any answer to Kuwait, quickly assented in March 1987 to forestall a larger Soviet role and presence in the Gulf. The United States could not afford to lose even more of its prestige and influence than it had already as a result of the shipment of arms to Iran. The aim was clearly to eliminate the Arab perception that the United States had become pro-Iranian, or had become irresolute and was therefore a less desirable guardian of the sheikdoms' security than Moscow. A refusal to protect Kuwaiti tankers would, in Washington's eyes, have had that result, with a corresponding increase in Moscow's prestige and influence.

A Soviet presence in the Gulf, located near two thirds of the world's oil reserves—probably the greatest geopolitical prize of the late twentieth century—had therefore to be opposed. The plain fact is that the United States cannot permit the oil kingdoms to fall under the influence of any hostile power, regardless of whether it is the Soviet Union or Iran. Thus the fallout of Irangate had a profound impact on U.S. foreign policy. To prove U.S. reliability to the Arabs, the administration rather quickly agreed to a major step, assuming that its escort service could be carried out with ships then present in the Gulf and that Iran would not dare provoke the American Navy.

If Washington's decision, therefore, was largely a response to a Soviet move in an area where Russia has historically sought control since tsarist days, it soon became clear that the Reagan administration had not thought this move through any more than it had its earlier intervention in Lebanon, where a small force of marines was sent in as part of an international peace-keeping force. As Lebanon's bitter civil war resumed, the United States took sides and supported the Christian-dominated government, which did not even control the capital city, against the Moslem opposition. The marines now became targets. The result was a tragedy and a timely but humiliating withdrawal by a humbled superpower. Would that sequence be repeated now, for reflagging Kuwaiti tankers and escorting them with U.S. warships would be taking sides in the Iran–Iraqi war? The issue of the Reagan admin-istration's policy-making processes—already prominent because of Iran-gate—came to be questioned even more closely as the U.S. frigate, *Stark*, was inadvertently attacked in May 1987 by an Iraqi jet with a French-made missile. Not expecting an attack by "friendlies," the ship took no defensive measures and suffered a loss of thirty-seven lives.

Now the Congress, which had previously not voiced any objections, became worried, for the new rules of engagement—shoot first, ask questions later—plus the U.S. intention to reregister eleven Kuwaiti oil tankers as U.S. vessels to be commanded by a U.S. captain and escorted by U.S. warships meant that the risks of conflict with Iran and more casualties had grown. What would happen if the Iranians would not be deterred by the likelihood of U.S. retaliation, as the administration contended they would? What kind of retaliation and risks did it have in mind? What if a Kuwaiti ship with a U.S. flag were attacked, or the escorting U.S. ships or planes? Would the United States then strike back at Iranian missile or air bases? If attacks be-came more frequent, would the United States continue to retaliate or strike preventively? Could U.S. warships defend themselves properly? Did they need air protection and, if so, how was that to be assured if none of the Gulf states would give the United States landing rights? And should the United States not insist on help from its allies to whom most of the Gulf oil was shipped? Obviously, while making its commitment to Kuwait, the ad-ministration had not thought through the consequences and prepared for them. For instance, on March 7, 1987, the secretary of defense announced the policy but only on May 24, after the Iraqi attack on the U.S. frigate on May 19, did Weinberger assert that air cover for U.S. ships was essential. Yet no agreement for land air bases for U.S. planes had been negotiated before the policy was announced; nor was such an agreement concluded afterward. Administration officials stated that they would examine the above questions and others *now*. This lack of preparation was dramatically illustrated when the Pentagon, having underestimated Iran's shrewdness and the danger of mines, was immediately confronted by the first tanker being hit by an Iranian-planted World War II mine, leading the U.S. naval ships to line up behind the damaged tanker to avoid hitting other mines. Having spent its money on high-technology weapons, the navy now found itself without the lowly minesweepers it needed, leaving the United States to plead with its European allies for help—which it got.

Despite the obvious risks of its policy, the administration refused to invoke the War Powers Resolution; the president contended that conditions at the time did not meet the resolution's description of a "situation where imminent involvement in hostilities is clearly indicated by circumstances." Yet the navy was giving sailors dangerous duty pay because they were "subject to hostile fire or imminent danger"! Indeed, there were a number of incidents in which American forces opened fire, sinking Iranian oil rigs and more than half of its navy. The Congress therefore repeatedly objected to the president's failure to invoke War Powers; indeed, over 100 congressmen took the issue to the courts to compel the president to invoke the resolution, although their suit was rejected. While Congress remained nervous about the entire Persian Gulf commitment, leading members stated that they realized that once committed, the United States could hardly withdraw without disastrous consequences in the area because such an action would reinforce the Persian Gulf countries' perceptions that the United States was an unreliable protector who could not be counted on, exactly the impression the administration wished to counter. That is why the administration remained suspicious of Congress' intention and tended not to believe the reassurances of support. It continued to believe that if there were a major Iranian attack on a U.S. naval ship with high casualties, Congress would seek a U.S. withdrawal. Indeed, the passage of the War Powers Resolution might provide precisely the incentive the Iranians needed for an attack.

A Reassessment: The Role of the Congress and the Military

The continuing debate about the War Powers Act touches on a number of issues: the wisdom or stupidity of the policies that involve the use of overt or covert force; the institutional struggle between the executive and the legislature; and not unexpectedly, partisan politics. The War Powers Act, then, requires the Congress to stand up and be counted—"Put blood on our hands, too," as Senator Jacob Javits (R-N.Y.) reportedly said—instead of hiding behind the president and letting him take sole responsibility.[45] But, of course, the Congress has always possessed the power to intervene in that it must approve of a president's actions by appropriating funds for the conduct of any hostilities. Events in Central America, Lebanon, and Grenada had made it clear that Congress no longer intended to be passive on matters of war and peace, and uncritically accept presidential explanations. Nonetheless, the limits of presidential discretion in the use of force remained cloudy. Perhaps only a major large-scale intervention abroad by U.S. forces will resolve the issue.[46]

What happens if the president and Congress differ in their respective definitions of what constitutes "imminent involvement in hostilities," that is, whether a crisis exists? Would the Congress have accepted Roosevelt's definition of the German threat after the fall of France as a menace to U.S. security and supported the transfer of destroyers to Britain, the convoying of British merchant ships by U.S. warships as far as Iceland, or the "shoot on sight" order against German raiders? The War Powers Act simply assumed the unassumable: that imminent involvement in hostilities is clear to any beholder and therefore does not need a definition. This may not always be true, as Lebanon, Grenada, and the Persian Gulf suggest. The president may simply refuse to recognize imminent involvement in hostilities is at hand to keep Congress from interfering and perhaps insisting on U.S. withdrawal.

Even if they agree on what an emergency is, how, from a practical point of view, can the president be given sufficient authority and flexibility to act without evading congressional involvement and responsibility to participate in key decisions affecting war and peace? In short, how can one find the spot halfway between authority that is too broad and that which is too narrow, between giving the president the flexibility he needs to protect American interests and handcuffing him so that he does not involve the country in needless conflict? In the weeks before the abortive rescue attempt of the American hostages in Iran in 1980, the Senate Foreign Relations Committee chairman and ranking minority members insisted that the Carter administration consult with the committee before any potential use of force. Rumors were rife that Iran's ports were about to be mined in an effort to increase economic pressure on Iran. But how can any administration consult the Congress in advance on plans for the use of force without placing the world on notice, giving its adversary time to mobilize international opinion (including American opinion) against such an effort, and placing its military forces on alert to foil the American effort? Is this any way for a great power to conduct its foreign policy and protect its interests?

A third problem remains equally vexing: How can Congress really participate in crisis decision making? President Ford after the *Mayaguez* said that it could not and cited several reasons, some of which President Kennedy before him and Carter after him also cited.[47]

1. Key legislators were out of town and communicating with them was difficult, slow, and in some instances impossible. (Kennedy had the air force pick up the important congressional figures and return them to Washington during the Cuban missile crisis.)

2. Congressmen have a multitude of concerns that prevent them from focusing over a period of time only, or primarily, on one issue.

3. Time is of the essence and this requirement is incompatible with developing a consensus among congressional leaders in case of disagreement, especially if they are not in town.

4. Even if a consensus were reached, many congressmen among today's independent-minded legislators might not accept it.

5. The likelihood of information leaking out from some members of Congress about a forthcoming military operation inhibits any executive consultation with the Congress or with more than just a very few members.

One might add to these reasons cited by President Ford that in the contemporary Congress it is doubtful that many members would consider presidential consultation with key congressional leaders sufficient. The days when a few men could speak for the Congress appear to be over. Paradoxically, however, one might question how many congressmen really want to know what the president is planning. It is one thing to blame him for failure afterward and suggest that had he consulted Congress this failure could have been avoided; it is another matter to also be held accountable for disaster. Perhaps it is for this reason that not too many voices were raised in protest about the lack of consultation after the failure of the hostage rescue mission in Iran.

The War Powers Act and the increasing concern of the Congress to limit presidential discretion on foreign policy ran into a major Supreme Court decision on June 23, 1983. The Court that day swept away the fifty-year-old congressional practice of blocking executive action with a "legislative veto" after it had delegated authority to the president. A legislative veto occurs when Congress gives provisional authority to the executive to make a decision, subject to ultimate legislative approval. In the case of foreign policy, the War Powers Act gives the president the power to dispatch troops as he deems necessary, but Congress reserves the right to reverse such decisions. Depending on how Congress has written the original legislation, a veto may be made either by one house or by both.

The Court ruled that once Congress delegated a decision to the executive branch, either the president or the bureaucracy, it could not simply decide to overrule that branch. Such an action would constitute a breach of the separation of powers between the two branches. The veto itself had come about because Congress has been willing to grant the president broad powers to set policy, whereas legislative initiatives require narrow and specific legislation. The idea behind the veto, then, was to permit the president or the bureaucracy to determine the specifics of policies, subject to congressional disapproval. The Supreme Court ruled, however, that Congress must make its specific decisions *before* the executive branch acts. The War Powers Act, the Arms Export Control Act of 1976, which gave Congress a veto over arms sales, and the Jackson–Vanik amendment of 1974 denying preferential trading status to communist nations that restricted Jewish emigration were the key foreign policy tools threatened by the decision. Since the Court ruled only on an obscure emigration case, it was not clear that these acts were immediately invalidated. Earlier, the House Foreign Affairs Committee attempted to evade the Court's decision by including a provision that permits Congress to vote on a joint resolution to suspend aid to El Salvador. A joint resolution of the two houses can be vetoed by the president, whereas a concurrent resolution, which had been used previously, was not subject to presidential approval.[48] Joint resolutions are virtually identical to ordinary bills, while concurrent resolutions merely express the "sense of Congress" that something ought to be done.

The Court decision does not affect the portions of the War Powers Act that require the president to report to Congress when American troops are sent overseas and face either combat or imminent hostilities that prohibit the president from keeping troops in such situations for more than ninety days unless Congress declares war or approves an extension. What Congress cannot do, at least according to the president's interpretation of the Court decision, is to force withdrawal of troops engaged in hostilities. The Congress has not admitted defeat on the War Powers issue, claiming that the Supreme Court decision on the immigration bill may not cover all aspects of the legislative veto. Yet there is little evidence that Congress has developed any alternatives to the current procedure that might work effectively.

Despite the ruling, however, the executive branch is not likely to regain more freedom to use force. A lawyer for the Reagan administration dealing with foreign policy commented: "From our point of view, nothing has changed. We never conceded the constitutionality of the legislative veto in the first place. But as a practical matter, we would be fools to thumb our noses at Congress now."[49] A president will still have to live with Congress, which clearly remains determined to participate in decisions involving the use of force, especially ones that unlike Grenada may lead to lengthier military interventions against more formidable opponents. It would be very impolitic for a president not to be sensitive to congressional opinion about issues of war and peace; the political cost would be too high. Presumably, this is the reason the executive has not challenged the War Powers Resolution in the courts and presidents have consulted with Congress if time permitted and have reported to Congress "consistent with the War Powers Resolution" while asserting that the president as commander in chief has the authority to use the armed forces.

Overall, the Reagan administration was in its way sensitive to congressional and public opinion when it contemplated the larger scale use of U.S. forces. Its resort to covert operations in Nicaragua reflected its awareness that it could not use U.S. troops; short, successful, and relatively cost-free operations in terms of situations like Grenada and the air strikes on Libya created their own public support and did not therefore pose a War Powers issue, as the Democrats discovered. Even with initial War Powers support in the Congress, Reagan was quick to cut losses in Lebanon after the deaths of 241 marines rather than escalate the relatively limited intervention of 1,200 marines, suffer a greater number of casualties, and risk public disaffection. In the post-Vietnam period, lengthy and costly interventions in losses of lives were to be avoided; whenever the possibility of the use of force was even discussed, concerns were expressed about another Vietnam.

Congress has, of course, as noted, always had power over U.S. involvement in military operations, namely, the power of the purse. But it has rarely exercised this power. Despite its growing vocal opposition to Vietnam, it cut off funds for military operations only once, in Cambodia in 1975 after the war in South Vietnam was already over. It did so again in the covert Nicaraguan war in 1984, fearing the use of American armed forces at some future point. However understandable Congress' desire to be involved in decisions involving the use of force, the War Powers Resolution has "done nothing to alleviate the ambiguity that now exists with regard to who in the government has the authority to use American armed forces abroad, short of a declaration of war. On the contrary, the War Powers Resolution has simply politicized the question more than was the case in the past."[50]

One contributory factor to the question of direct U.S. intervention is the military itself, which in a sense has become the dove among the major foreign policy actors. After Korea and especially after Vietnam, the military, particularly the army, became strongly opposed to *any* interventions. What is especially revealing during the Reagan years—the years of reasserting American prestige in the world and of the huge rearmament program—is that the Pentagon resisted the interventions in Lebanon, Grenada, and Libya, as well as a possible intervention in Nicaragua. It was Secretary of State Shultz who advocated the use of force in the three instances when it was used and Secretary of Defense Weinberger who resisted. In November 1984, Weinberger enumerated the conditions for the use of force in such a way that virtually proscribed such action: The commitment of troops must be vital to the national interest and made with the clear intention of winning; political and military objectives must be clearly defined and there must be the assurance that the public and Congress will support the intervention.[51] While on the one hand, none of these conditions would have prevented Vietnam, the clear intention of stating them after the last conflict was to avoid future interventions. Very few future crises are likely to fit all these prerequisites. Korea and Vietnam, besides being deemed vital security interests, had popular and congressional support when the United States first intervened, but this support eroded later. In short, initial support is not a sufficient condition for winning. Had Grenada been debated in the Congress before the intervention, it might not have received overwhelming approval; there certainly would have been strong opposition from the Democratically controlled House and perhaps even the Republican-controlled Senate. But Grenada's success created its own support. In short, even the absence of an initial consensus does not mean a successful intervention is impossible. For Weinberger to demand congressional support before intervention occurs and expect Congress to remain supportive regardless of how the situation evolves is to recommend against any intervention or decisions that might lead to intervention.* Since Vietnam, the

---

*In 1987, contradicting himself, Weinberger despite strong congressional opposition, defined reflagging Kuwaiti tankers as a national interest and thus recommended going ahead despite the risks of conflict with Iran.

military wants to intervene only when it is guaranteed such support and, once that has occurred, to have a free hand; even though war is a political instrument, it does not want to be politically restrained and "micromanaged." That simply is impossible. States go to war for political reasons and to achieve political goals; military operations must therefore be subordinated to the attainment of these goals, whatever they are. In fact, the U.S. military is organized and prepared only for the one war that is unlikely ever to occur—a war with the Soviet Union, including a land war in Europe. It has never adjusted its organization and doctrine for limited wars and the kind of Third World "pinpricks" that are far more likely to occur and in which force may have to be used. In its preoccupation with deterring the Soviet Union and protecting U.S. allies in Europe, it has not adequately prepared itself militarily and hardly at all psychologically and intellectually to cope with the kinds of political situations that will require the use of conventional forces. In a troublesome world that exists under the umbrella of nuclear deterrence and strategic stalemate, the United States will need to cope with the daily pinpricks of terrorism, subversion, and shifting geographical situations. Covert operations as in Nicaragua cannot be substituted for the Pentagon's antiinterventionist counsel if the president feels the use of force necessary and public opinion will support him.

Between the Congress and the Pentagon, other nations may wonder about what is still referred to as the world's most powerful nation. Was President Assad of Syria correct when he reportedly said that the United States was "short of breath," that Syria and its Moslem allies in Lebanon needed only to wait because once America had suffered some casualties, the Congress would clamor to bring the troops home? What is the message the United States is sending to allies and friends who depend on it? And what of its enemies when, after the first shot and casualties, congressional voices demand a pullout? It was to prove U.S. steadfastness that President Reagan refused to invoke War Powers Resolution in the Gulf. A risk-free foreign policy for a superpower is a contradiction in terms. "Certainly, the ability of presidents to support credibly U.S. diplomacy with American force if necessary has been weakened by the War Powers Resolution and the periodic debates that take place in Congress concerning its requirements. . . . What the War Powers Resolution does is to weaken a strong president and exacerbate the indecisiveness of a weak president."[52] The central issue, however, may not really be the War Powers Resolution but whether the United States still has the will to play its role of superpower. Public opinion remains divided in this post-Vietnam period on what kind of a role the United States should pursue and especially, on the use of force to advance American purposes.

The War Powers act is a symptom of this deeper problem, as revealed by Congress' attitude. On the one hand, the Congress insists on being consulted before the United States engages, as in the Persian Gulf; when this does not occur to Congress' satisfaction, as is usually the case, it can then place responsibility for what happens later on the president. In short, the act permits Congress to avoid taking responsibility for risky military action. On the other hand, by not normally invoking the War Powers (as in the major exception of Lebanon), using its appropriation power, or outrightly opposing the president's action (as in banning the reflagging), it also avoids assuming responsibility for the consequences of the United States *not* taking the action the president proposes. Rarely does today's Congress ever plainly say "yes" or "no."[53] If it says "yes," it may also be held responsible should a military clash and casualties result; if it says "no," it is fearful of being accused of interfering with the president's authority as commander in chief and of failing to support the nation's leader on a matter of national interest at a critical moment—indeed, of being responsible for humiliating the United States by forcing the president to "bug out" after he has already committed American power.[54] In short, Congress will not choose among what a retiring marine commandant in 1987 called "lousy options," all of which, whether the United States does anything or not, involve costs and risks.

NOTES

1. *New York Times,* January 21, 1961.
2. Aaron Wildavsky, "The Two Presidencies," *Trans-Action,* December 1966, p. 3.
3. Francis E. Rourke, Robert E. Osgood, Robert W. Turner, et al., "The Domestic Scene: The President Ascendant," in *Retreat From Empire?* (Baltimore: The Johns Hopkins University Press, 1973), p. 106. See also Leslie H. Gelb and Richard K. Betts, *The Irony of Vietnam* (Washington, D.C.: The Brookings Institution, 1979), pp. 223–24.
4. Robert S. Strauss, "What's Right with U.S. Campaigns," *Foreign Policy,* Summer 1984, pp. 3–22; and Stephen Hess, "Foreign Policy and Presidential Campaigns," *Foreign Policy,* Fall 1972, pp. 3–22.
5. Ibid., p. 19.
6. Cyrus Vance, *Hard Choices* (New York: Simon & Schuster, 1983), p. 13.
7. Gary Sick, *All Fall Down* (New York: Random House, 1985), pp. 363–77, especially 376–77.
8. Zbigniew Brzezinski, "NSC's Midlife Crisis," *Foreign Policy,* Winter 1987–88, pp. 91–92.
9. Duncan L. Clarke, "Why State Can't Lead," *Foreign Policy,* Spring 1987, pp. 108–42.
10. *New York Times,* January 25, 1983. See also Zbigniew Brzezinski, *Power and Principle* (New York: Farrar, Straus, Giroux, 1983), pp. 53–55.
11. Quoted in *New York Times,* May 21, 1980. Also see I. M. Destler, "A Job That Doesn't Work," *Foreign Policy,* Spring 1980, pp. 80–88; and Flora Lewis, "The Parts and the Whole." *New York Times,* September 30, 1980.
12. Alexander Haig, *Caveat* (New York: Macmillan, 1984), p. 352 ff.
13. Interview with Zbigniew Brzezinski, *New York Times,* January 6, 1982.
14. See the Tower Commission Report on the Iran arms for hostages deal, *New York Times,* February 27, 1987.

15. Norman J. Ornstein, "Regan's Mismanagement Style," *New York Times*, February 5, 1987. Also, Donald T. Regan, *For the Record* (San Diego, Calif.: Harcourt Brace Jovanovich, 1988).
16. *New York Times*, March 2, 1987.
17. Ronald Steel, "Shultz's Way," *New York Times Magazine*, January 11, 1987, p. 17 ff; Also see George W. Ball, "A Report Card on Secretary Shultz," *New York Times*, July 3, 1988.
18. Clarke, "Why State Can't Lead," pp. 141–42.
19. I. M. Destler, *Presidents, Bureaucrats, and Foreign Policy*, rev. ed. (Princeton, N.J.: Princeton University Press, 1974), pp. 298–319; and "Can One Man Do?" *Foreign Policy*, Winter 1971–72, pp. 28–40.
20. Clarke, "Why State Can't Lead," pp. 140–41.
21. Brzezinski, *Power and Principle*, pp. 536–37, and more recently, "The NSC's Midlife Crisis," *op. cit.*, pp. 94–99. For background on the NSC and NSA, see Karl F. Inderfurth and Loch K. Johnson, eds., *Decisions of the Highest Order* (Pacific Grove, Calif.: Brooks/Cole, 1988).
22. Richard K. Betts, *Soldiers, Statesmen, and Cold War Crises* (Cambridge, Mass.: Harvard University Press, 1977), pp. 4, 6.
23. Henry T. Nash, *American Foreign Policy: Response to a Sense of Threat*, 3d ed. (Homewood, Ill.: Dorsey Press, 1985), p. 151.
24. Henry A. Kissinger, "Bureaucracy and Policy-Making: The Effects of Insiders and Outsiders on the Policy Process," in *Readings in American Foreign Policy*, Halperin and Kanter, eds., p. 89.
25. Francis E. Rourke, *Bureaucracy and Foreign Policy* (Baltimore: Johns Hopkins University Press, 1973), p. 32.
26. Ibid.
27. Edward N. Luttwak, *The Pentagon and the Art of War* (New York: Simon & Schuster, 1984), pp. 19–20. On the new military reforms, see Arthur T. Hadley, "Military Coup," *The New Republic*, January 18, 1988, pp. 17–20. For this author's critique of the U.S. military, see *The Straw Giant* (New York: Avon Books, 1987).
28. Quoted by Robert A. Dahl, *Congress and Foreign Policy* (New York: Harcourt Brace Jovanovich, 1950), pp. 129–30.
29. Joseph Jones, *The Fifteen Weeks* (New York: Viking Press, 1955), pp. 138–41.
30. Arthur M. Schlesinger, Jr., *The Bitter Heritage* (Greenwich, Conn.: A Fawcett Crest Book, 1967), p. 47. (See also, Larry Berman, *Planning A Tragedy* (New York: W. W. Norton, 1982).
31. William Conrad Gibbons, *The U.S. Government and the Vietnam War*, Part II: 1961–1964 (Princeton, N.J.: Princeton University Press, 1986).
32. *New York Times*, October 18, 1979.
33. *New York Times*, October 2, 1981.
34. Ibid., October 27, 1981.
35. Guenter Lewy, *America in Vietnam* (New York: Oxford University Press, 1978), pp. 202–5.
36. J. William Fulbright, *The Crippled Giant*, (New York: Vintage Books, 1972), pp. 218–20; and *The Pentagon Papers* (New York: Bantam Books, 1971), p. 25.
37. Fulbright, *Pentagon Papers*, p. 79.
38. Arthur M. Schlesinger, Jr., "Congress and the Making of American Foreign Policy," *Foreign Affairs*, October 1972, p. 98.

39. Quoted by Joseph C. Goulden, *Truth Is the First Casualty* (Skokie, Ill.: Rand McNally, 1969), pp. 50–55. See also Eugene C. Windchy, *Tonkin Gulf* (New York: Doubleday Publishing, 1971).

40. See, for example, David Halberstam, *The Best and the Brightest* (New York: Random House, 1972); Stanley Karrow, *Vietnam* (New York: Viking Press, 1983).

41. Spanier, *The Truman-MacArthur Controversy and the Korean War,* rev. ed. (New York: W. W. Norton, 1965).

42. Fulbright, *The Crippled Giant,* pp. 188–91. On the intervention, see Larry Berman, *Planning a Tragedy* (New York: W. W. Norton, 1984).

43. Thomas F. Eagleton, "Whose Power is War Power?" *Foreign Policy,* Fall 1972, pp. 29–31. John H. Sullivan, *The War Powers Resolution: A Special Study of the Committee on Foreign Affairs* (Washington, D.C.: U.S. Government Printing Office, 1982).

44. Ibid.

45. Jacob Javits in the *New York Times,* February 14, 1972. See also Javits, *Who Makes War* (New York: William Morrow, 1973).

46. Pat M. Holt, *The War Powers Resolution* (Washington, D.C.: American Enterprise Institute, 1978); and Robert F. Turner, *The War Powers Resolution* (Philadelphia: Foreign Policy Research Institute, 1983).

47. Cited by Richard G. Head, Frisco W. Short, and Robert C. McFarlane, *Crisis Resolution* (Boulder, Colo.: Westview Press, 1978), p. 254.

48. "Panel Skirts Legislative Veto Ban," *Congressional Quarterly Weekly Report* 41 (July 30, 1983), p. 1,576.

49. John Felton, "Hill Weighs Foreign Policy Impact of Ruling," *Congressional Quarterly Weekly Report* 41 (July 2, 1983), p. 1,324.

50. Alan Ned Sabrosky, "The War Powers Resolution: Retrospect and Prospect," in *The Reagan Defense Program,* ed., Stephen J. Cimbala (Wilmington, Del.: Scholarly Resources, 1986), p. 132.

51. For Weinberger's speech to the National Press Club, see *New York Times,* November 29, 1984.

52. Sabrosky, "Retrospect and Prospect," pp. 132–33.

53. Timothy Noah, "War Power in Action," *The New Republic,* July 6, 1987.

54. Tom Wicker, "A Law That Failed," *New York Times,* January 7, 1988.

Chapter Three

The Presidency and Executive–Legislative Relations

THE BACKGROUND: 1940–41

It must be clear by now that no issue is of greater importance than the relationship between the executive branch and Congress in the conduct of foreign policy. Even before the United States became a world power, one observer noted:

> America has never yet devised a sound or efficient technique of diplomacy. . . . Nearly every important treaty the country has been called upon to make has become a bone of contention between the executive and the Senate. It is certain that in years to come if we are to go forward in the new paths and stand for a clear-cut world policy, we must devise some method of speaking to the world promptly and with an undivided voice. Our present system leads to utter weakness, muddle, and delay; it forces both sides to play politics, and instead of meeting the issue squarely, to indulge in a vast controversy over the prerogatives of two coordinate branches of the government. The deadlock between the executive and the senate every time we face a really critical foreign problem is intolerable. It not only disgraces us before the nations, but in some future world crisis may ruin us.[1]

Since the United States did become a superpower, executive–legislative relations have grown more important. In a Cold War situation, where presidents have come to wield virtually emergency powers that in the past they would have exercised only temporarily—mainly in wartime—they need the support of the Congress. Treaties require a two-thirds Senate vote, diplomatic appointments must be confirmed, control over the military is shared with the president as commander in chief and, most important, appropriations must be authorized for all sorts of foreign and defense policies. Nevertheless, all recent presidents have consistently and repeatedly complained about congressional restrictions and interference with their efforts to carry out U.S. policy. These criticisms have often been summed up by the comment that Congress is composed of 535 secretaries of state.

Actually executive–legislative conflict is as old as the Republic and institutional rivalry and partisanship are its principal causes. If mounting U.S. involvement in world affairs is the main reason for the growth of presidential power, another important cause has been congressional obstructionism. Three phases of U.S. policy in this century need to be mentioned if one is to understand not only why the presidency has established preeminence in the conduct of foreign policy, but, equally important, why until Vietnam, this trend received popular approval and academic blessings.

The starting point is the Versailles Treaty of 1919, which concluded World War I and established the League of Nations. The intensity of the conflict between President Wilson, a Democrat, and the Senate, controlled by the Republicans and directed by Senator Henry Cabot Lodge (Mass.), resulted in the treaty's defeat. Executive–legislative rivalry, partisan considerations, and personal hatred of the two men toward each other thus contributed to the U.S. withdrawal from an active world role after the war. This return to isolationism, many Americans later felt, was partly responsible for the outbreak of World War II. The defeat of the Versailles Treaty thus dramatically raised the question of America's ability, with its institutions, to conduct a foreign policy to protect its interest.

The second period, from the German defeat of France in the spring of 1940 to Pearl Harbor in late 1941, reinforced this concern.[2] This was a period in which the president had to confront the threat of an increasingly powerful Germany while Congress remained in the grip of isolationism. Indeed, during the 1930s the Congress had passed a series of neutrality laws that were supposed to keep the United States out of any future European war. On the eve of that war in 1939, when the administration asked for changes that would allow the government to sell arms to the allies who seemed less well prepared than the Nazis, Senator William Borah (R-Idaho), chairman of the Foreign Relations Committee and himself an ardent isolationist, not only rejected the request, but asserted that *his* sources of information were superior to those of the State Department, and that they had told him there would be no war!

After hostilities erupted, the problem for President Roosevelt was how to do the "right thing" and be able to do it despite the continued isolationist sentiment in the Congress. For Roosevelt, the right thing meant supporting Britain after the fall of France, the low countries (the Netherlands, Belgium, and Luxembourg), and Denmark and Norway. American policy makers have historically considered the domination of Western Europe by a single power as a potential threat to American security. Even Thomas Jefferson, a Francophile, voiced the possibility of aligning with England as Napoleon proceeded to conquer Europe. In Roosevelt's words, the defense of American democracy would be difficult and would certainly result in the sacrifice of the democratic ingredient if the United States were to become a lone island of peace surrounded by a world of brute force (German, Italian, and Japanese). America would have to turn itself into a garrison state; the Atlantic

Ocean was no longer a barrier to attack but a highway to the Western Hemisphere.

The president therefore wanted to help Britain, first of all, to defend itself against a possible German invasion. But despite entreaties by Prime Minister Churchill for some old World War I-vintage destroyers, Roosevelt, at a time of great emergency, procrastinated. The Congress, anticipating him, had imposed a legal barrier by decreeing that the president could not transfer the destroyers unless the chief of naval operations certified that such ships were not needed for U.S. defense. The distrust of the president was abundantly clear. Roosevelt finally outflanked the Congress with an executive agreement but only after four months of hesitation. The president had to secure a pledge from the Republican presidential nominee that he would not make the transaction a political issue; at the same time, the Committee to Defend America by Aiding the Allies had mobilized domestic support through intensive propaganda, and Churchill had agreed that in return for the destroyers the United States could lease bases on British islands in the Atlantic and Caribbean. This deal allowed Roosevelt to present the destroyer transfer basically as an American acquisition of bases and thus a means of enhancing American security; nonetheless, the destroyers were hardly mentioned in Roosevelt's speech to the country. What would have happened had the Germans invaded, as expected, during these months?

After his reelection in 1940, Roosevelt was successful in obtaining congressional support for the Lend-Lease Act by which Britain, soon unable to pay for American arms and ammunition, could acquire these on a lease basis. The United States was to become "the great arsenal of democracy." The Congress went along with the president because of the view—probably shared by Roosevelt too—that the best chance of staying out of the war was by helping the British to strengthen themselves and win the war. "Give us the tools and we will finish the job" was Churchill's cry. But the key problem was getting the supplies to Britain. In the battle of the Atlantic, the Germans were sinking British and Canadian merchant ships faster than they could be built. But Britain's survival remained the critical issue. Yet, what was the point of giving the arms to the British if their ships were sunk? Roosevelt felt inhibited, however, from doing anything. He had, in the summer of 1941, sent the marines to Iceland to prevent the Germans from stationing air reconnaissance and submarines there to cut Britain's lifeline to America. But he continued to hesitate in authorizing American warships, which were taking supplies and mail to the marines, from also convoying British and Canadian merchant ships to Iceland, even though that would relieve the already thinly stretched British navy (which would then have to convoy ships only the last half of their journey across the Atlantic). One senator had introduced a resolution specifically forbidding the president from authorizing convoys. Again, not until after several months of hesitation did Roosevelt as commander in chief of the armed forces authorize such protection.

He did so only after a German submarine had attacked the U.S. destroyer *Greer.* In publicly explaining that the navy would from then escort all merchant ships and "shoot-on-sight" at German submarines and raiders, the president was in effect involving the United States in a limited naval war in the western Atlantic. But he did not explain in his "undeclared war" speech that the destroyers had for several hours pursued the German submarine, that in desperation to escape the submarine had turned on the destroyer and fired its torpedoes, after which the destroyer had dropped depth charges on the submarine. Thus a German act, which could not have been anticipated, finally permitted the United States to do what was needed to ensure that the arms required by Britain—America's first line of defense— would get there. Had the submarine been able to slip away and had other German submarines not sunk several other American ships, what could the president have done? For congressional sentiment on the eve of World War II was clearly shown in two separate votes—one on extending the Selective Service Act, which passed the House by only one vote, and the other, finally repealing the last major neutrality-law constraint blocking American ships from carrying supplies directly to British ports, squeezed through a very narrow House majority of 212 to 194 and Senate majority of 50 to 37. These last two votes came right after a German submarine had torpedoed a U.S. destroyer near Iceland.

Franklin Roosevelt thus set a precedent for his successors. He felt compelled to resort to executive agreements to expand the powers of the commander in chief. His problem, as he saw it, was that if he did not undertake the various measures he used to help Britain, Hitler might win in Europe and then threaten the United States. If he had sought to gain congressional approval for such steps as the destroyer deal or the convoying of allied merchant ships by U.S. warships as far as Iceland, he might have failed, eroding his own authority and effectiveness as president and encouraging Hitler. Indeed, had he come out more openly for intervention, he might have lost his unprecedented third-term bid for the presidency.

It is interesting that even the critics of the president's war powers do not question Roosevelt's judgment of the peril to national security. But they do question the constitutional propriety of his actions. Thus, quite typically, Merlo Pusey, after admitting that had the president gone to Congress he would have been turned down even though "human freedom was gravely endangered on a global scale," says: "On grounds of expediency and of international power politics, the argument [for the actions Roosevelt took] is very impressive. But where does it leave us in terms of democratic principles and the maintenance of constitutional government?"[3] By the juxtaposition of such loaded terms as *expediency* and *power politics* with *principles* and *democracy,* Pusey stacks the odds and avoids the issue of (1) what Roosevelt should have done, and (2) how to reconcile American democratic government, with its separation of powers, with the protection of national security. Pusey dismisses this concern as "one of the inescapable risks in democratic government."[4] The worst, he says, that would have happened had Roosevelt gone to Congress for support and been rejected, would have been more aggressive behavior by the Nazis on the assumption that the United States would do nothing to stop them; they might even have struck the first blow, as Japan finally did.

In short, what Pusey argues is that U.S. institutions could not cope with the critical situation in 1940 and 1941; they could not take the initiative to protect U.S. security, but could only react to the enemy's initiatives. But no matter. America's paralysis would have provoked its enemies so that after they had attacked this country Congress could legally have declared war.[5] The integrity of the Constitution in these circumstances could have been preserved. In other words, American democracy—separation of powers style—unable to act wisely would be saved by its enemies' stupidity.

But Pusey's argument avoids the central issue of the effectiveness of American institutions in meeting critical foreign policy situations and of the ability of the political process to produce the best policy outcome. What would have happened had the Japanese bypassed Hawaii and had Hitler not declared war on America? Could Roosevelt have mobilized sufficient congressional and public support to declare war on the Axis powers? It is doubtful, even though by late 1941 Germany had conquered all of Western Europe except Britain, stood at the gates of Moscow and Leningrad, had captured much of North Africa, and was soon to move within sight of the Suez Canal, while Japan was poised for the conquest of British, French, and Dutch colonies in the Far East with a possible linkup via India with the Germans in the Middle East. But for German *and* Japanese mistakes, these two powers might have finished off their opponents and then confronted a psychologically and militarily unprepared America at the peak of their power and self-confidence. The ultimate decision—to make war on the United States—was made by Japan and Germany. The United States did not make this decision for itself despite the fact that the balances of power in Asia and Europe were at stake. As Robert Divine has aptly said:

> From the first signs of aggression in the 1930s to the attack on Pearl Harbor, the United States refused to attack until there was no other choice. . . . Although it was the single most powerful nation on the globe, the United States abdicated its responsibilities and became a creature of history rather than its molder. By surrendering the initiative to Germany and Japan, the nation imperiled its security and very nearly permitted the Axis powers to win the war. In the last analysis the United States was saved only by the Japanese miscalculation in attacking Pearl Harbor.[6]

Given the experience of 1940–1941, it is not surprising that students of American foreign policy have often seen the executive–legislative relationship as a chief obstacle to the formation of a sound American foreign policy in the postwar era.

PRESIDENTIAL PRIMACY, BIPARTISAN SUPPORT, AND THE COLD WAR

The triumphant victories over Germany, Italy, and Japan under Franklin Roosevelt's majestic leadership only reinforced the trend toward strong presidential leadership. This strong leadership would allow the United States to act with authority, speed, steadiness, and, when necessary, flexibility. An active congressional role raised the possibility that U.S. foreign policy would be characterized by divided counsel, frequent policy changes, if not occasional paralysis, slow reactions, and inability to exploit rapidly changing situations—all of which would raise questions as the Cold War began about U.S. leadership and reliability. Under the new circumstances of American–Soviet conflict, the country could not afford constant executive–legislative quarrels; indeed, as noted earlier, it was in recognition that such conflict would be harmful that the policy of bipartisanship or "nonpartisanship" was born. The aim of a bipartisan foreign policy, is, in the words of a former State Department official, "to make it virtually impossible for 'momentous divisions' to occur in our foreign affairs" and to provide a "continuity and consistency" in decision making from one administration to another.[7]

The bipartisan formula, which accepted presidential primacy and congressional acquiescence, was probably unavoidable during the Cold War, even had the memories of Versailles faded and those of 1940–1941 been less vivid. For the Cold War was attended by an almost universal American perception that the country's security was under threat. It was not called *Cold War* for nothing. The United States was engaged in a war, even if it was not a hot one. But the adversary was as much, if not more, of a threat than Germany had been. The Soviet Union was the other superpower, the only nation in the world that could threaten our security—indeed, our survival. It was a threat not only because the Soviets were a great power but because they were also a totalitarian state, representing beliefs and values completely antithetical to those of American and Western democracy. The Soviet challenge, like the German one that preceded it, constituted a menace to America's physical and political survival.

This perception of threat was reinforced by frequent high tensions. Each superpower watched the other carefully to preserve the precarious balance of power. Frequent confrontation and crises were the result: Greece and Turkey (1946–1947), Berlin (1948–1949), the Korean War (1950–1953), Quemoy–Matsu (1954–1955), the Suez War and Hungarian uprising (1956), Quemoy–Matsu (1958), Berlin (1958–1962), Cuba (1961–1962), and the deepening Vietnam involvement after 1961 and finally, war after 1965. Lack of time and the need to make rapid decisions often meant that presidents spent most of their time consulting with their advisers; they then usually informed Congress of their decisions. When there was more time for consultation between the two branches of government, policy might be modified.

Congress frequently put its imprint on the president's policy, but the essence of executive policy remained intact. In any event, the recurrence of crisis brought home the perceived danger to America and reinforced the popular and congressional rallying-around-the-flag phenomenon that external danger always encourages.

During this period, Congress also recognized the executive's expertise in foreign policy. The president has at hand a large bureaucracy to help him. Senators and congressmen, therefore, rely on executive officials for information and interpretation of events. In foreign affairs, members of Congress lack the confidence they have on domestic matters. As citizens and representatives, they hold views on many of the problems their constituents experience, whether inflation, unemployment, busing, education, subsidies, or health care. Whatever their own professions, they presumably have wide acquaintanceship, via their constituencies, with individuals in other walks of life and their specific problems as doctors, farmers, or workers. Moreover, they can call on a whole range of interest groups for other views of the facts and alternative policy views. But foreign problems—the question of Sino–Soviet relations, Soviet intentions, Third World nationalism, military strategy, force levels, and weapons systems—are for most congressmen just that—"foreign." This is also true for most interest groups; their expertise is essentially domestic. Deference to executive judgments followed logically. Congress tends to be not only supportive, therefore, but permissive in giving the executive a good deal of leeway.

Congressional subordination, the result of a consensus on foreign policy, was also very important. For over two decades after World War II, the president and Congress shared a common set of beliefs about the role and objectives of the United States in the world. The central conflict in international politics was the conflict between the Communist world led by the Soviet Union and the free world led by the United States; that any expansion of Communist influence and power was a loss of influence and power for the free world; that the fundamental role for American and Western policy, therefore, was to oppose such expansion; that the United States, by far the strongest Western power, had the primary responsibility for containing communism; that military power was a principal tool for preserving the strategic balance between the superpowers and deterring a Soviet first strike against the United States and its European allies as well as for opposing any limited Communist aggression around the Sino–Soviet periphery; that firmness in negotiations was essential because concessions only whetted the unlimited ambitions of the totalitarian rulers of the Soviet Union and China and would not therefore resolve key issues but lead to further demands; that other means for waging the struggle against communism—ranging from economic aid and arms sales to subversion—were legitimate in what was essentially a global competition between two giants whose rivalry would determine which of the two antithetical ways of life would dominate the world—freedom or despotism. Permeating this consensus was the feeling that this conflict between despotism and democracy was a struggle between the forces of good and evil. This set of "shared images" between the two branches of government meant that conflict between them largely revolved around the problem of means. The ends or objectives of American policy were agreed on; controversy was focused on implementation.

One other critical reason for the success of bipartisanship—a reason not present after the Vietnam War—was the advice and support that the Truman, Eisenhower, and Kennedy administrations enjoyed from a relatively small group of individuals, collectively referred to as the Eastern Establishment.[8] Its members were white, Anglo-Saxon, Protestant, and by profession, largely Wall Street lawyers and investment bankers, with a few international corporation executives and academics, especially from M.I.T. and Harvard. They were generally well off, though not necessarily rich, for wealth was not a membership requirement; Dean Acheson and John Foster Dulles, secretaries of state to Presidents Truman and Eisenhower, respectively, and men who had served the government in important positions before that, were both sons of clergy. All, however, were members of "good" families and had received an elite education at private preparatory schools, most notably Groton (where the ethic of public service was strongly emphasized), and at elite private Universities such as Harvard, Yale, and Princeton. Few of them were New Dealers or liberal Democrats; indeed, the most prominent were Republican. In addition to Acheson and Dulles, there were distinguished figures such as Robert A. Lovett, John J. McCloy, Paul Nitze, Thomas K. Finletter, and Averell Harriman (one of the few members who ran for public office and won—the governorship of New York state). Around them were a small number of soldiers, such as Generals Marshall (the architect of the military victory in World War II), Eisenhower (victor in Europe, the first NATO commander, and later president), Bradley, (Eisenhower's deputy in Europe during the war and later chairman of the Joint Chiefs of Staff), and diplomats such as George Kennan, and Charles Bohlen (the government's chief experts on the Soviet Union), and Allen Dulles, (first deputy director and later, director of the CIA), all of whom were nonpartisan.[9]

The core group of lawyers and bankers was essentially New York based. The members were generally from the prestigious Council of Foreign Relations. Also included was the publisher of *Foreign Affairs*, the distinguished quarterly journal.[10] Indeed, the Establishment and the council became synonomous. Council members were distinguished by their internationalist outlook and their rejection of prewar isolationism. They had become active in the period after France's defeat in 1940. At that time the key issue confronting the United States was whether to help Britain, who was fighting Hitler all alone and in jeopardy of invasion, or cling to the traditional policy of isolationism from Europe. These council members took the lead in arranging the famous Destroyer Deal and helped to mobilize public opinion in favor of aid to Britain. Once the United States was in the war, many of the younger members served in the Office of Strategic Services, the CIA's predecessor. After the war, they were united in opposing a return to isolationism. They also opposed any appeasement of Stalin, as the Soviet threat appeared to be growing. They remembered the British–French appeasement of Hitler which, together with American isolationism, they held to be the chief cause of World War II. They were committed to containing the Soviet threat, by force if necessary. Having served Roosevelt, they now remained to help Truman, or to be available if called on. They became "ins" and "outers." Individual members would join an administration, later leave, and then if requested, rejoin the same or another administration in a different capacity, each time occupying a higher position. These individuals were among the post-war presidents' most reliable and capable advisers.

It should be noted that isolationism was still strong on the far left and right after the war. Henry Wallace, vice president during World War II, who abandoned the Democratic party to run for president on his own ticket, was the most prominent of the leftists. He charged that there was no Soviet threat, that Stalin's actions in Eastern Europe were limited to that area and basically defensive, and that U.S. meddling in that area was provoking Moscow. Wallace believed that the United States should stop interfering abroad and concentrate on its domestic and hemispheric affairs. At the other extreme, the conservative wing of the Republican party, dominant in Congress, remained strongly committed to its historic opposition to European involvement. Senator Arthur Vandenberg, an isolationist before Pearl Harbor, an internationalist afterward belonged to a minority in the party. Largely composed of easterners, this group, often referred to as Republican liberals or moderates, supported the Truman foreign policy toward Europe.

Bipartisanship thus served several important functions. First, it ensured that U.S. foreign policy would be centrist, containing both extremes. Second, it ensured a high degree of continuity in policy, despite changes of administrations every four years and possible shifts in the public mood. In 1948, when Truman was expected to lose his bid for the presidency, Vandenberg made it clear to Moscow that a Republican president would be as committed as was Truman to the United States staying in Berlin and that the airlift to the western half of the city, under blockade by the Soviets, would be continued. Third—and most important—in 1952, when conservative Republican Senator Robert Taft, was the leading presidential candidate, prominent members of the internationalist wing recruited General Dwight Eisenhower, who became the Republican nominee. Eisenhower was brought in to maintain continuity in foreign policy and to convert the party, out of power since 1933, to a responsible internationalist position. Finally, the cooperation that bipartisanship produced between the executive and legislative branches provided for stability and avoided the kinds of separation of powers conflicts that typically had accompanied domestic policy making.

All of the above reasons favored presidential leadership and Congress' willingness to accept, or at least acquiesce in a secondary—if not at times peripheral—role in foreign policy making. Ironically, therefore, the problem of executive–legislative relations, which many observers in the mid to late 1940s expected would obstruct the formation of a policy responsive to America's international needs, was largely—although not completely—avoided.[11] Bipartisanship, it should be noted, involved the use of various techniques. President Franklin D. Roosevelt had, as early as 1940, named Republicans Henry Stimson and Frank Knox as secretaries of war and of the navy, respectively. By appointing members of the opposition party to high-level government positions, Roosevelt sought to dramatize the idea that foreign policy decision making involved the welfare of the entire nation and transcended any partisan lines. Truman continued the bipartisan foreign policy after World War II. James Forrestal and Robert A. Lovett, both Republicans, served as secretary of defense under Truman; Lovett also served as under secretary of state. Among Republicans appointed by Kennedy were McNamara as secretary of defense, William C. Foster as head of ACDA, John A. McCone as head of the CIA, and Henry Cabot Lodge as ambassador to Saigon. Democrats have followed this pattern of bipartisanship more than Republicans, probably because Democratic presidents have been more concerned with warding off charges of being too "soft" on communist regimes than have Republicans (the charges having come mainly from Republicans). A Democratic administration with Republicans playing a major role in the formation of foreign policy, Democrats believed, would be less susceptible to such attacks.

The appointment of opposition party members was just one method presidents used to gain bipartisan support for their foreign policy. Truman, as well as Acheson, as we know, worked closely with Vandenberg, particularly during 1947–1948, when the Republicans controlled Congress. The White House openly brought Congress into the decision-making process on foreign policy. The Marshall Plan and the establishment of NATO probably marked the high points of congressional involvement in foreign policy making. Truman pursued a bipartisan foreign policy not only because he believed that the international stakes were extremely high and that they transcended partisan grounds, but also because his party simply did not have the strength in Congress to adopt his proposals without Republican support. In 1947–1948 particularly, cooperation with the Republicans was a necessity.

In this respect, Republican chief executives also resemble their Democratic counterparts. Eisenhower had to deal with a Democratic Congress during six of his eight years in the White House, and he found Senate Majority Leader Lyndon B. Johnson's support of his foreign policy more dependable than that of his own party leaders. Democrats have generally been more cohesive on foreign policy votes in Congress than have Republicans. Furthermore, Eisenhower's dealings with his own party majority in 1953–1954 were rather strained. Senator Robert Taft (R-Ohio) was Eisenhower's first majority leader; Taft had been Eisenhower's main competitor for the

1952 Republican nomination, and the two men sharply disagreed on certain foreign policy questions. Following Taft's death in 1953, the president received only slightly more support from Majority Leader William Knowland (R-Calif.), who had presidential ambitions of his own. In 1953, the bipartisan foreign policy of more than a decade was almost upset by the efforts of Republican Senator John W. Bricker (Ohio). Bricker wanted to limit severely the president's authority to conduct foreign policy by amending the Constitution to prohibit the executive from entering into any agreement that committed American troops to any foreign conflict without specific congressional approval. Knowland, in a rare spirit of cooperation with Eisenhower, agreed to be the floor leader for an administration-sponsored substitute to the Bricker amendment. All three of these Republicans belonged to the right wing of the party. In general, bipartisan foreign policy is accentuated when control of the White House and Congress is split between the two parties.

Indeed, bipartisanship during the Cold War seemed a necessity if the nation were to have any type of coherent foreign policy in a situation of divided control. When one party controls both the executive and legislative branches, as occurred in 1949–1955 and 1961–1969, arguments over foreign policy may increase because bipartisan support is no longer strictly necessary. Conversely, when the opposition controls Congress, it may well be reluctant to oppose the president outright, for he can then accuse it of subordinating the nation's interests to partisan politics and advantage. Yet a president cannot be sure in advance from which direction criticism will come. Eisenhower received the bulk of his criticism from fellow Republicans, Johnson from other Democrats. Kennedy and Truman, on the other hand, found their own parties more united in their support and the opposition split.

PARTISANSHIP AND DOMESTIC POLITICS IN FOREIGN POLICY: THE EXAMPLE OF U.S.–ASIAN POLICY

One exception to this largely bipartisan Cold War consensus ultimately developed: American policy in Asia. Its occurrence was a constant reminder of what could happen to U.S. foreign policy in a situation of congressional assertiveness and partisan rivalry, for its effects on policy was twofold: (1) to transform U.S. policy in Asia into a rigid anti-Communist Chinese mold, deepen Sino–American enmity and delay until 1972 a reconciliation between the two countries. From the early 1960s on, they had shared a common interest in containing the Soviet Union; and (2) to help precipitate the tragic American intervention in Vietnam. Whether Vietnam was avoidable is debatable; what is not debatable is that congressional pressures, and the anticipation of such pressures by Presidents Kennedy and Johnson, made Vietnam inevitable.

Since presidents run for office, wish to be reelected, or want successors elected who will keep control of the White House in their party, foreign policy cannot be divorced from domestic politics. This is not to say that foreign policy positions are adopted only, or primarily for, domestic political reasons, but it does say that the last may, to varying degrees, depending on the president and international and domestic circumstances, influence the conduct of the nation's international behavior.

Nowhere was this more clearly demonstrated than in America's post-World War II Asian policy.[12] After three defeats of Republican presidential nominees in 1940, 1944, and 1948–elections in which the Republicans were led by candidates from the moderate-liberal eastern wing of their party— Republican conservatives felt that only a presidential candidate from their wing of the party could regain control of the White House. A conservative candidate would give the country (to quote the 1964 Republican nominee) "a choice, not an echo." Since the party of Herbert Hoover and the Depression was hardly likely to attract a popular majority on domestic issues, foreign policy became their target. The collapse of Nationalist China in 1949 presented one such opportunity. Until then the Republicans had supported containment in Europe and had not been very critical of U.S. policy toward China. But when Nationalist China disintegrated because of its war weariness, corruption, inefficiency, and brutality and the country "fell" to the communists, the loss was exploited by Republican conservatives and led to vicious attacks on Democrats. China, it was charged, had been sold out; the administration had "coddled communism" and "appeased" the Kremlin; communists and "communist dupes" in the State Department and other high places in government—whether they had infiltrated or been appointed by Roosevelt or Truman—had betrayed an ally and friend as well as their own country. China, in brief, had not fallen because the Nationalists had been incompetent or because communist morale, organization, and fighting ability had been superior; it was "lost" because of a deliberate conspiracy within the Democratic administration to lose Nationalist China. These charges of a deliberate betrayal and conspiracy within the U.S. government are still associated with its principal proponent, Senator Joseph R. McCarthy (R-Wisc.), even though other leading Republican figures like then Senator Nixon were also involved.

The results of these vicious and continuing attacks had profound consequences for U.S. policy. They particularly affected the Democrats whenever they controlled the White House. To avoid further charges of betrayal or of selling out allies, they were disposed to preempt such a charge with policies that tended toward strong anticommunism, military intervention, and (until Jimmy Carter), no diplomatic recognition of Communist China. Thus, during the Korean War, once the North Koreans had been driven back to the 38th parallel where they had begun their attack on South Korea, an end to the war based on the prewar status quo was attacked as appeasement by Republicans. Undoubtedly, such attacks on a solution short of total victory influenced the Truman administration's decision to advance into North Korea. Its neighbor, Communist China, seeing American armies march toward its frontier, then intervened and enlarged the war. When the Korean War began in 1950, the Republicans exacted a price from the Democrats for political support and domestic unity: the protection of the island of Formosa (Taiwan), to which the Nationalist leader Chiang Kai-shek had fled. Thus, the United States, which had finally washed its hands of Chiang and his losing cause in January 1950, had, in effect, reintervened in that civil war by June. No wonder the new China, seeing the United States protect the rival claimant to legitimate authority over all of China, and American armies advancing toward its borders, defined the United States as its enemy and intervened to protect itself. This intervention embittered U.S.–Chinese relations for two decades and played into the hands of those opposing any reconciliation.

One can only speculate about whether the Chinese intervention in the Korean War, the escalation of the hostilities, and the subsequent rancorous Sino–American relationship could have been avoided had the United States had its own diplomatic representatives in China. Chinese warnings of intervention if the United States advanced toward the Korea–China frontier were dismissed in Washington as a bluff. Would American personnel in China not have told Washington that these warnings had to be taken seriously? If one cannot argue with certainty that two costs of American nonrecognition of the People's Republic were the intense fighting in Korea and the political alienation of the two countries, there is much less uncertainty that two *real* costs were the Vietnam War and the failure to recognize and exploit the Sino–Soviet dispute by the late 1950s. Instead, even as late as the early to middle 1960s, any moves toward the diplomatic recognition of the People's Republic of China were politically dangerous—indeed, for the Democrats, suicidal. Not surprisingly, without U.S. personnel in China, the differences between the Soviet Union and China were often dismissed as tactical rather than fundamental, and North Vietnam viewed as essentially a tool of an expansionist oppressive China. Hanoi was not understood to have any degree of independence or nationalism outside the orbits of both Moscow and Peking. Surely, American observers in Peking would have known better and so advised the U.S. government. The Vietnam War may thus have been one of the highest prices the United States paid for the congressional hard-line attitude toward recognition of Peking.

The decision to intervene with U.S. military forces in Vietnam was made by President Johnson. He did so because by early 1965 U.S. options regarding the fate of South Vietnam had run out. His predecessors had stalled and done only what each had judged necessary to prevent the fall of South Vietnam to the communists. For each postwar president, increasing involvement in Indochina was calculated as *less* costly domestically than doing nothing and writing it off as an unwinnable situation in the long run. In the context of American domestic politics and a government characterized by a separation of powers, the acceptance of defeat was believed to be unacceptable. The costs of nonintervention in the loss of congressional and public support was measured as exceeding the cost of intervention. The basic rule was "Don't lose Indochina." As Daniel Ellsberg summed up this imperative for each White House incumbent: "This is a bad year for me to lose Vietnam to communism."[13] Thus, each time the possibility of disaster stared an administration in the face, it escalated the involvement and its commitment to *not* losing Vietnam.

Note the negative nature of the goal: to prevent a disaster. It was hoped that if they could not win, the North Vietnamese would eventually desist. Even before the French defeat in 1954, the Truman administration, by the time of the Korean War, was sending aid to help the French and prevent a communist victory. The Eisenhower administration, while not intervening militarily, talked a great deal in public about the strategic importance of Vietnam, raised the U.S. financial contribution to the French conduct of the war, and organized and supported the new anticommunist Diem government in Saigon politically, economically, and militarily. The Kennedy administration fortified this commitment with U.S. military "advisers" and tacitly consented to the South Vietnamese military's overthrow of the increasingly despotic and ineffective Diem regime. Hence the link was provided between the United States and the U.S.-encouraged military government in Saigon, which Washington hoped could conduct the war more effectively than its predecessor. But it was Johnson who sent in the military to prevent the collapse of South Vietnam. The intervention was the logical culmination of the acts of his predecessors; with the exception of Eisenhower, none of them had had to make a decision about the use of force in Vietnam to prevent communist domination. Johnson did; he could not avoid it. Each of Johnson's predecessors was responsible for an increasing commitment and escalation in Vietnam; but if each one was an architect of intervention, each was also a "part, and prisoner of the larger political system that fed on itself, trapping all its participants in a war they could not afford to lose and were unable to win quickly."[14]

Why was it that charges of appeasement from the opposition party made it impossible to recognize the People's Republic after its birth, negotiate with it on a continuing basis on outstanding issues, and later exploit China's quarrel with the Soviet Union? Why was American diplomacy frozen into a rigid anticommunist posture that finally led the nation into the quagmire of Vietnam? Because if nation X collapses, a president lays himself open to political attack by the opposition party. One of the resulting casualties may be his prestige and reputation. For a man who has sought the presidency, worked and sacrificed for it, and perhaps long dreamed about it, a major failure is a blow to the strong ego that drove him to the top and made him believe that he could be a successful president. Even after they leave office, presidents are not forgotten; they becomes immortal because their heads appear on postage stamps, and their records go into the history books. So major political criticisms of alleged failure that might endanger their reputations, so to speak, are not desirable. To paraphrase Johnson, he was not going to be the first president in American history to lose a war.

But more than personal prestige is at stake for any president. He has to be concerned with his own reelection or, if he does not run again, his successor's election. In a democracy, the president's focus on his own political fortunes and those of his party cannot be neglected; to suggest that there is something immoral about such considerations is to ignore how U.S. politics works. Even if the public does not "punish" the president at the polls for the "loss" of country X, the president's calculations about the possible electoral impact of such a setback are understandable. Of crucial importance is what presidents believe might happen. Laurence Radway has said that "American incumbents tend to overinsure against even a remote possibility of defeat. They can be sobered to the point of paranoia by the realization that quite a few congressional elections and fully 50 percent of all presidential elections since World War II have been decided by only a handful of votes."[15]

Closely related is another cost: the president's domestic program. The fall of China, followed by the Korean War, helped slow Truman's Fair Deal, which was followed by a Democratic defeat in 1952. Kennedy's perceived setbacks in Laos, Cuba (Bay of Pigs), and Berlin at the time the Berlin Wall was built hurt his chances of achieving his New Frontier. Johnson did not want to jeopardize his Great Society program but also did not want to be tagged as the president who "lost Indochina" as Truman had "lost China." Until 1966, he was able to convince Congress to give him both social spending and military escalation in Vietnam.

Despite frequent invocations of "bipartisanship" in the postwar era, an administration's foreign policies have been fair game for attack. Thus a loss of a China or Vietnam or other countries was portrayed as a serious blow to U.S. interests in other areas. No wonder, confronted by such electoral pressures and partisan attacks, the president calculates that tough foreign policy postures, including intervention or nonrecognition of an "evil" government, are preferable to more accommodating and noninterventionist postures, and frequently will cost *less* politically at home. Even before congressional or partisan pressures are exercised, the mere anticipation of such pressures will have a prenatal effect on the president's conduct of foreign policy, leading to rigid policies ranging from the pretense that Nationalist China's government on the island of Taiwan was still the government of all of China to the escalation of U.S. involvement in South Vietnam. During both of the limited wars the United States has fought in Asia—Korea and Vietnam—Truman and Johnson felt that they were pressured from the right to escalate even further. It has been said with great perceptiveness that Congress, like the Strategic Air Command, possesses both the power of deterrence to prevent the president from doing what Congress feels he should not do (such as recognizing the new regime in Communist China) and the threat of "massive retaliation" if he does what Congress wants him not to do (such as lose South Vietnam, which Congress in the early-middle 1960s was as much opposed to as the president).*

By contrast, conservative presidents were able to withstand domestic pressures for intervention and escalation (although they might also do so for international reasons) and could meet and negotiate with communists. Thus Eisenhower could sign a Korean peace treaty based on the *status quo ante bellum*, which Truman had been unable to do. Confronted by the possible collapse of the French position in Indochina in 1954, Eisenhower threatened intervention but then decided against it, and no one accused him of a sell-out. In 1955, he became the first Cold War president to meet the Soviet leaders and was not labeled "procommunist" for so doing. Nixon, while escalating the air war in Vietnam, could bring U.S. ground forces out and eventually disengage the United States from that war. Above all, he initiated a détente with Moscow to negotiate seriously over a whole range of issues, including strategic arms limitation, and he began the American rapprochement with Peking. The last, particularly, would have been impossible under a more liberal president. More conservative presidents, immune to attacks from the right of appeasement and coddling communism, have far greater flexibility in the conduct of foreign policy.

Not that they are immune to such attacks. To protect himself from the right wing of his own party, Eisenhower resorted to tough talk of "liberation," "unleashing Chiang," and "massive retaliation." Initially, he permitted Senator Joseph McCarthy (R-Wis.) a free hand in his general witch hunt for alleged security risks in the State Department, the U.S. Information Agency, and the army, among other institutions of government. Eisenhower also allowed congressional Republican leaders in the Senate occasionally to constrain his foreign policy options. Even in Indochina, although Eisenhower did not intervene there in 1954, neither did he disengage the United States. Rather, he substituted an American presence for that of France; American dollars, military equipment, and men to train South Vietnamese forces flowed to the new country, and the SEATO alliance was formed to permit unilateral U.S. intervention if it failed to deter future "communist aggression." Eisenhower, in Gelb and Betts' neat summation, "kept America out of war, and he kept America in Vietnam."[16]

---

*Even in areas other than Asia, presidents are susceptible to doing whatever is necessary to avoid such political attacks. Thus, after becoming president, John Kennedy discovered the CIA plans for the Bay of Pigs operation. He felt uneasy about the feasibility of the operation but proceeded anyway lest he subsequently be accused of weakness and cowardice when compared to his predecessor, Eisenhower, who had conceived of the operation and presumably would have carried it out (or left that to his heir apparent, Richard Nixon). Similarly, when, in 1965, "pro-Castro communists" were allegedly involved with the opposition in an attempted overthrow of the Dominican Republic's right-wing military-supported government, Lyndon Johnson intervened. The Democrats had to avoid the accusation of having allowed "another Cuba" in the hemisphere.

Similarly, when Eisenhower's former vice president, Nixon, came into office in 1969 at a time of growing disillusionment with anticommunism as a rigid foreign policy, he made the initial moves toward opening relations with China secretly and presented his trip as a fait accompli so that any opposition would not have time to organize itself. And the reality of the final withdrawal from Vietnam and the peace negotiations were well disguised by the heavy bombing of North Vietnam, including a pounding of Hanoi by B-52s during the 1972 Christmas season. Even Nixon and Kissinger were haunted by the fear of another right-wing, appeasement-type of attack at home if they "sold out" in Vietnam. It is surely a devastating comment on executive–legislative relations and American political institutions that the overture to China, the prerequisite for the détente of the 1970s, could probably not have been accomplished through normal diplomatic channels. From the time he entered government, Kissinger's secretive, closely held style of making policy was often condemned for creating confusion and low morale—if not bad policy—in the bureaucracy. However, who can doubt that without it, the new and strategic American–Chinese relationship could not have been achieved when it was? Another critical commentary is that a conservative administration was fearful of attacks from its own party's right, in and out of Congress. Thus, one reason for the Christmas bombing was to preempt such attacks. The United States had to disguise its leaving of Vietnam with an act of toughness.

WHAT HAS HAPPENED TO EXECUTIVE–LEGISLATIVE RELATIONS SINCE VIETNAM?

Before Vietnam, Congress, public opinion, and the press had all looked to the president for leadership in foreign policy. He and his leading foreign policy advisers defined the situation facing the United States, the key issues, and what the nation should do about them. Bipartisanship, with the one significant exception of Asian policy, ensured the president's ability to mobilize legislative support. Public opinion was also supportive. All in all, presidents until Vietnam took and held initiative and leadership while public opinion not only supported their decisions and actions, but gave them a high degree of freedom and maneuverability. Rarely, as noted earlier (Chapter 1), was a president defeated because of foreign policy issues, unlike the situation surrounding domestic policies.

After Vietnam the bipartisan consensus disintegrated. The fact that the two presidents who came to power following the collapse of South Vietnam in 1975 were "outsiders," governors who ran against Washington and were inexperienced in foreign policy, is itself revealing. The collapse of bipartisan foreign policy making was strikingly embodied in Carter's and Reagan's personal visions of what U.S. policy should be.[17] Not only did Carter denounce past policy as an over-reaction to an exaggerated Soviet threat, but he specifically condemned it for its lack of morality. In the name of anticommunism, Carter believed, the United States had linked itself with too many right-wing dictatorial regimes. Carter's vision of morality led him to reject the SALT II ceilings on weapons which Kissinger had almost finished negotiating, but Ford had put off a decision about until after his expected reelection. As the newly elected president, Carter thought these ceilings were too high, that they sanctioned the arms race. He was going to seek "real" arms control, that is, very deep arms reductions. The result was a Soviet rejection of the Carter proposals, three more years of negotiations, and a postponement of SALT II until a time when détente was in decline and the president could not mobilize two thirds of the Senate in support of the treaty.

Morality also demanded a concern for human rights. But since Carter could do little to ensure against the violation of human rights in the Soviet Union (his one attempt to denounce Soviet violations delayed the arms control negotiations, whose successful conclusion was also demanded by morality), the president enforced the human rights policy on the weaker U.S. allies who were dependent on this country, thus causing turmoil within the nation's various alliances.

Reagan's morality, by contrast, was so intensely anticommunist that during his initial years in office, he repeatedly and undiplomatically denounced the Soviet leadership. More importantly, he strongly opposed negotiations, especially arms control, with the Soviet Union, seemingly preferring (at least in his rhetoric) confrontation with an enemy he condemned in religious terms as evil and the source of all sin in the world. Carter viewed his predecessor as not having vigorously enough pursued radical arms reduction. Reagan believed his predecessor had not been tough enough on Moscow. The Reagan diplomatic legacy was thus rather bare. Its one outstanding exception—on medium- and short-range missiles in Europe—was the result of a U.S. plan deliberately conceived in such a way that Moscow would reject it, which initially was the case. When, to Washington's surprise, Moscow later turned around and announced its readiness to accept Reagan's offer, the president could hardly say "no." Even more illustrative of Reagan's morality was his personal vision of a strategic defensive shield to protect America's population. This shield was to replace the deterrent policy that had given the United States and its allies security and peace for four decades. That policy was now denounced as immoral and bound to break down some day, causing nuclear war. These were the same arguments the antinuclear movement was making at the time.

Apart from these breaks with preceding policies—and, of course, the widespread skepticism in Congress and society about superior presidential wisdom and expertise in foreign affairs—an additional critical change in the post-Vietnam period was the decline of the Establishment's influence and the usurpation of its role by think tanks and their staffs, which have been called the *professional elites.* Many of these think tanks, often also referred to as *beltway bandits* provide basically technical services, especially for the Pentagon. Living on government money, they are concerned with everything from personnel policies to management and logistical problems to seeking ways of joining high technology to weapons systems. Our focus will remain with those whose preoccupation is strategy and foreign policy, and the shift of power from the former Establishment to these "professional service industries."

This shift was perhaps most aptly symbolized by the attacks on the Council of Foreign Relations. The Establishment, which had supported the containment policy, including the intervention in Vietnam, became divided by the war and lost much of its prestige.[18] Former Secretary of State Henry Kissinger, who had first achieved prominence in his famous book *Nuclear Weapons and Foreign Policy*, sponsored by the council, was rejected in 1981 when he was renominated for the board of directors. During his 1980 campaign for the presidential nomination, George Bush, a moderate Republican, had resigned his council membership so as not to further alienate his party's conservatives; the resignation no doubt made it easier for Ronald Reagan to choose Bush as his vice presidential running mate. After the Reagan–Bush victory, Republican Senator Jesse Helms' standard question for foreign policy appointees was whether they were council members; not being a member became a test of the ideological purity of a true conservative. (The council was allegedly too liberal.) This type of reaction to the council was not limited to the right wing. In Jimmy Carter's campaign for the presidency, his close adviser and future White House Chief of Staff, Hamilton Jordan, stated that he would not serve in an administration that appointed council members to leading positions. Later, when Cyrus Vance became the secretary of state and Zbigniew Brzezinski the NSA, Jordan suppressed his concerns and stayed on, but the council's elitism and reputed conservatism from the left side of the political spectrum clearly made it a target from this direction too. The later Vance–Brzezinski disputes over policy were symptomatic of the council's inner divisions. Its pre-Vietnam reputation was one of being tough minded and hard nosed,[18] but the war transformed many members from hawks on foreign policy issues to doves; those who remained hawks like Brzezinski became a minority. *Foreign Affairs* articles reflected this shift in the middle to late 1970s.

The Establishment's prestige and prominence as a centrist organization were now taken over by the professional elites on the left and right.[19] Foreign policy had become increasingly complex and specialized, requiring expertise in topics ranging from arms control to currency exchange, from trade issues to population control. Full-time experts were needed; as the new "ins" and "outs", they tended to identify more with either the Democrats or Republicans. While Establishment figures usually were Republicans, they served both Democratic and Republican administrations; in fact, since the Democrats were more vulnerable to attacks for being "soft" on foreign policy, they were more visible when Democrats controlled the executive. The new elites were not only full-time professionals as political, military, or economic experts, but they were more ideologically inclined and loyal. They gained their prominence—as council members Kissinger and Brzezinski had done—by being university professors at the right schools (mainly Ivy League, but no longer as exclusively as before). They wrote articles and books, gaining their fame this way and thereby becoming consultants to government agencies and making contacts, largely in the Boston–New York–Washington area.

Both Kissinger and Brzezinski were immigrants. Kissinger became close to Nelson Rockefeller, governor of New York and a liberal presidential aspirant in the Republican party; it was Rockefeller who recommended Kissinger for the NSA's position to President-Elect Nixon. Brzezinski latched onto David Rockefeller, Nelson's brother, and became a member of the Trilateral Commission, which was organized to promote closer U.S.–European–Japanese ties; while serving on the commission, Brzezinski, who also wrote a column for *Newsweek*, met Governor Carter of Georgia, another member. Less-famous figures followed basically the same path. The Establishment shunned publicity; they had access in Washington and used their influence quietly. The new professional elites had to gain public visibility first, then promote themselves to find their political connections and acquire influence. This required time, patience, push, a large ego, party identification—and often picking the winning candidate even before the primaries.[20] In short, expertise was not enough; being a good combatant was at least as important.

When they were not in an administration, the new professional elites usually returned to a think tank, if they did not (re)join a university faculty, or, on occasion, a Wall Street firm. Rarely did they go into business or law. If they did so to make money, they kept themselves in the limelight with articles and frequent television appearances. They hoped they were "outs" only temporarily. Perhaps the best known think tank, often referred to as the Democrats-in-exile, was the Brookings Institution. "Its principal purposes are to aid in the development of sound public policies and to promote public understanding of issues of national importance."[21] A moderately liberal, slightly left-of-center organization, Brookings is staffed by experts who publish actively. One of its strong suits is the defense-arms control field, in which it offers considerable and alternative expertise outside of the Pentagon. The Republican equivalent, slightly right of center, is the American Enterprise Institute, although it publishes less than Brookings and focuses more on helping Republican legislators bolster their arguments against their usually more numerous Democratic colleagues. A more actively liberal institution is the Carnegie Endowment for International Peace, which publishes the quarterly *Foreign Policy* journal. Many of its editors and contributors became members of the Carter administration, devotees of interdependence and "world order" politics, and critical of the power politics outlook. A very ideologically conservative and Republican organization is the Heritage Foundation, which was to sponsor General Daniel Graham's High Frontier advocacy of strategic defense, one of the early, although not the most influential, forces in what was to become President Reagan's Strategic Defense Initiative (SDI) or Star Wars. A prestigious conservative center for foreign-defense policy expertise is Georgetown University's Center for Strategic and International Studies, among whose members are such luminaries as Kissinger, Brzezinski, former CIA Director and Secretary of Defense James Schlesinger and other distinguished "outs," mainly Republicans.

Almost all these institutions hold regular conferences and take a generally scholarly approach to issues. Interestingly, many Democrats—often officials in past administrations—who remained faithful to the containment policy and continued to place priority on the U.S.–Soviet rivalry (instead of favoring an interdependence policy) now found new outlets for their growing criticisms, especially of the Carter administration. Calling themselves *neoconservatives*, these people, often former liberals, finding themselves without a voice in the Democratic party, formed a lobby, the Committee on the Present Danger, and regularly published their critiques in *Commentary*, a monthly magazine historically devoted to Jewish affairs. Many of the committee's members and *Commentary*'s authors were later to join the Reagan administration.

These think tanks are all Washington based. While there are some think tanks outside of Washington, such as the conservative Institute for Foreign Policy Analysis in Cambridge, Massachusetts, and the Hoover War and Peace Institute in Stanford, California, most are in the nation's capital because this is where most of their consumers are and where they can gain influence and hopefully power by staffing an administration. These and other less well-known think tanks illustrate the fragmentation of the pre-Vietnam consensus while simultaneously ensuring that a variety of views about the role and purposes of U.S. foreign policy will continue to be aired. Administrations may at election time move toward the proverbial center of American politics, but the experts who increasingly identify ideologically with one party or the other often take sharply contrasting views of, for instance, the desirability and character of an arms control agreement, how much emphasis should be placed on human rights in American policy, or the importance of Nicaragua to U.S. security interests.

The greater "ideologicalization" of foreign policy issues is more basically a reflection of the shift from bipartisan agreement to a more partisan stance on foreign policy between the two parties, as well as within each party[22] in the post-Vietnam period. When President Nixon resigned and Gerald Ford assumed the office and ran for the presidency in 1976, Ronald Reagan challenged and nearly beat an incumbent president in the primaries, an almost unheard of occurrence when a party controls the highest office in the land. Reagan attacked his own party's president for his pursuit of the Nixon–Kissinger détente with the Soviet Union. Ford dropped the word *détente* entirely from his vocabulary during the primary season and told his secretary of state (Kissinger, whom he had already removed as NSA) to maintain a low profile until the nomination was his. Ford, in fact, ran on a platform that included a plank inserted by the Reagan conservatives repudiating his détente policy! After Ford's defeat at the polls, the conservatives captured the party and the moderate or liberal Republicans, who had played such a key role in the 1940s and 1950s, now became a shrinking minority as the party swung to the right. It had been the conservatives who, in the days of bipartisanship, had dominated the congressional Republican party. From 1946 to 1952 they had tolerated the liberal wing's support for Truman's containment policy. Only after their fifth consecutive loss of the presidency in 1948 did they reject what was now called *me-tooism* and try to capture the presidential nomination for one of their own kind, Senator Taft. Defeated again as the moderates continued to control the Republican presidential party with the nomination of General Dwight Eisenhower, a popular hero, the conservatives finally achieved their first success in 1964 with the nomination of Senator Barry Goldwater. After his defeat, former Vice President and 1960 Republican standard-bearer Richard Nixon was renominated in 1968. Conservatives were not to forgive him in the late 1970s and early 1980s for what they considered his naiveté at best, and betrayal at worst, in adopting a policy of détente with the Soviet Union.

Indeed, the conservatives who during the Truman years had largely clung to their historic nationalist/isolationist stance and opposed the Democrats' alliance with the states of Western Europe and intervention across the Atlantic to contain Soviet power, now ironically adopted the liberal Democrats' Cold War policies. Labeled Cold War internationalism or conservative interventionism, the Republicans gave priority to the East–West struggle. In their perception the central conflict remained the one with the Soviet Union; national security was still the key consideration; the chief threat to the United States was Soviet expansionism and growing military might; and the motivating drives behind this expansionism were Communist ideology and Soviet totalitarianism. In short, the Republican party in the post-Nixon/Ford period shifted to an antidétente and promilitary orientation until the late Reagan years. Kissinger's prodétente and proarms control perspective was anathema to the conservatives. This explained not only why Kissinger could not get an appointment in the Reagan administration, but it was one reason why his former deputy in the NSC, Alexander Haig, was probably doomed from the start when Reagan appointed him secretary of state.

The Democrats too had flip-flopped from Cold War liberalism to post-Cold War internationalism or liberal internationalism. Presidents Truman and Kennedy/Johnson had pursued vigorous anticommunist and interventionist policies. These policies reflected the liberal Democrats' basic commitments to individual dignity and freedom, racial equality, and social justice. These were not only considered good values for America at home, they were to be promoted overseas as well. Communism and totalitarianism were the antitheses of these values; therefore, Soviet expansion had to be resisted. It was precisely because the Democratic party—certainly the presidential party—was liberal that it initiated the containment policy and became strongly interventionist. After Vietnam, this stance was condemned and Cold War liberalism became a term of condemnation because of its anticommunist and militarist character. As the Cold Warriors became a small minority that now found their voice largely outside of the Democratic party, as in The Committee on the Present Danger (Chapter 5) and *Commentary* magazine, post-Cold War liberal Democrats now divorced themselves from the party's earlier hard-line stance.

The new liberal internationalism viewed the nations of the world as increasingly interdependent. The key issues were social/economic/humanitarian: overpopulation, hunger, poverty, ill health, ignorance, lack of resources, and environmental issues. The Democrats' chief concern was not the East–West axis, but the North–South axis (which was also consistent with the party's commitment to the New and Fair Deals, that is, welfare issues at home). National security issues were regarded as subordinate to the transnational problems confronting all of humanity. The Democrats especially identified themselves with the less-developed countries' (LDCs) demands in the 1970s for economic justice: they called for a new international economic order between the West and the LDCs. The Democrats were also opposed to the status quo within the LDCs because it was often associated with American-supported, politically repressive, regimes. Wanting to be on "the right side" of history, the party favored social change, called *national liberation*. Liberal internationalism did not ignore the Soviet Union, which was considered merely a traditional great power, not a militant revolutionary state. Russian expansion was seen mainly as defensive, the product of a deep sense of insecurity produced by frequent past invasions (and defeats). American–Soviet arms control, plus nuclear nonproliferation, was therefore desirable to help defuse the American–Soviet conflict and to take a first step toward a new world order.

The Democrats' main thrust was antimilitary, antiinterventionist, and pro-human rights. Vietnam had seared the party's conscience. "No more Vietnams" became the party's motto whether the issue was Angola or Nicaragua. While the party recognized that in principle military power remained an instrument of policy, in practice it abhorred the use of violence and opposed its use in any actual situation anywhere, just as fervently as the Founding Fathers had counseled against "entangling alliances." When Reagan invaded the tiny Caribbean island of Grenada in 1983 to overthrow a pro-Cuban and pro-Soviet regime, leading Democrats both in and out of Congress immediately voiced their concern and opposition until this operation gained widespread popular approval, leaving them little choice but to join in praise of Reagan's action. In 1988, Dukakis, who had been critical of Grenada, was weakened by what was widely seen as his inexperience and softness on defense; Bush had experience and claimed to be tough on defense.

These different post-Vietnam Republican–Democratic views of the world, with one party swinging more to the right and one more to the left, emerged fully after the Nixon administration. Characterizing belief systems by outlining the differences between them may somewhat exaggerate actual partisan differences; nevertheless, these characterizations do represent genuine differences. (In fact, there was a third position, called *semiisolationism*. It emphasized that the main threats to the United States were internal ones, such as inflation, unemployment, racial conflict, and so on, and that genuine superpower conflicts of interests were few and could be resolved. According to this view, the Soviet Union represented no genuine threat to the United States, and Soviet fears and insecurities could be assuaged by a friendly United States policy. This position was largely identified with the Reverend Jesse Jackson in the Democratic party.) Interestingly, congressional Republicans had supported the Nixon administration despite its prodétente, although also promilitary (as well as proarms control) outlook. This was due in part, of course, to the fact that the administration was Republican. It can also be explained by noting that while the administration pursued détente it pursued the Vietnam War, refusing to "bug out" despite a great deal of political pressure to do so. By Ford's time, however, the hearts of these congressional Republicans were with Reagan, even if their heads warned them against dumping an incumbent president. Thus, when Carter won and later signed the Strategic Arms Limitation Treaty (SALT II), Republicans in large numbers opposed it despite Ford's and Kissinger's endorsements and the fact that negotiations for it had started with Nixon, who had fathered SALT I. SALT II was now the Democrats' treaty. The same held true for the Panama Canal treaties, concluded during the Carter years.

By contrast, the Democrats favored détente but they opposed Vietnam. Once they were out of office, it became "Nixon's war," although it was Kennedy and Johnson who had militarily intervened in Vietnam. When the war was over, they became more vocal about the Republicans' alleged lack of concern for human rights, as well as their effort to modernize U.S. strategic forces, which was often criticized for provoking a new arms race and being antiarms control. Partisanship now became the order of the day and foreign and defense policies tended to become enmeshed in controversy. Because partisans in both parties were convinced of their rightness, indeed the morality of their particular perspective, these controversies often became tinged by ideological convictions that embittered foreign policy debates in and out of Congress. Policy issues became matters of "right" and "wrong," of "morality" and "immorality."

Public opinion also changed (see Chapter 5).[23] Once rather passive and willing to allow the president to lead while it was quite content to follow, the public had grown increasingly distrustful and suspicious of political leadership. It thus tended to swing from left to right to the other end in response to current concerns and anxieties and could no longer be discounted as in the Cold War days. Whereas bipartisanship had once protected presidents against the extremes on the left and right and volatile changes in the public mood, its decline meant that there was little to prevent wild swings in foreign policy.[24] These changes in party outlooks and public opinion are nowhere more visible than in the Congress, which no longer was willing to play "president knows best."

THE PRESIDENT AND CONGRESS: A TROUBLESOME RELATIONSHIP

The relationship between the president and Congress is an ever-changing one. In the 1930s, the Congress was clearly the dominant partner. During World War II and the Cold War the president was supreme. Since Vietnam, the Congress has reasserted itself and sought to restrain the president's conduct of foreign policy lest he get the country involved in another war. This has created the situation many feared in the early postwar years of a president and Congress pulling in different directions, either paralyzing U.S. policy or undermining the possibility of the wise, long-range, and steady course required of a leader of a coalition of nations. This worry was well taken; executive–legislative conflict and partisan differences between Republicans and Democrats were the norm.[25] The peace treaty with Spain at the turn of the century after the United States had emerged on the international stage—for a brief performance, as it turned out—squeaked through by two votes with a majority of Republicans supporting it and the Democrats opposed. The 1919 Versailles peace treaty, which involved U.S. entry into the newly organized League of Nations, went down to defeat in the bitter rivalry between Democratic President Woodrow Wilson and Republican Senate Majority Leader and Chairman of the Senate Foreign Relations Committee Henry Cabot Lodge. Both men, besides disliking each other personally, were also strong partisans. The interwar period was one of isolationism but executive–legislative differences surfaced again even before President Roosevelt began moving to help Britain in 1940. In 1935, Roosevelt barely mobilized enough votes—helped by telephone calls from the postmaster general threatening a cutoff of patronage from recalcitrant Democrats—to defeat the Ludlow amendment 209 to 198, requiring a popular referendum before Congress could declare war.[26] After France's defeat, the president, with the major exception of the Lend-Lease Act, preferred using executive agreements for his policies rather than going to Congress. The reason is obvious. On August 10, 1941, the Congress passed by only one vote the renewal of the Selective Service Act. "In favor were 203 House members (182 Democrats, 21 Republicans); opposed were 202 members (65 Democrats, 133 Republicans). But for a single vote the nation might have been left with an army in dissolution, only a few months before Pearl Harbor."[27] Another historian noted that "fundamentally the close ballot indicated that the American people were not convinced that Germany and Japan truly endangered the security of the United States."[28]

Given this historical pattern, it appears that the twenty years of bipartisanship after 1945 were an exceptional period rather than a norm that must be restored. Only a "clear and present danger" appears to unite the nation and the two branches of government. Otherwise there is conflict. That was, of course, the intention of the Founding Fathers in establishing the separation of powers, a rather ill-termed phrase because the reality is a separation of institutions sharing powers. It is this sharing that produces the sparks.

The Founding Fathers' design was deliberate. They expected institutional conflict. Their aim was to prevent domestic tyranny and ensure individual freedom. The question today is whether an institutional arrangement of checks and balances designed for that purpose is capable of making policy to deal with external threats to American security and prosperity at a time when there is no agreement on what the U.S. role and aims should be in the world, how those goals should be achieved, and at what risk and cost. Further, the American margin of safety and wealth has shrunk drastically as a result of the emergence of the increasing Soviet nuclear strength and the decline of U.S. economic capability and competitiveness in the world. In any event, the current executive–legislative relationship is probably nearer the norm than the now largely defunct bipartisanship.

The split in the post-Vietnam consensus is also a major cause of today's institutional conflict. Liberal Democrats had earlier been the strongest advocates of presidential preeminence and leadership. First the New Deal and then the vigorous prosecution of the Cold War had led the party to champion executive power. It was conservative Republicans, who had opposed the New Deal and later the European orientation of U.S. foreign policy, who became the spokespersons for a more vigorous Congress that would limit presidential power. The liberal Democratic/conservative Republican reversal on policy after Vietnam also led to a flip-flop on executive–legislative relations. The Republicans, who controlled the White House from 1972 to 88 (with the exception of 1976–80), were now the Cold War party, focusing their attention on the continuing Soviet threat and need for U.S. containment. Thus, they became the champions of presidential leadership. In fact, the Republicans have controlled the presidency for twenty-four of the thirty-six years since Eisenhower. The Democrats, badly hurt by Vietnam and unable to forget it, did not share this perspective and became especially wary of new commitments and any use of force. Since they tended to control at least one of the Houses, if not both, they pressed for a strong congressional role to restrain the conduct of U.S. foreign policy vis-à-vis the Soviet Union. The Democrats have controlled both houses of Congress for twenty-eight of the thirty-six years since 1952, and at least one house for six more years. Executive–legislative conflict thus reflected more than the institutional prerogatives and sensitivities of the two branches.

Examples of the presidency and the Congress pulling in different directions are legion since Vietnam: on assistance to two quarreling NATO allies—Turkey, favored by the executive and Greece, favored by the legislative—in the 1970s; on U.S. interventions to counter Soviet moves in the Third World (Angola in 1975 and Nicaragua in the 1980s); on the Middle East where presidents have tried to be more evenhanded between Israel and the Arabs while Congress leans strongly toward Israel; and on sanctions against South Africa, to name but a few. But more prominent and consistent has been the arms control issue. In 1979, the Senate refused to give its consent to SALT II; President Carter had earlier barely managed to receive the Senate's consent on the two Panama Canal treaties. The Congress, however, reversed itself during the Reagan years because (1) the administration was initially hostile to arms control, including the SALT II limitations on strategic weapons; and (2) it sought to shift U.S. strategy from one of deterrence, which had provided the basis of American and Western security for four decades, to one of strategic defense (see Chapter 8). The Democratically controlled House was in favor of arms control and therefore sought repeatedly to prevent U.S. nuclear testing over one kiloton for the eighteen months during which the Soviets had declared a unilateral moratorium on testing. It also sought to prevent antisatellite testing and to compel the administration to adhere to the provisions of the unratified 1979 treaty on strategic arms. When the Democrats recaptured the Senate in 1986, forty-seven Democrats joined by ten Republicans sent the president a letter urging him to reverse his decision to exceed the limits set by SALT II. SDI has been a particularly contentious issue, much of the fighting revolving around the preservation of the 1972 ABM treaty (also see Chapter 8). The other critical issue, as already discussed at length, has been the use of force. Nevertheless, it is worth repeating one critical point. In the post-Vietnam era, the model for military intervention appears to be a Libya or Grenada, that is, a quick, almost cost-free, and an acclaimed successful operation against a fifth-rate power (if that high).

The United States in terms of its relative strength and influence, remains a superpower despite its economic decline. The question, however, as noted in the discussion of the War Powers Resolution, is whether it is capable of acting like one, and perhaps more fundamentally, if it wants to do so. One observer has noted that the pre-World War II pattern seems to be repeating itself. Presidents either constrain themselves in response to congressional insistence on a more circumscribed world role and less risk taking, especially militarily, or they seek to find a way around such constraints, resulting in potential constitutional crises in the post-Vietnam period.[29] More specifically, except for situations of quick interventions, which when successful have been popular, a president confronts three choices: (1) to use force, if he can mobilize congressional support; (2) to do nothing, if he cannot use force; and (3) to find a way around the various post-Vietnam congressional efforts to restrain him (as most recently and notably in Nicaragua). Since the first choice is only likely for extreme circumstances and the third choice of precipitating a constitutional confrontation is used only if he is caught, choice two is the most likely outcome. If contemporary circumstances can be projected backward, it is legitimate to ask whether President Roosevelt would have been able to lead the country to Britain's support in 1940–41. Or would his resort to executive agreements to circumvent restraints imposed by the Congress' strong isolationist sentiment have led to extensive Senate and House hearings and the passage of an amendment constraining the president's leadership? Indeed, had the War Powers Resolution been in place, what could Roosevelt have done?

In retrospect, no one quarrels with the fact that Nazi Germany constituted a threat to U.S. security, but in 1939–41 that was not as clear; it was not even take for granted after France's defeat in 1940 when Britain stood alone. Today, the possibility that the Sandinistas constitute a threat to American security—at least a sufficient threat so that the use of U.S. force to overthrow them would be acceptable—is not widely acknowledged. But what if Reagan will some day be proven correct in his assessment? There is, to be sure, an enormous difference between the way Roosevelt and Reagan acted. Roosevelt acted openly, not hiding his deeds from either Congress or the public, although he did frequently bypass the first while trying to educate the last. Reagan acted secretly, deliberately misleading the Congress. Roosevelt maneuvered shrewdly by invoking legal executive agreements. Reagan simply claimed that in the final analysis the law did not apply to him; as president he had plenary powers.

Nevertheless, despite these contrasts, Charles Krauthammer of *The New Republic* has raised an interesting issue that, in conclusion, is at least worth considering. In commenting on Irangate, he wrote that it was not so much "a Reagan crisis nor a presidential crisis, but a recurring crisis, rooted ultimately in the tension between America's need to act like a great power and its unwillingness to do so. Into the breach between will and necessity have stepped people willing to violate the law. The result is disaster."[30] In Roosevelt's time, one might add, the president could still expand his powers as commander in chief, but by Reagan's time, the Congress had reined the president in. Fearful of what a president might do, Congress had written into law a number of restraints and, as presidents saw it, sought to micromanage his conduct of foreign policy. As the restraints mounted, was the attempted privatization of foreign policy not perhaps inevitable, even if illegal? It might be well to remember that before Reagan, presidents did not hesitate to intervene—especially in this hemisphere—when they deemed U.S. interests to be at stake. Eisenhower acted covertly in Guatemala in 1954; Kennedy acted covertly in Cuba in 1961; and Johnson used the marines in the Dominican Republic in 1965. Reagan could not use overt or covert intervention; the news was soon all over the front pages and the television screen.

THE PRIVATIZATION OF FOREIGN POLICY:
THE IRAN–CONTRA AFFAIR

The scandal that enveloped the Reagan administration in late 1986 was initially likened by many to President Nixon's Watergate debacle. Although the nation clearly was unwilling to go through such a wrenching experience again so soon, President Reagan remained personally popular, even though most Americans thought he was lying about his involvement.[31] Nixon had sought to deal with certain domestic problems, including his 1972 reelection, in extralegal ways by misusing the CIA and other agencies, deceiving Congress, and engaging in efforts to cover up crimes. Collectively, these matters led to the drawing up of the articles of impeachment. At the heart of the resulting impeachment proceedings was the finding that President Nixon had violated the duty of his office that, according to the Constitution, the president "take care that the laws be faithfully executed."

The abuses of power by the Reagan administration were considered more serious and fundamental because of their effects on U.S. foreign policy. Through the National Security Council the White House had organized a "shadow government" that secretly sold arms to Iran to gain the release of six U.S. hostages held in Lebanon in violation of the Arms Export Control Act banning arms shipments to states that sponsor terrorism (which had been applied to Iran by a Reagan executive order). The Reagan administration also violated a requirement to notify Congress' intelligence committees if the president authorized covert arms sales (done only retroactively). It further established a network of private individuals, mostly former government officials, some of rather unsavory reputation (because of their earlier association with Edmund Wilson, who had supplied Libya's Colonel Muammar Qaddafi with terrorist capabilities, including arms and training by former Special Forces personnel),[32] as well as foreign personnel, including Iranian, Saudi, and Israeli arms dealers. It employed these men as agents of the U.S. government to carry out an arms-for-hostages exchange with Iran. It then used some of the profits from this deal to supply arms to the U.S.-organized and supported Contras against the Nicaraguan government. This was done in clear violation of a congressional cutoff of military aid for the Contras from mid-1984 to late 1986. (Indeed, after it became clear that the hostages still held would not be released, the arms sales continued to fund the Contras.) Money for the Contras was solicited from wealthy private individuals in the United States and from foreign governments, thus violating the constitutionally approved method requiring a president to seek approval and funding from the Congress for his policies. As revelations of these activities surfaced in November 1986, the White House and NSA, together with the director of the CIA and the attorney general, attempted a cover-up by constructing a false chronology of events to protect the president by minimizing his role. Incriminating documents were altered and shredded to conceal extralegal covert activities—enough "to fill up half a box car"—as well as smuggled out of their files.

The president himself changed his story about when he first learned of the initial secret shipment of U.S. arms to Iran via Israel in September 1985 and about whether he had authorized it to gain the release of the U.S. hostages. He claimed a loss of memory on this radical shift of policy from his own earlier and repeated insistence that the United States would never deal with terrorists. Reagan denied ever having been told of the Contra diversion. The president's stated unawareness of important details and the factual errors in his public accounts of the Iran affair led the Tower Commission, established by the president to investigate the matter, to be highly critical of his hands-off "management style."* One of its members, former Senator and Secretary of State Edmund Muskie, said that he and his two colleagues on the commission "were all appalled by the absence of the kind of alertness and vigilance to his job and to these policies that one expects of a president.[33] On circumventing the Congress' restrictions on aid to the Contras, the president first asserted that he had obeyed the law and had not solicited funds. As the evidence piled up during the congressional investigation of this matter that Reagan and several members of the NSC staff had done precisely that, he changed his defense and asserted that helping the Contras with private and foreign funds was his idea, that he had been kept fully informed (undoubtedly true for the Contras were his favorite cause), and that the legislative restraints did not apply to him and the NSC staff. In fact, Reagan claimed that the restraints were an unconstitutional encroachment on the president's right to conduct foreign policy.

Yet, throughout the period of Congress' cutoff of military aid, the administration had repeatedly deceived Congress when questions were raised about what it was doing to help the Contras. It never challenged the congressional restrictions in the courts. Reagan had, in fact, signed the law he now claimed he was above! Consistent with that claim, the NSA and others involved with both policies systematically and deliberately lied and deceived not only Congress, but the secretaries of state and defense and other NSC members, in order to keep secret what they were doing to implement what they had every reason to believe were President Reagan's policies.

Reagan became president the day the U.S. hostages, held by Iran for 444 days, were released. From the beginning of his administration he vowed to deal firmly with terrorists, whether sponsored by states like Iran or not. His administration would not bargain with terrorists since that would only encourage further acts of terrorism. But as terrorist actions multiplied throughout the Middle East and Europe—especially in Lebanon, a state disintegrating in civil war—the administration remained passive. These actions included the 1983 blowing up of the U.S. embassy with over 50 lives lost and some months later the blowing up of 241 marines who were in Lebanon as part of an international peacekeeping force. Similar attacks on Israeli and French troops led to quick retaliation on the terrorist camps. But after several more terrorist attacks in which Americans were killed, the United

---

*President Reagan appeared to feel relieved by this critical assessment, for it seemed to support his contention that he had been unaware of what was being done in his name. That a president would feel pleased by being publicly told that he was not doing the job expected of a chief executive is a commentary in itself.

States attacked Libya in response to what was said to be a Libyan-planned attack on a West Berlin discotheque frequented by U.S. service personnel. The president's actions were finally forging a Western consensus on how to deal with the terrorists. Up to this time Western Europe had been reluctant to act against Libya because it was economically profitable to maintain good relations with Libya and because of the fear that Qaddafi would retaliate on their territory, not in the United States. Following a wave of bomb explosions in Paris and a reported Syrian-sponsored attempt to plant a bomb on an Israeli airliner in London, Europeans, who had already begun to watch Libyan personnel at their people's bureaus or embassies more closely, adopted a British plan for an arms embargo and diplomatic sanctions against Syria.

Apparently because the president was deeply moved by the plight of the U.S. hostages taken by Iranian-sponsored terrorist groups in Lebanon, the administration approached Iran to gain their release (the midterm election in 1986 may have increased the incentive for an early release). Iran, at war with Iraq since 1979, needed spare parts for its largely American military equipment purchased by the Shah's pro-American regime (which had preceeded the Ayatollah Khomeini's militantly anti-American government). While the president was later to explain the U.S. shipment of arms in geo-political terms—as an approach to so-called *moderates* with whom the United States could, after Khomeini's death, establish better U.S.–Iranian relations—a memorandum written by CIA Director William Casey showed that this was a rationalization to be used as a cover story if the hostage swap were discovered. The U.S. was concerned not with strategic goals, but with the hostages' release.* In fact, NSA Robert McFarlane, and NSC staffer Lt. Col. Oliver North accompanied one shipment of arms, bringing their Iranian hosts not only antitank missiles, but a Bible signed by Ronald Reagan and a cake in the shape of a key (to unlock the door of U.S.–Iranian friendship). When his hosts did not release all the hostages, McFarlane recommended ending the exchange. (The secretary of defense, when first informed, contemptuously remarked that the whole idea was too absurd even to comment on.) Shortly thereafter McFarlane resigned as NSA, but the White House went ahead with additional shipments of arms.

U.S. interest in continuing to deal with the Iranians was triggered by the fact that the more cash that was brought in by the arms transaction, the more could be diverted to the Contras. In any case, only one hostage was

---

*The original "finding" authorizing shipment, signed by the president only after the arms shipment had started, stated this purpose only. But this original copy has disappeared and in at least two subsequent findings, the broader reasons to disguise the arms for hostage trade were stated: the geopolitical "strategic initiative," to establish relations with "moderate elements" and so on. The initial cover-up got lost in the later congressional hearing, which focused more on the diversion of funds for the Contras and on whether the president knew about it.

released after each of three shipments. But three more U.S. hostages were seized in Lebanon! It was clear that the administration's decision to trade arms for hostages gave the terrorists an incentive to replace the ones released. Depressed by the failure to gain the hostages' release and feeling in general that he had let the president down, former NSA McFarlane attempted suicide.

Quite apart from not gaining all the hostages' freedom and violating U.S. laws, the Reagan administration exposed itself as hypocritical and undermined its own tough antiterrorist public posture of never surrendering to terrorist blackmail. It sanctioned the usual European approach of bartering for hostages and undermined the British effort to lead Europe to adopt Reagan's publically stated position of not dealing with terrorists. Arms for Iran violated not only the administration's prior proclamation of neutrality in the war but, if it helped the Iranians to defeat the Iraqis, would endanger all the Persian Gulf oil sheikdoms, which controlled two thirds of the non-communist world's oil reserves (a key reason why in 1987 the United States committed itself to naval protection of some Kuwaiti oil tankers). An Iranian victory might also spread Islamic extremism to Egypt and Jordan, as well as to the Shiite Moslems in southern Lebanon on Israel's northern frontier, thereby endangering moderate pro-American Arab regimes and placing Israel in greater jeopardy (which is why questions might at least have been raised in the NSC about Israel's policy of helping the Ayatollah's Iran against Iraq). In return for the arms, the administration had not even gained concessions on terrorism or the war.

It was hard to understand how the president could place the lives of a few individuals over America's broader and longer-run national interests. At the very least it jeopardized the nation's and his own authority, reputation, and credibility at home and abroad. To trade arms in a war in which it is against America's national interest for Iran to win, and to do so in a way that would encourage further hostage taking—all this with a regime that had only recently humiliated and mocked the United States and blown up over 200 American marines and diplomats in Lebanon—raised serious questions about the president's judgment and competence and the whole manner in which the Reagan administration made policy. The Iran decisions appear to have been made by the president and the director of the CIA, with the support of the NSA, first McFarlane and then Poindexter, over the protests of the secretaries of state and defense, who were then cut out of the decision-making process. The government's experts on Iran in the State Department, Defense Department, and the CIA were never brought into the process to evaluate whether the arms deal would gain the release of the hostages and strengthen the so-called *moderates* in the Iranian government— if they existed. Nor were any outside experts consulted about whether the shipment of arms was indeed a sound way to move toward the laudable objective of improving U.S.–Iranian relations and helping to bring about an Iranian–Iraqi peace, an additional justification stated by the president for his move when it was embarrassingly revealed. Iran's leaders—radicals, not moderates—still virulently denounced the United States, continued to sponsor and finance the groups carrying out terrorist actions against the United States in Lebanon, and were in fact using the hostages to manipulate the U.S. approach for their own purpose of acquiring arms. In the secretary of state's word's "we got taken to the cleaners." The Reagan administration's behavior in these circumstances could only enhance their contempt for the "Great Satan," as they called America, and incite them further to undermine U.S. interests throughout the Middle East–Persian Gulf area rather than moderate or change their behavior. The White House officials running the Iran operation clearly knew little about Iranian politics and personalities. Good intentions thoughtlessly pursued, subject to no checks and balances, could only end in disaster—and did.

For the administration, the revelation of its dealing with Iran was bad enough since there probably was no country—not even the Soviet Union— more despised by American public opinion. Even worse, however, was the additional revelation that some of the profits from the arms sales to Iran had been diverted illegally to fund the Contras in Nicaragua. From its first days in office, the Reagan administration had focused on what it perceived and defined as the communist threat in this hemisphere. In El Salvador, the government was fighting against left-wing guerrillas and the administration contended that Nicaragua was transmitting Soviet and other Eastern bloc weapons shipped via Cuba to the rebels. It therefore organized the rag-tag remnants of former American-supported dictator Anatasio Somoza's National Guard into a Contra guerrilla force, ostensibly to pressure Nicaragua's Sandinista government to halt these arms deliveries. In reality, the aim was to overthrow the Marxist Sandinista regime. Having come into power in a genuinely popular revolution against Somoza, the Sandinistas, once in control of the government, squeezed its former partners (the Roman Catholic Church, the business community, trade unions, intellectuals, student groups and others) out of the coalition. It became increasingly authoritarian in its rule at home and shifted toward the Soviet Union in foreign policy, betraying its previous promises of political democracy, a mixed economy, and nonalignment in world politics. The Reagan administration, admittedly, stated that its goal for Nicaragua was free elections. But once in power the Sandinistas, already convinced that they represented the popular will, were hardly likely to allow such "bourgeois" practices, especially as they began to alienate segments of the population with their policies of economic austerity, political suppression, Miskito Indian resettlement, and military conscription. The administration, determined to prevent a "second Cuba" in this hemisphere and the "first Cuba" on the mainland, and convinced that the Sandinistas, committed to a "revolution without frontiers," would seek to undermine not only El Salvador but other Central American countries, therefore committed itself to the support of the Contras. The president rather generously called their leaders the "moral equals of our Founding Fathers."

Central America was seen as part of the East–West struggle, a new front in the Cold War opened up by Somoza's overthrow and the resulting Soviet–Cuban–Nicaraguan decision to exploit this opportunity to weaken the United States in its own backyard. In a sense, the administration viewed the area and the possibility of spreading the Sandinista revolution to Nicaragua's neighbors as creating an "Eastern Europe" for America on its southern border, a result it sought to avoid. American foreign policy, in extending U.S. power across the Atlantic and Pacific Oceans, had always taken its security in this hemisphere for granted; it could extend American power precisely because it did not have to worry about enemies close to home. Thus, despite Nicaragua's small size and population, and the overwhelming military power the United States exercises in this hemisphere, the administration was convinced that U.S. security was at stake in Nicaragua. Besides SDI, there was no issue about which President Reagan felt more strongly.

The administration was, however, constrained in how to deal with the Sandinistas. The memory of Vietnam was still vivid and the use of U.S. forces to topple the Nicaraguan regime was therefore not a genuine option, even though the administration kept this possibility alive by building airstrips in Honduras, transporting U.S. troops for "exercises" on Nicaragua's borders, deploying warships on Nicaragua's east and west coasts, and invading Grenada. Another option it rejected was the diplomatic solution. While, on occasion it pretended to support the Contadora process (the effort by Mexico, Venezuela, Colombia, and Panama to arrange a peaceful settlement), the United States remained opposed because such a settlement would have left the Sandinistas in power. The issue was not defusing the situation by having the Sandinistas send the Soviet bloc and Cuban military personnel home, reducing the size of the Sandinista army so that it could not be a threat to its neighbors, having the regime promise not to support revolutionary groups in neighboring countries or permitting the establishment of a Soviet base in Nicaragua. The issue was eliminating the Sandinistas. Thus the Contras were the administration's principal alternative. CIA Director Casey and United Nations Representative Jeane Kirkpatrick, both influential in the Reagan inner circle, believed that the support of the Contras would lead to the Sandinistas' collapse.

Thus the United States escalated the covert war. The CIA organized the Contras into more of a fighting force, which eventually grew to approximately 15,000 men; and CIA personnel became involved in the mining of Nicaraguan harbors, the blowing up of oil storage depots, and other operations. The Congress was outraged. Its intelligence oversight committees, which are supposed to supervise covert actions, had not been informed of these American-run operations. Apart from the sense of being deceived, the principal congressional concern was that the growing U.S. sponsorship of the war would eventually draw the country into another Vietnam. Even if no Americans were involved, once U.S. prestige was committed, could it avoid not "finishing the job" itself if the Contras failed to overthrow the Sandinista regime? Congress—led by the Democratically controlled House—

therefore cut off military aid to the Contras in the spring of 1984 for that year and for 1985, although it restored $27 million in "humanitarian aid" (allegedly, food, bandages, and the like) when the Sandinista leader traveled to Moscow. Not until 1986 did the Congress—nervous about administration charges that if Nicaragua were "lost" it would be their fault—vote $100 million once again for military assistance to the Contras. In the meantime, Congress' intent was clear. It was not a question of whether President Reagan approved. He did sign the law, no doubt with misgivings, but Congress had enacted it. Undoubtedly, the president would try to get Congress to change its mind. Until that happened, however, he did not have the right to subvert the law by implementing the rejected course of action in secret. Specifically, the Boland amendment prohibited the CIA, Pentagon, or any other entity of the U.S. government involved in intelligence from "directly or indirectly" aiding the Contras militarily. At the time, neither the president nor anyone close to him in the administration claimed that the amendment did not apply to the president or the NSC staff; and no one denied that it prevented administration officials from encouraging other nations to finance and arm the Contras. In 1985 Robert McFarlane, as he did in 1987 during the Iran–Contra congressional hearings, stated that it was always his belief that Congress' intent was that the Contras were not to receive U.S. assistance and that therefore the NSC was not exempt from the Boland amendment. Even more specifically, Robert Motley, the assistant secretary of state in charge of Central American affairs, said the amendment prohibited the entire administration from giving any help, direct or indirect for the Contras, and that this implied soliciting or encouraging foreign money. The fact that the administration did raise funds and organize military help so furtively suggests that it was well aware that it was circumventing the will of Congress, whatever its rationalizations once the whole matter had been exposed. It is hardly surprising that the Boland amendment did not include the NSC, for the NSC had not been established to be an intelligence, let alone a paramilitary organization, but an advisory body to the president.

That is, however, what it became as Reagan, frustrated with the results of democracy at home, decided to work for democracy in Nicaragua by transforming the NSC into a secret government. The president's commitment to the Contras—whom he called *freedom fighters*—was firm. But the CIA, which normally runs covert operations, could no longer do so; top officials expressing their skepticism of the arms deal, had opposed the agency's involvement. Thus its director, a close confidante of the president, shifted the operation to the NSC, which had not been listed in the Boland amendment;*

---

*North's testimony about Casey's role, while very persuasive, was offered to exculpate North and could not be contradicted by Casey, who had recently died. Yet a book by *Washington Post* reporter Bob Woodward of Watergate fame on Casey's directorship of the CIA makes North's testimony plausible. See Robert Woodward, *Veil* (New York: Simon Schuster, 1987).

and Casey's zealous point man in the NSC, a "can-do" officer par excellence, later to be called the only five-star lieutenant colonel in the U.S. military, was a marine officer, Oliver North. The NSA, certainly McFarlane, appeared almost irrelevant, outflanked by the Casey–North alliance (although Admiral Poindexter supported the policy and was thus included in the small circle of men who ran the Iran and Contra operations). North, a relatively junior officer whose authority came from Casey, could command help from officials in the CIA, State Department, and Pentagon. The NSC thus became the shadow government to ensure the Contras' survival until Congress would hopefully change its mind and fund the Contras again.

Perhaps it would be more appropriate to call the NSC a shadow CIA. North organized a network of operatives led by retired Major General Richard Secord. Most were veterans of the failed 1961 Bay of Pigs operation to overthrow Castro in Cuba and the disastrous 1980 Desert One rescue operations of U.S. hostages in Iran (hardly a good omen for success this time). It was this "private aid" group that took over the purchasing of weapons, their shipment to the Contras, and the training and direction of the Contra war. Secord and his men organized, among other things, an air service to supply the rebels; the main air base was in El Salvador, but airstrips were laid in other countries as well. Ships were also acquired to help this supply operation. U.S. government help, usually through Lt. Col. North in the form of CIA maps, intelligence information, tactical advice about military strikes and—causing quite a stir at the time—a CIA-prepared manual on assassination, was, however, never far away. Administration officials were always at the other end of a telephone line: calls were placed from El Salvador to Lt. Col. North's private line at the NSC. The U.S. ambassador in Costa Rica was ordered to help this clandestine operation, reportedly run by North with the help of Assistant Secretary of State for Inter-American Affairs, Elliott Abrams, and the CIA official heading the Central American Task Force; calls were also made to Stanford Technology Trading Inc., an arms firm half owned by General Secord.

This shift of field operations from the CIA to the NSC to General Secord's warriors—this privatization of covert action—left the NSC mainly in the role of fund-raiser. North and his cohorts were not only a shadow CIA, but became a shadow Treasury, raising millions to buy arms for the Contras. Secord and another retired major general, John Singlaub, played key roles. Secord opened a Swiss bank account and deposited $30 million earned from selling arms to Iran in it. As chairman of the World Anti-Communist League, Singlaub had many overseas contacts and he collected large funds from, for instance, South Korea and Nationalist China. Both men were in frequent contact with North and occasionally even met with CIA Director Casey. When in 1986 funds reportedly began to dry up after potential donors realized that the United States would resume funding after Congress had appropriated $100 million, Abrams successfully solicited $10 million from the ruler of Brunei. (These funds disappeared until May 1987 when it was discovered that Abrams had deposited the money in the wrong account!)

North also contacted private fund-raisers in the United States. Conservative anticommunist organizations like the tax-free National Endowment for the Preservation for Liberty (later indicted for tax fraud) raised more millions for arms. North himself often addressed Endowment meetings, talking about the Contras. While he did not himself solicit funds, others did so after his speeches. In addition, North arranged for large contributors ($300,000 minimum) to be taken to the White House to meet the president, who thanked them for their donations (which he later claimed he thought would be used for television spots supporting the Contras, although the private donors knew their contributions went to buy arms). The president, too, addressed some conservative groups, stopping just short of asking for funds. While administration officials pressured or enticed the Central American democracies with economic and military aid to assist the Contras, the president himself reportedly talked to Saudi King Fahd when the king visited the White House. The Saudis, who had paid $1 million per month after the congressional cutoff in mid-1984, raised that sum to $2 million a month after the king had talked to the president in early 1985 for a total of $32 million. While Reagan denied soliciting these funds or doing anything illegal, Saudi generosity is hard to explain except as a contribution to Reagan's favorite "charity" in return for the president's past help in obtaining AWAC surveillance planes—never before sold to non-NATO countries—and other advanced weapons despite strong congressional resistance and favorable consideration in the future. Still, someone at some point must have suggested a contribution to the Contras; and someone must have proposed doubling the contribution.[34]

In fact, the line between public and private assistance for the Contras is difficult to draw; the two were inextricably merged. For operators like Secord, the 50 percent markup of weapons sold provided a sufficient profit to make his participation more than just the matter of patriotism he presented in his defense. Secord did not consider himself financially accountable to the government, although the cash raised by his company was from the sale of U.S. arms bought with taxpayers' money. He and his partner made $4 million from the arms sale; the Contras received only $3 million. On the other hand, Secord could enlist the cooperation of the NSC, CIA, or State Department, or show Iranian visitors through the White House's private quarters and the Situation Room, where the most secret military planning is done, when the president was away. Thus he was also an agent of the U.S. government. Where was the line between private citizen and U.S. representative, when North, virtually assuming the powers of the president, Secord, and his Iranian-born business partner tried to sweeten the pot for the Iranians by promising that the United States would go to war against the Soviet Union if it invaded Iran, help depose President Hussein of Iraq, and pressure Kuwait to release seventeen pro-Iranian terrorists who, among their deeds, had attacked the U.S. embassy? As Senator Daniel Inouye (D-Hawaii) commented, it was a "sad state of affairs" when a lieutenant colonel and two private citizens without security clearances could conduct such sensitive negotiations.

> We find an American general who should know better, an American lieutenant colonel who everyone suggests is second only to the president of the United States, committing this country, its power and majesty to defend Iran is just unbelievable.
>
>   And then to come out that we will participate in deposing a chief of state of a country, and we're supposed to be neutral in that area.[35]

North and other government officials also pressured officials among Nicaragua's neighbors to permit "private operations."

But the U.S. Constitution intended that the basic foreign policy of the country be decided by the president and Congress after consultation and debate; foreign policy, like domestic policy, needed public support and confidence, and these could not exist if policy were made secretly. Nowhere does it say that private groups can conduct the nation's foreign policy in secret. If this were permissible, a president could at any time propose a controversial policy to Congress and if Congress turned him down, he could then ask wealthy individuals or foreign countries to finance his policy. The State Department would hardly be needed anymore. And who, for that matter, would need Congress? The president could franchise his diplomacy and raise money privately. However, it is a fundamental principle of the American political system that Congress decides whether to support a policy by appropriating funds.

Placing the NSC in charge of carrying out what everyone knew was the "old man's" favorite cause, then, was intended to do an end run around Congress. The NSA and NSC staff appointments are not subject to Senate confirmation. Therefore, an administration zealously committed to a cause, distrustful of Congress, and filled with a passion for secrecy and covert operations turned to the NSC, thumbing its collective nose at the Constitution. The White House communications director articulated this mood when in praising Lt. Col. North he said that North's "distracted and indifferent" countrymen could not be counted on to recognize what U.S. interests were in Nicaragua. North's loyal secretary put it more succinctly: "Sometimes you have to go above the written law."

Indeed, as a kind of logical culmination to this effort, CIA Director Casey reportedly had planned to use the profits from the arms sales to Iran not just for the Contras, but to establish a privately funded "off-the-shelf, self-sustaining, standalone" fund (to use Lieutenant Colonel North's description) to pay for covert operations beyond *all* governmental controls. Thus, the resumption, at inflated prices, of arms shipments had its own incentive, despite McFarlane's recommendation to call the hostage deal off and the opposition from cabinet members: The CIA director wanted money to support a super-secret, self-financing intelligence operation outside the CIA to fund programs that were either not known or not authorized by Congress and had they been known, might have been rejected by Congress.[36] Neither the president nor the vice president was told about the fund; the Congress too was not informed. Casey, who was not even in the NSC chain of command, would direct operations of this private spy agency with NSC staffers like North and perhaps even CIA personnel—all away from the watchful eyes of the Congress.

President Reagan had for six years, despite his enormous budget deficits, the bungled 1983 intervention in Lebanon, and frequent policy misstatements at press conferences, survived with his reputation and popularity high. Mistakes just bounced off him, and he became known as the "teflon president." But the Iran–Contra affair scratched that teflon and left him badly damaged as he faced his last two years in office. To be sure, as the president had said, "There ain't no smoking gun," but that was hardly the point. He was the president, he should have known what was going on. Even if he did not, he is responsible for his administration's actions. Reagan had wanted to avoid being a lame duck president, as most presidents are when they do not run for reelection; and he had already lost the Senate to the Democrats in the 1986 midterm election. His judgment, sense of competence, and credibility with the Congress, the press, and public were now badly hurt. A large majority of Americans believed that he was lying about what he knew of the diversion of funds. His approval ratings dropped sharply, reportedly affecting his sense of self-confidence, placing him on the defensive, and affecting his ability to lead the nation for the rest of his term.[37]

NSA Admiral Poindexter later testified that he had not informed the president of the diversion of funds. However, he did say that had he asked for the president's approval, he was certain he would have had it. The president, of course, denied that he would have approved, but Poindexter's point was that the policy had been established: to support the Contras. Therefore, using profits from the arms sales was only an "implementation" of this basic policy. Poindexter did admit that he also did not ask the president for his approval because, if this use of funds ever became public knowledge, it would be politically damaging. He wished to protect the president and provide him with "future deniability." Indeed, Poindexter emphasized that in no other decision of equal importance had he failed to bring a matter to the president's attention and get his approval or disapproval. Only on this decision had he decided that "the buck" stopped with him, rather than with the president. This was a rather incredible decision for a subordinate official, a quintessential staff officer, to make, given its significance and political importance and the fact that, if discovered, the president would have had to take the responsibility for it. Equally as obvious, the president was the kind of man who did not ask the questions his predecessors would have asked. Thus, given his general lack of interest in policy details, he let his NSAs make decisions that he should have made. A staff officer does not usually make such critical decisions; elected and accountable officials do. The picture that emerged from the congressional investigation into these matters certainly raised questions about whether the president was capable of managing the foreign policy of a world power. Ironically, however, more Americans were upset by Reagan's dealings with the Iranians than the Contras. As Senator Dole, Republican minority leaders said, the only way the American people wanted arms delivered to the Ayatollah is from a B-1 bomber. But most ironically, the president had by his actions probably jeopardized future support for the Contras in Congress.

In the longer run, apart from having stained his historical reputation and leaving the question open of whether Poindexter offered himself as the "fall guy,"* the president's modus operandi in this matter may also have created a new issue about which to fight with Congress:

> The strange two-year episode of the private covert war may have uncovered a power of the presidency that has never before been fully illuminated: the power to persuade private citizens and friendly governments, each eager to cultivate Washington, to do what Congress will not. It is a blunt and unwieldy instrument, but it is not easily susceptible to legislative restriction—and that alone may recommend it to future presidents and open a new field of conflict between the executive and legislative branches.[38]

This prediction may well be correct because one of the results of the Iran–Contra affair was to confirm the importance of the checks and balances system, the necessity of both branches being involved in policy making. The tendency toward abuses of power and mistakes in policy requires that each branch keep watch on the other while simultaneously insuring that any U.S. policy will first be properly debated and have the support of the American people. No important foreign policy moves can be sustained without it. The problem is that as the executive has sought to evade congressional restrictions, Congress has increased the restrictions and sought more and more to micromanage policy, leading the president to seek new ways of evading legislative supervision.

---

*Lt. Col. North had offered himself, but CIA Director Casey had told North that the administration might need a figure with higher rank. He specifically named Admiral Poindexter. His testimony, therefore, raised a serious credibility question and almost as many Americans believed he had told the president despite his denial, as believed he had not told him.

Poindexter said he withheld the information to protect the President.

One key reason many congressmen on the investigating committees did not believe the admiral was that he testified that on the day he resigned, neither the president, vice president, chief of staff, nor attorney general, all present when he submitted his resignation, asked him any questions about the diversion. Had they not known anything about the diversion, which was one of the principal reasons for the scandal, they surely would have asked the admiral to explain what happened. The fact that they did not suggests that they already knew, either from Poindexter or Casey, or both.

THE DILEMMAS REVISITED: THE PRICE OF POWER

The purpose of the separation of powers has been to guard against executive concentration of power. Such a concentration, it was feared, might constitute a threat to the liberties of American citizens. Yet the conduct of foreign policy requires just such a concentration; a powerful president is a fundamental prerequisite. But as even Alexander Hamilton, an advocate of a strong executive, said in *Federalist 75*, history did not warrant such an "exalted opinion of human virtue" that it would be wise for the United States to leave its relations with other nations to "the sole disposal of a magistrate created and circumstanced as would be the President of the United States."[39] The first dilemma might therefore be rephrased as "What does foreign policy do to American democracy?"[40] Former Senator Fulbright and chairman of the Senate Foreign Relations Committee was pessimistic on this question. "The American Constitution was never meant to operate in a condition of permanent warfare and crisis." The effect would be to transform the United States into a "presidential dictatorship" for it would gradually erode established constitutional procedures. Foreign policy "has become subversive of the very ends it is meant to serve."[41] Writing in 1972, Fulbright said that in protecting democracy, presidents had seized the authority to initiate war from the Congress, as well as the Senate's treaty power by the extensive use of executive agreements and by interpreting existing treaties in unwarranted ways.

One reason isolationists resisted international involvement was precisely this: the domestic effects. Becoming a major player in world politics meant big government and a shift of power from Congress to the presidency; it meant vast appropriations for a large military establishment. The resulting tax increases, isolationists feared, would stifle private enterprise. In brief, the cost of foreign policy would be freedom; the American promise would be betrayed. "An extreme sensitivity to, and consequently an obsessive fear of, the domestic effects of foreign policy has been one of the hallmarks—perhaps the hallmark—of the isolationist outlook."[42] A war, hot or cold, to preserve democracy elsewhere would result in the destruction of democracy in the United States.

Obviously, America's global involvement over four decades has yielded some of the results about which isolationists were concerned: the centralization of power in Washington, the enormous expansion of the executive branch, the growth of presidential power, the rise of a large military establishment and military-industrial complex, the violations of civil liberties during the infamous McCarthy period of the 1950s, the distortions of priorities as domestic needs gave way to defense concerns, and the widespread use of secrecy in the conduct of many government activities such as covert operations by the CIA. The isolationists were correct in this respect: there is a price to be paid for being a world power. The privatization of foreign policy to help the Contras is a recent, very disturbing, and blatant example.

It does demonstrate the danger that in fighting an undemocratic adversary a democracy may become like its enemy. In Nicaragua, the Reagan administration stated that its aim was to bring about democracy—apparently by ignoring democratic processes at home. This potential cost of the attrition of the prescribed constitutional methods for making policy, even covert operations, is the inherent possibility that worried Senator Fulbright.

The isolationists were wrong, however, on one fundamental point, namely, that the United States could survive as a democratic state in a world of hostile antidemocratic states. Nazi Germany and the Soviet Union were both totalitarian states that represented a threat to the balance of power and democratic values. The survival of democratic values in the United States depends on their survival in other nations as well, especially in Western Europe. That is why when France and Britain were threatened twice by Germany, the United States came to their assistance and made a commitment to Western Europe's defense after World War II. Moreover, the fact remains that despite occasional associations with authoritarian regimes, the basic thrust of U.S. foreign policy since World War II has been the support and promotion of democratic values.

Similarly, the expansion of presidential-bureaucratic power has not seriously jeopardized America's democratic liberties or the executive–legislative balance. The institutional balance seems very much alive and well and it cannot seriously be argued that the United States is a less free society today than it was before its deep involvement in world affairs. Whatever infringements there have been from time to time on civil liberties during wartime or during the Cold War, the American people have obviously accepted the trade-off between tolerating some violations of American democratic norms at home and the defense of the United States against antidemocratic threats from abroad. In wartime, democracies usually abandon democracy temporarily. Power is basically concentrated in the executive and everything is subordinated to the conduct of the war and the achievement of victory. Freedom of speech or assembly, the right to strike, and other normally accepted rights may be constrained or set aside temporarily. Such "democratic Caesarism" ends when the last shot has been fired. What is, therefore, remarkable about the lengthy Cold War is that despite the growth of executive power and the need for a strong presidency to conduct U.S. policy, Americans enjoy more freedoms today than ever before. As an increasing number of citizens have involved themselves on various foreign policy issues, including such issues as nuclear weapons, which had previously been left to the experts, the United States has indeed become more of a "participatory democracy" than before. The insistence that this country support human rights abroad as one of its objectives has also grown stronger. All in all, the United States has been able to flourish as a democratic society while simultaneously concentrating power in the executive, despite the historical fear of such power; power has been held accountable. The very fact that in the 200th year of the Constitution, congressional hearings were publicly exposing Irangate suggests that however embarassing all this was, U.S. democracy remained alert and vital.

The issue of presidential power is directly related to the third dilemma, the character of the policy process: elite policy making versus broad democratic participation. At the beginning of the Cold War, George Kennan, a respected foreign service officer and a specialist in Soviet affairs who provided the rationale for America's postwar containment policy, reviewed the first fifty years of U.S. foreign policy in this century and concluded:

> A good deal of our trouble seems to have stemmed from the extent to which the executive has felt itself beholden to short-term trends of public opinion in the country and from what we might call the erratic and subjective nature of public reaction to foreign policy questions. . . .
>
> . . . I firmly believe that we could make much more effective use of the principle of professionalism in the conduct of foreign policy. . . . However, I am quite prepared to recognize that this runs counter to strong prejudices and preconceptions in sections of our public mind, particularly in Congress and the press, and that for this reason we are probably condemned to continue relying almost exclusively on what we might call "diplomacy by dilettantism."[43]

This plea for leaving foreign policy to an elite small group of officials and experts because public opinion and the Congress could not be trusted was not novel. The conduct of foreign policy has traditionally been the province of the executive, absolute kings and their ministers before the rise of democracy, and prime ministers and presidents responsible to elected legislatures after. But even in Britain, a democracy, the House of Commons did not become continuously and closely involved in foreign affairs until after the enormous casualties suffered by that island-nation during World War I. After that disaster, foreign and military policy experts were no longer trusted to be always wise enough or to care enough to avoid war. Representative legislative bodies claimed that foreign, like domestic, policies must be publicly debated and approved. The public was to be informed and participate in making policy. Persons professionally engaged in the conduct of international politics were no longer to do so by themselves.

Consistent with the tradition of executive primacy in foreign policy making, presidents have long claimed to be the spokesmen for the national interest. They are the only nationally elected officials and therefore feel they have a popular mandate. The Constitution grants them the authority as the nation's leading foreign policy official; they are the country's chief diplomat and commander in chief. And as the single figure in the U.S. government to whom the public in an increasingly dangerous and changeable world looks for leadership and solutions—indeed, public expectations are probably too great to be fulfilled—presidents not unnaturally believe that they should be given wide latitude to conduct foreign policy as they, advised by experts, see fit.

On the whole, even Congress has recognized the need for presidential leadership, but it does insist on being informed and consulted on foreign policy issues. Given institutional differences, which are strengthened by conflicting partisan views, executive–legislative cooperation has been difficult and frequently frustrating. Yet, obviously, democratic norms give the Congress that right to participate. The Contra issue vividly demonstrates, however, what may happen if the two branches of government disagree and the executive is unwilling to live with the resulting stalemate.

The conservative Reagan administration, with its strong Cold War outlook, was obviously absolutely convinced that Nicaragua was part of the superpower rivalry and that the Sandinistas represented a "Soviet beachhead" on the mainland of the Western Hemisphere. Therefore, the Congress, under the leadership of a liberal Democratic House, was totally wrong when it banned military assistance to the Contras. Whether that mistake was due to incompetence, shortsightedness, Democratic control, or any combination of these, the conclusion the administration drew was that Congress had to be cut out of the decision-making process because it was a nuisance and impediment. Those in the executive branch who were competent to judge what U.S. interests were and how to advance them had therefore to continue the policy, regardless of what Congress wanted. Congress did not seem to know what it wanted, they argued. It changed its mind six times in five years, first favoring aid, then opposing it, and finally favoring it again. Only in one year did Congress absolutely ban assistance to the Contras, for even in 1985 it voted for humanitarian aid. That appropriation came as the Sandinista leader slapped Congress in the face after it had banned assistance for the Contras by immediately flying to Moscow to consolidate Nicaragua's links with the Soviet bloc. Thus, Congress half changed its mind, voted funds for the Contras, but insisted that they could not be used to buy arms. In short, this vote represented not a clear act of legislative conviction, but indecision and embarrassment.

In these circumstances, the president considered it his duty to hold the Contras' "body and soul together" until the Congress changed its mind once more. The long-term security interests of the United States demanded no less. In the meantime, as Lt. Col. North repeatedly insisted during his testimony from July 6 to 14, 1987, the president and the NSC had the *right* to withhold information from the Congress, deceive it and lie to it repeatedly, and to destroy records and alter documents as the whole covert operation started to unravel. In fighting the "good fight," North represented the attitude of the NSC well when he characterized the Contra affair as a conflict between good and evil, between a small band of patriots and hostile forces in Washington as well as Moscow.[44] Without remorse or any sense of guilt, he defiantly stated that he and his colleagues had acted as they had only because Congress seemed blind to the threat; although they felt beleaguered, they had carried on against what should have been a readily visible security threat to everybody. North indicted Congress. Doubting that Congress would conclude it had been wrong in restricting the executive or that it would commend the executive for sustaining the Contras, he said

> Plain and simple, the Congress is to blame because of the fickle, vacillating, unpredictable, on-again-off-again policy toward the Nicaraguan democratic resistance. . . . The Congress of the United States allowed the executive to encourage them to do battle and then abandoned them. . . . When the executive branch did everything possible, within the law, to prevent them from being wiped out by Moscow's surrogates in Havana, in Managua, you then had this investigation to blame the problem on the executive branch.[45]

Even if this affair was a rather extreme case, the product of a group of men who believed that the ends justified the means, who did not for a moment entertain the thought that they might be wrong, that the conflict with Congress over the Contras represented a legitimate expression of differences of opinions, the fact remains that since 1940 presidents have repeatedly sought to bypass Congress with executive agreements. They have acted by not informing it at all, telling it only part of the story, or mobilizing the Congress by exaggerating the threat the United States faced and/or going over Congress' head directly to the people. If Congress is part of the solution—indeed, must be part of the solution—it has also been a major part of the problem from the Versailles peace treaty to SALT II.

As we saw earlier, one major reason for the presidential growth of power has been the obstructionist character of Congress on foreign policy issues. It was in recognition of this that Congress until Vietnam was willing to accept a subordinate role in foreign affairs. But Vietnam's destruction of the Cold War consensus, conflicts over what the U.S. role in the world should be, a continued public cautiousness, if not unpredictability, about foreign commitments have led Congress to once more reassert itself. On the whole, Congress represents caution and skepticism about commitments, especially ones that involve risks and costs, while the presidency, because of its responsibility, tends to be more activist and willing to define U.S. security interests broadly. Congress has therefore tried to restrict the president's freedom of maneuver, from the War Powers Act to specific issues such as the Boland amendment or attempts to block funds for arms exceeding SALT II limits. On occasions, it even seeks to upstage the president and make policy, as in 1987, when House Speaker Jim Wright intervened between the administration and the Sandinistas and, acting as secretary of state, sought to mediate between them. Indeed, he and the secretary later made their own peace pact after the furor died down. Congress is also concerned with executive evasion, and when it catches the executive doing so, it tries to micromanage, in turn leading the presidency to try all the harder to evade legislative restraints. The result is conflict and, on occasion, paralysis—unless the president decides to ignore congressional opinion, as President Reagan decided to do, go ahead with his policy, and lie to the Congress. But deception hardly provides a sound basis for policy; nor does lack of public support.

Thus, finally, we return to the second dilemma, process versus output, which as should be clear by now, is intimately linked to the third dilemma. More specifically, the issue is whether democratic policy making yields the "right" decisions on crucial issues. Another way of phrasing this is by reversing our initial question—What does foreign policy do to democracy?—to What does democracy do to foreign policy? It is the lack of confidence that broad popular participation will produce the correct policies required to deal with particularly troublesome issues that provides the rationale for elite decision making. Since the public remains largely uninformed on most foreign policy issues despite television and newspaper coverage, and since most of these issues are not really of major concern to most citizens, the impact of democratic participation in foreign policy making has generally been regarded negatively. The public has been criticized for relaxing its vigilance, ignoring rising threats, and being unwilling to spend the funds necessary to ensure the nation's defense. Therefore, while the public may be rational in its response to foreign policy events retrospectively and over the long run, it is not a good guide for action in the shorter run. While in wartime public fervor tends to be aroused and engages in ideological-military crusades, this jeopardizes the emergence of a stable postwar balance. Furthermore, once peace has been reestablished, the public prefers to focus its energy and resources on domestic issues, thereby endangering the preservation of the balance of power against its adversaries.

In a classic formulation of the resulting democratic dilemma, Walter Lippmann, journalist, philosopher, and man of affairs, said many years ago that "The rule to which there are few exceptions . . . is that at the critical junctures, when the stakes are high, the prevailing mass opinion will impose what amounts to a veto upon changing the course on which the government is at the time proceeding. Prepare for war in time of peace? No. It is bad to raise taxes, to unbalance the budget, to take men away from their schools or their jobs, to provoke the enemy." The people, Lippmann continued "have compelled the governments, which usually knew what would have been wiser, or was necessary, or was more expedient, to be too late with too little, or too long with too much."[46]

One does not have to believe that this statement is necessarily true or at least always true to recognize that tensions may arise between democracy and its international role. Britain and France were two of the great powers in Europe in the interwar period (1919–39). After 1933, when Adolf Hitler assumed power in Germany, and the Nazi leader began to undermine the status quo as he built up his military machine, it was in Britain and France's self-interest to preserve the balance of power. But the two Western democracies failed in this task and war resulted because public opinion in the 1930s preferred to appease Germany in the hope of avoiding war rather than rearm and take a firm stand against it. British leaders were particularly reluctant to tell the public what needed to be done. A conservative party prime minister refused to make rearmament an issue in the mid-1930s because he thought he would lose the election; he won the election but Britain remained unprepared. The policy of appeasement was clearly popular. A later conservative prime minister was wildly cheered in the House of Commons when he announced that he would meet Adolf Hitler, Germany's leader, to settle differences over Czechoslovakia; he achieved this by giving in completely to Hitler's demands. Peace was preserved and the nation felt relieved. Not until Hitler attacked Poland in 1939 did the two Western democracies make a stand; but from 1933, when Hitler gained power, to 1939, they did not, making war unavoidable. Both failed. Worse, France was defeated in 1940 and Britain was saved from defeat by the English Channel, the bravery of its own people, and especially its ability to fall back on the United States to save it from defeat and help it achieve victory. That makes the issue of American democracy's performance all the more critical. Democracy can, as in the 1930s, fail to make the "right" decisions, and it can be fatal.

During the Cold War, we noted the collapse of bipartisanship on the China issue. Had the United States recognized The People's Republic when it was established and had American diplomats been present in China when the Korean War broke out in 1950, would not U.S. intelligence on Chinese concerns about the U.S. advance to China's border have been received with more credibility in Washington? And might diplomatic arrangements not have been worked out or the advance halted short of China's frontier, thus avoiding China's intervention with the bitter consequences it had on Sino–American relations for twenty years? Even more pertinently, had the United States been represented in Beijing, China's capital, would the United States not have been dissuaded from its belief that North Vietnam was a Chinese puppet and that a North Vietnamese victory would therefore be damaging to U.S. interests since it meant an increase in the power of China, then still seen as an enemy and a member of the Sino–Soviet bloc? It was these beliefs that led to the intervention in Vietnam's civil war, a war that ended in the damaging collapse of the consensus underlying the nation's postwar foreign policy.

The rational or right policy toward Communist China after Nationalist China's collapse was never in doubt. What was in doubt was the rationality of public opinion and the Congress on the issue of recognition. After the Democrats' accusations of being "soft on communism" and "appeasement" following Nationalist China's demise, it is not surprising that President Johnson did not want to be accused of "having lost" Indochina. Johnson did not want to jeopardize his domestic program and his ability to conduct foreign policy, as Truman's had been after the vicious attacks on him for "having lost" China. No president, not even a conservative Republican like Eisenhower, wanted to be attacked by the anticommunist right. None therefore disengaged from Vietnam. Each did just enough by sending economic aid, military assistance, and finally, military advisers to prevent South Vietnam's collapse and avoid domestic attacks. President Johnson, faced with an imminent South Vietnamese defeat, was not so lucky. He could not procrastinate as had his predecessor, deferring any final decision on what to do if the crunch came. He had to make a decision and he followed his predecessors by escalating U.S. commitment and involvement. He paid dearly for that intervention.

This Asian pattern of grievous errors in policy, admittedly, must be set against the European pattern of correct decisions. The Truman Doctrine, the Marshall Plan, the Berlin Airlift, and the North Atlantic Treaty Organization were among a series of imaginative and daring policies adopted by the United States, a novice in international politics, to resurrect Western Europe after World War II. These created a framework of security for all the Western democracies that still stands over forty years after the end of that conflict. Still, the undeclared war with China, after its intervention in Korea, remains a serious and avoidable blunder. After the late 1950s the growing Sino–Soviet schism was becoming quite clear, but until 1972 the United States failed to exploit this schism for its own security benefits. A rational great power confronts only its primary enemy. It does not get bogged down fighting secondary enemies in areas of secondary importance, wasting its resources. It husbands these to defend areas of vital importance against its principal adversary. The United States was unable to follow these simple but cardinal rules in its conduct of foreign policy. It is worth repeating for the sake of emphasis that when he decided to play "divide and rule" and attract China into strategic cooperation against the Soviet Union, President Nixon did not first consult his vice president or cabinet, let alone Congress. He kept his decision secret to prevent leaks to the news media, sent his NSA to China to open relations with it and prepare for a presidential visit, and confronted the nation with a fait accompli.

Thus the question raised by Charles Krauthammer and, indeed, by Merlo Pusey earlier in our discussion of President Roosevelt's policy during 1940–41, remains: Can a democracy, if it is a great power, deal responsibly with the threats and problems it confronts? Above all, can it mobilize the will to carry on over a long period of time when it is at peace? There is really only one answer in a democracy: if a particular course of action, like helping the Contras, is unacceptable to the Congress, a president has no choice but to take his case directly to the public. If he cannot persuade the Congress or the public, the policy cannot be pursued. Thus if Congress forbids military aid to the Contras, that is the law. It is not a license to substitute the president's will for the popular will, however strong the temptation to act covertly and illegally. If the result turns out to be an error, that remains one of the inescapable risks of democratic government. Although in some instances it is very clear what should be done, as in the case of helping Britain in 1940–41 or dealing with China after 1949, in most cases the correct policy is not clear at all. We tend to know only afterward. Public opinion certainly judges afterward, rewarding or punishing its political leaders. In a democracy, in any case, established and legitimate democratic policy making procedures cannot be ignored in the search for the "right" policy. Totalitarian states do that; self-appointed leaders, claiming to know what the correct policies are, arrogate to themselves the right to rule. But the difference between democracy and totalitarianism lies precisely in the method of decision making. Just as economic systems, seeking to provide certain goods and services to satisfy human wants and needs, are distinguishable from one another by *how* economic decisions are made, political systems are distinguishable by how public policies are made and justified. Democratic theory rejects the concept of the right answer or that a few know what is best for the country. It suggests instead that in a free society there may be many versions of the right answers on any issue. Confrontation and debate before the public ought to decide which is the best solution to a specific problem. Democracy is a method of seeking the best solution. Failure, as France and Britain demonstrated, is always an inherent possibility. The basic test of any political system is surely its ability to protect itself. The Western democracies' failure was precisely their unwillingness to pay sufficient attention and invest the necessary resources to protect themselves. Thus Congress may have been in error on the Contras, but as democracy can fail, it can, however, also correct its mistakes and change policy. Senator Warren Rudman (R-N.H.) said at the Iran–Contra hearings, "The American people have the constitutional right to be wrong." Public opinion did not favor the Contras. This was the reason, he said, Congress had vacillated on Contra support.[47] Therefore, we return to the beginning. U.S. foreign policy aims to protect the security of a democratic United States. But to quote Congressman Lee Hamilton from the same hearing: "I cannot agree that the end has justified these means . . . that the threat in Central America was so great that we had to do something, even if it meant disregarding constitutional processes, deceiving the Congress and the American people. The means employed were a profound threat to the democratic process. We've weakened our country, not strengthened it."[48]

NOTES

1. Ray Stannard Baker, quoted by Cecil V. Cabb, Jr., *Bipartisan Foreign Policy* (New York: Row, Peterson and Company, 1957), p. 9.
2. Robert A. Divine, *The Reluctant Belligerent* (New York: John Wiley & Sons, 1965): and Diriner, *Roosevelt and World War II* (Baltimore: Penguin Books, 1969).
3. Merlo J. Pusey, *The Way We Go to War* (Boston: Houghton Mifflin, 1971), p. 74.
4. Ibid., p. 75.
5. Ibid.

6. Robert A. Divine, *The Illusion of Neutrality* (Chicago: University of Chicago Press, 1962), pp. 280–81.
7. Ernest A. Gross, "What Is a Bipartisan Foreign Policy?" *Department of State Bulletin* (October 3, 1949), pp. 504–5.
8. Godfrey Hodgson, "The Establishment," *Foreign Policy,* Spring 1973, pp. 3–40; and I. M. Destler, Leslie Gells, and Anthony Lake, *Our Own Worst Enemy* (New York: Simon & Schuster, 1984), pp. 102–6.
9. Walter Isaacson and Gran Thomas, *The Wise Men* (New York: Simon & Schuster, 1986) tells the story of six of these men: Harriman, Lovett, Acheson, McCloy, Kennan, and Bohlen.
10. Hodgson, "The Establishment," p. 13.
11. For example, Daniel S. Cheever and Field H. Haviland, Jr., *American Foreign Policy and the Separation of Powers* (Cambridge, Mass.: Harvard University Press, 1952); and James M. Burns, *Congress on Trial* (New York: Harper & Row, 1949).
12. See Foster Rhea Dulles, *American Foreign Policy Toward Communist China* (New York: Thomas Y. Crowell, 1972); John W. Spanier, *The Truman–MacArthur Controversy and the Korean War,* rev. ed. (New York: W. W. Norton, 1967); and Leslie H. Gelb and Richard K. Betts, *The Irony of Vietnam* (Washington, D.C.: The Brookings Institution, 1979).
13. Daniel Ellsberg, *Papers on the War* (New York: Simon & Schuster, 1972), pp. 101–2.
14. Gelb and Betts, *The Irony of Vietnam,* p. 25.
15. Laurence I. Radway, "Electoral Pressures on American Foreign Policy," prepared for delivery to the International Studies Association convention, Los Angeles, March 21, 1980, p. 6.
16. Gelb and Betts, *The Irony of Vietnam,* p. 68.
17. James R. Schlesinger, "The Eagle and the Bear," *Foreign Affairs,* Summer 1985, p. 957.
18. Hodgson, "The Establishment," p. 15.
19. Destler et al., *Worst Enemy,* pp. 110–26. For a parallel fragmentation of foreign policy magazines, see Ousa Sananikone, "The World of Journals," *The Washington Quarterly,* Spring 1988, pp. 209–14.
20. See, for example, "Democrats in Exile Count the Days," *New York Times,* June 4, 1987.
21. Statement printed in Brookings Institution books describing its purposes.
22. Ole R. Holsti and James N. Rosenau, *American Leadership in World Affairs* (Boston: Allen & Unwin, 1984), especially pp. 130–32, for a table summarizing the three foreign policy belief systems: Cold War internationalism, Post-Cold War internationalism, and semiisolationism. Also see update of Holsti and Rosenau, "Consensus Lost. Consensus Regained?: Foreign Policy Belief of American Leaders, 1976–1980," in *International Studies Quarterly,* December 1986, pp. 375–409.
23. See Michael Mandelbaum and William Schneider, "The New Internationalisms"; and Schneider, "Conservatism, Not Interventionism: Trends in Foreign Policy Opinion, 1974–1982"; and " 'Rambo' and Reality: Having It Both Ways" in *Eagle Entangled* (New York: Longman, 1979), *Eagle Defiant,* and *Eagle Resurgent?* (Boston: Little, Brown, 1983 and 1987), eds. Kenneth A. Oye, Robert J. Lieber and Donald Rothchild, pp. 34–88, 33–64 and 41–72, respectively.

24. Destler et al., *Worst Enemy,* p. 126.

25. Daniel S. Cheever and H. Field Haviland, *American Foreign Policy and the Separation of Powers* (Cambridge, Mass.: Harvard University Press, 1952), pp. 56–96.

26. Divine, *The Reluctant Belligeront,* p. 49.

27. William L. Langerand and S. Everett Gleason, *The Undeclared War* (New York: Harper & Row, 1953), p. 574.

28. Divine, *The Reluctant Belligeront,* p. 131.

29. John R. Silber, "Presidential Handcuffs," *The New Republic,* February 19, 1985, pp. 14–16.

30. Charles Krauthammer, "Divided Superpower," *The New Republic,* December 22, 1986, p. 16.

31. Based on the Tower Commission Report, *New York Times,* February 27, 1987; Doyle McManus, "Dateline Washington: Gipperdämmerung," *Foreign Policy,* Spring 1987, pp. 156–72; Robert Parry and Brian Barger, "Reagan's Shadow CIA," *The New Republic,* November 24, 1986, pp. 23–27; the daily *New York Times* throughout the congressional hearings of Irangate, the final congressional committee's report, *The Iran–Contra Affair* (Washington, D.C.,: U.S. Government Printing Office, 1987); Robert Woodward, *Veil* (New York: Simon & Schuster, 1987); and Jane Mayer and Doyle McManus, *Landslide* (Boston: Houghton Mifflin, 1988).

32. Peter Maas, "Oliver North's Strange Recruits," *New York Times Magazine,* January 18, 1987, p. 20 ff.

33. *New York Times,* March 2, 1987.

34. It was later revealed that the Saudis had contributed billions of dollars since the early 1970s to governments and movements to further anti-Marxist, Western interests, often at the suggestion of the United States, although this was also clearly in the Saudi interest. *New York Times,* June 21, 1987. The newspaper's report, titled "Prop for U.S. Policy: Secret Saudi Funds," however, omitted Saudi policies contrary to U.S. interests such as support for the Palestinian Liberation Organization, isolating Egypt in the Arab world after its peace agreement with Israel, and the 1973 oil embargo against the United States.

35. *New York Times,* June 6, 1987.

36. *New York Times,* July 7, 1987; Woodward, *Veil,* p. 467.

37. Ibid., June 28, 1987.

38. McManus, "Dateline Washington," p. 172.

39. Quoted by J. William Fulbright, *The Crippled Giant* (New York: Vintage Books, 1972), p. 216.

40. Charles Krauthammer, "The Price of Power," *The New Republic,* pp. 83–85.

41. Fulbright, *Crippled Giant,* pp. 178, 193, 208.

42. Robert W. Tucker, *A New Isolationism* (New York: Universe Books, 1972), p. 35.

43. George Kennan, *American Diplomacy 1900–1950* (Chicago: University of Chicago Press, 1951), pp. 93–94.

44. *New York Times,* July 9, 1987.

45. Ibid., July 10, 1987.

46. Walter Lippmann, *The Public Philosophy* (Boston: Little, Brown, 1955), pp. 19–20.

47. *New York Times,* July 14, 1987.

48. Ibid., July 15, 1987.

Chapter Four

Congress: How Silent a Partner?

THE FIRST BRANCH OF GOVERNMENT

The president is the major actor not only in foreign policy but in domestic policy as well. But the intentions of the Founders of the American republic had not envisaged this. The legislative branch is the first one discussed in the Constitution, and this was not accidental.[1] The type of government planned by the Founders was one of legislative dominance. The Constitution gives the Congress a large number of specifically enumerated powers and a wide-ranging grant of "implied powers." In contrast, as noted earlier, the president has constitutionally been given only three specific powers: (1) the position as commander in chief of the armed forces and as the principal officer in each of the executive departments; (2) the power to negotiate treaties and to appoint ambassadors, in each case with the advice and consent of the Senate; and (3) the power to make executive appointments during periods when the Senate is in recess.

Two of the three powers specifically granted to the president deal with questions of foreign policy, but this hardly is evidence that the Founders expected the executive branch to dominate policy making in this arena. George Washington's farewell address to the nation warned against the country becoming involved in *entangling alliances,* and the Founders generally expected the president to execute the laws of the country as passed by the Congress in domestic policy. The scope of foreign policy making was viewed as quite limited—and not terribly important to a new nation thousands of miles away from the European powers. Foreign policy was simply too inconsequential to take up much of the time of the Congress, the first branch of government. In the unlikely event of armed conflict, however, the legislature retained the sole power to declare war on foreign countries.

Two centuries later, however, presidential preeminence in foreign policy was an established fact. The impetus of decision making had shifted dramatically, and many members of the Congress after Vietnam sought to reclaim their historical role as at least a coequal policy maker on foreign questions. The arguments raised in this debate over which branch should be most powerful have been reminiscent of those which marked the original debate over the Constitution. The Founders selected a president rather than a king because they did not want one individual to hold excessive and unchecked power. The powerful president, so highly regarded when people respected the men occupying the office, became in the 1960s and 1970s the "imperial presidency,"[2] an American king. Congress, in contrast, was the "voice of the people," the men and women directly elected by the mass public. As such, a representative government should place great emphasis on reflecting public opinion in policy making.[3]

A president, sitting in Washington, might become too isolated from public opinion and carry out policies which do not have widespread support. The Congress, on the other hand, might prove to be too parochial: members of the House of Representatives are elected from Legislative districts and thus have little incentive to consider the great issues of international politics. There are two senators representing each state and, initially, senators were chosen by state legislatures rather than by popular vote. The Senate possesses more formal foreign policy powers than the House because the Founders feared what a political body so closely linked to mass opinions might do. The House, with its smaller districts and elections held every two years, would tailor its policies to the popular sentiment of the moment. The Senate, chosen for six-year terms and supposedly the more elite body, would be more concerned with the long-term consequences of its decisions. For it is, or at least calls itself, the "world's greatest deliberative body."

How, then, should policy be made? Should it follow the will of the public, or are the masses too uninformed and unconcerned to be trusted? What differences are there between foreign and domestic policy formation? These are the large issues which concern us in this and succeeding chapters. Furthermore, since the Congress has taken many steps to reassert its power in foreign policy, what is the actual balance between legislative and executive initiatives on foreign policy? Can a bicameral legislature with 535 members formulate any sort of policy? If not, what is the most appropriate role for the legislature to play?

The constitutional theories of legislative supremacy, or at least equal sharing of decision making by the two branches, are discussed more these days in the literature on Congress than on foreign policy making. Indeed, the dominant model of foreign policy decision making is that of the concentric circles.[4] In these circles (see Figure 1–1), the central decision making locus on foreign policy is the president and his key advisors. In the second circle are the bureaucracies in the major foreign policy agencies and the armed services, the second-rank and less influential foreign policy departments, presidential advisers, and cabinet members whose primary responsibility is in the domestic sphere but who may be consulted on foreign policy questions, and scientists. The innermost circle is composed of a select few members of the administration; the outer circles have successively more members and correspondingly less impact on foreign policy decisions. We have placed Congress in the third circle. The fourth, outer circle comprises public opinion, and the media, political parties, local activists, and interest groups.

Foreign policy decision making has been viewed, as represented in the concentric circles, as basically hierarchical. There is one president and then there is everyone else. Occasionally, as the situation warrants, an adviser might move into the first circle from the second. But the norm is that the president, as the only nationally elected politician, chooses whomever he wishes to occupy the innermost circle with him. The outer circles are expected to be at the beck and call of those in the inner circle, thus establishing the hierarchy. The difference is highlighted by a story involving President Johnson and Senator Frank Church, a ranking Democrat and future chairman of the Senate Foreign Relations Committee, at a White House reception. Johnson queried the senator, an early opponent of the Vietnam War, about where he was getting his information on the war effort. Church replied that his information came from the columns of the noted journalist Walter Lippmann. The president reportedly replied, "Well, the next time you want a dam in Idaho, ask Walter Lippmann for it."

The concentric circles analogy stands in sharp contrast to the decision-making process in domestic policies. Here lines of authority cut across the national, state, and local levels and across the executive, legislative, and judicial branches as well. The stakes are generally perceived as less critical and policies are, at least in principle, more easily reversible. The actions taken are viewed as the results of bargaining and coalition building by actors who are intensely interested in their own priorities and often could not care less about other issues. Thus a legislator from the Midwest will fight long and hard for agriculture subsidies to wheat farmers and work with representatives of farmers' groups and the Department of Agriculture to ensure that their programs are protected. These well-structured relationships among legislators, bureaucrats, and interest groups have been called *policy subsystems*[5] and, somewhat less admiringly, *cozy triangles.*[6] The dilemma that the agriculture subsystem has to face is that the farm bloc in the legislature is not large enough to provide a voting majority on the floor of either the House or the Senate to get its programs enacted. Thus, it is forced into seeking out votes from "uninterested" members[7]—such as legislators from New York City or Cleveland, who may want public housing projects or government-backed loans to their cities to prevent imminent bankruptcy. Intermestic policies are much like domestic policies, at least with respect to decision-making patterns. Indeed, the number of actors may be greater on some intermestic policies because the decisions involved affect more than a single nation. This is particularly true on energy politics as well as on most trade issues.

Legislators thus trade votes and, ideally, interests are not in direct conflict, so that most major groups can get what they want from the Congress. When interests do conflict, a group that feels very intensely about its position can often block the passage of a bill adverse to its position. The political processes of domestic politics hardly guarantee good policies. Instead, they are designed to ensure that each important group gets heard before a decision is reached.[8] The power of an interest lies in how often it can get its way and how strong its ties are to legislators and bureaucrats who formulate and administer the policies which affect the routines of the interest. Bargaining takes place among equals, although as George Orwell has reminded us, some are more equal than others. But every member of Congress, no matter how much power or seniority he or she might have, still has to face the electorate every two or six years. Once elected, or reelected, each has the same mandate as every other.

The concentric circles, then, indicate the amount of centralization or hierarchy in decision making on foreign policy. Restriction of foreign policy initiatives to the innermost circle, the president and his closest advisers, fits the hierarchical model nicely and best describes crisis decision making (Chapter 7). On the other hand, congressional action on foreign policy necessarily includes more actors, and since the legislature is itself not hierarchically structured, the potential for widespread participation by legislators and their supporting and opposing constituents (interest groups, political parties, public opinion, and the media) is enhanced. But what does this do to the quality of decisions made on foreign policy?

We note that in contrast to the executive branch, congressional decision making is parochial rather than national or global in focus, with members rarely putting their districts' concerns out of mind; indeed, because members rely so heavily on constituency contacts rather than strong national parties for reelection, this local focus may be inevitable in the Congress. Second, the executive branch can respond quickly to changing events; the legislature is a "deliberative" body (or, as critics might have it, an obstructionist one which succeeds by employing delaying tactics). Third, the Congress is only intermittently interested in foreign policy, does not have the staff expertise on international questions that the administration does, has had weak foreign policy committees in the House of Representatives, and has not developed the resource base in information that the executive branch has on foreign policy issues. We shall examine each of these issues. But we first turn to a discussion of perhaps the most important occurrence of recent years: the increased activism of Congress on international issues.

CONGRESS AND FOREIGN POLICY: REVIVAL FIRES

The Congress has become more involved in foreign policy in recent years. The most celebrated action it has taken, as noted earlier, is the War Powers Act. Other actions have also been largely directed toward amending, or restraining, executive initiatives. Congress has not taken upon itself the problem of formulating alternative policies. That is, as we shall see shortly, simply impractical. But the legislature can be an effective check on the executive branch. In 1974, for example, it passed what has been called the Hughes–Ryan amendment, after Senator Harold Hughes (D-Iowa) and Representative Leo Ryan (D-Calif.), which significantly restrained the president's leeway to use the Central Intelligence Agency as he wished.[9] The bill forbade the CIA to use public funds for foreign operations, excluding the gathering of intelligence, unless the president decides that the activity is important to the national security. Even in that event, the chief executive was required at one time to report such actions to as many as *eight* committees in the House and the Senate. This was finally limited to two (House and Senate Intelligence) in 1980. Furthermore, the Case–Zablocki Act of 1972, named after Senator Clifford Case (R-N.J.) and Representative Clement Zablocki (D-Wis.), established new requirements for the reporting of executive agreements to the Congress. A 1974 amendment sponsored by Senator Gaylord Nelson (D-Wis.) and Representative Jonathan Bingham (D-N.Y.) established procedures for reporting arms sales to the Congress and provided for a legislative veto over some sales. Although this legislation had a large loophole (only sales of over $5,000 had to be reported, so that multiple sales of $4,999.99 could go undetected) and there were relatively few instances of administration proposals actually being defeated, the impact of the amendment should not be underestimated. Despite an unsuccessful effort to prevent the sale of jet fighters in 1978 to Egypt and Saudi Arabia by leading Jewish groups and many members of Congress, arms sales to Turkey, Chile, Argentina, Libya, Iraq, and other nations were either defeated or stalled in committee and not pressed further by the administration. In some cases, such as Libya and Iraq, the issue was not strictly over military sales but about the purchase of aircraft that had potential military applications. In several cases, including Turkish aid, the increased congressional role threatened to disrupt the NATO alliance, while in others, such as the cutback of aid to Nicaragua in 1980 following the revolution in that country, the legislative actions ran directly contrary to the Carter administration's announced foreign policy toward developing nations.

Other legislative initiatives include an amendment, sponsored by Representative Thomas Harkin (D-Iowa) in 1975, which established criteria for determining aid eligibility based on a nation's human rights record. Except in a few cases (mostly in Latin America), the Congress did not exercise the veto power it granted itself over executive decisions that could waive this provision. In 1973, Senator Henry Jackson (D-Wash.) and Representative Charles Vanik (D-Ohio) shepherded through the Congress an amendment that linked favorable trade relations with the Soviet Union to more liberal emigration procedures by that country, particularly for Jewish dissidents. Many of these actions occurred during the Nixon administration and constituted a congressional assault on the president's refusal to be forthcoming on both foreign and domestic questions with the Democrats who controlled the Congress. Nixon strongly believed in the command style of decision making and was also much more interested in foreign policy than domestic issues.

The foreign policy clashes thus were part of a pattern of poor legislative–executive relations that marked his administration. But the roots of the congressional resurgence and assertiveness go deeper—to Vietnam and a reluctance to have the United States too widely committed throughout the world and especially to become involved in wars that might not be winnable (Angola in 1976) or in countries where the leadership may have been only marginally more popular than that in Vietnam. The cry was "No more Vietnams."

While the examples point to attempts by Congress to regain control over foreign policy and indicate that the president may well face strong constraints (as demonstrated especially by the two very close Senate votes on the Panama Canal treaties in April 1978), the greatest challenge to presidential preeminence on foreign policy occurred in 1979 on the second Strategic Arms Limitation Treaty or SALT II (see Chapter 8 for a detailed analysis). The second SALT treaty was favorably viewed by the Senate Foreign Relations Committee, but faced considerable opposition from the Senate Armed Services Committee, a much more hawkish group of legislators. Jackson, a senior member of Armed Services who had been offered the position of secretary of defense in the Nixon administration, joined several conservative senators from both parties in opposing the treaty. Some moderate Republicans, including ranking minority member of Foreign Relations, Jacob Javits, supported the treaty, and press reports variously indicated that the treaty would either pass with several votes to spare or be soundly defeated. The administration's political problems were compounded by the decision of then-Minority Leader Howard Baker to oppose SALT II. Baker had been a key, if not decisive, backer of the Panama Canal treaties, maintaining the tradition of bipartisanship in foreign policy that dated back to at least the administration of Franklin D. Roosevelt. But in 1979 Baker specifically argued that it was time to reassess the wisdom of restraining partisan criticism of presidential foreign policy decisions. After Baker announced his position, press estimates of vote counts in the Senate tilted heavily toward defeat of SALT II. The minority leader may not have made his decision based on the desirability of bipartisanship in foreign policy; Baker was on the verge of announcing his own bid for the Republican nomination for president and had been roundly criticized by GOP conservatives for supporting the Panama Canal treaties. Following the Soviet Union's invasion of Afghanistan in December 1979, President Carter asked the Senate to defer further consideration of SALT II. While it was a presidential initiative that took the treaty off the Senate calendar, there was little doubt that Carter's action was taken as much to prevent his own political embarrassment as to punish the Soviets.

The bipartisan consensus on foreign policy, which had crumbled during the Johnson administration as political conflict over Vietnam crossed party lines and deeply divided the Democrats, has not been restored. When Nixon had assumed office in 1969, the Asian war had become a "Republican war," which was widely criticized by Democrats of various political persuasions.

Splits within both parties developed over Reagan's Central American policy as well. The administration sent 55 "advisers" to El Salvador to train government troops battling Cuban-backed insurgents. Members of Congress, as well as the public, feared "another Vietnam," however, and were worried that the United States might be supporting militarily a government it could not justify supporting politically. Many members of Congress believed that the cause of the rebellion in El Salvador was not just Cuban or Soviet provocation, but poverty and a long history of political repression. Terrorism had been widespread in that country on both the left and the right and critics charged that the government cared little about stopping the rightist "death squads" that carried out political assassinations throughout the country. In late 1980, four American churchwomen, three of them Catholic nuns, were murdered, and in 1981 two other Americans serving as labor advisers were killed. It took some time for the government to begin an investigation, and the trial of the El Salvador national guard members charged in the former murders was delayed several times until 1984. An election held in 1982 replaced a right-center government with an interim government dominated in the constituent assembly by a far-right coalition. Until the election of 1984, a negotiated solution was thus impossible.

By then, however, Congress had already acted to restrict the scope of American involvement, albeit weakly. In 1981 it enacted legislation that forced the president to report every six months on the progress of land reform, the movement toward democracy, the capacity of the El Salvadoran government to control the "death squads," and compliance with "internationally recognized human rights." The press reported 5,331 civilian "death squad" casualties in 1981 and 2,630 in 1982.[10] Future U.S. aid would depend on reports of satisfactory progress.

The early opponents in Congress to Reagan's El Salvador policy were Democrats, particularly those from the party's liberal wing. In 1983, however, the president began to lose support among moderates in both parties. In May of that year the House Foreign Affairs Committee adopted a proposal to withhold half of the foreign aid granted to El Salvador until after the government prepared a plan for unconditional negotiations, created an effective judicial system, brought the accused murderers of Americans to trial, and completed land reforms. Furthermore, within ninety days of enactment of the legislation, all military aid would be suspended unless the government had begun negotiations with the opposition over participation in new elections. However, the proposed legislation provided no *automatic* cutoff in aid; Congress would have to vote anew any such restriction. The Senate Foreign Relations Committee proposed much milder restrictions on administration policy limiting the amount of aid El Salvador could receive and demanding that the United States push the government toward negotiations.

The Congress has been even more assertive on other aspects of Reagan's Latin American policy. As far back as 1977, during the Carter administration, it had suspended military assistance to Guatemala because of human rights violations. In 1983 the House Select Committee on Intelligence voted strictly along party lines to cut off covert CIA assistance to American-backed insurgents attempting to overthrow the left-wing government in Nicaragua. Overt aid had already been cut off in December 1982 by the Boland amendment, named after House Intelligence Committee chairman Edward P. Boland (D-Mass.). An Intelligence Committee report in 1983 concluded that American assistance to the insurgents was actually strengthening internal support for the Nicaraguan regime.[11] Thus, the entire House, in July, followed the Foreign Affairs Committee and voted to bar covert aid. The vote was largely on party lines, although House Democrats were more split than their Republican colleagues. To a considerable extent, the vote was viewed as a rebuke to then-National Security Adviser William P. Clark, who had not revealed details of American military maneuvers in the Caribbean to Congress.[12]

Many Democrats strongly opposed the president's policy of attempting to overthrow a government and were also anxious to rein in the Central Intelligence Agency. The Congress had last paid close attention to the CIA in the late 1970s and was fearful that the agency might become a mechanism for an administration to evade legislative scrutiny of foreign policy. However, Democrats were also concerned that the president might charge them with being "soft on communism" and demand to know "who lost El Salvador or Nicaragua?"[13] Thus, the Congress went along with Reagan's decision to appoint a bipartisan commission on Central America, headed by former Secretary of State Henry Kissinger, to recommend a new course of action for that troubled area.

Reagan regained much of the initiative in foreign policy making compared to many recent presidents. Much of his success can be attributed to his large margins of victory in the 1980 and 1984 presidential elections and his high approval ratings in public opinion polls. Carter appeared to be a weak president following the Soviet invasion of Afghanistan and the taking of hostages by the Iranian government. There was considerable public support for increased defense spending and a more aggressive foreign policy, especially toward the Soviet Union. Defense spending sharply increased in 1981–82 even as many domestic programs were drastically curtailed. In 1984 Congress agreed to provide assistance to anti-Soviet rebels in Afghanistan and Cambodia. It also repealed the Clark amendment prohibiting aid to the South Africa-backed guerrillas fighting the Angolan regime, despite strong opposition from American oil companies that were still operating in Angola. The legislative branch further approved "nonmilitary" assistance to the Contras in Nicaragua and, following the 1984 reelection of moderate President Jose Napoleon Duarte against right-wing opposition, the Congress once again approved assistance to El Salvador. The invasion of Grenada in 1983 and the bombing of Libya three years later were both popular moves that confirmed to the public the president's assertion that the United States was once again "standing tall" in the eyes of the world.

However, Reagan's foreign policy proved contentious even before the Iran–Contra affair (see Chapter 3), which in late 1986 demonstrated to Congress that its worst fears about secret foreign policy making within the administration were well grounded. In contrast to previous administrations that tried to maintain some form of bipartisan spirit, if not consensus, on domestic as well as foreign policy, the Reagan team proposed a radical program of budget and tax cuts, deregulation, and an aggressive foreign policy that it hoped would create a new Republican majority in the country. Reagan's strategy, then, was less to seek congressional support for his programs than to pursue what he believed was right and what he thought the public might approve (in hindsight if not immediately). Gaining control of the nation's policy agenda from the Democratic party and from the House of Representatives in particular was paramount to this strategy of long-term political gain. The Republican victory in 1980, based much more on foreign policy concerns than most previous contests (see Chapter 5), led many in the administration to believe that they had a mandate for a new direction in policy.[14]

The sale of arms to Iran and the diversion of funds to the Contras is the prime example of administration officials pursuing policies that they believed to be correct, even when Congress had dictated otherwise. When Congress recessed for a week without acting on the president's aid for El Salvador Proposal in 1984, the administration announced that it would bypass the legislature and use a special emergency defense fund to send the aid.[15] The administration also attempted to politicize the historically nonpartisan Foreign Service, which staffs American embassies and consulates overseas. Traditionally, 75 percent of American ambassadors have been career Foreign Service officers; this figure fell to 60 percent under the Reagan administration. Some Foreign Service officers charged that there had been a "wholesale purge" of career diplomats in the Bureau of Inter-American Affairs, which handles Central American policy.[16] The administration also charged the House and Senate Intelligence committees with jeopardizing the nation's intelligence through their investigations of covert actions in the Third World.[17] It and its friends in the Congress clearly viewed foreign policy formation as a presidential preserve. Representative Richard Cheney (R-Wyo.), a key ally of the president, argued that the president has "to put up with every member of Congress with a Xerox machine and a credit card running around the world cutting deals with heads of state."[18]

The Congress has not stood still in the face of these administration initiatives toward reasserting executive prerogatives. The legislature's responses to the Reagan administration predated the Iran–Contra affair. As the economy slipped into a severe recession in 1982, public support for increased defense spending fell sharply (see Chapter 5) and Congress reacted accordingly. The unpopularity of aid to the Contras (see Chapter 5) meant that every year the president had to struggle to get his requests through the legislature, usually by the narrowest of margins. In 1986 the Congress passed a strongly protectionist trade bill that did not become law only because of a presidential veto.

The administration had actually lost much of its initiative before the revelations of the Iran–Contra affair. The Democrats recaptured control of the Senate in November 1986, shortly before the initial revelations of the secret arms deals. These events, however, weakened support for the president within the Republican party as well, as many legislators charged that the president had not told them the entire truth. Emboldened Republican members of Congress, including their Senate leader Robert Dole (who had announced his intention to seek the presidency), were much more ready to criticize the president on other foreign policy initiatives such as protecting Kuwaiti ships from Iranian fire in the Persian Gulf. The congressional mood was said to be "bold and bitter."[19]

These challenges not only reflect a willingness of Congress to assert itself more vigorously on foreign policy (during the entire eight years of the Nixon and Ford presidencies the Congress was controlled by Democrats), but also indicate that some of the traditional differences in congressional determination to participate in policy making between domestic and foreign policy are weakening. Domestic policy has traditionally involved multiple groups and interests. All of these forces are represented in the Congress, where their spokespersons argue forcefully for their positions. There is no presumption of greater administration experience and expertise on domestic policy as on foreign policy. A member of the House Education and Labor Committee, interviewed by Richard F. Fenno, Jr., in the 1960s, made a dramatic (and still valid) point:

> Hell, everyone thinks he's an expert on the questions before our committee. On education, the problem is everyone went to school. They all think that makes them experts on that. And labor matters are so polarized that everyone is committed. You take sides first and then you acquire expertise. So no one accepts anyone as impartial.[20]

In contrast, there is still the "we–they" attitude on foreign policy issues, with the United States pitted against other nations. A president's popularity increases whenever he is involved in a major foreign policy achievement or a crisis. There were virtually no critics of Carter following the Camp David accord between Israel and Egypt; a confrontation with the president over the handling of the Iranian hostage issue was viewed as unpatriotic. Indeed, Vice President Mondale charged Senator Edward Kennedy with a lack of sufficient patriotism when the Massachusetts senator told a San Francisco television station that the president should not have let the Shah back into the United States for cancer treatment when there were indications that such a decision might lead to problems at the American embassy in Teheran. As the Congress moves toward greater activism in foreign policy, we must consider its institutional capacity to take concerted action in this arena.

THE REELECTION IMPERATIVE: "AFGHANISTAN'S NOT IN MY DISTRICT"

As foreign policy making moves beyond the innermost circle to include participation by the Congress, more actors and perspectives become involved in making decisions. While Congress has become more active on foreign policy to check any potential "imperial president," greater participation has its costs as well. In particular, members of the House and Senate tend to see policy alternatives in the districts and states they represent. Representatives and senators see the stakes based on the people they represent; the views of a Midwest farmer are not necessarily similar to those of a New Yorker or a Floridian.

Unlike most parliamentary systems, the American Congress is elected by congressional districts in the House and by states in the Senate. Representatives face constant reelection battles, while senators, because of their six-year terms, are more insulated from the mass public. House members always face the electorate at the same time as the president, but they also must run in even-numbered years when the president is not on the ballot. Only one third of the Senate is elected at the same time as the president. This type of electoral system puts even stronger pressures on legislators to pay more attention to local issues than to national concerns and to define national issues in local terms. Furthermore, the United States does not have strong political parties at the national level (Chapter 5). There is no country in the world where individual legislators are as free of pressures from national political parties and where the ties to local constituencies are as strong as the United States. The electoral system and weak parties reinforce localism in American politics. And it is difficult, if not impossible, to conduct a coherent national foreign policy if decision makers do not see the stakes in the same way.

In international crises, support for the president by the public and the Congress is generally strong and lasts for a considerable amount of time. On more routine foreign policy issues, legislators from different regions with different types of constituencies will, as on domestic policy questions, see questions in terms of alternative stakes. Consumers want lower prices at the grocery stores, farmers want protection from meat and vegetables which sell at lower prices in other nations. Steel and automobile workers also fear foreign competition and clamor for protection against cheaper imported materials and products from Europe and Japan. Automobile manufacturers—who might favor higher tariffs on foreign cars—might fight any move to restrict imports of less expensive steel. Legislators from the steel-mining area of Pittsburgh and the automotive center of Detroit, although representing the same political party and both espousing the "national interest," will see the stakes in foreign policy decision making quite differently. It is unlikely that they will perceive the issues as involving primarily foreign policy, since the economic well-being of their constituents is at stake.

The electoral cycle and the weak party system explain much of the parochialism of members of the Congress, but so do the attitudes of members toward their jobs and their constituencies. Former Representative Frank Smith (D-Miss.) stated: "All members have a primary interest in being reelected. Some members have no other interest."[21] For representatives, the reelection drive begins the day after the previous contest ends. The overwhelming majority of members of Congress, and particularly the House, not only seek reelection but attain it. And, as we shall see below, they realize what former Speaker Thomas P. O'Neill said: "In all my years, I have yet to meet a politician who was elected to anything on the basis of his foreign policy."[22] In 1986 almost 99 percent of House members seeking reelection won. Fewer than one in eight won by less than 55 percent of the vote, compared to one in five in 1956. In 1988 once again almost 99 percent of incumbents on the ballot won, and this time fewer than one in eight received less than 60 percent of the vote. However, incumbent safety is not a completely new phenomenon. The *lowest* percentage of incumbents who were reelected since 1950 was 87.1 in 1974 when many Republicans were ousted in the Democratic landslide that followed the Watergate scandal.

How do members get reelected? In the past, congressional elections were referenda on the standings of the political parties. Within Congress, the parties and their leaders dominated the Congress in the late nineteenth and early twentieth centuries. In the House, the speaker appointed members of all standing committees and controlled the flow of legislation; members voted the party line in the vast majority of instances. But in 1910–1911, a revolt against the strong speakership by the progressive wing of the Republican majority and the minority Democrats stripped the leader of the House of much of his power and transferred it to committees. Since then, committee and party leaders have struggled for dominance in the Congress, with the former being victorious much of the time. The growth of subcommittee government has further weakened the congressional parties, as members are free to pursue their own policy interests without much concern for formal positions of power. When a member cannot obtain some jurisdiction over a bill in subcommittee, he or she is likely to propose an amendment to it on the House or Senate floor. This is a role that was proscribed for junior members in the past. But today independence is valued more highly than party or committee discipline. As the congressional parties have weakened, so have the parties in the mass electorate. There are more ticket splitters and fewer strong attachments among voters to political parties today than at any time in our recent history; to many, political parties are anachronisms.[23]

Taking the place of parties are single-interest groups representing a wide spectrum of issues: proabortion and antiabortion forces, antigun control activists, environmentalists, antinuclear groups, and so forth. While it is unclear what impact such forces have on actual election returns, the proliferation of these political action committees (PACS) has changed the political landscape. Although candidates for office no longer can depend on strong party organizations to turn out loyal supporters, many do not lament the passing of the parties. The increased incumbency advantage for members seeking reelection can be traced to some of the perquisites of office that members have provided for themselves: in 1954, the Congress had a staff of about 5,000 people; by 1978, the figure had risen to over 17,000, where it has stabilized. Thirty years ago, House members were limited to five members on their personal staffs; senators were allowed six. These figures are very generous by comparison to almost any other legislative body in the world. In Britain, for example, all but the most senior members of the majority party have their correspondence handled by a typing pool. The contemporary House, however, allows members to hire up to twenty-two personal staff members at a cost to the public of about $370,000 for each representative. Senators' staffs are based on the population of the states the members represent, but allocations today range from a low of $650,000 to a high of $1.3 million. In addition to personal staffs, members of both chambers who chair committees or subcommittees have access to several more staff assistants through their committee positions.

These staff assistants do work on legislation, to be sure, but many concentrate on "casework," providing such services to constituents as finding lost social security checks, writing letters of congratulations or condolence, or sending out copies of government publications. Many staffers do little more than answer mail from constituents. The cost of official mail from Washington to constituents has risen almost tenfold from 1971 to 1984: from $11.2 million to over $107 million, while the average cost of each item mailed has increased by just over 50 percent: from 8 to 12.3 cents. And this massive postal bill is not paid for by the members themselves. Correspondence dealing with the "official" business of the Congress can be mailed without postage under the member's signature (called the *frank*); other mail, much of it oriented toward reelection, does require stamps, but the members have very generous postage allowances.

In the quest for reelection, there is no place like home. Even while in Washington, legislators maintain a considerable presence back in the district. Over one third of House employees worked in district offices in 1983, compared with just over one fifth a decade earlier. Almost 28 percent of Senate staffs worked in state offices in 1983, more than double the 1972 percentage.[24] Not only has the percentage of staff assigned to the district increased, but so has the total number of staff members. This at least doubles the impact of the increase. But going home is also important.

Members of the House are authorized twenty-six trips back to their districts at government expense every year, but most members go back every weekend or at least three out of four weekends a month. Senators, who go home less frequently, are authorized forty trips home each year. Many senators believe that they do not have to pay such close attention to their constituents because they face the electorate only once every six years.

Furthermore, most senators would clearly prefer to be interviewed on "Face the Nation" or "Meet the Press" than discuss some constituent's personal problem at a garden club meeting back home. Yet, senators who neglect this advice are becoming increasingly vulnerable to challengers who promise better constituency service.[25]

Such close attention to the constituency no doubt helps the members gain reelection, but it also reinforces parochialism in congressional decision making. To members of the Senate and particularly the House, the national interest is usually defined in terms of local priorities. The reelection imperative as well as the success that members have in exploiting these advantages work against the development of a national or international perspective. In a rare burst of introspection, a survey of representatives conducted by the House in 1977 found that 57 percent of the legislators believed that constituent demands interfere with other aspects of the job, especially the legislative role.[26] By contrast, the president is the only nationally elected political leader and thus has greater leeway to balance competing interests in both domestic and foreign policy. The chief executive can thus take a more detached view of policy alternatives and can—indeed must—consider the reactions of our allies and enemies to foreign policy decisions as well as the long-term consequences of decisions.[27] The vast foreign policy bureaucracy serves the president and his secretary of state—who, in turn, can be dismissed at any time the president chooses.

Reelection is not the only goal of members of Congress, however. Fenno examined three other major goals which characterized legislators to varying degrees: (1) seeking influence within the House or Senate; (2) making good public policy; and (3) a career in politics beyond the House or Senate.[28] (For House members, this career generally means the Senate or a governorship, for senators the goal is the White House.) Indeed, some members, a minority to be sure, try to strive for the making of sound national and international policy without excessive concern for the parochial interests of their own districts or even the political consequences of their decisions. A somewhat jaundiced member of the House commented to Fenno:

> All some House members are interested in is "the folks." They think "the folks" are the second coming. They would no longer do anything to displease "the folks" than they would fly. They spend all their time trying to find out what "the folks" want. I imagine if they get five letters on one side and five letters on the other side, they die.[29]

The goal of making good public policy is held in varying degrees by all members. But what is good policy? For many, it is meeting the needs of the district. It is hardly surprising to find that a member from the Midwest or South would be primarily concerned with agriculture policy or that a black representative from New York or Chicago would be most interested in civil rights and labor policy. For most members, what is good for the district is good for the country—and, to a certain extent, each is correct. But the bal-

ance between district demands and the nation's priorities is difficult to determine. The policy oriented member must not neglect his or her district,
but he or she is also compelled to consider the claims of other members.
Domestic policy making is generally not discussed in these terms. Legislators, who must face constituencies back home as well as among their fellow
members, prefer policies which produce only "winners" and "nonwinners,"
the politics of the pork barrel and the agriculture and housing subsidies.
Probably only a small minority of elected officials are concerned with resolving the issues involving "winners" and "losers," the sorts of questions that
arose when over 100,000 Cuban refugees entered the United States during
the 1980 recession. When unemployment is rising, how do you distribute
jobs to the new Americans? An even smaller number direct their attention
to foreign affairs. Those who do often have studied international relations
in college and traveled extensively.[30] In the House, they tend to come from
urban areas and have relatively safe seats, and they are also more likely to
be members of ethnic groups particularly concerned with foreign policy
(Jews regarding Israel and blacks on Africa). In addition, as noted earlier
(Chapter 2), many members of the foreign policy committees have ambitions
beyond the Congress.

These diverse goals may often come into conflict. Particularly on questions of foreign policy, legislators recognize that concern for foreign policy
is often not appreciated back home. A Democratic member of the House
Foreign Affairs Committee in the 1950s and 1960s told Fenno:

> The first few weeks I was here I would go home on the weekend to see con-
> stituents. One night, there must have been 45 people waiting to see me, this
> big ward leader came in, big fat guy, a head taller than me. He said, "What's
> the big idea keeping me waiting?" I tried to explain to him that, gee whiz,
> we had a committee meeting, Berlin was falling apart, the Secretary of State
> was briefing the Committee on Berlin, and I didn't feel that I, as a new mem-
> ber, should be rude to him by walking out. I said, "John Foster Dulles ap-
> peared before the committee, the meeting went a little overtime, and I
> missed the plane." He said, "John Foster Dulles. Hell, he wasn't even with
> us last time out!" There's no relation between your committee work and back
> home.[31]

A member of the Senate Foreign Relations commented similarly:

> It's a political liability, . . . You have no constituency. In my reelection cam-
> paign last fall, the main thing they used against me was that because of my
> interest in foreign relations, I was more interested in what happened to the
> people of Abyssinia and Afghanistan than in what happened to the good
> people of my state.[32]

Foreign policy is often not very salient to many candidates either. In 1950
the Democratic challenger to Senator Robert A. Taft (R-Ohio) was asked his
position on two controversial islands off the coast of China, Quemoy and
Matsu. He reportedly replied: "I'll carry 'em both."[33] More recently, only

the Republican candidate in the 1986 Maryland Senate election could answer correctly more than half the questions on foreign affairs posed to them by reporters. Among the answers missed by most was the name of the prime minister of Israel. Among those who fared poorly in the "pop quiz" were the state's governor and two sitting members of the House, one of whom chaired the Foreign Affairs Committee's Subcommittee on the Western Hemisphere.

Do the generalizations of the 1950s and 1960s apply to the 1980s? The answer is a most emphatic "yes." If anything, politics is more locally oriented than it was two to three decades ago. Senators who concentrate on foreign affairs or who cast controversial roll calls against vocal groups in their constituencies may suffer electorally for their decisions. The fate of two senators on the Panama Canal treaty is instructive. Thomas McIntyre (D-N.H.) was castigated by conservative groups in his state for supporting the treaty and eventually lost his seat. Jennings Randolph (D-W.V.) waited until a sufficient number of senators had cast "yea" ballots to ensure the adoption of the treaty and then voted against it. He won reelection. Other senators who played key roles on the Foreign Relations Committee also went down to defeat. Included in this list were Dick Clark (D-Iowa), chair of the African Affairs Subcommittee of Foreign Relations; George McGovern, the Democratic nominee for president in 1972; Richard Stone (D-Fla.), who also went down to defeat in the 1980 election after supporting the Canal treaty; J. William Fulbright (D-Ark.), the longtime chair of the committee; Frank Church (D-Idaho), who sought the Democratic nomination for president in 1976 and then assumed the chair of Foreign Relations in 1979; and Jacob Javits (R-N.Y.), the ranking minority member. Of the five members of the committee seeking reelection in 1980, only John Glenn (D-Ohio) won another term. The 1980s have been kinder to Foreign Relations members; only one, Chairman Charles Percy (R-Ill.), has lost. But two others had very close calls: Jesse Helms (R-N.C.) in 1984 and Alan Cranston (D-Calif.) in 1986. All were accused by opponents of spending too much time on foreign policy and not enough time courting their constituents. Percy and Helms also faced criticism over their stand on the Middle East and had to confront major campaign contributions to their opponents by pro-Israel groups (see Chapter 6). Yet Cranston, despite all of his seniority and the high name recognition it brings, did not benefit substantially from strong *support* from pro-Israel groups. Cranston ran for president briefly in 1984 and, as with McGovern and Church, he had to contend with an image that this foray into national and international politics showed he had lost touch with his state's interests.

By contrast, the House Foreign Affairs Committee remains classified as a "minor" committee by the party organizations which assign members to committee positions. A member on a minor committee can also serve on another committee. The additional committee assignment of most House Foreign Affairs members is more politically beneficial to them; unlike senators, therefore, they do not become infamous for their foreign policy concerns. Furthermore, the lower profile of the House on foreign policy also helps to protect members in this regard, as does the greater attention House members give to their constituents compared with senators.[34]

For senators, then, the goal of making good foreign policy may often conflict with that for reelection. This is not quite the case in the House, but probably because those members attracted to the House Foreign Affairs Committee are among the most electorally secure. The Senate Foreign Relations Committee is a high-profile committee; Foreign Affairs in the House is almost invisible. Indeed, in an attempt to call greater attention to its role, the committee changed its name in 1971 to International Relations. A senior committee member commented: "We were sick of that old (former senator and vice president) Alben Barkley joke, the House committee only had affairs, not relations. Basically, we were considered a throwaway committee—our only bill was foreign aid. So we changed our name to fit our image."[35] But, despite the increasing activism of the body, the House did not stand up and take notice, so the name was changed back to Foreign Affairs in 1979 because members found the new title confusing and "difficult to remember."

Perhaps because so many senators seek (or wish to seek) the presidency, the Senate Foreign Relations Committee has served to help members attain institutional power. The House Foreign Affairs Committee is not the road to power in the House. When foreign policy activism was first renewed in the Congress, the committee did serve as an incubator for emerging politicians. Five of the thirty-eight members serving during 1970 ran for the Senate, three successfully during the 1970s. Once the role of the committee as a critic of administration foreign policy had been institutionalized, however, its attractiveness declined. On the one hand, it was no longer producing as many potential senators. Only three of thirty-seven members serving in 1980 had run for the Senate by 1988 and all lost. The attractiveness of the committee had greatly declined as very few members were willing to leave more desirable assignments to serve on Foreign Affairs. Freshman members comprised two thirds of all new appointments to the committee from 1973–1981, almost twice the percentage of a decade earlier. No other committee had such a large increase in junior membership.[36] In contrast to previous years when a large percentage of the committee's membership had considerable seniority and was generally reluctant to challenge the administration, the new junior-dominated committee is composed of members anxious to make their mark. They do not have "institutional memory"; since few legislators served in the pre-Vietnam War days, there are not many who recall the era of bipartisan foreign policy.

The Senate, long the bastion of both reasoned and unprincipled opposition to—and support for—administration foreign policy, is becoming more and more like the House. Senators are finding foreign policy concerns to be politically costly. The goals of members of Congress may often be conflicting and legislators may be called on to decide whether to cast a vote in favor of a controversial foreign policy issue supported by the president or to ensure their reelection or quest for higher office. In a parliamentary system, Howard Baker, who was to become the Senate Majority Leader, would have been the odds-on choice to gain the Republican nomination for president (or party leader) in 1980. Instead, an outsider to the legislative party, Ronald Reagan, captured his party's nomination with ease and Baker took considerable criticism within his own party for supporting the Canal treaties. In 1988, an informal poll of House Democrats indicated that their clear first choice was House Majority Leader Thomas Foley (D-Wash.), but Michael Dukakis, also an outsider to national politics, prevailed in the primaries.

The ideological attacks by conservative groups on senators who supported the foreign policy of the recent Democratic *and* Republican administrations have increased Senate parochialism on foreign policy. Foreign policy is less important in House contests because representatives have paid more attention to their constituents than have senators and because House members have not expressed a very strong concern for foreign policy issues. The prevailing attitude has been: Let sleeping dogs lie. When the House has taken initiatives on foreign policy, it has generally done so in response to some sort of a constituency pressure—from the demands of ethnic lobbies to economic interests in the district. One of the ultimate ironies of recent Congresses has been the tremendous increase in size of House and Senate staffs, but the lack of new efforts to challenge the executive branch in staff expertise on foreign policy. Congressional staffs concentrate on public relations activities designed to aid reelection efforts but, when they are concerned with policy, it is with domestic issues. The reason is straightforward: most members of Congress do not have a primary or even a strong interest in foreign policy. The issues raised stand in the way of reelection and often institutional power. Since each member can allocate staff resources, time and interests as he or she wishes, the Congress is capable of producing 535 separate foreign policies, each based on a different conception of national and local interests with no strong organizing force such as political parties to produce more coherent choices.

The Congress, then, represents primarily domestic interest groups and its members have a responsibility to protect the economic well-being of their constituents. A president can afford to ignore the views of many citizens. For expeditious decision making, this may be a virtue. But such a president cannot claim to represent "all of the people" any more than can a collection of representatives and senators. The president, to be sure, is in a better strategic position to take into account the global interests of the country. But someone must look after the constituencies in a democracy. Thus the president, but particularly the Congress, faces the dilemma posed at the beginning of the *Talmud*, the vast compilation of the Oral Law of the Jews: "If I am not for myself, who will be for me? If I am for myself alone, what am I?"

COMMITTEES: CENTERS OF CONGRESSIONAL POWER

A camel, it is said, is a horse designed by a committee. Congressional government is committee government—and, in recent years, government by subcommittees, the littlest legislatures of them all. The camel analogy is quite appropriate, for committee government does not move much faster than that desert animal. Whereas foreign policy, or at least crisis decision making, is marked by the need for action that is both *unified* and *quick*, responsiveness to public opinion and allowances for maximum feasible participation in decision making are characterized by a slow process of bargaining, negotiations, and compromises. Senators particularly like to call this process *deliberation.* Others might see it as an attempt to stalemate the opposition by responding so slowly that the opponent in the policy-making process may simply give way because of exhaustion.

Congressional government by committees is also parochial government. In the Congress, committees are organized largely based on constituency interests: Education and Labor, Agriculture, Interior, Public Works and Transportation, Energy and Commerce, Judiciary, and Small Business are typical House committees. Public Works is a much sought-after body, especially for junior members who want to engage in pork-barrel politics for their districts; it is the committee that constructs dams and produces hydroelectric energy. Judiciary, of course, handles civil rights legislation but also the more politically salient questions of resolving claims against the government and expediting immigration and naturalization procedures. Interior is the guardian of the national parks, as well as the protector of the environment. Energy and Commerce handles much, although not all, energy legislation, but also virtually everything that can be sold, bartered, or regulated—from the nation's airwaves to health care to railroads. These committees attract members from districts most directly affected by their principal subjects. While jurisdictions are not always clearly defined, membership on a committee that seems most relevant to one's district concerns can be of great benefit in reelection drives. Precisely because jurisdictions are not always clear-cut, the potential for slowing the progress of a major bill—or even stopping it completely—is very real in the Congress. A bill selected at random for all of those introduced in any given Congress (almost 20,000 now in the House alone) may not have as good a chance of passage as a camel trying to find an oasis in the desert. The long and tortuous path that a bill must take, involving at least one committee and one subcommittee in both the House and the Senate, makes its enactment into a public law a major event.

The "big three" committees in the House are Appropriations, Ways and Means, and Rules. Members assigned to any of these committees are generally not given any additional committee assignments. They are considered "power committees," bodies where members who want to gather institutional power jockey for positions. These committees are important because they handle the key aspects of legislative decision making: money and procedure. All bills that provide for the direct spending of money must go to the House and Senate Appropriations committees. The money, in turn, must come from taxes, which are handled by Ways and Means in the House and Finance in the Senate. In the House, but not the Senate, most important bills *must* be sent to the Rules Committee, which determines which amendments (if any) can be offered on the floor and what the ground rules (including time limitations) for debate will be. The Rules Committee also serves as the arbiter when there are conflicting claims among committees over alternative bills—or simply which body ought to have jurisdiction over a specific piece of legislation. Some bills are "privileged" in that they can go directly to the House floor without getting a rule. These include appropriations bills, but the power of the Rules Committee to restrict the amendments that might be offered provides strong incentives for virtually all committees to seek rules for debate for their bills. The situation is different in the Senate. Time limits can only be established by unanimous consent (the norm) or by a motion of cloture to break a filibuster, a prolonged period of "debate" designed to kill a bill. During a filibuster, members may argue the merits of a piece of legislation for days, weeks, or even months; in earlier days, the quality of Senate debates during filibusters varied widely as some members cited the arguments on their side of the bill and others read from telephone books merely to consume time. Senate procedures restricting amendments are so weak that a powerful committee such as the House Rules Committee could never develop. There is a Rules Committee in the Senate, but it deals with internal housekeeping (like the House Administration Committee), not the resolution of critical procedural issues.

The slow pace of congressional decision making is perhaps best illustrated by a change in House procedures in 1974 to permit greater participation in its decision making by junior members. In previous years, committees had been dominated by strong chairs. The seniority system—and indeed the entire committee system—was systematically weakened through a series of reforms (which we shall discuss later). But the change in referral procedures in the House in 1974 to make this chamber's procedures similar to those in the Senate dramatically demonstrates how the drive for power by a large number of actors can lead to a legislative stalemate. The situation is made even more cumbersome by the constituency politics that marks the fight over which committees and subcommittees get control over a piece of legislation.

The change in referral procedure permitted more actors to get involved in the processing of each bill. Previously, a bill was filed by a member; then the clerk of the House, acting through the speaker, would assign it to a committee. In several key instances, this referral procedure permitted the leadership to avoid recalcitrant chairs. The reform of 1974 in the House, following similar action in the Senate, permitted several different types of bill referral, including joint, sequential, and split referrals. The first permitted several committees to consider a bill simultaneously; the second allowed several committees to handle a bill in sequence; while the last let the speaker break a bill into several components and assign them to different committees.

While the rationale behind this proposal was to increase participation by all House members on legislation in which they were particularly interested, the reform had one major drawback: politically, the speaker could hardly reject the demand of any committee (or of a subcommittee through the full committee) as long as jurisdiction, determined by House rules, gave the committee a legitimate claim to the subject matter of the bill. The new participatory environment gave virtually every member the opportunity to have some say on a policy decision of concern to him or her. What ensued over the next several years was a series of jurisdictional conflicts that Representative Toby Moffett (D-Conn.) called *jungle warfare*.[37] Thus virtually every committee could claim jurisdiction over energy policy (Chapter 8). The situation is even worse on health policy, where national health insurance is the concern of the Health Subcommittee of Energy and Commerce and a similar subcommittee on Ways and Means (which has primary jurisdiction over medicare, a social security program financed through taxes); in addition every special interest committee (Veterans' Affairs, Small Business, Merchant Marine and Fisheries, Education and Labor, Interior, and so forth) controls decision making on health care within its general jurisdictions. The situation is no better on foreign policy, where questions of restrictions on foreign trade were matters of concern to Ways and Means (primary jurisdiction over trade policy), Foreign Affairs, Government Operations (oversight of both commerce and national security), Agriculture (food exports), Small Business, and Energy and Commerce—at a minimum. Should any of these committees, or the relevant subcommittees, refuse to report the bill to the Rules Committee, the legislation would die unless extraordinary measures were taken to rescue it.

The increasing use of multiple referral procedures in both the House and the Senate and the greater emphasis on the reelection goal have both served to weaken congressional initiatives in policy making. Approximately 10 percent of all bills filed in the House of Representatives are referred to more than one committee. However, these tend to be among the most controversial pieces of legislation. Multiply referred legislation is about half as likely to be enacted as bills that are sent only to one committee. Neither the Foreign Affairs nor the Armed Services Committee are among the panels with the largest number of multiple referrals. However, both fall right in the middle of the list of committees.[38] Their legislation is thus controversial enough to cause other panels to want to get a piece of the action.

The Foreign Affairs Committee shares the Food for Peace program with the Department of Agriculture; foreign intelligence activities with Armed Services and the Select Committee on Intelligence; international banking with Banking, Finance, and Urban Affairs; the ACTION program (including the Peace Corps) and other educational programs, as well as the United Nation's International Labor Organization, with Education and Labor; immigration, claims, and passports with Judiciary; international fishing rights and environmental legislation (as well as the Panama Canal) with Merchant Marine and Fisheries; and trade with Ways and Means, among other committees (see Chapter 8). The committees that have the most multiple referrals are those dealing with intermestic issues such as energy (Science and Technology, Energy and Commerce, and Interior) and agriculture.

The referral system clearly adds many delays to the congressional process and may be particularly problematic in foreign policy, where quick responses to changes in the international system may often be required. Additionally, the Congress often uses temporary select committees to investigate the executive branch, as the Senate did to examine Watergate and as both chambers did in the Iran–Contra affair. These temporary committees are only permitted to conduct investigations and to suggest possible legislation. They may not refer bills to the floor. Only permanent committees may do so, so these temporary investigative bodies may add to legislative fragmentation. The more actors who become involved in foreign policy, the less expeditiously the nation can act.

TOO MANY COOKS?

Congressional decision making is also slowed down by the lack of any committee similar to the House Rules Committee in the Senate, where debate may continue at great length on virtually any subject. The lack of a strong procedure limiting amendments in the Senate means that a foreign policy question can be attached as a "rider" (an amendment not directly connected to the bill under consideration) to any other piece of legislation. There are rules in both houses prohibiting new legislation in an appropriations bill, so that it should not be possible to constrain, say, foreign trade on a foreign aid appropriation. However, virtually every subject imaginable involves the expenditure of money. All programs require someone to manage them at the least, and these managers must be paid salaries, so the jurisdictional lines become even more blurred and the process can be delayed at virtually any time for almost any reason.

Multiple referral of bills complicates the policy process; so does a 1971 reform that greatly eased the requirements for roll-call votes. Before that action, there were approximately 150 to 200 recorded votes a year; now there are about 800 such votes. Each vote takes between fifteen minutes and half an hour (often longer in Senate, where computerized voting has been resisted), adding yet further delays to the slow process. It is small wonder, then, that members often do not know the details of the bills on which they are voting. Much of the time, they do not even know what the basic substance of the bill is and rush to the floor from their offices or committee meetings, ask a trusted colleague who has followed the proceedings what the bill is and how he or she is voting, and vote accordingly.[39]

The concern for maximum possible participation, then, clearly slows down the legislative process and gives many more outside interests, as well as members themselves, the opportunity to block legislation before it can be adopted. But the commitment to a greater role for individual members, which led to the change in House referral procedures, is a hallmark of the open politics of the Congress of the 1970s and 1980s. Until 1980 the president, as cited earlier, had to report covert CIA activities to eight committees of the Congress, four each in the House and the Senate. No member trusted the others in making policy decisions for the country. Speed and coherence became clearly secondary goals to those of openness and participation. Critics charged that such a philosophy of policy making might prevent an "imperial presidency," but would also militate against a chief executive who could command enough authority and respect within his administration, as well as his own congressional party, to demand the attention and loyalty of our allies in international politics. The bill referral reform is but one of the factors that makes legislative decision making on foreign policy so much less expeditious than executive policy formation. The congressional reforms of the 1970s led to an increased policy activism in both the House and the Senate. We shall discuss these reforms shortly. But here we stress that this very activism and the longer deliberations that precede any final action on behalf of the nation have led foreign leaders, both in friendly and adversary countries, to wonder who exactly is in charge of our foreign policy—if anyone. A former British foreign minister reportedly once suggested, and not completely in jest, that foreign embassies ought to be built across from the Congress. More recently, and certainly not in jest, Representative Lee Hamilton (D-Ind.)—second in seniority on the Foreign Affairs Committee, formerly chair of the Select Intelligence Committee, and chair of the House Select Committee on the Iran–Contra affair—stated: "When I first came to Washington a head of government would visit the president, the secretary of state, the World Bank, and go home. Today, it's rare for a head of state to come to Washington without meeting members of Congress."[40] In 1987, as the Congress grew critical of American policy in the Persian Gulf following the Iraqi attack on the U.S.S. *Stark*, the Congress dispatched Senator James Sasser (D-Tenn.) to prepare its own report on the situation even as the administration sent an investigative team to the same site. Later that year, the administration clashed with House Speaker Jim Wright (D-Tex.) when the Democratic leader met with Nicaraguan officials to try to arrange for peace talks with the Contras. Administration officials, including the president himself, charged the Speaker with violating the separation of powers.

In 1979, both the House and the Senate voted to restore diplomatic relations with Taiwan after the administration broke such relations to recognize the People's Republic of China; the fight over congressional prerogatives in this area was finally settled in the administration's favor, but not until the Supreme Court refused to overturn a decision by the U.S. Court of Appeals that supported the contention that while initial recognition of Taiwan was accomplished by legislative action, the president could reverse that decision without congressional assent. Had the Court ruled otherwise, the newly established relations with China might well have been broken; they surely would have been very strained. During 1978 and 1979, the Congress wrestled with an amendment proposed by Senator Jesse Helms (R-N.C.) that would have repealed American participation in the United Nations trade embargo on the white minority government of Rhodesia, a policy endorsed by every other nation except South Africa. Rhodesia, now the black majority-controlled nation of Zimbabwe, had been involved in a civil war for over a decade since the small white minority had unilaterally declared independence from Britain. The Carter administration, working with the British government under a United Nations mandate, was attempting to resolve the impasse in that African nation. Repeal of the embargo would certainly have set back such efforts, but in the eyes of the Senate supporters it would also have freed the United States from virtually complete dependence upon the Soviet Union for chrome imports. The Helms amendment cleared the Senate by a wide margin, but administration and party leadership pressure finally prevailed as the House refused to go along with the upper chamber. In 1986, the Congress approved, over President Reagan's veto, a package of sanctions against the apartheid regime in South Africa. Reagan had strongly opposed such actions, arguing that the United States would be better off pursuing the policy of "constructive engagement." This policy was aimed at using moral persuasion rather than economic boycotts to convince South African authorities to change their policies. However, a bipartisan majority in Congress believed that Reagan's policy had failed to make any meaningful changes in South African policies to date and overrode the president's veto to impose the sanctions on South African imports. In 1987 Congress wrestled with a proposal to reduce or eliminate foreign aid to Pakistan, which had reportedly constructed an atomic bomb that some members of Congress believed might be shared with Libya. Successive administrations have perceived Pakistan as a strong American ally in southern Asia and as a particularly critical base for insurgents fighting the Soviet-backed regime in Afghanistan. In a funding bill for the Department of State in 1987, the Senate sought to initiate a wide spectrum of foreign policy objectives, ranging from condemnation of China for its policies in Tibet to closing the office of the Palestine Liberation Organization in the United States to demanding reimbursement from Persian Gulf nations for American protection of shipping in the waterway. The House concurred in the movement to close the PLO offices, but a federal court ruled that the legislature could not take such action. For good measure, the Senate also expressed its disapproval of the long honking motorcades and heavily armed guards established by the State Department for foreign officials visiting its chamber.

Most of these issues took many months of congressional time. The legislative process is designed to be deliberative rather than expeditious. There is a far greater premium placed on hearing diverse points of view and reflecting constituency opinion than on quick coordinated action. The Senate, even though it has fewer members and a smaller number of committees (eighteen), is even slower than the House. First, Senate procedures are designed to be more reflective. Second, House members generally serve on only one or two committees; senators, on the other hand, serve on three to five committees and often have eight to ten subcommittee positions. A Senator running from one meeting to another, having to ask what the subject of today's hearing is, is commonplace. The heavy work load necessarily slows down the pace of action. The 535 members of the Congress rarely speak with a single voice and that makes decisive action on "crisis" issues much more difficult. Congress, on the other hand, excels at reflecting constituency opinion—and performs reasonably well at deliberative decision making. Whether it does as well as the executive is not readily resolved. Many of our views of process are colored by the decisions actually reached. Those who favored establishing relations with China would regret congressional "interference" with the foreign policy process, while supporters of sanctions against South Africa might hail the actions of the legislature against a recalcitrant chief executive. It is not implausible for people to hold both views— to be thankful for a Congress when one believes the president is wrong and to argue that the legislature is being obstructionist when one agrees with executive decisions. The democratic dilemmas stress these difficulties, but do not have ready answers to them.

One area in which the executive does have considerable advantages over the Congress is information about international politics. While both representatives and senators have large staffs, and the Congress has provided itself with three research organizations, the General Accounting Office, the Office of Technology Assessment, and the Congressional Research Service of the Library of Congress (as well as the Congressional Budget Office), even these facilities are dwarfed by the administrative bureaucracies of the Executive Office of the President, the Office of Management and Budget, and the State Department. Also each congressional research unit serves all 535 members of the House and Senate and examines not only foreign policy questions, but domestic ones as well. Furthermore, the congressional research service does many studies of internal congressional organization and fulfills specific research requests from members' offices which may have been forwarded from constituents needing information.

Could the Congress establish a research and investigative arm for foreign (and domestic) policy that would rival that of the executive branch? Probably not, given the vast resources of the entire federal bureaucracy available to the White House. Even with its recent increases of staff and the strengthening of its research organizations, jurisdictional conflicts have arisen to weaken the potential for real coordination. The subcommittee system, a set of governments numbering over 300 in the House and Senate, which has replaced committees as the center of congressional power further fragments authority. The growth of subcommittee autonomy, together with other reforms of the 1970s, has meant that policy specialists are now not only competing with the executive branch but also with each other. We turn now to an examination of these reforms and their impact.

THE NEW CONGRESS: THE IMPACT OF REFORMS

In the 1970s, committee government gave way to subcommittee domination. A series of reforms in the 1971–1975 period radically changed the way in which the House of Representatives conducted its business. Committee chairs were no longer automatically selected by seniority. Democratic party members were no longer to be assigned to positions by the Ways and Means Committee; instead, a party organization, the Steering and Policy Committee, a third of whose members are appointed by the Speaker, controlled appointments to committees and the naming of chairs. The Democratic caucus, composed of all party members in the House, then voted on the recommendations of Steering and Policy, and agreement was not automatic. Furthermore, in an attempt to control the agenda, the Rules Committee was brought under party control. The Speaker was given the authority to appoint all Democratic members of Rules directly. In 1974, Appropriations also fell prey to the party leadership when its subcommittee chairs were to be appointed by Steering and Policy, subject to caucus approval.

Other reforms of even greater import include the "subcommittee bill of rights" and the creation, in both the House and the Senate, of budget committees which were designed to rationalize the relationship between spending and revenue raising. The first has had the greatest impact and is the most widely discussed.[41] In 1971, the Democratic caucus began the process that liberated junior members from the tyrannical chairs. The initial reforms restricted Democratic members from chairing more than one legislative subcommittee (although a member could retain a second chair of an investigative body that did not report original legislation) and guaranteed subcommittees the power to hire their own professional staff members. The biggest block of reforms occurred two years later when the selection of subcommittee members was made the responsibility of the full committee caucus and could not be dominated by the committee chairs; subcommittees were also guaranteed fixed jurisdictions, so that full committee chairs could not create new subcommittees at will to reward friends and punish enemies; committee members were guaranteed their choice, based on seniority, of subcommittee assignments; and subcommittees were forced to have ratios of party members which reflected the full committee party balances, so that conservative chairs could not stack certain subcommittees, for instance, with Republicans and overbalance less powerful ones with liberal Democrats.

In December 1974, in addition to the change in Appropriations subcommittee chairmanship appointments, the caucus mandated the following reforms: committees with more than twenty members (Ways and Means) but with no subcommittees would have to establish at least four such bodies; numbered subcommittees, such as those on Armed Services, were abolished so that the conservative chair could no longer prevent some of the new liberal members of the committee from serving on subcommittees that were examining racial and sexual discrimination in the armed forces through the assigning of bills to subcommittees without specific subject jurisdictions; committees were required to establish an oversight subcommittee; and members would be restricted to membership on two subcommittees in each full committee on which they serve (four years later, they would be restricted to five subcommittees in total—at least in principle).

These reforms encompassing the "subcommittee bill of rights" were not intended to "punish" all chairs of full committees, and, in fact, many were very highly regarded by the other members. The major objective of this reform, which was enormously successful, was to disperse power within the House. The focal point of activity shifted from the twenty-two standing committees to the approximately 120 subcommittees. The prestige of the title "Mr. (or Madame) Chairman" was somewhat reduced since almost two thirds of the Democrats in the House now hold it. The days of the strong chairs were over. The younger members who had been entering the House since the late 1960s found their cause bolstered by the Democratic landslide of 1974, which brought into the Congress a large bloc of post-Vietnam politicians distrustful of highly structured decision making.

The demise of the strong committees opened up two possibilities for future congressional decision making: an increased role for the two parties or an extreme decentralization so that each member would, in essence, become a sovereign. In the mid-1970s a resurgence of party government seemed possible. The Democratic caucus had gone on record three times (1971, 1973, and 1975) calling for a withdrawal of American troops from Vietnam and many in the party saw the prospect of using the caucus as a forum for coordinating policy making in Congress. But the old-line conservatives, including many chairs of full committees who had seen their power eroded, feared that the caucus would impose a liberal orthodoxy on the congressional party. The newer, more progressive members, on the other hand, were distrustful of any hierarchical decision-making structure, and they, too, opposed an increased role for the caucus. Thus, in early 1975, the caucus forbade itself from binding members to specific voting stands on the House floor and then voted to open future meetings to the public to stem any possibility that party leaders might try to resurrect the caucus as an internal forum for policy decision.

One measure designed to centralize decision making in the Congress was the Budget and Impoundment Control Act of 1974, which created Budget committees in the House and the Senate and also a Congressional

Budget Office to formulate an alternative budget to that of the president and to coordinate spending and revenue raising in the Congress. The idea of a legislative budget was initiated as one of the anti-Nixon reforms of the Democratic Congress, but it drew support from liberals and conservatives alike. Each saw the potential for the Congress to put its budgetary process in some sort of order, for the new law required the budget committees to propose and enact a legislative budget. The limits established for expenditures in the final act passed each year could not be exceeded by the Appropriations committee of either House for any of the approximately twenty categories of federal spending.

The existing expenditure process was a classic example of group politics designed to produce many "winners" and few real "losers." Before any money could be expended, it must first be *authorized*, that is, made legal. Authorizations are determined by the substantive policy committees of the House and the Senate, so that Armed Services in each chamber would determine a maximum (and also possibly a minimum) amount to be spent on the military, while Education and Labor (House) and Labor and Human Resources (Senate) would set spending limits for federal aid to education, and so forth. Should the two houses disagree, as they usually do, a *conference committee* would be appointed by the Speaker of the House and the Senate party leadership (generally the majority and minority leaders working together) to work out a compromise within the limits of the original House and Senate bills. The conferees are, virtually without exception, members of the (sub-) committee(s) that handled the original legislation. House and Senate conferees each had to vote as a bloc and no bill would be enacted unless both groups reached agreement. Once agreement was reached, the House and Senate could only vote to accept or reject the conference report; no amendments are allowed. Failure to pass the report by either House would require the convening of another conference.

Even assuming that the conference report is accepted by the two houses, the spending process is far from over. Authorizations do not provide for the expenditure of any money; all they do is to make it legal for the appropriations committees in the House and Senate to propose actual expenditures, as restricted by the authorizations bills' maximum (or minimum) amounts. But at this point tension arises: The appropriations committees are faced with authorizations that, when added up, would break any conceivable budget. Thus they work to cut back the authorized amounts from the special interest committees to produce a more coherent relationship between taxing and spending. The House Appropriations Committee, therefore, has historically served as the budget cutter in the expenditure process, with the Senate body as a "court of last resort" for the authorizing committees and their supporting constituency groups.[42] The armed services committees have been notably active in pursuing their claims for more money and, in an extremely unusual move in 1980, Carter's chairman of the Joint Chiefs of Staff of the armed services, David Jones, opposed his own president's budget recommendations and supported the authorizing committees' recommendations for further increases in military spending. While the appropriations committees did, then, serve to restrain spending somewhat, the entire budget was never discussed in overall priorities. The new budget committees were designed to remedy this flaw in fiscal planning. To date, however, the success of these committees has been greatly limited. Budget resolutions often did not pass the Congress and the norm became a system in which spending limits on particular programs were simply waived by legislative acts. The early resolutions of the budget resolutions supported by President Reagan in 1981 suggest that the process can indeed work when disciplined majorities exist in the House and Senate. But it was the very lack of such discipline that led to the formation of the budget committees in 1974.

While the reforms of the 1970s could have produced either a more centralized or a more decentralized Congress, the weakness of the party system and the reluctance of the members to subordinate their newly liberated subcommittees to party leadership tilted the balance strongly in favor of fractionalized allegiances. Individual members, motivated by power, sought the overthrow of the committee barons who replaced the strong Speaker of the late nineteenth and early twentieth centuries. The upshot of this move toward greater participation in decision making within the Congress has led to a situation in which the only real power is the ability to block consideration of proposed legislation. If domestic authorizations and appropriations are not passed, highly salient political programs (such as agriculture, housing, and transportation subsidies) will come to a sudden halt and federal paychecks will bounce. In contrast, failure to act on key foreign policy issues will leave the executive unchecked; diplomacy will not cease. Enormous costs may, therefore, result from congressional failure to act, but these will not be directly borne by angry constituents in most instances. Foreign policy has a much smaller and less organized constituency than do most domestic programs. However, when Congress does not act on foreign policy, the president might gain so much leverage that the policy does not reflect popular opinion. What Congress does best is to represent the views of organized groups within the electorate. We can debate the wisdom of making policy, either domestic or foreign, through such group demands, but the American system has been based on this concept of politics.[43] We shall turn to an examination of how well Congress might perform this representation function after discussing the structure of foreign policy decision making in Congress.

THE FOREIGN POLICY COMMITTEES

Table 4–1 presents the full range of dispersion of foreign policy decision making in the Congress. Jurisdictional lines are often not as clear-cut as the table indicates, but the very large number of bodies with significant foreign

TABLE 4-1 Committees of Congress Dealing with Foreign Policy Issues

Committee	Subjects
Foreign Relations (Senate)	General conduct of foreign policy; declarations of war; executive agreements; treaties
Foreign Affairs (House)	Same as Senate Foreign Relations except for treaties
Armed Services (Senate and House)	Military affairs; defense budget; national security; arms exports
Energy and Commerce (House)	Energy; international economic policy; telecommunications; transportation; shipping
Commerce, Science, and Transportation (Senate)	International economic policy; telecommunications; transportation; shipping; ocean and fishing rights; nonmilitary space programs; merchant marine
Merchant Marine and Fisheries (House)	Merchant marine; ocean and fishing rights; offshore oil; law of the sea; Panama Canal
Appropriations (Senate and House)	All programs requiring funding; defense budget; budget for running bureaucracies
Budget (Senate and House)	Overall spending levels and spending within specific categories
Banking, Housing, and Urban Affairs (Senate)/ Banking, Finance, and Urban Affairs (House)	International monetary policy; international commerce; authorizations for Export-Import Bank, and World Bank

Committee	Jurisdiction
Intelligence (Senate and House)	Oversight of intelligence agencies (Select committees)
Science and Technology (House)	Space program; energy research and development
Energy and Natural Resources (Senate)	Energy policy; energy research and development
Environment and Public Works (Senate)	Environmental policy; water resources; nuclear energy regulation
Interior and Insular Affairs (House)	Environmental policy; nuclear energy regulation; coal mining
Public Works and Transportation (House)	Aviation; water resources; hydroelectric energy; transportation
Finance (Senate)/Ways and Means (House)	Reciprocal trade agreements; tariffs; import quotas; customs
Agriculture, Nutrition, and Forestry (Senate)/ Agriculture (House)	Price supports; international food policy; food exports; Food for Peace
Governmental Affairs (Senate)	General oversight; nuclear energy and export; executive branch organization
Government Operations (House)	General oversight; energy policy; trade oversight (including embargos)
Rules (House)	Setting of legislative agenda for House bills
Education and Labor (House)/Labor and Human Resources (Senate)	ACTION (including Peace Corps); International Labor Organization; migration and immigration
Judiciary (Senate and House)	Immigration policy
Joint Economic Committee (Senate and House)	International economic policy (no legislative authority; research function only)

policy authority is staggering. It is small wonder that Congress rarely takes the lead in initiating foreign policy. The key foreign policy committees are Foreign Relations (Senate), Foreign Affairs (House), Armed Services and Appropriations in each chamber, Governmental Affairs (Senate), and Government Operations (House). In addition to these standing committees, there are *select* intelligence committees in both the House and the Senate. Select committees usually are established within each house for a specified time period and are restricted to either general oversight of the administration or the reporting of very few pieces of legislation. The intelligence committees, however, have been established (as of 1977 for both houses) as permanent select committees.

The key committees are Foreign Relations in the Senate and Foreign Affairs in the House, and an examination of each highlights the different ways in which senators and representatives perceive foreign policy. Foreign Relations is a highly desired committee slot; members have waited years to obtain a seat on it. Some analysts consider it the most prestigious committee in the Senate. The body has attracted the "best and the brightest" of the Senate and, historically, both chairs and ranking minority members have achieved great stature. Prominent Foreign Relations members have included Arthur Vandenburg (R-Mich.), J. William Fulbright, Frank Church, and Jacob Javits. The current chair is Claiborne Pell (D-R.I.), who has served on the committee since 1961 and spent seven years in the Foreign Service before that. He is a thoughtful and widely respected senator, of a patrician background but nevertheless among the most liberal members of the committee. Like his predecessor, Richard Lugar (R-Ind.), he strives for a bipartisan consensus to the extent possible, especially on such contentious issues as arms sales to Arab countries and sanctions against South Africa.[44] However, this has become a more difficult task. First, the historic prestige of the committee has suffered serious reversals in recent years. As in the House Foreign Affairs Committee, members no longer seek out assignment to Foreign Relations. Indeed, it is below the mean in seniority for all Senate committees. The body has been marked by increasingly bitter partisan bickering. Armed Services has gathered more of the spotlight as military sales become an increasingly contentious item on the nation's foreign policy agenda. The electoral costs of serving on Foreign Relations have made new members reluctant to seek positions on the committee. The weakness of Charles Percy (R.-Ill.), who had served as chair from 1981 to 1985, further diminished Foreign Relations' luster; ironically, so has the consensus-building style of Pell. The spotlight now goes more to headline grabbers such as Jesse Helms (R-N.C.) and less to the leaders. Thus, Foreign Relations no longer occupies its formerly privileged place among Senate committees, and party leaders have even found it difficult to recruit new members.[45]

Second, when the Democrats retook control of the Senate in 1986, a bitter struggle emerged among Republican members. Helms, the self-proclaimed leader of the Christian right in the Senate, was next in line to succeed Percy as chair of the committee in 1985. He honored a pledge to his constituents and remained chair of the Agriculture Committee, which is of great importance to his state's tobacco farmers. To do so, however, he had to forgo chairing Foreign Relations since Senate rules prohibit anyone from heading more than one standing committee. Even an administration as conservative as Reagan's felt relieved at Helms' decision. The North Carolina senator has attempted to block many ambassadorial appointments of the Reagan administration on the ground that they were not sufficiently conservative. (As chair, he would have been more than just a lonely voice of obstructionism.) Instead, the moderate Lugar assumed the chair and rebuilt much of the committee's prestige. While generally a dependable supporter of the president, he broke with Reagan on two key issues in 1986: he pushed for more decisive action on pressuring Ferdinand Marcos to resign as president of the Philippines, and was a strong supporter of sanctions against South Africa. In 1987, with his party no longer in the majority, Helms reassessed his commitment to his constituents. Arguing that service as ranking minority member of the Agriculture Committee would not provide particular benefits to North Carolina, he opted for the same position on Foreign Relations. It was highly unusual at best for any challenge to succeed, but Helms convinced his Republican colleagues that seniority ought to be followed. In a very close vote he toppled Lugar from the position of ranking minority member, leaving the president without a reliable ally of either party in positions of committee leadership. Many Republican senators voted for Helms because of his policy positions, but others, including liberals such as Lowell Weicker (R-Conn.), supported him because party moderates wanted to preserve their own seniority rights.

In contrast, the leadership of the House committee reflects the lower prestige of that body within the chamber. More senior members generally opt for chairmanships of other committees. The committee has a reputation for concentrating on only one piece of legislation a year—foreign aid—and there are few less salient or popular issues among the mass public. The committee has eight subcommittees, four dealing with general issue areas and four arranged on geographic locales. For many years the dominant premise was to resist conflict with the administration, even to the point of inaction. One member told Fenno in the 1960s:

> I've been on the Europe subcommittee for five months and I haven't even heard NATO mentioned, haven't even heard the word. I read my hometown newspaper to find out what's happening to NATO. . . . The subcommittees have displayed absolute irrelevancy in foreign affairs, amazing irrelevancy.[46]

The chair from 1958 to 1977 was Thomas "Doc" Morgan (D-Pa.), who was succeeded by Clement Zablocki. Morgan believed that the proper role of the committee was to pass the president's foreign aid request and little more.[47] He rarely interfered with subcommittee chairmen and gave them considerable leeway in the 1970s when several members, including Zablocki, became more activist. Zablocki in 1972 cosponsored (with Senator Clifford Case) a successful move to require prompt reporting to the Congress of executive agreements. But the greatest degree of activism in the 1970s came from other members, mostly representatives from relatively safe seats. These younger members, mostly Democrats, were quite ambitious. Stephen J. Solarz (D-N.Y.) now chairs the committee's Subcommittee on Asian and Pacific Affairs. In 1986, he was the leading congressional actor in moving the Reagan administration to press for the resignation of Marcos in the Philippines. Paul Sarbanes (D-Md.) moved on to the Senate; John Brademas (D-Ind.) became the House Democratic Whip before his defeat in the 1980 Republican tide; Pierre duPont (R-Del.) became governor of his state and in 1988 sought the Republican nomination for president; Hamilton rose to second in seniority among Democrats on the panel and chaired both the Select Committee on Intelligence and the Iran–Contra Select Committee; and Benjamin Rosenthal (D-N.Y.) mounted an unsuccessful challenge to Zablocki in 1977, arguing that he was not dynamic enough.

Zablocki got along reasonably well with William Broomfield (R-Mich.), the quiet ranking minority member who continues to serve in that position. The Wisconsin Democrat died in 1983 and was succeeded by Dante Fascell (D-Fla.), a moderate with a wide base of support and respect among members of both parties in the House. While a supporter of aid to the Contras, he was otherwise quite wary of committing troops abroad, having opposed the Vietnam War as early as 1970. He is regarded as a shrewd bargainer, especially in shepherding the controversial foreign aid bill through the legislative arena.[48] One liberal colleague praised him for having "an instinctive sense of where the middle lies and how to get there."[49]

The challenges to the war in Vietnam, especially the War Powers Act, originated in the Senate committee. During the late 1960s and early 1970s, several attempts were made by Foreign Relations members to cut off funds for the war in Vietnam, notably by Senators Church, McGovern, Case, and John Sherman Cooper (R-Ky.). This bipartisan effort, in various forms, passed the Senate many times but always failed in the House, where members were reluctant to challenge presidential authority. Whereas Fulbright was a leading spokesman on behalf of these efforts, Morgan quietly led the opposition in the House. An amendment to forbid funding for military operations in Cambodia did pass both houses in 1975, but by that time the troops had already been withdrawn. The only real success of a congressional amendment to terminate the American involvement in Vietnam occurred *after* the Paris peace agreement of 1973, when all U.S. combat forces had been withdrawn from Vietnam and all prisoners of war returned to America. Only then did *both* houses cut off funds for the administration's continued bombing in Cambodia, where no cease-fire had yet occurred. Yet, the legislative success was qualified, because Nixon vetoed the appropriations bill to which the cutoff on funds was attached. The president's need for funds for several executive agencies led to a compromise delaying the end of the bombing for several weeks. This gave Washington and Hanoi another chance to negotiate a Cambodian cease-fire and await the onset of the monsoon season, which would make further fighting very difficult.

The Senate, through the Foreign Relations Committee, consistently took the lead in the efforts to restrain the executive in Vietnam in the 1960s and 1970s. But the most prominent House committee initiative on foreign policy occurred on an issue that in many ways resembles the classic constituency politics of domestic policy more than the global issues of foreign policy: aid to Turkey. In July 1975, Turkey intervened militarily in Cyprus, a Mediterranean island populated by people of Turkish and Greek descent, after the Greek military government had attempted to unite Greece and Cyprus. The two countries were historical rivals, but both were NATO members. The situation was further complicated by the fact that Turkish troops used American-supplied arms in their attack. The dilemma posed to American interests was readily resolved when two factors were taken into account: (1) Turkey had not been cooperative with the United States in restricting the growth of poppy seeds, the source of heroin, despite repeated American overtures and assistance on this issue; and (2) there are many more Greek-Americans than Turkish-Americans, and these Greek-Americans tend to live in the larger cities and vote Democratic. Greek-Americans established the American Hellenic Educational Progressive Association (AHEPA) and the American Hellenic Institute Public Affairs Committee (AHIPAC) to lobby for a boycott of military aid to Turkey.

The initial move on the boycott came in the Senate but the Appropriations Committee of that body weakened the language introduced in the House to permit the president to restore aid when Turkey showed good faith in attempting to reach an agreement with Greece. The House clearly took the lead in responding to this foreign policy initiative with strong constituency politics elements. From a position of strength, the House insisted on its position and won in the conference with the Senate, although it agreed to delay the embargo until February 1976, when arms shipments were finally cut off. The success of the House in foreign policy making was, however, short-lived. By the fall of 1976, the good-faith effort language of the Senate was adopted by both houses. The ban was finally lifted in 1978, when Carter was basking in the glory of the Camp David accord between Israel and Egypt. The president's foreign policy leadership had been clearly established, and the Congress was in no mood to reject such a foreign policy initiative, particularly one with such clear-cut implications for NATO.

Throughout the 1970s, then, the House Foreign Affairs Committee was no match for either the president or the Senate Foreign Relations Committee. The 1980 election changed that dramatically. The Republicans not only captured the White House, but also the Senate—for the first time since 1953. The House Foreign Affairs Committee in 1981 became the focal point of Democratic opposition to many of the president's initiatives—especially aid to the Contras, the imposition of sanctions on South Africa, movements toward democracy in the Philippines and South Korea, the blocking of arms sales to Arab countries, and human rights issues. It was not so much that the committee itself had changed; it had not. Instead, it became the only governmental forum in which the Democratic party could air its views. When the committee could force the administration to change policy—as in the South African, Philippine, and South Korean instances—it instantly became a major actor in foreign policy.

While the Foreign Affairs/Foreign Relations committees have generally pushed the president to the left, the Armed Services Committees have tilted to the right. Following the 1986 elections, Sam Nunn (D-Ga.) assumed the chair of the Senate committee. Widely considered the expert in Congress on military matters, he has been a strong supporter of increased defense spending, as have virtually all of his predecessors. Yet Nunn emerged in 1986 as a persistent critic of the Reagan administration's position on the SALT II treaty (see Chapter 8). He argued that the treaty prohibited testing of a "Star Wars" defense system. The ranking minority member, Senator John Warner (R-Va.), served as under secretary and then secretary of the navy from 1969 to 1974. A consistent supporter of increased military power, Warner is nevertheless a low-key legislator without the clout of either Nunn or the four senators who chaired the committee before the Georgia senator took the reins: Republicans Barry Goldwater (Ariz.) and John Tower (Tex.) and Democrats John Stennis (Miss.) and Henry Jackson (Wash.). All have been vocal supporters of defense spending; Jackson was sometimes called the "senator from Boeing" since the defense contractor was a major employer in his state.

The House committee traditionally has been an equally strong defender of the military. Additionally, its members have sought to ensure that their districts receive their fair share (or more) of defense contracts. The most venerable chair of the committee, Mendel Rivers (D-S.C.), who headed the body in the 1950s and 1960s, came from Charleston, which is a veritable armed fortress with every conceivable type of military base. Rivers reputedly once said that "I didn't come to Congress to preside over the demise of the first congressional district." In the 1970s, however, a new group of legislators joined the committee. They were less committed to high levels of defense spending and were often highly critical of the military, especially on the recruitment of women and minorities.

One, Patricia Schroeder (D-Colo.), contemplated running for president in 1988; another, Les Aspin (D-Wis.), shocked the House when he toppled Melvin Price (D-Ill.) as chair in 1985 despite ranking only seventh in seniority. Aspin was just the opposite type of what one would expect as chair of the House Armed Services Committee. He did not spend years working in local politics before his election to the House; instead, he was an economics professor in Wisconsin. He did not practice the inside strategy of bargaining with his colleagues on the committee; instead, he wrote lengthy, scholarly, yet often quite partisan articles in national newspapers and magazines criticizing the committee's policies. He did not concentrate on doling out military contracts to his colleagues; instead, he called for Pentagon reorganization.[50]

Aspin achieved power because a growing majority of the full Democratic caucus—if not the Armed Services Committee itself—wanted a more dynamic leader than the aging and moderate Price to challenge the president's proposed defense buildup. The Wisconsin Democrat pledged to fellow Democrats to do just that—as he had done as a member of the panel—and to oppose military assistance to the Contras and the MX missile. However, he voted for *both* programs favored by the president and in late 1986 the Democratic caucus stripped him of his position for violating his pledge to it. Aspin immediately set out to win back his position and in early 1987 eked out a narrow victory in a four-member race. He won his seat back because he publicly apologized for his errant votes and because his principal rival was a Texas legislator who also had voted for Contra aid.[51] Neither party in the House or the Senate routinely punishes legislators for voting against the majority of their fellow partisans. What made the Aspin case so different is that the legislators sought to send the Armed Services Committee a message in selecting a more activist chair and wound up with a spokesman who sounded like more of the same. If there was to be leadership on Armed Services, it would have to come from the Democrats; ranking minority member William Dickinson (R-Ala.) is low key and hardline on defense.

The remaining foreign policy committees have substantially less clout than do Foreign Relations/Foreign Affairs and Armed Services. The subcommittees on Defense on the House and Senate Appropriations Committees have considerable power over the defense budget. But the balance of power has shifted away from these panels. The House Appropriations committee, as already noted, is expected to play a different role than as booster for the armed forces or for constituency benefits. Before 1981, when the Republicans took control of the Senate, John Stennis chaired both the Armed Services Committee and the Appropriations Defense Subcommittee—something not permitted under House rules restricting any member to one major committee.

The Budget committees in each chamber have major influence on overall levels of spending, but: (1) since their scope is so general, these panels can devote limited attention to foreign policy related expenditures; and (2) more often than not, Congress fails to enact binding budget resolutions, thus circumscribing the committees' influence. Periodically, issues such as energy, trade, and agriculture play a prominent role in the legislative debate over foreign policy. But such instances are intermittent and do not dominate the arena of international politics within the American system. Each of the committees that handles these issues is primarily concerned with domestic affairs.

Finally, the Select Committees on Intelligence have largely faded from the public view. They arose from the abuses of CIA and FBI power in the 1970s, but failed to write a charter for the CIA in 1979–80. They did prevent outright repeal of many of the Hughes-Ryan provisions, as urged by members who thought that the restrictions might have contributed to the failure of the government to respond to the revolutions in Iran and Nicaragua. These committees briefly returned to public view in 1986 when they conducted hearings on the Iran–Contra affair. But they were quickly upstaged by special panels that took over the investigative function. Both the House and the Senate panels have rotating memberships—and shifting chairs—so that legislators have few incentives to develop expertise on intelligence operations. Indeed, Senate Chair David Boren (D-Okla.) is better known for his proposals to control campaign expenditures and House Chair Louis Stokes (D-Ohio) has received more publicity for his prior service in chairing the body's ethics panel.

The many different committees that have jurisdiction over aspects of foreign policy weaken the ability of Congress as an institution to propose and carry out an alternative foreign policy. But they also provide opportunities for the administration to seek support from different constituencies within the Congress for its foreign policy as well as pitfalls for the implementation of some policies. In many instances, the administration only needs to block a restive committee effort to undermine the president's program, and, as stressed before, it is much easier to defeat something in Congress than to pass a bill. But when congressional *support* is required, the battle may become more difficult to win, as the examples of SALT II, the Panama Canal treaties, and even the Turkish arms embargo indicate. Trade-offs on other questions of foreign policy or on domestic issues may have to be employed, and in this sense foreign policy formation by—or with—Congress comes to resemble the constituency politics of domestic policy.

CONGRESSIONAL FRAGMENTATION: CONGRESSIONAL CAUCUSES

In the beginning there was the floor of the Congress. Then things got a little complicated, so the legislature established a system of standing committees to help divide the work load among many people, each of whom would specialize in particular areas. Then, as the subjects of legislation became more complex, the number of committees proliferated so that by 1946 the Congress had to take some action to curtail their growth. In turn, subcommittees bloomed—to as many as 140 in each chamber at one time in the late 1970s and early 1980s. Then members realized that the subcommittee system so compartmentalized decision making that there was no way to get an overall perspective on a particular problem. The multiple referral process further complicated the situation. Rather than coordinating action on a particular problem, this procedure merely divided the work load further. Trade, for example, is such a broad-ranging issue that nine committees in the Senate alone must consider any legislation proposing changes in federal law; energy is even worse (see Chapter 8).

The congressional response, beginning in the 1960s but becoming very important in the 1970s and 1980s, has been the establishment of caucuses dealing with particular policies. (These are not to be confused with party caucuses in the House and Senate, which include all members of each party.)[52] These caucuses focus on particular topics—some broad (energy, trade, black issues, regional concerns), some narrow (footwear, travel, ports). They bring together members from many committees and often both houses. Some are partisan, but most include both Democrats and Republicans. Legislators contribute part of their allowances to support these caucuses. These bodies do not write legislation as committees do; they have no official legislative status, but they often hold their own informal hearings and their members can propose legislation that arises from caucus interactions.

In 1985, there were ninety-three caucuses in the Congress; sixty-three of them (or more than two thirds) had some foreign policy concerns. A list of these caucuses is presented in Table 4–2.[53] Some of the caucuses dealing primarily with foreign policy are concerned with the great issues of war and peace: the Arms Control and Foreign Policy Caucus; the Members of Congress for Peace Through Law, founded during the Vietnam War to seek a legal (rather than confrontational) resolution of that conflict; the Members of Congress for Peace Through Strength, established to support the prosecution of the war; and the Senate Human Rights Caucus. Others are concerned with ethnic or regional politics: the Congressional Coalition for Soviet Jews; the Ad Hoc Committee on Irish Affairs, which advocates support for the Catholics in the religious conflict in Northern Ireland; the Friends of Ireland, which proposes a more moderate approach; and the Ad Hoc Congressional Committee on the Baltic States and Ukraine, among others. The Congressional Black Caucus concerned itself primarily with domestic issues until 1985–86, when it led the fight for sanctions on South Africa. Some are quite narrow—the House Task Force on Coal Exports and the Task Force on the Devaluation of the Peso.

Other caucuses are not primarily concerned with foreign policy issues, but do address them. Eight of these in Table 4–2 deal with energy at least in part; eighteen deal with trade. The Grace Commission Caucus investigates waste in federal spending, including that of the military. While the caucuses do provide members with the possibility of taking detailed looks at questions that might not interest committees (or subcommittees) and let legislators from different panels join together to discuss issues of common interest,[54] they also further fragment congressional policy making. Even nine Senate committees pale by comparison to eighteen caucuses dealing with trade that fall into our list of informal groups only partially dealing with trade with foreign policy. At least eight, and possibly more, of the first group of caucuses fall into the trade category. While these bodies do not consider legislation, they can reinforce the parochial interests of their members. They certainly do not make it any easier for Congress to speak with one voice— so as to convey a straightforward message either to the president or to foreign countries.

The committee system has not only been losing power to subcommittees (see above) and caucuses, but also it has been self-destructing. Simply stated, bills come to the floor of the House and Senate from committees and are no longer "safe" from attack by legislators not on the committee. As late as 1977 the House Armed Services Committee proposed a military spending

TABLE 4–2 Congressional Caucuses Dealing with Foreign Policy

Caucuses Dealing Primarily with International Issues	Chamber
Arms Control and Foreign Policy Caucus	House/Senate
Members of Congress for Peace Through Law	House/Senate
Coalition for Peace Through Strength	House/Senate
Vietnam Veterans in Congress	House/Senate
Coalition for the Peaceful Uses of Space	House/Senate
Congressional Friends of Human Rights Monitors	House/Senate
Senate Human Rights Caucus	Senate
Congressional Space Caucus	House
Military Reform Caucus	House/Senate
Nuclear Non-Proliferation Task Force	House/Senate
Ad Hoc Committee on Irish Affairs	House/Senate
Friends of Ireland	House/Senate
Congressional Coalition for Soviet Jews	House/Senate
Ad Hoc Congressional Committee on the Baltic States and Ukraine	Senate
Congressional Task Force on Afghanistan	House/Senate
Congressional Ad Hoc Monitoring Group on South Africa	House/Senate
Export Task Force	House
Senate Caucus on North American Trade	Senate
House Task Force on North American Trade	House
Pacific Northwest Trade Task Force	House/Senate
Task Force on Devaluation of the Peso	House
Congressional Border Caucus	House
Border Caucus	Senate
Congressional Territorial Caucus	House
House Task Force on Coal Exports	House

TABLE 4–2   *(concluded)*

Congressional Caucuses with Significant Foreign Policy Jurisdiction (Chamber)	Areas of Interest
Democratic Study Group (H)	General
House Democratic Research Organization (H)	General
Senate Steering Committee (S)	General
Senate Wednesday Group [Republicans] (S)	General
House Wednesday Group [Republicans] (H)	General
Conservative Democratic Forum (H)	General
Congressional Clearinghouse on the Future (H/S)	General
Congressional Alcohol Fuels Caucus (H/S)	Energy
Congressional Coal Group (H)	Energy
Senate Coal Caucus (S)	Energy
Congressional Wood Energy Caucus (H/S)	Energy
Environmental and Energy Study Conference (H/S)	Energy
Renewable Energy Congressional Staff Group (H/S)	Energy
Tennessee Valley Authority Caucus (H)	Energy
Task Force on Industrial Innovation and Productivity (House)	Trade
Congressional Steel Caucus (H)	Trade
Senate Steel Caucus (S)	Trade
Congressional Automotive Caucus (H)	Trade
Congressional Textile Caucus (H)	Trade
Senate Textile Steering Committee (S)	Trade
Senate Copper Caucus (S)	Trade
Congressional Travel and Tourism Caucus (H)	Trade
Senate Tourism Caucus (S)	Trade
Senate Wine Caucus (S)	Trade
Congressional Agricultural Forum (H)	Trade
House Footwear Caucus (H)	Trade
Senate Footwear Caucus (S)	Trade
Congressional Port Caucus (H)	Trade
Congressional Populist Caucus (H/S)	Trade
Conference of Great Lakes Congressmen (H)	Trade
Northeast-Midwest Congressional Coalition (H)	Trade/Energy
Northeast-Midwest Senate Coalition (S)	Trade/Energy
Western State Coalition (S)	Energy
Congressional Black Caucus (H)	Africa
Congressional Hispanic Caucus (H)	Latin America
Senate Drug Enforcement Caucus (S)	Drug Enforcement
Grace Commission Caucus (H)	Expenditures

H: House; S: Senate; H/S: Both House and Senate.

SOURCE: Samuel Kernell, *Going Public* (Washington, D.C.: CQ Press, 1986), pp. 28–32.

bill that passed the House after three days of debate with no amendments added to it. Ten years later a military funding bill came to the floor with over 200 amendments proposed.[55] This bill may be somewhat unusual, but it is not atypical. Members of Congress no longer respect committee lines in proposing amendments. Truly, today everyone is an expert on everything— not just education, as with the member cited earlier in the chapter. The number of amendments per bill in the Senate has increased by almost 60 percent in the past three decades. The number of amendments to bills from the Senate Armed Services Committee increased from three during the en- tire decade of the 1950s to seventy-one during the 1970s and 1980s, while on Foreign Relations the jump was less drastic though still notable: from fifty-five to eighty-two.[56] The number of amendments similarly increased in the House. In the Eighty-fourth Congress (1953–54) there were just 14 amendments to Foreign Affairs bills; by the Ninety-sixth (1979–80), the fig- ure had jumped to 183. Furthermore, 83 of those 183 proposals were offered by legislators who did not serve on the committee. For Armed Services, the increase was not quite so dramatic: from thirty-eight to sixty-two. Of the last figure, twenty-seven amendments were proposed by members not on the panel.[57]

CAN CONGRESS MAKE AN EFFECTIVE FOREIGN POLICY?

For all of the increased activism of Congress in recent years, it would be a mistake to conclude that the legislative branch has assumed a role in foreign policy on the magnitude of its concern for domestic policy. The stakes are too different for that to happen, and the data would not support such a conclusion. We present in Table 4–3 a comparison of the number of treaties and executive agreements between 1930 and 1986. While the num- ber of treaties has not increased dramatically, executive agreements have become much more frequent.[58] A study of executive agreements formulated between 1946 and 1972 found that the overwhelming majority of them (87 percent) had been authorized by congressional statute.[59] But this analysis indicates only a greater procedural role for Congress in enacting legislation which permits the agreements to be signed. An agreement signed in 1988 may have been authorized by statute twenty years earlier. Furthermore, the study produced no evidence—and, indeed considerable skepticism—that such statutory grants were based on a knowledge of what types of agree- ments were to follow. Indeed, Carter threatened to implement the Panama Canal legislation as an executive agreement had the Senate defeated the treaties. This suggestion led to heavy criticism of the president and was promptly withdrawn—although Carter's threat may have alleviated some momentum building at the time among treaty opponents. In any event, the idea was unrealistic since the treaties required implementing legislation which appropriated funds to pay Panama for the operation of the canal in

TABLE 4–3   Treaties and Executive Agreements, 1930–1982

Year	Treaties	Executive Agreements	Year	Treaties	Executive Agreements
1930	25	11	1974	13	230
1935	25	10	1975	13	264
1940	12	20	1976	13	402
1944	1	74	1977	17	424
1945	6	54	1978	15	417
1946	19	139	1979	28	378
1950	11	157	1980	26	321
1955	7	297	1981	12	322
1960	5	266	1982	17	343
1965	14	204	1983	23	282
1970	20	183	1984	15	336
1971	17	214	1985	8	336
1972	20	287	1986	17	400
1973	17	241			
Totals, 1946–1986				615	10,542

the years before the land reverts to Panamanian sovereignty. The critical House roll call on this funding in 1979 passed by only a single vote. The administration had assumed that the battle had been won after the Senate consented to the treaties. It could not have been more mistaken. On the other hand, the Congress in 1979 refused to approve the SALT II treaty negotiated with the Soviet Union by the Carter administration despite the president's strong push for ratification. Carter announced that the United States would abide by it anyway and Reagan, despite his strong criticism of the treaty in the 1980 presidential campaign, also agreed to follow its dictates. By 1986, when Reagan argued that SALT II stood in the way of the testing of his "Star Wars" missile defense program, it was the Congress that pressed for continued adherence to the treaty's terms (see Chapter 8). The assertiveness of the Congress on foreign policy questions may not occur often, but at least often enough *on important issues* that the legislative branch can no longer be consigned to a third circle of decision making.

Can Congress make foreign policy? Not by itself, to be sure. Should Congress make foreign policy? The members themselves have answered that question in the affirmative. The president is still the leading spokesman on foreign policy questions, but there is little doubt that his power will not be unchecked in the future. Congress had become more assertive in challenging the president through the use of the legislative veto, especially on foreign policy through the War Powers Act and through stipulations on military sales permitting either or both houses of Congress to block arms transfers after the president had proposed them. However, the 1983 Supreme Court decision invalidating the legislative veto (see Chapter 2) has limited this form of congressional intervention in the foreign policy process.

While the Court has not ruled on the War Powers Act itself, President Reagan has interpreted the 1983 decision as implying that the act *is* unconstitutional. At times he has complied with it anyway—as when marines were sent to Lebanon—but he has also resisted congressional dictates on other occasions (when American ships were sent to the Persian Gulf to protect Kuwaiti oil tankers). The Congress is reluctant to give up the War Powers Act. It is even more concerned that it will be restricted to using joint resolutions, which the president can veto, to assert itself on foreign policy. When the administration refused to invoke the act in September 1987 after an American helicopter fired on an Iranian ship in the Persian Gulf, many in Congress were irate. But they had no clear idea what to do, so the Congress responded by establishing a commission to study how to make the act work.

Yet, even if the War Powers Act is overturned, Congress will continue to assert itself on international affairs. On arms sales, for example, it might—as it has in the past—put forward such strong objections that the administration is compelled to withdraw these proposals. On other areas of international politics, the Congress can be more confrontational by putting limits on what types of aid or military action the administration might pursue *before* any presidential decisions are made.

How desirable is such a trend? Crisis decision making is unlikely to be affected, since the Congress, as well as the mass public, tends to rally around the president during such moments. However, for noncrisis decision making, the question comes down to a very difficult choice which lies at the heart of the problem of foreign policy decision making in a democracy: How can we reconcile the need for swift and united national action and the demand for a set of policy goals that are responsive to public opinion and also meet the requirements of constitutional government? There are inherent tensions here, and every increase in speed and flexibility leads to a decrease in public participation. On the other hand, the greater the degree of public and legislative initiatives in foreign policy, the more difficult it might be for the administration to negotiate (particularly when secret talks are required) with foreign governments and conduct its foreign policy.

The issue of expeditious action versus reflection of public preferences is, however, more complex. The Congress certainly does reflect what its members believe to be public opinion in their districts (or states for senators). Some legislators go so far as to make such opinions the deciding factor in their policy decisions, as Senator Edward Zorinsky (D-Nebr.) did on the Panama Canal treaties in 1978. Zorinsky pledged that he would be bound by poll results he obtained and even went so far in support of the treaties as to convince Carter to invite 250 Nebraska residents to the White House to increase support among influential citizens in the state.[60] The polls consistently showed a majority against the treaties, and Zorinsky reluctantly followed public sentiment. This localism in congressional foreign policy making is clearly aided by the large staffs and tremendous expenditures for offices, supplies, and trips back home. The resources available to members have changed dramatically. Contrast this with the concern of Robert A. Dahl more than thirty years ago over how to make foreign policy making in Congress more consistent with public opinion:

> Representative Jacob Javits employed the Roper agency to poll opinion in the Twenty-first congressional district of New York prior to the 1948 elections. But this is not a readily available technique; the expense rules it out as more than a rare device. One polling agency estimates that it would cost $2,000 to $2,500 to poll a "typical" Congressional district—pretty clearly an expense not many Congressmen or local party organizations can often afford.[61]

In contemporary politics, virtually every candidate for Congress conducts polls which are a regular part of the campaign. Even at inflated prices, polls are now regarded as necessities and well within campaign budgets, which are well over $200,000 for most challengers in the House (and even greater for incumbents) and considerably more than $1.5 million in the Senate.[62] This increased use of polling certainly induces more localism into decision making, including that on foreign policy.

However, it would be all too facile to assume that presidents are immune from public pressure in the conduct of foreign policy. Indeed, in his first major speech after resigning in protest as secretary of state in the Carter administration, Cyrus Vance charged in June 1980 that the administration's policies regarding SALT II, Afghanistan, the Middle East, and human rights were based more on election year political considerations—public opinion—than on global political considerations.[63] Carter spent the better part of his early campaign in the White House during the 1980 Democratic party primaries, in which Kennedy challenged him, stressing his role as president. To be sure, the president argued that he was preoccupied with the crisis in Iran, but when he felt that political pressures forced him to resume active campaigning, the hostages were still not free. During the campaign, Reagan roundly criticized Carter for refusing to take decisive action and preferring to negotiate with Iran for the hostages' release. This made for good press and studies of the 1980 election indicate that Reagan benefited from the public's perception of Carter as a weak leader, especially on issues of national defense (see Chapter 5). Yet, six years later the revelations that Reagan had in fact approved negotiating with the Iranians for the release of American hostages showed that even the most strident of candidates was actually seeking more leeway than popular sentiments might permit. The Iran–Contra affair tested the limits of public opinion and severely constrained the Reagan administration's initiatives in foreign policy thereafter.

In 1972, before the Republican convention, Nixon made his historic trip to China and traveled to Moscow to sign SALT I. Presidents, no less than members of Congress, are political animals and have a keen sense of how to use the advantage of incumbency to increase their standing in public opinion polls. Foreign policy initiatives—or even crises—are particularly useful in this regard because they focus directly on the president in a "we–they" perspective. The chief executive is seen dealing with other heads of state, thus avoiding a direct confrontation with political rivals. To a certain extent, a president serving his second term is shielded from such political pressures, but we should not overestimate the impact of the two-term limitation mandated by the Twenty-second Amendment to the Constitution. For no president wants to leave office unpopular—and perhaps charged with contributing to the election of a successor of the opposite party because his policies were out of step with public opinion.

The question, in the final analysis, is which institution better represents public opinion? In turn, we must ask: Is there a single national opinion to be represented, as defenders of the strong presidency maintain, or is the nation composed largely of groups of citizens with different interests? The answer we give largely determines which institution should dominate foreign policy decision making, assuming that one wants to argue that foreign policy, like domestic policy, should be subject to such public concern and influences. Perhaps the major questions each of us must ask ourselves are whether the two types of policy making require basically similar or different approaches and whether the benefits of participation by the legislative branch in foreign policy making, thus checking a potential "imperial president," are greater, equal to, or less than the costs imposed by the concern of Congress with issues of interest to the constituencies and by the delays (deliberations) involved in participatory decision making.

NOTES

1. Alfred deGrazia, ed., *Congress: The First Branch of Government* (Washington, D.C.: American Enterprise Institute, 1966).
2. Arthur M. Schlesinger, Jr., *The Imperial Presidency* (Boston: Houghton Mifflin, 1973).
3. Hanna Fenichel Pitkin, *The Concept of Representation* (Berkeley: University of California Press, 1967), chap. 4.
4. Roger Hilsman, *The Politics of Policy-Making in Defense and Foreign Affairs* (New York: Harper & Row, 1971), pp. 118–20.
5. J. Lieper Freeman, *The Political Process*, rev. ed. (New York: Random House, 1965).
6. Roger H. Davidson, "Breaking up Those 'Cozy Triangles': An Impossible Dream?" in *Legislative Reform and Public Policy*, eds. S. Welch and J. G. Peters, (New York: Praeger Publishers, 1977), pp. 30–53.
7. David R. Mayhew, *Party Loyalty among Congressmen* (Cambridge: Harvard University Press, 1966).
8. Robert A. Dahl, *Polyarchy* (New Haven: Yale University Press, 1971), esp. p. 120.

9. Thomas M. Franck and Edward Weisband, *Foreign Policy by Congress* (New York: Oxford University Press, 1979), pp. 283–84.

10. John Felton, "Reagan Again Finds El Salvador 'Making Progress' on Rights; Critics in Congress Skeptical," *Congressional Quarterly Weekly Report,* January 29, 1983, p. 218.

11. John Felton, "Democrats Falter on Nicaragua Covert Aid Ban," *Congressional Quarterly Weekly Report,* May 21, 1983, p. 1,009.

12. Steven R. Weisman, "Nicaragua Vote: How White House Ran Aground," New York *Times,* August 1, 1983, p. A3.

13. David S. Broder, "New Potential for Dividing Democrats," *Washington Post,* May 8, 1983, pp. A1, A9.

14. For a detailed explication of this thesis, see Eric M. Uslaner, "The Decline of Comity in Congress," paper presented at the American Politics Group of the Political Studies Association of the United Kingdom, London, January 1987.

15. Joanne Omang, "Reagan to Bypass Congress to Fund El Salvador Fight," *Washington Post,* April 14, 1984, pp. A1, A14.

16. John M. Goshko, "Appointing Loyalists as Envoys" and "Clout and Moral Decline: Reaganites' Raid on the Latin Bureau," *Washington Post,* April 28, 1987, pp. A1, A16, and April 26, 1987, pp. A1, A12.

17. David B. Ottaway and Patrick E. Tyler, "New Era of Mistrust Marks Congress' Role," *Washington Post,* May 19, 1986, pp. A1, A10.

18. Quoted in Steven V. Roberts, "Foreign Policy: Lot of Table Thumping Going On," *New York Times,* May 29, 1985, p. A16.

19. Steven V. Roberts, "The Mood in Congress Is Bold and Bitter," *New York Times,* June 2, 1987, p. B6.

20. Richard F. Fenno, Jr., *Congressmen in Committees* (Boston: Little, Brown, 1973), p. 103.

21. Frank Smith, *Congressman from Mississippi* (New York: Pantheon, 1964), p. 127. Cf. David R. Mayhew, *Congress: The Electoral Connection* (New Haven: Yale University Press, 1974), esp. chap. 1.

22. Warren Weaver, Jr., "Books of the Times: Review of *Man of the House: The Life and Political Memoirs of Speaker Tip O'Neill,*" *New York Times,* September 3, 1987, p. C24.

23. Walter Dean Burnham, *Critical Elections and the Mainsprings of American Politics* (New York: W. W. Norton, 1970).

24. The above figures were drawn from Morris P. Fiorina, *Congress: Keystone of the Washington Establishment* (New Haven: Yale University Press); and Norman J. Ornstein et al., eds., *Vital Statistics on Congress, 1984–1985 Edition* (Washington, D.C.: American Enterprise Institute, 1984).

25. Eric M. Uslaner, "The Case of the Vanishing Liberal Senators," *British Journal of Political Science* 11 (January 1981), pp. 105–113.

26. Data from the House Commission on Administrative Review, 1977, survey of members of the House of Representatives.

27. Samuel P. Huntington, "Congressional Responses to the Twentieth Century," in *The Congress and America's Future,* 2d. ed., ed. D. B. Truman (Englewood Cliffs, N.J.: Prentice-Hall, 1973), pp. 6–38.

28. Fenno, *Congressmen in Committees,* chap. 1.

29. Richard F. Fenno, Jr., *Home Style* (Boston: Little, Brown, 1978), p. 160.

30. Fenno, *Congressmen in Committees,* p. 110.

31. *Ibid.*, p. 12.
32. *Ibid.*, p. 141.
33. Mark Shields, "One Man's Dynasty," *Washington Post*, September 10, 1986, p. A19.
34. Uslaner, "The Case of the Vanishing Liberal Senators."
35. Quoted in Norman J. Ornstein and David W. Rohde, "Shifting Forces, Changing Rules and Political Outcomes," in *New Perspectives on the House of Representatives*, 3d. ed., Robert L. Peabody and Nelson W. Polsby, eds., (Chicago: Rand McNally, 1977), p. 222.
36. See the remarks of the Honorable Bob Carr (D., Mich.), *Congressional Record*, Daily Edition, Ninety-sixth Congress, First Session (March 5, 1978), p. E838; and Bruce A. Ray. "Committee Attractiveness in the U.S. House, 1963–1981," *American Journal of Political Science* 18(August 1982), pp. 609–13.
37. Testimony before the United States House of Representatives Select Committee on Committees, November 14, 1979; quoted in Uslaner, "The Congressional War on Energy," paper prepared for the Conference on Understanding Congressional Leadership sponsored by the Everett McKinley Dirksen Congressional Leadership Research Center, Washington, D.C., June 10–11, 1980, p. 2.
38. Roger H. Davidson, Walter J. Oleszek, and Thomas Kephart, "One Bill, Many Committees: Multiple Referrals in the House of Representatives" (Washington, D.C.: Congressional Research Service, Library of Congress, 1986).
39. See Donald R. Matthews and James A. Stimson, *Yeas and Nays* (New York: John Wiley, 1975).
40. Roberts, "Foreign Policy."
41. For a general discussion of these reforms, see Leroy N. Rieselbach, *Congressional Reform in the Seventies* (New York: General Learning Press, 1977).
42. Fenno, *The Power of the Purse* (Boston: Little, Brown, 1966), esp. chap. 11.
43. Theodore J. Lowi, *The End of Liberalism*, 2d ed. (New York: W. W. Norton, 1979).
44. John M. Goshko, "For Pell, Tests Await on a Resurgent Panel," *Washington Post*, November 11, 1986, p. A19.
45. Leslie H. Gelb, "For Senate Foreign Relations Panel, More Partisanship and Less Influence," *New York Times*, November 27, 1984, p. A27; and Jonathan Fuerbringer, "Senate Foreign Relations Committee: Some Political Chasms That Await the Arms Treaty," *New York Times*, December 7, 1987, p. B6.
46. Fenno, *Congressmen in Committees*, p. 108.
47. *Ibid.*, pp. 71–72 and 134; see also Ornstein and Rohde, "Shifting Forces," p. 223.
48. Christopher Madison, "Foreign Aid Bill Will Put Fascell's Old-School Legislative Skills to the Test," *National Journal*, March 16, 1985, pp. 572–76.
49. John Felton, "Fascell Gives New Life to Foreign Affairs Panel," *Congressional Quarterly Weekly Report*, April 28, 1984, pp. 967–70.
50. Michael Barone and Grant Ujifusa, *The Almanac of American Politics 1986* (Washington, D.C.: National Journal, 1985), pp. 1,458–60.
51. Jacqueline Calmes, "Aspin Makes Comeback at Armed Services," *Congressional Quarterly Weekly Report*, January 24, 1987, pp. 139–42.
52. Only the Democrats have caucuses. The Republicans call their organizations of all members in each house *conferences*.

53. The source, as noted in the table, is Samuel Kernell, *Going Public* (Washington, D.C.: CQ Press, 1986), pp. 28–32. Kernell, however, does not list the Members of Congress for Peace Through Law.

54. Arthur G. Stevens, Jr., Daniel P. Mulhollan, and Paul S. Rundquist, "U.S. Congressional Structure and Representation: The Role of Informal Groups," *Legislative Studies Quarterly* 6 (August 1981), pp. 415–37.

55. John H. Cushman, Jr., "Amending Military Spending," *New York Times*, May 5, 1987, p. A32.

56. Barbara Sinclair, "The Transformation of the U.S. Senate—Institutional Consequences of Behavioral Change." Presented at the 1987 Annual Meeting of the Midwest Political Science Association, Chicago, April 1987.

57. Steven S. Smith, "Revolution in the House: Why Don't We Do It on the Floor?" Table 12. Brookings Discussion Papers in Governmental Studies, number 5 (Washington, D.C.: Brookings Institution, 1986).

58. This table is taken from Majorie Ann Browne, "Executive Agreements and the Congress: Issue Brief Number IB75035" (Washington: Congressional Research Service, Library of Congress, 1980), p. 2. We are grateful to her for providing unpublished updated and revised figures.

59. Loch Johnson and James M. McCormick, "The Making of International Agreements: A Reappraisal of Congressional Involvement," *Journal of Politics* 40 (May 1978), pp. 468–78.

60. Thomas M. Franck and Edward Weisband, *Foreign Policy by Congress* (New York: Oxford University Press, 1979), p. 277.

61. Robert A. Dahl, *Congress and Foreign Policy* (New York: W. W. Norton, 1950), p. 37.

62. Norman J. Ornstein, Thomas E. Mann, Michael J. Malbin, Allen Schick, and John F. Bibby, comps., *Vital Statistics on Congress, 1984–1985 Edition* (Washington, D.C.: American Enterprise Institute, 1984) p. 65; and Thomas Edsall, "$450 Million Was Spent in '86 Hill Races," *Washington Post*, May 10, 1987, p. A15.

63. *New York Times*, June 6, 1980, p. A12.

Chapter Five

The Fourth Circle I:
Public Opinion, Political Parties,
and the Media

One of the key differences between foreign and domestic policy making lies in the power of the president. Domestic policy formation is always a matter of give and take between the legislative and executive branches. In foreign policy crises, however, the smallest inner circle (see Figure 1–1) makes the decisions and the other actors simply react. Before the 1960s, the executive dominated other aspects of foreign policy decision making as well. Now, however, other actors such as the Congress, public opinion, the political parties, the media, local political leaders, and interest groups play a much larger role in foreign policy decision making than in the past. This is particularly the case on intermestic policies that are a mixture of foreign and domestic issues such as energy, trade, and agriculture (see Chapter 8).

The actors in the outermost circle, who have become increasingly active on foreign policy in the past two decades, highlight the democratic dilemmas. On the one hand, foreign policy has become much more participatory and thus more like domestic politics. On the other hand, the stakes of foreign policy in a nuclear age have remained much higher than those of domestic issues. The distrust of presidential authority that began during the Vietnam War lasted through the Carter administration. Faith in a strong presidency was restored early in the Reagan administration, only to plunge again during the Iran–Contra affair. World leaders looking to the United States for action on foreign policy found not only no central authority, but also conflicting policy initiatives. During the televised hearings, some key witnesses testified that Congress and the actors in the two outer circles were confounding effective policy making by opposing aid to the Contras. Outraged senators and representatives responded that the United States is, after all, founded on a respect for law, whether one agrees with the specific statute or not.

The role of the outer circles is crucial to any discussion of foreign policy making and the democratic dilemmas. Since the Vietnam War, the old politics of consensus crossing the two major parties has given way to one of multiple factions. Some will see a danger in this trend, much as James Madison did in *Federalist Papers* 10 and 51 on domestic political issues over 200 years ago. Others will argue that democratic decision making requires a give and take and that it is more important that a policy be arrived at democratically than that it be correct. In international crises, after all, the executive still retains the flexibility to act expeditiously. And should not the people have a say in forming the very policies that will decide whether they live or die? We examine these questions in this and the next chapter.

POPULAR CONTROL OF FOREIGN POLICY

At the heart of any discussion of democratic government is popular control of decision making by the citizenry. Parties, interest groups, and the media serve to shape public opinion, which is the foundation of legitimacy in democratic politics.[1] Without popular control of decision making, democratic government becomes little more than a myth. Yet the question remains of how competent the public is to make the difficult decisions on complex issues such as nuclear deterrence. It is also unclear that the public is sufficiently interested in these issues to take an active role in ensuring that government leaders adopt the positions that a majority of the public wants. If the public does not give the actors in the first three circles clear cues about what it wants, the leadership will have few incentives to follow what is called *public opinion*. In turn, however, the public may complain that its leaders—whether in government or the opinion leaders of political parties, interest groups, or the media—do not present these complex issues in terms the ordinary citizen can understand.

These issues in popular control of government were less salient twenty years ago because there were few lines of cleavage on most foreign policy questions. Political parties did not take divergent stands on foreign policy questions. Foreign affairs intruded less frequently on the domestic scene in the era before the world economy became so interconnected. Thus, the press did not focus on the international arena except during crises. And there were very few interest groups active on these issues.

The Vietnam War changed all of this in two important ways. First, television coverage of the war brought home a new dimension of international conflict. New technology made it possible, for the first time, for viewers to see the war fought as it happened. Second, and more critical, as the war dragged on, so did public cynicism. In the late 1960s there were sharp increases in the percentages of citizens who felt that the government was unresponsive and could not be trusted. Furthermore, the high levels of faith in the political system in the early 1960s have not been restored.[2] The conflict over the war translated not only into public cynicism, but also into the breakdown of the prewar consensus on the proper role of the United States in world affairs.

This is not to say that there were no disagreements in the United States on foreign policy issues before the Vietnam War. There has always been a sizable portion of the American public who have pointed to President George Washington's warning in his farewell address about "entangling alliances." Yet this isolationist segment of public opinion has been a distinct minority; it did not succeed in preventing American entrance into either world war. But in the post-Vietnam period, a new attitude of noninternationalism has arisen and now accounts for almost half of the electorate. It is skeptical of international involvements of any kind.[3] Elites, who had always been more united than the mass public, were now split on even more complex lines than they were before the war in Vietnam. Some of these opinion leaders remained ready to use American military power wherever needed (the Cold War internationalists). Others, especially those who opposed the Vietnam War from the beginning, were either outrightly skeptical of the use of force (the semiisolationists) or at least much more wary of where military action would do any good (the post-Cold War internationalists).[4]

The Vietnam War brought an end to the era of bipartisanship on foreign policy. No longer was it clear that the United States was united on the goals of "making the world safe for democracy," the expressed purpose for entering World War I. The breakup of the consensus led to increasing partisanship and the formation of a large number of interest groups taking part in international issues. Foreign policy had, in short, become democratized. Yet, for all of the din, it was not at all clear that the public was terribly concerned with international issues.

As in domestic issues, a debate has arisen about whether the public responds rationally to international affairs or is readily manipulated by executive leadership.[5] Yet, in contrast to domestic issues—which are often very salient to the everyday lives of citizens—foreign affairs often seem remote. One view of public opinion on foreign policy is that the bulk of the citizenry cares little about foreign policy and thus may easily be manipulated.[6] People respond to external events, but they tend to rally behind the president in an international crisis *even when it is clear that the president's policy has failed.* Only when policy failure clearly extends over a long period of time does the public turn fickle. It then does so with a vengeance, demanding that the government refrain from any similar initiatives, no matter how well intentioned. Public opinion thus offers little guidance to elected leaders about what they should do. Rather, it serves to set limits about what is prohibited.[7] In either case, however, "the reaction has no depth and no structure."[8]

There is another perspective that does perceive the public as acting rationally on foreign policy. It acknowledges that there are different patterns of public responses to domestic and foreign policy—public opinion shifts more abruptly and by larger amounts on foreign policy—but that the public is rarely misled by its leaders. Instead, it responds in predictable, and thus rational, ways to external events.[9] These differing perspectives are based on alternative views of what popular control of foreign policy means. The first view requires that the public understand events, formulate opinions about them, and hold consistent belief systems across a range of foreign policies. Furthermore, for public opinion to be really effective, citizens should translate their policy preferences into voting decisions. As we shall see below, there is little evidence that any of these conditions hold. The alternative view, however, only requires that people react *retrospectively* to foreign policy decisions. It stems from a conception of democracy that places less emphasis on detailed knowledge than on the ability to form judgments about what the government has done. The leading proponent of this view, E. E. Schattschneider, argued almost three decades ago that one doesn't have to be an obstetrician to have a baby, just as one doesn't have to be a policy expert to form a rational opinion about government decisions.[10]

IS PUBLIC OPINION ON FOREIGN POLICY RATIONAL?

What does the evidence show about a "rational public"? Since public opinion has been measured, public opinion has been responsive to presidential leadership on foreign policy. It supported hardline anti-Soviet and anti-Chinese policies when they were official policy (as from Truman's day through Johnson) and it supported moves toward a relaxation of tensions and the negotiating of conflicts (as during the Nixon and Carter eras). The public looked to the president for its cues. During international crises the public rallies behind presidential leadership even when the chief executive's policy is widely viewed as a failure. The Japanese attack on Pearl Harbor boosted Franklin D. Roosevelt's popularity from an already high 72 percent to 84 percent. The communist invasion of South Korea led to a nine-point gain for Harry S Truman (from 37 to 46 percent). Kennedy's popularity jumped sharply after the abortive Bay of Pigs invasion by Cuban emigrés, while Ford's surged by eleven points immediately after the *Mayaquez* incident. The seizure of the American embassy in Teheran resulted in a nineteen-point gain for Carter. Public approval of President Reagan increased after the hijacking of TWA flight 847 to Beirut.[11]

Even more dramatic are the effects on specific actions taken by the government. Just before Nixon's decision to send American troops into Cambodia, only 7 percent of the respondents to a national survey approved of such a move. Afterward, support had increased to 50 percent. The initial reaction to the invasion of Grenada was mixed at best, with just a bare plurality supporting the president's initiative. After the president made a televised speech defending his policy there and in Lebanon, support for the Grenada invasion increased by nine points in one poll and thirteen points in another. In Lebanon, where the marines had been killed in a terrorist attack, the president registered an eleven-point increase in public approval of his handling of the crisis, even though there was no change at all in the public's disapproval of maintaining troops in that beleaguered country.[12]

Why do presidents seem to benefit from setbacks in foreign policy? In such crises, the public tends to "rally around the flag" because it sees international conflicts in "we–they" terms.[13] People place the blame for international crises on the opposition—and this is quite understandable since the "they" is almost always a hostile power such as the Soviet Union. If presidents benefit from setbacks, they also gain when things seem to go their way. Even as the Grenada intervention and the bombing of Libya in early 1986 were widely condemned internationally and by many members of Congress, both events were viewed as shows of American strength by the American public and led to sharp increases in the president's popularity. The bombing of Libya resulted in Reagan's second highest public support rating during his presidency. Even staged events such as summits—even summits that fail to reach accords—can lead to significant increases in presidential popularity.[14]

Yet presidents are hardly unconstrained by public opinion. First, the quick jumps in presidential popularity are usually short-lived. Presidents can gain some support from international events, but since the public's attention span on foreign policy is limited, soon other factors will intervene to shape its view of presidential performance. Foreign policy is different from domestic policy in its impact on popularity. Domestic issues rarely have measurable impacts on the public's approval of the incumbent chief executive. However, the second constraint shows that international events can be double-edged swords. As crises drag on and the continued high costs appear increasingly pointless given the disappearance of the expectation of victory, public support for the president declines. In Korea, five months after the American intervention public support for Truman dropped sharply. The drop took longer in Vietnam: public support for the president did not reach a low point until more than two years after the initial troop commitment. The communist Tet offensive in early 1968 led to a temporary rebound for Johnson. As the number of casualties increased in each contest, public support for the policy and for the president decreased dramatically; the impact of the casualty rate was sharper for Vietnam than for Korea.[15]

Following the seizure of hostages by Iran, Carter's approval more than doubled from its nadir of 30 percent. Approval of the president's handling of the hostage crisis stood at almost 80 percent in December 1979. But as the situation wore on without resolution, public confidence in Carter declined. By April 1980 support for the way he was handling the crisis dropped to 39 percent, his overall job performance to 40 percent, and foreign policy performance to just over 30 percent from 50 percent approval five months earlier.[16] Carter's descent was much more precipitous than Truman's or Johnson's. As with Vietnam, however, the constant media attention served to highlight the president's inability to resolve the issue.

Presidents tend to lose their popularity slowly, except when some major event intervenes. Nixon lost considerable popularity in 1973 over the Watergate scandal and Ford's popularity declined sharply in just six weeks following his pardon of Nixon the next year. Truman, battling a hostile Congress controlled by the opposite party, gradually lost popular support in 1947. However, Reagan's drop of twenty-one approval points in one month following the revelations of illegal arms sales to Iran set a contemporary record. Some argued that the quick fall occurred because news travels faster than it did twenty years ago.[17] Yet television is only part of the story. The long-term decline of public confidence in American institutions and authority figures has produced a citizenry ready to turn on its leaders with striking rapidity. Furthermore, Reagan had done much to restore public confidence in the presidency, so it is hardly surprising that the public would react with such severity against the rescuer of the mantle of the White House.

So far, we have a paradox. On the one hand, the public does respond to events. Declines in presidential popularity follow a pattern pretty much like that described in the theory of rational public opinion. Citizens respond retrospectively to policy failures by the chief executive. Yet they also react positively to what seem to be policy successes, at least as revealed in the polls. What, then, are we to make of public opinion on foreign policy?

One constraint on viewing public opinion as rational is that the public does not always speak with one voice. Sixty-four percent of a November 1965 sample of Americans did *not* think that American involvement in Vietnam was a mistake, as compared to 21 percent who believed that it was. By October 1967, the balance had shifted to the position that the war was a mistake (44 percent in favor, 46 percent opposed). By the summer of 1968 a sizable majority took the latter position.[18] Yet the pattern of support for proposals to end the war—including both a stepped-up military posture and total withdrawal—had not changed accordingly from 1965 to 1968. Mueller has thus argued that, at any given time, "support should be considered a chord rather than a note."[19] This was no less true of the Iranian situation, where citizens critical of the president nevertheless did not offer a mandate about what should have been done.[20] The president can use this pattern of inconsistency to indicate that there is not enough support for any alternative policy to warrant a shift in his position.

A second constraint on rationality in public opinion about foreign policy is the citizenry's lack of interest in and knowledge about international events. A 1986 poll found that only 38 percent of Americans knew that the United States was supporting the Contras as opposed to the government in Nicaragua. Yet this represented a virtual tripling of knowledgeable Americans from three years earlier. In 1986, an equal number of respondents thought that the Nicaraguan government was right wing as did those who thought that it was Communist. Similarly, only 34 percent of a national sample knew that "Star Wars" referred to Reagan's space missile defense; 28 percent could only remember the movie. And two thirds of the public admitted knowing "nothing at all" about the SALT II treaty in 1986.[21] Only 20 percent of a sample reported that they had followed the news about Central America "very closely." Four of the five most important foreign goals cited by the public were intermestic issues; two of the top three goals concerned protecting American jobs and exports.[22]

Third, American public opinion on foreign policy is much more fickle than attitudes on domestic issues. Attitudes changed by a mean of 31 percent a year on international questions, compared to just 12 percent for domestic issues. While Shapiro and Page argue that these abrupt changes are rational responses to the changing international environment,[23] the quick shifts we discussed earlier—after a presidential address, for example—indicate that the public often forms opinions on the spot. The retrospective (looking backward) perspective on rationality does not require the same level of information as the more demanding "democratic citizen" model. Yet, even with the retrospective model, it is difficult to come up with the picture of a reasoned citizenry. The public does make "rational" retrospective judgments on the state of the economy, even relatively sophisticated ones that punish the president's party more for inflation than for unemployment.[24] People are confronted with the same economic problems again and again and thus can make reasoned judgments easily. On the other hand, many (if not most) foreign policy issues are new (Grenada, Libya, the Iran hostage crisis) and catch the nation unaware. It is far more difficult for citizens to make rational retrospective evaluations on international issues.

Yet, for all of the difficulties with the concept of rational thinking on foreign policy by the American public, there are some signs that point the other way. Most critical, attitudes on foreign policy are still shaped primarily by presidential initiatives, but the chief executive no longer has the free hand that he did before Vietnam. Schneider argues that the inattentive public has nevertheless been guided by two overriding themes over the past two and a half decades: peace and strength. Furthermore, the primacy of one idea over the other follows quite closely from events in the international arena. From 1964 to 1974, the public was preoccupied with issues of peace as opposition mounted to the war in Vietnam; from 1974 to the early 1980s, growing Soviet militarism as well as the Iran hostage crisis focused people's attention on reasserting American strength in the world. Yet after the initial military buildup achieved by the Reagan administration, public attitudes turned away from increased defense spending and toward the nuclear freeze. One member of the House of Representatives said that the drive for a freeze was "the most powerful, spontaneous grass-roots movement I have seen since I was elected to Congress."[25]

Public opinion has served to constrain the president on a wide variety of issues. Most generally, the president can afford to be cooperative rather than aggressive with the Soviet Union only in periods when the public's attention is not focused on international affairs. Contrary to the widely held belief that an executive can use international conflict to shore up lagging popularity—as did British Prime Minister Margaret Thatcher in the Falklands War before the 1983 British elections—unpopular presidents generally fear using force abroad.[26] Presidents in the post-Vietnam era find that they can no longer dominate the agenda on international affairs. The public, as noted, strongly favored the nuclear freeze and lower defense spending by 1982, despite strong efforts by Reagan to convince them otherwise. Poll after poll showed consistent public opposition to aid to the Contras—among those who knew which side the United States government was supporting *and* among those who did not, and among both liberals and conservatives and Democrats and Republicans. Even citizens who approved of the way Reagan was handling his job did not favor support for the Contras.[27] Polls do not show this kind of clear-cut evidence on sanctions against the apartheid regime in South Africa, but it appears that support for such measures—which were strongly opposed by the Reagan administration yet supported by bipartisan majorities in the Congress—was increasing during the period leading to the congressional action in 1986.[28]

RATIONAL PUBLIC OPINION AND THE IRAN–CONTRA AFFAIR

Not only does the public no longer simply follow presidential initiatives, but citizens also more readily criticize the president now than in the pre-Vietnam era. Vietnam, Watergate, the Iran hostage crisis, and the Iran–Contra affair have all left deep scars on presidential popularity and reputations. Unlike Vietnam and the hostage crisis, the Iran–Contra affair resulted in an immediate loss of popularity for Reagan. The clear reason for this is that there was no external enemy to blame. Iran did nothing to the United States in this example; the administration, rather, shot itself in the foot. A substantial percentage of the American public, up to a third, was uninterested in the affair as late as February 1987 and even the chairman of the House committee investigating the incident found his constituents wishing that the Congress would move on to more weighty matters.[29]

Yet the considerable majority that did follow the affair was able to make reasonably sophisticated judgments. In Figure 5–1 we present graphs from several polling sources of trends in presidential popularity and show the percentage of respondents who believed that the president was telling the truth about the matter. We see that Reagan's popularity was near its peak before the revelation of the problem in early November and that it quickly plummeted. When the president made a televised speech in which he agreed to name an independent counsel to investigate the affair in early December, his popularity continued to decline as people evidently felt that where there is smoke there is fire. Following the testimony of former National Security Council Chairman Robert McFarlane in early December, Reagan's popularity did not fall further, but the share of people saying that the

FIGURE 5–1   Public Opinion on President Reagan during Iran–Contra Affair

president was telling the truth increased by 5 percent. While McFarlane did not specifically exonerate the president, he did accept much responsibility himself.

Following the January release of the Tower Commission report indicating that the president didn't know of the diversion of funds to the Contras, Reagan's popularity slightly increased. It fell sharply in mid-February, following McFarlane's attempted suicide. Other events such as the replacement of Chief of Staff Donald Regan by Howard Baker in late February and Reagan's television speech in early March admitting that "mistakes were made" had little impact on either the president's popularity or the percentage of people who believed he was telling the truth. The first was of little interest "outside the Washington Beltway" and, presumably, Reagan's television speech made so little impact because most people already realized that mistakes *had* been made. However, the beginning of televised hearings on May 5 led to a sharp drop (seven percentage points) in the share of the public believing that the president was telling the truth, even as Reagan's personal popularity marginally increased. By early June, however, no major new revelations had damaged the president and Reagan's popularity and truthfulness ratings each increased by approximately 5 percent.

While the testimony of Lt. Col. Oliver North dramatically changed the tenor of the hearings, as North became something of a national hero, Reagan did not appear to benefit personally from the boomlet of public support for the colonel. There was little change in the percentage of Americans who thought the president was not telling the truth in early July. Some surveys indicated that the public believed that North was simply "taking a fall" for

the president. Yet, when Admiral John Poindexter testified that he had en-
gineered the diversion of funds to the Contras and there appeared to be no
"smoking gun" linked to the White House, the public turned a deaf ear.
Most believed that Poindexter was not telling the truth. While there was a
sharp increase in just one week in the percentage of Americans who believed that Reagan was telling the truth, the conversion came primarily from
the ranks of citizens who previously had had no opinion. There was but a
modest drop in the share of the public (still a majority) who believed the
president to be lying. More generally, the president appeared no more popular than two months earlier. Ironically, the major shift in public opinion as
a result of the hearings—in particular, of North's testimony—was a dramatic
increase in public support for aid to the Contras, as reported in most (but
not all) polls. Supporters of the president's policy argued that the hearings
made the American people more aware of the stakes involved in Central
America, so Nicaragua no longer seemed like just a remote place where
American soldiers might be sent to be killed. Opponents charged that these
results would prove fleeting, representing little more than patriotic zeal and
"Olliemania."

Reagan never fully recovered his popularity after the Iran–Contra affair.
The percentage of people who approved his performance was generally
about the same as that who disapproved for the remainder of 1987, with just
a few exceptions. Two raids on Iran in September and October (each of
which was supported by over 75 percent of Americans) led to surges in
presidential popularity, but each time Reagan fell back to the break-even
point shortly thereafter. Reagan did finish the year on a high note, with
approval rising form 50 percent to 58 percent following the summit with
Soviet leader Mikhail Gorbachev. Even worse for the president, support for
his Central American policies quickly evaporated. Within one month, all
polls indicated that the public's opposition to aid for the Contras was once
again in the 50–60 range, the same level as before North's testimony. Public
resistance to aid to the Contras stabilized at this level throughout the year.

The Iran–Contra affair, the hostage crisis, and the wars in Vietnam and
Korea had profound effects on presidential popularity. Yet other presidential
failures such as the Reykjavik summit with Gorbachev in 1986 did not. Richard A. Brody and Catherine R. Shapiro noted that Reagan's popularity actually increased by 4 percent following the failed summit. They argued that
the difference between the two situations is found in the president's ability
to control the flow of information. When events are moving quickly, as in
the summit, the administration effectively controls the news and opposition
political leaders hesitate to criticize the president for fear of appearing unpatriotic. The press behaves similarly. When a crisis begins to drag out,
however, the president becomes a target for all sorts of opposition.[30] The
message for presidents, then, is: Prevent a crisis from getting out of hand to
minimize damage to your popularity. This, of course, is much easier said
than done.

PUBLIC OPINION AND THE DEMOCRATIC DILEMMAS

The pattern of public opinion on the Iran–Contra affair indicates that the public, when it is sufficiently interested in a foreign policy issue, can respond quite rationally to events—even events that are not dramatic. And the public certainly found the Iran–Contra affair disturbing: there were as many people who believed that it was at least as serious as Watergate as there were people who thought that Watergate was worse.[31] Events such as the Iran–Contra affair, the hostage crisis, and wars such as Korea and Vietnam occur over months and years. The public's attention is focused on such issues and thus citizens can respond "rationally" to even relatively minor incidents. Issues such as peace and strength also appear on the nation's agenda continuously. On the other hand, short-lived international crises such as the Bay of Pigs, the Tet Offensive, the *Mayaquez*, Grenada, Libya, and hostage takings vanish from public attention quickly. People are unfamiliar with these international scenarios. Indeed, sometimes so are the State Department and even the Central Intelligence Agency, both of which were caught unaware regarding the fall of the shah and the hostage crisis that ensued. In those circumstances people follow the only cue that is available—presidential leadership. Indeed, so does the Congress. The "we–they" conflict inherent in such crises provides the president with a key advantage. More so than at any other time, there is a need to focus on a single actor to reinforce the "we" in domestic politics.

Issues that linger in the background—especially the American role in world affairs—form a middle ground. For the most part they are not terribly salient to the average citizen. Furthermore, the public is skeptical of getting deeply involved in world affairs, fearing another protracted conflict such as Vietnam; it worries more about protecting the United States—both militarily and economically. Here the nature of the debate on foreign policy and the democratic dilemmas shifts. Even those who argue that the public does not closely follow all of the issues in world politics do not argue that the public is irrational. Noninternationalism is based on clearly articulated fears of becoming too entangled in international conflicts. Thus, the debate shifts from the desirability of broad participation (the third dilemma) to the need for the president to maintain flexibility in dealing with other nations (the first dilemma) and to process versus output (the second dilemma). In dealing with other countries, the president needs to be able to respond quickly to international crises, on the one hand, and to pursue policies that are acceptable to our allies on the other hand. Public opinion can act as a strong constraint on both. There is no guarantee, as we stated in Chapter 1, that foreign policy guided by public opinion will lead to policies that are "right" in either sense.

The "correct" policies, as seen by presidents, are sometimes held to be those of elites who, unlike the public, confront international issues on a regular basis. These elites are more likely to be internationalists, to favor a more active role in world affairs, and to be willing to place short-term domestic gains for the United States at bay in favor of what they believe to be wise policy in the long run. Periodically, the Chicago Council on Foreign Relations surveys both the mass public and elites, including representatives and senators, State Department officials, business leaders, representatives of the media, educational institutions, labor unions, ethnic and religious groups, and the like. The results of the most recent survey, conducted in 1986, are presented in Table 5–1.[32]

The data do indicate that the public is less interventionist than the elites. On every issue in the table the public is more favorable to economic retaliation against other nations on trade issues and a less active role in international affairs, especially on the question of the use of American forces abroad. The gaps are particularly wide on trade issues: 69 percent of the elite favor eliminating all tariffs, compared to just 35 percent of the public. Conversely, 79 percent of the public believes it is critical to protect the jobs of American workers, while the elite shows a majority supporting the

TABLE 5–1   Foreign Policy Orientations of the Public and Elites: Chicago Council on Foreign Relations Surveys, 1986

	Public	Elite	Gap (Elite Minus Public)
Best to take an active part in world affairs	71	99	+28
Favor economic aid to other nations for economic development and technical assistance	60	93	+33
Favor eliminating tariffs and restrictions	35	69	+34
Favor sanctions against South Africa	65	82	+17
Favor giving military aid—and arms—to other nations	36	78	+42
Favor increasing or maintaining commitment to NATO	82	86	+4
Protecting jobs of American workers "very important"	79	44	−35
Favor exchanging scientists with Soviet Union	59	86	+27
Believe U.S. military aid to Central America is not likely to lead to U.S. military involvement	20	52	+32
Favor use of U.S. troops if North Korea invaded South Korea	28	67	+39
Favor use of U.S. troops if Arabs invaded Israel	38	60	+22
Feel Vietnam War was not wrong or immoral	29	57	+28

Entries are percentages agreeing with each statement; figures exclude respondents saying "don't know."

free-trade alternative. The elites are more ready to use American influence and military might to protect the nation's interests abroad, ranging from the 78 percent favoring military foreign aid to percentages in the 60s favoring the use of troops if South Korea or Israel were invaded. The public opposes all of these initiatives—and by considerable margins. Only 29 percent of the public believes that the Vietnam War was not immoral, compared to 57 percent of the elites. This does not mean that elite respondents favored the war in Vietnam, only that they are less reluctant to use American military might in general. A survey in 1982 found that over 60 percent of the public would *oppose* sending American troops to intervene in each of the following additional situations: (1) if the Arabs cut off oil to the United States; (2) if the Soviets invade Poland; (3) if Iran invades Saudi Arabia; (4) if the Soviets invade China; (5) if leftist guerillas win in El Salvador; or (6) if China invades Taiwan.[33] A surprisingly high 49 percent opposed sending troops to Japan if the Soviets invaded. The public was more supportive of American involvement should the Soviets invade Western Europe; only 35 percent opposed sending troops in that case. The elites were also wary of intervention; on four items they were even less supportive of sending troops than the mass public (Soviet invasions of China and Poland, an oil cutoff, and El Salvador). But for the most part they were far more selective about possible military action and emphasized both defending the security of allies and imposing restraints on the CIA.[34]

These data confirm the view of elites as more internationalist than the public. Presidents are likely to look on public opinion with disdain or to ignore it completely when confronted with an international crisis. They do so with the expectation that following decisive action, they can count on public support. Thus, to reiterate, only on those issues that consistently occupy a prominent place on the nation's agenda—especially "crises" that extend for months or years—will public opinion have a marked effect on public policy. Otherwise, presidents will listen primarily to elites, who share the same basic internationalist perspective. Chief executives thus can retain the flexibility to act decisively because they are convinced that ultimately the "process versus output" dilemma will be submerged as the public rallies behind the president.

Members of Congress, who must run for reelection every two years, are more likely to respond to citizen attitudes on international affairs. This sets up a direct confrontation between the executive and legislative branches. Congress has been decidedly more protectionist on trade (see Chapter 8) and, at least since Vietnam, less interventionist on security issues. In the post-World War II/pre-Vietnam consensus era, a decision such as Reagan's to place Kuwaiti oil tankers in the Persian Gulf under American protection in 1987 would have met with bipartisan support. Instead, it met with bipartisan opposition, including that of Senate Minority Leader Robert Dole (R-Kans.). Congress, as noted in Chapter 4, took the lead in restricting aid to right-wing insurgent movements in Latin America and in imposing sanctions on South Africa. In its battle with the executive for control over foreign policy, Congress can use public opinion to force changes in administration decisions.

THE ELECTORAL CONNECTION

The battle for control of foreign policy between the legislative and executive branches implies a struggle for the hearts and minds of the American people. But popular control of government is hardly a one-way street. Public opinion can affect policies in two ways. The first occurs when politicians simply decide to do what the people want. This is a less powerful means of control because public attitudes do not sanction errant behavior on the part of the president or Congress. The second is through elections. If citizens do not like the policy decisions of their officials, they can vote them out of office. For the message to be clear, however, it is imperative that there be some connection between electoral outcomes and policy preferences—or at least between retrospective evaluations of leaders' performance on foreign policy and vote choice.

There are thus two views of electoral accountability. The stronger argues that public opinion should be "converted" into public policy by the representative system of government. These theorists expect leaders to "re-present" the views of the public. How well the public's viewpoints are translated into public policy gives us an idea of how well the democratic system is working. This conversion function assumes that it is the task of officeholders to represent faithfully the majority position (for Congress in their constituencies, for the president of the nation) between elections as well.[35] The weaker theory of retrospective voting maintains that voters can replace an officeholder whose views or simply whose performance they do not like at the next election.[36] We shall examine both views of the function of public opinion in elections in this section.

Popular Control of Foreign Policy

In no recent election was there as clear-cut a choice on competing policy choices on both foreign and domestic policy as 1972. George McGovern as the Democratic nominee proposed to withdraw American troops from Vietnam unconditionally, whereas President Nixon still held out hope for a negotiated solution. Uncharacteristically, foreign policy issues became a central focus of the presidential campaign. In other contests, public unease over foreign policy problems might lead to the defeat of an incumbent political party even if the challenger offers only a vague promise of change. This is what happened in 1952 as the public tired of American involvement in Korea and in 1968 as concern over our role in Vietnam mounted,[37] as well as in 1980 when there was a sharp negative reaction to the Iranian hostage crisis.

In general, however, there appears to be no great amount of policy voting on either domestic or foreign policy issues. On the one hand, the two parties have not usually offered the voter a clear-cut choice on policy alternatives. On the other hand, there is even less evidence that voters are aware of whatever differences there may be between two candidates for an office.

In most cases, voters tend to be less interested in questions of foreign policy than in domestic policies. Most Americans are more concerned with their local communities than anything else. A survey in 1982 found that 61 percent of Americans said that they were "very interested" in news about their local communities, compared to 51 percent in national news, 45 percent in news about American relations with other nations, and only 28 percent in events abroad. Even these figures sharply overestimate people's interest in specific events.[38] Thus, it is not surprising to find that policy voting on foreign affairs questions is rather rare. A study of voters in the 1956 and 1960 presidential elections led Warren E. Miller to conclude that, at an absolute maximum, the net contribution of the parties' foreign policy stands toward changes in voting behavior from one election to the next was one half of 1 percent.[39] In an election as close as the 1960 contest, this margin may have significance. When looked at by itself, however, the effect of policy stands on voting is negligible. A Roper poll reported that in the 1976 election, voters saw domestic issues as more important in their voting decisions than foreign policy issues by a margin of more than 12 to 1. The results for foreign policy of more recent studies are no more heartening for the advocate of a political system that converts public opinion on foreign policy into public policy through elections. A study by Gerald M. Pomper found that, from 1956 to 1972, voter attitudes and partisan affiliation became more strongly associated in five areas of domestic policy but did not change for the one foreign policy measure (foreign aid) he examined.[40] There remained in 1972, as there had been in 1956, 1960, 1964, and 1968, virtually no relationship between public opinion and party identification on this foreign policy measure.

The 1980 election was more complex than previous contests. The conflicts were muted as Carter had supported a defense buildup in response to the Soviet invasion of Afghanistan. Two very sophisticated analyses differed about the meaning of the election. One found that defense issues were very important in citizens' vote choice, responsible for 8.5 percent of Reagan's vote and ranking behind only general economic conditions in the nation. Ideology ranked third, followed by a general desire for policy change and the perception of Reagan as a more competent president.[41] The other argued that ideology had no effect at all on the electoral outcome and that Reagan's issue stands on both foreign *and* domestic policies gained him no more than one percentage point of the votes nationally.[42] On the other hand, foreign policy issues generally, national defense, and the Iranian hostage crisis were among the five most most salient issues that voters thought the government should handle, the others being inflation and unemployment.[43] The strongest determinant of the outcome of the election was dissatisfaction with Carter's performance. Disapproval of Carter's handling of his job increased sharply on the issues of inflation, unemployment, and the hostage crisis from February to October 1980; the greatest rise occurred on the hostage crisis. The percentage of respondents who "strongly disapproved" of Carter's performance on the hostage crisis jumped form 30 to 49, compared to increases from 37 to 47 and 23 to 36 on inflation and unemployment, respectively.[44] Thus, even if foreign policy issues did not directly affect vote choice in 1980, they had an impact on the election through their effects on Carter's overall performance.

In 1984 the contrast between the candidates was virtually as great as it had been in 1972. Former Vice President Walter F. Mondale made the nuclear freeze one of the major issues in his ill-fated campaign, while Reagan repeatedly chastised the Democratic-controlled House of Representatives for cutting defense expenditures. Some analyses pointed to a prominent role for foreign policy in the election. A *Los Angeles Times* poll found that foreign relations generally and nuclear arms control were, at 19 and 18 percent respectively, of concern to the electorate. Yet Reagan's two-to-one advantage on foreign affairs was exactly balanced out by an edge for Mondale on the nuclear arms issue.[45] Other analyses indicated that by the eve of the election in October, Reagan had surged ahead, even if barely, on *all* salient foreign policy issues except that of keeping the United States out of war.[46] These poll results, however, do not consider the *relative* importance of foreign policy compared to other factors in the voting decision. One analysis that did so noted that the strong relationship between attitudes on defense spending, détente with the Soviet Union, and American involvement in Central America and vote choice vanished once other factors were taken into account. The same study that found strong effects for foreign policy in the 1980 election concluded that these issues played a distinctly minor role in the 1984 Republican landslide. Indeed, the Central American issue was Mondale's fifth strongest source of votes other than a general desire for policy change. Yet this aversion to involvement added only 2.4 percent to Mondale's vote; defense issues added an additional 1 percent to the Democratic total, while defense spending accounted for no more than one tenth of 1 percent in Mondale's direction. Reagan's victory was largely a ratification of the public's satisfaction with his overall policies, his leadership, and his performance in the White House. The fading of defense issues as important determinants of the Reagan vote can be explained by the virtually complete reversal of public opinion on the defense issue: the 4 to 1 majority favoring more public spending in 1980 had become a 3 to 1 majority supporting cuts in expenditures. The key issues in 1988 were largely economic: 41 percent of voters most liked the stands of their favored candidates on these issues, compared to 25 percent on social issues and 22 percent on defense and foreign policy. However, it was on defense and foreign policy questions that George Bush derived his largest margin over Michael Dukakis. The Democratic candidate had a lead of over 12 percent on social issues. Bush had a modest 2-point advantage on economic questions, but a margin of almost 17 points on defense and foreign policy. Bush's supporters were almost as likely to select foreign policy issues as their reasons for supporting the vice president as economic ones, while only 6 percent of Dukakis's voters selected such concerns. Dukakis tried to use the Iran–Contra affair against Bush. He did gain considerable backing on this issue for those voters who were concerned about it, but only the same percentage of voters cared about Iran–Contra as did about the flaps over the pledge of allegiance to the flag and the prison furlough issues (both of which heavily favored Bush).[47]

In presidential elections, voters seem to look for some indication that the candidate they prefer is capable of handling foreign policy and will not adopt extreme policies which might provoke a world war or other major international confrontation. Negative perceptions on both concerns hurt McGovern in 1972,[48] while positive responses helped John F. Kennedy in 1960 and Carter in 1976. The latter candidates gained the upper hand on this issue by scoring very well in televised debates with their "more experienced" opponents. Despite the increased salience of foreign policy among members of Congress, there is no indication that foreign policy plays a role in congressional elections. In 1978, fewer than 1 percent of voters cited foreign policy issues as the most important questions facing the nation, while none cited foreign policy as the most important campaign issue.[49] Foreign policy plays a role in races for Congress when candidates pay *too* much attention to international affairs and not enough to those important locally. As noted in Chapter 4, service on the Senate Foreign Relations Committee can be an electoral liability, as three successive chairmen have been defeated in either primary or general elections. Rarely have members of the House Foreign Affairs Committee or other (sub)committees dealing with international affairs been defeated for identifying too closely with transnational problems and not paying sufficient attention to their constituents. Congressional elections are becoming increasingly local events, less tied to national trends than in the past, especially in presidential election years.[50] National trends still do affect some congressional elections, but when they do they are more likely to be referenda on the state of the economy and political scandals than specific issues such as foreign policy.[51]

There is, then, very limited potential for policy conversion on foreign policy issues. Only in 1972 was there clear-cut evidence that these concerns had an impact on the presidential elections. In 1980 the evidence is mixed, but at a minimum in that contest, as in 1952, there is strong support for retrospective evaluations of foreign policy having had a major impact on the electoral outcome. The conclusion is straightforward: only when the nation is involved in either a war or a prolonged crisis will even evaluations of the presidential candidates be related to international events. The situations under which even a "rational" foreign policy public can exert effective control are infrequent. And even when the public chooses at least partly based on foreign policy considerations, the message it sends is far from clear. Retrospective evaluations simply indicate that the public is satisfied, or more likely dissatisfied, with the conduct of foreign policy. When voters are upset, they do not offer a competing vision of what policies ought to be followed.

The situation is even less promising for popular control of congressional initiatives over foreign policy. The small number of voters who base their electoral choices on foreign policy issues makes the linkage between the public and legislators difficult to establish. If voters are not interested in these issues, the chances are quite high that they will not make up their minds in the voting booth based on those policies. Furthermore, many legislators themselves do not devote much time to international relations because they do not see much of an electoral payoff in tackling these issues. On the one hand, they risk charges that they have forgotten the problems of their constituents. On the other hand, foreign policy has become a lightning rod for activists in the district to attack legislators who do not support their preferred policy positions. In Seattle, Washington, Representative John Miller, a liberal Republican, has been roundly criticized by the local press and activists in the Mayor's Commission on Central America and the Catholic Church for his support for aid to the Contras. His margin of victory in 1986 fell five points to just 51 percent. Florida Representative Kenneth H. "Buddy" MacKay, a moderate Democrat, was similarly chastised by local activists for opposing Contra aid. Much of the criticism came from Cuban exiles committed to blocking communists from making further inroads in Latin America,[52] yet only 2 percent of the voters in MacKay's district are of Hispanic origin.[53] As we discussed in Chapter 4, members of Congress try to keep a very low profile on controversial issues. Foreign policy issues are peripheral to the general problem of representation because neither the representatives nor the represented give it a high priority.

POLITICAL PARTIES: DO THEY PROVIDE THE BASIS FOR LINKAGE?

Why is the linkage between voters and foreign policy not stronger? There are clear lines of partisan cleavage on many domestic issues, both among the electorate and within the Congress. Domestic policies that are primarily distributive—general appropriations measures, agriculture price supports, public works bills, and legislation relating to the size of the bureaucracy and the overall level of spending—are highly partisan. These issues involve the spending of money by the government. Democrats have traditionally supported domestic spending programs, while Republicans have emphasized fiscal restraint. The differences between the parties on these issues are quite real and long standing. As the North–South split within the Democratic party dissipated in the 1970s, issues concerning civil liberties and social welfare also became very partisan, while differences on the new intermestic issues such as energy and agriculture became more re-gional. After a period during which the ideological distance between the parties on domestic policy was declining, the Reagan years were marked by dramatic rises in partisanship.[54]

A system of strong political parties would resolve much of the tension in foreign policy making and the democratic dilemmas. If the president were the leader of a party, he could count on the support of fellow partisans in pursuing his foreign policy objectives. If the president's partisans controlled both houses of Congress, this backing would provide solid majorities for the initiatives of the chief executive. The electorate could then decide between competing visions of what the nation's foreign policy should be. Such a sys-tem would provide for democratic accountability for the decisions of govern-ment and for executive leadership. It is the hallmark of parliamentary government.

However, the United States has not been marked by strong political parties, as most parliamentary systems are. American parties have not been very distinctive ideologically from one another or internally cohesive. Most roll-call votes in the House of Commons in Great Britain are strictly along party lines. A member who deviates from the party position on a major vote can be denied renomination for another term in Parliament. In the United States, however, the only votes that can be safely predicted to come out along strictly partisan lines are those that choose the leaders of each house of Congress. Parties do not demonstrate the cohesiveness that we find in parliamentary systems because the American public has never been enam-orated with the idea of majority rule that goes hand in hand with strong parties. Majority-rule politics means that whichever party gains control of the government can implement any policies it chooses. Instead, Americans place a higher value on individual rights and set limits on what the govern-ment can do (the Bill of Rights in particular). The division of powers be-tween separately elected legislative and executive branches reflects the American aversion to majoritarian institutions. Parties have always been looked on with guarded skepticism by Americans.[55]

On no issue is this apprehension about the role of political parties so evident as foreign policy. There has been a search for a consensus that crosses party lines. As noted in Chapter 3, bipartisanship ensures continu-ity in policy making across administrations.[56] Bipartisan support for foreign policy was very strong in the Eisenhower administration. Modest cleavages arose during the Kennedy and Johnson presidencies. It was under Nixon that foreign policy became the focal point of partisan conflict, as most Dem-ocratic hawks reassessed their prior support for the Vietnam War. They sought to blame the Republican president for dramatically escalating the conflict beyond the confines of Vietnam and into Laos and Cambodia. The Congress enacted the War Powers Act over Nixon's veto, even as the presi-dent threatened not to comply with it. A new, more partisan era in foreign policy formation had begun.[57]

During the Carter and Reagan administrations, partisan cleavages on foreign policy issues became more pronounced, although regional differences continued to persist within each party.[58] During the Reagan administration, when all issues facing the Congress were marked by high partisanship, foreign policy was marked by almost as much party-line voting as economic issues and by just about the same amount of partisanship as social welfare votes.[59] Yet one effect of the breakdown of consensus crossed party lines: the fifteen members of Congress who served in Vietnam were united in opposing sending American troops to Lebanon—liberal Democrats because they were skeptical of further international involvement in what they believed were "lost causes" and conservative Republicans because they doubted the nation's willingness to defend the marines.[60]

Partisanship has been the most intense on foreign policies that more closely resemble domestic issues. The parties have been traditionally divided over the size of the defense budget, with the Republicans supporting increases in military spending and the Democrats calling for cutbacks. (This is not to suggest that the Democrats have been traditionally less hawkish than the Republicans on many foreign policy issues.) Recent years have witnessed a reversal of this pattern of behavior. The defense budget is no longer viewed as just another part of the budget, but rather as a major element of the nation's foreign policy as well as a key issue of foreign/domestic priorities. Another area of foreign policy that has often (though not always) divided the congressional parties is reciprocal trade legislation.[61] The Democrats have historically supported lower tariff barriers, with the Republicans taking the opposite position. However, recent years again indicate a shift in this polarization. American companies have been hurt by many imported goods that are sold at prices below their own. Strong pressure from labor has resulted in a shift and a strong increase in protectionist sentiment in the Democratic party. While there are divisions in each party by region over trade legislation, Democrats now overwhelmingly favor protectionist policies while Republicans have a slight majority backing free trade. In 1985 party leaders attributed a Democratic victory in a special congressional election in Texas to the trade issue and argued that it was a harbinger of trends to come. The next year Democrats ousted Republican incumbents in several House and Senate elections; while a host of factors contributed to those victories, including mobilization of the black vote, many Democratic leaders perceived a mandate for stronger trade legislation (see Chapter 8).

If the parties are becoming more distinctive on foreign policy issues, why have not elections been reflective of this clash of ideologies? In other words, why have not foreign policy issues become more important in elections? One answer is that to some extent, they have. At least in a retrospective sense, foreign policy concerns did play a prominent role in the 1980 presidential contest. Yet, as we have argued, 1980 was unusual at least in part because the parties were so clearly divided on questions of international affairs. In most other contests, the electorate would have a hard time separating the parties on key foreign policy issues *even if it were predisposed to do so.* Consider the 1984 Democratic and Republican campaign platforms. While Reagan and Mondale certainly had very different views about how foreign policy should be conducted and Democrats and Republicans in both houses of Congress sharply differed with each other on these issues, the platforms offered little guidance on what each party would do differently from the other if elected.

This is not to say that each party's platform was vague. Yet where one party was specific, the other was not. The Republican platform, for example, pledged continued economic and military aid to the Contras; the Democrats called for an increased reliance on a negotiated solution to the problems of Central America, but did not specifically propose a cutoff of Contra aid. On the other hand, the Democrats endorsed tough sanctions on South Africa in a detailed policy statement; the Republicans simply condemned apartheid and urged support for "well-conceived efforts to foster peace, prosperity, and stability." Both parties endorsed a strong defense, human rights, support for anti-Soviet Afghan forces, arms control, American peace efforts in the Middle East (including an undivided Jerusalem), and even efforts to restore free trade. The Democratic platform overall was far more specific, the Republican quite general. Yet this is what one would expect from an out party, trying to garner new votes, and an in party, attempting to alienate as few previous supporters as possible, respectively. On domestic issues, the differences between the parties were far more dramatic.[62] In 1988, with a streamlined Democratic platform and a much more detailed Republican document, the same basic pattern emerged. Only on Contra aid did the parties take clearly distinguishable positions on foreign policy.

The inexplicit statements on foreign policy reflect the coalitional problems within each party. More so on foreign policy than on domestic issues, there are regional and ideological clashes within each party. As noted in Chapter 3, presidents have continually had to cope with dissenters within their own parties on foreign policy issues, especially treaties. Carter was plagued by objections from his own southern Democrats on SALT II. Most recently, Reagan faced opposition on the Intermediate-range Nuclear Force (INF) reduction treaty with the Soviet Union from the very conservative Republicans who were initially so critical of his gaining the 1980 nomination of his party. Furthermore, party ties no longer mean quite so much in people's vote choices as they did in the past. Other factors such as incumbency, performance evaluations, personalities, and salient issues have become more important in recent years. Election analysts call this the *dealignment* of the American party system rather than a realignment in which the two parties and their supporters in the electorate are clearly identifiable by their policy stands.[63] If voters no longer are firmly attached to parties, the parties would rationally emphasize only those issues they believe would bring them votes from nonsupporters. Foreign policy issues do not qualify because they are of little salience to most voters. Thus, we face another paradox: parties might use foreign policy issues to attract voters if they believed that the electorate would respond to them. Yet, because parties and candidates (correctly) perceive that voters are not strongly motivated by international issues, they do not offer the electorate the divergent policy stands that might actually make people pay attention to foreign policy. The parties in Washington do differ from one another even as their supporters seem to wander from one electoral coalition to another. We now have, in the words of one observer, a "realignment at the top [and a] dealignment at the bottom."[64]

THE MEDIA FACTOR: YOU ARE WHAT YOU WATCH?

If parties do not mobilize the citizenry, can the media do so? Certainly the media have played a critical role in shattering the pre-Vietnam consensus. Public support declined more precipitously for the war in Vietnam and Cambodia than for the Korean conflict in no small part because the fighting was brought home to Americans' living rooms every night. The violence, including massacres such as that in My Lai, turned many viewers against the war. So did the public opposition to the war from America's great folk hero, CBS anchor Walter Cronkite. In earlier wars, including Korea and World War II, people learned about fighting through newspapers and radio, neither of which could provide the explicit graphics of television. Visual portraits were available only through highly edited newsreels shown at movie theaters.

As with Vietnam, the constant media exposure served to highlight the president's inability to resolve the issue. To be sure, Carter focused attention on himself by holding many press conferences and insisting that he could not leave the White House to campaign or even to meet with other public officials outside Washington. But the media also paid a great deal of attention to Iran, with ABC television news scheduling a nightly program on the events (or nonevents) of the day. (The program, hosted by Ted Koppel, later became "Nightline.") Americans became very familiar with the militants holding the hostages at the embassy; their spokeswoman, called Mary, generally had higher late-night ratings than Johnny Carson did on NBC. Meanwhile, on the top-rated "CBS Evening News," Cronkite ended each broadcast counting down the number of days that Americans had been held hostage in Iran. The evaporation of public support permitted other sources of information to gain a public following.

The two principal alternative sources are congressional hearings and the media. Lacking the power to change the president's Vietnam policies, Senator Fulbright used the mechanism of his Foreign Relations Committee hearings to dramatize opposition to the war. At times, the major television networks would carry live coverage of these hearings. At a minimum, the hearings would be covered on the evening network news programs and in the major newspapers across the country. The influence of such hearings— which are often long and tedious and may not bring out any new information—may be slight, but it is often almost all that opponents of a policy have in their attempt to affect public opinion. With the growth of the medium of television, the roles of the congressional committee hearings and the media have become ever more closely intertwined. Television gives opponents of a policy a more direct line to the public than do newspapers or radio, and it provides for visual contact as well. However, the gains that opponents of a policy have made through this newest medium have also accrued to the president. Indeed, the chief executive can almost always obtain free network time for an address to the nation, and he can use such speeches to rally public opinion behind his policies. On balance, the advent of television probably has meant more to opponents of a president's policy than to the chief executive himself. Since public opinion is generally permissive and supportive of presidential initiatives, any gain in exposure of the opposition's point of view may well enhance the opponents' strength. A president frequently needs *less* exposure to rally support for his position than does the opposition.

The media are more than just vehicles for presenting alternative views of public officials to the public or, in turn, representing the public to the foreign policy establishment. The media also have their own impact on public opinion. Although most voters are usually not terribly concerned with foreign policy issues, the nightly television coverage of events in Vietnam brought an overseas war into millions of American homes each night as did the reports on Iran a half decade after American involvement in Vietnam ended. Furthermore, the media have not always presented presidential decisions in a favorable light. Virtually every president of the United States in recent years has believed that the press was hostile. Indeed, the Nixon administration brought its hostilities toward the media—the television networks and national news magazines as well as the newspapers—out into the open. Johnson was less hostile to the press but did criticize several reporters and nationally syndicated columnists for their opposition to his Vietnam policies. And both Carter and Reagan, at various times, lamented the treatment they received from the press.

Presidents respond in different ways to criticism from the press. At one extreme, Nixon was so angered by the *Washington Post's* coverage of the Watergate affair that he threatened to have the Federal Communications Commission deny the applications for license renewals of two television stations the *Post* owned in Florida. At the other extreme was the reaction of Kennedy, who canceled his subscription to the New York Herald Tribune following a series of uncomplimentary articles the paper ran about him. The subscription was quietly renewed after the incident proved embarrassing to the president. Carter, withdrawing from criticism of his handling of foreign and domestic policy before the hostage crisis, refused to hold press conferences in Washington for several months, traveling to distant locales where the local press might be somewhat more sympathetic to his situation. After the hostages were seized, however, Carter actively sought out the press, even as his popularity was declining.

Reagan, a former actor quite at home with cameras, established a reputation as the "great communicator." He used press conferences and televised addresses to build support for his programs and to disarm the opposition with his quick wit. Reagan is the master practitioner of a presidential strategy born of the television age: "going public," circumventing negotiations with the Congress and directly appealing to the public to pressure their elected representatives to support the president's program. Such tactics bring about a more confrontational relationship between the president and the Congress as each attempts to appeal to the public. Nixon and especially Carter used the same strategy, but since neither was a master of the media— indeed, Carter generally performed poorly on television—they were not as successful at it as was Reagan. Direct appeals to the people played a critical role in convincing many members of Congress to vote for Reagan's program of tax and budget cuts in 1981. As the president's popularity sagged in 1982 and again in 1986–87 during the Iran–Contra affair, his use of the media declined—as did positive public responses to his infrequent appearances (see above). Television has also become the medium of choice for foreigners, from the leaders of the Soviet Union, China, and Iran to terrorists. They seek to affect public opinion—and thus to "go public" over the heads of the president, the Congress, and the State Department.[65]

The media focus people's attention on foreign policy issues beyond those such as hearings on the Vietnam War, the Iranian hostage crisis, or the Iran–Contra affair. Many members of Congress argued that the U.S. government was ultimately compelled to take action forcing Philippine President Ferdinand Marcos to resign because of television. The extensive coverage of the Phillipine election of 1986 and the widespread allegations of vote fraud against Corazon Aquino were in sharp contrast to television's usual one-shot two-minute stories about international politics. Furthermore, the Filipinos interviewed were usually middle-class English speakers with whom Americans could identify. Almost 60 percent of respondents to a poll said that they followed the contest very or fairly closely, and by a 5 to 1 margin they believed that Aquino, not Marcos, was the legitimate victor.[66]

Television has had a major impact on electoral politics as well. Media expenditures constitute the largest share of candidates' disbursements.[67] Negative advertising has come to play a prominent role in campaigns. Candidates for both the presidency and Congress emphasize "looking good" over substance.[68] In the 1984 presidential primaries, Senator Gary Hart (D-Colo.) traversed the country, stopping only at airports where he met with television reporters for interviews that would be taped for the local evening news. The stories would make it appear that the candidate actually spent time in each city, although following the interviews he would reboard his campaign plane to fly to the next set of waiting reporters. Three years later, while running once more for the presidency, Hart found the press to be more of an adversary. Allegations of sexual impropriety by the *Miami Herald* and the *Washington Post* led Hart to withdraw from the race for the Democratic nomination for the presidency.

Television has replaced newspapers as the primary source of news: 64 percent of Americans rely on television for news, as compared to just 44 percent for newspapers.[69] Television news differs radically from print news. First, viewers are unlikely to skip stories in which they are not vitally interested, such as foreign affairs. Flipping the page in a newspaper is easy; turning off the television or changing the channel generally requires that people get out of their chairs. Second, as previously noted, televised news is more dramatic than print stories. Third, television news covers stories quickly and without repetition. Reading a newspaper permits one to return to a story at leisure. Fourth, newspapers must be purchased—and in fact have never been purchased by a majority of citizens. Television news comes into people's homes for free and virtually every American home has a television set. Fifth, televised coverage of news, including but not limited to congressional hearings, gives the viewer a keener sense of the adversarial nature of contemporary politics. The public thus becomes less patient with and more cynical about their leaders, whom they perceive as divided.[70]

In another sense, however, television and newspapers are very similar. Both tend to give short shrift to issues of substance in presidential elections, particularly during the primaries. Even "prestige" newspapers and news magazines give the same disproportionate coverage to the "horse race" aspect of the campaign as do local papers and mass-circulation dailies that emphasize "lifestyle" stories. During the conventions and the general election campaign, quality newspapers and news magazines do put greater emphasis on issues than the network newscasts and other press outlets, but on balance even then the elite press focuses more on the "game."[71]

How responsible is television for the breakdown of the pre-Vietnam consensus? Some observers have attributed the growth of television to the loss of trust among the American public as well as to the waning of partisan attachments.[72] Yet, while not denying that television has become a major factor in how we perceive international politics, it seems dubious to maintain that television is the *cause* of many of our contemporary problems. Rather, it is more reasonable to argue that it is a *symptom* of the state of public attitudes in the nation. For one thing, television coverage of major American political figures does *not* emphasize the "blow-dried" politicians seeking thirty seconds of notoriety on the major networks; congressional leaders rather than "show horses" receive the bulk of coverage.[73] For another, if television coverage worked to undermine faith in the political system, we would expect that further media expansion would lead to less confidence in leadership. Yet just the opposite has occurred. As cable television grew dramatically in the 1980s, a master of the media (Reagan) presided over a nation in which trust in government was *increasing*.[74] Rather, media politics, including going public, reflect the breakdown of party coalitions in American politics rather than cause it. Without a dependable bloc of support in the Congress, presidents feel compelled to seek support outside the legislative branch.[75]

All of this is not to say that the media are impotent. They play a critical role in transmitting information to the public and the way the news is presented can make a difference in peoples' interpretations of it. Both news commentary on television and stories depicting alternative policies in a positive light can change public opinion by three percentage points or more—considerably more than presidents. Indeed, the impact of commentary is particularly strong when presidents are unpopular. Television can have a particularly strong effect in enhancing negative images of presidents. When Nixon took to the airwaves during Watergate to state, "I am not a crook," the very fact that a president of the United States had to plead his innocence added to beliefs that something really must be wrong. Carter's poor performance on television certainly led to the sharp decline in his popularity. His vice president, Walter Mondale, attributed his poor showing in the 1984 elections to his failure to master the medium of television. Even Reagan as the great communicator found that television was a double-edged sword. During the Iran–Contra affair, Reagan often appeared ill at ease on television. Many Americans put aside his geniality and began to concentrate more on the president's misstatements and inconsistencies.

Yet even these effects may reflect elite or public consensus rather than the unique influence of the media.[76] Most of the time television coverage *intensifies* views already held and makes them more volatile.[77] Yet negative advertising and stories about candidates' sex lives would not play such a prominent place in the media if viewers did not respond so favorably to them. If the electorate really preferred more debates on international affairs to more lurid stories, the networks would oblige and "Dallas" would be replaced by live debates from the Oxford Union. It would be truly remarkable, and regrettable, if citizens in a democracy abdicated the accountability of their political leaders to the press. It is reassuring that they do not.

There is a strong irony to the changing role of the media. On the one hand, there has been a veritable news explosion on the airwaves. All-news television and radio have become a staple of American life in recent years. Additionally, there are the Cable News Network's *two* all-news channels, the public affairs programming on the two C-SPAN cable networks, the growth of public radio news programming, and more news programming on the major networks. More and more local television stations and newspapers have opened Washington bureaus, and the foreign bureaus of both television/radio and newspapers have expanded greatly. There are also many more specialized magazines on politics and foreign affairs than there were just a decade ago. On the other hand, many newspapers have closed, ceding the news dissemination function to radio and television. And, for all the greater concern with public affairs on television, the growth of cable has created alternatives to informational programming. The rise of independent television stations and especially cable networks means that the American public is no longer a captive audience for the network news or even the State of the Union address. Many people tune instead to music videos, reruns of 1950s programs, or the "Wheel of Fortune."

The number of actors in the fourth circle is quite large—too much so to do justice to them in a single chapter. We therefore continue our consideration of these actors in Chapter 6, where we focus on the growing role of local political actors in foreign policy making and the impact of interest groups, long associated with domestic policies, in the international arena. We shall also delay our consideration until Chapter 6 of what this all means for the democratic dilemma. We do so because it is important to examine all of the actors in the fourth circle together. There are different aspects of public participation in decision making and these need to be compared systematically.

NOTES

1. See Giovanni Sartori, *The Theory of Democracy Revisited,* Part One (Chatham, N.J.: Chatham House, 1987), chap. 5.
2. See Warren E. Miller, Arthur H. Miller, and Edward J. Schneider, *American National Election Studies Data Sourcebook 1952–1978* (Cambridge, Mass.: Harvard Univ. Press, 1980), pp. 268, 283.
3. William Schneider, "Conservatism, Not Interventionism: Trends in Foreign Policy Public Opinion, 1974–1982," in *Eagle Defiant: United States Foreign Policy in the 1980s,* eds. Kenneth A. Oye, Robert J. Lieber, and Donald Rothchild (Boston: Little, Brown, 1983), pp. 33–64, esp. p. 41.
4. Ole R. Holsti and James N. Rosenau, *American Leadership in World Affairs* (Boston: George Allen and Unwin, 1984), esp. pp. 117–23, 141.
5. See, on the one hand, Angus Campbell, Philip E. Converse, Warren E. Miller, and Donald E. Stokes, *The American Voter,* abridged ed. (New York: John Wiley & Sons, 1960); and, on the other hand, V. O. Key, Jr., *The Responsible Electorate* (New York: Random House, 1966).
6. See Gabriel Almond, *The American People and Foreign Policy* (New York: Praeger Publishers, 1960); and Schneider, "Conservatism, Not Interventionism," p. 41.
7. Schneider, "Conservatism, Not Interventionism," p. 53.
8. Almond, *The American People and Foreign Policy,* p. 232.
9. See Benjamin I. Page and Robert Y. Shapiro, "Changes in Americans' Policy Preferences," *Public Opinion Quarterly* 46 (Spring 1982), pp. 24–42; and Shapiro and Page, "Foreign Policy and the Rational Public," mimeo, Columbia University, September 1986.
10. E. E. Schattschneider, *The Semisovereign People* (New York: Holt, Rinehart & Winston, 1960), p. 137.
11. See, among other citations, Adam Clymer, "Analyzing the Drop in Reagan's Ratings," *New York Times,* December 7, 1986, p. E5; and Lou Cannon, "What Happened to Reagan the Gunslinger?" *Washington Post,* July 7, 1985, pp. B1, B4.

12. David Shribman, "Poll Shows Support for Presence of U.S. Troops in Lebanon and Grenada," *New York Times,* October 29, 1983, p. 9; Barry Sussman, "Reagan's Talk Gains Support for Policies," *Washington Post,* October 30, 1983, pp. A1, A18; and Sussman, "Grenada Move Earns Reagan Broad Political Gains," *Washington Post,* November 9, 1983, p. A3.

13. See John E. Mueller, *War, Presidents, and Public Opinion* (New York: John Wiley & Sons, 1973).

14. Sussman, "Grenada Move Earns Reagan Broad Political Gains"; Sussman, "Seventy-six Percent of Americans Polled Back Bombing of Libya," *Washington Post,* April 30, 1986, p. A4; NBC News press release, May 12, 1986.

15. The Vietnam War cost Johnson seventeen points in popularity in 1968 alone, far more than it hurt Nixon later on and much more than Korea cost Truman. See Charles W. Ostrom, Jr. and Dennis M. Simon, "Promise and Performance: A Dynamic Model of Presidential Popularity," *American Political Science Review* 79 (June 1985), p. 351.

16. Adam Clymer, "Poll Finds Reagan-Carter Choice Unsatisfactory," *New York Times,* April 18, 1980, pp. A1, B5.

17. Clymer, "Analyzing the Drop in Reagan's Ratings."

18. Mueller, *War, Presidents, and Public Opinion,* pp. 54–55.

19. Ibid., p. 50.

20. Louis Harris, "Carter Rated as 'Failure' in Handling of Hostage Crisis," *Washington Post,* March 17, 1980, p. A18.

21. David Shipler, "Poll Shows Confusion on Aid to Contras," *New York Times,* April 15, 1986, p. A6; "Star Wars Status," *Public Opinion,* August/September, 1985, pp. 33–35; Barry Sussman, "Public Would Preserve SALT II Treaty, Not Help Nicaragua Contras," *Washington Post,* June 6, 1986, p. A16.

22. John E. Rielly, ed., *American Public Opinion and U.S. Foreign Policy 1987* (Chicago: Chicago Council on Foreign Relations, 1987), pp. 8, 13.

23. Shapiro and Page, "Foreign Policy and the Rational Public," pp. 8–9.

24. Voters react more strongly to inflation than to unemployment because the former affects all citizens, whereas unemployment affects only a small percentage of people. Furthermore, many unemployed people do not vote and, most critical, the average length of unemployment is a few months. See Kay Lehman Schlozman and Sidney Verba, *Injury to Insult* (Cambridge, Mass.: Harvard Univ. Press, 1979).

25. Schneider, "Conservatism, Not Interventionism," pp. 35, 43–48.

26. Ostrom and Simon, "Promise and Performance," p. 351; and Charles W. Ostrom and Brian L. Job, "The President and the Political Use of Force," *American Political Science Review* 80 (June 1986), pp. 541–66.

27. Shipler, "Poll Shows Confusion on Aid to Contras"; NBC News press release, May 12, 1986; Sussman, "Public Would Preserve SALT II Treaty, Not Help Nicaragua Contras"; Steven V. Roberts, "Tensions Grow When the Prize Is the Next Presidency," *New York Times,* January 31, 1988, p. E1.

28. "Americans Evaluate the Situation in South Africa," *Public Opinion* (August/September, 1985), pp. 26–28; Rielly, ed., *American Public Opinion and U.S. Foreign Policy 1987,* p. 27.

29. *Los Angeles Times* Poll press release, February 20–23, 1987; Kenneth B. Noble, "Iran Wave Is a Ripple Back Home," *New York Times,* May 26, 1987, p. A10.

30. Richard A. Brody and Catherine R. Shapiro, "Policy Failure and Public Support: Rekjavik, Iran, and Public Assessments." Paper presented at the 1987

Annual Meeting of the American Political Science Association, Chicago, August–September. The sources for the public opinion data cited above were the *New York Times,* the *Washington Post,* and *Newsweek.* All three used essentially the same question wording, so problems of comparability are minimized. When more than one poll was available for a particular week, the results were averaged.

31. *Los Angeles Times* Poll press release, February 20–23, 1987.

32. The data in Table 4–1 are compiled from Rielly, ed., *American Public Opinion and U.S. Foreign Policy 1987.*

33. John E. Rielly, "American Opinion: Continuity, Not Reaganism," *Foreign Policy,* Spring 1983, p. 99. The scenarios are listed in order of percentages opposed to sending troops, from 61 percent to 82 percent.

34. Ibid., pp. 90–99.

35. See Hannah Fenichel Pitkin, *The Concept of Representation* (Berkeley: Univ. of California Press, 1967), chap. 4.

36. See Key, *The Responsible Electorate;* and Austin Ranney and Willmoore Kendall, *Democracy and the American Party System* (New York: Harcourt Brace Jovanovich, 1956), chap. 4.

37. Warren E. Miller, "Voting and Foreign Policy," in James N. Rosenau, ed., *Domestic Sources of Foreign Policy* (New York: Free Press, 1967), pp. 215–16; and Mueller, *War, Presidents, and Public Opinion,* p. 227.

38. Rielly, ed., *American Public Opinion and U.S. Foreign Policy 1983* (Chicago: Chicago Council on Foreign Relations, 1983), p. 8.

39. Miller, "Voting and Foreign Policy," p. 229.

40. The five domestic issue areas studied were federal aid to education, medical care, federal job guarantees, fair employment legislation, and school integration. See Gerald M. Pomper, "From Confusion to Clarity: Issues and American Voters, 1956–1968," *American Political Science Review* 66 (June 1972), pp. 415–29.

41. J. Merrill Shanks and Warren E. Miller, "Policy Direction and Performance Evaluation: Complementary Explanations of the Reagan Elections." Paper presented at the 1985 Annual Meeting of the American Political Science Association, New Orleans, August–September, p. 84.

42. Gregory Markus, "Political Attitudes in an Election Year: A Report on the 1980 NES Panel Survey," *American Political Science Review* 76 (September 1982), pp. 558–59.

43. Warren E. Miller and Merrill Shanks, "Policy Directions and Presidential Leadership," *British Journal of Political Science* 12 (October 1981), p. 318.

44. Markus, "Political Attitudes During an Election Year," pp. 550, 558–59.

45. Scott Keeter, "Public Opinion in 1984," in *The Election of 1984,* Gerald Pomper et al. (Chatham, N.J.: Chatham House, 1985), p. 96. The percentages for each issue are based on respondents' mentions of up to *two* concerns that were most important to them in the election.

46. William Schneider, "The November 6 Vote for President: What Did It Mean?" in *The American Elections of 1984,* ed. Austin Ranney (Durham, N.C.: Duke Univ. Press, 1985), pp. 216–17, 226.

47. Shanks and Miller, "Policy Direction and Performance Evaluation," pp. 75, 32. In 1988 results were computed from data from ABC News exit polls graciously provided by John Brennan of ABC News. Candidate advantages reflect

the relative percentages supporting each candidate multiplied by the share of the electorate concerned with the issue.

48. Arthur H. Miller et al., "A Majority Party in Disarray," *American Political Science Review* 70 (September 1976), pp. 753–78.

49. Computed from the 1978 National Election Study of the Center for Political Studies, University of Michigan, Ann Arbor, Michigan.

50. Randall L. Calvert and John A. Ferejohn, "Coattail Voting in Recent Presidential Elections," *American Political Science Review* 77 (June 1983), pp. 407–19.

51. Calvert and Ferejohn, "Coattail Voting in Recent Presidential Elections," p. 417; and Eric M. Uslaner and M. Margaret Conway, "The Responsible Congressional Electorate: Watergate, the Economy, and Vote Choice in 1974," *American Political Science Review* 79 (September 1985), pp. 788–803.

52. Denis Farney, "In Seattle, Rep. Miller Is Drawing Fire for Support of Contra Aid. . .," *The Wall Street Journal*, October 13, 1986, p. 34; Monica Langley, "But in Florida, Rep. MacKay Takes Heat for Opposing Rebels," ibid.

53. Michael Barone and Grant Ujifusa, *The Almanac of American Politics 1986* (Washington, D.C.: National Journal, 1985), p. 261.

54. Barbara Sinclair, *Congressional Realignment 1925–1978* (Austin: Univ. of Texas Press, 1982), pp. 77–78; Steve Blakely, "Partisanship in Congress up Sharply in 1985," *Congressional Quarterly Weekly Report*, January 11, 1986, pp. 86–91.

55. Austin Ranney, *The Doctrine of Responsible Party Government* (Urbana, Ill.: Univ. of Illinois Press, 1962).

56. Ernest A. Gross, "What Is a Bipartisan Foreign Policy?" *Department of State Bulletin*, October 3, 1949, pp. 504–5.

57. Sinclair, *Congressional Realignment*.

58. Barbara Sinclair, "Agenda, Policy, and Alignment Change from Coolidge to Reagan," in *Congress Reconsidered*, 3d. ed., eds. Lawrence C. Dodd and Bruce I. Oppenheimer (Washington, D.C.: CQ Press, 1985), pp. 291–314.

59. William Schneider, "A Year of Continuity," *National Journal*, May 17, 1986, pp. 1,162–91.

60. David K. Shipler, "The Vietnam Experience and the Congressman of the 1980s," *New York Times*, May 28, 1987, p. B6.

61. For data on the 1940s and 1950s, see Leroy N. Rieselbach, *The Roots of Isolationism* (Indianapolis: Bobbs-Merrill, 1966).

62. For the texts of the Democratic and Republican platforms, see *Congressional Quarterly Weekly Report*, July 21, 1984, pp. 1,747–80 and August 25, 1984, pp. 2,096–117. The quote from the Republican platform on South Africa is on p. 2,113. Foreign policy issues occupied nine of thirty-four pages in the Democratic platform and seven of twenty-two in the Republican plank.

63. See Norman H. Nie, Sidney Verba, and John R. Petrocik, *The Changing American Voter*, enlarged ed. (Cambridge, Mass.: Harvard Univ. Press, 1979); and Walter Dean Burnham, *Critical Elections and the Mainsprings of American Politics* (New York: W. W. Norton, 1970).

64. James Q. Wilson, "Realignment at the Top, Dealignment at the Bottom," in *The American Elections of 1984*, ed. Austin Ranney (Durham, N.C.: Duke Univ. Press, 1985), pp. 297–310.

65. Samuel Kernell, *Going Public* (Washington, D.C.: Congressional Quarterly Press, 1986), pp. 3–35; and John Corry, "Even Revolutionaries Smile for the Camera," *New York Times*, October 4, 1987, p. H31.

66. Steven V. Roberts, "The Global Village: A Case in Point," *New York Times*, February 20, 1986, p. B8; and John M. Goshko, "Most in Poll Say Marcos Won by Fraud," *Washington Post*, February 25, 1986, p. A11.

67. Robert E. DiClerico and Eric M. Uslaner, *Few Are Chosen: Problems in Presidential Selection* (New York: McGraw-Hill, 1984), p. 59; and Edie N. Goldenberg and Michael W. Traugott, *Campaigning for Congress* (Washington, D.C.: Congressional Quarterly Press, 1984), p. 85.

68. Nelson W. Polsby, "The Washington Community, 1960–1980," in *The New Congress,* eds. Thomas E. Mann and Norman J. Ornstein (Washington, D.C.: American Enterprise Institute, 1981), pp. 7–31.

69. Schneider, "Conservatism, Not Interventionism," p. 61.

70. Ibid., pp. 61–62; Theodore J. Lowi, *The Personal President* (Ithaca, N.Y.: Cornell Univ. Press, 1985), pp. 63–70; and *The World Almanac and Book of Facts 1984* (New York: Newspaper Enterprise Association, Inc., 1984), p. 429.

71. Thomas Patterson, *The Mass Media Election* (New York: Praeger Publishers, 1980), p. 29.

72. Austin Ranney, *Channels of Power* (New York: Basic Books, 1983).

73. Stephen Hess, *The Ultimate Insiders* (Washington, D.C.: Brookings Institution, 1986); and Timothy E. Cook, "House Members as Newsmakers," *Legislative Studies Quarterly* 11 (May 1986), 203–26.

74. E. J. Dionne, Jr., "Government Trust: Less in Western Europe Than in U.S.," *New York Times*, February 16, 1985, p. 20.

75. Kernell, *Going Public*, p. 9.

76. Benjamin I. Page, Robert Y. Shapiro, and Glenn R. Dempsey, "What Moves Public Opinion?" *American Political Science Review* 81 (March 1987), pp. 23–43.

77. See Schneider, "Conservatism, Not Interventionism," p. 62.

Chapter Six

The Fourth Circle II:
Local Activists and Interest Groups

The role of public opinion in foreign policy formation has been a subject of concern since the very first days of democratic government. Disagreement over what the proper role for the public should be has formed the core of the debate not only on electoral sanctions, but also on bipartisanship and media coverage of international events. Yet there has been little attention paid to local activists and interest groups. Until recently, what we have called *local diplomacy* simply did not exist. Governors and mayors, not to mention city councils, were much more concerned with sewers than with Sandinistas. Similarly, interest groups—apart from a few on the fringes of both the left and right—were considered the stuff of which domestic, not foreign, policy formation was made. The shattering of the bipartisan consensus in the post-Vietnam era has changed all of this. Today, the fourth circle is bursting with participants. It may be the farthest removed from the centers of power in international politics, but it is becoming among the most important, especially as issues that formerly are purely domestic are now increasingly matters of concern in the international arena. As Secretary of State George Shultz stated in the Iran–Contra hearings, quoting the late entertainer Jimmy Durante, "Everybody wants to get into the act!"

THE NEWEST ACTORS: ALL POLITICS ARE LOCAL

In the pre-Vietnam period the focus of national policymaking on international affairs was just that: *national* policy formation. However, in the post-Vietnam era, new actors have emerged on the foreign policy scene: state and local governments. In one sense this is not surprising. As former Speaker of the House Thomas P. O'Neill was fond of saying, "All politics are local." Yet it is difficult for the nation to speak with one voice if presidents must contend with governors, mayors, unelected officials, presidential candidates, and even private citizens (as in the Iran–Contra affair) attempting to make foreign policy.

Concern with international relations is not new for local governments. However, as the consensus on what foreign policy should be has broken down, many local officials such as Larry Agran, mayor of Irvine, California, argue that they have an *obligation* to speak out against administrative policies they oppose so that citizens will have an alternative set of leaders. For years localities have established "sister cities" with localities in other countries; there are now more than 1,200 such arrangements. These relationships have traditionally been little more than signs of neighborliness, a sort of hands across the ocean. Now thirty-seven cities have established such relations with Managua, the capital of Nicaragua, in protest over the United States policy of providing aid to the Contras, and thirty-three other Nicaraguan cities have similar arrangements with American communities. Seattle, sometimes described as a "city with its own foreign policy," has eleven such sister cities and a Mayor's Commission on Central America.[1] San Francisco has declared itself a sanctuary for refugees from El Salvador and Guatemala, one of more than twenty cities to do so. It has instructed its police department not to cooperate with the Immigration and Naturalization Service, which seeks to deport many of the illegal aliens. Together with over seventy other cities, it has begun selling stocks of companies still doing business with South Africa.

Massachusetts, with a large Irish Catholic population, has prohibited state pension funds from investing in companies that sell arms to Great Britain for use in the religious conflict of northern Ireland. Michigan has limited university investments in companies trading with the Soviet Union. Over 130 cities, including Chicago, have declared themselves "nuclear-free zones." They ban the manufacture, transport, or disposal of nuclear weapons within city limits. Almost as many refused to participate in the federal government's program for test relocations in the event of a nuclear war. In 1982, twenty-eight out of thirty communities and eight of nine states conducting nonbinding referendums supporting the nuclear freeze adopted such proposals.[2]

One issue has pitted states against each other. The federal government has argued that the National Guard is part of the country's defense system and has assigned guard units to build roads (among other projects) in Honduras, which is battling left-wing guerrillas and which also serves as a launching base for raids by the American-backed Contras in neighboring Nicaragua. Ten states followed the lead of Minnesota and its Democratic governor, Rudy Perpich, in a challenge to a statute enacted in 1986 that prohibited governors from withholding their approval of the use of guards outside the country in the absence of an emergency within the states. These governors argued that the guard units are state organizations. Eight other states entered the legal fray as "friends of the court" *supporting* the guard's right to dispatch troops abroad.[3] Eight of the eleven states challenging the law have Democratic governors, while seven of the eight supporting the statute have Republican chief executives. One state in which the governorship changed parties in 1986—Arizona—has seen a reversal in policy on this issue. The former governor, Evan Mecham, reversed his Democratic predecessor's ban on sending guard members other than military police to Honduras.[4] A federal court ruled in late 1987 against the Minnesota challenge, maintaining that the National Guard fell under the jurisdiction of the Congress. One Illinois state legislator, upset at his state's policies, filed a bill to prohibit the guard from being sent abroad, visited the troops in Honduras, and reported on the trip in a newsletter to his constituents (reproduced in this chapter).

The new activism of subnational governments reflects the breakdown of the pre-Vietnam consensus on foreign policy. Yet it symbolizes something more. The good economic times of the 1950s and especially the 1960s and the great increase in the role of government in the nation's economy led to a new participatory environment throughout American politics—on domestic as well as foreign policy issues. The number of lobbyists in Washington increased from 2,000 in 1976 to over 9,000 in 1986; as far back as 1975, however, there were reported to be 15,000 individuals, including unregistered lobbyists, working on some form of foreign lobbying activity in Washington.[5] As noted in Chapter 4, the number of special interest caucuses in the Congress has also skyrocketed.

The slogan in the 1960s of radicals protesting the Vietnam War and the lack of progress in civil rights—"Power to the people"—was taken quite literally by Americans. The range of issues that excited people increased dramatically. Concern over the environment, civil rights, womens' rights, and other social issues (abortion, prayer in schools, etc.)—as well as foreign policy—changed the atmosphere in Washington. When the boom of the 1960s gave way to very high rates of inflation in the 1970s and the recession of 1982, local politicians—both mayors and governors—traversed the world to seek new outlets for investment in their communities and states. The emergence of an interdependent world economy—as well as the large budgetary surpluses run by exporting countries such as the oil producers and Japan—added greatly to local politicians' interest in the international arena. Concern with other foreign policy questions followed naturally. Indeed in 1987, at the annual meeting of the National Governors' Association, it was declared that state leaders must take an active role in foreign policymaking, especially on issues such as trade, to prevent economic wars among the states. Twenty-three states have established offices to provide financial assistance to firms in the export business and more than 200 cities have sent trade envoys abroad.[6]

Ellis B. Levin
Illinois State Representative

SPRING, 1987

REP. LEVIN INTRODUCES LEGISLATION TO GET THE ILLINOIS NATIONAL GUARD OUT OF CENTRAL AMERICA, FOLLOWING, TRIP TO HONDURAS AND NICARAGUA

REP. LEVIN WITH MEMBERS OF THE ILLINOIS NATIONAL GUARD IN NORTHERN HONDURAS

Dear Friend:

In late February and early March I traveled to Honduras and Nicaragua on a fact finding trip in connection with the deployment of the Illinois National Guard to Honduras. What we saw and heard demonstrated beyond any possible doubt that the Illinois National Guard does not belong in Honduras

This newsletter gives me a chance to report to my constituents and others in Illinois on what we saw and the conclusions we reached. While there, we had the opportunity to meet with all sides in both countries, including being helicoptered by the U.S. military to the base where the Illinois National Guard is deployed in Honduras, meeting with Contra leaders, members of the majority and opposition Honduran parties, as well as members of the Sandinistan Government in Nicaragua. Everyone we met with was extremely cooperative. This gave us an extraordinary opportunity to reach some hard conclusions as to what is really going on down there.

The Illinois National Guard does not belong there and it is our role as citizens to make this conclusion known to the legislators in the State. One wonders if it would have been possible to undertake a similar type of trip before the Vietnam War.

Sincerely,

Ellis B. Levin
State Representative

IN THIS ISSUE

The distrust of governmental authorities in Washington led people to become more actively involved in all sorts of issues; Americans have traditionally believed that the most representative governments are the ones closest to home. The activism, both through local politics and interest groups, reflects the reemergence of this motif in the 1970s and 1980s.

INTEREST GROUPS

Nothing has so directly challenged the idea of presidential dominance over foreign policy in the past two decades as the increase in the role of interest groups in foreign policy. In the pre-Vietnam period there was a scattering of groups on the ideological fringes, as well as some ethnic groups pressing for congressional statements of support for their causes, but little more. To be sure, interest groups were active on issues such as trade, but they were far fewer in number than today. Groups pressuring for free trade generally canceled out those demanding protection, so that presidents retained the upper hand in negotiating tariff agreements with other countries. As Bauer, Pool, and Dexter argued:

> The stereotype notion of omnipotent pressure groups becomes completely obsolete once there are groups on both sides. The result of opposing omnipotent forces is stalemate. But, even taken by themselves, the groups did not appear to have the raw material of great power. We noted shortages of money, men, information, and time.[7]

Interest groups on trade also tended to concentrate their efforts on legislators who agreed with their own stands; there was hardly unanimity even within the corporate and union sectors. Thus, much lobbying took the form of speaking to the already converted.

On domestic policies, where the stakes more clearly involve "winners" and "nonwinners" rather than "winners" and "losers," interest groups have been much stronger actors. Moreover, weak political parties generally indicate that interest groups are powerful.[8] Thus, farmers' lobbies have an important say on agriculture; veterans' organizations are forceful proponents of their demands for more government services; and business lobbies fight against government regulation and for tax deductions for investments. In contrast, on foreign policy there have been far fewer active interest groups. When there is a clearly perceived "national interest" at stake, it appears unseemly for groups to seek some private interest.

However, there are some important areas of foreign policy in which interest groups have traditionally been active. In addition to trade, one prominent issue has been the defense budget. Since defense expenditures are in the range of $300 billion, it is reasonable to presume that military contractors would attempt to play a major role in the defense budgetary process. And it is indeed the case that military contractors have supported specific services in their competition for funds and weapons. However, the military services are not themselves united over which weapons should be built: the navy wants more ships, the army more tanks, the air force more jets. Not all can be purchased, and rivalries among the services are fierce. Members of Congress do fight for military projects for their districts, but even in this realm there is no strong evidence to support a linkage between serving on the armed services committees and getting more than a "fair share" of military expenditures in one's district or state.[9] Legislators do a better job of protecting military installations already in their districts than in obtaining new bases. Cost effectiveness is one criterion. As military expenses increase so does inflation, and most of the military budget now is spent on personnel, so there is simply less flexibility in locating installations for political purposes. In 1988 Congress enacted legislation establishing a bipartisan commission to recommend the closing of unneeded military bases. Furthermore, there are some other restrictions that we tend to gloss over: you cannot locate a naval base in Kansas.

The intermestic policies of food and energy also involve group conflict, just as trade and the defense budget do. However, the policy-making process on these issues is considerably more complex. In addition to the range of domestic interest groups involved, there are foreign actors who can restrict the range of alternative policies from which a decision can be made. There are also multinational corporations, such as the oil companies or telecommunications giants such as AT&T, ITT, or IBM, which operate both in the consuming nations (particularly the United States) and the producing nations (such as the OPEC countries). These corporations are, of course, among the domestic interests involved in the policy-making process. But multinational corporations are not easily controlled by the American government. They can act in concert with the producing nations (as the oil companies cooperate with the OPEC nations) and are not subject to U.S. regulations outside the American borders. Pharmaceutical firms can market products abroad that have not been approved by American authorities. The leverage that the United States has over such companies is limited, since the multinationals can threaten to move their bases of operation abroad. The policy-making process on these issues becomes much more complex, and often the result is no coordinated policy at all.

The sharp rise in energy prices (up to $36 per barrel) and their rapid descent (to a low of $8 per barrel) within the course of a decade led to increased economic turmoil in the developing nations of the Third World. The nations that had relied on cheap energy to industrialize had to resort to borrowing instead during the 1970s, often at levels far beyond their capacity to repay the loans. Energy-rich countries such as Mexico and Nigeria profited mightily from the boom in oil prices and rushed to diversify their economies with massive building projects, again financed by loans. When prices plummeted in 1985–86, these countries were unable to pay back even the interest on loans. Together with other developing nations, they threatened not to repay the loans at all. Since popular support for foreign aid among the mass public has plummeted in the post-Vietnam era and because direct grants are more difficult to obtain, banks have taken the place of governments in financing Third World loans. Many of the banks are themselves multinational corporations. Traveling abroad, it is no longer surprising to see offices of Citicorp, the Bank of America, or the First National Bank of Chicago, among many others. These financial institutions have become the principal financiers of development and, in turn, have large deposits from Japan and of "petrodollars" from oil-producing nations. Banks have lent money not only to American friends in the Third World such as Mexico, Argentina, Brazil, Turkey, and Zaire (among many others), but also to the communist nations of Eastern Europe and even to the Soviet Union itself. By making these loans, the banks not only make calculated business decisions but foreign policy as well.

Such private loans often serve the same function as government loans or direct aid. Just as critical, many of these loans are made to facilitate purchases of American goods by foreign nations. The banks, then, control the flow of international commerce, and international banking regulations are few in number and difficult to enforce. When Carter froze Iranian assets in American banks in 1980 (including overseas branches) following the seizure of hostages, observers in the financial community wondered whether the banks would go along; many even doubted that foreign branches would comply. The banks did not challenge the president, however, and America's allies were quite supportive in permitting American branches in their nations to follow presidential orders. An international, financial, and political crisis might have developed otherwise. The issue was resolved without substantial difficulty, because most banks involved also were holding unpaid notes from the shah's government, and it was far from clear that the new Islamic government would honor past debts. The possibility that the government might have to bail out some banks that lost large amounts of money through loans to American allies was fortunately avoided in the Iranian case, but it is a question that worries both policy makers and bankers. It is far from clear what the government would do should a major nation such as Argentina, Brazil, or Mexico default or refuse to pay its debts. Nor is it immediately evident whether the government of the United States or the banks, which control much of the domestic money supply, would ultimately emerge from such a struggle as the dominant actor.[10] The government won the first round of what promised to be a protracted legal battle when the Supreme Court ruled unanimously in July 1981 that President Carter had had authority under the Constitution to conclude the agreement which finally won the hostages' release. In May 1987 the banks had to confront a far more serious problem. Several of the nation's largest banks, led by Citicorp, increased their reserve deposits to cover possible defaults on Third World loans. Citicorp put aside $3 billion, but its total outstanding loans to developing countries amount to $14.7 billion. The five largest American banks alone had losses in 1987 estimated at $7 billion.[11] These figures, of course, do not include obligations owed to financial institutions in Western Europe, Japan, and Canada. Should many Third World countries default, the major banks in North America, Western Europe, and Japan could be thrown into turmoil—and with them the economies of each nation. The federal government already has had to rescue one bank—Continental Illinois—from imprudent lending practices to the domestic energy sector. Some leading politicians, especially Senator Bill Bradley (D-N.J.), have recommended forgiving part of the loans if the debtor nations agree to restructure their economies.

The increased interdependence of the world economy has brought a whole new range of actors into the foreign policy process: foreign companies that have invested in the United States. Foreigners now own more than 10 percent of all U.S. government securities and often obtain special tax advantages for opening plants in the United States. Many states have engaged in bidding wars against each other to attract Japanese car manufacturers, for example. Altogether, the 850 foreign lobbyists who did register in 1985 spent $150 million on their activities. The political action committees (PACs) of American companies owned by foreign nationals donated more than $1 million to congressional campaigns in 1984, twice as much as two years earlier; two years later, the figure had more than doubled again to $2.3 million. While foreign nationals are prohibited from making contributions to American political campaigns, the Federal Election Commission has ruled that foreign-owned companies operating within the United States are the political arms of their employees rather than their stockholders.

Japanese firms have also donated large sums of money to California state legislative candidates who pledged to overturn a law that imposed taxes on the worldwide earnings of corporations operating in California. As Japan came under increasing criticism for its large trade surplus with the United States, it mounted a political offensive in Washington in an attempt to forestall stringent trade legislation in the Congress. Japan is estimated to spend $60 million a year in lobbying, more than twice as much as any other country, and to have hired as many as 300 lobbying firms to assist it. When a Japanese firm, Toshiba, was charged with selling advanced American technology to the Soviet Union in violation of American laws, the firm was able to mobilize not only the resources of the government of Japan, but also leaders of many American corporations doing business in the Far East to lobby (unsuccessfully) against a ban on the import of Toshiba products.

The Korean-based Unification Church has established daily newspapers in Washington and New York to compete with the *Washington Post* and the *New York Times*, as well as a news magazine to compete with *Time* and *Newsweek*. And former presidential aide Michael Deaver was accused in 1986 of using his influence with President Reagan on behalf of his employer, the government of Canada, to affect acid rain legislation. Deaver, who also worked for Saudi Arabia and South Korea, was just one example of prominent federal officials who went to work for foreign countries. From 1980 to 1985 at least seventy-six former high-ranking government officers worked for over fifty foreign governments, including former Vice President Spiro T. Agnew, two former secretaries of state (Dean Acheson and William P. Rogers), a former secretary of defense (Clark Clifford), the ex-director of the Central Intelligence Agency (William Colby), an erstwhile national security adviser

(Richard Allen), and many former representatives and senators, including one who chaired the Foreign Relations Committee (J. William Fulbright).[12]

Ideological interest groups, such as the Committee of One Million and the Women's Strike for Peace, played a prominent role in the foreign policy of the 1950s and 1960s. The first group consistently battled to prevent the recognition of the Peking government of China, whereas the last organization pressed for nuclear disarmament. Neither of these groups was successful in its goal, and both have disappeared from public view. During the 1970s and 1980s new and temporarily influential groups did arise. One such organization, The Committee on the Present Danger, arose in the 1970s to combat what it considered to be public apathy in the wake of Vietnam about the growing military threat of the Soviet Union. One of its major efforts was to prevent ratification of the SALT II treaty. Its principal impact, however, came during the Reagan administration, when many of the committee's most prominent individuals found themselves in positions in government.[13] Included were:

Ronald Reagan	President of the United States
George P. Shultz	Secretary of State (from 1982)
Richard V. Allen	National Security Assistant (1981–1982)
William J. Casey	Director of Central Intelligence
Fred Charles Iklé	Under Secretary of Defense for Policy
Richard N. Perle	Assistant Secretary of Defense for International Security Policy (Arms Control)
Eugene V. Rostow	Director, Arms Control and Disarmament Agency (1981–1982)
John F. Lehman	Secretary of the Navy
Jeane J. Kirkpatrick	Representative to the United Nations
Paul H. Nitze	Negotiator for European Theater Nuclear Forces
Kenneth Adelman	Deputy Representative to the United Nations and Director, Arms Control and Disarmament Agency (after April 1983)

Among the "ideological" interest groups that have emerged since the Vietnam War are religious organizations, especially churches. Churches have traditionally been active politically in the United States, fighting for the abolition of slavery before the Civil War, for Prohibition in the early twentieth century, for civil rights in the 1950s and 1960s, and on both sides of the new social issues of the 1970s and 1980s (abortion, prayer in schools, etc.). Church activism on foreign policy dramatically increased during the Vietnam War and has continued apace since then. In 1986, the National Conference of Catholic Bishops almost unanimously approved a pastoral letter calling for significant increases in foreign aid and a ban on the sale of military hardware abroad. The next year it announced that it would divest

$5.3 million of investments in American firms doing business in South Africa.

The Catholic Church has gone on record as opposing aid to the Contras, while the Presbyterian General Assembly has actively lobbied members of the Congress on the same issue. Together with the United Church of Christ, the United Methodists, the American Baptists, the United Council of Churches, and pacifist churches such as the Mennonites and the Society of Friends, they have formed the Inter-Religious Task Force on El Salvador and Central America. A few secular groups also lobby on the left on this issue, as do conservative organizations such as the Heritage Foundation, the American Security Council, the Council for Inter-American Security, and the Institute on Religion and Democracy. Most of these organizations have little or no staffs and only the religious groups have had much of an impact on Capitol Hill. Even the Bahai faith, whose members accept the principles of most of the world's major religions and who are prohibited from participating in partisan politics, have formed a lobbying organization to call attention to the persecution of their coreligionists in Iran.[14]

However, not all action takes place within the confines of the mile-long road that both joins and separates the Capitol and the White House. One organization, loosely affiliated with some Protestant and Catholic Church groups and deriving its inspiration from a Jesuit concept of the harmony that binds people together, pursues its goals through a more adversarial venue—the legal system. The Christic Institute filed suit in 1986 to force the Reagan administration to abandon its support for the Contras, charging that some of the antigovernment military operations in Nicaragua have been financed by illegal narcotics sales assisted by American officials.[15] Churches and synagogues have been at the forefront of the sanctuary movement. Evangelical churches, however, have mobilized their members in support of aid to the Contras. Jews have, in addition to their strong support for Israel (see below), lobbied heavily for penalizing the Soviet Union until it no longer restricts Jewish emigration. In 1974, they pressured Congress to enact the Jackson-Vanik amendment restricting trade with the Soviet Union.

Some ethnic lobbies have lost influence. The stereotypical "ethnic lobby" of the 1950s and 1960s was the Eastern European immigrant organization (representing Ukrainians, Latvians, Lithuanians, and Estonians) seeking demonstrations of congressional support for freedom for their fellow countrymen who reside in formerly independent states or regions that are now part of the Soviet Union. These groups still exist, but they no longer occupy the privileged position on Capitol Hill that they did during the Cold War days. These lobbies reasserted themselves in 1988 when nationalist movements in the Soviet republics demanded autonomy as part of Mikhail Gorbachev's policy of *perestroika* (restructuring).

Other ethnic lobbies are even stronger than they were in the 1950s and 1960s. More prominent ethnic lobbies include the American Israel Public Affairs Committee (AIPAC), and the Greek lobbyists, the American Hellenic Institute Public Affairs Committee and the American Hellenic Educational

Progressive Association. These groups are generally regarded as the most effective and well organized in Washington, particularly AIPAC. The Jewish organizations (AIPAC, the American Jewish Committee, and the B'nai B'rith Anti-Defamation League) are concerned almost exclusively with American policy toward Israel, although emigration of Soviet Jews has also been a major focus of their efforts. While these organizations have been unusually successful, they are not always victorious. The failure to block the sale of military aircraft to Egypt and Saudi Arabia in 1978 or to prevent the transfer of AWACs planes to the Saudis are two examples.

While AIPAC could not prevent an additional arms deal with Saudi Arabia in 1986, it did reassert its strength later that year and in 1987, when Congress forced Reagan to withdraw proposed arms sales to Jordan and the Saudis. Legislators feared that the arms might be used against Israel and believed that neither Jordan nor Saudi Arabia had been sufficiently forthcoming in furthering the Middle East peace process.[16] Additionally, many Americans were up in arms in 1987 against Saudi Arabia's refusal to shoot down the Iraqi plane that fired at the U.S.S. *Stark* in the Persian Gulf. Israel receives by far the largest amount of foreign aid from the United States—as much as $7.1 billion for 1986 and 1987—and has received other unique forms of aid. The United States and Israel signed a free-trade pact in 1985 that will completely eliminate all tariffs between the two countries. The United States has also permitted Israel to use some of the military credits it receives to develop its own technology; additionally, contributions by Americans to Israel, largely from the Jewish community, are tax-exempt.

The strength of ethnic groups is not a new phenomenon in American politics; they have played a major role in foreign policy debates throughout the twentieth century. Irish groups, opposed to Britain, argued against American participation in World War I and later opposed U.S. entry into the League of Nations. Italian and German groups were active opponents of American entry into both world wars. Indeed, German groups were extremely powerful in the Midwest throughout the century, helping elect several senators and members of the House. While often quite liberal on domestic policies, the midwestern members of Congress elected from districts with heavy concentrations of Germans were decidedly isolationist in their foreign policy. Their rationale for not fighting a war against Germany was that the United States should not attempt to resolve what essentially were conflicts between other nations. Isolationist strength reached its peak between the two wars, when Robert LaFollette, Sr. ran for president on a third-party ticket in 1924. Although LaFollette carried only his home state of Wisconsin, he ran a close second in several midwestern states and compiled what was then the second largest number of votes a third-party candidate had ever received for president. The strength of the LaFollette movement raised serious questions about American entry into World War II before Pearl Harbor. The Irish, Italian, and German groups failed because they each opposed the government's established policies, whereas the Jewish groups have been more successful at least partially because of the government's official position of support toward Israel. On those issues where AIPAC has been least successful, it faced strong opposition from the administration.

The AWACS Sale: A Case Study

The transfer of five AWACS planes to Saudi Arabia sorely tested relations between the Israeli lobby and both White House and congressional supporters. Neither AIPAC nor the president was accustomed to losing battles on Capitol Hill; moreover, the administration seemed an unlikely adversary for the Israeli lobby, since Reagan had actively campaigned in 1980 as a strong supporter of Israel. However, the security of Saudi Arabia, one of America's leading suppliers of oil, was also of prime concern to the president, who wished to create a security zone in the Middle East composed of all of America's friends. However, regional animosities were too strong for such a unified stance to come about, and the stage was set for a confrontation between the administration, which wanted to sell the planes to the Saudis, and the Israeli lobby, which feared that they would be used to spy on Israel's military moves. The constellation of forces involved in the fight was quite wide, and as such the AWACS sale provides a fascinating case study on the interaction of interest groups, the president, and Congress in foreign policy decision making.

Under the 1976 law which permitted Congress to veto major arms sales (since June 1983 of dubious constitutionality), a majority in both the House and the Senate had the power to kill the sale of the AWACS planes to Saudi Arabia. No president had ever lost an arms sales agreement before, even to nations for which the American public had little affinity. Americans, however, generally agreed that Saudi Arabia was vital to their interests; a 1982 poll indicated that 77 percent of the public felt so, compared to 75 percent for Israel. (Israel had a slightly higher overall favorable rating than did Saudi Arabia.)[17] Yet a wide variety of polls also indicated varying degrees of opposition to arms sales to the Saudis, with none showing majority support for such deals (including AWACS) or demonstrating that the sales would have even the level of support that supplying Israel did.[18]

Thus, the stage was set for a dramatic confrontation between the White House and the Congress. Many also interpreted it as a test between presidential power and the lobbying power of the friends of Israel. Israel contended that the sale would pose a threat to its existence, since the AWACS would alter the military balance of strength in the Middle East. The administration countered that the planes were to be used exclusively for defensive purposes against threats to the Saudi regime, although it was unable to persuade Saudi Arabia to agree to have both their own and American pilots operate the planes. Instead, the president sent a letter to key Republican senators promising to cancel the deal if the planes were not used exclusively for defensive purposes. This hardly mollified the opponents of the sale, since they believed that the deal could not be canceled retrospectively.

The pro-Israeli lobby strongly mobilized against the sale. AIPAC, with an annual budget of $5 million and a staff of about eighty operating a block from Capitol Hill, regarded blocking the AWACS as its top legislative priority in 1981. AIPAC operates mostly on Capitol Hill and carefully attempts to distance itself from the Israeli embassy uptown.[19] Also involved were the Conference of Presidents of Major American Jewish Organizations, an umbrella organization of forty groups; and the larger members of the conference, including the American Jewish Committee, the American Jewish Congress, B'nai B'rith, and the Union of American Hebrew Congregations, all of which have their own Washington offices. Most of these organizations focus on domestic issues or on raising funds for Israel rather than on lobbying for foreign policy issues. But the AWACS sale was viewed as too important an issue to ignore.

The effort appeared to be paying off in the summer of 1981. AIPAC secured a letter opposing the AWACS deal in June signed by 224 members of the House and 54 senators, enough to defeat the sale in both houses. The timing of the letter was fortuitous; it was circulated after the Israeli bombing of an Iraqi nuclear reactor and, hence, gave the impression that the signatures constituted the minimum basis of support for the Israeli lobby's position.[20] The power of the lobby has been attributed to its success in fundraising. Nonetheless, electoral reprisal from Jewish votes was feared even though it rarely, if ever, materialized. Many key members of Congress, including AWACS opponent Senator Bob Packwood (R-Oreg.), had raised substantial portions of their campaign funds from Jewish contributors.[21] Senator Charles McC. Mathias, Jr. (R-Md.), reflecting the congressional obsession with the disposition of the "Jewish vote," wrote in *Foreign Affairs* magazine that

> as a result of the activities of the lobby, congressional conviction [that Israel must remain strong] has been measurably reinforced by the knowledge that political sanctions will be applied to any who fail to deliver.[22]

AIPAC was clearly a formidable foe. Its reputation in Washington is comparable not to other foreign policy lobbies, but to domestic actors such as organized labor. Presidential candidates seek its advice, even though AIPAC itself does not endorse candidates for office, and administrations have often sought AIPAC's assistance in gaining congressional support among friends of Israel for other foreign policy issues. The organization has also mobilized local networks of supporters of Israel who meet with members of Congress when they are back in their districts, as well as with those candidates who seek to defeat incumbents.[23]

The "Arab lobby" consists primarily of the National Association of Arab Americans (NAAA). While openly modeled on AIPAC, it has far fewer resources, including a mailing list of only 80,000 names, most of whom are inactive, and a budget reported to be $500,000 annually.[24] While AIPAC has been able to maintain a separate identity from the Israeli government, much of the funding of NAAA (through advertisements in the organization's publication) comes directly from Arab governments and the Palestine Liberation Organization. NAAA leaders complain that many Arab Americans are apolitical, but a rival organization, the American Lebanese League, is harshly critical of the NAAA and views it as essentially anti-American.[25] There have been some efforts to get American businesses with interests in the Middle East, especially oil companies, to do more lobbying and fund raising for the Arab cause, but they have not yielded much success to date. One analysis concludes: "Most Arab embassies throw impressive parties, but have little day-to-day contact with Congress, according to lawmakers and aides. Israel, by comparison, has a staff of congressional relations counselors who keep in touch with Capitol Hill."[26]

With all of these advantages, then, it would appear that victory was almost guaranteed for the Israel lobby on the AWACS votes. The vote in the House was a ringing endorsement for its position; on October 1, 1981, it vetoed the sale by a margin of 301 to 111. But on October 25, the Senate upheld the president by the narrow vote of 48 to 52. The president had convinced eight senators—seven Republicans and one Democrat—to vote with the administration. What happened to turn what seemed to be a sure victory for the Israel lobby into a humiliating defeat?

First was the hard lobbying done by the president himself. Reagan had won rave reviews as a legislative persuader earlier in the year when he successfully maneuvered a very controversial domestic budget through a Congress which was initially skeptical. On the AWACS issue, he asserted the need for the Republican-controlled Senate to back a Republican president on a key foreign policy issue. The fact that a president had never lost an up-or-down arms sales vote before worked to his advantage, as did arguments that the United States would be embarrassed in the Arab world should the sale be vetoed. The specter of another oil embargo, although not specifically raised, was on many people's minds. Second, five days after the House vote Egyptian President Anwar Sadat was assassinated by Muslim radicals in Cairo. Many senators were worried about further instability in the Middle East and decided that they must rally around the president. Third, simple party loyalty played an important role. Many of the senators whom Reagan converted were elected in 1980 and identified with the "New Right." Most leaders of the religious right, particularly the Moral Majority's Jerry Falwell, have a strong affinity for Israel as the Holy Land and actively opposed the AWACS sale. But pressure to support their fellow conservative, the president, proved too strong to resist. Senator Roger Jepsen (R-Iowa), one of the earliest and strongest opponents of the sale, ended up voting with the president "after prayerful and careful deliberation."[27] Fourth, the letter that the president sent to wavering senators promising to cancel the sale if the planes were not used for defensive purposes permitted some senators to argue that the White House had made concessions. Finally, there were also charges that the president engaged in logrolling on the AWACS vote, promising a political appointment to an Iowa senator, a hospital for a Washington Republican, a power plant for a Montana Democrat, and even a pledge not to campaign in 1982 against an Arizona Democrat.[28]

Whatever the relative impacts of each factor, the senators assuaged their consciences and bolstered the Israel lobby five weeks later when the Senate Appropriations Committee voted to increase foreign aid to Israel by $475 million more than the administration requested. Ultimately, the administration prevailed on its original lower request for aid, but in 1983, following the accord between Lebanon and Israel on the withdrawal of foreign forces from Lebanon, the administration agreed to congressional action increasing assistance to Israel. Furthermore, the Congress dealt the administration a further setback when a House Foreign Affairs subcommittee voted to ban arms sales to Jordan until King Hussein publicly recognized Israel and agreed to negotiate with it under the terms of the 1979 Camp David accords.

A further test of AIPAC's effectiveness might have come had Reagan pushed his 1982 peace plan, under which the Israelis would withdraw from most of the West Bank and Gaza (captured from Jordan and Egypt in 1967) and permit a self-governing Palestinian entity to be formed in association with Jordan. The plan was proposed after the Israeli invasion of Lebanon in late spring 1982. To many, the invasion appeared not only as an effort to destroy the Palestine Liberation Organization (PLO), but as an attempt to destroy Palestinian nationalism and tighten Israeli control of the West Bank. While Israeli forces were in control of Lebanon's capital of Beirut, Christian Lebanese forces massacred Palestinians in two camps. As a result of the invasion and the massacre, Israel's position in America—both in the eyes of the public and the Congress— was seriously undermined.

American pressure on Israel to withdraw from Lebanon was initially resisted as the Israelis insisted on a long list of preconditions. In response, the United States postponed the transfer to Israel of U.S.-made fighter planes. Finally, Secretary of State Shultz journeyed to the Middle East and worked out a Lebanese–Israeli agreement under which the Israelis would withdraw if the Syrian and remaining PLO forces did so simultaneously. The Reagan administration's relationship with American Jews improved as a result of these mediation efforts. Responsibility for an Israeli failure to pull its forces out of Lebanon now lay clearly with the Syrians and PLO. A test of the strength of the Israel lobby was also avoided because the PLO and Jordan's King Hussein refused to negotiate a settlement of the Palestinian problem based on the Reagan plan after an initially cautious but favorable reaction. Had they accepted the plan, the administration would have had to pressure the Israeli government and the administration's relationship with the Jewish community, already badly strained by the AWACS deal, would have been severely tested.

The United States "brokered" an agreement for the withdrawal of Israeli troops from Lebanon between Israel and the government then dominated by Maronite Christians in Beirut. This further strengthened American-Israeli ties as most people in the United States viewed the American role as another step toward fostering peace treaties (which the Israel–Lebanon agreement was not!) between Israel and her neighbors. When Syria successfully pressed the Beirut government to abandon the agreement, Israel's stock in the United States rose even further; it was viewed as proposing a peace to unwilling or incapacitated neighbors.

ETHNIC LOBBIES[29]

The Greek lobby was "for years . . . widely rumored to have influence second only to the supporters of Israel" on foreign policy issues facing the Congress.[30] It was successful in gaining substantial foreign assistance as well as in enacting a partial arms embargo on Turkey following that nation's invasion of Cyprus in 1974. Historically, the Greek and Israeli lobbies worked together in providing support for each other's causes, thus making each more effective than either would be alone.[31] But the alliance broke down in 1978 when Israel feared that the embargo on sales to Turkey might lead to a loss of U.S. bases in that country, so many key supporters of Israel in the Congress, led by Representative Steven Solarz (D-N.Y.), supported President Carter's proposal to repeal the embargo. The election of a Socialist government in Greece and Greek threats to leave NATO have further weakened both the Greek–Israeli lobbying alliance in Washington (especially since Greek Prime Minister Andreas Papandreou is outspokenly pro-Arab) but also the efforts of the Greek lobby itself. In 1983, Turkey insisted that the traditional 7 to 10 ratio of American aid to Greece and Turkey be revised further in Turkey's favor. Greece in turn demanded far greater aid if the United States were to maintain bases there. The House insisted that the traditional ratio be maintained, a defeat for the administration and a victory for the Greek lobby, its first notable win in more than five years. Despite the belligerence of the Greek government, which periodically threatens to demand that the U.S. military base outside Athens be shut, Greek-Americans continue to be more successful in lobbying Congress than Turkish-Americans. One reason is the greater sophistication of the Greek lobby, which traditionally worked closely with the Jewish lobby and, indeed, was consciously modeled after AIPAC. Also, there are far more Greek-Americans—estimated to be between 600,000 and three million—than Turkish-Americans, who number only 200,000 and have no lobbying group of their own.[32] In 1987 the Congress not only reduced military aid to Turkey, but also stipulated that none of the arms could be used in Cyprus, which Turkey had invaded in 1974. The Congress also enacted a resolution condemning the massacre of hundreds of thousands of Armenians in Turkey in 1915—an event strongly disputed by the Turks themselves. Greek-Americans took a particularly active role in the 1988 presidential campaign as one of their own, Massachusetts Governor Michael Dukakis, sought the presidency.[33]

Hispanic Americans number between 15 and 23 million, or between 6 and 10 percent of all Americans. Yet, there is little unity among them. Mexican-Americans constitute 60 percent of all Hispanics, but many are not American citizens and even those who are have ambivalent feelings toward Mexico. The next largest group of Hispanics is Puerto Ricans, comprising 14 percent. Yet they too are divided over the status of Puerto Rico, some favoring statehood, others continuation of the commonwealth status, and some independence. Mexican-Americans and Puerto Ricans are generally less well off than many other Americans. They overwhelmingly identify with the Democratic party.[34] On the other hand, the third largest group of Hispanics, Cuban-Americans, are much better off financially and vote heavily for Republican candidates. They are strongly motivated by anticommunism and have contributed heavily to the Floridian Republican party and to anti-Castro groups throughout the nation. Cuban–Americans account for up to 10 percent of the Republican vote in Florida and elected a Cuban-American mayor of Miami. They helped to fund Lt. Col. Oliver L. North's legal expenses during the Iran–Contra affair and a lobbying effort to force Cuban troops from the African nation of Angola.[35]

Black lobbying groups have been active in urging increased aid to African nations, but in recent years have shifted their attention to the struggle to defeat apartheid in South Africa. The Congressional Black Caucus and Trans-Africa, an ethnic lobbying organization with a budget of $325,000 in 1982 and a membership of 10,000, played key roles in arranging demonstrations outside the South African embassy and in pushing Congress to impose sanctions on the apartheid regime.[36]

It is not surprising that Arab organizations have not been successful in tilting the American Middle East position away from Israel, even given the much greater resources of the American Petroleum Institute (API), which represents 350 corporations, and which has been lobbying for a shift in American Middle Eastern policy for about a decade.[37] The API is primarily concerned with oil politics, of course, but it has acted in the not unreasonable belief that American relations with the oil-producing nations are related to the willingness of the country to consider alternative political solutions in the Middle East. The oil companies have *not* been able to dictate foreign policy to the president or the Congress. Indeed, this poor record of influencing policies suggests that any view of foreign policy based on economic determinism is a vast oversimplification. Economic interest groups have been active on foreign policy issues, but Bernard Cohen found that they obtain what they want if these demands *do not conflict with preestablished policies of the government.*[38] An economic interest group may benefit from a foreign policy decision, but this does not imply anything about the role that the group actually played in the formulation of the decision. A good example of this is the economic boom that some farmers and grain speculators reaped from the decision of the United States to make major wheat sales to the Soviet Union in 1973, without having initiated or lobbied for the deal.

However, a threat to the traditional American support for Israel arose in 1979 when several major black civil rights leaders, including the Reverend Jesse Jackson, visited the Middle East and made statements in support of the PLO. The civil rights leaders were upset when United Nations Ambassador Andrew Young, the first black to hold a major foreign policy position in the American government, was forced to resign following an unauthorized meeting with a PLO representative at the United Nations. Jackson and others met with key Arab leaders, including Yasir Arafat of the PLO, but did not meet with Israeli Prime Minister Menachem Begin. On returning home, the black leaders made strong statements in support of Palestinian rights and on the need for a cease-fire in the areas under military threat. Black–Jewish tensions were exacerbated by some poll data showing a weakening in the traditional black support for Israel and by revelations that Arab groups had made donations to black civil rights organizations. The traditional black–Jewish alliance was in danger, and there were serious questions of what the impact on foreign policy in both the Middle East and Africa might be. Other black leaders reasserted traditional support for Israel and rejected the argument that blacks must be concerned with Palestinian rights because in any conflict involving American armed intervention in the Middle East, an interruption of oil supplies would most adversely affect the most disadvantaged economic groups, notably blacks.

Several factors worked to defuse the conflict, at least temporarily. One was the strong defense of Israel and the need for a continuation of the black–Jewish alliance made by Urban League President Vernon Jordan. A second was the revelation of financial inducements made by Arab groups and allegedly demanded by some black leaders in return for political support. Finally, the takeover of the American embassy in Iran by Islamic militants united black and white Americans in support of the president's policies, at least temporarily. It is thus far from clear that these issues between blacks and Jews have been resolved. A major conflict between these two important constituent groups, both strongly associated with the Democratic party, might affect policy through the ballot box: should the party lose the support of either group, it could not hope to gain a majority in presidential elections for years to come. The loss of both groups would virtually guarantee it perpetual minority status. In 1984 such a split did threaten the Democrats, as the simmering conflict for the first time spilled over into the electoral arena. The Reverend Jesse Jackson, who ran for the Democratic nomination for the presidency, not only vociferously supported the creation of a Palestinian state and welcomed the backing of Arab-Americans, but also admitted calling Jews *Hymies* and New York City *Hymietown* in private conversations with black reporters. Furthermore, Jackson refused to denounce one of his most vocal supporters, Minister Louis Farrakhan of the Nation of Islam, who had reportedly threatened the life of the *Washing-*

ton Post reporter who broke the Hymie story and who had called Hitler a "great man." Many key Jewish leaders denounced Jackson as a racist, while black leaders rallied to his support. Jews threatened to boycott the Democratic party if Jackson's views on the Middle East were reflected in the party's platform, while many in the Jackson camp said that they would do likewise if their perspective were *not* included. While most blacks were not as hostile to the Jewish perspective on the Middle East, the importance of Jackson's role in mobilizing black voters was not to be taken lightly by Democratic party leaders who had to confront a great dilemma about how to handle two of the party's most loyal voting blocs. The same conflict reasserted itself in 1988 when Jackson unsuccessfully proposed a Democratic party platform plank calling for an independent Palestinian state.

The potential power of economic and ethnic interests raises important issues related to the democratic dilemma on foreign policy decision making. Specifically, the question becomes: What price might our foreign policy pay for its openness? Does the opportunity for groups to participate mean that they might come to dominate the policy-making process and seek ends which only they find desirable (or profitable)? While most economic interests cannot dominate foreign policy making, some can. An argument for the thesis that economics may on occasion determine policy choices can be made by examples.[39] The attempt by the International Telephone and Telegraph Company to rig the 1970 election for president of Chile against the Marxist Salvador Allende to protect its financial interests there is a case in point. Although Nixon and Kissinger specifically rejected a plan that would have entailed the cooperation of the White House in what proved to be an unsuccessful attempt to prevent Allende from becoming president, in 1973 the CIA "destabilized" the Allende government. While there is no direct evidence that multinational corporations were also involved in the 1973 incident, Nixon did know about the CIA involvement. Thus, even if there was no firm conspiracy between business and the government, in this instance, at least, American foreign and economic policies certainly coincided. Such occurrences are, apparently, relatively rare. But we must always be concerned about the potential for a private interest to determine public policy. On the other hand, grass-roots organizations such as the Emergency Coalition to Save the Panama Canal do attempt to mobilize support in the Congress to persuade members to espouse certain policy positions based on public opinion. In such efforts, as in the ethnic lobbies, foreign policy making resembles domestic policy formation.

The actors in the fourth circle of decision making are strongest on foreign policy when they respond to the same pressures as found in domestic and even intermestic policies. However, a bipartisan foreign policy aids the executive branch in its battle with the Congress since the president can build a new coalition of his own on each foreign policy roll call. Furthermore, the leaders of both parties can generally be counted on to seek out support for the president's positions. As the traditional bipartisanship is threatened, so is the president's strategic advantage. Particularly when such consensus may be replaced by conflicts among traditional allies—the members of the Democratic coalition—and when American foreign policy might become more dependent on international economic conditions (as have the policies of Western Europe and Japan on Middle Eastern issues), the executive branch faces severe challenges ahead. The Congress is not in a position to fill any such leadership vacuum, because it has not resolved, and hardly seems willing to try to resolve, the difficult question of which interests are ultimately to be represented.

ARE INTEREST GROUPS DANGEROUS?

In *The Federalist* (#10) James Madison warned of the "mischiefs of faction."[40] The ambivalence early felt toward parties is analogous to current attitudes toward interest groups. On the one hand, everyone has interests, so certain interest groups are seen as legitimate. The ones that we tend to think of most positively are those with whose goals we agree. Certainly those groups which do not stand to benefit directly by their actions, such as the environmental lobby and the various ideological groups on both the left and the right, are often accorded the right to represent their members without suspicion. On the other hand, when groups do benefit directly, the public may regard them with suspicion. Particularly on foreign policy, when the stakes are so high, we may wonder whether these groups or the president is running the country. We have argued that various lobbying groups active on foreign policy questions generally have not succeeded in changing the policies of a government. But in instances where they have, was their influence in the interests of the nation as a whole? The argument against foreign policy lobbies has been framed by former Maryland Senator Charles Mathias in terms of ethnic lobbies. We must also consider the relationship between foreign policy lobbies and public opinion. A key theme in many critiques is that public opinion is a more appropriate determinant of foreign policy than lobbying pressure. But do they generally conflict with one another? Mathias argues:

> Factions among us lead the nation toward excessive foreign attachments or animosities. Even if the groups were balanced—if Turkish–Americans equaled Greek–Americans or Arab–Americans equaled Jewish–Americans— the result would not necessarily be a sound, cohesive foreign policy because the national interest is not simply the sum of our special interest and attachments. . . . ethnic politics, carried as they often have been to excess, have proven harmful to the national interest. . . . Public debate becomes charged with accusations of "betrayal" and "sellout," which is to say, of moral turpitude, when in truth the issues that divide us are, with few exceptions, questions of judgment and opinion as to what is best for the nation. . . . There is a clear and pressing need for the reintroduction of civility into our public discussions of these matters.[41]

We cannot resolve the question of whether lobbies are beneficial or harmful in the formulation of foreign policy but only determine to what extent the activities of these organizations conform to the broad outline of public opinion on a few issues. We examine here public attitudes toward the Middle East and El Salvador. Periodically, Gallup and other polling organizations survey the American public about its sympathies toward Israelis and Arabs. Should the poll reveal a generally pro-Arab sentiment among Americans, or indeed even a reasonable split, then the reputed power of the Israel lobby would be pernicious indeed, notwithstanding its loss on the AWACS vote. But the figures in Table 6–1 reveal that the American public has consistently been more pro-Israel than pro-Arab. The greatest Israeli advantage occurred, not surprisingly, following the Six-Day War in June 1967, when the ratio in favor of Israel was 14 to 1. It has now fallen to slightly more than 3 to 1 and, indeed, once fell to an almost even level (following the siege of Beirut during the 1982 Israeli invasion of Lebanon). Even with the increase in the overall level of support for the Arab nations, Israeli support within the United States remained very high indeed, especially considering the controversy surrounding many of Israel's actions and the level of the American commitment and involvement in events not of its making. In late 1987 young Palestinians on the Israeli-occupied West Bank and Gaza Strip began a prolonged "uprising." They attacked Israeli military and civilian personnel on the West Bank and threw stones at the police. Israel retaliated with tactics that many in the West, including the United States, believed were stronger than necessary. As a result, public support for Israel dropped sharply in 1988. Table 6–1 shows that in three polls there were pronounced drops in the level of popular backing for Israel. Two surveys show declines of 15–18 points, another a drop of 25 points. Yet, despite these results, two key factors are still important. First, the American public still supports Israel over the Arabs by a substantial margin, even as it disapproves of specific Israeli policies in handling the uprising. Popular backing for Israel is found for virtually every group among the American citizenry (data not shown). Second, even as Americans express less support for Israel, they are no more sympathetic to the Arab cause in 1988 than they were during the more peaceful times of the late 1970s. Indeed, the Arabs now appear to be less popular with the American public than they were during the Lebanon War, and no more favorably perceived than at the time of the Camp David peace treaty. Israel's supporters do have a very effective lobby and one that many in Congress fear can threaten electoral sanctions, although the data do not support this assertion. But even Mathias admits that the tactics of AIPAC consist largely of providing information as well as informational letters and visits from lobbyists and influential constituents.[42] These are the tactics of any lobbying organization. The threats of electoral sanctions, however, would appear to be far more disturbing if the lobbying organization were out of step with public opinion. Exactly the contrary seems to be the case with AIPAC. As in the AWACS sale, AIPAC "lost" the battle to block

TABLE 6–1   Public Sympathies in the Middle East Conflict

Date of Poll	More with Israel	More with Arab Nations	Neither/ Both	Don't Know
June 1967 (following Six-Day War)	56	4	25	15
December 1973 (following Yom Kippur War)	50	7	25	18
January 1975	44	8	22	26
March 1978	38	11	33	18
January 1979	40	14	31	15
July 1981	49	10	20	11
June 1982	52	10	29	9
September 1982 (following Lebanon invasion)	32	28	21	19
January 1983	49	12	22	17
February–March 1983	52	16	13	19
July 1985 (following TWA hostage crisis)	49	11	18	22
October 1985 (following *Achille Lauro* incident)	64	14	13	9
June 1986	62	13	13	12
January 1988 (during Palestinian uprising)	47	15	21	17
April 1988 (during Palestinian uprising)	37	11	37	16
May 1988 (during Palestinian uprising)	44	13	21	22

All polls up to January 1983 were conducted by the Gallup organization and are reported in Alvin Richman, "American Attitudes Toward the Middle East Since Israel's Invasion of Lebanon," Table 4B (paper presented at the Annual Meeting of the American Association of Public Opinion Researchers, May 1983). The remaining polls, except for the October 1985 survey, were conducted by the *Washington Post* and ABC News; the October 1985 poll was conducted by the Harris organization. They are reported in Eytan Gilboa, "Terrorism and Trust: How We See The Middle East," *Public Opinion*, November/December 1986, pp. 52–55. The January and May, 1988, surveys were prepared by Penn and Schoen Associates for the B'nai B'rith Anti-Defamation League and were reported in Penn and Schoen Associates, "Summary of National Survey for Anti-Defamation League," Penn and Schoen Associates, May 13, 1988. The April, 1988 survey was prepared for the American Jewish Committee by the Roper Organization and was reported in David Singer and Renae Cohen, "In the Wake of the Palestinian Uprising: Findings of the April 1988 Roper Poll" (Washington, D.C.: American Jewish Committee, April, 1988). Both 1988 polls included the option that respondents support both Israel and the Arabs. Respondents selecting this option (eight and six percent respectively in the Penn and Schoen polls and eleven percent in the Roper survey) are included in the "neither" category in the table.

the beginning of an American dialogue with the PLO in 1988 after Yasir Arafat recognized Israel's right to exist and renounced terrorism. Even though public opinion polls showed a plurality in opposition to this move, many American Jewish leaders differed with AIPAC and supported the Reagan administration's initiative.

Opponents of American policy in El Salvador may argue that the ideological and church-related interest groups opposing administration policy may have a salutory effect on the congressional attempts to limit American involvement there. Opposition on the part of interest groups to the war in Vietnam played a major role in turning public opinion against the conflict, a key ingredient in the final American defeat in Southeast Asia. A decade and a half later, various polls indicated that Americans fear that the United States will become entangled in Latin America much as it did in Vietnam. A Gallup poll in June 1983 found that 71 percent of Americans were concerned that the United States would become more deeply involved in El Salvador, compared with only 24 percent who thought otherwise. Three years later, even though no American troops had been committed to Latin America, 62 percent of Americans believed that Nicaragua would become the next Vietnam. The minority that knew which side the United States was backing was 17 percent more strongly opposed to aid to the Contras than were the citizens with less knowledge of the situation.[43]

If one can trace any impact of interest groups on attitudes toward present Latin American policy, it would seem that it has been to lead public opinion away from the president's program. But the widespread public opposition to a troop commitment in Central America has also been reflected in congressional skepticism about the appropriate role for the United States. Thus, groups opposed to U.S. involvement in Latin America have not only challenged the administration, but also strengthened the hands of the congressional majority opposed to the president's policy. It is precisely because the churches do not stand to benefit directly from any specific policy in Latin America that there have been relatively few charges that their role is illegitimate. There is, of course, substantial debate about whether these foreign policy questions are appropriate matters for church lobbying at all, but the simple fact that church sentiment is very much in line with public opinion in this instance militates against interest-group participation in foreign policy.

WHEN IS LOBBYING WORRISOME?

Lobbying on foreign policy becomes worrisome for the same reasons that lobbying on domestic policy does: when there is cause for alarm that policy formation is subjected to undue pressure or when there is a potential loss of accountability in policy formation. Let us consider one instance of each.

First, we have argued that ethnic lobbying on foreign policy generally succeeds when the group pursues policies that are in accord with public opinion and existing governmental decisions. The efforts of the pro-Israel lobby certainly meet both criteria. However, in recent years, pro-Israel groups have relied increasingly on electoral competition: they have tried to single out for defeat candidates who challenge the lobby or who make pro-Arab statements.[44] In 1980 and 1982 AIPAC focused on Representative Paul Findley (R-Ill.), who had called for recognition of the PLO. Findley was defeated in the last contest and argued plaintively that he was the target of the lobby. His view was not entirely unjustified: over 90 percent of his opponent's campaign expenditures reportedly came from Jewish sources. Two years later a Jewish donor from California contributed $1 million of his own money in independent expenditures that helped defeat Senate Foreign Relations Chair Charles Percy (R-Ill.), also a critic of Israel. Yet the largest recipient of pro-Israel money was North Carolina Governor James Hunt, who barely failed to unseat Senator Jesse Helms. After the election, Helms changed from a strong critic of Israel to one of its most determined supporters in the Senate.

In 1984, fifty-four pro-Israel political action committees contributed more than $4.25 million to House and Senate candidates—considerably more than was spent by the largest domestic political action committee, that of the real estate industry. Almost 80 percent of the contributions went to Democrats; more than a third of all money given to Republicans went to Senator Rudy Boschwitz (R-Minn.), who is Jewish and chaired the Senate Foreign Relations Committee's Subcommittee on the Middle East. In the 1986 contests, eighty pro-Israel political action committees spent $6.9 million, of which $3.9 million was contributed to candidates. In contrast, Arab-Americans have not been at all active in contributing to political candidates. One of their two political action committees neither raised nor spent any money in 1982; the other, which supports moderate candidates, gave only $5,500 to six campaigns in 1982. In 1986, the National Association of Arab Americans contributed just about $70,000 to congressional aspirants.[45]

Making foreign policy hostage to campaign contributions is at least as dangerous as buying votes on domestic legislation, for, if domestic groups can purchase influence, so can foreign companies. When confronted with demands by foreign companies to withdraw taxes on their worldwide earnings, Florida complied and California did not. Japanese companies responded, as noted above, with large donations to legislative campaigns in the first state.[46] In time this might provoke not only legal action, but more important, hostile public attitudes toward the companies that pursue such strategies. Similarly, the tactics of the pro-Israel lobby may result in a backlash against what has been relatively consensual support for Israel. Indeed, even as the pre-Vietnam consensus on foreign policy has broken down, the one issue that draws support across the ideological spectrum of elites is the moral obligation to prevent the destruction of Israel.[47]

Interest Groups and Accountability

Policy making through threats of electoral retribution can only serve to disrupt such a consensus. Pro-Israeli groups seemed to recognize this in 1985 and 1986 when they contributed heavily to Republicans, especially to those New Right senators who have backed Israel. Making contributions bipartisan does not depoliticize the issue. Focusing on an electoral strategy may make it appear that American Jews have no other concerns than the support of Israel—and can raise the issue that American Jews fear most: that of dual loyalty, not only to the United States but also to Israel. Furthermore, electoral support through campaign contributions, with the sanctions that are implicit in that strategy, will ultimately raise questions of private interests competing with national interests. When then-Representative (now Senator) John Breaux (D-La.) was asked if his vote could be bought, he responded, "No, but it can be rented."[48] Perhaps more than anything else, such a charge would destroy a policy consensus.

The other concern for interest group activity on foreign policy is with accountability. To be sure, electoral activity such as pro-Israeli groups have pursued *does* enhance accountability, even if it results in divisions within a policy community. This strategy works to limit presidential—and congressional—flexibility in foreign policy formation. Yet the privatization of foreign policy, as in the Iran–Contra affair, makes us worry about whether foreign policy can be conducted democratically. In a very different way, so does the Third World debt crisis. Because of public opposition to foreign aid, the funding of Third World loans has been left to banks, which are clearly private institutions. What happens if some countries default on their loans, as now appears increasingly likely? Will the government bail out the banks? Many argue that it should *not* do so. If government maintains a hands-off policy, it is effectively delegating foreign policy formation to the banks. Even if the banks were not to act against any conception of the public interest, even if they were to make what we might consider the "correct decisions," ought private institutions to be placed in the position of making foreign policy? Does the government, then, have the right to delegate foreign policy formation?

Similarly, foreign lobbying raises the question of accountability as well. While it is always difficult to hold interest groups "responsible" for governmental decisions, the problem is compounded for international lobbyists. Senator Lloyd Bentsen (D-Tex.) has proposed legislation that would outlaw any campaign contributions by foreign nationals. There are already laws that prohibit many former high-level government officials from working as foreign lobbyists and there are proposals that would further restrict such activities. Yet some opponents of this legislation argue that such statutes might lead highly qualified individuals to forego government service altogether. There is also the problem of balancing the interests of American firms and international corporations. Should foreign companies be put at a

disadvantage in influencing governmental policy when, other than owner-
ship, they are quite similar to domestic firms? Also, should other governments restrict American companies' political activities? Ought American
firms to refrain from such "mild" politicking as trying to change South Africa's apartheid laws through extensive minority recruitment?

THE PUBLIC AND FOREIGN POLICY

The democratic dilemmas of foreign policy making apply more to the
fourth circle than to any other. This is no accident, because the dilemmas
focus on whether a coherent foreign policy can result from democratic policy. Public opinion, elections, the media, and interest groups are the heart
of popular control of democratic institutions. We have seen that public opinion does affect foreign policy and that the post-Vietnam electorate can exercise some control over decision making on foreign affairs. Yet the people
remain largely uninterested in international issues. It takes a major crisis for
the public to become aroused and to make electoral decisions based on foreign policy. On the other hand, public opinion, when aroused, does respond
systematically to events in the international system. The people may not
provide detailed instructions to decision makers on what they ought to do.
Instead, they indicate what actions they do not like. This overall balance
gives political leaders considerable flexibility to respond to the actions of
other nations. Whether they have sufficient leeway—or too much—and
whether the constraints imposed by the public are wise are different questions altogether.

The role of the media has changed considerably. Gone are the days
when press barons such as William Randolph Hearst can play a major, if
not dominant, role in pushing the nation into intervening in, for example,
the Mexican revolution of 1913–14.[49] Nowadays the media are more likely to
terminate a war than to start one. Yet media impacts can be—and often have
been—overemphasized. There is little evidence that the media have actually
changed the balance of power on any policy area, foreign or domestic. Much
of the criticism of the media wants to have it both ways. On the one hand,
television is said to be too superficial; on the other hand, it is charged with
having too much power over public opinion. More likely, the media have
some effects—it would be truly remarkable if they had none—but hardly
enough to constitute a threat to either a democratic order or to presidential
government. Similarly, the activities of local political leaders may make it
difficult for presidents to claim that America speaks with one voice, but then
the congressional "voice" has the same effect.

More than anything else, the rise of interest groups in foreign policy
marks a sharp break with the past. Are interest groups dangerous? To the
extent that they promote fragmentation of decision making, they challenge
presidential authority. But again, so does the wide swath of congressional
decision making on foreign policy. Like the Congress, interest groups can-

not formulate their own foreign policy for the nation—unless, as in the case of the Third World debt crisis, the government abdicates responsibility to them. To the extent that foreign policy increasingly resembles domestic policy, however, there is a threat to coherent decision making and to the flexibility that chief executives require. The stakes are far higher in foreign policy than on domestic issues. International issues affect elections only when passions are high and there is widespread dissatisfaction with administration policy. Groups that actively seek to make foreign policy issues the focal points of political campaigns must contemplate the likely consequences of their acts.

NOTES

1. Larry Agran, "Local Officials Should Speak Out on Foreign Policy," *Governing,* December 1987, p. 74; and Denis Farney, "In Seattle, Rep. Miller Is Drawing Fire for Support of Contra Aid," *The Wall Street Journal,* October 13, 1986, p. 34.
2. David Brock, "Municipal Hue and Cry Makes Foreign Policy Waves," *Insight,* April 4, 1986, pp. 18–20; and William Schneider, "Conservatism, Not Interventionism: Trends in Foreign Policy Opinion 1974–1982," in *Eagle Defiant: United States Foreign Policy in the 1980s,* eds. Kenneth A. Oye, Robert J. Lieber, and Donald Roth (Boston: Little, Brown, 1983), p. 58.
3. Reuters, "11 States Seek to Bar Foreign Training of Guard," *New York Times,* June 17, 1986, p. A10. The ten states joining Minnesota were Arkansas, Colorado, Delaware, Hawaii, Iowa, Maine, Massachusetts, Ohio, Rhode Island, and Vermont. The eight states supporting sending the guard abroad were Florida, Illinois, Louisiana, Nevada, New Mexico, Oklahoma, South Carolina, and Wisconsin. Iowa, Maine, and Rhode Island had Republican governors, while Louisiana had a Democratic chief executive.
4. "Arizona Troops Deploy," *Washington Post,* May 31, 1987, A8.
5. Deborah M. Levy, "Advice for Sale," *Foreign Policy,* Summer 1987, p. 67.
6. William K. Stevens, "Governors Assert Key to Prosperity Is in Global View," *New York Times,* July 26, 1987, pp. A1, A22; Kathleen Sylvester, "Exporting Made Easy (or How States and Cities Are Selling Products Overseas)," *Governing,* January 1988, p. 38; and Agran, "Local Officials Should Speak Out on Foreign Policy."
7. Raymond A. Bauer, Ithiel de Sola Pool, and Lewis Anthony Dexter, *American Business and Public Policy,* 2d ed. (Chicago: Aldine-Atherton, 1982), pp. 300–1.
8. E. E. Schattschneider, *The Semisovereign People* (New York: Holt, Rinehart & Winston, 1960), esp. chap. 2.
9. Bruce Ray, "Congressional Losers in the U.S. Federal Spending Process," *Legislative Studies Quarterly* 5 (August 1980), pp. 359–72.
10. Jack Zwick and Richard K. Goeltz, "U.S. Banks Are Making Foreign Policy," *New York Times,* March 18, 1979, p. F14.
11. Leonard Silk, "Citicorp's Step: Mixed Effects," *New York Times,* May 22, 1987, p. D2; and Anne Swardson, "Losses Mount as Banks Cope with Bad Third-World Loans," *Washington Post,* July 14, 1987, pp. A1, A12.

12. "As Investments by Foreigners Surge, Their Influence in U.S. Politics Grows," *New York Times*, December 30, 1985; Martin Tolchin, "U.S. Elections Got More Foreign Cash," *New York Times*, May 24, 1987; Bill Whalen, "Japan Builds a Lobbying Leviathan," *Insight*, September 21, 1987, pp. 22–23; Susan F. Rasky, "Top U.S. Corporations Lobbying against Curb on Toshiba Imports," *New York Times*, September 14, 1987, pp. A1, D12; and Levy, "Advice for Sale," pp. 68–71.

13. *New York Times*, November 23, 1981.

14. Robin Toner, "Those Who Beg to Differ on Aid to Nicaragua," *New York Times*, March 14, 1986, p. A14; Bill Keller, "Interest Groups Focus on El Salvador Policy," *Congressional Quarterly Weekly Report*, April 24, 1982, pp. 895–97; and Lena Williams, "Bahais Open a Lobbying Operation," *New York Times*, October 22, 1987, p. A32.

15. Keith Schneider, "A Liberal Group Makes Waves with Its Contra Lawsuit," *New York Times*, July 20, 1987, p. A16.

16. Interestingly, the Israeli government itself did not object to the arms sale proposal to Jordan.

17. John E. Rielly, ed., *American Public Opinion and U.S. Foreign Policy 1983* (Chicago: Chicago Council on Foreign Relations, 1983), pp. 16, 19.

18. Connie deBoer, "The Polls: Attitudes Toward the Arab-Israeli Conflict," *Public Opinion Quarterly* 47 (Spring 1983), pp. 128–29.

19. Ben Bradlee, Jr., "Israel's Lobby," *Boston Globe Magazine*, April 24, 1984, p. 64.

20. Bill Keller, "Supporters of Israel, Arabs Vie For Friends and Influence in Congress, at White House," *Congressional Quarterly Weekly Report*, August 22, 1981, p. 1524.

21. Ibid., p. 1527.

22. Charles McC. Mathias, Jr., "Ethnic Groups and Foreign Policy," *Foreign Affairs* 59 (Summer 1981), p. 993. Mathias' home state has a substantial and very politically active Jewish population. (At the time he wrote the article the chairs of both political parties were Jewish, as was the state attorney general and the state treasurer.) It is hardly surprising that in 1986, after the article appeared, he chose not to run for reelection.

23. David K. Shipler, "On Middle East Policy, A Major Influence," *New York Times*, July 6, 1987, pp. A1, A4; and Robert Pear with Richard L. Berke, "Pro-Israel Group Exerts Quiet Might as It Rallies Supporters in Congress," *New York Times*, July 7, 1987, p. A8.

24. Keller, "Supporters of Israel," pp. 1,527–28.

25. Ibid., p. 1,528.

26. Ibid.

27. Richard Whittle, "Senate Supports Reagan on AWACS Sale," *Congressional Quarterly Weekly Report*, October 31, 1981, p. 2,098.

28. Ibid., 2,099.

29. Most of the discussion below follows Eric M. Uslaner, "One Nation, Many Voices: Interest Groups in Foreign Policy-Making," in *Interest Group Politics*, 2d ed., eds. Allan J. Cigler and Burdett A. Loomis (Washington, D.C.: CQ Press 1986), pp. 236–57.

30. John Felton, "Military Aid Requests Presented to Congress," *Congressional Quarterly Weekly Report*, February 12, 1983, p. 345.

31. Thomas M. Franck and Edward Weisband, *Foreign Policy by Congress* (New York: Oxford University Press, 1979), pp. 195–96.

32. Franck and Weisband, *Foreign Policy by Congress*, pp. 191–93.

33. Alan Cowell, "Turkish Leader Puts off U.S. Visit Over Anger at Congress," *New York Times*, May 9, 1987, p. 3; and Richard Berke, "Heeding Plato, Greek-Americans Aid in Effort to Raise Money for Dukakis," *New York Times*, December 27, 1987, A30.

34. Bernard Weinraub, "Wooing Cuban–Americans in G.O.P.," *New York Times*, May 22, 1987, p. A14.

35. Robert S. Greenberger, "Right-Wing Groups Join in Capitol Hill Crusade To Help Savimbi's Anti-Communists in Angola," *The Wall Street Journal*, November 25, 1985, p. 58.

36. Michae Beaubien, "Making Waves in Foreign Policy," *Black Enterprise*, April 1982, pp. 37–42.

37. Franck and Weisband, *Foreign Policy by Congress*, pp. 195–96.

38. Bernard C. Cohen, *The Public's Impact on Foreign Policy* (Boston: Little, Brown, 1973), pp. 98–104.

39. Detailed analysis of American imperialism may be found in, among other books, Carl Oglesby and Richard Shaull, *Containment and Change* (New York, Macmillan, 1967), and in any of the several volumes by Gabriel Kolko on U.S. foreign policy during World War II and since; a briefer statement of Kolko's view is presented in *The Roots of American Foreign Policy* (Boston: Beacon Press, 1969).

40. Alexander Hamilton, John Jay, and James Madison, *The Federalist Papers*, with an introduction by Clinton Rossiter (New York: Mentor, 1961), pp. 77–84.

41. Mathias, "Ethnic Groups and Foreign Policy," pp. 981, 997.

42. Ibid., p. 993.

43. Lindsey Gruson, "Poll Reveals Fear of a New Vietnam," *New York Times*, July 24, 1983, pp. A1, A6.

44. See Uslaner, "One Nation, Many Voices," pp. 252–54, for more details on this strategy.

45. On Findley, see Paul Findley, *They Dare To Speak Out: People and Institutions Confront Israel's Lobby* (Westport, Conn.: Lawrence Hill and Company, 1985). Also see Ed Zuckerman, "Pro-Israel PACs: What Role Do They Play?" *PACs & Lobbies*, September 2, 1987, pp. 1, 7.

46. "As Investments by Foreigners Surge, Their Influence in U.S. Politics Grows," *New York Times*, December 30, 1985.

47. Holsti and Rosenau, *American Leadership in World Affairs*, p. 206.

48. Thomas B. Edsall, "Democrats' Lesson: To the Loyal Belong the Spoils," *Washington Post*, January 14, 1983, p. A7.

49. Thomas A. Bailey, *The American Pageant*, 2d ed. (Lexington, Mass.: D. C. Heath, 1961), p. 701.

Chapter Seven

The Rational Actor Model and Crisis Decisions

TWO MODELS OF POLICY MAKING

How do the various actors who participate in foreign policy making interact? To examine this question, we will analyze two models of the policy-making process. The first model is the rational actor; the second is the bureaucratic/governmental politics model. These models are devices by which we, as outside observers and analysts, organize our perceptions about how decisions are made. We do not assume that the various actors necessarily "choose" one model or the other and then make their decisions based on that model. Rather, we describe possible methods of decision making when we posit the models. We will then examine several specific foreign policy decisions in light of these models.

The Rational Actor

The rational actor model is based on the assumption that the government is a unitary actor and that there is some agreed-on goal to be attained; the problem, then, is to find the most effective way to reach that goal. This model is most useful in studying crisis decision making, as we shall indicate later in the chapter. In contrast, the bureaucratic/governmental politics model assumes that there are a multiplicity of actors, each with different goals, who see the stakes involved in a situation in different terms. The outcome reached will be one that is most politically feasible, the result of a bargaining agreement among the parties involved. This model best fits non-crisis decisions involving security policies and particularly those policies that are intermestic—partly international, partly domestic. The characteristics of the policy-making process on each of these types of policies are detailed in Table 7–1.

TABLE 7-1 Policy Characteristics

Type of Policy	Chief Characteristic	Primary Actors	Principal Decision Maker	Role of Congress	Role of Interest Groups	Role of Public Opinion	Relationship among Actors
Crisis	Short run; bureaucracy and Congress short-circuited. Common stake: all win or lose together	President, responsible officials, and ad hoc individuals from in and out of government	Executive (Presidential preeminence)	Postcrisis legitimization	None	Supportive; legitimization	Cooperation
Noncrisis (security)	Long run; bureaucratic–legislative participation; winners and losers	President; executive agencies; Congress; interest groups; public opinion	Executive bureaucracy	Congressional participation	Low to moderate	Low to moderate	Competition and bargaining
Intermestic (welfare)	Long run; bureaucratic–legislative participation; winners, nonwinners, and losers	President; executive agencies; Congress; interest groups; public opinion	Executive-congressional sharing	High	High	High	Competition and bargaining

SOURCE: This table is adapted from Randall B. Ripley and Grace A. Franklin, *Congress, the Bureaucracy, and Public Policy* (Chicago, Ill.: Dorsey Press 1976), p. 17.

263

Crisis decision making involves a response to a perceived threat, a rational calculation of what to do given the actions of an opponent. Such situations involve relatively few actors, with the president preeminent, and require the capacity for both swift and careful planning. The group is normally small enough to arrive at quick decision while allowing vigorous debate on how the crisis ought to be managed. In that respect, crisis decision making approximates rational decision making. There is little or no time for bureaucratic infighting or the executive-legislative conflicts that characterize routine policy making.

There is also little time for prolonged discussion within the legislature or among the public about what the response to the crisis should be. All actors perceive—or are expected to perceive—a common stake in responding to the external threat and forming a united front. The focus of the decision-making process is on arriving at the most effective solution to the question of how to respond. Otherwise, the crisis may escalate into military confrontation and war. The rational actor approach and crisis decision making thus stress a strong executive, the ability to act swiftly, and domestic unity. This concentration of decision-making in a small circle of executive officials, generally unrestrained by congressional or public opinion during a critical and relatively short period, means that the normal shortcomings of decision making said to characterize the American separation of powers are downplayed or disappear altogether. The policy makers can focus on the means-end problem.

The bureaucratic/government politics model, on the other hand, emphasized the other values: checks and balances, fair opportunities for bargaining among diverse actors, and the need for widespread participation by as many interested parties as possible. The emphasis here is on the representation of diverse interests, each of whom may see the stakes involved in a decision-making situation differently. There is no "best" outcome. The decision is evaluated based on the opportunities that various actors have to influence the bargaining that produces some outcome—which may very well end up supporting the status quo, because each of the various participants may check and balance each other effectively and prevent anyone from emerging as dominant and thus changing the status quo. This model applies to noncrisis policies—security issues such as arms control policies within the United States—and even better, to intermestic policies (for instance, energy) since the origin of this model lies in the domestic policy process.

Let us return to the rational actor model. The term rational has a very specific meaning. It refers to a decision-making process and involves four steps: (1) selecting the objectives and values that a given policy is supposed to achieve and maximize; (2) considering the various alternative means to achieve these purposes; (3) calculating the likely consequences of each alternative course; and (4) choosing the course that is most likely to attain the objectives originally selected. Furthermore, as noted, the government is viewed as a unitary actor when the rational actor model is used.

This is implicit in the phrases we use or read: "The United States has decided . . . ," "It is believed that Moscow seeks . . . ," and "China has announced . . . ."

Decision makers have goals and attempt to maximize them in the policy-making arena. Deterrence of nuclear war, for example, assumes that a potential aggressor will not attack if the price of destroying the adversary is far higher than any conceivable gains taken.[1] Nuclear devastation is clearly a price totally disproportionate to any possible profit. Deterrence thus rests on the assumption that the party to be deterred is rational and will reject alternative courses of action—that is, not attack and commit suicide or choose a third course such as refusing to defend national interests and withdrawing into isolationism. Or, consider the rationale for limited war. In 1957, Henry A. Kissinger published a book, *Nuclear Weapons and Foreign Policy*, in which he argued that since the U.S. strategy of massive retaliation gave the president only two options—deterrence or, if challenged, fighting a total war—America's adversary (then still perceived as a united Sino-Soviet bloc) would be able to confront it with limited challenges in areas of vital interest to the United States.[2] This would then put Washington up against a dilemma: either respond completely and risk nuclear immolation, or don't respond and appease or yield. The rational alternative in these circumstances was to have a limited war capability to respond to challenges in a measured way.

The rational actor model has been dominant in explaining international politics to a far greater degree than in domestic politics.[3] Because most decisions studied in international politics have involved relations among nations, students of international politics have tended to view nations as unitary actors. It is our view that for crisis decision making, this assumption is a reasonable one. In a crisis, the scope of the decision-making arena is rather small. The inner circle makes the decisions and is almost invariably supported by Congress, the bureacracies, and public opinion. This is less true for noncrisis security decisions, and we shall see in the next chapter that these present a different model for explaining and understanding the decision-making process in more normal or everyday type of security policies.

Bureaucratic/Governmental Politics

In contrast to the rational actor model, the bureaucratic/governmental politics model does not assume that the government is a unitary actor.[4] It does not use phrases such as "the U.S.," or " the Soviet Union"; or refer to Paris or London as shorthand terms for their governments. Government is the sum of many parts. The executive branch of the U.S. government consists of more than the office of the presidency—it is also, as we know, composed of the senior foreign policy departments such as the State Department, junior foreign policy departments, such as the International

Communication Agency, Arms Control and Disarmament Agency; and such essentially domestic departments as the Departments of Commerce, Labor, Agriculture, and Treasury, all of whom have some interest in foreign policy, because they wish to enhance exports, protect U.S. labor, or seek a favorable balance of trade. Similarly, as we saw earlier, the Congress is composed of two houses, each of which is further decentralized into committees that in turn, fragment into a multitude of subcommittees. And in this context, a whole host of interest groups representing every conceivable group from business and labor to environmental and other self-styled public interest groups are additional actors.

Second, each of these actors—the presidency, executive departments, committees, subcommittees, and interest groups—approaches a problem or issue from a different perspective. This should not be surprising. They have different responsibilities; often they have received training to fulfill these responsibilities; they view the world from different perspectives and their stakes are different as well. It is surely understandable that all actors should believe that what they are doing is important otherwise, why bother?) and that they should actively seek to gain the adoption of their solutions for the problem being confronted. There is a phrase for this: where you stand depends on where you sit. State Department Foreign Service officers not unnaturally believe that given patience, and the kinds of skills they possess, almost any problem can be resolved by diplomacy. By contrast, military officers are more prone to dismiss the possibilities of a compromise settlement and feel that the use of force or threat of force is more likely to yield fruitful results. Similarly, a congressional committee concerned with foreign affairs may well see a specific issue quite differently than one concerned with military affairs.

Actually, government can be broken down even further. Thus the State Department, as noted earlier, is hardly a single actor, even if the secretary of state officially presents his viewpoint. For the department in turn is composed of desks representing each major area of the world. Thus, as often happened in the past, the European desk and the African desk would be at odds. If a colony were seeking its independence, as often happened after World War II, the African desk would urge U.S. support of the independence movement, even if it annoyed one of our European allies, while the European desk would recommend caution. Preserving the cohesiveness of NATO against the Soviet threat was from its point of view more critical. Similarly, the Defense Department is composed of the air force, army, and navy, each of which quite naturally feels that its contribution to the defense and security of the United States is the most important and, therefore, seeks the larger share of the budget to best equip itself for any tasks it might be called on to do. Therefore, not only are the three services rivals, but each is subject to further conflict, for example, between the Strategic Air Command, Tactical Air Command, and Military Air Transport (air force); armor, artillery, and infantry (army); and aircraft carriers, regular surface navy, and nuclear submarines (navy). The United States thus has three navies. The aircraft carrier navy, which has been dominant since World War II, believes that should war occur with the Soviet Union, it can best project U.S. naval power; and in limited war and crisis situations it can bring U.S. air power to bear even if land bases are absent. The surface navy is preoccupied with control of the sea lanes in case of war, so that American troops and munitions can be shipped to Western Europe and American industry can continue to have access to the raw materials it needs from all regions of the world. The nuclear submarine navy, of course, feels it is the most important of these three navies since its task is the deterrence of war and, should that fail, retaliation against the Soviet Union. To repeat: where you stand depends on where you sit.

Third, the inevitable result of so many executive and legislative actors, each with a different stake and viewpoint on an issue, is conflict. Making a decision is thus not a matter of selecting a particular value or goal, calculating the various means by which it can be attained, and then selecting the one means that will most fully realize it at the least possible cost. Rather than reflecting a calm, considered, dignified, and reasoned process, decision making resembles a brawl, usually an unseemly one at that. For the issue is not whose policy position and recommendation is correct. There is no single correct policy that, but for every actor's narrow and self-interested perspective, would clearly emerge. Let us be clear about this. There is no objective "national interest" that would be clearly visible to all policy makers if they would but give priority to a broader, unselfish, patriotic view and subordinate their own parochial and selfish perception of a problem and do "what's right for the country." The issue is not who is right but how to reconcile—if that is possible—many conflicting interpretations of what the correct policy should be.

The reason the term *bureaucratic politics* is used more frequently than *governmental* politics should be obvious from our earlier analysis: the executive branch has the primary responsibility in the formulation and implementation of foreign policy. Thus the focus of the policy struggle is among the many executive actors; the conflict is between the various bureaucracies. But, as is also clear from our earlier discussion, the Congress can never be neglected in noncrisis decisions. Since Vietnam, indeed, interested legislative actors have participated more consistently and assertively than before. Hence, our emphasis on governmental politics, encompassing all the decision-making circles. In nondemocratic societies such as the Soviet Union, of course, one focuses only on the executive.

Fourth, as noted, this pluralism of actors, interests, and views means that the policy process is one of attempting to reconcile these conflicting perspectives and building a consensus or majority coalition so that a decision can be made. This is not done by considering only whose policy recommendation has the most merit; it is also a question of which actor is the more powerful. Indeed, the degree of an actor's influence, skill in negotiating, ability to attract some actors and accommodate others, are probably more important than the wisdom of his or her position. Indeed, the reason for the use of the word *politics* in the terms *governmental politics* or *bureaucratic politics* reflects the fact that a policy emerges from a process of simultaneous conflict and accommodation among a multitude of actors with competing viewpoints and possessing different amounts of power. Policy making means bargaining; negotiations are required and compromises must be struck. Those *for* a policy and those *opposing* the policy negotiate with other actors, seeking to organize a coalition of a majority of the actors to advance their collective policy interests or oppose a change of policy. Negotiations thus occur throughout the executive branch as officials, bureaus, and agencies in one department seek support in another; attracting the president and/or some of his advisers is especially important and is, therefore, a cause of fierce struggle. Policy making is thus a matter of widening the base of support within the executive while also seeking allies within Congress. This occurs through the constant modification of the proposed policy as concessions are made to potential allies to satisfy their needs and overcome their objections in the hope of building a majority coalition. Coalition building, in short, crosses institutional lines.

Fifth, the characteristics of the conflict and the coalition-building process affect the policy output. One of the most important results of this continuous bargaining within the "policy machine" is that policy moves forward one step at a time and tends to focus on momentary concerns and short-range aims. This is usually called *incrementalism*. Another word is *satisficing*. This word suggests that policy makers do not, each time they have to make a decision, sit down and go through the rational procedure of decision making. Policy makers have neither the time nor the resources to go through this process. Instead, they pick the policy that is likely to be the most satisfactory; and they judge this by whether a policy has been successful in the past. If a policy has been satisfactory up to that point, why not take another step forward on the same path? The presumption is that what worked in the past will work now, as well as in the future. In addition, once a majority coalition has been forged after hard struggle, a winning coalition will normally prefer modification of existing policy decisions. This is not necessarily true. The negotiating process among different groups with conflicting perspectives and vested interests can produce a stalemate and paralysis of policy—that is, no policy at all.

Sixth, a further characteristic of the policy process, and implicit in our analysis so far, is its time-consuming nature. Incrementalism suggests a policy machine in low gear, moving along a well-defined road rather slowly in response to specific short-run stimuli. A proposed policy is normally discussed first within the executive branch. It then passes through official channels, where it receives clearances and modifications as it gathers a broader base of support on its way up the executive hierarchy to the president. The constant conferences and negotiations among departments clearly slow the pace. The process takes even longer when a policy needs congressional and public approval. Potential opponents can occupy many veto points to block legislation within Congress; such veto points are in the House Rules Committee, the House and Senate committees and a multitude of subcommittees, and on the floor during debates and votes in both chambers. The advantage normally lies with those who oppose a specific policy, because it is difficult to jump all the hurdles along its route of legislative enactment. An additional result, given this slow policy process, the formidable obstacles and great effort needed to pass major policy, is that old policies and the old assumptions on which they are based, tend to survive longer than the conditions that produced these policies initially.

Seventh, one further characteristic of American foreign policy decision making is that it is usually public in nature. In a democracy, this is inevitable. While policy may be made primarily by the executive, the confines of this policy are established by public opinion. No American government before the fall of France could have intervened in Europe to preserve the balance of power. During World War II and most of the Cold War, however, Congress and public opinion tended to be permissive and supportive as far as the presidential conduct of foreign policy was concerned. Aware of their lack of knowledge, information, and competence in an area remote from their everyday involvement—in the more familiar area of domestic policies, public opinion is much more structured and knowledgeable—the legislature and public looked to the president for leadership. Only when setbacks or painful experiences arose would Congress and public opinion react, broadly clarify the limits of its tolerance, and perhaps punish the party in power. But even if most of the time public opinion did not act as a restraining factor, policy makers were always aware of its existence. Because mass opinion does not tend to take shape until after some foreign event has occurred, it can hardly act as a guide for those who must make the policy. Nonetheless, the last will take into account what they think "the traffic will bear," because they know that if a decision is significant enough, there is likely to be some crystallization of opinion and, possibly, retribution at the polls. Since Vietnam, this has changed considerably. There is more widespread skepticism of presidential wisdom, greater congressional capability, more extensive public concern about dangerous involvements; and the emergence of intermestic policies with their pocketbook effects on voters arouses legislators and interest groups. Congress and public opinion tend to be both less permissive and supportive of presidents now; presidential capacity for leadership has become more constrained.

We shall examine the bureaucratic politics model as it relates to the antiballistic missile system (ABM), strategic arms limitation talks, and energy politics in the next chapter. But we shall first focus on the rational actor model and its application to crisis decision making on Cuba and Iran in this chapter.

THE CUBAN MISSILE AND IRANIAN HOSTAGE CRISES

Crises, as we have seen, are characterized by a number of features: a perceived threat to vital interests, usually surprise, and a sense of urgency to make decisions.[5] But the principal characteristic of crises in which one of the superpowers demands a change in the status quo and the other resists, is the threat of violence, possible nuclear war. This possibility of military action is also likely when the United States is involved with secondary states, whether they are communists (for instance, the unexpected North Korean attack on South Korea in 1950) or noncommunists (for instance, the Iranian seizure of the U.S. embassy in Teheran in 1979). Time may not be quite as critical a factor (Iran dragged on for 444 days) but the importance of the issues at stake for both sides virtually guarantees the use of the threat, if not the actual employment, of force.

Decision Making Flows Upward

It is these characteristics of a crisis that influence the decision-making process. The suddenness of a critical confrontation situation with vital interests perceived to be involved and the great danger of military confrontation guarantees that decision-making will become centralized and "go to the top," that is, the president and his closest advisers. Some will be his statutory advisers, such as the secretaries of his chief foreign policy agencies; others, who will come from both in and out of government, will be those whose judgment the president particularly trusts. During the potentially explosive Cuban missile crisis of 1962,[6] which occurred after the Soviets had sent approximately seventy intermediate and medium-range missiles to the island, the executive committee, which managed the crisis, included the president and vice president; the secretaries of state and defense and their seconds in command; the director of the CIA; the chairman of the Joint Chiefs of Staff; the president's special assistant for national security affairs; the secretary of the treasury; the attorney general (the president's brother) and his special counsel (perhaps the president's closest friend among his advisers); an ambassador just returned from Moscow; and President Truman's secretary of state.

After Islamic students had taken over the American Embassy and seized sixty-six hostages* in November 1979, President Carter was advised chiefly

---

*Fourteen were released because the Iranians wanted to divide the hostages and U.S. opinion by releasing minority members.

by his NSA, the vice president, and the secretaries of state and defense; he also consulted Hamilton Jordan, White House chief of staff, and Jody Powell, the White House press secretary, two men who were close to him and also actively directing his campaign for renomination and reelection. Carter consulted all these men frequently over the months the crisis dragged on.

Note a difference between Presidents Kennedy and Carter. Kennedy, who demanded that the Soviets dismantle the missiles, assembled a special group of advisers to help him manage this particular crisis; this ad hoc group's function would end with the resolution of the crisis. But for the duration, it was a full-time group. Members who were high officials of various departments were relieved of their regular responsibilities. Business unrelated to the crisis was left to lower level officials or remained undecided. The point was that confronting a situation of war or peace, Kennedy wanted a small group of able and trusted men to give him their best advice about what to do. To do this they were to concentrate totally on the crisis at hand; they were to check their regular departmental business at the door to the White House. Had these men been asked to assist the president in the crisis as well as carry out their normal duties, they could have given the Cuban situation only superficial attention—quite frankly, the kind of attention most high-level officials are able to devote to problems due to their frequent occurrence.

The Iranian crisis, which erupted in November 1979, and ended on inauguration day, January 1981, was quite different. One reason was that the use of force did not hang over this situation in the same way. The embassy was in downtown Teheran. A sudden use of force in a rescue attempt was impractical. Armed student guards were swarming over the embassy grounds, and tens of thousands—sometimes hundreds of thousands—paraded around the grounds screaming anti-American slogans and praising the Ayatollah Khomeini, the religious leader of the Islamic revolution.

A rescue mission in these circumstances was initially rejected; many of the hostages might be killed and the troops would suffer heavy casualties, if they could even get into the embassy. In one sense, this crisis does not fit our definition in a key respect, but given the intense concern in the United States about the safety of the hostages and the public outrage that their seizure stirred, President Carter and his principal foreign policy advisers had to give it immediate and full attention. Even as it became apparent that the hostages would not be released soon, the crisis maintained its sense of urgency.

Throughout much of the Iranian crisis, Carter's public opinion ratings stood at an all-time low. While widely perceived as an honest and decent man, the president was frequently portrayed in the media as incompetent, not capable of handling the demanding job he had so eagerly sought. Many members of his party in Congress were hoping Senator Kennedy would run for the nomination and become the Democrats' standard-bearer; the Kennedy magic, they hoped, would help them get elected at a time when the economy was in terrible straits, suffering simultaneously from high inflation and a recession. With Carter as its nominee, the fear was that the Democrats would lose both the presidency and many congressional seats against an attractive Republican candidate who was an effective campaigner. The seizure of U.S. hostages could not have been better timed for Carter. In such moments the country tends to unite, and the president is the beneficiary. A crisis focuses virtually everyone's attention on the president. Thus, Carter's handling of the hostage issue gave him an unexpected opportunity to erase his image as a bumbler and substitute for it that of a leader who deserved to be reelected. With the Soviet invasion of Afghanistan a few weeks later, Carter's handling of foreign policy now seemed to be his path for electoral salvation.

President Kennedy in 1962, of course, was not running for reelection. Yet he did confront the midterm congressional election. Cuba had been a hot issue since Castro came to power. It had been an issue in one of the Nixon-Kennedy TV debates; Kennedy's position was militantly anti-Castro. The failure of the 1961 Bay of Pigs operation, planned by the Eisenhower administration and reluctantly carried out by a Kennedy dubious about the feasibility of this covert CIA operation, hurt him as well as the nation's prestige. If nothing succeeds like success, nothing fails like failure. Kennedy was also under attack on the Cuba issue by Republican senators, who maintained that the Soviets were installing missiles. Since there were no hard intelligence data supporting this contention, the president denied it and issued a statement that the United States would not tolerate missiles in Cuba. When the rumors turned out to be fact, inaction would undoubtedly have hurt Kennedy's reputation in the nation, Congress, and within the executive branch. Thus, from a purely political standpoint, a tough U.S. response was required.[7]

Presidential Perceptions and Rational Choice

In a democratic system, awareness of the possible electoral consequences can hardly be avoided. This is especially true in a system like that of the United States, where some sort of election is always occurring or about to occur. How much awareness of domestic politics is allowed to intrude into foreign policy considerations and decisions, however, depends on the president. For if the first characteristic of crises is that decision making flows upward to the top, while at the same time being narrowed to relatively few participants, the second characteristic is the central role of the president. It is he who, more than anyone else, interprets events and evaluates the stakes in the crisis. Kennedy's and Carter's "readings" of the nature of the situations they confronted, and the consequences these situations might have on U.S. security and on their own political futures and ability to lead the nation were responsible for their actions. (The last two considerations can hardly be separated, for the external challenges, as presidents see them, do not really leave them with a choice of accepting a personal loss of prestige without accepting as well a loss of national prestige. For a president of the United States, personal and national cost calculations tend to become identical.

Kennedy saw the installation of Soviet missiles in Cuba as a personal challenge with damaging national effects. Since, in response to earlier congressional and public clamor about possible offensive missiles in Cuba, Kennedy had publicly declared that the United State would not tolerate offensive missiles on an island ninety miles off the Florida coast, he had to act. Kennedy's statement had clearly been understood in Moscow, which had responded that it had no intention of placing missiles in Cuba; the Soviet Union had more than enough missiles at home. Thus, with the president having initially deemphasized the possibility that the Soviets would install such weapons in Cuba, and Moscow having then signaled that it understood Kennedy's declaration, Kennedy was publicly pledged to act if the Soviets lied—as it turned out they had—unless he wished to be publicly humiliated. If he did not act in these circumstances, the Soviet leader, Nikita Khrushchev, so the argument went, would not believe other pledges and commitments the president had made. At least, this, apparently, is how Kennedy perceived the situation.

Kennedy also feared that Khrushchev would attribute previous acts of restraint to a lack of will, an absence of sufficient resolution and determination on the part of the United States to defend its vital interests. During the Bay of Pigs invasion in 1961, Kennedy had refused to commit U.S. forces once the invasion appeared doomed. During the building of the Berlin Wall the same year, American forces had stood by as the wall went up. Khrushchev began to talk openly of America's failure of nerve. The United States apparently talked loudly but carried a small stick. Thus failure to act in the Caribbean, which has traditionally been an area within America's sphere of influence (as Eastern Europe was the Soviet's) would have immense and damaging consequences.

It was not so much the effect of the Soviet missiles on the military equation between the two powers, although that was important; it was the political consequences of the appearance of a change in the balance of power that were deemed critical by Kennedy. The Soviet Union was supposed to be on the short end of the missile gap. But American inaction would, Kennedy feared, be widely recognized as a persuasive answer to the U.S. claims of missile superiority, would lead allied governments to fear that in the new situation, with America highly vulnerable to nuclear devastation, they could no longer count on the United States to defend them. In these circumstances the Soviets would be tempted to exploit the situation and seek to undermine America's alliances—especially NATO. Thus, while the risks of action in Cuba were obviously great, the risks of escalation as a result in *inaction* were also perceived as great. If Khrushchev got away with Cuba, why should he take seriously Kennedy's pledge to defend West Berlin? And if he did not, would not Soviet and American troops soon be clashing in an area where they would be hard to separate?

One irony of the Cuban missile crisis is that Kennedy was determined during his years in office to seek a more stable and restrained basis for coexistence with the Soviet Union. This long-range goal, which hardly had the massive support it had later, could not be realized if Khrushchev would not take Kennedy seriously or felt he could push Kennedy around; then serious negotiations, recognizing each other's legitimate interests, would be impossible. Thus a major change in the Cold War atmosphere was at stake, in addition, to America's reputation for power and willingness to keep commitments. If Khrushchev viewed him as weak, he would continue to pressure and push. Such a lack of respect for the United States could only be dangerous, for if he raised the pressure too much and pushed too far on the assumption that the president was too fearful of risking a confrontation, a Soviet miscalculation could well spark a military conflict. Aware of the fact that his prestige was identical with the prestige of the United States, that he, Kennedy—chief of party and government—was also the symbol of the United States, the president's prime considerations were clearly the foreign policy effects of his inaction. He would, in short, have reacted to the Soviet missiles even if domestic politics had not pointed in the same direction. His blockade of Cuba was basically a rational response to the demands of the external situation as he perceived and defined it.

Having personally made the key decision that the stakes were high and required the Soviet Union to dismantle its missiles and take them out of Cuba —this issue was never even debated between the president and his advisers—the president and his advisers focused their attention on how to gain Soviet compliance. The U.S. alternatives ranged from diplomatic pressure on Moscow, a secret approach to Castro, a surgical air strike on the missiles, invasion, and blockade. However, feeling strongly that he had to act to impress Khrushchev, Kennedy chose the blockade as the option most likely to attain the removal of the Soviet missiles. While the blockade could not by itself achieve this objective, it (1) was a sign of American determination; (2) permitted the United States the option of increasing the pressure on Moscow later if Moscow would not remove its missiles; (3) provided a relatively safe middle course between inaction and invasion or an air strike, which might provoke the Soviets; and (4) placed on Khrushchev the responsibility of deciding whether to escalate or deescalate. It is significant to note that, thanks to a U–2 spy plane, the administration had an entire week in which to debate the meaning and significance of the Soviet move, what its military and political effects were likely to be on U.S. security interests, what the different courses of actions open to the United States were, and which was most likely to achieve the removal of the Soviet missiles without precipitating nuclear war. Many crises simply do not allow such time for preparation and the careful consideration of the many alternative actions that can be undertaken. Even during the missile crisis, the initial reaction of most of the president's advisers was to bomb the missile sites. Slowing down the momentum of events becomes crucial if impulsive actions are to be avoided.

If Kennedy, like Carter in the Iranian crisis, did not deliberately define the Soviet missiles in Cuba as a crisis for domestic reasons, Carter, unlike Kennedy, confronted a much longer-term situation. The missile crisis was over in slightly less than a week after the president delivered his speech revealing the presence of the Soviet missiles in Cuba. Carter was not so lucky. The longer the hostages remained in Iranian hands, the more impotent and helpless the country appeared to many Americans and the greater the public impatience became; the president's standing in the polls dropped as well. Initially, however, Carter's handling of the crisis gained great domestic approval. Before the hostages' seizure, as noted earlier, the president's popularity had stood at an all-time low approval rating of only 30 percent. Senator Kennedy had led Carter by 54 to 20 percent among Democrats nationally. After the seizure, Carter's rating shot upward. By February 1980, 48 percent of the public approved of his conduct of foreign policy in general and 53 percent approved of his handling of the presidency.[8] By then, Carter asserted that he was personally not going to campaign actively for the Democratic nomination. The suspicion remains that he did so only partly for the reason he stated—to focus his full attention on the hostage situation and not appear to be "playing politics" while American citizens were being held hostages and their lives endangered. The real reason appears to have been that by staying in the White House and "being presidential," Carter felt he could best resurrect his fallen image. This "rose garden" strategy would also avoid the embarrassment of refusing to debate Senator Kennedy or being beaten on television by the senator, who in his campaign was heavily emphasizing the president's dismal economic record. The best politics for Carter, in short, was to pretend that he was not playing politics but being a statesman tending the nation's business at a critical moment.

There really was not much Carter could do to get the hostages freed. Since using force seemed to the president to be the most likely way to get them killed, his objective in this crisis dictated a policy of restraint, one of gradually applying sanctions to make it more costly for Iran to hold the hostages. This policy of "tightening the screws" bit by bit was widely hailed in the United States, as well as among our allies, as a responsible one. What were the objectives of this policy of patience and incremental pressure? One was simply to impress on the Iranians that the United State would not pay the price they set for ending the crisis. The ayatollah and the student militants demanded the return of the shah to stand trial for his "crimes against the Iranian people." He had been allowed into this country for the treatment of cancer. Indeed, the shah was hustled out of this country to Panama as soon as he had recuperated from his operation. This was supposed to impress on the Iranians that a deal would no longer be possible, but it failed to do so. The demands for his return, and after his death from cancer, for the billions of dollars he was supposed to have taken with him or sent over here in earlier years, continued until nearly the end of the crisis.

A second goal was the freeing of the hostages. Their lives were the key objective. Their fate in these dramatic circumstances gained the nation's attention. The president's determination to save the lives of American citizens—Americans who served the nations' government at that—was understandable. The media was obsessed by this human drama. But by making the hostages' lives the preeminent issue, it inflated their value to the Iranians. By saying he would not use force and thereby jeopardize the hostages' lives, the president in fact guaranteed that Iran would pay no price for continuing to hold the Americans. The policy of no military sanctions, to put it bluntly, allowed the Iranians to hang onto the hostages virtually cost free and use them to humiliate the United States, a world power whose prestige was already low in the post-Vietnam era. Yet there could be no doubt that if America's prestige required military action, the hostages' lives would be endangered. The president's dilemma was as painful as it was obvious.

A third objective was to protect the West's political friends and economic interests in the area. The conservative sheiks in Saudi Arabia and other oil kingdoms on the Arabian peninsula were badly shaken by the downfall of the shah. Most of these states, including Saudi Arabia, were also politically vulnerable to internal disturbances (including the growth of Islamic fundamentalism), coups d'états, or revolutions. The likelihood of such occurrences gave nightmares to the United States, Western Europe, and Japan, all of whom depended on the area's oil to maintain their economies. A U.S. attack on Iran might set off a strong wave of anti-Americanism, which might endanger these proWestern regimes. The ayatollah repeatedly condemned the United States as a "satanic power" and Western influence as corrupt and destructive of traditional Muslim values and religion. Although he was a Shiite Muslim and this sect was minority in the Islamic world, he was appealing to Islamic (mainly Sunni) masses to overthrow American political and cultural influence. Thus, a recourse to force was even less likely. Even if Carter had been willing to risk sacrificing the lives of the hostages, and even had U.S. forces been capable of an immediate large-scale military operation against Iran, the possible danger to the conservative Islamic governments friendly to the United States, and the protection of their oil—on which America's allies were far more dependent than the United States—counseled against using large-scale violence it if were at all avoidable.

But Carter's various maneuvers were all to fail over the next six months. He tried one thing after another. He cut off Iranian oil imports (a symbolic gesture since we did not import as much as the Europeans, and we could buy that amount elsewhere now while "our" oil would be sold to someone else). He froze all Iranian funds in U.S. banks at home and abroad (several billion dollars) and sought and gained a U.N. Security Council resolution (supported by the Soviet Union as well as several Islamic nations) calling on Iran to release the hostages; enlisted both the International Court of Justice and the pope for the same purpose; and agreed to an Iranian demand for a commission of inquiry to investigate the shah's rule and American support for him. (In fact, the Iranians did not want *any* report but clearly one that condemned both.) These and other efforts all came to naught. As economic sanctions were now organized and the United States pressured its industrial allies to cooperate, mostly without success; and, as the first reports that the United States might mine Iran's harbors became public, the administration attempted a rescue mission, which failed because of poor organization of the rescue force, several malfunctioning helicopters, and poor weather conditions.

The president had been patient but in vain; the polls showed a declining confidence in his handling of the Iranian situation. Indeed, the first time the polls had started to go down in late 1979, Carter was rescued by Afghanistan; his tough measures against the Soviet Union after its invasion of that country raised his standing again. But the public's sense of helplessness, humiliation, and patience ran out. Senator Kennedy was still contesting the president's renomination; in the eastern industrial states his emphasis on inflation and unemployment was being heard even though Kennedy won few primaries. And the chaos in Iran appeared to be spreading as various nationalities sought greater autonomy, Iran and Iraq clashed, left-wing students fought with Khomeini's "revolutionary guards" on the streets of Teheran, and the Revolutionary Council that governed Iran remained divided. Clearly, the hostages were being used by the various factions competing for power in Iran and they would, therefore, not be released soon. Under these circumstances, a rescue mission appealed to the president. Success would make him an instant hero, restore the nation's dignity and pride, and relieve our allies of cooperating with sanctions they only most reluctantly and slowly accepted. While most Americans agreed with the president's decision to attempt the rescue mission, the failure seemed to symbolize the widespread perception of the administration's ineptness. The polls plummeted again. The one thing the abortive rescue mission did accomplish was to bring the president out of the White House and onto the campaign trail again, although he had earlier said that he would not do so until the hostages' release. Carter clearly was seeking to maximize his delegate strength in the primaries as much as possible to ward off embarrassing and divisive challenges from Kennedy at the convention; the senator's delegate strength had to be kept down.

Carter won the nomination but the hostage issue came back to haunt him in the closing days of the presidential campaign. As the Iranians announced their terms for the hostages' release and hopes for their quick release rose again—only to be quickly dimmed—the nation was vividly reminded of the president's failure to secure their release. Whether fair or not, the postelection *New York Times*/CBS News poll showed a last minute change of mind on whom to vote for or whether to vote at all; three fifths of these voters decided to vote against Carter. Twenty-three percent of these switchers cited Iran.⁹

The Bureaucracy and Implementing Policy

Another characteristic of crises and the accompanying sense of urgency to make a decision, as well as the perception by the policy makers that the nation's security is at stake and the possibility of war looms, is the subordination of bureaucratic interests to the need to make a decision to safeguard the national interest. Crisis decision making takes place at the top level of the government, and those in these positions, while reflecting their departmental viewpoints, do not necessarily feel themselves limited to representing these perspectives. Organizational affiliation is not per se a good predictor of their stands.¹⁰ McNamara did not reflect the Joint Chiefs' impulse to bomb and invade during the 1962 missile crisis (as later in Vietnam, he was increasingly to disagree with their views and recommendations); instead, he became the leading advocate of the blockade.

While crisis decision making may approximate the rational model, the execution of the means chosen to achieve the nation's goal is left to the bureaucracies, mainly the military bureaucracy. In this context, standard operating procedures and departmental interests tend to rise to the fore, a potentially dangerous situation. A bureaucracy reflects a division of labor; it possesses an expertise in a certain area. Within this area, it manages problems according to standard ways that over time have been found successful. A bureaucracy cannot handle each problem as if it were a new one; it assigns each problem, therefore, to a certain category of problems that it handles and resolves regularly. These are called standard operating procedures (SOP). But in a crisis such SOP designed for the management of daily routines may cause trouble, even spark a conflagration. Thus the U.S. Navy wanted to place the blockade 800 miles away from Cuba, outside of the range of Cuban jet fighters. But Kennedy, while concerned about the safety of the U.S. ships, was even more concerned that the Soviet leaders should be given as much time as possible to consider their options and actions; too short a time might lead them to hasty and ill-considered action. He therefore insisted that the navy pull its blockade back to 500 miles to give the Kremlin extra hours in the hope it would realize the gravity and danger of the situation and do nothing rash.

Similarly, Kennedy refused to stop the first two ships that approached the blockade line. One was a Soviet ship and the other an East German one; neither carried missiles. The third ship to approach also carried no missiles, but the president did stop it—a U.S.-built World War II Liberty ship, Panamanian owned and registered in Lebanon under charter to the Soviet Union. Stopping that ship as the first one would be less provocative to the

Soviets. Kennedy applied the same reasoning to the air force. Asked by the president if it could carry out a "surgical strike" against the missiles, the air force dusted off an old plan, part of an invasion operation, requiring several hundred sorties and widespread bombing. Clearly, such on operation might have killed hundreds of the thousands of Soviet personnel in Cuba. Would this not cause Khrushchev to react militarily? Could he really tolerate such loss of life and do nothing?

In short, Kennedy not only made the key decision about the U.S. objectives, but supervised the implementation of the plans to achieve them in detail. He did not hesitate to interfere in the military chain of command. While this made some military officers, especially the chief of naval operations, unhappy with such political interference and micromanagement, the president knew that if he were not aware of all the plans and did not ask all the right questions, he could not be assured that his objectives could be achieved—the withdrawal of the Soviet missiles *and* the avoidance of a nuclear war. Since the military was in charge of operations, he wanted to be certain he knew as much as possible about what they were going to do to ensure that their military maneuvers and actions were consistent with his political aims.

President Carter, by contrast, did not similarly closely supervise the preparations for the Iranian rescue mission. While he did acquaint himself with the plans in advance, he left the details to the military professionals. Given the stakes a president has in a successful outcome of a crisis, however, he must become familiar with each facet of the operation. He cannot completely rely on either the experts or trusted advisers. Full details about the rescue mission remain unknown. But we do know that three of the eight helicopters broke down (the minimum required number was six); that the helicopters chosen had a poor mechanical service record and that probably twelve should have started the mission; that the navy maintenance for the eight helicopters appears to have been carried out in rather routine fashion; that the helicopters needed refueling on the ground and landed at a desert strip called Desert One (so close to a road that a busload of Iranians had to be detained to keep the mission secret); and that during this refueling stop one helicopter's propeller blades struck a C–130 transport plane filled with fuel, causing both to burst into flames. In addition, the president may have cut the operation back from a 400–man force and thirty-five helicopters because he was unwilling to risk a major military confrontation.

The fact is that as in every other military operation, interservice rivalry and bureaucratic consensus were the dominating elements.[11] Air force pilots with experience in long-distance flying, including air refueling and night flying, were not chosen (thus making that stop in the desert unnecessary); marine pilots, whose principal experience is shuttling between ship and shore, were chosen because every service demanded—and received—a role. Moreover, almost unbelievably, no full-dress rehearsal was ever held. Rehearsals were piecemeal only, each unit training for its assignment. Worse, the rescue force did not train together as a single unit; each component trained separately, at different training centers, under its service's command. When they all met at Desert One, there were three senior colonels (air force, marines, army) but no one had full operational authority! An investigation after the disaster by the military itself was critical of the planning, coordination, and training. Yet, perhaps to avoid the usual military charges of interference, President Carter did not insist on an independent review of the plan by a small group of professional officers and civilians with experience in special operations and no vested interest in the existing plans. Because of overly great concern for security, not even normal review processes had been followed. Indeed, not even the Joint Chiefs ever sat down to look at the details of the plan—because there was none. No final, overall, written plan existed because of the obsession with security.

The Peripheral Role of Congress

Finally, despite the War Powers Act, crisis decision making is characterized by minimal, if any, congressional involvement. Before Vietnam, congressional leaders were usually called in, merely as a matter of courtesy, and informed of the president's decision just before he announced it publicly. But their advice was not requested. Moreover, as the term *crisis* suggests, such occurrences were—and continue to be—perceived by one side as affecting vital interests and frequently happen suddenly and unexpectedly, leaving decision makers with a sharp sense that they have to make rapid decisions lest the situation deteriorate further. A lack of decision time tends to mean that Congress is bound to be bypassed, except for briefings *after* decisions have been made by the executive. The president has a full-time job at such times just consulting his staff and cabinet officers to obtain all possible information on what is happening and interpretations about the adversary's motives, canvassing the alternative courses of action among which he must choose, and exploring which of these is most likely to achieve his aims without triggering a nuclear exchange. The War Powers Resolution has not yet changed this pattern.

Congress may be bypassed for yet another reason. Superpower confrontations often begin with a test of each other's will and determination in some low-level action. Thus, in Cuba, Kennedy decided on the blockade as an initial move even though it could only prevent the further shipment of missiles to the island, not eliminate the ones already there. The hope was that Moscow would perceive the blockade as a demonstration of American determination to achieve that objective; if convinced by the blockade, the Soviet Union would withdraw its missiles before Kennedy had to escalate the crisis. He could, for example, have ordered an air strike on the missiles or an invasion, and these options remained available to him. Moscow knew that and was unwilling to risk such an escalation. In short, crises, precipitated by the attempt of one side to change the status quo and the other's equal resolution not to permit such a change, become elaborate maneuvers in which each side seeks to achieve its aim but simultaneously avoid a nuclear exchange. Thus it becomes vital first to start on one of the lower rungs of the escalation ladder, and second to give the opponent at each higher rung sufficient time to consider risks, costs and payoffs of either desisting, escalating, or settling the issue at stake through negotiations. These steps must be carefully timed, coordinated, and calculated, for the risks of miscalculation are ever present. It is interesting to note that the first counsel of Kennedy's advisers was to bomb the Soviet missile sites. Only after a week of deliberation did Kennedy and his advisers decide on the blockade. Normally, presidents do not have a week's grace to prepare their moves but must decide virtually overnight what to do when they unexpectedly confront a major challenge.

Significantly, however, when a delegation of legislators was called in to be told of the Soviet missiles and what the United States intended to do about them, the delegation's initial reaction was skepticism about the blockade's ability to compel the withdrawal of the missiles, and it urged an air strike (Fulbright advocated such a move). Presumably, had Congress been consulted, (and given its intensely hostile mood against Castro and Cuba at that time), it would have pressed the administration to bomb or possibly invade the island. The risks of these courses, in contrast to the blockade, would have been enormous. Consulting Congress, asking for a supportive resolution, would also have robbed the administration of the advantage of surprise and allowed the U.S.S.R. to take preemptive steps that might have made it difficult or impossible for Kennedy to act at all. In any event, it is clear that the president has much more room to maneuver if he is not subject to congressional pressures. Congress, on the whole, has not been a force for restraint—except in the late 1970s and early 1980s, when it began to resist many presidential initiatives in foreign affairs.

Carter, fearing a leak, did not consult Congress about the Iran rescue mission. Ironically, just before the mission, the chairman of the Senate Foreign Relations Committee and the ranking minority member, worried by the stories that the president was considering military moves against Iran, sent a letter to the secretary of state insisting on consultation under the War Powers Act before any force was used. The purpose of invoking this act—the first time Congress had done so—was clearly to discourage the administration from mining Iran's harbors or making similar moves. If such consultation occurred, it would obviously alarm much of the world by making it appear that action was imminent and, worse form the point of view of operational success, place on alert those against whom the mission was intended. Administration officials did say that military moves were months off since economic and diplomatic sanctions had just been agreed to by America's allies. Nothing was said about the forthcoming rescue effort, which the president later called a "humanitarian mission."

Congressional opinion after the mission was divided over the issue of consultation, but most, including the senate majority leader, were willing to give the president the benefit of the doubt. President Carter defined the mission as humanitarian, not military, since it involved the rescue of U.S. citizens and only a small force was involved. As the acting secretary of state had explained (after Secretary Vance resigned in protest over the mission): the "extraordinary circumstances" surrounding this operation forbade consultation with Congress before its start; if any details of the plan had been revealed, the operation might have been compromised. But had the first stage gone well, "the president had planned to advise appropriate congressional leaders before the next stage." Furthermore, "I want to emphasize," continued the acting secretary, "the administration does not regard the extraordinary circumstances of this case as a precedent for avoiding consultations with the Congress."[12]

Crisis Decision Making and the Democratic Dilemmas

Crisis decision making is predominantly characterized by a "rational" mode of operation. The fact that vital interests are considered to be at stake, that the decision makers are usually surprised by the occurrence of the crisis and feel under great pressure to make quick decisions ensures that crisis decisions will not be handled routinely. Decision making rises to the top and is narrowed to a few participants who may be organized for the duration of the crisis as a special task force. The president plays the key role; he has a greater opportunity in these circumstances to determine policy than he does in more normal security policies, let alone intermestic policies. He and his specially selected advisers are not hampered by an aroused Congress, irate interest groups, or an inquisitive public. The crisis itself tends to unite everyone. There is not enough time to stimulate sufficient opposition. The cabinet officers participating in the decision making process are usually not fundamentally motivated by the organizational and bureaucratic interests of their departments, as when "normal" policy is being made. In any case, there is normally little time for bargaining among actors with different perspectives.

Thus, in a way, there are no dilemmas. As Lowi said many years ago, "only command positions were involved; the public and its institutions were far removed. . . . In sum, there was hardly any politics at all." The men in these "command positions" are "institutional leaders . . . *without their institutions.*[13] Thus the U.S. political system ironically may work more efficiently when it acts in an authoritarian manner, when the normal democratic participation of the bureaucracy, Congress, interest groups, and public opinion is at a minimum. Some refer to this presidential dominance and freedom from political constraint as *democratic Caesarism.*

Yet while the consequences of surprise, high threat, and short time can be very functional by considerably reducing, if not eliminating, the "traditionally acclaimed disabilities and deficiencies of United States democracy in foreign affairs,"[14] one final point deserves to be discussed briefly: the possibility that when decision making is limited to a few individuals—as noted earlier regarding the Iran-Contra affair— they will not make rational decisions but will fall victim to *groupthink*.[15] This term refers to the tendency of a small group of decision makers to become a cohesive group and the possibility that individual members may silence their doubts and qualifications about the policy views the majority holds; those who disagree tend to be rejected. Thus the consensus reached may be superficial because it does not reflect the sound judgment of the group reached after critical examination; without the give-and-take of debate in which all options are carefully analyzed, this consensus may represent a collective misjudgment—or just plain bad judgment. Groupthink, claims Irving Janis, is a deterioration of the mental efficiency, reality testing, and moral judgment that is the product of group pressure to conform.[16]

In the Cuban missile crisis, the president avoided becoming a victim. First, he absented himself from the executive committee's discussions so that its members would be free to say what they wanted to. Had he been present and expressed his views, the tendency would have been for the committee members to take their cue from him. Who, after all, dares to challenge the president's views? Second, the committee was divided into smaller groups who debated and cross-examined one another. In this way, all members became thoroughly familiar with the pros and cons of the arguments for specific options. Robert Kennedy, the attorney general who was his brother's confidante, often played devil's advocate, probing and asking what some felt were rude questions that demanded a justification of their position.

If the Cuban missile crisis was handled so well that it has become a classic case study of crisis management, it is because the administration learned from the disaster of the Bay of Pigs operation a year earlier. This operation too has become a classic of sorts—of a "perfect failure."[17] The operation was launched on a series of assumptions, all of which proved wrong. Among these were: no one would discover that the United States was responsible for this invasion; the Cuban Air Force could be knocked out before the invasion started; Castro's army was weak; and the invasion would touch off uprisings that would probably lead to Castro's overthrow. How could such flimsy assumptions go unchallenged by a group of men who were considered "the best and the brightest"? A number of reasons have been cited, including the fact that the CIA's own intelligence experts and the State Department's Cuban desk people, who could have predicted the failure of sending 1,400 men to Cuba to topple the regime, were excluded, and the illusion of these able people that they were invincible and that they were unanimous in their support of the CIA plan. Doubts were not loudly voiced, silence was taken for consent, and any disagreements that surfaced were suppressed by a "mindguard" who guarded the consensus from intellectual assault as a bodyguard would protect an individual from physical injury.

Was Carter's Iranian rescue mission his Bay of Pigs? Were the plans for the mission extensively debated and subjected to rigorous scrutiny? Kennedy not only encouraged vigorous and frank debate in the executive committee but called in some of the "grand old men" who had been active in the early days of containment (Dean Acheson and Robert Lovett, for example). Carter does not appear to have asked for the opinions of such stalwarts of the previous Democratic administrations as Averell Harriman, George Ball, and Robert McNamara. Why were military people, possibly retired officers, who had no commitment to the specific plans made for this rescue mission, not consulted? Security considerations prevented even searching scrutiny within the government. How feasible really was this operation, however noteworthy and noble its intention? Could the operation have been carried out successfully had the helicopters not broken down, or was the mission itself conceptually faulty? Was its failure due to technical problems—what might perhaps be called bad luck—or was the plan itself a victim of groupthink? Incomplete evidence certainly suggest the last. The evidence also suggests that if widespread democratic participation in crisis decision making is not feasible, the failure to subject policy to critical evaluation has been greatest when the U.S. adversary was not a nuclear or even a major power. When the Soviet Union has been the opponent, U.S. policy makers have been cautious and careful, continuously reviewing their policies. The awesome cost of miscalculations and actions based on wrong assumptions have been the best antidotes to the pressures for group think.[18] One misstep could transform the superpowers' confrontation into a nuclear disaster for which the label World War III would be a misnomer. The scale of destruction would so greatly exceed those of World War I and II that new language and words would have to be found to describe it.

NOTES

1. Thomas C. Schelling, *Arms and Influence* (New Haven: Yale Univ. Press, 1966).
2. Henry A. Kissinger, *Nuclear Weapons and Foreign Policy* (New York: Harper & Row, 1957).
3. Most prominently, see Hans J. Morgenthau, *Politics Among Nations*, 4th ed. (New York: Alfred A. Knopf, 1967), esp. pp. 5–8.
4. The bureaucratic/government politics model is based on Graham T. Allison, *Essence of Decision* (Boston: Little, Brown, 1971); I.M. Destler, *Presidents, Bureaucrats and Foreign Policy* (Princeton, N.J.: Princeton Univ. Press, 1972); Morton Halperin, *Bureaucratic Politics and Foreign Policy* (Washington, D.C.: The Brookings Institution, 1974); and Roger Hilsman, *To Move A Nation* (Garden City, N.Y.: Doubleday, 1967): pp. 3–13, 541–76.
5. Oran R. Young, *The Politics of Force* (Princeton, N.J.: Princeton Univ. Press, 1968), pp.6–15; Charles F. Hermann, ed., *International Crises* (New York: Free Press, 1972); and Phil Williams, *Crises Management* (New York: John Wiley & Sons, 1976), pp. 59–93.
6. For the Cuban missile crisis, see Elie Abel, *The Missile Crisis* (New York: Bantam Books, 1966); Alexander L. George et al., eds., *The Limits of Coercive Diplo-*

macy (Boston: Little, Brown, 1971), pp. 86–143; and Robert F. Kennedy, *Thirteen Days* (New York: W. W. Norton, 1971).

7. J. A. Nathan, "The Missile Crisis: His Finest Hour Now," *World Politics, January 1975, pp. 262–64.*

8. New York Times, June 25, 1980.

9. *Ibid.,* November 16, 1980.

10. Morton H. Halperin and Arnold Kanter, eds., *Readings in American Foreign Policy* (Boston: Little, Brown, 1973), pp. 9–10.

11. Gary Sick, *All Fall Down* (New York: Random House, 1985), pp.352–56; and "Military Options and Constraints" in *American Hostages in Iran,* ed. Christopher Warren (New Haven, Conn.: Yale Univ. Press, 1985), pp. 144–73. See also Edward Luttwak, *The Act of War* (New York: Simon & Schuster, 1984); pp. 44–45; and most of all, Richard A. Gabriel, *Military Incompetence* (New York: Hill and Wang, 1985), p. 85 ff, especially pp. 103–16; and Arthur T. Hadley, *The Straw Giant* (New York: Avon Books, 1987), pp. 3–28. See also *New York Times Magazine,* May 17, 1981, in which the entire issue is devoted to the Iranian hostage crisis.

12. *New York Times,* May 9, 1980.

13. Theodore Lowi, "Making Democracy Safe for the World," in *Domestic Sources of Foreign Policy,* ed. James Rosenau, (New York: Free Press, 1967), p. 301 (italics in original).

14. Phil Williams, *Crisis Management* (New York: John Wiley & Sons, 1976), p. 72

15. Irving L. Janis, *Victims of Groupthink* (Boston: Houghton Mifflin, 1972).

16. Ibid., p. 9.

17. Ibid., pp. 14–49; and Theodore C. Sorenson, *Kennedy* (New York: Bantam Books, 1966), pp. 326–46.

18. Williams, *Crisis Management,* pp.79–80.

Chapter Eight

The Bureaucratic Politics Model and Noncrisis Decisions

The bureaucratic/governmental politics model described in Chapter 7 stands in sharp contrast to the rational actor model. Different participants see the stakes in different ways and there is no objective solution to be sought. Conflict occurs both within and across the branches of government and the outcome is the result of intense bargaining. Congress, the bureaucracies, interest groups, and public opinion all play key roles—as does, of course, the president—and there is no single actor who is determinative in most cases. By focusing on the broader governmental context rather than only on presidential leadership or the bureaucratic players, the governmental politics perspective is a reminder of the broader American political system and how it influences the conduct of foreign policy. In this chapter, we shall outline how decisions are made according to this model.

We first discuss Lyndon Johnson's decision to deploy an antiballistic missile (ABM) system—and contrast that briefly with Nixon's later decision to go forward, based on rational actor logic, with an expanded ABM and the ultimate governmental decision to dismantle the entire system. The emphasis in the ABM case is on the bureaucracy. Besides being a very interesting case study of what has been called "making a decision without really choosing" (to govern is supposed to be to choose among alternative courses of action), the ABM decision remains of current interest because in 1983 President Reagan called for a Strategic Defense Initiative (SDI), a major scientific effort to come up with defensive weapons that could shoot down incoming missiles. And during Reagan's second term, the ABM treaty itself became the issue as the administration sought to reintepret it to allow it to test components of this defensive system. Thus the issue of producing and deploying defensive weapons for protection against nuclear attack was not a new one. Indeed, the Reagan administration gave strategic defense an emphasis that it had not received before. "Star Wars" was the name the critics gave to this new stress on ABM defense, now renamed ballistic missile defense (BMD). While the focus of the original ABM is on conflict within the bureaucracy, there was none of this on SDI, for the president sprung it on the bureaucracy, Congress, and the nation; but SDI gave rise to an increasing confrontation with the Congress.

But between the ABM and SDI cases, we turn to the politics of arms control and strategy in which the emphasis is on executive–legislative relations. The Strategic Arms Limitation Treaty (SALT II), which had taken the Carter administration over two years to negotiate, was one of the most important treaties the United States had negotiated with the Soviet Union in the postwar period. It needed Senate approval; specifically, as a treaty it needed two thirds approval, which it undoubtedly would have failed to attain had it been put to a vote. Different opponents saw alternative stakes and found many conflicting reasons for their stands; some thought that the treaty compromised U.S. interests, others that it did not go far enough in reducing arms. Carter failed to win the Senate's consent and Reagan denounced the treaty when he came into office. Ironically, when Reagan sought approval for his Intermediate Nuclear Forces (INF) agreement with Moscow, he too had his difficulties gaining the Senate's consent.

Finally we consider the Byzantine politics of energy, farm, and trade policy, all examples of intermestic policy, where the stakes are perceived as very high by all actors and there is widespread participation in decision making (see Chapter 4) but virtually no coordination. In energy, this lack of coordination fails to produce international or national energy policy for the developed nations of the world, especially the United States. Energy politics typifies some of the more extreme aspects of the bureaucratic model, particularly because participation is so widespread, very few actors have common interests, and the capacity for not reaching a decision is great. Indeed, energy policy remains more of a domestic issue because the leading industrial nations—either collectively or individually—have not been able to come to grips with the international politics of oil and other energy supplies. The same is true for the other two policy areas.

THE EXECUTIVE BRANCH AND THE POLITICS OF THE ANTIBALLISTIC MISSILE

The Principal Actors and Arguments

In contrast to crisis decision making, more traditional security decisions such as the military budget and the development of new weapons systems typically involve a multiplicity of actors, different perceptions among the actors as to what is at stake, and a much longer time span in the decision-making process. There is a multiplicity of actors by the very nature of program policies. Such policies are initially developed in the bureaucracies, are sometimes of concern to interest groups (which might be helped or hurt economically by the decision made), and are finally resolved by Congress through an appropriations bill. In the first of the specific program decisions we are considering—Johnson's decision in 1967 to proceed with the procurement of some long-term lead items on an antiballistic missile system—the actors involved included not only the president, his advisers, and other members of the inner circle, such as the secretaries of defense and state and the chairman of the Joint Chiefs of Staff, but also lower level offices in Defense, members of Congress, and (albeit, indirectly) public opinion.[1]

Each actor saw the stakes differently. Indeed, Johnson was more of a neutral actor leaning against deployment. The strongest opposition to ABM came from Secretary of Defense Robert McNamara. Along with Secretary of State Dean Rusk and the ACDA, he felt that an American decision to deploy an ABM would mean a spiraling and costly arms race that would also destroy all chances for stabilization of the American–Soviet deterrent balance. McNamara contended that an American decision to deploy the ABM would virtually preclude any possibility of initiating arms limitations talks with the Soviets. While Johnson did not agree with McNamara on the likely effects of deployment,[2] he was willing to postpone a final decision until he had received word from the Soviets on the possibility of such talks.

McNamara was also skeptical of the feasibility of the proposed ABM. An early version of the ABM (the Nike-Zeus system) was rejected because of its inadequate radar facilities, and the Nike-X had been challenged on similar grounds. The defense secretary, however, was in a minority position within his own department on the question of feasibility. The Pentagon's Offices of Defense Research and Engineering and Systems Analysis both supported deployment. Within the Defense Department, only the Office of International Security Affairs joined McNamara in opposition to ABM.

The principal supporters of ABM were the services and key members of the Senate Armed Services Committee. In contrast to most defense budget situations, the ABM debate found the three services united in their support for a weapons system.[3] While the army, navy, and air force each "saw a different face of ABM and reached different conclusions,"[4] the very fact of this interservice agreement is worth noting. In the past, McNamara had used divisions among the services to prevail on issues of defense spending. However, the united front forced the secretary to appeal above the services directly to the president. General Earle Wheeler, chairman of the Joint Chiefs of Staff, made no attempt to hide his support for ABM. Even when the president was on record as opposed to the system, Wheeler made public statements supporting it and criticizing the administration.

Supporting the services were several senior members of the Senate Armed Services Committee, including the chairman, Richard B. Russell, and such other influential members as John Stennis and Henry Jackson. These senators were supporters of Johnson's Vietnam policy and had been friends of the president when he was Democratic leader in the Senate during the Eisenhower administration. Indeed, Johnson had served with them on the Armed Services Committee and trusted their judgment. He was particularly close to Russell.

In arguing their case, proponents and adversaries often stressed different factors. Supporters stressed the fact that the Soviets had already developed such a system, that it threatened America's deterrent capacity, and that ABM would save American lives. The issue of arms limitation talks was not paramount to them. To the extent that they even considered this issue, they argued that an ABM would provide the Americans with an extra bargaining chip in any negotiations on mutual defensive weapons limitations. Opponents, on the other hand, were less concerned about the possibility of Soviet possession of ABMs than they were about the potential for a new arms race. Another factor that concerned the opponents more than the supporters was the price tag. Estimates of the cost of an ABM system ranged from $30 billion to $40 billion. By 1966, even with an unusually large congressional majority, Johnson was experiencing difficulties mobilizing Congress to approve funding for many of the social welfare programs of his Great Society package. With a sharply reduced Democratic majority in Congress after the 1966 election, even greater difficulties were anticipated. Many opponents of ABM—and, indeed, even Johnson—realized that any increase in the military budget could come only at the expense of decreased spending for social welfare programs. Since most of the supporters of ABM were opposed to Johnson's Great Society package, this aspect of the problem did not trouble them.

President Johnson and Minimal Decision Making

Johnson was thus torn between the arguments made by his friends in the Senate that ABM was needed for the national security and those of McNamara and Rusk that the system was likely to initiate a new arms race. Therefore, he was willing to postpone a decision. Two factors seem to have been particularly important in this respect. The first was that Johnson believed that an arms limitation agreement with the Soviets could change the opinion of the public on the foreign policy of his administration. Johnson's years in office had been dominated by a seemingly endless war in Vietnam, and the president was hoping for a major breakthrough in some area of international reconciliation. Second, the president wanted to avoid, if at all possible, a direct break with McNamara. The two men were already at odds over Vietnam, but Johnson still valued his secretary of defense too highly to reject his advice out of hand. Since McNamara viewed the ABM choice as a direct confrontation between himself and the Joint Chiefs of Staff, a decision to deploy the system would be taken as a direct rebuff to the secretary. On the other hand, a negative decision on ABM would alienate key senators who might proceed to wreak havoc with Johnson's domestic program. While these senators probably opposed much of the Great Society

legislation anyway, a negative decision on the ABM might serve to antago-
nize them still further and thus provide a sustained effort to cut back domestic programs. Not surprisingly, then, Johnson's instincts "led him to
search for a compromise which would minimize the damage to his relations
with his advisers."[5]

Ideally, the president would have preferred to let the supporters and
opponents reach some kind of compromise among themselves. This was
very much the Johnson style—that of the ultimate bargainer—which had
been responsible for his tremendous popularity as Senate Democratic leader.
It was also the style of Johnson's political mentor, Franklin D. Roosevelt. On
this issue, however, such a course was simply not possible. As Hilsman has
argued, a major consequence of "the multiplicity of constituencies involved
in [foreign and defense] policy making is that more and more problems are
thrown into the White House. It is only the presidency . . . that can consider
the whole broad range of interconnections between conflicting interests and
demands."[6] The president's only recourse was to make a "minimal decision," one that would not identify either side as a "winner" or a "loser" but
would represent some compromise among the competing positions.[7]

The critical question thus became: What would be the nature of this
compromise? At least a part of the answer became clear in a meeting Johnson and McNamara had with Soviet Premier Kosygin at Glassboro, New
Jersey, in June 1967. Johnson pressed the Soviets for a date for the opening
of arms limitation talks but did not receive an answer. Kosygin, in a meeting
with both Johnson and McNamara, described the Soviet ABM as a defensive
weapon and therefore unobjectionable, hence not a proper subject for arms
limitation talks. McNamara's principal objection to the ABM had now been
refuted by the Soviets. Consequently, Johnson no longer saw the American
ABM as a possible stumbling block to beginning arms limitation talks.[8]

The president was also worried about the possible electoral consequences of a negative decision on ABM. In late 1966, Michigan Governor
George Romney—then believed to be the front-runner for the Republican
presidential nomination in 1968—discussed the ABM gap with the Soviet
Union on national television. He also indicated that it would be a major
issue in the 1968 campaign. Other Republicans made similar charges in Congress. Johnson wanted to quell these complaints. As the vice presidential
candidate on the 1960 ticket that had charged the Eisenhower administration
with neglecting the problem of an offensive missile gap, he knew that the
issue could be powerful.

Even though the pressure for an ABM from the military and Congress
far outweighed the countervailing pressure from McNamara and Rusk, the
president was still committed to seeking a compromise. Although the secretary of defense understood the pressures for a decision to deploy ABM,
he remained steadfastly opposed to an anti-Soviet system, which he believed might affect the possibility of an arms control agreement. On Septem-

ber 18, 1967, McNamara announced the administration's opposition to any major ABM deployment.

> The [Soviet ABM] system does not impose any threat to our ability to penetrate and inflict massive and unacceptable damage on the Soviet Union. In other words, it does not presently affect in any significant manner our assured destruction ability. . . . While we have substantially improved our technology in the field, it is important to understand that none of the systems at the present or foreseeable state-of-the-art would provide an impenetrable shield over the United States . . . the $40 billion is not the issue. The money in itself is not the problem. . . . The point for us to keep in mind is that should the [arms limitations] talks fail—and the Soviets decide to expand their present modest ABM deployment into a massive one—our response must be realistic . . . if the Soviets elect to deploy a heavy ABM system, we must further expand our sophisticated offensive forces.[9]

In brief, not only could an ABM not protect the public, but it could be overcome by saturating the defensive missiles' capability with a large number of ICBMs. If the United States could overcome a Soviet ABM system in this way, presumably the U.S.S.R. could do the same should the United States deploy a "thick" shield. On the other hand, McNamara came out for an anti-Chinese ABM—in case the Chinese, who were at the time perceived as militantly ideological and revolutionary, might be just irrational enough to attempt a nuclear attack upon the United States or its allies in Asia. The new system, called the Sentinel, would have as its major function the defense of American cities.

McNamara's speech clearly indicated that any American reaction to an increased Soviet buildup of the ABM system would be countered by an American increase in offensive missiles. This was a major victory for the secretary against the Joint Chiefs of Staff and ABM supporters in Congress, who favored the more extensive (and more expensive) ABM. The projected cost of Sentinel was approximately $5 billion. The very fact that McNamara made the speech announcing the administration's support for ABM indicated that he had by no means suffered a major defeat on this issue. He could view the president's decision as leaving open the possibility that the system would never be deployed at all if the Soviets would agree to a mutual defense weapons limitation. The administration had *not* come out in support of deployment, but only for increased funding for the procurement of certain ABM parts, which would require a long lead time. On the other hand, the very fact that the administration had publicly changed its position represented a victory for ABM supporters in Congress and the Joint Chiefs. Proponents of a more extensive "thick" system viewed the administration's change in position as a hopeful sign and expected that they could accomplish their goal later.

Johnson had indeed made another minimal decision, a decision that on the one hand, postponed the real decision, and, on the other, left each side

feeling it had won a partial victory. This is evident from McNamara's arguments on behalf of Sentinel. The interjection of the Chinese threat into the
argument seemed to belie the administration's real reasons for supporting
ABM. The Chinese nuclear threat was practically nonexistent in the fall of
1967: The first atomic bomb was detonated by China in 1964, the next one a
year later. In 1965, the Chinese were reported to have detonated two hydrogen bombs, and a third in the spring of 1967. For someone as committed to
programs with demonstrated cost effectiveness, it certainly appeared
strange to find McNamara proposing a multibillion dollar system to oppose
what was essentially a minor threat. Clearly, the real purpose of stressing
the anti-Chinese nature of the American ABM was to restrict the overall
scope of any possible future deployment and especially to prevent the creation of a thick anti-Soviet shield. McNamara was particularly anxious to
impress the distinction between an anti-Soviet and an anti-Chinese system
on American public opinion and mobilize support for the "thin" system. He
was also very concerned to communicate this difference to the Kremlin, lest
it continue to oppose strategic arms limitation talks and initiate a new offensive arms spiral. Another argument in McNamara's speech is worth noting:
the secretary's statement that "the $40 billion is not the issue." Why was it
not the issue? Not because Johnson would have been willing to spend that
much for an ABM if necessary, but rather because the Sentinel decision no
longer required massive outlays of funds. The new program did not dramatically increase the level of defense spending; the estimated cost of $5 billion
would not become a major issue until a decision to deploy the Sentinel was
made.

The critical point is that McNamara's speech did not address the main
arguments of either proponents or opponents of the ABM: The threat of the
Soviet ABMs was simply denied in two sentences; the impact of the new
system on the potential for arms limitation talks was not even mentioned;
the question of national priorities was barely alluded to (by the reference to
the $40 billion cost of Nike-X), and the feasibility of the Sentinel system was
totally ignored. Under a rational actor model, we would have expected these
questions to form the basis for a speech either accepting or rejecting the
ABM. They did not. Instead, a side issue—the Chinese "threat"—was made
the central concern. Neither the proponents nor the opponents had used this
argument in earlier debates over the ABM. The introduction of this argument for Sentinel clearly represented an attempt to find an *ex post facto* rationale to fit a decision that had been arrived at based on domestic political
considerations rather than strategic ones. The Chinese nuclear threat was
clearly a "minimal" problem that could be solved by a "minimal" decision.
The compromise Johnson was able to reach was hardly satisfactory to any
side—but compromises never are. By letting participants outside the executive branch play a major role in determining defense policy, the president
had skillfully maneuvered a compromise that neither the supporters nor the
opponents of the ABM could reject without risking further losses.

The ABM decision under Johnson thus is a good example of the bureaucratic model. There was, indeed, a multiplicity of actors in the decision-making arena. In contrast to crisis decision making, not only did Congress play a role on ABM, but the legislative branch was able to reverse the position the president himself had held. Second, the program decision took a considerable amount of time to be reached. An ABM system had first been proposed in the mid-1950s; Johnson did not act until 1967. Many program policies are resolved in shorter periods. Since the defense budget is annual, at least some programs are reevaluated in a relatively short time span. On the other hand, domestic programs may take even longer: comprehensive federal aid to education and a system of government-subsidized health care for the aged had each been under consideration in Congress for more than fifty years before Johnson maneuvered them through the Eighty-ninth Congress in 1965. And finally, the various actors may view the stakes in different ways, a situation that makes compromises possible and minimal decisions likely. The 1967 decision by Johnson let McNamara still believe that the arms race could be limited and let the Joint Chiefs still hope for an expanded ABM. As in all bargaining situations that are successfully terminated, neither side saw itself as a clear loser. In the process of reaching a compromise, however, the value-maximizing approach of the rational actor model was left behind. The 1967 decision did not appear to maximize any of the original values posed by either supporters or opponents of the ABM. Indeed, factors that have no place in a strategic decision made on the basis of rational calculations—such as domestic political considerations—appear to have been dominant in the bureaucratic politics of the Johnson decision.

President Nixon and the ABM Bargaining Chip

Ironically, two years later Nixon used the Johnson decision to proceed with an ABM to press for a larger system designed to protect American missiles. Less than two months after he took office, Nixon proposed the expanded Safeguard system and provoked a sharp confrontation with the Democratic Congress. The president presented the issue as one involving key stakes in our confrontation with the Soviet Union (not China) and refused to bargain at all with the Congress. The decision was presented as the conclusion of a rational calculus, and thus the debate in the Congress followed the lines of the rational actor model much more than the bureaucratic politics model.[10] Senator Edward M. Kennedy led the opposition and both sides gathered testimony (and has books published) on why ABM should (not) be constructed. The debate grew acrimonious, and a close vote, at least in the Senate, was expected. So much media attention was given to the debate that Gallup polls taken on April 6 and July 27, 1969, indicated that 69 percent of the respondents had either heard about or read about the ABM—a rather high figure. The surveys also showed, however, that many people were confused about the issue: only 40 percent of each sample had formed an opinion on the Safeguard system.

Nixon thus employed the decision that Johnson thought he had avoided, at least temporarily—building an ABM system.[11] Despite the heated arguments from liberal Democrats, Nixon easily prevailed in the House (223 to 141) and narrowly won with a two-vote margin in the Senate on August 6, 1969. The overall conditions had not changed markedly since 1967. But the ABM melodrama was not over.

The strategic arms limitation talks with the Soviets were on the agenda. The United States had no major offensive weapons system for a trade-off at a time when the Soviets were leading in the arms race in the number of missiles. ICBMs with multiple warheads, known as MIRVs, were specifically rejected for bargaining purposes because they were seen as the major way of keeping up with the Soviet's growing number of missiles. (In fact, Moscow in SALT I rejected a trade-off between a reduction of a U.S. *defensive* weapon for a Soviet reduction of *offensive* ICBMs.) Furthermore, U.S. deterrence depended on the "assured destruction" of Soviet society—its cities, industries, and population. It would have been suicide if they launched an attack on the United States. They, however, had already installed ABMs around Moscow. It was not known whether Moscow was working on a more effective second-generation ABM and might in the future extend it to protect the U.S.S.R.'s other major urban areas. But the United States could not presume that this might not occur, for obviously, if they could protect the majority of their population, the American threat to retaliate and destroy the Soviet Union as a viable society would lose its credibility. Thus an ABM tradeoff was a more likely possibility. SALT I in 1972 did exactly that, limiting each side to two ABM sites for a total of 200 ABMs; in 1974, this figure was cut in half and, for all practical purposes, this indicated the end of ABM defenses and meant the continuing ability of each superpower to destroy the other's population centers. For the next few years, the emphasis was on offensive weapons, creating equal ceilings for both powers and stabilizing the mutual deterrent equation.

EXECUTIVE–LEGISLATIVE CONFLICT, SALT II, AND THE INF TREATIES

When the Carter administration came to power in 1977, it was committed to the continuation of SALT negotiations.[12] Three problems had been inherited from its predecessor. One was that SALT I had not been able to provide an agreement on a limitation on offensive weapons. The two powers had simply agreed to freeze the numbers of ICBMs each side had in early 1972. The Soviets by then had several hundred more ICBMs than did the United States. The United States, however, had already begun MIRVing (multiplying the number of warheads on many of its ICBMs); and since in addition intercontinental bombers, in which the United States had a considerable quantitative lead, were excluded from SALT I, a rough equality or parity existed. This agreement was to be an interim one, to be replaced after five years by a long term agreement. The Senate, prodded by Senator Henry Jackson, had gone on record demanding that in SALT II, the United States should not accept force levels lower than those of the Soviet Union. Second, by the late 1970s the strategic balance had changed. Soviet technology, which in the past had not been as sophisticated as that of the United States, had relied on very large missiles. Their size compensated for their inaccuracy. Their warheads were sufficiently big so that when detonated they could destroy their targets even though they might hit a mile or more away. The United States concentrated on smaller, more sophisticated, and more accurate missiles. However, once the Soviets had overtaken the United States in the *number* of missiles, the fact that they could carry more throw-weight turned out to be very dangerous. Specifically, as the Soviets began to MIRV their new generation of missiles after SALT I, they could potentially place more and far bigger warheads on them than the United States could on its ICBMs; the Soviets also caught up with the United States in the accuracy of their missile terminal guidance systems. These much larger warheads, plus this enhanced accuracy, meant that Soviet ICBMs could strike at America's land-based missiles. Thus while a U.S. *Minuteman* missile carried three 180,000-ton warheads (later doubled in yield on 300 of the missiles), the U.S.S.R.'s SS–18 carried eight to ten separate megaton (million-ton) range warheads, and the SS–19 six separate 360,000-ton warheads. The SS–18, indeed, had the potential to carry thirty-four to forty smaller warheads. There was, therefore, great concern in Washington that the Soviets might be seeking a first-strike counterforce capability rather than a second-strike or retaliatory capability against cities. The experts agreed that the U.S. deterrent would become vulnerable in the 1980s. (It was estimated that 95 percent of the land-based *Minutemen* would be destroyed in a first strike.)

President Ford had laid the basis for SALT II with the Vladivostok agreement, which set a total upper ceiling of 2,400 launchers (including bombers, land-based ICMBs, and sea-launched ballistic missiles or SLBMs), of which 1,320 could be MIRVs. While high, the 2,400 ceiling was lower than the total number of Soviet ICBMs and SLBMs, although higher than the U.S. force levels. Although he was on the verge of an agreement, Ford was never able to conclude SALT II. The major reason was that in seeking nomination for the presidency in 1976 he faced a major challenge from the party's right wing in the candidacy of Ronald Reagan. Reagan attacked détente vigorously and Ford, who barely scraped by to beat Reagan for the Republican nomination, dropped the word *détente* entirely from his political vocabulary, replacing it with the phrase "peace through strength." Under the circumstances, Ford did not dare sign the SALT II agreement. Détente had lost much of its appeal by 1976.

Upstaging Kissinger

Once in office, Carter, who was personally committed to SALT, had to decide whether to sign a SALT II agreement based on the Vladivostok guidelines. Indeed, he stated before his election that if he became president, he would quickly sign SALT II on that basis. Once in power, however, Carter and his national security assistant, Zbigniew Brzezinski, decided to go for deeper cuts. This was to be the first of many changes of mind by Carter that over the years were to irritate the Soviets as well as allies and give the president a reputation abroad for unreliability. A principal reason for the reversal in this instance was that the two men wished to separate themselves from Kissinger, whose personality and achievements loomed over his successor's. Should they now sign an agreement whose outlines had already been negotiated by him? They appeared to want to show they could do better than Kissinger—and, by implication, their Republican predecessors. The last had accepted ceilings that were at or about U.S. force levels. Instead of these high ceilings, they would make real cuts. Such personal and partisan considerations were reinforced by the new secretary of defense and others concerned with the Soviets' growing first-strike capability and achievement of nuclear superiority. Deep cuts in Soviet ICBMs, allowing them only as many MIRVs as we had (550 Minutemen were MIRVed), and cutting their huge SS–18s down from the 300 allowed under SALT I to 150, would presumably decrease the Soviet threat to America's 1,000 ICBMs. The new secretary of state, Cyrus Vance, thought that the Soviets would not go for such a proposal. They had agreed to the Vladivostok ceilings and their entire thinking and negotiating posture was tied to Vladivostok. The Soviet bureaucracy would reject the sudden change of terms that had already been agreed on. The new chief of ACDA and chief SALT II negotiator, Paul Warnke, added that if the Soviets rejected the new Carter deep cuts, and the United States then fell back to the Vladivostok position, the administration would be criticized for retreating.

The Soviets, angered by Carter's early and frequent human rights pronouncements, which they saw as largely aimed at them, quickly rejected the deep cuts as a "cheap and shoddy" maneuver to seek a unilateral U.S. advantage. The administration, first defiantly declaring that it would "hang tough," finally changed its mind again and retreated. The final agreement, initialed by Brezhnev and Carter in the spring of 1979, twenty-nine months after Carter had come into office, was based on Vladivostok. It was an agreement that the president could presumably have had earlier, that, in turn, would then have allowed him to negotiate major reductions in SALT III. Had he done so, Carter, still popular, would have received Senate consent for SALT II. In any event, under the agreement signed two and one-half years after Carter had taken office and by which time he was already quite unpopular, each side would have 2,400 launchers, to be cut down to 2,250 by December 31, 1981 (Kissinger had already gained this Soviet concession).

All sorts of subceilings were agreed to: 1,320 MIRVs, of which 1,200 were to MIRVed ICBMs and SLBMs (which meant that the United States gained an advantage: 120 of its B–52 bombers could each be armed with 20 long-range air-launched cruise missiles, which the Soviets did not yet possess. Each B–52 so armed would count as one MIRV); and 820 MIRVed ICBMs, of which 308 could be the SS–18 (this 820 subceiling was an effort to limit any attempt by the Soviets who had most of their throw-weight on their ICBMs, to place even more of their warheads on their big land-based missiles). But the details of the entire SALT II treaty and its pros and cons need concern us less than what happened to the treaty once it was submitted to the Senate for its "advise and consent." But because of Carter's initial misstep in the negotiations and the consequent delay, Senate ratification was in doubt.

The "Treaty Trap"

The first hurdle was the treaty procedure, rightfully called by two critics the *treaty trap*. An earlier secretary of state, John Hay, had once likened the fate of an administration seeking Senate approval of a treaty to a bull going into an arena: "No one can say just how or when the blow will fall, but one thing is certain—it will never leave the arena alive."[13] It is not that the Senate has defeated most treaties; indeed, only eleven treaties have failed to gain the Senate's consent since 1789. It has, however, defeated a few important ones, the most famous of which was undoubtedly the Versailles Treaty ending World War I and establishing the League of Nations. Worse, the possible defeat of a treaty hangs over any administration, making treaty approval an arduous and risky process.

The treaty process was written into the Constitution at a time when the Founding Fathers conceived of the Senate as a wide, deliberate, appointed, and presumably conservative body, not a popularly elected house reflecting the ups and downs of popular passion. In a democracy that does almost everything else by a majority vote—including the declaration of war and the appropriation of billions for defense—the two-thirds provision stands out. It could even be said to be undemocratic in two senses. One, the Senate is composed of two senators from each state regardless of population. This means that the one third plus one vote would come largely from rural America, representing a minority of the nation's population. Two, the extraordinary size of the Senate majority allows a minority of senators to block a treaty favored by a majority of their colleagues. Not surprisingly, the treaty trap has tempted presidents to either bypass the Senate with executive agreements or simply to do nothing. This last phenomenon has been referred to as the "prenatal effect" or "anticipatory reaction"; fearful of what might happen to a treaty, they will kill it off before it is born. In the post-Vietnam era, when the Congress reasserted itself, executive agreements to bypass the legislature were not in favor. Indeed, when President Carter once floated the idea that he would sign SALT II as an executive agreement and then seek majority approval in both houses by means of a joint resolution, he was quickly rebuffed.

The problem is clearly that in a Senate of 100, it takes only thirty-four votes to defeat a treaty. On any important treaty, there is likely to be some opposition. It does not take many additional votes to add up to thirty-four. Indeed, the treaty provision places a premium on opposition. The incentive to come out against the treaty is strong because if the administration desperately wants Senate approval, it will have to "buy" those votes by satisfying senators' pet projects (a dam, nuclear power plant, a new weapons system, or some other appropriation). The extra votes—those needed in excess of a simple majority—may be sought not only among senators from one's own party but also among the opposition. Given the lack of party cohesion in the United States, mobilizing support from the opposition party is hardly novel; but a treaty may need more than the usual amount of support from the out-party. This presents an obvious problem for an opposition that hopes to become the in-party by criticism of an administration's record. It may be patriotic to support a treaty but will it not also be politically suicidal for the opposition party? It is the in-party that will claim and gain most of the popular approval for a treaty perceived to be beneficial to the nation.

The international repercussions of the treaty process are even worse. The fact that a president who has negotiated a treaty on behalf of the United States may be repudiated by the Senate undermines the president's prestige and authority to speak for the United States to the world, weakens America's leadership ability in the world, and raises serious questions among both friends and foes about both the desirability of negotiating with the United States and the reliability of this country. Having arrived at a mutually satisfactory agreement, the United States is presumably thereafter bound to live up to the provisions of that agreement. In which other country can the nation's chief of government be repudiated by another part of the same government? SALT II had been negotiated by three U.S. presidents—Nixon, Ford, and Carter—suggesting both the seriousness and continuity of U.S. purposes. How assured can other nations, especially those with whom the United States has negotiated a treaty, feel that once agreement has been attained, it will be final and receive Senate consent—rather than being renegotiated if the Senate attaches amendments to the treaty? One has only to wonder how Americans would view a treaty with the Soviets that, once negotiated and signed, Moscow would then either want to change or repudiate. Said a Soviet observer:

> With whom in America can we have dealings? If the president needs to coordinate his actions and stand with the Congress, why isn't this done before any international agreement is concluded? Is it really so . . . that for more than six years of talks the U.S. authorities have been unable to decide among themselves what in SALT II they can agree to and what they cannot? . . . Opinions in our government on this or that question may differ, too. But

when our representative at negotiations agrees to something, he does so on behalf of the country. . . . In the case of the United States, however, it appears that agreement with the administration even having a majority in the Congress often counts for little. It comes out that having reached agreement with the administration, one ought then to enter into separate external relations with the American Congress, and renegotiate, as it were, the agreement reached.[14]

Whether SALT II would finally have received Senate approval or not, had the Soviets not invaded Afghanistan in late December 1979, will never be known. But most observers feel that the reason President Carter "temporarily" withdrew the treaty from Senate consideration at that time was not to punish Moscow for its aggression but to save himself from probable defeat and a stunning political setback in the Senate. From the time the treaty was submitted to the Senate, if not before, the administration appeared on the defensive. The heart of the opposition came from the Armed Services Committee. Although the treaty did not fall within its main jurisdiction, ten of its members issued a report very critical of SALT II over the opposition of its venerable chairman, something that could never have happened a decade earlier. Jackson, one of the committee's members, was one of the Senate's most respected members and known as its leading expert on strategic affairs. Indeed, Jackson had been a strong advocate of deep cuts for SALT II and, when asked by Carter, had submitted his guidelines for the SALT negotiations to the president. Carter was aware that he needed Jackson's support. If he decided to adopt parts of the senator's proposal, Jackson would bring with him hardline senators and the Joint Chiefs of Staff. When Carter had to retreat to the Vladivostok ceilings, Jackson accused the president of retreating, as Paul Warnke had predicted. Indeed, Warnke's appointment as director of ACDA and, in that capacity, chief SALT negotiator, had been an early bitter battle in the Senate, forecasting trouble for the administration on SALT II. Forty senators—six more than needed to defeat a treaty—had voted against Warnke because he was felt to be too soft on arms control; that is, he would not bargain hard enough (fifth-eight senators voted for his appointment). The signal sent to the White House was clear: take a firm stance during the negotiations to get a fair and equitable agreement. The Warnke vote "was a statement of the Senate's determination to exercise independent judgment in assessing the SALT II accords."[15]

Mobilizing Bipartisan Support

As the treaty was being concluded and about to reach the Senate for its consent, the senators could be divided into three main groupings. About twenty senators were completely opposed to any treaty with the Soviet Union; fifteen additional senators could be classified as arms-control skeptics. Approximately forty-five senators could be classified as arms controllers because of their support of the SALT negotiations and belief that an agreement constraining the arms race was preferable to an unrestrained one.[16] A third category of around twenty senators were the swing votes who would be wooed intensely by the administration to make up the needed sixty-seven votes, and by the opposition to stop the vote short of the magic number.

Those opposed to or skeptical about, SALT II were so because of their anxiety about the mixture of expansionist Soviet–Cuban behavior in Africa and the growing Soviet military arsenal. The Soviets had since SALT I replaced their old missiles with an entire new generation of missiles. Although the SS–19 was considered by the Defense Department as the more dangerous missile because of its greater accuracy, the critics focused on the huge SS–18 and the administration's failure to get Moscow to accept far fewer than just over 300 heavy missiles. By contrast, Carter had canceled the B–1 bomber intended as a replacement for the again B–52, slowed down the development of the new Trident submarines and the Trident I and II SLBMs, remained undecided about the development of a new, larger, mobile MX land-based missile to replace the increasingly vulnerable Minuteman, and had also canceled—after seeming for a while to be unable to decide—the neutron bomb for NATO forces. SALT II, according to its critics, did not reverse what they saw as a strategic balance shifting in favor of the Soviet Union. The last had the momentum while the American president canceled and slowed down necessary replacements or improvements in U.S. weapons. This suggested that the president was unreliable on defense issues.

The treaty was to be managed on the Senate floor by the chairman of the Foreign Relations Committee, Senator Church; but its most effective proponent was the majority whip, Senator Alan Cranston (D-Calif.), who had earlier organized an informal study group of approximately twenty senators, mainly Democrats and arms control supporters, although not all were enthusiastically pro-SALT II. This group received briefings from the president's national security assistant, secretaries of state and defense, director of the CIA, and others, and most of them took a major role in replying to the critics' views and presenting the administration's case for SALT II. SALT supporters pointed to the fact that the Soviets would have to scrap several hundred older missiles to reach the 2,250 ceiling; limit themselves to one new ICBM (the Soviets have tended to introduce several missiles of a new generation at a time); promise not to produce and deploy the SS–16 ICBM; and limit the number of warheads on ICBMSs to ten and SLBMs to fourteen. In addition, SALT would not prevent the eventual deployment of the U.S. mobile MX missile (the limit on the number of warheads on Soviet missiles and the proposed deployment of 200 large U.S. MX missiles—to which Carter finally agreed—would greatly reduce the vulnerability of the American deterrent) and would exclude American forward based systems, such as those in Europe and on aircraft carriers in the Mediterranean, North Sea, and Atlantic, from which aircraft with nuclear bombs could reach the Soviet Union. In short, SALT II would be better than no SALT at all. "Passing the

SALT" would avoid a new era of uncertainty, accelerated arms competition, and greater defense spending.

Not all senators were either for or against SALT II. There were some liberal senators strongly for arms control who felt that the high ceilings merely legitimated the arms race, neither stopping nor reversing it. To win sufficient support, as just noted, President Carter had committed himself to the MX at an estimated cost of $40 billion (some estimates were considerably higher). This group even threatened to vote against SALT. There were other senators, many of them members of the swing vote, who generally favored arms control as well but shared the concern of many critics about the momentum of the arms race in which the Soviets were doing the racing and the United States the ambling. The Carter budgets had not increased defense spending as rapidly as domestic expenditures, leading critics to charge that the U.S. strategic posture was vulnerable. Led by Senator Sam Nunn from Georgia, they wanted a commitment from the administration for a 5 percent real increase (over inflation) in the defense budget over the next five years. Nunn in his few years in the Senate had established a leading reputation in the military area, especially in conventional armaments. He was greatly concerned with NATO's conventional ability to defend itself now that the Soviets had neutralized America's strategic power. Such increases for "guns" rather than "butter" only further annoyed the liberals, intensifying their threat to defect.

The alignments were even more complicated by the time of the 1980 presidential elections. Clearly, a SALT treaty would be a major achievement for the president; such a treaty could be equated with ensuring U.S. security and peace. But the year before a presidential election is not exactly ideal for important but controversial foreign policy moves if the aim is not to lose votes. The Republicans were opposed to many of Carter's foreign policies. By and large, they considered his foreign policy a failure. On the Warnke appointment, twenty-eight of the Senate's thirty-eight Republicans had voted negatively. This early attack was significant, reflecting both partisanship and genuine concern about the trend of Carter's policies.[17] Simultaneously, they felt that Carter had acted as a strong partisan from the beginning, not only with the deep cuts proposal, but also since he did not give the Republicans the credit they felt they deserved for saving Carter from defeat several times—most importantly on the Panama Canal treaties. Bipartisanship thus was nearing its end; responsible partisanship, as Fred Iklé, former ACDA director under Ford and undersecretary of defense for policy under Reagan, argued in a new Republican journal called *Commonsense*, might well be "the best medicine with which to cure an ailing foreign policy."[18]

Minority Leader Howard Baker, whose support for the Panama Canal treaties had been critical to their successful passage, and on whose support Carter had again counted for SALT II, had a special problem: he wanted to be president. His vote for Panama had angered many Republicans; if he wanted to be the party's nominee, he had to oppose SALT II. His rivals were all in favor of a treaty but with major changes. Baker thus found SALT II "seriously flawed" and expected to lead his party in the Senate into battle. Especially if the hearings could be televised, Baker would gain a great deal of publicity. The treaty was, therefore, bound to become a key political issue between the parties; and the debate would raise the issue of the broader U.S.–Soviet political context within which SALT II was occurring.

A simple rejection was one way of defeating the treaty. The Senate could also achieve this in another way; by amending the terms of the treaty. This would require renegotiation. The Soviets had already said they would not renegotiate. On the other hand, "understandings" or "interpretations" could be attached without killing the treaty. They clarified to the other contracting party the terms on which the treaty was being signed; they were unilateral declarations not requiring renegotiating. A reservation, that may limit rather than clarify the consequences of a treaty is also possible; they may, of course, lead the other state to make its own reservations.

What was striking during the Senate debate, and even before, was the activity of pressure groups. The advocate of SALT II was a group called Americans for SALT composed of many distinguished former government officials; the group kept in close touch with the White House and was, in a sense, its unofficial arm. The principal spokesmen and lobbyists for the administration, of course, were the president, Brzezinski, and the secretaries of state and defense; Hamilton Jordan headed the overall public relations effort from the White House, assigning responsibilities to those who were to be in charge of congressional liaison, the general public, and the media. Even though they had no spokesman to match the prestige of the president, the anti-SALT groups, which organized earlier, were the most vocal and gained much of the publicity. Unlike the administration, which waited until the agreement had been completed to start rallying support, the emerging treaty had already been heavily criticized by the anti-SALT forces. The American Conservative Union, the American Security Council, the Coalition for Peace Through Strength, and perhaps most prominently, the Committee on the Present Danger, whose members included many former high officials who had influence with conservative and moderate members of Congress, all possessed money. Mostly raised by conservative organizations and large corporate contributions, the amount could buy newspaper advertisements and time on television. The Coalition for Peace Through Strength reportedly estimated that it might spend $10 million to defeat SALT, and the American Conservative Union had already raised $400,000 by attacking the treaty on over 350 television stations before the superpowers had even announced agreement on SALT II.[19] Influential individuals, like President Ford and Henry Kissinger, initially kept quiet but later were critical of the agreement and/or what they perceived to be the Carter administration's weak resistance to the Soviet Union's expansionist policies.

Carter on the Defense

The administration, then, was on the defensive from the very beginning. Even as the treaty came to the Senate floor, it did so only after coming out of the pro-SALT Foreign Relations Committee by a bare 9 to 6 vote. The president's prestige had sunk to a low point in 1979. As the economy grew worse in a year when oil prices rose 100 percent, the public perception of President Carter's competence declined sharply. This perception had preceded OPEC's frequent price rises and was independent of these increases, although not his management of the economy as inflation rose into the double-digit column—soaring up to 20 percent. The sense that the president held a job beyond his capabilities was not limited to domestic affairs; while the Camp David agreement preceding the Egyptian–Israeli peace treaty brought the president great acclaim, this foreign policy achievement was the exception. The normalization of relations with China, the Panama Canal treaties, and SALT II gained Carter few points in the public opinion polls. By the time of SALT II, it was clear that the president was going to be challenged for renomination by a member of his own party, Senator Kennedy, who characterized the administration foreign policy as one of "lurching from crisis to crisis." The Kennedy name had long possessed a magic and wide appeal. Reportedly, many senators and legislators appealed to Kennedy to run; they felt that running with Carter they might go down to defeat. Carter, by the time he was halfway through his first term, stood at a lower popular rating than had Richard Nixon at a comparable point. Kennedy leading the Democratic ticket would be more likely to aid their reelection.

Carter lost further ground when intelligence reports sighted a Soviet combat brigade in Cuba. He had been cruising down the Mississippi River, relaxing as well as campaigning, followed by a vacation at his home in Plains, Georgia. Instead of releasing the information and leading the discussion of its meaning and the proper actions to be taken, the administration informed the chairman of the Senate Foreign Relations Committee, Senator Church, normally a dove, who was running for reelection in Idaho. So Church took the initiative with a hawkish stance, denouncing the Soviet move and demanding that the Senate put off negotiations on SALT II until Moscow had removed the brigade. He was soon followed by Senator Richard Stone (D-Fla.), also preparing to run for reelection in a state very conscious of Cuba's presence because of its proximity. Carter was caught by surprise and followed suit, calling the Cuba situation "unacceptable." Since he did not want another missile crisis type of confrontation, which was hardly warranted by the presence of a brigade, he had to retreat from his publicly taken stance when the Soviets denied that they had a combat brigade in Cuba. The brigade was merely a training brigade taking its regular field exercises. The president accepted this reassurance.

The episode seemed to be another example of a president not in charge, and his reputation went down a few more notches. Thus, an issue that did not affect the strategic balance almost torpedoed an issue of far greater priority because of the administration's ineptness, and the president, still short of the needed votes, probably lost one or two more. Above all, the administration lost time—about a month—while SALT II was caught up in the larger issue of Soviet policy, a linkage Carter had resisted from the beginning of his administration; Afghanistan came shortly thereafter. By raising the issue of the Soviet brigade, two senators (each of whom went down to defeat in 1980) cost Carter four weeks and may have destroyed the president's final chance for gaining Senate approval. For the Soviet invasion of Afghanistan was too blatant an act. SALT II, a complex treaty negotiated over a two-year period, finely tuned to both United States and Soviet interests, thus faced ultimate defeat and was withdrawn. An election year was hardly a year for its revival unless Moscow pulled its troops out of Afghanistan—which it did not do.

The surprising thing is that despite all this the Carter administration almost gained Senate approval by commitments to: (1) a 5 percent real increase in defense spending for several years; (2) the $40 billion MX; and (3) a major reduction of strategic arsenals in SALT III (while in the meantime both sides would presumably improve their arms in an arms race that had already become qualitative rather than quantitative). President Carter had, to be sure, made more than his share of mistakes, including the initial decision to go for deep cuts rather than sign SALT based on Vladivostok and, later, the timing of the U.S. recognition of Communist China. Each of these moves at the time antagonized Moscow and stalled negotiations. Carter could have had SALT II early on in his administration while his popularity and prestige were still high; the March proposals thwarted the effort and compelled him to retreat to the Vladivostok guidelines. In the final analysis, however, despite the president's errors, the fact remains that three administrations had negotiated with the Soviets on SALT II and shaped the agreement, a reflection that they believed such a treaty was in the national interest. A majority existed in the Senate for the treaty, at least until Afghanistan, and public opinion polls consistently showed a sizable majority of the American people favored SALT II.

Yet the two-thirds Senate majority proved too high an obstacle to overcome. Admittedly, Carter's ways with the Congress, as on other issues, left something to be desired. Many of the president's aides had no experience in Washington and, therefore, no experience in how to deal with Congress. "They didn't know anything about the Congress, and they don't like the Congress. The price for their amateurism and hostility has been too high.

They are learning, but maybe not soon enough," said a sympathetic Democrat who had served in the Congress for many years.[20] Some less sympathetic probably felt Carter never learned. "Carter does good things badly," admitted a member of the administration.[21] In addition, the president was consistently inconsistent, one day aligning himself with his secretary of state who believed that nothing must stand in the way of a SALT agreement and the next day sounding like his national security assistant who, concerned by Soviet behavior, was seeking to link SALT to Soviet foreign policy moves. On the one hand, SALT was important enough to stand by itself and, on the other, SALT was to be viewed as an integral part of the broader pattern of U.S.–Soviet relations.

Still, President Carter did a number of things that should have won him the necessary votes. First, as already noted, was soliciting Jackson's proposals for SALT II. Second, he appointed Lt. Gen. Edward Rowny as representative of the Joint Chiefs of Staff to the SALT delegation. This appointment was striking because Rowny was the first military man to be part of the SALT team and because the general was close to Senator Jackson. In short, Carter was trying to reassure the hardliners that the Joint Chiefs of Staff would be fully represented. Well intended, this move backfired when Rowny resigned and became an articulate critic of SALT II during the Senate hearings (and was later appointed by Reagan as chief strategic arms control negotiator). Third, Vice President Mondale, more knowledgeable of the ways of Congress, appointed a group of fourteen representatives and twenty-five senators to serve as advisers to the SALT delegation. Over a third of this group were to spend time with the U.S. delegation at the negotiations in Geneva, Switzerland, and participate in both formal and informal discussion with the Soviet delegation. Clearly, the administration was seeking to involve the Congress and strengthen some senators' vested interests in SALT II in hopes they would become its defenders and proponents in the upper chamber. Indeed, for the Senate as a whole, according to Steve Flanagan, senior Carter officials addressed SALT issues at almost fifty hearings from February 1977 to the 1979 Carter–Brezhnev Vienna summit, where the SALT II treaty was signed. A variety of officials briefed senators on 140 occasions and Senate staffers about 100 times. Together, with informed contacts, administration officials kept the Senate fully informed of the state of negotiations.[22] And fourth, in early 1979, in an attempt to defuse conservative critics, Carter replaced Warnke with retired Lt. Gen. George Seignious. A member of a lobby opposed to SALT II, he became an articulate spokesman for the treaty and, unlike his more combative predecessor, got along well with both liberals and conservatives.[23]

The Soviets, of course, share the blame for the demise of SALT II. In 1972, SALT I had been acclaimed as symbolic of—and an essential ingredient in—détente. But as American–Soviet relations declined over the following years and SALT II dragged on, disillusionment with détente and arms control set in. Soviet actions, often with Cuban military help, in Angola, Ethiopia, South Yemen, and Afghanistan (where there was a Soviet-supported coup in 1978 before the invasion by the Soviet army a year later) all appeared to American perceptions as attempts to exploit détente in the Soviet Union's favor. The rapid, enormous, and continuing growth of Soviet strategic as well as conventional power raised widespread concern over Soviet intentions and growing fears of what they might do with all this new military hardware. Thus by the time SALT II had been agreed on, there had been a large-scale erosion of confidence in détente and expectations about its benefits. Still, despite all this, SALT II could have received Senate approval.

The president, to be sure, was error prone and proved to be a major obstacle to achieving his desire for SALT II by repeatedly antagonizing the Soviets or the Senate with his decisions. And the Soviets refused to restrain themselves from any opportunities to advance their influence, even temporarily, to ensure Senate approval of SALT II. In the final analysis, however, responsibility for the failure of SALT lies clearly with the Senate and the treaty process. A treaty that, from the time the negotiations had begun during the Nixon administration, had taken a total of fifty months to conclude (twenty-nine under Carter) and had been judged to be in the national interest of the United States by three presidents, a majority in the Senate, and public opinion, fell victim to the institutional conflict between executive and legislative branches of the federal government and the American political process. Even sixty-five senators for the treaty—fourteen more than the simple majority required for any other piece of legislation, including the federal budget—was not sufficient. Clearly, one conclusion is that congressional participation in the SALT negotiations is no guarantee of its political support for the final agreement.

The Electoral Cycle

Note, finally, three impacts of democratic elections. First, confronting competition within the Republican party from Governor Reagan and the right, President Ford dropped détente and SALT II as a hot potato during his campaign for nomination in 1976. Then, accused by Carter in the subsequent presidential contest of not having been tough enough with the Soviets, he never picked up SALT II again, although Kissinger was close to a final agreement. In short, the year of a presidential election campaign tends to be a year in which controversial foreign policy issues are, if not jeopardized, at the very least placed in limbo.

Second, when the "new team" takes over if the "outs" are elected, another year may be wasted as the members of this team get to know one another, each other's strengths and weaknesses, how to get along with bureaucracy, and to what extent to trust and follow its experts' advice. In addition to personnel not being familiar with one another, each administration arrives in office thinking it can do things better than its predecessor. Thus it is committed to innovation. The first year of a new administration, then, tends to be like a shakedown cruise for a new ship, to see how shipshape it is and to work out the bugs and make it a more efficient vessel. Almost invariably, this is the year of the mistakes, for instance, Kennedy's sanctioning of the Bay of Pigs operations in 1961 and Carter's 1977 SALT II proposals and simultaneous human rights attacks on the Soviet Union.

Only in the second and third years can a new administration expect to get much done as the desire to innovate is tempered and illusions give way to pragmatism in the real world.[24] By year four, it is back to the presidential primaries and election. SALT II's demise, while obviously heavily influenced by the increasing disillusionment in the country with Soviet behavior as a result of Soviet–Cuban moves in Africa, Soviet–Vietnamese moves in Cambodia, the Cuban "Soviet brigade," incident, and Soviet moves in Afghanistan, was also the result of U.S. domestic politics and the four-year presidential cycle. Carter's early moves lost critical time. When the treaty reached the Senate, election politics were already beginning and, given that only thirty-four votes were needed to defeat the treaty, the president's task became formidable although not impossible. The Soviet invasion of Afghanistan saved the president from a possible defeat in the Senate and ended hopes for SALT II.

Third, a new administration may be tempted to improve on its predecessor's proposals or strike out on an entirely new course. The Carter administration wished to do things better than Kissinger had; it was seduced by the idea that it could achieve genuine arms control by attaining deep reductions, not just sanction the high levels of armaments both powers already had. Carter could have gained Senate approval of SALT II had he wrapped it up quickly based on the terms basically already negotiated by Kissinger (which is essentially what Carter did accept in 1979). In a country with frequent elections, and a presidential one each four years, each administration wants to present its policy as different from, and better than, its predecessor's. This is especially difficult when the issues and problems confronting any new administration are the same as the previous one and when policy continuities stand out. Still, the temptation to do it differently is there. Carter paid for this as the treaty was not finalized until American–Soviet relations had become embittered and support for SALT II had eroded.

Ronald Reagan's election is the evidence. He condemned SALT II as "totally flawed." Concerned with the growth of Soviet influence during the 1970s, and perceiving a shift in the strategic balance, the new administration was in no hurry to revive the SALT process. In fact, it blamed the arms control process for what it claimed to be America's strategic inferiority. Thus the Reagan administration preferred unilateral rearmament to bilateral arms control to ensure U.S. security. Yet while public opinion favored Reagan's arms buildup during the first three years, it also favored arms control. Therefore, Reagan agreed that he would not undercut SALT II. Ironically, having denounced SALT II, the president now found himself observing its limits. This was a new wrinkle in the treaty process: the Senate does not give its consent to a presidential agreement but the president acts as if it has become a treaty! There was another difference as well. In November 1986, the president announced that the United States would exceed the limits established by SALT II, but the Congress then threatened to use its power of the purse to compel the administration to maintain the unratified SALT agreement.

There is, therefore, an irony to the fact that Reagan was to run into considerable opposition when he sought the Senate's approval for his Intermediate Nuclear Forces (INF) agreement in 1988. In fact, INF was something of a misnomer. Not only did Reagan and Soviet General Secretary Gorbachev agree to eliminate all existing intermediate-range nuclear forces (600 to 3,000 miles), but they agreed to eliminate all short-range missiles as well (300 to 600 miles). Hence, the term *double zero.* In any event, when the most conservative post-World War II anti-Soviet president signed an arms control agreement—after years of attacking Moscow and arms control—he was suddenly denounced by the "Reaganauts" or right-wing Republican conservatives, both in and out of the Senate. One of his most zealous former supporters called the president "a useful idiot for Soviet propaganda" and strategy! Having cried for years "Let Reagan be Reagan"—for they always blamed what they saw as Reagan's lapses from orthodoxy on the president's staff—these former Reaganauts could not believe that their hero had committed such a heretical act. They were opposed to any agreement with the "evil empire." Yet Reagan's record as governor of California and president would suggest that despite firmly, if not tenaciously held conservative views, he was in the final analysis a pragmatist who would compromise when he felt it desirable or necessary.

The ratification process in the Senate occurred in an election year. But in contrast to the situation when Republicans and some conservative Democrats attacked Carter's SALT II, INF was attacked by some conservatives, although by no means all, but received overwhelming Democratic support. In a series of presidential debates, four of the six Republican candidates criticized the INF agreement; only Vice President Bush was strongly in favor. Senator Robert Dole, the minority leader, seeking to attract Republican conservatives, initially hedged his position, stating that he first wanted to examine the agreement and learn more about it during the Senate debate. But he quickly changed his mind and, as senate minority leader, asked and was given the right to read into the record a strong statement of support for INF before the Foreign Relations Committee called the secretary of state as its first witness. By contrast, all of the Democratic candidates supported the INF agreement.

To cut his losses among his followers, Reagan, on the eve of Gorbachev's visit to Washington to sign the INF agreement, released a report charging the Soviet Union with a new technical violation of the 1972 ABM treaty. The paradox was startling. The president was about to sign his only arms control agreement; it would be his only significant accomplishment with the Soviets, one that he had to hope would provide a place for him in history and recoup his reputation after the Iran–Contra affair. For years, the administration had opposed signing arms control agreements, citing past Soviet violations. Now it accused Moscow of another violation, yet it was signing a new agreement with Gorbachev. On the one hand, Reagan was giving his critics, who had opposed the treaty, additional ammunition. On the other hand, by coming out with a tough report, he was trying to reduce criticism and opposition by reminding his old followers that since he was well aware of past Soviet violations, his administration would remain fully alert to future ones. To reiterate, there could have been no greater irony than that Ronald Reagan should have been attacked by some of his most devout followers for a treaty negotiated by Max Kappelman, the chief arms negotiator, and Paul Nitze, the chief arms control adviser, both hawks, both former Democrats, both disillusioned by what they saw as their party's post-Vietnam dovishness, and both leaders of the Committee on the Present Danger, a chief critic of past arms control agreements. Yet polls on the eve of the signing of the agreement showed that Republicans approved the prospective treaty by the same 2 to 1 margin as the general public; even Republican conservatives approved by 5 to 3.

It was late May before the Senate finally approved it on the eve of President Reagan's summit trip to Moscow. A number of obstacles delayed Senate approval. There were questions about verification, which had presumably been settled, which needed further clarification from the Soviets. The Senate also sought assurances that futuristic intermediate-range weapons were also banned under the INF agreement. In addition, the administration also created a major problem with the Democrats. Having earlier sought to reinterpret the 1972 ABM treaty to allow it to test components of the anti-missile defense shield of the United States (see below), the Senate insisted that Reagan officials provide it with assurances that the interpretation of the treaty provided by them will be binding on future administrations. In the final analysis, however, once these issues were settled it was conservative Republicans, especially Senator Jesse Helms (R-N.C.), who delayed Senate support so long that Senate Minority Leader Dole denounced them for embarrassing their own president. Confronted with a bipartisan determination to shut off further debate, the critics of the treaty gave up, and the Senate, by a vote of 93–5 gave its consent to the INF agreement.

REAGAN AND STAR WARS

The Reagan administration's preference for unilateral rearmament was also the opposite side of the coin of its initial hostility to arms control.* The president and his secretary of defense were the first high officials in the

---

*The INF treaty stemmed from a U.S. propaganda proposal made in 1981. The zero proposal was not intended to be accepted but to make possible the U.S. deployment of INF. The Soviets did reject it, but when Gorbachev reversed the Soviet position and accepted the U.S. proposal, President Reagan could hardly reject it. Moreover, by 1986–87, Reagan needed an agreement to help repair his reputation, battered by the Iran–Contra affair.

postwar period to state categorically that the Soviet Union had achieved strategic superiority and that as a result of the momentum of the 1970s Soviet arms buildup the United States was already in second place. In making this claim, the president and secretary of defense were alone, as they were in attributing this condition mainly to the arms control process.[25] The Soviets, Reagan and Weinberger contended, signed agreements that lulled the democracies—which identified arms control with peace and improved U.S.–Soviet relations—relaxing their vigilance and letting down their guard. In addition, Reagan was perhaps the most anticommunist and anti-Soviet president of all the U.S. presidents since the beginning of the Cold War. Critical of the previous decade's détente, he was committed to containment and confrontation. The president was harsh in his denunciations of the Soviet Union. Its leaders, he said rather undiplomatically, would "lie, steal, and cheat" to advance their goals; communism was "the focus of evil in the modern world," which the scriptures and Jesus obligated the United States to oppose with all its might. Arms control agreements with the Soviet Union were therefore among the last things the administration favored. Even Reagan's Republican predecessor, President Nixon, and Henry Kissinger, his NSA and later secretary of state, were suspect because they had pursued détente and arms control.

SDI and the Antinuclear Movement

Among the reasons for Reagan's 1980 election was public concern about the arms balance; a majority of Americans by the late 1970s felt that the nation should spend more on defense.[26] Interestingly, in the 1980 election, Carter led Reagan by twenty-five points as the best candidate for keeping the United States out of a war; Reagan had a similar lead as the best candidate for strengthening U.S. defense and enhancing respect for the United States overseas. But as spending for the armed forces rose significantly after Reagan's election, this defense buildup gradually eroded support for continuing defense increases. By 1984 that was clear.[27] On the other hand, during Reagan's first years in office, the public was concerned that the president's tough rhetoric and assertive stance might get the nation involved in war. The mood of post-Vietnam isolationism might be fading, but the memories of Vietnam remained strong. Anxiety about Reagan as a trigger-happy cowboy remained high until it became clear that the president was a hardliner in rhetoric but cautious in policy and not impetuous or reckless. When he got into trouble, as in Lebanon, he cut his losses. When he used force, he did so quickly, successfully, and with minimal losses—and always against miniopponents, never the Soviet Union. But this too was not apparent until 1984.

The military buildup was thus both reassuring and worrisome because it was accompanied by rhetorical confrontation and increased Soviet–American tensions. The administration's course in Central America was particularly worrisome; so was its negative attitude toward arms control. The arms race thus became a matter of widespread concern. In the administration's lobbying for the MX (Missile Experimental), called *peacekeeper* by the president, a wholly new rhetoric was being introduced that frightened many people. The entire rationale for strategic deterrence had been to deter nuclear war; and the appeal of arms control was to ensure that deterrence would not break down. Now, however, the administration talked not only of modernizing these forces to strengthen deterrence, but of what might happen if deterrence failed. "Nuclear war fighting," "limited nuclear war," and "prevailing" in a nuclear exchange became commonly heard phrases in Washington. "Counterforce strategy," "preemptive strikes," "launch-under-warning" (or attack) were mixed with strong denunciations of the former deterrence policy, called *mutual assured destruction* (MAD). MAD was a strategy in which deterrence had relied for its effectiveness in preventing the enemy's first strike by threatening to destroy the opponent's society—economy and people—in a *second* strike. This strategy of "assured destruction" would cause such disproportionate losses to any conceivable gains that it would deter any enemy not bent on committing national suicide. The administration criticized this strategy as being immoral because it was genocidal and no longer credible since the Soviet Union could not destroy the United States as well.

The constant denunciations of the Soviet Union, the lack of arms control negotiations, the new arms race, and the accompanying explanations stimulated a strong antinuclear movement by 1982 as fears of war increased.[28] Numerous books appeared reminding everyone that nuclear war was bad for one's health. Then the Catholic bishops, followed by the Methodist bishops, condemned nuclear weapons as immoral, even if used only in retaliation. Nuclear weapons were thus bad for the soul as well.[29] The Catholic bishops had also let it be known that they would oppose MX, the missile the president felt was critical for the modernization of the U.S. deterrent. More fundamental, the effect, if not the intention, was to undermine moral support for deterrence. Several television films focused on the gruesomeness of the "day after" (never explaining how or why the deterrence that had worked the "day before" for four decades had suddenly broken down). In the midst of all this, as if the effects of blast, heat, and radiation stemming from a nuclear explosion were not bad enough, a new report emphasized that another result would be a nuclear winter.[30] Sunlight would be blotted out by the soot rising from burning cities, resulting in a long and deep freeze, threatening all vegetation and animal life. The extinction of humanity itself, not just the combatants and their allies, was a real possibility.

It was in these circumstances that President Reagan, confronted with a major and mounting political problem for his defense buildup, proposed his Strategic Defense Initiative (SDI) to render missiles "impotent and obsolete."[31] Reagan simply stole the antinuclear movement's clothes. He too condemned nuclear weapons as immoral; he too was committed to peace and the abolition of all nuclear arms. Instead of waiting for deterrence to fail, why not switch from strategic deterrence to strategic defense? Would it not be better to replace mutual assured destruction with mutual assured survival? Was it not better to save lives than to avenge them? From being on the defensive, the president seized the initiative in the nuclear debate and reduced the fears that had been initially aroused by his administration's arms buildup and emphasis on a war-fighting strategy. From being widely perceived as a warmonger, he had now cloaked himself as the leading peacemonger, although that did not prevent the Catholic bishops from opposing SDI as well five years later.

SDI, whatever its strategic rationale, was a politically shrewd move.[32] Interestingly, it came at the end of a speech to the nation. The president added the last paragraph himself after the rest of the speech had been put together by his speech writers. Thus, SDI was hardly the product of an initial research and development effort to resolve technical uncertainties, followed by a long thought-out process to reach conclusions about military strategy and force structures, the normal pattern. MAD, for example, had been the result of considerable debate within the government and the academic community interested in military issues. It had evolved over a number of years as participants thought hard about the impact of such revolutionary and destructive weapons as nuclear arms on foreign, defense, and arms control policies.[33] Before Reagan's speech, the Defense Department had done no feasibility study. After all, the president was talking of exotic space-based weapons such as the laser and particle beams, which were soon to give the name "Star Wars" to SDI. None of these weapons and the accompanying computerized battle-management systems was a reality, or likely to be so until well into the twenty-first century. Reagan was proposing a vision, not a strategy. Research would be needed to demonstrate whether what the president said should happen would ever occur. Indeed, until the March 1983 speech, the Pentagon had dismissed the possibility of defending the population with a space-based defense. Bureaucratic politics on SDI was notable only for its absence.

None of this is to say that the president's proposal was just a whim. In 1967, when Reagan had just been elected governor of California and again during his presidential campaign, he had asked what could be done about incoming Soviet missiles. He had been shocked to hear "nothing."[34] (The threat of retaliation was supposed to prevent Soviet missiles from flying to U.S. targets.) After that, Edward Teller, the father of the hydrogen bomb, became a lobby of one—although in early 1982 he had received help from Reagan business friends, including beer magnate Adolph Coors—and his persuasive arguments for strategic defense fell on receptive ears. Another retired general, Daniel Graham, who promoted space defenses that relied more on current rather than future exotic technologies, was also active but his ideas were generally dismissed as impractical and uneconomical.[35] It was Teller's vision that Reagan included at the end of his speech, almost as an afterthought. The president's plan had not been submitted to any of the appropriate departments and therefore received neither technical nor policy analysis from the Departments of Defense or State, despite their obvious interest in such a dramatic strategy shift for the United States and the consequences it held for the nation and its allies. SDI was largely a rational response to the president's concern about defending the American people and, not least, it was intended to placate domestic opposition to his defense program.

SDI 1–SDI 3

SDI was controversial from the beginning.[36] However shrewd a move in the context of U.S. politics, it also suddenly undermined the deterrent basis on which United States and Western security had rested for four decades. Moreover, it turned out there were not one but three SDIs. SDI 1—the president's proposed nonnuclear population defense shield based in space—was quickly dismissed by many technologists and arms controllers. Such a future oriented system would be so complex and technically demanding that it was doubtful it could offer the 100 percent protection the president had promised. Even if it were 80 or 90 percent effective—which was dubious— enough Soviet missiles would be able to penetrate the "space shield" to destroy the United States. The reasons why such a high kill rate was doubtful were many: (1) the best time to destroy missiles was in their boost or takeoff phase, which did not last more than 300 seconds and could be shortened to 60 to 90 seconds; (2) once the warheads separated from their missiles in the mid-course phase, the multiplication of warheads would so greatly increase the targets that to destroy them all would be virtually impossible; and (3) whether a sufficient number of the remaining warheads could be destroyed in the terminal reentry phase was unknown. The point was that no matter how good U.S. technology might eventually be, it was questionable whether, if the first-time SDI had to work perfectly, it would. No tests could be carried out in advance to check each item of this space-based defense and to ensure that each would interact properly with all other components.

Moreover, since the Soviets were hardly likely to accept the president's assurance that he would share this new technology with them so that both powers could substitute SDI for their offensive missiles simultaneously, SDI was likely to stimulate not one but two arms races. One way the Soviets could seek to overcome SDI was by flooding it with more warheads than it could possibly handle. This meant a further Soviet offensive buildup, just as the United States had responded to the Soviet ABM in the 1970s by MIRVing or multiplying the warheads on its missiles to inundate and thereby overwhelm any Soviet defenses. Simultaneously, the Soviets would accelerate their own SDI research. Thus, the critics said, SDI would result in offensive and defensive arms races, which would be enormously expensive and in the end would leave both powers less secure than before.

SDI 2 did not create such intense controversy. Relying largely on then or soon-to-be available technology, basically ground based, SDI 2 was limited to missile protection. Ironically, the MIRVing of missiles in the 1970s to overcome the opponent's ABM defenses and still deliver the assured destruction blow to deter them had unforeseen results. Together with increasingly accurate guidance systems, the huge numbers of warheads now available make it possible to attack the enemy's retaliatory forces to try to cripple them *before* they could strike back. In these circumstances, SDI 2 made sense. It would reduce the potential vulnerability of land-based missiles, thereby ensuring the deterrent balance. Since such a defense was not mainly predicated on exotic space-based technologies, it would also be more affordable and feasible.

Unlike population defense, even a 50 percent defensive capability would suffice for missiles. If the potential attacker knows that even half the enemy's missiles will survive to retaliate against him, he will remain deterred. Not surprisingly, many in the Pentagon and Congress, skeptical about SDI 1, were attracted to SDI 2, and the Senate Armed Services Committee specifically went on record as favoring this more attainable goal. But note its critical difference from SDI 1, whose assumption was that with SDI's deployment, offensive missiles would be eliminated. They would be impotent and obsolete and could therefore be scrapped. SDI 2's assumption was that offensive missiles would remain. Deterrence, rather than being abolished, would be made safer to ensure against a breakdown by reinforcing the message to the other side that it could not prevent a devastating second strike even if it struck first. SDI 2 was also compatible with further arms control efforts.

SDI 3 was the Soviet's perception of the president's proposal as an offensive, not defensive system. If SDI 1 could not be made "leakproof" against an attack by thousands of warheads, a certain number of which would still be able to penetrate it to create enormous destruction, it could be effective against a retaliatory force already weakened by the opponent's first strike. The Soviets cited the Reagan administration's doctrinal emphasis on a counterforce strategy and the host of accurate warheads it was beginning to deploy: MX, cruise missiles, the B–1 bomber (which is supposed to penetrate Soviet air defenses, and which in the 1990s is to be supplemented by a new generation of so-called *Stealth Bombers,* which will be undetectable by radar), the Trident submarine, and the Trident II missile. MX and Trident II especially are potentially first-strike weapons.

Interestingly, the Soviet objection to SDI was thus the same as America's early 1970s objection to Soviet ABM deployment. Washington viewed the Soviet ABM as part of a first-strike strategy, since Soviet military doctrine emphasized preempting if nuclear war appeared likely and destroying as much of the U.S. retaliatory capability as possible to limit damage to itself. The deployment of a new generation of Soviet missiles after SALT I reinforced that fear, despite the ABM limitation in 1972 and reduction in

1974 to insignificant numbers. Soviet missiles were bigger and carried larger numbers of warheads than U.S. missiles and presumably, like American warheads, they were being fitted with ever more accurate guidance systems.

Incentive or Obstacle to Arms Control?

SDI, ironically, gave the Soviets an incentive for a major strategic arms reduction agreement. The Reagan administration, worried that U.S. ICBMs were becoming more vulnerable to a Soviet attack, had sought such a radical reduction of Soviet ICBMs and warheads to reduce this danger from the beginning. But it offered the Soviets little in return, not even the scrapping of the fifty MXs Congress finally allowed the administration. Even if it had gotten the 100 MXs it asked for, and even had it been willing to trade all 100 with their 1,000 warheads, MX was a weak bargaining chip to gain a major reduction of the over 600 Soviet ICBMs (of approximately 1,400) that the administration was worried about. But SDI proved—no doubt to Reagan's surprise—a powerful bargaining chip.

In part, this was undoubtedly due to the Soviet fear of SDI as part of an offensive strategy. Still, while the Soviet Union has always had great respect for U.S. technology, and because Soviet leaders may have feared that American scientists and engineers could do what they proposed to do, Soviet scientific advisers must also have expressed some doubts to their political leaders about the feasibility of SDI 1. Why then were the Soviets so worried that they resumed arms control negotiations from which they had walked out some months earlier? And why were they to offer the type of radical cuts the administration had been seeking? Why did Gorbachev, at the summit meeting in Iceland in 1986, offer a 50 percent cut in strategic forces when Brezhnev only a few years earlier had angrily rejected a much smaller cut proposed by the Carter administration?

It may well be that what frightened the Soviet leadership, beset with a stagnating economy at home and already unable to keep up with Western technological advances, was that SDI research—whether it would succeed in creating a population defense or not—would result in a quantum leap forward in the very area in which the United States had been successful and the Soviet Union had not: technological innovation.[37] The Soviets feared that the consequences of such a leap forward would be to set them even further behind with profound consequences for their standard of living, their military power, and their claim of being a model for the economic development of the less-developed countries, a claim already badly tarnished.

The Soviet interest, then, was in preventing an SDI deployment or, at least, in slowing it down and allowing Soviet science to catch up. The research could continue in the laboratories; that could hardly be prevented. But there was to be no testing or deployment of any SDI technology in space, as the two powers had agreed in the 1972 ABM treaty. SDI had thus given the Reagan administration the lever with which to gain the reduction of Soviet first-strike capability. SDI, like the U.S. ABM, was potentially a very powerful bargaining chip. However, while Nixon had been willing to use ABM in that way, Reagan was unwilling to do so. The president clung to his vision, talking of SDI as if it were already a reality instead of a research program that would take ten to twenty years to reveal whether it was even technologically feasible. Unwilling to accept any limitations on U.S. research and *testing,* he rejected Gorbachev's "grand compromise."

Thus, instead of being a bargaining chip, SDI became an obstacle to an arms control agreement on strategic weapons. The Soviets repeatedly stated that they should not be expected to radically lower the numbers of their strategic missiles when they did not know whether they even had enough to cope with SDI. Again, they were taking the American argument of the early 1970s. How could he accept limits on U.S. offensive missiles, President Nixon had asked, until he knew whether the Soviets intended to deploy a nationwide ABM system? If they were going to deploy such a system, the United States would need large numbers of missiles to penetrate these defenses; if not, the United States was willing to accept an upper ceiling on missile deployment. The president, now that Gorbachev presented him with the Nixonian argument, would not accept this linkage between the offensive and defensive arms races.

It is hard to understand why the president was not more compromising on SDI. He was not being asked to abandon his vision; and the Soviets were willing to make him a good offer while SDI research continued in the laboratories. But what the Soviets were unable to achieve, Congress might, for SDI stimulated governmental politics in the form of an executive–legislative confrontation. The Congress, especially the Democrats who controlled the House and, after the 1986 midterm election, the Senate as well, had never been enthusiastic about SDI, about whose purposes, feasibility, and costs the administration appeared divided. The enormous cost of SDI at the time of a huge budget deficit—the result of the Reagan administration's cutting of taxes while vastly increasing military spending—and sizable cuts in social services, was an additional factor. Last, there was the arms control impact. That SDI was likely to accelerate the defensive and offensive arms competition was very critically regarded by those favoring arms agreements. Indeed, there was a good deal of skepticism about the shift from deterrence to defense. The Senate specifically has insisted that SDI concentrate on protecting missiles, contending that population protection is impossible. The Office of Technology Assessment, in a 1988 report, concluded that SDI would suffer a "catastrophic failure" in defending the nation because it was simply too complex. Congress, in any event, cut funding for SDI every year after 1985.

The biggest fight, however, came over the 1972 ABM treaty. The Reagan administration, determined to go ahead with SDI, wanted to test elements of SDI in space rather than just confine its research to the laboratories. The administration could, of course, give six months notice that the United

States was withdrawing from the treaty, as required by its provisions. But that would have stirred enormous amounts of political trouble from Congress and the allies. The ABM treaty had more than any other agreement become a symbol of arms control and the restraint of the arms race (the deployment of defensive arms would have led to an offensive arms race to overcome them). Thus, instead of denouncing the treaty, the administration asserted that a broad interpretation would allow such testing.

This led to a confrontation with Congress, especially the Senate and Senator Nunn, who had become chairman of the Senate Armed Services Committee after the Democrats regained control of the Senate. Nunn, the Senate's leading expert on military affairs, reviewed the record of the ABM treaty negotiations and found that it supported the narrow or restrictionist interpretation.[38] All but one of the American negotiators of the treaty supported Nunn, but none of them had been asked for their views by the administration. Paul Nitze, the one exception, worked for the Reagan administration. Nunn informed the administration that the Nixon administration had submitted the narrow treaty and that it was this treaty to which the Senate had given its consent. Therefore, for the administration to unilaterally change the treaty that had been signed with Moscow and ratified by the United States would lead to a constitutional crisis with the Senate.* Just to make sure, the Senate Armed Services Committee voted an amendment to the 1988 defense authorization bill that blocks any testing that violates the traditional reading of the ABM treaty and the subsequent defense budget bound the president until the end of his term. While Republicans argued that this represented an unconstitutional restriction of presidential authority, Democrats replied that they were protecting the Senate's role in making treaties.

Faced with congressional reductions in funding, and a possible confrontation over the ABM treaty, the president might have accepted Gorbachev's offer. Instead, as his term was drawing to a close, Reagan tried to commit his successor and the Congress to SDI by pushing for early deployment. Funds were reportedly shifted in a crash effort from laser and particle-beam research to more immediately realizable kinetic-energy weapons that would destroy missiles in the initial boost phase by hitting them at extremely high speeds. These space-based kinetic-kill vehicles, as they were called, would be supplemented by 400 to 1,000 earth-based interceptor rockets to destroy the remaining warheads in the middle and late stages of their flight, since even the kinetic projectiles would be deployed only in token numbers. Such a system could stop no more than a small percentage of incoming warheads

---

*Somewhat to the surprise of his Senate colleagues, Nunn later came out for developing a limited antimissile defense system to protect the United States from accidental missile launchings by other nations—an argument reminiscent of Robert McNamara's 1960s argument that a limited ABM system would defend the nation against a Chinese attack. *New York Times*, January 20, 1988.

during a large-scale strike and, when first proposed by General Graham's 1982 High Frontier report under the lovely name of BAMBI (Ballistic Missile Boost Intercept), had been dismissed by the president's science adviser as a "mad scientist's dream." The concern after 1986, however, was mainly to start some deployment, even though it would not be the SDI the president had proposed and early deployment required a lowering of the system's performance requirements. The fact that in 1987 a panel of the American Physical Society, composed of leading physicists on exotic weapons technologies (including top scientists from the government's own weapons laboratories, all of whom had access to the research and development being done on SDI) stated that it would be ten or more years, perhaps the next century, before it would be known if these technologies were even feasible, did not deter the administration.[39] The administration was clearly concerned that if deployment had not started, SDI would be downgraded after it left office, becoming a bargaining chip and a long-term research program. The fear was probably correct. The House in 1987 rejected by a vote of 302 to 121 an amendment to begin deployment by 1994. But the 1987 budget cuts, which compelled the administration to cut back sharply in key development projects, set such a date back. Reagan's successor may perhaps be more tempted to negotiate the grand compromise—which might not replace deterrence but make deterrence safer. From the beginning, SDI had been the president's personal "baby." There had been no bureaucratic or congressional lobbying within or major think tank support outside the government for SDI. But it obviously mobilized support among military officials placed in charge in the SDI office, among industries that became involved in the funded research and development, and among Republicans loyal to the president. But even in the Defense Department, there was some skepticism about the value of SDI, the Joint Chiefs of Staff favoring a limited shield protecting land-based missiles. In any case, Bush will face a Democratic Congress opposed to early deployment.

Ronald Reagan is gone. The reason for this emphasis of the obvious is that despite his self-appraisal as a conservative, the president was in fact a populist utopian on nuclear weapons. However strong a part domestic politics and the freeze movement played in the presentation of SDI, Reagan's interest in strategic defense predated March 1983. His proposal to abolish offensive nuclear arms and rely on a defensive system was hardly a conservative concept. Conservatism stands for tradition, restraint, caution, and continuity. Deterrence was by 1983 a tradition of almost forty years. As strategic and technological changes occurred, deterrence adapted to these changing conditions. SDI 2 was consistent with this principle. But SDI 1 was a radical utopian proposal. Scrapping nuclear missiles was not only straight out of the antinuclear movement's plans, but to prove that it was not just a one-shot idea, Reagan at a 1986 weekend summit meeting with Gorbachev in Iceland proposed the total abolition of all nuclear weapons by 1996, with SDI now relegated to an "insurance" system in case anyone cheated and hid a few missiles. Deterrence, which had provided the United States and its Western allies with their basic security, was to be exchanged for Soviet acceptance of the mutual deployment of SDI. Gorbachev rejected SDI for the same reason his predecessor had denounced it. The point here is that one man's vision had changed the strategic debate. Deterrence was now immoral, replaced by an untried idea whose technology had not yet been developed. Its appeal as a means of saving the American people from nuclear destruction provided its populist component; its total break with deterrence was radical and its promise of secular salvation was utopian.

The second reason why the 1988 election will determine what happens to SDI is shorter. It will depend on how committed Bush will be to which SDI, the progress in the ongoing negotiations about the 50 percent cut in strategic missiles, and what the Soviets will offer in return for confining SDI research and development to the laboratory. Such an offensive cut would greatly reduce the potential threat to U.S. deterrence by the Soviet Union's large number of increasingly accurate warheads. It had originally been Reagan's aim to gain such a reduction. But by the time the Soviets were willing to negotiate such a deal, the president was wedded to his vision. A new president has no such commitment. He might prefer to continue in the best conservative tradition to preserve deterrence, perhaps supplementing it with elements of SDI 2, and reduce the budget deficit instead.

ENERGY POLICY: AN INTERMESTIC ISSUE

In examining energy policy at the international and national levels, we see the democratic dilemma in very straightforward terms. This intermestic policy clearly demonstrates bureaucratic/governmental politics to the ultimate degree, because virtually no participants see the stakes in the same way others do, and each is in some position to check the actions of most others. What we are studying, then, is nonpolicy making. There are no energy policies, but also there are too many such policies. We find ourselves in the situation of Buridan's ass, which found two bales of hay each so attractive that it starved to death trying to decide which one to devour. On energy policy, however, there are more actors, and few mind starving others if that means more of a scarce commodity for themselves. Alas, it does not, however, and what we see is a classic lack of coordination across and within the developed nations—and particularly in the United States. When so many actors become so intensively involved in an issue, conflict resolution becomes virtually impossible. When we have both national and international stakes involved, hopeless may be the only way to describe the situation that begs for international coordination.

In any event, in an increasingly interdependent world, the traditional distinctions between foreign and domestic policy making break down. For many years, policy making in such areas as energy and food was viewed as domestic in scope. To be sure, there were some international implications of these policies—such as the Food for Peace program, trade quotas on specific food commodities particularly when American markets were weak, and the problem of taxing multinational oil companies. But most of the supplies of both energy and food were both produced and consumed in the United States. The energy imported from abroad was extremely cheap—and plentiful. Thus, there was little concern with the foreign policy implications of resource policy.

The price explosion for oil that followed the outbreak of the Yom Kippur War in the Middle East in 1973, when Arab members nations of the Organization of Petroleum Exporting Countries (OPEC) imposed an embargo on nations supporting the political position of Israel, setting the stage for international concern for energy prices and availability. The realization in that year that supplies of oil could be shut off and that once supplies were resumed the cost would more than quadruple transformed energy into an international issue. One direct effect was to change the positions of Japan and most Western European nations to favor the Arabs in the Middle East conflict. These countries are far more dependent on Arab oil that is the United States. Six years later, following the fall of the shah, Iran cut off oil supplies to the West and the price spiral resumed.

However, the worldwide recession of the 1980s and increased conservation led to an abundance of petroleum and the price of oil fell to as low as $8 a barrel in 1986 from the high of $36 in the early 1980s. Some producing countries that had benefited so much from the boom of the 1970s found themselves saddled with enormous debts to Western (mostly American) banks. Many could not pay even the interest, producing a different type of international crisis (see Chapter 6). Domestic producers also suffered and the economies of Alaska, Texas, Louisiana, and Oklahoma that had also boomed during the 1970s plunged into deep recessions. Prices rebounded somewhat in 1987 to about $20 per barrel.

Still, some analysts warned of another oil crisis looming in the 1990s as consumption and imports both increased.[40] It is almost beyond question that oil resources will be exhausted much sooner than anyone had forecast before the 1970s. Unlike food, oil is not a renewable resource—there is not a "new crop" every year. Furthermore, while new areas of arable land can be created by irrigation or other technological breakthroughs, one cannot so easily will another oil field.[41] Energy resources are clearly now an issue of intermestic policies. The scarcity of energy resources had led Western nations to establish the International Energy Agency to pursue a joint strategy for reducing energy consumption and sharing burdens in the event of future shortages. However, domestic political considerations within each of the member nations have precluded effective action. No government can risk facing an electorate after it has agreed to give up some of its scarce energy resources. When Iran expanded its war with Iraq in 1987 and attacked neutral ships in the Persian Gulf, threatening much of the world's oil supply, the Reagan administration put eleven Kuwaiti tankers under American protection in the Gulf. However, America's Western European allies, who get far more of their oil from the Gulf than the United States does, refused to join the patrols.

The most disturbing element in facing an uncertain energy future is the set of political problems in domestic politics that dwarfs the problems in reaching agreement in international politics. One cannot expect an international energy program to be developed in the absence of agreement on a national energy strategy. But, within the United States, the political problems in confronting this issue are overwhelming. The problem is largely one of stakes. The stakes are large indeed, because energy affects everything we do—from driving to school or work to producing the energy itself and the food that sustains us all—as well as shipping that food to where we live. The amount of gasoline wasted simply when Americans throughout the country waited in gasoline lines in 1973–1974 and 1979 is staggering. There also are virtually no winners in energy shortages—only different levels of losing. To be sure, the oil companies may be profiting immensely as might some other speculators or inventors. But there are few who benefit from shortages; even the oil companies might prefer greater supplies and somewhat lower prices, if for no other reason than to improve their public image. Even such diverse "capitalist" nations as Canada, Mexico, and the countries of Western Europe have either nationalized oil companies or established government controlled corporations to oversee imports because they view the issue of energy shortages as one of overwhelming importance.

But such coordination has eluded the Americans. There have been no major movements to nationalize the oil companies, but Presidents Nixon, Ford, and Carter each proposed at least one comprehensive national energy policy. None met with much success in the Congress. The reason for this lack of action is straightforward: if all politics are local, as former House Speaker Thomas P. O'Neill has maintained, then energy politics are the most local of them all. The producing areas of the South, especially Texas and Louisiana, have little in common with the consumers of the North and the West. In the first states, temperatures are mild and oil consumption is not nearly so great in the winter as it is in New England. One can drive on the wide Texas freeways and see many cars with bumper stickers reading, "Drive faster, freeze a Yankee!" In 1986–87, when oil prices fell, the bumper stickers' message was different: "Please Lord, Give Us One More Oil Boom. We Promise Not to Abuse It This Time." In the meantime, consumers in the producing states, which benefited strongly from the drop in energy prices, proclaimed that the North had risen again.

CONGRESSIONAL COMMITTEES AND ENERGY POLICY

Not surprisingly, the Congress has reflected these divergent local concerns. Furthermore, the jurisdictional battles in the Congress make a coordinated attack on energy virtually impossible. Congressional committees are based on jurisdictions that affect major interests in the country: Agriculture, Armed Services, Education and Labor, Banking, Veterans' Affairs, and so forth. These interests are largely, but not exclusively, unaffected directly by each other. Few farming lobbies are concerned with the fate of a housing project for New York or Cleveland. But energy is different. As stated above, it affects everyone. A gallon of gas allocated to New Hampshire means a longer wait on a line in California. So almost every committee in the Congress has some jurisdiction over energy policy. In the Ninety-fifth Congress (1977–78), eighty-three committees and subcommittees actually held hearings on some aspect of energy policy in the House of Representatives, encompassing every member of the House who serves on a committee.[42] Five committees share jurisdiction over the Department of Energy authorization—Energy and Commerce, Science and Technology, Interior and Insular Affairs, Public Works and Transportation, and Foreign Affairs. The last body has not exercised its jurisdiction, but executive spokesmen still must repeat the same testimony to four different authorizing committees in the House and then appear before the Appropriations and Budget Committees in that chamber and the Appropriations, Budget, and Energy and Environment Committees in the Senate.

An attempt to restructure and rationalize energy jurisdictions in the House failed in 1980 because key legislators did not want to yield their power over various aspects of energy legislation and convinced others that power, that goal of all politicians, was not something they should be forced to yield.

The House of Representatives generally has had a more proconsumer tilt because it better represents the more populous consuming states of the East, the Midwest, and the West Coast. The Senate provides the producers a more congenial forum since Louisiana, Oklahoma, and Alaska are entitled to the same two senators per state as are New York and California. These regional splits were reflected in many legislative battles. In 1977–78 Carter, newly inaugurated, sent to Capitol Hill the most ambitious energy program ever proposed. The new president recognized that he faced severe political problems. When he proposed the program in a televised address to the nation in April 1977, he warned: "I am sure each of you will find something you don't like about the specifics of our proposal. . . . We can be sure that all the special interest groups in the country will attack the part of the plan that affects them directly."[43] He was correct. Business leaders and conservatives generally opposed the program's emphasis on conservation rather than on production. Environmentalists found the level of support for solar energy pitifully low and objected to plans for the development of nuclear technology. Labor thought the program would cut back the number of jobs in energy related fields and feared that the proposed gasoline tax of 50 cents a gallon would affect only the middle and lower classes; it also argued that further taxation of gas-guzzling cars would take jobs away from the automobile industry—not yet fully recovered from the recession following the oil embargo and certainly not yet anticipating the even worse slump of 1980. Rural members thought the taxes would discriminate against their constituents, while urban legislators believed that the administration's plan to rebate some of the proposed energy taxes signaled an abandonment of the president's commitment to mass transit. The oil companies viewed the program as a consumer plot to keep petroleum prices regulated, but consumer groups felt that the modest energy savings that would be accomplished at great costs to everyone but industry constituted a giant ripoff by the oil companies and OPEC. The House of Representatives quickly passed the president's bill but the Senate tore the legislation to shreds. Ultimately the two chambers reached an accord much closer to the Senate's bill—a far cry from the comprehensive legislation that Carter sought.

Little changed in the next couple of years. Many pressures on Carter and the Congress to produce some national energy program continued, but no one could produce a program that was acceptable to 435 members of the House and 100 senators. Senate Majority Leader Robert Byrd (D-W.Va.) summed up the dilemma: "Energy is so divisive, because here all of the parochial—all of the parochial and regional interests surface."[44] Following the long summer of 1979 when residents of California and major cities throughout the country spent thankless hours on gasoline lines, the president proposed a *standby* gasoline rationing plan that could be implemented in the event of a national emergency—not a plan to implement rationing itself, which he opposed (and Kennedy espoused in his bid to deny Carter renomination the following year)—but again parochial, local interests prevailed on the first Carter proposal despite a most unusual plea by the speaker to members to put aside parochial interests and vote for the plan. In contrast, Representative Tom Hagedorn (R-Minn.) stated:

> I care less about supplies in the Washington area and more about the citizens of the Second District of Minnesota who would be forced to wait for their ration checks in the mail. . . . I care about the citizens of the Second District who would be forced to pay the white market value for extra coupons that could be sold in downtown Manhattan and brought out to the Midwest and sold for three to four times as much.[45]

The Energy Policy Roller Coaster

The Reagan administration came into office with a commitment to letting the open market resolve the problem of energy supply. In 1981 the memories of gasoline lines of the summer of 1979 faded as an oil glut developed throughout the world. Reagan announced in his inaugural address that the price of gasoline, subject to regulation since the cutoff of supplies following the Yom Kippur War in 1973, would now be free to find its market level. Congress in 1978 had authorized the president to take this step, but Carter felt it would be both bad policy and politically too risky in any event. As the oil companies cheered "Free at last!" they proclaimed that the days of shortages were over, since the additional revenue would allow them to tap previously undiscovered or unprofitable sources of oil. For a short time exploration efforts skyrocketed, but these were washed away by the oil glut. There were now abundant supplies and the price of gasoline actually went down considerably.

The decline in oil supplies was not the result of decontrol, but rather of the worldwide recession brought about by the fiscal policies of the Reagan administration and some Western European governments. As the oil glut grew the incentives to develop other sources of fuel vanished. Synthetic fuel experimental projects were canceled in the United States and cut back in Canada, even though they were backed by governmental loan guarantees. The Reagan budgets dramatically cut back funding for research and development of solar energy. Yet, despite the glut in both oil and natural gas, gas prices actually were increasing in many parts of the country. The Natural Gas Policy Act of 1978, part of the compromise legislation reached in that year, had produced a strange result. Even as gas was in surplus in 1981–82, gas pipelines were permitted to sell their highest cost supplies to consumers, so prices were increasing at levels almost as great as those of the years of shortages. Reagan proposed deregulating the price of natural gas, but with prices rising it is no surprise that the attempt to do so failed.

In 1986–87 when prices for all energy products plummeted, the very same producer-state representatives who had clamored for decontrol of pricing now were back in Washington begging the government to save the oil industry. A decade ago—and much later—these producers would respond to the laws of supply and demand. If prices were lifted, more supplies would become available since producers would have incentives to seek higher profits. Yet by the late 1980s producers were arguing that energy was a distinctive commodity. The wells that had been "shut in" because they were no longer profitable could not simply be reopened. Oil wells were not like shoe stores; you could not simply reopen them when the public wanted more shoes. To shut in a well, one had to block it with cement and it was terribly expensive to blast out the cement and start pumping again. Energy was vital to national security. Producers demanded taxes on imported oil so that those supplies would become more expensive. In turn, people would use more domestic energy. This brought cries of foul play from northerners, who use more foreign than domestic oil. Northerners felt that the producing states had gouged them during the shortage years and they were not about to become suckers again. They now argued vigorously in favor of letting the market take its course. The issues had not changed—only which participants were on each side.

The crux of the domestic problem lies in the constituency politics of energy policy and in the supporting base for this type of politics in Congress. Thus, to a very large extent, international energy politics is a captive of the localism of energy policies in the nation and states. We also refuse to acknowledge that sacrifices might have to be made in the face of shortages.

Half of Americans still believe that the country does not face a serious energy shortage and only slightly more than a third believe that another energy crisis will be very likely to occur in the next decade, so that most Americans report not conserving much energy at all.[46] These responses are perhaps understandable in the midst of an energy glut, but they do not augur well for a more reasoned response to the next crisis compared to the previous ones. The United States is the world's largest importer of oil and the biggest exporter of food. We could perhaps reach agreement on some national energy policy if there was any evidence that we could use the food weapon as OPEC has employed the oil weapon, but this is highly questionable because such a small portion of our food exports go to OPEC nations. If such a strategy existed, we could find some way of reaching agreement on a national policy to determine how to allocate the new gains from our agricultural surplus, and we could reconcile such a strategy with the international political environment, since we export so much of our food to our allies and to Third and Fourth World nations, which would then face very high prices for both fuel *and* food. Could such a strategy bankrupt the national economy on which all nations, but particularly the dominant economic powers such as the United States, Europe, and Saudi Arabia, depend for their prosperity or simple survival? The international energy problem is not likely to be resolved in the immediate future despite the compelling need to do so. But the interconnections between domestic and international considerations makes the political problem seem even less tractable than the technological one.

AGRICULTURE: A DOMESTIC ISSUE GONE INTERNATIONAL

There have been hard times on American farms in the 1980s. Movies starring Jane Fonda, Jessica Lange, and Sissy Spacek have described the new traumas of farming families much as *The Grapes of Wrath* did for the Great Depression of the 1930s. The farm economy has not been as depressed at any time since the 1930s as it was in the 1980s. Fifteen years ago we heard threats of imminent famine throughout much of the developing world. Yet today the problem is not one of shortages, but one of *surpluses.* Saudi Arabia is giving away wheat it cannot store, China is exporting corn, and the small African state of Malawi is trading maize.[47]

The world has experienced a "green revolution" over the past two decades. New technologies have led to dramatic increases in production of many food commodities. When countries grow their own foodstuffs, they have less need to import them. As recently as the 1970s, agriculture was the largest single contributor to America's trade surplus.[48] Since 1981 agriculture exports have declined from their high of $44 billion to about $26 billion in 1986. In that year the United States imported more food than it exported for the first time this century. The American share of the market for all agricultural commodities has fallen by more than 20 percent. Wheat, feed grains, and soybeans have been hit particularly hard.[49] Increased production is only one reason for the decline in American food exports. A second cause is the Third World debt. Countries that have severe financial constraints simply have to cut back on their export purchases. Often they lack the Western currency to make the purchases. These developing countries had been the fastest growing market for American agricultural exports.

A third cause is more aggressive pricing policies by other nations. Japan, Canada, Argentina, Australia, and the European Economic Community all subsidize their agricultural products to make them more competitive in the international market. In 1985 the United States began using farm export subsidies as well, although the government had been indirectly subsidizing agriculture for many years.[50] Fourth, during the 1970s the high inflation induced by spiraling energy costs actually worked to the benefit of farmers. Their prices also dramatically increased, aided in part by poor Soviet grain harvests. The United States Department of Agriculture urged farmers to augment their own production. To do so, many farmers bought more land and expensive equipment to aid in planting and harvesting. When world supplies surged and demand remained steady—or declined in the developing countries—farmers were faced with massive debts. By 1986, 20 percent of farm loans had been declared "nonperforming" (or essentially uncollectible), as opposed to just 5 percent three years earlier. Farm income had plummeted and the average value of farmland dropped by almost 30 percent.[51] Movies about farmers once again focused on bankruptcy foreclosures.

There were calls for the government to step in to save the family farm. There was nothing new about this proposal. Government has been involved in the agricultural economy for three quarters of a century. The philosophy of government assistance for the farmers was to stabilize prices, the same logic that led originally to government controls on natural gas prices a half century ago.[52] By paying farmers to withhold excess supplies from the market, the government ensured that prices did not fluctuate wildly from one year to the next. This strategy not only provided farmers with a secure income, but also protected consumers from large swings in their grocery bills. By 1986, however, the disarray in world markets had resulted in a government bill of $26 billion compared to just $4 billion in 1980. Yet the depression in the agricultural sector continued. There were signs of improvement in 1987, but the prognosis for a long-term recovery was poor.[53]

Agriculture stands in contrast to energy, then. Most experts predict a sharp rise in energy prices in the 1990s, but farm exports are expected to remain depressed. The difference is one of shortage versus surplus. Yet, despite these distinctions, the politics of the two intermestic issue areas are rather similar.

Both energy and agriculture traditionally have been regarded as domestic issues. Throughout American history, most of our energy has been produced domestically. This is still the case. Energy analysts worry that we might approach the 50 percent level for oil imports at some point in the 1990s (see the sources in note 40 above). We have historically produced most of our own food. Indeed, even though we now import slightly more than we export, the United States still sells about 30 percent of its farm production abroad. Both commodities have now been internationalized. While the United States has long imported energy from abroad, the price was so cheap that nobody paid any attention to the issues of international politics that might be raised. Indeed, there were few such questions to be answered, as price fixing for energy is a phenomenon of the 1970s. Similarly, before the 1980s the major question that Americans confronted in the agricultural arena was how to maintain the country's position as the world's dominant exporter. For both sets of commodities, all of this changed dramatically.

Additionally, like energy, agriculture has produced a politics in which traditional coalitions have broken down. Historically, agricultural politics in the Congress have been marked by cooperation. Legislators from agricultural districts, particularly those in the South, have supported urban aid programs for northern Democrats in return for the lasts' votes on government price supports for commodities. It was particularly critical for the farm bloc to maintain a united front. In recent years, however, northern Democratic support for farm programs has slipped and the farm coalition itself has fallen apart.[54] Consider the following remarks by two Democratic members of Congress, the first from the urban Northeast and the second from the farmbelt in the Midwest:[55]

> In my part of the country, if an industry can't cut the mustard they close down. Do we have too many farmers? Do we have $25 billion a year thrown at a problem that has no solution?
> We should reduce the exposure to the taxpayer. And the way you do that is to increase the exposure to the consumer. God forbid that the consumer should have to pay 1 percent more of his disposable income for food.

Not only has the urban-rural coalition for farm support split, but so has the farm bloc itself.

Different commodities face disparate problems—and a host of alternative farm programs has been proposed ranging from massive new subsidies to the Reagan administration's suggestion that all federal farm aid be phased out. These alternative policies have split the commodities that had been essential for the enactment of previous farm bills. Cotton, rice, dairy, tobacco, peanuts, and sugar interests, for example, opposed legislation that would limit how much farmers would be permitted to grow, while wheat farmers strongly backed the idea. The dairy interests themselves lost many of their subsidies in a 1981 bill; corn growers (who produce sweeteners that compete with sugar) joined the chorus of interests who argued for sharp cutbacks in sugar subsidies that were set at three times the world price.[56]

AGRICULTURE IN THE MIND OF AMERICA

Why did the American public go along with such high levels of farm supports at all? How did the $26 billion get approved in the first place when on energy the Congress seemed tied up in knots? The answer is simple: while Americans have little love for oil companies, they idealize farmers. They cling to the myth of the "yeoman farmer" who played such a prominent role in the development of the American frontier.[57] The same Americans who refused to believe that the energy shortages of the 1970s were real expressed concern that farm failures might lead to inadequate levels of food; they were willing to assist farmers if it meant increasing taxes; they said that farmers were more honest than other Americans; and half of the public even expressed the desire to live on a farm. Furthermore, people from the city were even more likely to support aid to farmers than were rural residents.[58] However, as the problem got worse with no end in sight, the coalition began to fall apart. Despite the sympathy for the farmer, people and their representatives in Congress quickly began to worry about the costs of this policy, particularly at a time when the federal deficit was such a problem.

The farm problems, however, were not restricted to the United States. World agriculture was in crisis and other countries that compete for markets with the United States were sending similar amounts to protect their own farmers: $23 billion by the twelve-nation European Economic Community and $15 billion by Japan alone.[59] In 1986, with the Republicans facing difficult Senate races in the farm states, the president overrode his own philosophical objections and agreed to sell the Soviet Union 3.85 million tons of subsidized American wheat. Reagan certainly recalled how unpopular the wheat embargo imposed by Carter in 1979 following the Soviet invasion of Afghanistan had been. Indeed, repeal of the embargo was one of the new president's first acts on taking office in 1981. But such actions only reinforce the same problem of collective action as in world energy supplies.

Each national leader looks after his or her own constituents. Thus, although every leader recognizes that all would do better by eliminating subsidies, each worries that his/her country might be the only one to do so. This would lead to a loss of market share for the country following "wise" policy and an increase in sales for the other countries. Only if everyone agreed to cooperate to eliminate subsidies would *anyone* agree to do so. But the political costs of doing so, especially if others fail to comply, would be very high indeed. Since world leaders have no way to ensure that even their allies would stand by any agreement reached, no accord is likely. This is precisely what didn't happen at the Venice economic summit in 1987. All seven of the leaders of the major Western economies—the United States, Great Britain, France, Canada, West Germany, Japan, and Italy—went into the meeting promising an agricultural agreement. With little fanfare, they emerged without one. American farm organizations have also banded together to challenge the World Bank, which provides development loans to

Third World countries. They charged that American farmers are being hurt by these credits to developing countries and called on Congress to withdraw its financial support for the bank and three other similar institutions. Domestic policy considerations led to the inability to resolve a critical problem in the international political economy among America's allies and could lead to all-out economic war between the developed and developing nations.

TRADE: THE TIES THAT BIND EVERYONE UP

Few issues have been as divisive in the 1980s as trade. The energy crisis of the 1970s led to billions of dollars sent abroad to pay the increasing petroleum bills of American consumers. The problems of agriculture in the 1980s led, as noted above, to decreased American exports of foodstuffs. There were depressions in sectors of the economy such as timber, lead, aluminum, and zinc. American raw materials and manufactured goods were no longer competitive either in world markets or even in the United States. Wages in the United States are among the highest in the world and the costs of extracting raw materials and producing manufactured goods are correspondingly great. In contrast, in developing nations both sets of costs are much lower. In other developed nations, especially Japan, government subsidizes much of the research and development costs of manufacturing.

In both cases, the producing countries have what economists call a *comparative advantage* over the United States. Because their costs are lower, so are their prices. As Third World nations have been developing their industrial bases, they have become more important players in the international political economy. Their emergence has hurt the United States in two important ways. First, the simple fact of cost advantages makes American raw materials and manufactured goods less competitive. Few have failed to notice the flood of imported electronics consumer goods, clothing, and shoes—among other products—in American stores. Second, increasing production by developing countries means that more goods are entering the marketplace. In several important arenas, there already was more than sufficient production to meet world demand. The entry of new producers glutted the market. The high inflation and the booming economy of oil producers in the 1970s spurred tremendous growth in the manufacturing sectors.[60] This alone would be sufficient to depress prices. Automobiles, steel, semiconductors, and petrochemicals are among the industries that have been particularly hard hit, with excess production in the range of 15 to 30 percent in the mid 1980s.[61] However, because American costs of production are higher than those of most other nations, the overcapacity hurts the United States more than most.

In 1950 the United States produced 40 percent of the world's goods and services. Three decades later the percentage had dropped almost in half—to 22 percent. Germany had replaced the United States by 1986 as the world's leading exporter, with Japan close behind.[62] The United States had lost as many as two million jobs related to exports from 1980 to 1986, even as total employment in the nation increased by 10 percent. What had been trade surpluses turned into trade deficits. In 1985 the United States imported $140 billion more than it exported; the deficit jumped to $166 billion in 1986, six times what it had been in 1981. In the last year the United States became a debtor nation for the first time this century: the amount of money owed abroad was greater than the money other countries were obliged to repay to America.

WHY THE TRADE DEFICIT?

The causes of the trade deficit are hotly debated. Some argue that the very large budget deficits are the most important factor in the imbalance of trade. The budget deficits mean that the United States government has to borrow money to pay the interest on the debt. This increases interest rates by the financial institutions that lend the money. In turn, inflation rises, making foreign goods relatively cheaper than goods produced in the inflated American economy. A related explanation is the high value of the American dollar relative to other currencies. When the American dollar is overvalued, it is cheaper for consumers to purchase goods produced abroad. Third, a frequently heard argument is that American workers are not as productive as their counterparts in other countries. There are cries that both workers and corporations care more about maximizing their salaries and profits than they do about the quality of their products. Consumers who want excellent quality, then, will seek out goods made abroad. Fourth, the decline of manufacturing in the United States is held to be part of a more general shift in the world economy. Developing countries will continue indefinitely to have cost advantages in manufacturing. The economies of the developed nations, and especially that of the United States, have been moving for at least two decades toward service industries. This service sector includes technology (computers, computer programming, and other high-tech areas), information/entertainment (publishing, television, movies), and recreation (restaurants, hotels, resorts, etc.), among others.

Fifth, many countries have been accused of unfair trade practices. The United States has charged that Japan was "dumping" semiconductors on the American market—subsidizing these computer chips so that Japanese companies could sell them to American wholesalers and retailers below the cost of production. In addition, Japan and other countries have not opened their markets to exports in the same way that the United States has done. Some domestic industries in these countries are directly subsidized by the government. Other practices include either outright bans on importing commodities or manufactured goods and very high tariffs on these goods that would make imports noncompetitive with domestic products. Both Japan and West Germany, for example, restrict the import of telephone equipment. Japan also places barriers on rice, while Norway, Sweden, and Finland, worried over plant parasites, ban American softwood.[63]

Each of these explanations has its supporters and detractors. We shall not consider them here. But just as there is little agreement on why the trade deficit has grown, there is also no consensus on what to do about it. There are noncontroversial proposals to establish commissions that would study how to make America more competitive by producing superior products. No one is against better quality. Yet few would agree that making American products better would resolve the trade deficit. There is less consensus on what to do about the other possible "causes." Noting that there has been a long-term shift in the nature of the American economy away from manufacturing jobs does not tell us what we can do to redress the balance of trade. Should we attempt to preserve our manufacturing base, as some have argued,[64] or ought the United States to "recognize reality" and find a new way to compete?

Politicians find it far easier to place the blame on other nations than on themselves. Almost all elected officials agree that it is important to reduce the nation's budget deficit, but few want to curtail programs that would hurt their constituents. Thus members of Congress seek ways to reduce the trade deficit without cutting the budget deficit. Similarly, bringing down the value of the dollar in relation to other currencies would certainly bring about inflation. Americans would have to pay more for imported goods simply because the dollar buys fewer yen than it previously did. So a video cassette recorder made in Japan with salaries and production costs paid in yen will cost more in dollars when the dollar's value fails. Consumers thus would react *against* the sort of policies designed to reduce the value of the dollar. Yet the expectation is that a dollar that is no longer overvalued would entice other countries to increase their purchases of American products. This would stimulate the economy and reduce unemployment. What is unclear is that the drop in the value of the dollar will be sufficient to have a measurable impact on the balance of trade.[65] Could the United States wind up with inflation without more trade?

The idea of other countries' subsidizing their industries and restricting imports is also controversial. Many in the Congress argue that without import barriers, other nations would import much more from the United States than they already do. On the other hand, Japanese Prime Minister Yashurio Nakasone maintained that Japanese consumers do not purchase American products because the United States does not produce the type of goods that his nation's consumers want. Should the United States impose tariffs on other nations to redress the trade balance or might this make the situation only worse? Representative Dan Rostenkowski (D-Ill.) stated:

> Trade is becoming very, very parochial. It's employment, it's our jobs. Legislators, whether they want to be international or national, when there's nobody working at home, become very local[66]

It is, as noted, far easier for politicians to place the blame for the trade imbalance on other nations than on America's own problems. Television advertisements featuring prominent entertainers exhort Americans to look for labels stating that the product was made in the United States. Even President Reagan, who has been a strong opponent of trade barriers, imposed restrictions on the number of Japanese cars imported into the United States and placed tariffs of up to 100 percent on electronics components in 1987. As noted above, he responded to political pressures in 1986 and agreed to subsidize American wheat sales to the Soviet Union.

While placing the blame abroad *appears* to be a politically astute thing to do, the consequences are not always so beneficial to all Americans. Senator Robert Packwood (R-Ore.) noted that 10,000 people in his state work in the automobile import business in such jobs as unloading Japanese cars from ships: "When anyone talks about restricting imports, they are talking about losing jobs in Oregon."[67] American attitudes toward trade are marked by ambivalent feelings. A variety of polls point to support for restricting imports from Japan and other countries. Most show rather large majorities— in the range of 60 to 70 percent—favoring such action. Yet they also reveal a kind of grudging admiration for Japan rather than outright hostility. And when Americans are asked whether they would support sanctions if this meant that they would face fewer choices in the marketplace or higher prices for imported goods, support for restrictions drops precipitously. Only 12 percent of a national survey in 1985 favored restrictions if prices were to rise and there were to be fewer choices. By 1987, however, almost two thirds of Americans were willing to support import restrictions even if this meant higher prices.[68]

Those who worry about the impact of sanctions do so because they fear a spiraling trade war. Sanctions imposed by the United States on Japan would lead to similar actions by Japan on the United States; this would lead to further restrictions by the United States on Japanese products and the process would continue indefinitely. In 1986 the United States and the European Economic Community narrowly averted such a trade war over agricultural goods, including Italian pasta. Sanctions make goods more expensive for consumers so that continued rounds of such reactions would raise inflation for all consumers. What we have is another problem of collective action much as we found on energy and agriculture. Everybody would be better off if there were no trade barriers at all, that is, if there were what economists call *open markets*. However, once one nation imposes some restrictions—be they government subsidies on computer chips or agricultural products or tariffs or even outright prohibitions on imports (as Japan bans American baseball bats to protect its own domestic industry)—then every other nation will see its best interest in doing likewise. Thus, we are likely to wind up with all countries imposing barriers on each other—making everyone worse off than if all markets were open. (High tariffs might also make some products for export too expensive for many developing nations, thus serving to hurt the importer.) As in other intermestic policies, there is a clear-cut strategy for actors in international politics to pursue: open markets. Yet pressures from domestic constituents lead politicians to deviate from that course.

OPEN OR CLOSED MARKETS?

American trade policy has wavered between promoting open markets and seeking protectionism through trade restrictions and high tariffs. The last major protectionist legislation was the Smoot-Hawley tariff of 1930, which many said caused the Great Depression. Since then, Congress has followed the presidential lead in pushing for more open markets in the world economy. American trade policy has taken as its principal objective the lowering of existing tariff barriers. After World War II, the industrialized nations formed the General Agreement on Tariffs and Trade in 1947 to co-ordinate trading practices and to work toward open markets. The support for these policies from 1930 through the 1970s was often overwhelming.[69] Congressional decisions reflected the prevailing consensus among econo-mists that open markets promoted economic growth.[70] The nation's business executives, strongly influenced by the prevailing economic theories, also provided consistent support for free trade. Yet as the U.S. position in the world economy shifted, so did the views of many business executives. While only 15 percent favored some type of import restrictions in 1980, this figure jumped to 38 percent in 1982 and to 44 percent three years later.[71] Obviously, elite opinion reflects the regional split in public opinion. Those people living in states such as the industrial Midwest where manufacturing has been par-ticularly hard hit by imports were much more likely to support restrictions on trade than those in states that have been the pioneers in the service industries (the Southwest and some southern states).[72]

The critical point is that the post-1930 consensus on free trade has bro-ken down and legislators are struggling to find a way out of the trade di-lemma. The import deficit may reach as much as $700 billion by 1990 and the problem may be the greatest threat of all to maintaining the standard of living of Americans.[73] With no apparent resolution to the American budget problem, legislators have turned their attention to restricting imports. Dem-ocrats have taken the lead in pushing for retaliation, arguing that workers in industries in America's heartland—the Northeast, the industrialized Mid-west, and manufacturing communities in some areas of the South (espe-cially the Carolinas and Tennessee)—have been hurt by foreign competition. Labor, a traditional ally of the Democratic party, has been at the forefront of the movement to impose tariffs and other sanctions on countries with low-paid work forces and nations that block American imports. This is a reversal of the party's historic role in the post-1930 era. Under Kennedy, some of the sharpest cuts in tariff rates in American history took place. The Republicans have been split, largely along regional lines. Reagan, as noted, has strongly opposed any restrictions on free trade. Yet Republican members from states or districts that have been adversely affected by imports have joined the Democratic chorus for strong legislation. Indeed, when a subsidiary of the Japanese electronic firm Toshiba sold sensitive military equipment to the Soviet Union, Republican members of Congress took the lead in pursuing retaliatory measures against the parent company. Senator Jake Garn

(R-Utah) proposed banning all imports of Toshiba products into the United States, while three Republican House members staged a demonstration outside the Capitol in which they smashed several Toshiba electronics products. The restrictive trade bill that passed the Senate in July 1987 (see below) garnered unanimous Democratic support, but also 40 percent of the votes of Republican legislators.

The Congress enacted a protectionist trade bill in 1986 with support from both the Democratic-controlled House of Representatives and the Republican-controlled Senate. The president vetoed it and the issue came up again in 1987 after the Democrats had won control of the upper house. While some Democrats interpreted this victory as a mandate to enact a strong trade bill—and polls showed the public as more supportive of restrictions than even two years ago—they nevertheless feared that the situation could get out of hand. First, they worried about retaliation from exporters. Should there be an all-out trade war and the worldwide economy go into a deep recession, Democrats feared that they might be blamed for this downturn. Second, they worried about specific industries attempting to write the bill to their own specifications. Steel, oil, textiles, and footwear firms, for example, were seeking special protection. Were they to succeed, they might set off a massive scramble for a similar action by many other industries and thus lead to a bill more protectionist than anyone wanted.[74] The conflict became exquisitely complex as sectors that a protectionist bill was designed to protect found themselves worrying about possible adverse affects. Wheat growers, for example, complained about subsidized exports from Canada and Argentina, yet feared that tariffs on other items might provoke European retaliation against American wheat. So did the Computer and Business Equipment Manufacturers Association, which also found itself straining under competition from Japan and Korea.[75]

Trade affects everything. The intermestic issues that are particularly contentious share this trait. So everyone has a position and every congressional player wants to get a piece of the action. In the Senate in 1987, nine committees considered the legislation. The Finance Committee has primary responsibility for trade legislation. The Judiciary panel prepared a section protecting American patent rights overseas; the Governmental Affairs Committee was concerned with reorganizing the executive branch to place a greater emphasis on competitiveness; the Department of Agriculture sought to expand farm subsidies; Labor and Human Welfare proposed to assist workers who lost their jobs through layoffs; the Foreign Affairs Committee examined proposals to enhance Third World investment through international agencies; the Banking, Housing, and Urban Affairs Committees restricted the right of foreign (almost exclusively Japanese) brokers to act as the primary agents in buying and selling government securities unless American agents receive reciprocal rights; the Department of Commerce wrestled with blocking foreign takeovers of American corporations; and the Small Business Committee added segments directing itself to place more emphasis on exports. The large number of actors indicates just how complex the politics of trade are—and how difficult it is to enact legislation that would command a majority of both houses of Congress. The bill that passed the Senate in 1987 was filled with special interest provisions such as (1) $300 million in rebates to sugar refiners for tariffs paid between 1977 and 1982; (2) $39 million for tobacco export promotion; (3) restrictions on imports of lamb, pork, strawberries, and steel fence panels; and (4) an amendment requiring that all imported food products be labeled as such.[76]

What is even more difficult is to enact trade legislation that also appeals to the president. Both the House and the Senate bills would restrict the chief executive's leeway to negotiate on trade issues. The president has traditionally had the authority to reject the recommendations of the International Trade Commission, which rules that specific industries have been hurt by unfair trade practices, if he felt that the nation's economic interest dictated otherwise. Congress sought to force the president to impose restrictions. The House enacted its provision, authored by Representative Richard Gephardt (D-Mo.)—himself a presidential candidate—by just five votes. This provision, which sets the boundaries between executive and legislative control of trade policy and between open markets and protectionism, more than any other shows the level of conflict on the issue. While the Democrats made trade their chief priority in 1987, some of the party's key leaders—including the two major actors on trade in the House[77]—broke to support the president.

Because trade has traditionally been both a domestic and international issue, unlike energy and agriculture, there has been a more long-standing legislative–executive conflict over who controls this policy area. When the economy was prospering, and especially when open markets were seen as furthering economic expansion, Congress and the president worked together in considerable harmony. However, as the economy weakened and trade stood out prominently as the source of many of the woes, the issue was marked by a clash of ideologies, interests, and prerogatives. Domestic considerations dominated over foreign ones and the role of the executive (the key actor on foreign policy) on trade came under challenge.

Ironically, it took a major crisis—the stock market crash of October 19, 1987—to lessen the pressures for tough trade legislation from the Congress. Many economists were concerned that a trade war with nations that had fewer economic worries might send the market into a free-fall that would invoke a recession or possibly even a depression; they recalled the effects that a protectionist trade policy had in 1929. Many members of Congress remained to be convinced that this logic was correct, but they worried more about what might happen if they were wrong and the consensus of economists was correct. In 1988 the Congress finally enacted a trade bill that was much less protectionist than originally proposed. However, Reagan vetoed it anyway, claiming that a provision to give workers in plants scheduled to close a 60-day termination notice would hurt the economy. The Congress failed to override the veto, but the president ultimately let both the trade and plant closing provisions become law.

BUREAUCRATIC/GOVERNMENTAL POLITICS AND THE DEMOCRATIC DILEMMAS

Crisis politics is marked by executive-led politics. It also provides the strongest public support for presidential leadership. Most of the citizenry perceives one policy as the "correct one." In crises, then, the democratic dilemmas are often resolved by default. Yet it is the strong presidency of crisis politics that gives rise to the "imperial presidency" of noncrisis periods. The weak Congress of crises becomes the bulwark of public opinion against the president who has gone too far. In bureaucratic politics, however, things are rarely that straightforward. Few people see the stakes in the same light. On issues that are primarily international, presidents must confront a fragmented bureaucracy. On intermestic issues, they must deal with a Congress divided along the lines of constituency interests. It is difficult to determine what the "correct" policy is—and even if one can do that, achieving it might not be so easy.

Even on strategic issues such as the ABM, SALT II, and the Strategic Defense Initiative, there is no consensus on what ought to be done. Different actors see the stakes in alternative ways—and these cannot be divorced from the domestic political issues involved in the decisions. Not only do the various services and branches of the foreign policy bureaucracy (the State Department versus the Defense Department, for example) have alternative perspectives, but so do members of the Congress and candidates for the presidency. In 1980, Carter responded to the Soviet invasion of Afghanistan with a ban on wheat sales to the U.S.S.R. Reagan, usually the hawk, reacted sharply in a bid for the farm vote and promised to repeal the embargo if he were elected. He did so on inauguration day in 1981, pleasing midwestern farmers whose markets had otherwise been shrinking.

In 1986, Nunn—also generally regarded as a hawk—led the opposition to the administration's interpretation of SALT II that would permit SDI deployment. Many observers argued that what motivated Nunn was not simply a concern for an arms control agreement, but also domestic political factors. On the one hand, the Democrats had regained control of the Senate in the 1986 elections and as chair of the Armed Services Committee, Nunn would be acting as a party spokesman. On the other hand, Nunn was considering running for the presidency in 1988 and his overall conservative voting record would not sit well with many Democratic activists. By taking a strong stand on the SALT II limitations, he could take a major step in establishing better relations with the mainstream of his party.

While crisis policy making points to the benefits—and potential dangers—of a strong executive leading the way on foreign policy, bureaucratic/governmental politics emphasizes checks and balances. The more bureaucratic policy making resembles domestic bargaining, as on intermestic issues such as energy and agriculture, the less powerful a president is to dictate the outcome. The chief executive is stronger on those issues—including the intermestic policy of trade—that more directly involve other nations. Yet even on these the chief executive must confront an often unruly bureaucracy or a divided Congress. The president becomes less a dictator and more a referee.

When we cannot readily agree on what the "right" policy is, the question of process versus output may be reduced to which actor we wish to have more power. Do we favor open markets because we believe that the president should have the flexibility to negotiate tariff rates—or because we oppose protectionist policies? Similarly, might we favor some restrictions because we believe that Congress better reflects public opinion than the chief executive rather than because we expect other nations to adjust their trade policies to America's? Would Democrats be so concerned with the conditions under which a president followed—or did not follow—a treaty that a Democratic-controlled Senate had refused to ratify (SALT II)?

Crisis decision making is of necessity policy formation by a small elite. Bureaucratic decisions, on the other hand, involve a wide range of actors. Again, intermestic issues on which the public might become energized involve an even larger number of actors than policy decisions that focus on more bureaucracies. Does either one lead to better policy making? It may seem that the potential for stalemate on bureaucratic policies is so strong that there should be a clear preference for crisis decision making. Yet the failure of participants to reach agreement on contentious issues, especially intermestic ones such as energy and agriculture, should not lead us to conclude that crisis decision making would work better on those questions. During the 1970s we called the policy problems on energy *crises.* But this didn't do much to affect the way we made—or didn't make—energy policy. Nor did the labels *agricultural crisis* or *trade crisis* result in fewer groups demanding to have a say. Bureaucratic/governmental politics are clearly more democratic, but is more democracy always more desirable on foreign policy? If one responds quickly in the negative, one only need recall how during Watergate the expansion of presidential authority beyond the crisis arena led to a long ordeal in which the basic aspects of presidential accountability underwent severe challenge.

NOTES

1. Morton H. Halperin, "The Decision to Deploy the ABM: Bureaucratic and Domestic Politics in the Johnson Administration," *World Politics,* October 1972, p. 83. On decision making on the ABM, also see Halperin, *Breaucratic Politics and Foreign Policy* (Washington, D.C.: Brookings Institution, 1974); and Alton Frye, *A Responsible Congress: The Politics of National Security* (New York: McGraw-Hill, 1975), esp. chap. 2.

2. Ibid., p. 74.
3. Ibid., pp. 67–69.
4. Ibid., p. 69.
5. Ibid., p. 76.
6. Roger Hilsman, *To Move a Nation* (Garden City, N.Y.: Doubleday, 1967).
7. Warner R. Schilling, "The H-Bomb Decision: How to Decide without Actually Choosing," in *Readings in American Foreign Policy*, eds. Halperin and Kanter, no. 3, chap. 3, p. 255.
8. Halperin, "Decision to Deploy," p. 87.
9. Robert S. McNamara, "The Dynamics of Nuclear Strategy," *Department of State Bulletin*, October 9, 1967, pp. 443–51.
10. Abram Chayes and Jerome B. Wiesner, eds., *ABM: An Evaluation of the Decision to Deploy an Antiballistic Missile System* (New York: Harper & Row, 1969), pp. 259–64. Nixon's speech is reproduced on pp. 254–59.
11. Carnes Lord, "The ABM," *Commentary*, May 1980, pp. 31–38 and *New York Times*, August 14, 1980; *U.S. Arms Control Objectives and the Implications for Ballistic Missile Defense* (Center for Science and International Affairs, Harvard Univ., 1980); Jan M. Lodal, "Deterrence and Nuclear Strategy," and *Daedalus*, Fall 1980, pp. 155–76; and William Schneider Jr., Donald G. Brennan et al., *U.S. Strategic-Nuclear Policy and Ballistic Missile Defense: The 1980s and Beyond* (Cambridge, Mass.: Institute for Foreign Policy Analysis, 1980).
12. This analysis of SALT II is based on Strobe Talbott, *Endgame: The Inside Story of SALT II* (New York: Harper & Row, 1979); Thomas W. Wolfe, *The SALT Experience* (Cambridge, Mass.: Ballinger Publishing, 1979); Stephen J. Flanagan, "SALT II," in *Superpower Arms Control*, Albert Carnsdale and Richard N. Haass, eds. (Cambridge, Mass.: Ballinger Publishing, 1987), pp. 105–38, and "Stalemate: The Domestic Politics of SALT II," in *Congress, the Presidency and Foreign Policy*, eds. John Spanier and Joseph Nogee (New York: Pergamon Press, 1981); and Report of the Committee on Foreign Relations, United States Senate, *The SALT II Treaty* (Washington, D.C.: Government Printing Office, 1979).
13. Quoted by Thomas A. Bailey, *A Diplomatic History of the American People*, 7th ed. (New York: Appleton-Croft, 1964), pp. 487–88.
14. Genrik Trofimenko, "Too Many Negotiators," *New York Times*, July 17, 1979.
15. Flanagan, "Congress, The White House and SALT," p. 36.
16. Ibid., pp. 34–35.
17. Quoted by Alton Frye and William D. Rogers, "Linkage Begins at Home," *Foreign Policy*, Summer 1970, pp. 50–51.
18. Ibid., p. 52.
19. *New York Times*, April 13, 1979.
20. Frye and Rogers, "Linkage," p. 55.
21. Ibid.
22. Flanagan, "The Domestic Politics of SALT II."
23. *New York Times*, July 6, 1979.
24. Brzezinski, p. 544; William B. Quandt, *Camp David* (Washington, D.C.: The Brookings Institution, 1986), pp. 14–27.
25. Strobe Talbott, "Playing for the Future," *Time*, April 18, 1983, p. 16 ff; *The Russians and Reagan* (New York: Vintage Books, 1984), pp. 51–53; and *Deadly Gambits* (New York: Alfred A. Knopf, 1984).

26. Samuel P. Huntington, "Renewed Hostility," in *The Making of America's Soviet Policy,* ed Joseph S. Nye, Jr. (New Haven, Conn.: Yale Univ. Press, 1984), pp. 272–74.

27. Scheider, *Eagle Resurgent* (Boston: Little, Brown, 1983 and 1987), pp. 41–45.

28. Robert W. Tucker, *The Nuclear Debate* (New York: Homes & Meier, 1985); "The Nuclear Debate," *Foreign Affairs,* Fall 1984, pp. 1–32.

29. National Conference of Catholic Bishops, *The Challenge of Peace* (Washington, D.C.: United States Catholic Conference, 1983).

30. Paul R. Ehrlich, Carl Sagan et al., *The Cold and the Dark* (New York: W. W. Norton, 1984).

31. *New York Times,* March 24, 1983.

32. For a similar interpretation received after my case study was written, see Arthur A. Stein, "Strategy as Politics, Politics as Strategy; Domestic Debates, Statecraft and Star Wars," in *The Logic of Nuclear Terror,* ed. Roman Kolkowicz (Boston: Allen & Unwin, 1987), pp. 184–210.

33. See, for example, Lawrence Freedman, *The Evolution of Nuclear Strategy* (New York: St. Martin's Press, 1981); Arthur Schlesinger Jr., and "The Eagle and the Bear," *Foreign Affairs,* Summer 1985, p. 959.

34. *New York Times,* March 4, 1985.

35. Gregg Herken, *Counsels of War* (New York: Oxford Univ. Press, 1987).

36. Hans H. Bethe, Richard L. Garwin et al., "Space-Based Ballistic Missile Defense," *Scientific American,* October 1984, pp. 39–49; Keith B. Payne, *Strategic Defense* (Lanham, Md.: Hamilton Press, 1986); Union of Concerned Scientists, *Why Space Weapons Can't Protect Us* (New York: Vintage Specials, 1984); Sidney D. Drell, Philip J. Farley, and David Holloway, *The Reagan Strategic Defense Initiative* (Cambridge, Mass.: Ballinger, 1985), and Philip M. Boffey, William J. Broad, Leslie H. Gelb, Charles Mohr, and Holcomb B. Noble, *Claiming the Heavens* (New York: Times Books, 1988).

37. Jeremy Azrael and Stephen Sestanovich, "Superpower Balancing Acts," *America and the World 1985,* pp. 481–82.

38. For Senator Nunn's arguments, see "The ABM Reinterpretation Issue," *The Washington Quarterly,* Autumn 1987, pp. 45–57. For the administration's case, see Abraham D. Sofarer, State Department legal counselor, "The ABM Treaty: Legal Analysis in the Political Cauldron," Ibid., pp. 59–75. See also Raymond L. Garthoff, *Policy versus the Law: The Reinterpretation of the ABM Treaty* (Washington, D.C.: The Brookings Institution, 1987).

39. *New York Times,* April 23 and 24, 1987.

40. These predictions came from both the administration and the Congress. See National Petroleum Council, *Factors Affecting U.S. Oil and Gas Outlook* (Washington, D.C.: National Petroleum Council, Department of Energy, 1987); and Joint Economic Committee, *The 1987 Joint Economic Report,* 100th Congress, First Session, March 5, 1987.

41. There are some new developments in the field of superconductivity that promise great energy savings and hence may revolutionize the field of energy.

42. These data were compiled by the United States House of Representatives Select Committee on Committees, 1979–80, and are reported in Eric M. Uslaner, *Shale Barrel Politics Energy and Legislative Leadership* (Stanford: Stanford University Press, 1989), ch. 1.

43. Quoted in *Congressional Quarterly Almanac 1977* (Washington, D.C.: Congressional Quarterly, 1977, p. 710.

44. Remarks made on the National Broadcasting Company's "Meet the Press" February 10, 1980 (Washington, D.C.: Kelly Press, 1980), p. 8.

45. *Congressional Record,* Daily edition, Ninety-sixth Congress, First session, May 10, 1979, p. H2997.

46. NBC News poll news release, April 23, 1986.

47. Wendy Wall, "World's Grain Output Surges as Nations Seek Food Self-Sufficiency," *The Wall Street Journal,* April 6, 1987, pp. 1, 10.

48. Art Pine, "Agricultural Subsidies Would Be Jointly Cut under U.S. Trade Plan," *The Wall Street Journal,* April 7, 1987, pp. 1, 26.

49. M. Ann Tutwiler and George E. Rossmiller, "External Events and the Recovery of U.S. Agricultural Exports," *Resources,* Winter 1987, p. 20.

50. Ibid.

51. Joint Economic Committee, *The 1987 Joint Economic Report,* p. 127.

52. See M. Elizabeth Sanders, *The Regulation of Natural Gas* (Philadelphia: Temple Univ. Press, 1981).

53. William Robbins, "Farmers Are Reaping Optimism by the Bushel," *New York Times,* May 5, 1987, p. A16.

54. On the coalitional strategy, see David R. Mayhew, *Party Loyalty Among Congressmen* (Cambridge, Mass.: Harvard Univ. Press, 1966); for more recent results, see Barbara Deckard Sinclair, "Agenda, Policy, and Alignment Change from Coolidge to Reagan," in *Congress Reconsidered,* 3d ed., eds. Lawrence C. Dodd and Bruce I. Oppenheimer (Washington, D.C.: CQ Press, 1985), pp. 291–314; and David Rapp, "For the Farmer, It's a Question of Necessity," *Congressional Quarterly Weekly Report,* February 21, 1987, pp. 303–8.

55. The first is Representative Frank Guarini (D-N.J.), the second the late Senator Edward Zorinsky (D-Nebr.). Cited in Rapp, "For the Farmer, It's a Question of Necessity," p. 303.

56. Sen. Rapp, "Hill Fervor for Farm Bill Changes Died Slowly," *Congressional Quarterly Weekly Report,* November 1, 1986, pp. 2,725–26; Martha Derthick and Paul J. Quirk, *The Politics of Deregulation* (Washington, D.C.: Brookings Institution, 1985), p. 231; and Ward Sinclair, "USDA Targets Domestic Sugar Production," *Washington Post,* March 8, 1987, p. A4.

57. Richard Hofstadter, *The Age of Reform* (New York: Vintage, 1955), pp. 23–59.

58. William Robbins, "Surge in Sympathy For Farmer Found," *New York Times,* February 25, 1986, pp. A1, A22; and Adam Clymer, "Poll Finds Most Americans Cling to Ideals of Farm Life," *New York Times,* February 25, 1986, p. A22.

59. Peter T. Kilborn, "U.S. Will Stress Farm-Aid Issues in Global Talks," *New York Times,* March 23, 1987, pp. A1, D4.

60. While much of the new demand occurred in energy-producing nations, the energy crises of the 1970s led to the development of a new market for smaller cars in the United States. See Bruce Stokes, "Coping With Glut," *National Journal,* November 1, 1986, p. 2,608.

61. Ibid.

62. Stuart Aberbach, "America, the 'Diminished Giant'," *Washington Post,* April 15, 1987, pp. A1, A18.

63. John Cranford, "Trade Bill: Partial Remedy for Complex Problem," *Congressional Quarterly Weekly Report,* April 25, 1987, p. 771.

64. Stephen S. Cohen and John Zysman, *Manufacturing Matters* (New York: Basic Books, 1987).
65. Peter Behr, "Is America Running Out of Steam?" *Washington Post,* April 17, 1987, pp. A1, A18.
66. *Washington Post,* "The Evolution of a Trade Bill," March 22, 1987, p. H3.
67. Anne Swardson, "Senate Panel Takes up Trade Bill," *Washington Post,* January 14, 1987, p. F4.
68. See, among other sources, Susan Chira, "Poll Blames U.S. on Japan Trade," *New York Times,* August 13, 1985, pp. A1, D6; Clyde Farnsworth, "U.S. and Japan: Fraying Ties," *New York Times,* June 5, 1987, pp. D1, D5; and David S. Broder, "Iran–Contra Concerns Hurting Bush, Poll Finds," *Washington Post,* June 4, 1987, pp. A1, A6–A7.
69. Robert A. Pastor, *Congress and the Politics of U.S. Foreign Economic Policy,* Berkeley: Univ. of California Press, 1980), pp. 196–99.
70. See, among others, Mancur Olson, *The Rise and Decline of Nations* (New Haven: Yale Univ. Press, 1981).
71. See William Schneider, " 'Rambo' and Reality: Having It Both Ways," in *Eagle Resurgent: The Reagan Era in American Foreign Policy,* eds. Kenneth A. Oye, Robert J. Lieber, and Donald Rothchild (Boston: Little, Brown, 1987), p. 6. Note that the last survey cited asked a somewhat different question than the two earlier ones, so comparisons must be made with caution.
72. Clyde Farnsworth, "Most in Poll Found to Favor Import Limits to Protect Jobs," *New York Times,* June 9, 1985, pp. A1, A40.
73. Behr, "Is America Running out of Steam?"
74. Jonathan Fuerbringer, "Congress Seeking Harmony on Trade," *New York Times,* February 6, 1987, pp. D1, D4.
75. Clyde Farnsworth, "One Day as a Trade Lobbyist," *New York Times,* June 16, 1987, p. A32.
76. "The Senate Trashes Trade," *New York Times,* July 24, 1987, p. A34.
77. They are Rostenkowski, who chairs the Ways and Means Committee, and Sam Gibbons (D-Fla.), who chairs the Trade Subcommittee on Ways and Means.

Chapter Nine

Balancing the Scales?

WHERE DOES THE BALANCE LIE?

The Great Depression, followed by the New Deal and the Nazi and Japanese threats, followed after Japan's and Germany's defeat by the Cold War, all contributed to the steady growth of presidential power. But for the Vietnam War, this unchallenged growth might have continued. This trend toward increasing presidential power had gone unchallenged because crisis after crisis, domestic and foreign, required strong action and often speedy reaction. The need for a powerful presidency seemed obvious. More than that, the growth of presidential power was identified with the use of this power domestically for progressive social legislation (the New Deal, Fair Deal, New Frontier, and Great Society programs) and externally for the defense of what used to be called the *free world*, although it included nondemocratic societies. The confrontation of Stalin's Soviet Union—which, not surprisingly so soon after World War II, looked a lot like Hitler's Germany to Western eyes— with the United States, Britain, and France, made the Cold War appear to be fundamentally a continuing struggle of totalitarianism against democracy. Thus the expansion of presidential power was identified with liberal causes, with domestic changes to help the underprivileged and to correct social injustices and a foreign policy to protect liberal values that had first been assaulted by Hitler and then by Stalin. In fact, it had simply come to be assumed that the president is a liberal and that, therefore, he can, like the kings of old, do no wrong.

During those days it was conservatives who opposed the trend toward increasing presidential power. As exponents of small government and congressional supremacy, the opposed New Deal and other domestic reforms as well as the conduct of a vigorous foreign policy, all of which required big government, especially "big executive government." Liberals championed the last. But Vietnam reversed the liberal attitudes toward presidential power. Liberals, who had always expected "their" presidents to back good causes whether eliminating poverty, doing away with racial injustice,

or stopping totalitarian aggression, became schizophrenic as the war escalated. Johnson's domestic record surpassed that of John F. Kennedy, whose
style and charm attracted liberals but who by the time of his death had not
managed to get Congress to pass any major social legislation; Johnson, unlike Kennedy, was able to achieve the passage of a vast amount of social
legislation. But Vietnam disillusioned many liberals. A war in defense of an
undemocratic government, often fought by methods that repelled people of
humane sentiments and springing from commitments made by Presidents
Eisenhower and Kennedy and transformed into major war by Johnson, not
only seemed incompatible with the very values America proclaimed to the
world but was carried on in a way that seemed unconstitutional.

The Gulf of Tonkin Resolution, the blank check Congress gave Johnson
but did not expect him to use to initiate a large land war in Asia, only made
the war an even more bitter experience. Vietnam, a "presidential war," was
perceived to be the culmination of the trend toward increasingly powerful
presidents who were not subject to the legislative restraint envisaged by the
Founding Fathers. Had they not with good reason, in the Constitution, specifically provided against the danger of locating absolute power in the hands
of one man by assigning to Congress the authority to "declare war" and the
president the authority to "make war"? In the future asked critic and *New
York Times* journalist Tom Wicker, "could a president, for example, bomb
Lima in order to forestall or retaliate for some act of expropriation by Peru?
If Fidel Castro refuses to help put an end to airline hijackings to Cuba, can
Mr. Nixon constitutionally bomb Havana to make him negotiate seriously?"[1]

If the Vietnam war traumatized many liberals, the Iran–Contra affair
had the same effect on many conservatives. It was those to the right of center who had so strongly stressed that the United States was founded on a
respect, indeed a reverence, for law. Yet there were former representatives
from what was arguably the most conservative administration of this century arguing before national television audiences that it was acceptable to
disobey some bad laws. Some even testified that there were so many different Boland amendments that National Security Council officials did not
know which one to follow at any given time—a view that *New Yorker* col-
umnist Elizabeth Drew regarded as somewhat disingenuous since the administration did not tell people to file their income taxes under the old rules
if they found the new reformed law too complicated to understand.[2] The
Iran–Contra affair, perhaps more than anything else in recent American diplomatic history, is a classic example of putting outcomes ahead of process
and thereby losing respect for law. It leads one to an interpretation that the
Constitution, amended by years of presidential practice and congressional
acquiescence, reads in effect: "The president may conduct a war unless Congress halts him." Hence, to redress the balance between the executive and
legislative, to prevent another Vietnam and avoid a second costly disaster
and strain of the American social fabric, a flood of proposals has been put
forward, almost all of which aim at a greater role in the making of foreign

policy, and especially the use of force, for Congress—and, through it, presumably, "the people."

The belief that the presidency—when occupied by bellicose presidents—needs to be restrained by a pacific Congress, acting as the representative of the people, assumes that Congress, especially the Senate, would demonstrate wisdom, moderation, and virtue, qualities that have frequently been lacking in the postwar period.

> This spring the land is filled . . . with a resounding chorus demanding that the United States Senate reassert its "right" over foreign policy. . . .
>
> But hold on a moment. Which Senate are we speaking of? Are we talking of the Senate which has over and over again balked at constructive foreign initiative, crippled foreign efforts, ignored foreign opportunities? Are we talking of the Senate which blocked American entry into the League of Nations, held back full support for the World Court, is presently cutting back further and further on foreign aid, which has no hesitation over passing resolutions mixing in the affairs of other countries for political rather than diplomatic reasons?
>
> Of course, this is not the Senate which today's "strengthen-the-Senate" advocates have in mind. They visualize an upper chamber full of wisdom and goodwill, a bulwark of reason and foresight in a reckless world. In short, they dream of a Senate which will hew to their own concept of where foreign policy should go and how it should be conducted.[3]

However, these expectations are of a Congress whose foreign policy stance for most of the postwar period has been intensely anticommunist and nationalistic. Presidents have therefore moved with great caution, if and when they have moved at all, in their relations with communist countries lest they be tainted as "soft on communism."

But the fall of pro-American governments in Nicaragua and Iran, as well as the weakness of other friends and allies such as Guatemala, El Salvador, Zaire, Turkey, and Morocco, led to increased demands that the country take a more activist role in international politics. Many of these arguments were heard most loudly in the Congress. The nomination of Ronald Reagan by the Republicans intensified the political debate on foreign policy, especially the growing concern with defense policy. The congressional activism, in contrast to that of the late 1960s and early 1970s, was now once more directed toward an interventionist foreign policy that conflicted with the policies of the president. The Congress of the 1970s was concerned with too much presidential power *and* prowess, while that of the early 1980s, especially the Republican-controlled Senate, was determined to reassert American power. Few members of the Congress during the Vietnam War period could have imagined that a president would not win universal acclaim for pronouncing that no American soldiers had died in overseas combat during his term of office, as Carter often reminded the country. The Iran–Contra affair led to another change of direction. The public feared that support for antigovernment rebels in Nicaragua would lead to another

American embroglio in Latin America. Memories of the hostage crisis, Iranian-backed terrorism throughout the world, the killing of American marines in Lebanon, and the attack on the U.S.S. *Stark* in the Persian Gulf led many Americans to argue that the United States need not make itself a sitting target for anyone would dare to attack. The Congress quickly picked up on this theme. It joined the chorus for restraint in government policy.

There is an irony to the post-Vietnam appointment of Congress as the watchdog of presidential temptations to go to war. For it overlooks the fact that Congress approved U.S. participation in both limited wars. Had President Truman requested a declaration of war after North Korea's invasion of South Korea, he would have received it; support for Truman's decision to intervene militarily with U.S. forces received virtually unanimous congressional and popular support. Only after the war became domestically unpopular did a few conservative senators raise the question of its constitutionality. Similarly, President Johnson had the support of large majorities in Congress and the country not only at the time of the Gulf of Tonkin incident during the summer of 1964, but also when the sustained bombing of North Vietnam began in the spring of 1965. If a War Powers Act had existed at the time, it would not have prevented either of the two limited wars in which the United States has become engaged since 1945. These actions would also not be blocked by the rule that, sixty days after intervening, the president must desist if he does not receive legislative support after explaining his reason for intervening have changed these outcomes. For this would have been too short a period for any congressional investigation to turn up facts beyond those—as in the North Korean invasion—already evident or explained by the president. Congress' Tonkin Gulf investigation did turn up additional information—three years after the events. Similarly, even in the Iran–Contra affair, where foreign policy appeared to have been privatized, many legislators argued that Congress had to shoulder some of the blame. The legislative branch had not been diligent enough in its oversight to prevent the affair.[4] Indeed, James Sundquist has argued that the power of the contemporary presidency can be traced to the actions of the Congress. The legislature has, until the 1970s, delegated much responsibility to the chief executive, generally to achieve more coordination and coherence in policy formation.[5]

If there is one rule that has become clear in the post-World War II period, it is that during real or alleged crises, Congress and the public turn to the president for information and interpretation. For example, it was Kennedy's interpretation of the impact of Soviet missiles in Cuba that precipitated the Cuban missile crisis. Put in different words, the president has a superior ability to manipulate the picture of reality in the short run; this advantageous presidential position is reinforced by an emotional fact of life—namely, that if the president sends troops into action, be it in the name of freedom or security or both, the patriotic feelings that are aroused will make it extremely difficult to oppose him and refuse him the troops and money he requests. In fact, it will take a great deal more willingness on the part of Congress to accept responsibility for its decisions in case history should vindicate the president.

WHY THINGS ALWAYS APPEAR TO GO WRONG

Our concern in this chapter is with reconciling the democratic dilemmas of foreign policymaking with the argument, advanced by many, that we seem to be trapped in a cycle of strong and weak presidents and congresses that leads to frustration and a sense that things seem to go wrong more often than they go right. The ideal balance seems to elude us. If Vietnam taught us that foreign policy making needed to be made more accountable to both Congress and the public, the Iran–Contra affair reminded us that we have not learned that lesson well enough.

What is the source of our difficulties? Are our presidents too strong or is the Congress too weak? Do we have too much partisanship on foreign policy or too little? Or is there a mismatch between our expectations of the president and the occupants of the Oval Office? All of these possibilities have been raised by serious observers. We shall consider each of them.

Deadlocked Democracy

In 1987, the bicentennial anniversary of the Constitution of the United States, a bipartisan group of distinguished citizens issued a report warning that the distinguished document might be in need of revision. The Committee on the Constitutional System was cochaired by Senator Nancy Landon Kassebaum (R-Kans.), former Secretary of the Treasury C. Douglas Dillon (a Republican who served in the Kennedy and Johnson administrations), and Lloyd Cutler, former counsel to President Carter. The committee's membership included sitting and former members of Congress from both parties, current and past governors and mayors, others who had served in the cabinet, as well as representatives from business, labor, and universities. It argued that the increasing responsibilities placed on modern governments were putting severe burdens on the contemporary political order. The committee argued:

> Consistency in our foreign and national security policies is . . . frustrated by an institutional contest of wills between presidents and shifting, cross-party coalitions within the Congress. Over forty treaties submitted to the Senate for ratification since World War II have either been rejected or have never come to a vote. . . . Meanwhile presidential concern over "leaks" and frustration with congressionally imposed restrictions have led presidents and their staffs to launch important diplomatic, military and covert activities in secret and without consulting Congress.[6]

The report rejected the notion that the problem lay with the quality of national leaders: "Our public officials are no less competent, either individually or as a group, than they used to be."[7]

The committee viewed the period before World War II as one in which the legislative and executive branches got along reasonably well. The "dealignment" of the party system since the 1930s has served to weaken the ability of legislative leaders to deal with the president. When party ties were strong, voters typically chose a legislature and a chief executive of the same party. Before World War II, the voters selected a president of one party and a Congress with at least one house controlled by the opposition less than 25 percent of the time. Since 1956, this has happened 60 percent of the time and since 1968 it has occurred over 80 percent of the time.[8] Moreover, as noted in Chapters 4 and 5, legislators no longer rely so heavily on political party ties when forming coalitions in Congress. Thus, even a president such as Carter, who had ample majorities of Democrats in both the House and the Senate, had difficulties in obtaining agreement with the Congress—as attested by his defeat on SALT II and his narrow victory on the Panama Canal treaties.

The Committee on the Constitutional System saw the need to try to put the genie back in the bottle, to achieve some greater coordination between the legislative and executive branches. Yet the past that it wanted to replicate was not one of bipartisan cooperation between the parties, but rather a time of renewed vigor for the parties. Strong parties, in its view, advance accountability. On the one hand, the people would know which party they could hold responsible for the decisions of the government. On the other hand, if the legislature and the executive were in the same hands, there would be added incentives for each branch to cooperate with the other. There would be no repetition of the long and arduous impeachment hearings of the Nixon administration or of the Iran–Contra hearings, though less momentous, of the Reagan era.

Reformers such as those in the Committee on the Constitutional System take the parliamentary form of government as their model for legislative–executive cooperation. In such systems, which are found in Great Britain, Canada, and many Western European nations, strong party government is possible. The prime minister is not elected by the people at large, but by the party (or coalition of parties) that wins the most seats in the legislature. Divided control of the legislative and executive branches is thus impossible. Furthermore, the prime minister must tailor policies to the wishes of the parliamentary party. A major defeat on a policy question can lead to the formation of a new government. Anthony Eden was replaced as prime minister of Great Britain in 1957 by Harold Macmillan after a major foreign policy blunder in the Middle East. Eden had committed British troops during the Egyptian–Israeli war to a joint effort with the French to recapture control of the Suez Canal from the Egyptians, who had seized the waterway.

The British–French attempt failed and Eden resigned. In the United States, on the other hand, Woodrow Wilson argued that:

> Our system is essentially astronomical. A president's usefulness is measured not by efficiency, but by calendar months. It is reckoned that if he be good at all, he will be good for four years. A prime minister must keep himself in favor with the majority; a president need only keep alive.[9]

American presidents can afford to take actions that risk failure early in their administrations. Because they have as long as three and a half years to recover from their "mistakes," they are virtually unchecked. When presidents ignore congressional criticism, as did Johnson in Vietnam, Nixon in Cambodia and on Watergate, and Reagan on the Iran–Contra affair, they lose popularity but retain their offices. What we have is a weakened presidency but a leader who cannot be dislodged from office.

How did the Committee on the Constitutional System propose to restore a sense of partisanship to the American political system? The reforms it suggested included four-year terms for House members and eight-year terms for senators, so that legislators would always be elected at the same time as presidents. In midterm elections the party of the president almost always loses seats in the Congress, often in substantial numbers. This situation provides incentives for legislators to divorce themselves from the president's policy initiatives and hinders legislative–executive cooperation. The committee also proposed permitting cabinet members to serve in the Congress to foster a less confrontational attitude between the bureaucracy and the Congress. Recognizing that the president's party would rarely achieve the two thirds of the Senate needed to ensure treaty ratification, it proposed that this requirement be lowered to 60 percent. The committee also noted a series of proposals on which its membership could not reach a consensus, but nevertheless deserved further consideration. These included encouraging the president to appear before the Congress to answer legislators' questions about administration policies, as prime ministers do at question time in parliamentary systems; permitting the states to make straight-ticket voting—at least for the president and Congress—compulsory rather than optional as it currently is; and permitting either the president or Congress to call a new election in the event of prolonged deadlock, as prime ministers in most parliamentary systems can do.[10]

A CONSTITUTIONAL DILEMMA?

To what extent are the sources of America's difficulties in forming a coherent foreign policy (not to mention a domestic policy) found in our Constitution? To be sure, the document does provide for a division of powers between the legislative, executive, and judicial branches. The separate elections for the president and Congress do permit the members of Congress to vote to establish their own political bases as opposed to contests in parliamentary systems where all candidates for office run based on party appeals and where the prime minister is selected from the ranks of legislators. Mid-term contests also provide voters with ready opportunities to select a Congress in which the dominant party is different from that of the president.

It is facile to blame all of the problems of deadlock on the constitutional system. First, the Constitution *permits* but hardly *requires* voters to choose divided government. In the presidential elections of 1968, 1972, 1980, 1984, and 1988, the electorate cast ballots for a president of one party and a Congress in which at least one house was controlled by the opposite party. Two of these contests, those of 1972 and 1984, were landslides of historic proportion in American electoral history, yet the Republicans did not gain control of both houses of Congress in either one. In 1988, when Republican George Bush carried 40 states to win the presidency, the Democrats gained strength in both houses of Congress. In the 1930s and 1940s only about 10 to 15 percent of congressional districts produced a plurality with one party for president and the other for Congress. In the 1970s and 1980s this figure had increased to a range of 30 to 40 percent.[11]

Further, the behavior of voters gives members of Congress ample reason to assert their independence from the White House. Not only do a third or more districts divide their vote between the parties for the legislative and executive branch, but even in districts carried by the president, the chief executive more often than not does not fare as well as the district's representative. When presidents do not score overwhelming victories (as in 1960 and 1976), members of the House run ahead of the president in more than 90 percent of congressional districts.[12] To reiterate, the Constitution does not dictate such behavior. There is deadlock between the parties because the people seem to prefer it that way. In several polls citizens have expressed the belief that split control of the legislative and executive branches is good for the country.[13]

The other devices suggested by the committee similarly might not achieve their objectives. Placing the secretary of state or defense in the Congress would not necessarily improve relations with the members of the legislature. First, there are already many opportunities for consultation between the secretaries and key congressional leaders.[14] Second, the lack of party discipline among legislators is not likely to increase simply because key White House officials sit among them. Even the idea that the president go before Congress to answer legislators' questions, as worthy as it is, might not lead to greater support for the chief executive among his own party. Question time in parliaments is useful mostly when prime ministers want to make some type of policy statement or might be trapped into explaining controversial programs. In the United States the press conference accomplishes the same goal with as much adversarial tenor as we would find in any parliamentary system.

The party system has been weakened without any change in the constitutional order. Indeed American presidents have had difficulties even when their parties controlled the Congress, as Carter's tenure demonstrated clearly. We should also recall that Johnson's Vietnam policy appeared to draw more unified support among Republicans than among his fellow Democrats in the Congress. In such cases it is highly unlikely that either the president or Congress would seek to resolve deadlock by calling a new election, if this proposal were to be adopted. When the president is unpopular, so too will be his party. Its members will be very reluctant to call for an election that would likely benefit the opposition party. When deadlock is between the parties, it is unclear who would be responsible for calling a new election, and the wrangling over who could do so might exacerbate the conflicts between the parties rather than resolve them. The United States does not have strong parties because Americans have always had ambivalent feelings toward these organizations. As Sundquist argues:

> The revitalization of political parties cannot be willed. If it could be, it already would have been; party leaders have not lacked the desire to preside over stronger organizations.[15]

Instead, the tendency toward deadlock in the American political system is "normal" and "irresistible."[16]

There are additional problems in the search for accountability in foreign policy. To have strong parties, voters must perceive clear-cut differences between the Democrats and Republicans on issues and must care enough about those concerns to cast ballots based on them. We saw in Chapter 5 that neither condition holds in the United States. The party platforms do not provide any but the most concerned voters with clear-cut information about where the parties differ on most foreign policy issues. Indeed it is quite rational for candidates *not* to stress their differences with the other party, so as to alienate as few voters as possible.[17] If parties do not present voters with clear-cut differences on policy issues, it would be difficult to expect the electorate vote based on the issues. Even if the parties did take divergent positions on foreign policy issues, citizens would only use such postures as as cues to voting if they were aware of the distinctions. This presumes an interest in foreign policy issues that we found is often lacking on the part of voters. When international problems become campaign issues, this usually happens through retrospective evaluations by voters—approval, or more likely, disapproval of an administration's policies. Voters rarely are so concerned with foreign policy that they give political leaders ideas about what *ought* to be done.

Finally, it is unclear that restoring the comity between the legislative and executive branches involves strengthening political parties. One can make a good argument that it might be desirable to have the two parties taking divergent stands on many policy issues, both domestic and foreign. It might be preferable to have one party take a hard line on dealing with the Soviet Union and the other a position more favorable to deténte, so that the electorate might be able to choose which course it prefers. But this is not the same argument as restoring legislative–executive cooperation. The "good old days," if they were that, were marked by *bipartisanship*, not by ideologically distinctive parties. With the pre-Vietnam consensus broken down, it is very difficult to restore it. Constitutional reform seems an unlikely method for altering public opinion.

Government by strong political parties might not be possible within the American context for another reason. Americans often express foreign policy attitudes that do not form the consistent basis for party appeals. For example, we found in Chapter 5 that strong majorities of both parties opposed aid to the Contras in Nicaragua, yet they overwhelmingly supported the invasion of Grenada and expressly back Israel over the Arab states in the Middle East conflict. Other policy proposals, such as the level of defense spending, have shifting majorities. At times a plurality of Americans support more money for the military and at other times it favors reduced expenditures. These data suggest that there may be no single set of policies that voters prefer.[18] Would the country be better off if one party endorsed lower defense spending, criticized the Grenada episode, opposed aid to the Contras, and supported the Arab cause in the Middle East while the other party took the opposite positions? It is far from clear that this would be desirable. In the era of the post-Vietnam dissensus, it is equally unlikely that both parties would adopt the same positions on all foreign policy issues.

IS THE PRESIDENT THE PROBLEM?

If the constitutional order is not the problem perhaps it is the presidency itself. We consider two arguments that focus on the White House. Both criticize the current selection process for presidential nominations, but they come to very different conclusions. The second thesis posits that the system of primary elections produces candidates who are better qualified to run for office than to serve once elected. The thesis we shall consider first presents a more damning conclusion: many of the people who have been elected president do not have the proper temperament to serve in the job. Furthermore, through appropriate analysis, it is possible to isolate such potential misfits and call their unsuitability for public office to the public's attention. Presumably the electorate would then reject such candidates for the nation's highest office.

PERSONALITY AND THE SEARCH FOR A PRESIDENT: WHY NOT THE BEST?

Increasing presidential power has spawned a heightened interest and concern about the type of individuals who have occupied—and will occupy—the highest office in the land and perhaps the world. Most schoolchildren can recite a list of "great" presidents such as Washington, Jefferson, Lincoln, Wilson, and the two Roosevelts. We hear substantially less about other presidents—from those who were simply not successful to those we consider outright scoundrels—and virtually nothing at all about vice presidents. In 1972, the McGovern presidential campaign suffered a major setback when it became known that the vice presidential nominee, Senator Thomas Eagleton (D-Mo.), had undergone psychiatric treatment earlier in his life. Eagleton was ultimately forced to withdraw from the ticket although he has continued to serve quite effectively in the Senate. Vice President Quayle's qualifications to serve as chief executive were severely questioned in 1988. In an era of the strong presidency, the nominees' personal traits are being critically scrutinized by the press, the public, and scholars.

The tensions of Vietnam and Watergate have made Americans somewhat fearful of presidential power. In turn, these events have called attention to the problems of determining in advance who might be an exceptional president, or at least a very good one. Could there be a prescreening, a sort of presidential leadership test that might not guarantee us great leaders but perhaps could save us from our previous errors? At least one school of thought leads to a positive answer to this question. Called *psychohistory* or *psychobiography*, this approach to studying leadership is based on the development of personality in potential leaders and the use of psychoanalytic methods of investigation to determine what brought some leaders to success and others to failure. The 1970s did not mark the beginning of psychohistory, but rather a renewed and enlarged concern for the capacity of academic research to guide us in screening out potentially bad presidents.

Psychobiography has been applied to such diverse figures as Martin Luther and Woodrow Wilson. But in 1972, James David Barber's book, *The Presidential Character*, the first psychohistory of American presidents, was published.[19] Barber's analysis dealt with presidents comparatively, presented a framework for classifying presidents, claimed to have predictive utility, and specifically and strikingly predicted the ultimate failure of the Nixon presidency. Barber's argument is itself complex, so we shall necessarily oversimplify it here.

Barber clearly maintains that the early development of a president's personality is the key to understanding how he will perform in office.[20] In examining this personality through the tools of psychoanalysis, we must be careful to avoid accounts that are too popular (press reports or biographies that may be overly critical or flattering) and obtain detailed information on the future leader's early development. What is one to look for in examining whether someone will be a successful leader? *Style* involves the way the president balances rhetoric, personal relationships, and detailed "homework"—ranging from the very intense patterns of Nixon, Johnson, and Wilson to the more relaxed style of Eisenhower and particularly Coolidge, who would not miss his daily nap. *World view* consists of the president's perception of what the great issues of the time are and what forces shape them, including both Franklin Roosevelt's dictum that "We have nothing to fear but fear itself" to Nixon's (and Johnson's) identification of such struggles as involving, among other things, elements of good and evil, white and black, the forces of incumbency versus the challenge from without and sometimes even from within from what Dan Rather has called "the palace guard."[21] Finally, there is the element of *character*, the president's outlook on life and his role in the world "not for the moment, but enduringly."[22] From these considerations Barber outlines two basic dimensions of the presidential character: activity-passivity and positive-negative affect toward one's activity. On the question of activity, style is stressed. Affect toward activity reflects world view and character; more specifically, affect poses the question: Does the (potential) president enjoy the job and have a positive outlook on his capacity to handle the problems he confronts?

Putting these two dimensions together, Barber constructs four types of presidential character. The active-positive chief executive puts much effort into the job and enjoys doing it. He values productivity and sees himself as developing over time to meet new challenges within well-defined personal goals. There is an emphasis on rationality; such a president sees events in terms of diverse factors and the political battles that must be won, within the contexts of rational action, to achieve productivity.[23] Among the active-positive presidents have been Franklin Roosevelt, Harry Truman, John Kennedy, Gerald Ford, and Jimmy Carter. In contrast, the active-negatives have a conflict between a very strong effort to succeed and low emotional reward for that attempt. Activity is compulsive, the president himself ambitious and aggressive. Unlike the active-positive, who relates well to others who may oppose his policies, the active-negative retreats from opposition, often into a lonely inner struggle that produces confrontation and despair for the leader and isolates him from the nation.[24] Such presidents include Wilson, Johnson, Herbert Hoover, and Nixon.

The passive-positive president is simultaneously optimistic and agreeable, friendly and compliant. Such a leader has a positive outlook on the job of being president but does not believe that much is demanded of him personally in commitment to new programs or national leadership. The emphasis is on personality, as Barber argues regarding the ever-smiling William Howard Taft and later about Warren Harding during the "return to normalcy" after World War I, a period of relative calm in the country. A passive-positive is popular because of what he does not do and because of what he is—either a hero to the nation or a likable sort of person (Harding). A passive-negative, in contrast, would rather be almost anything but president. He is in politics because he believes he ought to be. The job is unrewarding and this type of leader has little patience for it. The classic case is Coolidge, who cultivated the image of someone sleeping through his administration; another, less clear-cut example, is Dwight Eisenhower.[25] Neither appeared to want the position. Coolidge simply walked away from renomination when he said, "I do not choose to run." Eisenhower turned down the Democratic nomination in 1948, while the battle on his behalf for the Republican nomination was largely waged without his seeming involvement.

In the era of strong presidents, however, passive chief executives are increasingly unlikely to be selected. Rather, Barber sees the major struggle in American politics as one between active-positives and active-negatives.

The former are, of course, almost ideal types. The great presidents were all active-positives and others who fit into this category are viewed at least as reasonably successful. All were well adjusted and did not allow the office of the presidency to insulate them from the nation, whatever their other failings may have been. Active-negatives, on the other hand, are self-destructive and thus potentially fatal to the nation. Their world vision is limited by their concern for their respective places in history and their insistence that each of them has the answers to the nation's problems. Their opponents are simply wrong. Barber predicted in 1972 that Nixon's presidency would come to an unhappy end, and the utility of his framework was established for many.[26] In 1980, he predicted that if elected, Reagan would be a "jelly bean"—a softie—rather than the danger that President Carter was trying to portray him as. Reagan, according to Barber, would be a nine-to-five president. His passivity had been shown by his lifetime practice of taking it easy; his positive side is evident in his generally cheerful optimistic attitude. Reagan hates to fight and seeks to please and may cave in to pressure; the greatest danger will be that the president may be done in by his friends, as were many of his passive-positive predecessors. Who presidential friends are is thus critical and a considerably more important issue to consider than it would be for a president possessing a different character.

The strengths of the approach of psychohistory are its comparative evaluation of president and its recognition of the role of childhood development on a leader's personality. The active-positives are well adjusted and the active-negatives poorly adjusted. But historical records, even psychoanalytic ones, are subject to multiple interpretations. The same evidence can be used to adduce either a positive or a negative evaluation of even childhood experiences.[27] Often value judgments are a function of hindsight. Truman seems to be a much better president now than he did when he was in office. Revisionist psychohistory has, in fact, leapfrogged Eisenhower from a borderline passive-negative to a passive-positive.[28] Reagan's high profile and very effective bargaining style during his first several months in office seemed to dispute predictions of his passivity. Psychohistory is certainly a useful way of generalizing about leadership that has previously been beyond the political scientists' scope. But what happens when not just the journalists but the specialists, the psychohistorians, disagree on what the evidence means? Furthermore, Barber's linkage of the presidential character to early childhood experiences and teenage development seems to belie the traditional notion of a president "growing into the job." How much more likely is someone with earlier emotional problems to develop into an active-negative president? Has the country actually been better served by ensuring that an Eagleton will never be elected to either the presidency or the vice presidency? How do we determine the most appropriate methods of evaluating the evidence? Psychoanalysis is hardly an exact science.[29]

What kind of foreign policy president will a particular personality type make? It is in this area that there is the greatest potential for further development, because handling foreign affairs from the White House necessarily involves on-the-job training. Two classic active-negatives, Wilson and Johnson, failed on key foreign policy issues important to them. Wilson lost a pitched battle with the Senate over American entry into the League of Nations while Johnson was overcome by events in Vietnam. Both presidents had been primarily interested in domestic politics—and, despite Barber's analysis, Wilson is often listed in both public and academic surveys as one of the nation's great presidents.[30] The disparity lies in Wilson's remarkable achievements in social welfare legislation, his New Freedom, mostly accomplished during his first administration (1913–1917). Johnson was also a leader in domestic politics, where he sought "to heal and to build" and was a compassionate champion of civil rights and war against poverty. Probably more social legislation was passed during 1965–1966 than in the rest of this century (including the New Freedom and Franklin Roosevelt's New Deal). Could Johnson have been an active-positive president on domestic policy but not on foreign policy? On the other hand, Nixon's foreign policy accomplishments kept his personal popularity at levels that let him retain the presidency for at least several months longer than would otherwise be the case (Chapter 5). As much as Wilson and Johnson were bedeviled by foreign policy and sought refuge in social welfare legislation, Nixon believed that his world centered around international events. Reagan was even more complex. His management style was not so neatly broken up into foreign and domestic realms. Rather, he seemed to be an active-positive when he was popular—in the first years of each of his terms and in the last year of his first term. When public opinion was less supportive, Reagan seemed to fall into a much more passive phase. His presidency, as much as any other since Johnson, demonstrated the difficulties of attempting to sum up a president's style so simply. It is indeed difficult to understand the makeup of a president who took charge with such vigor and success in 1981 and 1985 but who seemed content to delegate so much of his authority in most other years.

These questions are not meant to disparage the contributions of psychohistory, but only to recognize the limitations of any approach that seeks to determine who might be a "great" president or even an "acceptable" one. A president successful in foreign policy is not necessarily the same as a strong leader in domestic policy. Perhaps the personality types involved in each are sufficiently different so that we expect the impossible. Traditional foreign policy leadership requires a command style, the establishment of a hierarchy so that there is a single leader for the nation. Domestic policy success, on the other hand, requires strong bargaining skills, an ability to deal with legislators on their own terms, and, most critically, an understanding of the complex political relationships among members of Congress and the president. One style emphasizes almost complete control over a situation; the other tremendous flexibility. It is a rare president, particularly in these days of an increasingly interdependent world, who possesses both traits. Perhaps only Franklin Roosevelt achieved such success.

How could we adopt presidential screening even if we had so few reservations about putting candidates on the couch? Would candidates submit themselves to a board of psychiatrists? How much about the personal background of candidates do we really need to know? And how much are we likely to learn even if we don't hanker to find out about it? The 1988 presidential contest has answered some of these questions for us. The revelations about former Senator Gary Hart's alliances with model Donna Rice and other women forced him out of the race. Following those divulgences by the *Miami Herald* and the *Washington Post*, the *New York Times* asked all active presidential candidates to supply written answers to a detailed questionnaire about their personal backgrounds. The *Times'* questions covered the gamut—from tax returns to health to personal relationships. Almost all of the candidates refused to answer at least some of the questions and the *Times* apologized for its poor taste. Yet the very fact that a major American newspaper felt that it could even broach the subject indicates that every aspect of the private lives of candidates is a matter for public examination. The sudden rise to celebrity status of Donna Rice also indicates that the press is hardly the sole culprit. As noted in Chapter 5, if the electorate preferred stories about arms control positions—as Hart indicated that it did— the media would have filled its pages and air time with these items rather than stories about sex in high places.

It seems that we are destined to know virtually everything that can be learned about presidential candidates. It is no surprise that even candidates who might have nothing to hide might decide to forego the trauma of having every aspect of their personal lives dragged before the network audiences of the nightly news. It is far from clear that only the least qualified candidates are the ones who withdraw from the fray. Yet the information garnered by the press is not likely to permit the detailed type of psychiatric investigation that Barber recommends. At most it will provide a pseudoscientific analysis that many citizens might be willing to accept as a substitute for more sophisticated studies. The very politicians who feel hounded by the press are unlikely to subject themselves to detailed analysis by a panel of psychiatrists so that the public might be better informed. Even if psychohistory were more reliable, they could rightly argue that leaving the decision to a panel of experts is undemocratic. The people have every right to select whomever they wish. The specter of experts quarreling among themselves in a field that has not reached anything like consensus would hardly dignify the presidential selection process.

THE TROUBLED PRESIDENCY: THE SELECTION PROCESS IS THE PROBLEM

It was Jimmy Carter who asked "Why not the best"? He also promised to give the United States "a government as good as its people." When he did so, governing as an outsider not born of the "Washington establishment," the people roundly rejected his administration in the 1980 elections. Yet they chose as his successor another outsider, Ronald Reagan. There are some who argue that the difficulty lies not so much with the psychological makeup of the candidates, but with their lack of experience in dealing with national and international affairs. This is especially problematic in a country that has come to look to the White House for the solution to all of its problems.

This perspective agrees with the constitutional reformers that the president no longer serves as party leader. It offers little hope that the party system can be restored and sees the real root of the problem with the people who occupy the office and the public's expectations of the president. On the one hand, the system of primary elections that has dominated the presidential nominating system since 1972 has put a premium on candidates who make good impressions on television, who simplify issues, and who run against the establishment in Washington. A wheelchair-bound Franklin Roosevelt, a short and stocky Harry Truman, or a tall and sometimes vulgar Lyndon Johnson would not fare well in the media age where everyone seeks to be the next John F. Kennedy. On the other hand, the electorate now has a very high set of expectations of what the president should do, so that even superhumans might not be able to fulfill them, much less the "outsiders" who fare so well on television.

The problem is not simply the abuses of power in an "imperial presidency," but rather a combination of poor presidents and overly optimistic views by the public about what the president can accomplish. In the nineteenth century, when the federal government had few responsibilities compared to the present and when the conduct of foreign affairs consisted largely of appointing ambassadors, the Congress rather than the president was the center of the federal government. The legislature was a part-time job whose members served but a few terms in Washington.[31] The popular view was that governing was anything but an art.

> We are too apt to think both the work of legislation and the work of administration easy enough to be done readily, with or without preparation by any man of discretion and character. No one imagines that the drygoods or hardware trade, or even the cobbler's craft, can be successfully conducted except by those who have worked through a laborious and unremunerative apprenticeship, and who have devoted their lives to perfecting themselves as tradesmen or as menders of shoes. But . . . administration is regarded as something which an old soldier, an ex-diplomatist, or a popular politician may be trusted to take by instinct. No man of tolerable talents need despair of having been born a presidential candidate.[32]

Another keen observer, Lord James Bryce, argued that intelligence and eloquence were useful, but perhaps superfluous traits for a president. Instead, the nineteenth-century president's job was such that the skills needed to perform the job were similar to those of "the chairman of a commercial company or the manager of a railway": firmness, common sense, and, most critical, honesty.[33] In the twentieth century, however, the role of the central government grew tremendously. The New Deal brought Washington into the lives of most American citizens. The two world wars, the conflicts in Korea and Vietnam, and, most important, the growing internationalization of the world economy made the central government the focal point of people's attention. So did the rise of national media, especially television networks, that led to a more homogenous culture throughout the nation's regions.

DO WE EXPECT TOO MUCH OF OUR PRESIDENTS?

The new focus on Washington, the growth of national media to spread the word about what was happening in the Capitol, and the declining power of political parties meant that people looked more and more to the president as the single source of authority in the country. The presidency thus became an almost mythical institution. The people viewed the occupant of the White House as the single person who could coordinate the activities of the government and who thus could solve the nation's problems. Presidents in turn encouraged this lavish attention by constantly appealing for popular support through the act of "going public." The people and their chief executive built up a rapport that excluded the Congress or other actors in the government. The parties were not left out. It was their weakness that led presidents to seek out a direct relationship with the public.[34]

This "special relationship" between the people and their leader is not a simple love story. One suitor, the public, is often quite fickle in its feelings toward the other, the president. Given the great expectations that people initially have of their leaders, it is only natural that disappointment sets in at some time during the president's administration. Even partial successes can become failures if the people expect too much; thus presidents appear doomed to failure. Contemporary presidents have succeeded for the most part in making their successors look better than they did while in office.[35] During the Iran–Contra hearings, many Americans came to upgrade their evaluation of Carter who, after all, took full responsibility for the hostage crisis. During the Carter administration Ford's hapless tenure in office, marked primarily by overridden vetoes, seemed a happy memory. And witness not only the rehabilitation, but the revival of Nixon's fortunes, including a 1986 cover story in *Time* magazine showing the former president making the "V for Victory" sign of happier days.

What factors contribute to the roller-coaster contour of presidential popularity in the post-Vietnam era? Clearly our expectations of presidential performance are critical, but suggestions that we lower our sights are unrealistic.[36] The presidency occupies too important a role in our political system. If we cannot convince the public that they are demanding the impossible, perhaps we can find presidents who are up to the task. When we look to recent history, we find that those presidents who have failed sought the office as "outsiders." They ran against the Washington establishment, promising a whole new way of doing business. More than any other recent presidents, they went public. Carter established a reputation as the "people's president" by carrying his luggage into the White House himself. Reagan continually pressed viewers to write their representatives and senators to demand support for his policies. Both gave short shrift to their party leaders in Congress. As Meg Greenfield argued:

> We have developed something new in our politics: the professional amateur. It is by now a trend, a habit, a cult. You succeed in this line of activity by declaring your aversion to and unfitness for it. That will bring you the cheers of the multitude. It will also bring in time . . . the kind of troubles the Carter presidency has sustained and seemed, almost perversely, to compound.[37]

Both Carter and Reagan, as well as "amateur" candidates who failed to win the presidency (George McGovern in 1972, John Anderson in 1980) ignored the traditional party organizations through which presidents used to be selected.

Presidential candidates focus on the media instead of the parties. They spend their time going public and confer with a handpicked set of personal advisers, many of whom have had no contact with politicians in Washington. At the 1980 Democratic convention, only 14 percent of the Democratic members of the House and Senate attended as delegates.[38] The party recognized the error of its ways when it provided for additional "superdelegates" who would comprise 14 percent of the 1984 convention delegates. This group would consist of party members and elected officials, two thirds of whom might be members of the House and Senate. However, the party's ties to its Washington base had long been weakened. Between 1968 and 1980 the number of primaries doubled from seventeen to thirty-five and the percentage of delegates selected through this route increased from forty to seventy-five. The focal point of Washington politics had shifted back to the heartland of the country.

The backgrounds of Carter, Reagan, and Michael Dukakis are also no accident. Presidential candidates no longer come primarily from the Senate. Both Carter and Reagan were *former* governors who became full-time presidential candidates. In 1984 Walter F. Mondale's background in the Senate and as vice president were considered by many to be handicaps, and a legislative outsider with few accomplishments in the Senate (Hart) captured the imagination of many Democrats and almost the nomination as well. In 1988, only three of the candidates had won statewide races for national office on their own more than once: Robert Dole, Paul Laxalt, and Joseph Biden. Just three had risen to positions of leadership in their parties: Dole as majority (and later minority) leader of the Senate and Gephardt as chair of the Democratic Caucus in the House. Three prominent candidates (Jesse Jackson, Alexander Haig, and Pat Robertson) had never been elected to any position. Two senators ran in their first terms (Albert Gore and Paul Simon). What is even more remarkable is the large number of trial balloons sent up by rather ordinary political figures who had virtually no name recognition beyond their own states. The presidency had become democratized, so that the refrain one learned in elementary school—that any little boy or girl could grow up to become president—seemed quite true indeed.

Presidents get into trouble, this thesis goes, because they come to Washington as enemies of the government and bring their own staffs—be they from California or Georgia—with them. This is the "cult of the amateur" that the public seems to reward. Yet chief executives must confront congressional leaders still chosen largely in accord with the seniority system, and heads of other countries who rise through the ranks of their political parties and legislatures. How do we get such presidents—those who disdain the type of bargaining that past leaders recognized as necessary to accomplish the successful enactment of their legislative programs, and their dealings with foreign heads of state?

According to many, the villain is the nomination system. The proliferation of primaries and caucuses places a premium on candidates' willingness to spend two to three years traversing such states as Iowa and New Hampshire, shaking hands with potential supporters rather than developing ties with party leaders who in previous years could deliver delegate support at the nominating conventions. The British magazine, *The Economist*, expressed this view succinctly.

> America gets bad presidents because it gets bad candidates, and it gets bad candidates because they are now chosen chiefly in a series of primary elections in which voters put a premium on superficial qualities televisually conveyed, with little consideration of the attributes needed to run the most powerful country in the world.[39]

Since many of the delegates themselves are attending conventions for the first time, there are few ties that bind the presidential candidates to the party, or the party to its eventual nominee.[40] The delegates are nowhere to be found when the winner takes office.

The new president must deal with the "entrenched Washington establishment," in the Congress and in the bureaucracy. After having run against these same people—and having run behind most congressional candidates even in districts carried by the victorious party—the president cannot rely on them for support. Thus, the only alternative is to go over their heads and demand that the public put pressure on these officials to support the administration's policies. This leads presidents not only to chastise the Congress, but ultimately to ignore it. In turn this produces either an isolated chief executive such as Carter or an irate one such as Reagan, whose hand-chosen advisers feel free to take policy initiatives into their own hands when Congress seems obstructionistic. The Iran–Contra affair thus can be seen not as a unique event, but as the culmination of a political crisis between the two major branches of government. In turn, it produces a downward spiral in public confidence in the presidency that can only be reversed by the same type of anti-Washington appeals that led to the difficulties in the first place. Thus, the cure for the ills of amateurism—to paraphrase the late Robert LaFollette, the Progressive party candidate for president in 1924—is more amateurism.[41]

Is there a way out of this seemingly vicious cycle? Some have suggested that if the primary system is the cause of the problems, taking the nomination out of the hands of the public might resolve the predicament of "the cult of the amateur." One proposal would make all of the party nominees for the House and Senate in addition to senators not due for reelection automatic delegates to the party conventions. This proposal is designed to increase the ties that bind the presidential candidate to the party's congressional delegation.[42] A more radical suggestion would abolish primaries altogether and rest the nominations with the party's membership in Congress, as was the case before 1824. Not only might this bring more harmony to legislative–executive affairs, but it would also make the nomination of an outsider extremely unlikely.[43] Legislators would hardly be apt to select as their party's standard-bearer someone who refused to acknowledge any ties to the caucus. Both of these reforms, it should be noted, do not require any legislation. The national parties could adopt them.

The difficulty with the first suggestion is that it has already been substantially adopted without much effect on the nominating process. In 1984, the Democrats provided that up to two thirds of the sitting members of the House and Senate would be delegates to their convention. Even with the same system in place for 1988, a whole raft of unknown and untested candidates sought their party's nomination. Merely adding a handful of additional members, plus party nominees for the Congress who have not yet served in Washington and may never be elected, is unlikely to have a measurable impact. This "reform" would not do away with the long arduous nominating system that places a premium on outsider strategies. The second, more radical proposal *would* do away with primaries and caucuses. However, for that very reason, it is not likely to be adopted. It is especially unlikely that the very amateurs who gather at conventions would vote to eliminate their base of power and give it back to party leaders.

In any event, there is reason to doubt that the primary system itself is the cause, rather than the effect, of the decline of parties. Many of the trends of the new long campaign, with its numerous candidates, actually predated the 1972 reforms that made the nominating system for the Democratic party so wide open.[44] As noted in Chapter 5, the decline of party strength dates back to the 1930s. A more proximate cause of the success of the outsider strategy than the primary system is the decline in political trust in America that began in the 1960s (see Chapter 5). This makes perfect sense. Candidates for the White House succeed with the outsider strategy because people see the Washington establishment as not trustworthy. Each new crisis of the presidency further erodes trust in government—and makes it more difficult for an "insider" to gain a nomination. This perspective also explains both the capture of the Democratic nomination by Mondale in 1984 and the proliferation of candidates seeking the presidency in both parties four years later. In 1984, Mondale benefited, albeit perversely, from the upsurge in trust that Reagan generated. Four years later the decline in confidence resulting from the Iran–Contra affair made amateurism the vogue once again. President George Bush appears to be an exception. However, he never won a statewide election on his own prior to 1988, in contrast to his major opponent for the Republican nomination, Senate Minority Leader Robert Dole.

If this argument is correct, there is little we can do to stop the cult of amateurism. To get better presidents, we need a successful presidency. Yet presidencies seem doomed to failure, if for no other reason than because the public expects more of the office than any human being can deliver. The nominating system puts a premium on successful politicians rather than on men and women who can govern well, so our leaders are sure to fall very short of public expectations. We do indeed have a vicious cycle. Perhaps we can gain some solace from recognizing that this is not a novel problem of the television age. Writing of the "mediocre" candidates of the nineteenth century, Bryce argued that "the merits of a president are one thing and those of a candidate another thing."[45] The stakes, especially in international politics, have increased enormously and thus it is more crucial than ever that we find some way to balance executive and legislative power and responsibilities.

WHAT KIND OF FOREIGN POLICY DOES THE PUBLIC WANT?

If the search for better presidents is not likely to be fruitful, perhaps one way to avoid the cycles of presidential popularity is for the legislative branch to become stronger. A more active role for the Congress might restrain the president from engaging in the sort of policies that ultimately and it seems inevitably lead to failed presidencies. A stronger Congress might also make legislators less parochial and more willing to view foreign policy from a global perspective.

Whom does the public believe makes foreign policy in the United States and whom does it trust the most to formulate the great issues of international affairs? Surveys by the Chicago Council on Foreign Relations in 1982 provide some insight into these questions.[46] Interviewing both a national sample of the public and 341 elite opinion leaders, the council asked each who had the most power on foreign policy decision making and who *ought* to be the most important. The results of the surveys are presented in Table 9–1.

It is hardly surprising that the president is seen by both samples as the most important actor, although 70 percent of the general public has this perception compared to almost the entire elite sample. Almost equally pow-

TABLE 9–1   The Importance of Various Actors in Foreign Policy Making: The Chicago Council on Foreign Relations Mass and Elite Surveys, 1982

Actor	Actor Perceived as Very Important*		Actor Should Be Important	
	Public	Elite	Public	Elite
President	70	91	39	17
Secretary of state	64	83	33	22
State Department	47	38	34	34
Congress	46	34	44	34
Military	40	36	26	3
Public opinion	23	15	54	36
United Nations	29	2	37	33
American business	35	22	23	22
Labor unions	17	3	17	14
Private organizations	9	3	10	21
Central Intelligence Agency	28	20	16	9
National security adviser	35	46	31	13

*In percentages.

erful from the public's perspective—and still a strong second in the eyes of the elite—is the secretary of state. Slightly less than half of the public sample and just about a third of the elite sees an important role for Congress. This represents a considerable shift from a 1974 set of surveys when only 20 percent of the elite sampled and 40 percent of the public perceived Congress as playing an important role on foreign policy. However, it also represents somewhat of a decline, at least among the elite, from the 45 percent who saw Congress as very important as recently as 1978–1979, the most recent survey taken after the legislature began to challenge the executive during the Nixon years on domestic and foreign issues. What is striking from this table is that most of the actors, ranging from the bureaucrats at the State Department to the United Nations to labor and business as well as the military and the CIA, are perceived as less important by the elite than they are by the public at large. The elite thus tends to view the foreign policy-making process in dominance by the president and the secretary of state, with some power for the Congress and more limited influence by the bureaucracy, the military, and public opinion. The elite, however, does perceive the president's national security adviser as more powerful than does the general public. Ordinary citizens may be less likely to understand the unique role of this adviser, much less to know who he is, than the more attentive elite. But the public does acknowledge executive dominance on foreign policy while perceiving substantial roles for most other actors. Most of the public, however, does not view public opinion as a particularly powerful voice on foreign policy when compared to Congress, the military, the State Department, business, or even the United Nations.

While the public does not see its own opinions as having a major impact, it does believe (by a margin of 54 percent) that it should be the most important determinant of foreign policy making. Congress is second, ahead of the president, who barely edges the United Nations and is not far ahead of the State Department, the secretary of state, or the national security adviser. Indeed, the public seems to have lost confidence in all actors— including public opinion itself—since 1978–1979. Thirteen percent more of the public (67 percent in all) felt that its attitudes should be very important in 1978–1979, while 46 percent believed that the president should be important. Of the other actors, there were drops of between 3 and 7 percent except for the Congress and labor unions, which stayed at almost similar levels to four years earlier. The elites became somewhat less trustworthy as well of most actors. Public opinion fell 8 points, the most of any actor, while the military dropped 7.5 percentage points. On the other hand, there were small increases in elite opinions about the roles that Congress, the State Department, and labor ought to play. The opinion leaders remain distrustful of presidential dominance, perhaps because of the lack of foreign policy experience that the men who have recently become president had before assuming office. The Iran–Contra affair demonstrates that perceptions of poor performance lead to crises of trust in *all* institutions. Although more people lost confidence in the executive branch (24 percent) than in any other institution, 20 percent reported losing faith in the Congress and about 16 percent each in the press, business, and labor.[47] The elite seems to prefer a more dispersed pattern of authority on foreign policy than does the public, although the difference is not nearly as sharp as it was in earlier surveys. The public is more willing to entrust policy making to business than to labor or other private organizations, but it already sees business as having more power than is desirable. The elites recognize that business is powerful, but do not seem to think that it is quite as strong as the public believes it to be. Indeed, its influence is seen as "just about right," while both labor and private organizations ought to be more powerful.

The key message of the surveys is that the elite prefers a foreign policy conducted by the unusual coalition of Congress, the State Department, public opinion, and the United Nations. On the other hand, the public prefers more of a partnership among its own opinions, the Congress, and the executive. In essence, it calls for a more evenly distributed balance of power between the legislative and executive branches than we now have, with somewhat more power given to the legislature.

How might the Congress take on a more assertive role in foreign policy? The institutional barriers we discussed in Chapters 3 and 4 remain. It is simply unrealistic to expect the 435 members of the House of Representatives and the 100 members of the Senate to coalesce in support of a single foreign policy. It might even be too much to demand that the major foreign policy committees in each house reach agreement. Even if they could, who would negotiate with international leaders, the president, or the Congress?

When the two branches agree on key issues, this question is of little consequence. However, the entire question of which branch should predominate
is predicated on the idea that the legislative and executive will generally *not*
agree. This, of course, is the heart of the democratic dilemmas. If whatever
process we used had the same outcomes, the problem of making foreign
policy in a democracy would not exist.

THE PRESIDENT PROPOSES, THE CONGRESS REACTS?

Perhaps we should admit that the Congress is not well suited to formulate an independent foreign policy and that it is unlikely to impose its
own views on the president in many instances. Is there an alternative role
for Congress? The answer is "yes." Like the role of public opinion in a democracy, the Congress can—and often does—evaluate foreign policy retrospectively. That is, it responds to administration proposals and actions by
examining them, holding hearings, and proposing alternative policies. The
Legislative Reorganization Act of 1970 indeed mandated increased oversight
for all committees in the Congress.

The prospects for oversight can perhaps best be summed up by the
traditional refrain. The word *oversight* has two meanings: critical evaluation
of executive performance and a passing thought. In the Congress, where
many committee hearings are routine and not very investigative, there has
been an overemphasis on the meaning not intended by those who want
more of a balance of power in the national government. The difficulty is that
in too many cases, the regulators (congressional investigators) become the
accomplices of the groups or organizations they are supposed to investigate
and control.[48] Furthermore, as Morris Ogul argues, the oversight function is
not terribly salient to most members of Congress.[49] Even when members do
become concerned with their oversight duties, the close working relationships that develop among the legislators, bureaucrats, and interest groups
("those cozy triangles"[50]) are not conducive to critical examinations of the
behavior of each other.

Yet there has been an increase in critical oversight in recent years. In
particular, both the House and the Senate established oversight committees
to investigate the abuses of power of the Central Intelligence Agency and
the Federal Bureau of Investigation in the Ninety-fourth Congress (1975–
1976). Yet, the very fact that such committees were established points to one
of the weaknesses in the congressional oversight procedure. Institutional
loyalties prevailed, so that no thought was given to a joint committee—
which would have saved duplication of effort. In each House, a select committee (as opposed to one of the more traditional standing committees) was
formed for the investigations. Yet there existed committees on foreign relations, armed services, government operations, and judiciary (in the case of
the FBI) in each House that could just as effectively have conducted the
oversight. Why were select committees employed? Again, the question of

institutional loyalties arose within congressional committees, and there was also a problem of where the ultimate jurisdiction was to be placed.

Once established, the intelligence committees did not function smoothly. In the Senate, many critics claimed that Chairman Frank Church was headline hunting and was trying to conclude the hearings as quickly as possible to enter the Democratic presidential primaries. The committee in the House, known as the Pike Committee, drew better "press notices," but the lower house produced a spectacle of its own. The original House Intelligence Committee was chaired by Representative Lucien Nedzi (D-Mich.). A conflict within the committee developed when maverick Representative Michael Harrington (D-Mass.) leaked to the press classified material on the CIA's role in destabilizing the Allende government in Chile in 1973. Nedzi demanded that Harrington be removed from the committee, and there was a movement within the House to censure Harrington. The Harrington case was overshadowed by further leaks to the press and the entire matter was finally closed on a rather obscure technicality that saved Harrington from possible action by his fellow House members. Speaker Carl Albert finally resolved the dispute between supporters of Nedzi and those of Harrington by reconstituting the committee without either member. Like its Senate counterpart, the House Intelligence Committee was established as a permanent committee in 1977.

What did the intelligence committees accomplish? They did bring to public attention a large number of abuses of power by the FBI and particularly by the CIA. Yet much of this publicity arose through leaks and much of what we learned about the intelligence agencies came from newspapers and magazine follow-up stories rather than from congressional testimony. Indeed, Pike and Ford were at loggerheads on what the committee could or could not release. The full House ultimately sided with the president against a moderate Democrat. Much of the impetus for reform was slowed when Richard Welch, a CIA operative in Greece, was assassinated. Many people thought that the congressional hearings were divulging too much information about the agency, thereby making the intelligence operations of the United States vulnerable throughout the world. Ultimately, the Congress did take some action: It forbade the CIA from engaging in domestic intelligence operations, and it also passed a law that made the assassination of foreign leaders illegal—an action that undoubtedly would make a few foreign chiefs of state sleep more soundly at night. Attempts to make the CIA budget available to at least the relevant congressional personnel failed. No wide-ranging reorientation of foreign intelligence was mandated by Congress. The decision in 1977 to place all intelligence operations dealing with foreign policy under a single agency, headed by CIA Director Stansfield Turner, was made in the White House, not on Capitol Hill.

In 1980 the Congress voted to restrict the number of committees to which the president must report any covert action to two, the intelligence chambers in the House and the Senate. A congressional move, backed by the Carter administration, to formulate a charter for the CIA failed to win approval, but so did a conservative bid in the Congress to repeal the provisions of the Hughes-Ryan amendment and "unleash" the intelligence community. The actions of 1980 were taken by many as a sign that the CIA and other agencies had learned to live with the new requirements, indeed that the reporting procedures were not particularly onerous. There had been considerable concern that if the president reported to eight committees, leaks of national security information from the Congress would occur, which was the case with the single committee in the House in 1973. Thus, the administration had simply not informed all relevant committees and subcommittees of foreign intelligence operations.

There were few congressional complaints until the attempt to rescue the hostages from Iran in 1980 failed, and some members of Congress claimed that they had not been given advance notice. However, this did not prevent them from restricting the Hughes-Ryan amendment shortly thereafter. Oversight of the CIA, particularly in a period of international tensions when the American will was being severely tried, was not a politically beneficial issue in 1980, so few members pressed for it. Oversight on foreign policy has thus tended to become regularized since the early 1970s but is not nearly as rewarding as many members thought it might be. Thus, it has taken a lesser role in congressional politics than domestic policy or even other foreign policy issues; and the permanent select committees have not been made standing committees, a move that would indicate greater importance for these bodies within the Congress.

Congressional oversight on foreign policy has not been totally ineffective. Congress did interrogate Kissinger to a greater extent than during any other recent period on the details of the 1975 Sinai accord. As discussed earlier, Congress passed, over Nixon's veto, a War Powers Act; and, against the wishes of the Nixon administration, the legislature required the secretary of state to submit the final text of any executive agreement on foreign policy to Congress within sixty days. In 1983, the House attempted to rein in the CIA once again by voting to prohibit covert aid to insurgents trying to overthrow the Nicaraguan government.

This was clearly one of the most conspicuous failures of the oversight process. Three years later the Iran–Contra affair broke and the Congress had to admit that it did not make the sanctions strong enough to block covert assistance. The Reagan administration's policies in both the Middle East and Latin America stood in shambles as the Congress merely stood by in anger. Similarly, the War Powers Act has not given Congress the new tool it sought to control the executive. Critics of the Grenada invasion, the bombing of Libya, and the reflagging of Kuwaiti tankers in the Persian Gulf found themselves acting too late with too little authority to reverse the Reagan administration policies. More critical, however, they found themselves with insufficient support on Capitol Hill and lacking alternative programs with which to reverse course.

However, these examples of frustration should not obscure the substantial initiatives of the Congress on foreign policy. Congress has reversed the administration course of action on South African sanctions and in providing aid to the Contras. It blocked aid to Angolan rebels in the 1970s. Since the founding of Israel, it has been the legislature rather than various presidents that has insisted on strong American support for the Jewish state.[51] This backing has included not only economic and military aid, but also several successful attempts to block arms sales to Arab countries. Presidents virtually always win on these arms sales, so the magnitude of the victories of pro-Israeli groups should not be underestimated. These are but a few of the examples of congressional initiatives that have succeeded. To be sure, the legislature is more active on domestic policy. These issues permit greater legislative initiatives and, indeed, the Congress has often taken the lead on domestic questions.[52] On foreign policy, however, the legislature is consigned to act in response to executive initiatives. This is not because of inherent weaknesses of Congress, for the same institutional structure that takes the lead on domestic policy must take a back seat on foreign policy. Rather, the distinction lies in the nature of the issue areas. The foreign policy agenda is set not by legislators' constituents exclusively, but by other nations as well. Country-to-country negotiations necessarily take place at the level of executives. When domestic legislatures do react to executive initiatives on foreign policy issues, especially intermestic ones, they protect the interests of their own citizens (see Chapter 8). This is the case even in strong party systems in parliamentary regimes.

Those who want to strengthen the role of Congress in determining what the foreign policy of the United States *will be,* as opposed to what it should have been, may seek a more active role for the legislature than oversight. However, they must answer the question, do legislators want to do more policy initiation? One study has found that rational members of Congress would not devote all of their time to examining the minute details of any policy area. In this "police-patrol" model of oversight, legislators examine a sample of executive activities in a search for violations of legislative dictates. Alternatively, the Congress might pursue a "fire-alarm" model, in which the legislature delegates much of the oversight responsibility to interest groups and citizens who ring "fire-alarm boxes" to indicate to Congress that the executive has breached its congressional mandate. Sometimes the legislature responds directly to its own indications of transgressions. The analogy is to community protection agencies. Police patrols drive around neighborhoods more or less at random and keep their eyes open for unusual occurrences. Fire departments, on the other hand, respond only to calls from citizens, unless they notice fires themselves.

The fire-alarm strategy of responding primarily to crises—and often through the assistance of interest groups or citizens—is a rational use of legislators' time and resources.[53] Police-patrol oversight cannot examine every issue area; it must sample and in doing so it is likely to miss some important violations of congressional intent in administrative practices. Fire-alarm oversight, in contrast, is less likely to miss any important transgressions because it delegates responsibility to interested groups in the public. While this strategy dictates a more limited role for the legislature than do police patrols, it may actually provide Congress with more leverage over executive decisions by highlighting questions that the legislators believe are critically important. Ironically, then, the Congress can have a greater say in foreign policy formation by acting selectively than by trying to compete with the administration on every front.

One explanation for this conclusion is that legislators are not as accountable for their actions, especially on foreign policy, as the president.[54] Legislators will thus focus their activities on policy questions on which they can make electoral gains. These do not generally include foreign policy. Devoting too much time to international issues can, as was argued in Chapter 4, lead to electoral problems. Instead, the fire-alarm approach permits legislators to delegate foreign policy concerns to interested constituents. By the time these issues trickle up to the Congress, legislators already know that there is at least some group who might reward them for taking an active role on such questions. How large the group is will determine the amount of effort legislators will expend on foreign policy oversight.

Once an issue catches the public's imagination many legislators will become involved in it. As noted in Chapter 5, however, there are a few issues on which the public is so aroused—or even where there are sufficiently powerful interest groups to entice members of Congress to devote considerable attention to international problems. Yet those issues that do arouse the public's attention for more than fleeting moments—in contrast to short-lived events such as the Grenada invasion and the bombing of Libya—are those on which the president's position proves unpopular. Here the Congress can have the greatest effect. It can reverse administration policy on South African sanctions, aid to the Contras, and putting pressure on Marcos to leave the Phillippines. It can reinforce American support for Israel in the Middle East even as successive administrations have sought to reverse course.

Even when public opinion is not mobilized, interest groups may well be. When groups are well organized *and* have no powerful opposition, they can prevail on foreign policy just as they do on domestic issues—even in the face of presidential opposition to their points of view. The blocking of arms sales to Arab countries, as sought by the pro-Israel lobby, is perhaps the most striking example of this effect. However, very few of the examples of the "effects" of foreign policy rest entirely on the reactions of the unorganized citizenry. The most vocal exponents of any point of view are the interest groups. Groups, however, would not get their way, especially on foreign policy, if they did not begin with at least potential support among the mass public and a predisposition by most members of Congress to agree with their positions. In effect, what Congress can do is bring public concerns to bear on American foreign policy. When congressional initiatives fail, it is either because public opinion supports the administration more than the legislature or simply because there is no clear mandate from the electorate. This was the case in Vietnam. As unpopular as that war was, critics could not convince the public that withdrawal was preferable to a stepped-up military presence. Those who demand that Congress play a greater role in the initiation of foreign policy must confront the incentives facing legislators. That brings us back to a reconsideration of the democratic dilemmas.

THE DEMOCRATIC DILEMMAS RECONSIDERED

We have seen that one way of resolving the problem of how much power each branch of the government should have on foreign policy is by strengthening the power of Congress, which can at least in part be accomplished by reforms such as the War Powers Act or increased oversight. But this will not necessarily lead to further congressional *control* over foreign policy decisions. On the other hand, a change that would give Congress more power on foreign policy, strengthening political parties to the point of sharing responsibility with the executive, might not be possible to initiate.

Is there an answer to the problem of foreign policy decision making in a democracy? Probably not, if one insists on a panacea for failures in foreign policy and a guarantee that successful policies will continue to be chosen. The decision-making process on foreign policy questions appears to work best in crisis situations, when immediate and decisive action is required. Perhaps leaders function best in crises—or perhaps the "followers" are simply more likely to support the leaders. On security and intermestic policies, the system appears to work less well. These issue areas may have high stakes, but they are not perceived as external threats. Furthermore, there is not always agreement about what the stakes are for all actors or what the most desirable outcome is. A democratic political system appears to handle foreign policy decisions best when the fewest actors—the inner circle—are involved in the process of decision making. As more and more actors in all four circles become involved, the conflict between presidential formation of foreign policy and the desires of other actors to have a say in foreign policy becomes intense. In crisis decision making, the administration chooses a course of action designed to maximize a given goal. The decision that is reached is directly related to that goal. Students of the foreign policy-making process have praised the decisions made in crises and concluded that democratic governments can indeed rival monolithic dictatorships in response to external threats, citing the pattern of rational decision making in such situations as the reason why the American political system has fared so well in crises. Lowi has stated:

Crisis decisions in foreign policy are made by an elite of formal, official officeholders. Rarely is there time to go further . . . the people who make decisions in times of crisis are largely those who were elected and appointed to make such decisions. That is to say, *in foreign affairs crises our government has operated pretty much as it was supposed to operate.* There is a normative corollary as well: Since our record of response to crisis is good, then the men in official positions have been acting and are able to act rationally. . . . Indeed, a fundamental feature of crisis decisions is that they involve institution leaders (holders of the top posts) *without their institutions.* Only when time allows does the entire apparatus of the foreign policy establishment come in play.[55]

On security and intermestic policies, however, the decisions reached through bureaucratic/governmental politics are often "minimal" ones; they do not resolve issues one way or the other and often cannot be justified on the basis that they maximize any particular foreign policy goal. Indeed, it is possible that, as in energy policy, bureaucratic/governmental politics may lead to no decisions at all—if the contending forces are each strong and obstinate enough to prevent a compromise acceptable to all (or even most) parties.

In addition, in security policies—including limited wars—the objectives of the policy as well as the proposed ways of handling them often lack the clarity of crisis decision making.* In Vietnam, for example, the objectives of American policy were never clearly delineated. On the one hand, a policy of total war was never seriously considered by the Johnson or Nixon administrations. However, neither was the policy of withdrawal of all American troops. Both administrations flatly rejected what might appear to have been a "rational" compromise first suggested by other nations and then advocated by North Vietnam: a coalition government in South Vietnam. The result was a sequence of minimal decisions: to increase American troop strength during the Johnson administration, but to continue to press for a negotiated settlement to the conflict. By contrast, Nixon reduced American troop strength but increased the bombing of North Vietnam, again continuing to search for a negotiated settlement. Yet the strategies of both administrations involved contradictory policies, producing what Burns has called an *immoderate moderation.* The United States finally extricated itself from the war without ever having resolved the question of what goals were accomplished by the many years of costly fighting.

If it is then concluded that decision making works best—produces the best results or garners the most public support—in crisis situations, we

---

*Limited wars are much like program policies in that both types of foreign policy decisions (1) involve multiple actors; (2) take a considerable amount of time to reach a conclusion; (3) involve conflicting goals on what a policy is supposed to accomplish; (4) involve bargaining—generally among the combatants rather than domestically—and are ultimately resolved by a negotiated settlement; and (5) are often marked by minimal decisions.

must, in conclusion, address ourselves again to the democratic dilemma posed at the beginning of the study. To ensure its security in the essentially anarchical international system, a state must have a concentration of executive authority so that it can respond quickly and with unity of purpose to events in the international political system. A democratic state, on the other hand, requires a restraint on executive power to preserve the constitutional system. This tension between the needs of international and domestic systems spills over into the distinction between crisis decision making on the one hand and security and intermestic policies on the other. Decision making in crisis situations very much resembles authoritarian decision making: policies are determined by a relatively small number of actors who must act with dispatch and unity. Democratic politics, on the other hand, is often marked by the necessity to compromise, to consider issues at great length in the attempt to reconcile conflicting interests, and to highlight the different goals of the actors involved rather than to assume that the decision makers all agree on the goals to be maximized.

What Role for Democratic Institutions?

The three aspects of the democratic dilemmas pervade all aspects of policy making, but are particularly difficult to resolve on foreign policy issues, where the stakes are so high and the actors all share at least one common goal: the survival and defense of the nation. The need to act quickly on foreign policy issues means that the president, as chief diplomat and commander in chief of the armed forces, must be able to respond to events in the international environment. But presidents may claim many things in the name of national security. (Nixon went as far as to include conversation with his aides on the Watergate scandal) and the question remains of how democratic the nation will be so that the president must protect these claims. What should the proper role of Congress be in foreign policy decision making—particularly when the Founding Fathers expected the legislature to dominate domestic politics and domestic policies to dominate the nation's agenda? If the Congress should have some role in foreign policy making, how great should that role be? Should other actors, such as interest groups, public opinion, and the media, also have their interests represented, as is the case with domestic policy? Does the Congress, with its more limited resources compared to the vast foreign policy bureaucracy of the executive branch, have the capacity to reach the "correct" foreign policy? In this same regard, how do we determine what the "correct" decision is—and how might we reconcile what we believe to be the proper course of action on an international issue with what popular sentiment might be? When the public is supportive of administration policies, this issue does not arise. But the public and the administration may both be right or may both be wrong. Hindsight is a great teacher, but it gives us little guidance about how widespread the scope of participation should be for present decisions.

The irony of foreign policy decision making is thus that the American political system appears to function best when decisions are made in the very way authoritarian states formulate policies.[56] When foreign policy decisions become more "democratic" by encompassing more actors, the policies selected may not have as clear a relationship to the strategic problem at hand. The democratic dilemmas do not admit of a ready answer. The framers of the Constitution did indeed produce a document with "missing powers," allowing for the growth of presidential power to meet changing needs. And by consciously creating a form of government that was inimical to responsible party government,[57] the framers of the Constitution ensured that the legislative branch could not take the foreign policy initiative away from the executive—an initiative they had given him. Believing that the nation would engage in no "entangling alliances," against which George Washington was to admonish the country in his farewell address, the Founding Fathers expected the war-making powers given to Congress in the Constitution would provide an adequate check on presidential dominance of the foreign policy process.

The president will, however, remain the dominant actor in foreign policy decision making. The conduct of an activist foreign policy—as distinct from a neoisolationist one—will continue to require a strong foreign policy president. Thus, the basic dilemma remains. What is a virtue internationally may be a vice domestically, and what is virtue domestically—a restraint on executive power—may become a vice internationally. The basic question is whether the United States can grant its government sufficient authority to safeguard the nation while preserving its democratic system. In the final analysis, the purpose of America's foreign policy is to protect the country's democratic way of life. Yet, will the policy subvert the very purposes it was intended to serve?

After Vietnam, it appeared that presidents would be less willing to seek out the sort of confrontations with Congress that led to Nixon's surprising defeat on the Cambodian and War Powers issues in 1973 and the refusal of Congress to authorize funds for Ford's requests on Vietnam and Angola. Yet the Iran–Contra affair indicates that administrations continue to challenge congressional dictates on foreign policy—indeed, even to defy them. The Congress has found itself always having to play catch-up with the executive. By the time the Congress took action prohibiting further aid to Vietnam in 1975, the South Vietnamese government had fallen and public support for continued American aid had virtually evaporated. Not until the Iran–Contra affair broke—and even then not expeditiously—did the Congress follow public opinion and stop aid to the Contras. Getting Congress to take a more assertive role in formulating foreign policy is no small task.

Indeed, it appears that the American people and their Congress, who have become less internationalist, have learned the lesson of restraint from the Vietnam experience more than have presidents. Yet the public's very high expectations of American presidents may lead chief executives to be *more* adventurous than in the past. Since the people demand so much of their presidents, and because it is becoming increasingly difficult for leaders (especially outsiders) to live up to these expectations, presidents may well be tempted to do something dramatic to shore up lagging popularity. There is nothing new in such presidential initiatives to build up popular support. However, in a period when presidential popularity can fall very far very quickly—and do so several times within an administration—the potential for adventurism by the chief executive may be much greater than even in the years before Vietnam.[58]

An irony of the post-Vietnam breakdown in the foreign policy consensus is that, even in what are called *crises,* there may be no agreed on course of action for the nation to take (see Chapters 2 and 3). What should the United States' response have been to the situations in Grenada and Libya? While the invasion of Grenada and the bombing of Tripoli both were very popular, there was also widespread criticism of each action—in a manner that we would not have seen before Vietnam. Much of the difficulty faced by foreign policy makers can be traced to the breakdown in consensus in the nation. Yet as the Iran hostage crisis demonstrated, the changing international environment also plays a critical role. Policy makers simply did not know what to do in response to a regime that practiced international terrorism. Some believed that quiet diplomacy was the best course, while others favored a military solution. Carter tried both. Reagan chided Carter in the 1980 elections for being too soft on terrorist regimes, but he himself approved arms sales to the same regime in the attempt to resolve another hostage crisis. Another reason, then, why crises do not automatically unite the nation is that it is simply unclear how to deal with the aggressor other than to get angry.

When there is no agreement on what the nation should do, questions of the best policy become intertwined with issues of who should decide what the country's policy ought to be. The Iran–Contra affair brought the issue into striking relief. As we argued in Chapter 3, members of the House and Senate committees investigating the affairs stressed the importance of following democratic procedures in enacting foreign policy. Even supporters of aid to the Contras, such as Senator Warren Rudman (R-N.H.), were highly critical of the diversion of arms sales profits. Yet many present and former administration officials—especially Lt. Col. Oliver North and Admiral John Poindexter—emphasized that support for the Contras was so vital that it justified misleading the Congress regarding what the executive branch was doing. While polls showed that the American public strongly disapproved of the entire affair, there is no clear pattern showing which offense Americans thought was worse: conducting a bad policy or violating legislatively mandated procedures. One survey found that 81 percent objected to selling arms to Iran, while 80 percent were upset that "a small group of unelected representatives [made and carried out] foreign policy without Congress or the public knowing about it."[59] In the case of the Iran–

Contra affair, the public response was so overwhelmingly negative that there hardly seemed a tension between outcomes and process. Yet that crisis highlights the potential conflict that might arise and the public concern with both process and outcomes.

On other policies, the roles of the presidency and Congress will depend on at least three circumstances. One is the future course of relations with the Soviet Union. The increasing disillusionment in the United States with what is seen as the Soviet Union's expansionist behavior as exemplified by Ethiopia, South Yemen, Afghanistan, and the Soviet support of Vietnam's invasion of Cambodia, has weakened support for détente in this country. The recent American anxiety about the continuing rapid growth of Soviet military strength, and the increases in American military spending for new weapons systems are but two symptoms of a renewed concern with checking Soviet influence and matching Soviet power. Second, events in the developing world may also have an enormous impact. Events in the Persian Gulf–Indian Ocean area—the fall of the shah in Iran and the subsequent Islamic revolution, the signs of potential internal instability in Saudi Arabia and other oil sheikdoms, and the Iran–Iraq war—have led an energy-dependent United States to commit itself to the protection of the oil kingdoms. This is one of several signs that instead of withdrawing from many of its commitments, which it is unable to do, the United States has discovered that it has become more involved than during the pre-Vietnam era. Third, because of the Vietnam War and the subsequent cries of "No More Vietnams," the question is how long the mood of the country, as expressed in this slogan, will constrain a foreign policy that is becoming activist once more and might again include the possibility of military action.

World War I was the "war to end all wars." World War II started only twenty-one years after the earlier conflict had ended. The United States was propelled into this war against Germany and Japan despite congressional attempts to constrain presidential freedom of action to maintain America's isolationist stance. It was not to be the last time that, despite a preference for peace, the country found itself at war. This long war ended with the detonation of two atomic weapons over Japan and was supposed to underline the dangers of any future international conflict. A few years later, General Douglas MacArthur, commenting on the Korean War, stated that it was sheer folly for the United States to fight a land war in Asia; but his warnings did not prevent Vietnam. As George Santayana noted, any nation that doesn't learn from history is doomed to repeat it. The question is: Which lesson should it learn—the lesson of 1940–1941 or that of Vietnam?

NOTES

1. Tom Wicker, *New York Times*, January 14, 1973.
2. Elizabeth Drew, "Letter from Washington," *The New Yorker*, June 22, 1987, p. 82.

3. "Will the Real Senate Stand Up?" *Christian Science Monitor,* May 29–June 1, 1970.
4. David Ignatius, "Contra-Funding Affair Illustrates Failure of Oversight Process," *Washington Post,* December 16, 1986, p. A16.
5. James Sundquist, *The Decline and Resurgence of Congress* (Washington, D.C.: Brookings Institution, 1981), esp. p. 155.
6. Committee on the Constitutional System, *A Bicentennial Analysis of the American Political Structure* (Washington, D.C.: 1987), p. 3. For a similar analysis that contrasts "the freebooting adventurism of a go-it-alone executive" with the "535 secretaries of state who cannot resist any opportunity to . . . microman-age foreign policy" with the result of "mutual suspicion and a state of flux," see the comments of two senators: David L. Boren [D-Okla.] and John C. Danforth [R-Mo.], "Why This Country Can't Lead," *Washington Post,* December 1, 1987, p. A21.
7. Ibid.
8. Ibid., p. 5.
9. Woodrow Wilson, *Congressional Government* (Cleveland: Meridian Books, 1967), pp. 167–68. Originally published in 1885.
10. Committee on the Constitutional System, *A Bicentennial Analysis,* pp. 10–16.
11. Norman Ornstein et al., *Vital Statistics on Congress, 1984–1985 Edition* (Washington, D.C.: American Enterprise Institute), p. 56.
12. Computed from ibid., p. 57.
13. James Sundquist, *Constitutional Reform and Effective Government* (Washington, D.C.: Brookings Institution, 1986), p. 87.
14. Sundquist, *The Decline and Resurgence of Congress,* p. 470.
15. Ibid., p. 477.
16. Ibid., p. 476.
17. See Anthony Downs, *An Economic Theory of Democracy* (New York: Harper & Row, 1957).
18. This is the problem of the "cyclical majority" in which there is no clear-cut set of policies that can garner majority support among the full set of citizen voters. See Kenneth J. Arrow, *Social Choice and Individual Values* (New York: John Wiley & Sons, 1951).
19. James David Barber, *The Presidential Character* (Englewood Cliffs, N.J.: Prentice-Hall, 1972). Further citations are to the second edition (1977).
20. Ibid., chaps. 1 and 10.
21. Dan Rather and Gary Paul Gates, *The Palace Guard* (New York: Harper & Row, 1974).
22. Barber, *The Presidential Character, p. 8.*
23. Ibid., chaps. 2–3.
24. Ibid., chap. 5.
25. Ibid., chap. 5.
26. Barber, *The Presidential Character,* pp. 345–442.
27. See Alexander George, "Assessing Presidential Character," *World Politics* 26 (January 1974), pp. 234–82; and James H. Qualls, "Barber's Typological Analysis of Political Leaders," *American Political Science Review* 71 (March 1977), pp. 182–211; see Robert C. Tucker, "The Georges' Wilson Reexamined," *American Political Science Review* 71 (June 1977), pp. 606–18.
28. Fred I. Greenstein, *The Hidden-Hand Presidency* (New York: Basic Books, 1982).

29. Robert E. DiClerico, *The American President* (Englewood Cliffs, N.J.: Prentice-Hall, 1979), p. 305.
30. Ibid., chap. 9, esp. p. 332.
31. Theodore J. Lowi, *The Personal President* (Ithaca, N.Y.: Cornell Univ. Press, 1985), p. 25; and Nelson W. Polsby, "The Institutionalization of the U.S. House of Representatives," *American Political Science Review* 62 (March 1968), pp. 144–68.
32. Wilson, *Congressional Government,* p. 170.
33. James Bryce, *The American Commonwealth,* vol. 1, rev. ed. (New York: Macmillan, 1915), p. 80.
34. This is the thesis, very briefly stated, of Theodore J. Lowi, *The Personal President* (Ithaca, N.Y.: Cornell University Press, 1985).
35. Ibid., p. 11.
36. Richard Neustadt, *Presidential Power* (New York: John Wiley & Sons, 1980), pp. 204–5. For a set of proposals, including the adoption of a multiparty system in the United States, that are based on lower expectations, see Lowi, *The Personal President,* pp. 191–210.
37. Meg Greenfield, "The Cult of the Amateur," *Washington Post,* June 11, 1980, p. A19.
38. William Crotty, "Two Cheers for the Presidential Primaries," in *Rethinking the Presidency,* ed. Thomas Cronin (Boston: Little, Brown, 1982), p. 68.
39. "Only Freaks," *The Economist,* May 9, 1987, pp. 12. See also David S. Broder, "Would You Prefer a Mondale-Baker Race?" *Washington Post,* June 4, 1980, p. A19.
40. Lowi, *The Personal President,* pp. 107–8.
41. LaFollette's statement was that the cure for the ills of democracy is more democracy.
42. Committee on the Constitutional System, *A Bicentennial Analysis of the American Political Structure,* p. 8.
43. Robert E. DiClerico and Eric M. Uslaner, *Few Are Chosen: Problems in Presidential Selection* (New York: McGraw-Hill, 1983), chap. 6.
44. See Howard L. Reiter, *Selecting the President* (Philadelphia: Univ. of Pennsylvania Press, 1985).
45. Bryce, *The American Commonwealth,* vol. 1, p. 79.
46. The data in Table 7–1 are reported in John E. Rielly, ed., *American Public Opinion and U.S. Foreign Policy 1983* (Chicago: Chicago Council on Foreign Relations, 1983). No similar questions were posed in the 1986 surveys cited in Chapter 4.
47. *Los Angeles Times* poll press release, February 20–23, 1987.
48. Seymour Scher, "Conditions for Legislative Control," *Journal of Politics* 25 (August 1963), pp. 526–51.
49. Morris S. Ogul, *Congress Oversees the Bureaucracy* (Pittsburgh: University of Pittsburgh Press, 1976), esp. chaps. 1, 6, and 7.
50. Roger H. Davidson, "Breaking Up Those 'Cozy Triangles': An Impossible Dream?" in *Legislative Reform and Public Policy,* eds. Susan Welch and John G. Peters (New York: Praeger, 1977), pp.30–52.
51. Steven L. Spiegel, *The Other Arab–Israeli Conflict* (Chicago: Univ. of Chicago Press, 1985).
52. See David E. Price, *Who Makes the Laws?* (New York: Schenkman, 1969).

53. Mathew D. McCubbins and Thomas Schwartz, "Congressional Oversight Overlooked: Police Patrols versus Fire Alarms," *American Journal of Political Science* 28 (February 1984), pp. 165–79.

54. Sundquist, *The Decline and Resurgence of Congress*, p. 454.

55. Theodore J. Lowi, "Making Democracy Safe for the World," in *Domestic Sources of Foreign Policy*, ed. James N. Rosenau (New York: Free Press, 1967), p. 301.

56. Contrast this argument with the one made by Kenneth N. Waltz that democratic institutions in the United States *do not* hinder foreign policy decision making. See Waltz, *Foreign Policy and Democratic Politics* (Boston: Little, Brown, 1967), esp. chap. 11.

57. See Richard Hofstadter, *The Idea of a Party System* (Berkeley: Univ. of California Press, 1970), p. 68.

58. We owe this insightful argument to a June 1987 graduate seminar paper by Walter Schaefer at the University of Maryland.

59. "A Distinct Sense of Unease," *U.S. News and World Report,* July 13, 1987, pp. 22–23.

Further Readings

Chapter 1

Art, Robert. "Bureaucratic Politics and American Foreign Policy: A Critique." *Policy Sciences,* December 1973.

Henkin, Louis. *Foreign Affairs and the Constitution.* Mineola, N.Y.: Foundation Press, 1973.

————. "Foreign Affairs and the Constitution." *Foreign Affairs,* Winter 1987/88, pp. 284–310.

Hilsman, Roger. *The Politics of Policy Making in Defense and Foreign Affairs.* New York: Harper & Row, 1971.

Hughes, Barry. *The Domestic Context of American Foreign Policy.* San Francisco: W. H. Freeman, 1978.

Lowi, Theodore, J. "American Business, Public Policy, Case Studies, and Political Theory." *World Politics,* July 1964.

Manning, Bayless. "The Congress, The Executive and Intermestic Affairs: Three Proposals." *Foreign Affairs,* January 1977.

Neustadt, Richard. *Presidential Power.* New York: John Wiley & Sons, 1980.

Peppers, Donald. "The Two Presidencies: Eight Years Later." In *Perspectives on the Presidency,* ed. Aaron Wildavsky. Boston: Little, Brown, 1975.

Wildavsky, Aaron. "The Two Presidencies." *Transaction,* December 1966.

Chapter 2

Brzezinski, Zbigniew. *Power and Principles.* New York: Farrar, Straus, Giroux, 1983.

Campbell, John. *The Foreign Affairs Fudge Factory.* New York: Basic Books, 1972.

Clarke, Duncan L. "Why State Can't Lead." *Foreign Policy,* Spring 1987, pp. 108–42.

Fulbright, J. W. *The Crippled Giant.* New York: Random House, 1972.

George, Alexander. *Presidential Decision Making in Foreign Policy.* Boulder, Colo.: Westview Press, 1980.

Haig, Alexander. *Caveat.* New York: Macmillan, 1984.

Inderfurth, Karl F., and Loch K. Johnson, eds. *Decisions of the Highest Order.* Pacifica Grove, Calif.: Brooks/Cole, 1988.

Kissinger, Henry A. *White House Years.* Boston: Little, Brown, 1979.

Rubin, Barry. *Affairs of State: The State Department and the Struggle over U.S. Foreign Policy.* New York: Oxford University Press, 1985.

Sick, Gary. *All Fall Down.* New York: Random House, 1985.

Spanier, John. *American Foreign Policy since World War II.* 11th ed. Washington, D.C.: CQ Press, 1988.

Vance, Cyrus. *Hard Choices.* New York: Simon & Schuster, 1983.

Chapter 3

Cheever, Daniel S., and Field H. Haviland. *American Foreign Policy and the Separation of Powers.* Cambridge, Mass.: Harvard Univ. Press, 1952.

Crabb, Cecil V. *Bipartisan Foreign Policy.* New York: Row, Peterson, and Co., 1957.

Destler, I. M.; Leslie Gelb; and Anthony Lake. *Our Own Worst Enemy.* New York: Simon & Schuster, 1984.

Hodgson, Godfrey. "The Establishment." *Foreign Policy,* Spring 1973, pp. 3–40.

Holsti, Ole R., and James N. Rosenau. *American Leadership in World Affairs.* Boston: Allen & Unwin, 1984. (Also see the update in the December 1986 issue of *International Studies Quarterly.*)

Isaacson, Walter, and Gran Thomas. *The Wise Men.* New York: Simon & Schuster, 1986.

Quandt, William B. *Camp David: Peacemaking and Politics.* Washington, D.C.: The Brookings Institution, 1986.

Spiegel, Steven L. *The Other Arab–Israeli Conflict.* Chicago: The Univ. of Chicago Press, 1985.

The Iran–Contra Affair. Washington, D.C.: U.S. Government Printing Office, 1987.

Woodward, Robert. *Veil.* New York: Simon & Schuster, 1987.

Chapter 4

Fenno, Richard F., Jr. *Home Style: U.S. House Members in Their Districts.* Boston: Little, Brown, 1978.

————. *Congressmen in Committees.* Boston: Little, Brown, 1973.

Fiorina, Morris P. *Congress: Keystone of the Washington Establishment.* New Haven: Yale Univ. Press, 1977.

Franck, Thomas M., and Edward Weisband. *Foreign Policy by Congress.* New York: Oxford Univ. Press, 1979.

Jacobson, Gary C. *The Politics of Congressional Elections.* 2d ed. Boston: Little, Brown, 1987.

King, Anthony, ed. *Both Ends of the Avenue.* Washington, D.C.: American Enterprise Institute, 1983.

Mayhew, David R. *Congress: The Electoral Connection.* New Haven: Yale Univ. Press, 1974.

Smith, Steven S., and Christopher J. Deering. *Committees in Congress.* Washington, D.C.: CQ Press, 1984.

Spanier, John, and Joseph Nogee, eds. *Congress, the Presidency and Foreign Policy.* New York: Pergamon Press, 1981.

Uslaner, Eric M. "The Case of the Vanishing Liberal Senators: The House Did It." *British Journal of Political Science* 11 (January 1981), pp. 105–113.

Wilcox, Francis O. *Congress, the Executive, and Foreign Policy.* New York: Harper & Row, 1971.

Chapter 5

Abramson, Paul R.; John H. Aldrich; and David W. Rohde. *Change and Continuity in the 1984 Elections.* Rev. Washington, D.C.: CQ Press, 1987.

Chubb, John E., and Paul A. Peterson, eds. *The New Direction in American Politics.* Washington, D.C.: The Brookings Institution, 1985.

Holsti, Ole N., and James N. Rosenau. *American Leadership in World Affairs.* Boston: George Allen and Unwin, 1983.

Kernell, Samuel. *Going Public.* Washington, D.C.: CQ Press, 1986.

Lowi, Theodore J. *The Personal President.* Ithaca, N.Y.: Cornell Univ. Press, 1985.

Mueller, John E. *War, Presidents, and Public Opinion.* New York: John Wiley & Sons, 1967.

Page, Benjamin I., and Robert Y. Shapiro. "Changes in Americans' Policy Preferences." *Public Opinion Quarterly* 46 (Spring 1982), pp. 24–42.

Patterson, Thomas E. *The Mass Media Election.* New York: Praeger Publishers, 1980.

Pomper, Gerald M., ed. *The Election of 1984.* Chatham, N.J.: Chatham House, 1985.

Ranney, Austin, ed. *The American Elections of 1984.* Durham, N.C.: Duke Univ. Press, 1985.

Rielly, John E., ed. *American Public Opinion and U.S. Foreign Policy 1987.* Chicago: Chicago Council on Foreign Relations, 1987.

Schneider, William. "Conservatism, Not Interventionism: Trends in Foreign Policy Public Opinion, 1974–1982." In *Eagle Defiant: United States Foreign Policy in the 1980s,* eds. Kenneth A. Oye et al. Boston: Little, Brown, 1983.

Chapter 6

Bauer, Raymond A. et al. *American Business and Public Policy.* 2d ed. Chicago: Aldine-Atherton, 1972.

Cigler, Alan J., and Burdett A. Loomis, eds. *Interest Group Politics.* 2d ed. Washington, D.C.: CQ Press, 1986.

Gilboa, Eytan. *American Public Opinion toward Israel and the Arab–Israeli Conflict.* Lexington, Mass.: Lexington Books, 1987.

Mathias, Charles McC. Jr. "Ethnic Groups and Foreign Policy." *Foreign Affairs* 59 (Summer 1981), pp. 975–98.

Schattschneider, E. E. *The Semisovereign People.* New York: Holt, Rinehart & Winston, 1960.

Schlozman, Kay Lehman, and John T. Tierney. *Organized Interests and American Democracy.* New York: Harper & Row, 1986.

Spiegel, Steven L. *The Other Arab–Israeli Conflict.* Chicago: Univ. of Chicago Press.

Talbott, Strobe. *Endgame.* New York: Harper & Row, 1979.

Uslaner, Eric M. "One Nation, Many Voices: Interest Groups in Foreign Policy Making." In *Interest Group Politics,* 2d ed. eds. Allen J. Cigler and Burdett Loomis. Washington, D.C.: CQ Press, 1986, pp. 235–57.

Wolfe, Thomas, *The SALT Experience.* Cambridge, Mass.: Ballinger Publishing Co., 1979.

Chapter 7

Brown, Harold. *The Strategic Defense Initiative* (Boulder, Colo.: Westview Press, 1987).

Doran, Charles F. *Myth, Oil, and Politics.* New York: Free Press, 1977.

Flanagan, Stephen J. "Congress, the White House and SALT." *The Bulletin of Atomic Scientists* (November 1978), pp. 34–40; and "The Domestic Politics of SALT II: Implications for the Foreign Policy Process," in Spanier and Nogee, *Congress, the Presidency and Foreign Policy,* pp. 44–76.

Halperin, Morton. "The Decision to Deploy the ABM: Bureaucratic and Domestic Politics in the Johnson Administration." *World Politics,* October 1972.

———— . *Bureaucratic Politics and Foreign Policy.* Washington, D.C.: Brookings Institution, 1974.

Herkin, Gregg. *Counsels of War.* New York: Oxford University Press, 1987, especially pp. 331–57.

Holland, Lauren and Hoover, Robert. *The MX Decision.* Boulder, Colo.: Westview Press, 1984.

Payne, Keith. *Strategic Defense.* Lanham, N.Y.: Hamilton Press, 1986.

Smoke, Richard. National Security and the Nuclear Dilemma. 2d ed. New York: Random House, 1987, especially pp. 247–82.

Talbott, Strobe. *Endgame.* New York: Harper & Row, 1979.

Wolfe, Thomas. *The SALT Experience.* Cambridge, Mass.: Ballinger Publishing Co., 1979.

Chapter 8

Cohen, Stephen S., and John Zysman. *Manufacturing Matters.* New York: Basic Books, 1987.

Congressional Quarterly. Energy Policy. Washington, D.C.: Congressional Quarterly, 2d ed., 1981.

Davis, David. *Energy Politics,* 2d ed. New York: St. Martin's Press, 1983.

Doran, Charles F. *Myth, Oil, and Politics.* New York: Free Press, 1977.

Drell, Sidney D.; Philip J. Farley; and David Holloway. *The Reagan Strategic Defense Initiative.* Cambridge, Mass.: Ballinger, 1985.

Flanagan, Stephen J. "Congress, the White House and SALT." *The Bulletin of Atomic Scientists,* November 1978, pp. 34–40; and "The Domestic Politics of SALT II: Implications for the Foreign Policy Process," In *Congress, the Presidency and Foreign Policy,* eds Spanier and Nogee, pp. 44–76.

Halperin, Morton. "The Decision to Deploy the ABM: Bureaucratic and Domestic Politics in the Johnson Administration." *World Politics,* October 1972.

———— . *Bureaucratic Politics and Foreign Policy.* Washington, D.C.: Brookings Institution, 1974.

Holland, Lauren, and Robert Hoover. *The MX Decision.* Boulder, Colo.: Westview Press, 1984.

Jones, Charles O. "Congress and the Making of Energy Policy." In *New Dimensions to Energy Policy,* ed. Robert Lawrence. Lexington, Mass.: Lexington Books, 1979, pp. 161–78.

Landsberg, Hans H. "Energy," chap. 4. In *Setting National Priorities: Agenda for the 1980s,* ed. Joseph A. Pechman. Washington, D.C.: Brookings Institution, 1980.

Nivola, Pietro. *The Politics of Energy Conservation.* Washington, D.C.: The Brookings Institution, 1986.

Pastor, Robert A. *Congress and the Politics of U.S. Foreign Economic Policy.* Berkeley: Univ. of California Press, 1980.

Schurr, Sam et al. *Energy in America's Future: The Choices Before Us.* Baltimore: Johns Hopkins University Press for Resources for the Future, 1979.

Stein, Arthur A. "Strategy as Politics, Politics as Strategy; Domestic Debates, Statecraft and Star Wars." In *The Logic of Nuclear Terror,* ed. Roman Kolkowicz. Boston: Allen & Unwin, 1987, pp. 184–210.

Uslaner, Eric M. *Shale Barrel Politics: Energy and Legislative Leadership.* Stanford: Stanford University Press, 1989.

Chapter 9

Crabb, Cecil V. Jr. *Bipartisan Foreign Policy: Myth or Reality?* White Plains, N.Y.: Row, Peterson and Co., 1957.

DiClerico, Robert E., and Eric M. Uslaner. *Few Are Chosen: Problems in Presidential Selection.* New York: McGraw-Hill, 1984.

McCubbins, Mathew D., and Thomas Schwartz. "Congressional Oversight Overlooked: Police Patrols versus Fire Alarms." *American Journal of Political Science* 28 (February 1984), pp. 165–79.

Polsby, Nelson W. *Consequences of Party Reform.* New York: Oxford Univ. Press, 1983.

Reiter, Howard L. *Selecting the President.* Philadelphia: Univ. of Pennsylvania Press, 1985.

Robinson, Donald L., ed. *Reforming American Government: The Bicentennial Papers of the Committee on the Constitutional System.* Boulder, Colo.: Westview, 1985.

Rockman, Bert A. *The Leadership Question.* New York: Praeger Publishers, 1984.

Sundquist, James L. *The Decline and Resurgence of Congress.* Washington, D.C.: The Brookings Institution, 1981.

———— . *Constitutional Reform and Effective Government.* Washington, D.C.: The Brookings Institution, 1986.

Wilson, James Q. "Does the Separation of Powers Still Work?" *The Public Interest,* Winter 1987, pp. 36–52.

Index

ABOUT THE AUTHORS

John Spanier is a professor in the Department of Political Science at the University of Florida in Gainesville. He received his B.A. and M.A. from Harvard University, and his Ph.D. from Yale University. He has been a visiting professor, lecturer, and consultant, including serving as Professor of Strategy at the Naval War College (1983–84), and as a member of the Advisory Board of the Foreign Policy Research Institute (1980–88).

He is the author of *The Truman-MacArthur Controversy and the Korean War* (one of the 2,000 books selected for the official White House library), *American Foreign Policy since World War II* (the first officially translated and published book on U.S. foreign policy in the People's Republic of China), *World Politics in an Age of Revolution,* and *Games Nations Play: How to Analyze International Politics.* He is also the co-author of several books and numerous articles.

Eric M. Uslaner is Professor of Government and Politics at the University of Maryland—College Park. In 1981–82 he was Fulbright Professor of American Studies and Political Science at the Hebrew University of Jerusalem (Israel).

Professor Uslaner is a specialist in American government, especially the Congress, elections, and energy policy. He is the author of *Shale Barrel Politics: Energy and Legislative Leadership,* and co-author of *Few Are Chosen: Problems in Presidential Selection,* and *Patterns of Decision-Making in State Legislatures.* His articles have appeared in such journals as the *American Political Science Review,* the *American Journal of Political Science,* the *Journal of Politics,* and the *British Journal of Political Science.* He has testified before both Congress and state legislatures, and in 1979–80 was a consultant to the House of Representatives Select Committee on Committees (Energy Task Force).

A NOTE ON THE TYPE

The text of this book was set in 10/12 Palatino using a film version of the face designed by Herman Zapf that was first released in 1950 by Germany's Stempel Foundry. The face is named after Giovanni Battista Palatino, a famous penman of the 16th century. In its calligraphic quality, Palatino is reminiscent of the Italian Renaissance type designs, yet with its wide, open letters and unique proportions it still retains a modern feel. Palatino is considered one of the most important faces from one of Europe's most influential type designers.

Composed by Weimer Typesetting Co., Inc.

Printed and bound by R. R. Donnelley & Sons Company